Daily
Learning
Drills

Grade 6

 **Children's Publishing**

Columbus, Ohio

 **Children's Publishing**

Copyright © 2004 McGraw-Hill Children's Publishing.

Printed in the United States of America. All rights reserved. Except as permitted under the United States Copyright Act, no part of this publication may be reproduced or distributed in any form or by any means, or stored in a database or retrieval system, without prior written permission from the publisher, unless otherwise indicated.

Send all inquiries to:
McGraw-Hill Children's Publishing
8787 Orion Place
Columbus, OH 43240-4027

ISBN 0-7696-3096-0

1 2 3 4 5 6 7 8 9 10 MAZ 08 07 06 05 04 03

The *McGraw-Hill* Companies

Table of Contents

Language Arts 1–90

Math 91–177

Science 178–232

Social Studies 233–288

Answer Key 289–320

Language Arts Review 321–342

Math Review 343–363

Science Review 364–384

Social Studies Review 385–403

Review Answer Key 404–412

Name _____

All About Cats . . . and Sentences

Rule All sentences need a punctuation mark at the end.

Exercise Finish each sentence with the correct word(s).

1. A **declarative sentence** ends with a
   _____ .

2. An **interrogative sentence** ends with a
   _____ .

3. An **exclamatory sentence**, which shows excitement or strong feeling, ends with
   an _____ .

4. An **imperative sentence**, which makes a request or gives a command, ends
   with a _____ .

• Read each sentence and punctuate it correctly. Write what kind of sentence it is on the line: **declarative, interrogative, imperative,** or **exclamatory**.

1. The cat was the most sacred of all Egyptian animals _____

2. Amazingly, Egyptians even mummified their cats _____

3. Long ago, people thought witches could turn into cats _____

4. Did you know cats were often burned for this reason _____

5. Incredibly, some people are still frightened of black cats _____

6. Cats perform a useful service in China and Japan _____

7. They protect silkworm cocoons from rats _____

8. Are cats really such independent animals _____

9. Domestic cats enjoy the companionship of people _____

10. Give your cat a lot of care and attention _____

11. Watch the pupils of a cat's eyes contract in bright light _____

12. Do cats' eyes reflect light _____

13. I'm amazed that a cat can walk easily on a two-inch-wide surface _____

14. Look your cat over carefully before buying it _____

15. Has your kitten had all the shots it needs _____

16. Pick your cat with care and train it well _____

Name _____

A Perfect Gem

Rule A sentence has a **complete subject** and a **complete predicate**. The most important word in the complete subject is the **simple subject**. The most important word or phrase in the complete predicate, the verb, is the **simple predicate**.

Example

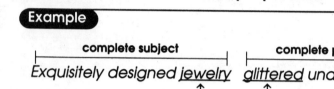

complete subject	complete predicate
Exquisitely designed _jewelry_	_glittered_ under the glass.

simple subject   simple predicate

Exercise Put a slash between the **complete subject** and the **complete predicate**. Then circle the **simple subject** and underline the **simple predicate**.

1. People used stones and gems as a source of protection long ago.
2. People thought they were protected and helped by these stones.
3. Stones called birthstones were supposed to bring the wearer good fortune.
4. A stone associated with one's birth month is a birthstone.
5. Different lists of birthstones are used today.
6. We are not certain which stones were used by the ancients for which months.
7. The aquamarine is associated with wisdom.
8. Birthstones are set in rings or carried in some other way on the person.
9. Both men and women wear birthstones.
10. Either rings or pins can be set with these stones.

- Finish the following sentences by adding complete predicates to the complete subjects.

1. The brilliant emerald _____

2. Rubies and garnets _____

3. The three-carat diamond _____

4. Her new ring _____

- Write the simple subjects and the simple predicates here from the sentences you just completed.

	simple subject	simple predicate		simple subject	simple predicate
1.	_____	_____	3.	_____	_____
2.	_____	_____	4.	_____	_____

Name _____

Prepare Yourselves

Rule **Reflexive pronouns** reflect the action of the verb back to the subject. **Myself, yourself, herself, himself, itself, ourselves, yourselves,** and **themselves** are reflexive pronouns.

Example

*Roger made **himself** a model of the space shuttle.*

*The shuttle landed **itself**, using only gravity to pull it down.*

Exercise Complete each sentence with the appropriate reflexive pronoun.

1. "You should take _____ to the launch, Cheryl," her parents said.

2. The Davenport children congratulated _____ on the good spot they found.

3. We sure found _____ a good viewpoint from which to watch the shuttle landing.

4. David imagined _____ trying to maneuver in a space shuttle that was hurtling toward earth.

5. "I told _____ that I will become a commander someday," Earl said.

6. Deborah settled _____ to wait for a glimpse of the space shuttle.

7. David Davenport enjoyed _____ at the shuttle launch.

8. "You could train _____ for space travel if you built a model simulator," Bobbie and David's parents suggested.

• Write the reflexive pronoun from the Word Bank that matches each subject listed below.

1. Peter _____

2. The dog _____

3. Gwen _____

4. Monica and I _____

5. Heather and Kimberly _____

6. You and Carolyn _____

7. I _____

8. You _____

Word Bank
myself
yourself
himself
yourselves
themselves
itself
herself
ourselves

Name _____

Honeybees Buzz

Rule A verb's tenses are formed by its principal parts: the **present**, the **past**, and the **past participle**.

Example

Present: Honeybees **live** in colonies inside a hive.
Past: The honeybees **lived** inside a tree.
Past Participle: The honeybees **have lived** in the bee-keeper's hive a long time.

Exercise Write the tense of the underlined verb: **present**, **past**, or **past participle**.

1. About 50,000 honeybees <u>followed</u> the scouts to the new location. _____

2. The queen <u>lays</u> about 2,000 eggs in one day. _____

3. She <u>has produced</u> many fertilized eggs that will become female worker bees.

   _____

4. The unfertilized eggs that she <u>has placed</u> in the brood nest will become male drones.

   _____

5. Worker bees <u>work</u> very hard during their lifetime of about 6 weeks. _____

6. Worker bees <u>dance</u> to tell the others in the hive where the flowers are containing the nectar and pollen they need for food. _____

7. Some workers <u>danced</u> in a circle to explain that the food was nearby. _____

8. Others <u>have danced</u> in a different direction to let the other workers know where to find the flowers farther away. _____

9. The youngest worker bees in the hive <u>cleaned</u> the empty cells. _____

10. They <u>feed</u> "royal jelly" to the larvae in the hive. _____

11. Young worker bees <u>build</u> the honeycomb. _____

12. A worker bee <u>guarded</u> the hive. _____

13. During the last three weeks of the worker bee's life she <u>has collected</u> much pollen and nectar. _____

14. Honeybees <u>have helped</u> us by making honey and wax and by fertilizing flowers.

    _____

Name _____

Camel Trivia

Rule Verbs that show action are called **action verbs**.

Example *The camels **walked** across the desert.*

Rule **Linking verbs** do not show action. Instead, they link the subject with a word or words in the predicate that tell something about the subject.
Linking verbs are forms of the verb **be** and verbs such as **seem** and **become**.

Example *Camels **are** desert animals.*

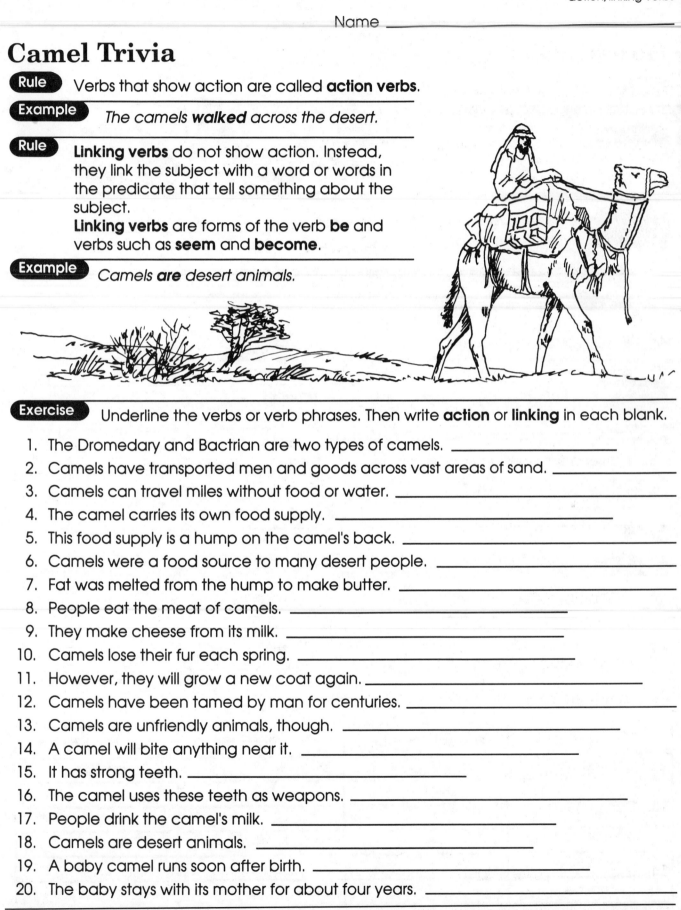

Exercise Underline the verbs or verb phrases. Then write **action** or **linking** in each blank.

1. The Dromedary and Bactrian are two types of camels. _____
2. Camels have transported men and goods across vast areas of sand. _____
3. Camels can travel miles without food or water. _____
4. The camel carries its own food supply. _____
5. This food supply is a hump on the camel's back. _____
6. Camels were a food source to many desert people. _____
7. Fat was melted from the hump to make butter. _____
8. People eat the meat of camels. _____
9. They make cheese from its milk. _____
10. Camels lose their fur each spring. _____
11. However, they will grow a new coat again. _____
12. Camels have been tamed by man for centuries. _____
13. Camels are unfriendly animals, though. _____
14. A camel will bite anything near it. _____
15. It has strong teeth. _____
16. The camel uses these teeth as weapons. _____
17. People drink the camel's milk. _____
18. Camels are desert animals. _____
19. A baby camel runs soon after birth. _____
20. The baby stays with its mother for about four years. _____

Name _____

Action!

Rule A **verb phrase** is made up of a **main verb** and one or more **helping verbs**.

Example *Our class **is studying** the Roman Empire.*

Exercise Find the **verb phrase**. Circle the **main verb** and underline its **helpers**.

1. The passenger must have forgotten his ticket.
2. He had carried his luggage to the airport in his trunk.
3. The airplane must have been delayed by the severe storm.
4. The travelers were touring the country by bus.

Rule **Action verbs** show action. **Linking verbs** link the subject with a word or words in the predicate.

Example

(Action verb)	(Linking verb)
*Harold **ran** into the field.*	*He **was** a fast runner.*

Exercise Underline each **verb**. Then tell if it is an **action verb** or **linking verb**.

1. Today is Tuesday. _____
2. We practiced today. _____
3. Jim was late. _____
4. The coach teased him. _____
5. Jim was embarrassed. _____
6. Next time he will run. _____

Rule Verbs have simple tenses: **past, present,** and **future**.

Exercise Draw a line under each **verb phrase**. Tell if the tense is **past, present,** or **future**.

1. The hockey team will be playing a game in two weeks. _____
2. They are practicing every afternoon after school. _____
3. They have skated many hours on the practice rink. _____
4. Soon the crowd will cheer their teams. _____

• Complete this chart.

Verb	Present/Singular	Past	Past with helpers
Ex. *talk*	*talks*	*talked*	*has talked*
go			
buzz			
move			
take			
choose			

Name _____

The Staff of Life

Rule A **transitive verb** is followed by a direct object.
An **intransitive verb** is not followed by a direct object.

Exercise Underline the verbs or verb phrases. Circle the direct object if there is one. Identify the kind of verb by writing **transitive** or **intransitive** in the chart below.

1. Bread is often called the staff of life.
2. Bread, in different forms, has been eaten for thousands of years.
3. Man has made bread longer than any other manufactured food.
4. The earliest breads were made in a hard, flat form.
5. A mixture of ground grain and water formed the dough.
6. The sun or hot rocks baked the mixture into bread.
7. A wide variety of breads are eaten by people around the world.
8. Farmers grow many kinds of grains for the various flours.
9. People in other countries may prefer different kinds of bread.
10. Asian people eat bread made from rice.
11. In Scotland, oatcakes and barley breads are preferred.
12. Central Americans enjoy flat cakes of cornmeal dough.
13. The roots of the cassava plant provide flour in the West Indies.
14. The first leavened bread was made by the Egyptians.
15. Hard, flat loaves changed into soft, air-filled loaves.
16. The Egyptians built the first ovens, too.
17. The lighter, leavened bread couldn't be baked on hot rocks.
18. An enclosed, heated area was needed to bake the larger masses of dough.
19. We still use the principles of early bread-making today.
20. We all enjoy many forms of bread in our daily diets.

Transitive or Intransitive

1. _____	8. _____	15. _____
2. _____	9. _____	16. _____
3. _____	10. _____	17. _____
4. _____	11. _____	18. _____
5. _____	12. _____	19. _____
6. _____	13. _____	20. _____
7. _____	14. _____	

Name _____

Show Time

Rule The past and past participle forms of irregular verbs are not formed by adding **-ed**.

Example **Present:** The talent show **begins** at 6:30 p.m.
Past: It **began** right on time.
Past Participle: The show **has begun** with a smash hit by Joey on the piano.

Exercise Complete each sentence with the correct form of the irregular verb in parentheses.

1. Many guests have (ate, eaten)_____ the hors d'oeuvres which were served on trays.

2. Samuel (sang, sung) _____ a very funny song accompanied by piano.

3. Joey, dressed in a gorilla suit, (fell, fallen) _____ down twice while reciting his poem.

4. Katelyn Dawn (stole, stolen) _____ the show when she sang "God Bless America."

5. Mark has (wrote, written) _____ a song to play on his saxophone.

6. The choir has (chose, chosen) _____ to sing a song that the director arranged.

7. They all (rose, risen) _____ together at the director's signal.

8. The audience has (gave, given) _____ Heather the loudest applause of all.

• Complete the chart below:

Present	Past	Past Participle
1. Bill *chooses*	chose	(has, have) *chosen*
2. Alexa *says*		(has, have)
3. Eva *speaks*		(has, have)
4. David *throws*		(has, have)
5. Monica *teaches*		(has, have)
6. Gwen *swims*		(has, have)
7. Cheryl *rides*		(has, have)
8. Thomas *writes*		(has, have)

                   Daily Learning Drills Grade 6

Name _____

Hats Off to You

Rule and Example

1. A singular subject takes a singular verb.
   Bill <u>washes</u> the dishes.

2. A plural subject takes a plural verb.
   They <u>watch</u> television.

3. A compound subject connected by **and**
   takes a plural verb.
   Mary and Bill <u>read</u> books.

4. For a compound subject connected by
   either/or or **neither/nor**, the verb agrees
   with the subject closer to it.
   *Either my aunt or my uncle <u>takes</u> us
   to games.*
   *Neither my grandfather nor my
   grandmothers <u>are</u> over 85 years old.*

5. A singular indefinite pronoun as the subject
   takes a singular verb. (anybody, anyone,
   everybody, everyone, no one, somebody,
   someone, something)
   Everyone <u>enjoys</u> games.

Exercise
Write the correct present tense form of each verb on the line. Write the
number of the rule that was followed after the sentence.

1. Everyone _____ wearing interesting hats. (enjoy) ____

2. Many people _____ hats for various activities. (wear) ____

3. One factory _____ only felt hats. (make) ____

4. The coney, rabbit, and hare _____ the fur for felt hats. (furnish) ____

5. Either England or Scotland _____ the fur to the U.S. (ship) ____

6. Neither the fur of the squirrel nor the chipmunk _____ the best felt hats.
   (make) ____

7. Either bamboo grass or the leaves of a pine tree _____ wonderful straw
   hats. (make) ____

8. Someone _____ to wear straw hats. (prefer) ____

9. Factories _____ straw hats, too. (produce) ____

10. Somebody _____ the straw material. (braid) ____

11. Either machines or a worker _____ the braided material. (bleach) ____

12. Chemicals and gelatins _____ straw hats. (stiffen) ____

13. Ironing _____ the hat-making process. (finish) ____

14. Everybody sometimes _____ hats that are interesting. (see) ____

Name _____

The Ball Bounces

Rule and Example   A verb must agree with the noun or pronoun in the subject part of the sentence.

- **Singular nouns** take **singular verbs**.
  *The **dog runs**.*

- A **collective noun** usually uses a singular verb.
  *The **crowd laughs**.*

- **Plural nouns** take **plural verbs**.
  *The **girls work**.*
  *The **children play**.*

- The verb **be** is treated differently.

I am.	*You are.*	*He is.*
I was.	*You were.*	*He was.*
We are.	*They are.*	
We were.	*They were.*	

Exercise   Read the sentences below. Then underline the subject and circle the correct verb. Write **S** in the blank if the subject is singular. Write **P** if it is plural. Write **C** if it is collective.

1. _____   The boys (is, are) members of the hockey team.
2. _____   They (practice, practices) daily during hockey season.
3. _____   The quarterback (pass, passes) the ball to the wide receiver.
4. _____   The girls' team (play, plays) hard every Saturday morning.
5. _____   You (was, were) lucky to be able to see that terrific game.
6. _____   Tired runners (race, races) across the finish line.
7. _____   The crowd (stand, stands) up for the national anthem.
8. _____   The skiers (finish, finishes) the slalom run in record time.

- Fill in the blank with the singular or plural form of the verb. Then complete the sentence.

1. I _____ (am, are) _____

2. Players _____ (try, tries) _____

3. The skier _____ (race, races) _____

4. We _____ (is, are) _____

5. The cats _____ (hisses, hiss) _____

6. The team _____ (plays, play) _____

7. Henry _____ (laughs, laugh) _____

8. You _____ (is, are) _____

Name _____

Spaghetti and Meatballs

Rule A **subject complement** is a word which follows a linking verb and refers to the subject of the sentence. Adjectives, nouns, and pronouns can be used as subject complements.
Remember: Linking verbs do not show action.

Example The papaya is a fruit grown in the tropics.
          ↑   ↑   ↑
      subject linking noun
              verb complement

That turkey was the smallest one on the counter.
   ↑   ↑   ↑
 subject linking   pronoun
        verb   complement

The food-tasting party seemed successful.
          ↑   ↑   ↑
      subject linking adjective
             verb complement

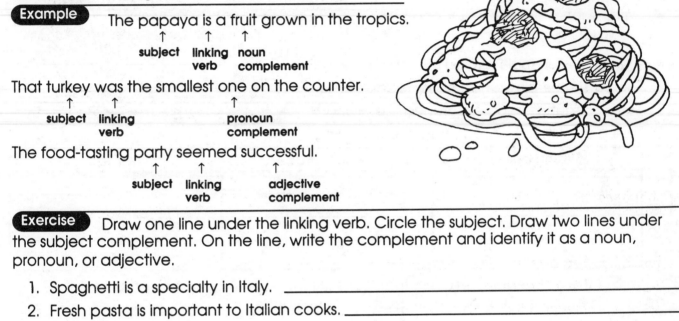

Exercise Draw one line under the linking verb. Circle the subject. Draw two lines under the subject complement. On the line, write the complement and identify it as a noun, pronoun, or adjective.

1. Spaghetti is a specialty in Italy. _____
2. Fresh pasta is important to Italian cooks. _____
3. The pasta pot is hers. _____
4. The tomatoes look fresh today. _____
5. Fresh oregano and garlic are necessary for the sauce. _____
6. The spaghetti sauce tastes delicious after simmering for hours. _____
7. Their favorite dish is spaghetti. _____
8. The dinner looks wonderful. _____

• Complete the following sentences with adjectives as subject complements. Underline the subject and circle the linking verb.

1. The freshly baked bread smelled _____
2. The pickles tasted _____
3. The famous chef is _____
4. The saltine crackers were _____
5. The Swiss chocolate cake appeared _____
6. That recipe looks _____
7. Each meal at her house seems _____
8. The table setting was _____

Name _____

The Cute, Little Clown

Rule Adjectives modify nouns or pronouns. Adjectives answer these questions: **Which one? What kind? How many?**

Exercise

- Underline the adjectives in the four sentences below.
- Circle the nouns they modify.
- Write each adjective in the chart under the question it answers about the noun.

1. One graceful eagle circled overhead.
2. The cute, little clown had a big, reddish nose.
3. Several excited people watched the game.
4. That black kitten jumped at the moving string.

	Which one?	What kind?	How many?
1.			
2.			
3.			
4.			

- Underline the adjectives and circle the nouns they modify. Draw a box around the adjectives that are in the predicate part of the sentence.

1. The little country mouse was scared.
2. Her city cousin seemed braver.
3. The house cat appeared enormous.
4. Her country home is quiet and safe.
5. The spicy food here tastes delicious!
6. The happy mice are glad.

Rule Special forms of adjectives are used to show comparison. These are called the **comparative** and **superlative forms.** The comparative form is used to compare two nouns. The superlative is used to compare three or more nouns.

Example

*John rode his bike **faster** than Tom. (**comparative**)*
*Jean rode her bike the **fastest** of all. (**superlative**)*

Exercise Add **-er** or **-est** to make a comparison. Then write **C** for comparative or **S** for superlative in the box.

☐ 1. Mark ran the (long) _____ distance of all the runners in the race.

☐ 2. Josh is much (tall) _____ than Hank.

☐ 3. That apple I gave you is (red) _____ than mine.

☐ 4. The white house is the (close) _____ one to the playground of the three houses.

Name _____

A Glimpse at Gorillas

Rule Adverbs can show comparison. The **comparative** form of the adverb shows comparison between **two** actions. Use the suffix **-er** or the words **more** or **less** to form the comparative.

The **superlative** form of the adverb compares **three** or more actions. Use the suffix **-est** or the words **most** or **least** to form the superlative.

Some words have special forms for the comparative and the superlative.

Example

Adverb	Comparative	Superlative
high	higher	highest
sadly	more sadly	most sadly
politely	less politely	least politely
well	better	best
little	less	least

Exercise Underline the verb and circle the adverb that shows comparison. On the line, write if the adverb form is comparative or superlative.

1. The gorilla was the most feared of all the apes in the past. _____

2. More recently we have understood the gorilla's true nature. _____

3. People have enjoyed best the stories about gorillas. _____

4. For some time, we knew less about them than other primates. _____

5. However, men knew better than to try to fight them. _____

6. The males acted fiercer than the females. _____

7. Those brave explorers tried the hardest of all explorers to catch a glimpse of them.
_____

8. Some ventured closer to the gorilla's habitat than others. _____

9. Others behaved less adventurously than that. _____

• Rewrite each sentence twice. The first time, use the comparative form of the underlined adverb. The second time, use the superlative form.

1. The male gorilla ran <u>fast</u>. _____

_____

2. The baby swung <u>high</u> on the vines. _____

_____

3. That mother tended her baby <u>carefully</u>. _____

_____

4. The gorillas chattered <u>little</u> at night. _____

Name _____

Hawks Flying High

Rule In addition to modifying verbs, adverbs modify adjectives and other adverbs. The adverb strengthens or weakens the adjective or adverb it modifies.

Example

*I bought a **very** delicate figurine.*
(***Very*** *strengthens the adjective **delicate**.)*

*He skated across the ice **extremely** carefully.*
(***Extremely*** *strengthens the adverb carefully.)*

Exercise Underline each adverb that modifies an adjective or another adverb. Circle the word that is made stronger or weaker.

1. Hawks fly very quickly across the sky.
2. They have slightly rounded wings.
3. Hawks have thickly feathered heads and necks.
4. Their light-colored eyes give them a rather fierce look.
5. Hawks are seen quite often in many parts of the world.
6. When disturbed, they utter extremely piercing whistles.
7. Hawks have amazingly sharp eyesight.
8. The female hawks quite often are larger than the male hawks.
9. Their rather extensive diet includes most small mammals and birds.
10. Hawks are extremely private birds.
11. They prefer living in quite secluded nests.

• Add an adverb to modify each adjective or adverb.

1. _____ beautiful hawk   4. _____ heavily
2. _____ rough nest   5. _____ cleverly
3. _____ helpless chick   6. _____ carefully

• Use each phrase in a sentence of your own.

1. _____
2. _____
3. _____
4. _____
5. _____
6. _____

Name _____

The Pond Scene

Rule **Adjectives** describe or modify nouns.
They tell **what kind, how many**, or **which one**.

Example a *tall* building (what kind)
three buildings (how many)
that building (which one)

Rule **Adverbs** usually describe or modify
verbs. They tell **how, when**, or **where** the action
of a verb is performed.

Example He ran *quickly*. (how)
He ran *today*. (when)
He ran *away*. (where)

Exercise Circle the adjectives and underline the adverbs. In the blank, write what each one tells about the noun or verb it modifies.

1. a fast sailboat _____
2. rapidly blinked _____
3. ran outside_____
4. the speckled egg_____
5. seven tailors _____
6. discussed later _____
7. that rose _____
8. quickly covered _____
9. a clumsy step _____
10. played again _____
11. four kittens _____
12. fell forward _____
13. woke early _____
14. the tired worker _____
15. several pages _____
16. softly whistled _____
17. hidden nearby _____
18. a sporty car _____

• Rewrite each sentence adding an adjective and an adverb. Circle all of the adjectives and underline all of the adverbs in the new sentences.

1. The pond melted in the sunshine. _____

2. Frogs croaked while sitting on the lily pads. _____

3. Birds warbled in the trees. _____

4. A robin searched for a twig. _____

5. Turtles sunned themselves on the rocks. _____

6. Ducklings waddled behind their mother. _____

Name _____

Anyone Want a Legume?

Rule A **prepositional phrase** is a group of words that begins with a preposition and ends with a noun or pronoun. It can act as an adjective or adverb.

Example *Pineapple is also grown **outside of Hawaii.** (adverb)*
*The sandwiches **with the peanut butter** were the best ones. (adjective)*
*We ate the peanut butter sandwiches **at night.** (adverb)*

Exercise Underline the prepositional phrase in each sentence.

1. Peanuts are enjoyed around the world.
2. Peanuts are native to South America.
3. Peanut pods develop beneath the ground.
4. The pegs, which are the pod stems, push their way under the soil.
5. In the southern United States, people enjoy eating boiled peanuts.
6. Peanuts are part of the legume family.
7. Most peanuts are grown in Africa and Asia.
8. Do you grow peanuts in your garden?

• Tell whether each prepositional phrase acts as an **adjective** or an **adverb**.

1. Wait until choir practice is over to eat peanut butter. _____
2. Peanut butter on a spoon is a delicious and quick snack. _____
3. Have you ever enjoyed celery with peanut butter and raisins? _____
4. Peanuts are a favorite treat across the United States. _____
5. Try your peanut butter sandwich with cold milk. _____
6. Roasted peanuts in a shell are my favorite! _____
7. I love peanut butter on toast. _____
8. I enjoy eating peanuts at a ball game. _____

Name _____

Who's the Party For?

Rule   **Who** generally is used as a subject.
Whom is used as an object.

Example

Who would like to organize the surprise party?

For *whom* will the party be given?

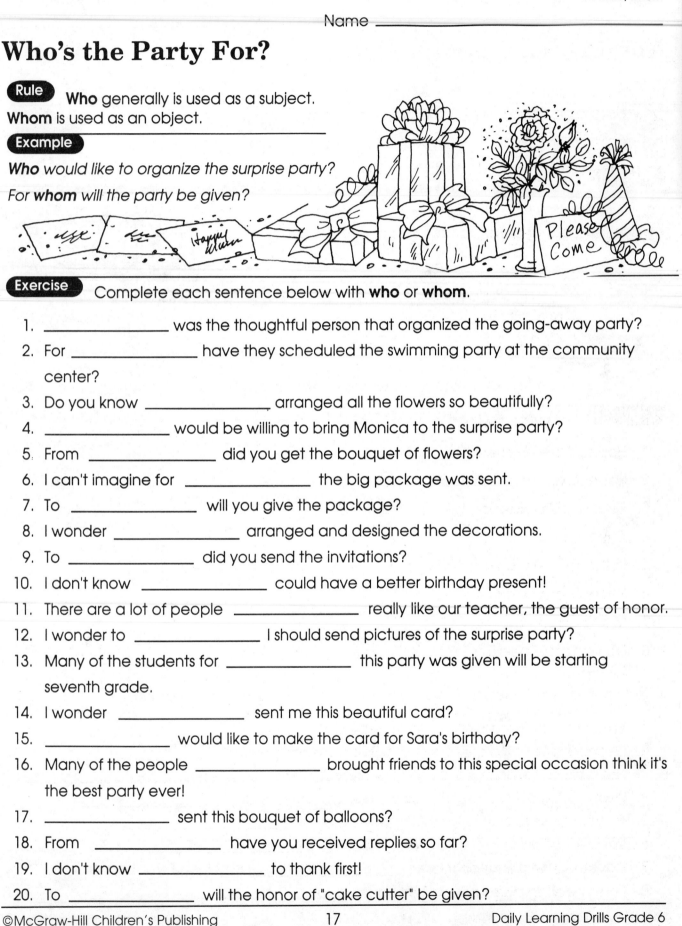

Exercise   Complete each sentence below with **who** or **whom**.

1. _____ was the thoughtful person that organized the going-away party?

2. For _____ have they scheduled the swimming party at the community center?

3. Do you know _____ arranged all the flowers so beautifully?

4. _____ would be willing to bring Monica to the surprise party?

5. From _____ did you get the bouquet of flowers?

6. I can't imagine for _____ the big package was sent.

7. To _____ will you give the package?

8. I wonder _____ arranged and designed the decorations.

9. To _____ did you send the invitations?

10. I don't know _____ could have a better birthday present!

11. There are a lot of people _____ really like our teacher, the guest of honor.

12. I wonder to _____ I should send pictures of the surprise party?

13. Many of the students for _____ this party was given will be starting seventh grade.

14. I wonder _____ sent me this beautiful card?

15. _____ would like to make the card for Sara's birthday?

16. Many of the people _____ brought friends to this special occasion think it's the best party ever!

17. _____ sent this bouquet of balloons?

18. From _____ have you received replies so far?

19. I don't know _____ to thank first!

20. To _____ will the honor of "cake cutter" be given?

Name _____

Don't Be So Negative!

Rule   Use only one negative word when you mean **no**.

Example

Incorrect: It **isn't** proper for **nobody** to use two negatives in one sentence.
(negative)   (negative)

Correct: It **isn't** proper for **anyone** to use two negatives in one sentence.
(negative)   (positive)

Incorrect: You **wouldn't** tell **nobody** to use two, would you?
(negative)   (negative)

Correct: You **wouldn't** tell **anybody** to use two, would you?
(negative)   (positive)

Exercise   Circle the correct word from the pair in parentheses.

1. I haven't (never, ever) heard a newscaster use double negatives.

2. There aren't (no, any) radio broadcasters in New York who use negatives incorrectly.

3. Didn't (anyone, no one) jump up and down when he or she heard me use negatives correctly?

4. Don't (ever, never) use double negatives when speaking to an audience.

5. Wasn't (no one, anyone) a little shocked to hear the speaker use double negatives?

6. There weren't (no, any) double negatives in his song.

7. We couldn't find (no one, anyone) who spoke improperly.

8. No one (nowhere, anywhere) heard the host use negatives improperly.

9. There wasn't a double negative (nowhere, anywhere) in the President's address to the nation.

• Rewrite each sentence, correcting the double negatives.

1. We haven't heard none of the guest speakers use improper negatives.

_____

2. Don't you never cringe when you hear someone use double negatives?

_____

3. I couldn't tell nobody that I used to use double negatives when I was young.

     Daily Learning Drills Grade 6

Name _____

Aviator Firsts

Rule A noun, noun phrase, or pronoun that follows a noun and gives additional information about it is called an **appositive**. Use a comma before and after the appositive.

Example *John Prins, **a head mechanic**, worked on the plane.*
*Our flight instructor, **Mr. Lopez**, is very helpful.*

Exercise Place **X's** in front of the sentences that contain appositives. Add commas as needed.

_____ 1. Amelia Earhart a brave woman flier made her first flight from Newfoundland to Wales.

_____ 2. She was accompanied by two other people on this eventful flight.

_____ 3. In 1932, Amelia Earhart the first woman to fly across the Atlantic Ocean alone flew from Newfoundland to Ireland.

_____ 4. Five years later Amelia one of the greatest female pilots started a flight around the world.

_____ 5. Amelia Earhart and her navigator were flying toward Howland Island a tiny island in the Pacific Ocean when they disappeared.

_____ 6. No one knows what happened to this courageous pilot, the plane, or her navigator.

_____ 7. Charles Lindbergh an American aviator was the first man to fly solo non-stop across the Atlantic Ocean.

_____ 8. "Lucky Lindy" a nickname the press gave him was suddenly famous in both America and Europe.

_____ 9. Lindbergh took off in his plane the *Spirit of St. Louis.*

_____ 10. He taught his wife Anne Morrow Lindbergh to fly soon after they were married.

_____ 11. Lindbergh was criticized by many Americans when he campaigned against voluntary American involvement in World War II.

_____ 12. Lindbergh died of cancer in 1974 in his home on Maui one of the Hawaiian islands.

Name _____

The World of Books

Rule   Sometimes a word or phrase will interrupt the main thought of a sentence. It may be an added thought of the writer, or it may be a word or phrase used to make the meaning of the sentence clearer. These words or phrases are called **interrupters**. Use commas to separate interrupters from the rest of the sentence.

Example

*This book, **in my opinion,** is very exciting.*
*I would, **by the way,** recommend that author.*

Exercise   Place X's in front of the sentences that contain interrupters. Add commas as needed.

_____ 1. Robert Louis Stevenson was a Scottish writer of novels, poems, and essays.

_____ 2. He is however best remembered for *Treasure Island* and *A Child's Garden of Verses.*

_____ 3. Many people on the other hand remember him for his novel *Kidnapped.*

_____ 4. *The Strange Case of Dr. Jekyll and Mr. Hyde* was in my opinion one of his best books.

_____ 5. A.A. Milne of course is an English writer of children's stories.

_____ 6. He wrote for example *Winnie-the-Pooh* and *House at Pooh Corner.*

_____ 7. Most children have read something written by A.A. Milne.

_____ 8. Louisa May Alcott as a matter of fact is the author of *Little Women* and *Little Men.*

_____ 9. She also wrote another great book called *Jo's Boys.*

_____ 10. I think that *Little Women* is the most popular book for girls ever written.

_____ 11. Her books I believe were usually written about people she actually knew.

_____ 12. She wrote children's stories by the way as well as stories and articles that were for adults.

_____ 13. Did you know that she was born in 1832?

_____ 14. *Little Women* was published in 1868.

Name _____

The Slow Turtle

Combine the sentences in each group by adding an important word or two to the first sentence. Change the form of a word when necessary.

Example: The turtle moved through the grass. It was <u>slow</u>.
The turtle moved <u>slowly</u> through the grass.

The dog ran after the cat. The dog barked.

_____

Jason liked the bacon. It was crisp.

_____

It is hard to hear the phone. It rings softly.

_____

The door needs oil. It creaks.

_____

Sheila's hand was cut. It was broken.

_____

They chopped down the tree. It was an accident.

_____

Jane stopped the ball with her arm. Her arm already had a bruise.

_____

The police car raced around the corner. It sped.

_____

The ball rolled under the car. The ball was blue. The car was moving.

_____

The dog was asleep on the bed. He snores.

_____

The boy won first place in the science fair. He shows promise.

_____

The rainbow rose above the trees after the rain. It had lots of colors. The trees had damage.

_____

_____

The books have been counted. They have been dusted. They are rare.

_____

I will be at the park after school. I will skate.

_____

21

Name _____

Compound It!

Compound sentences contain two or more
independent clauses and are joined together
with such words as *and*, *but*, and *since*.

Write compound sentences by adding endings to
the sentences begun below.

We will eat now since _____

The boys played soccer, and _____

Ted wanted to go to the movies, but _____

Our class received a letter, and _____

Bill will play the violin, or _____

The scouts raised over $100, and _____

The girls went to recess, but _____

Paint was tracked everywhere, and _____

Computers are fun, but _____

We put our books away since _____

The cats tore the curtains, and _____

We had to have the door repaired, or _____

The morning had been pleasant since _____

The trees need trimming, or _____

Write compound sentences by writing beginnings for the partial sentences
below.

_____ since the water is so high.

_____ and lemons cost twenty-five cents.

_____ but it rained all day.

_____ but the fire kept us warm.

_____ since we just came back from vacation.

_____ and the baby slept all day.

_____ or the grass will die.

_____ but she did not ask me.

_____ and he forgot his homework.

_____ or weeds will take over.

_____ since the boys threw the yarn away.

_____ but the door was left open.

_____ and we had three pieces of cake.

_____ but no one answered our call.

Name _____

The Girl Raced Home

Some verbs create more vivid pictures than others.
Patty raced home after school to see Grandma creates a
better mental picture than Patty ran home after school to
see Grandma.

Substitute the verbs in the sentences below. Rewrite each sentence using a
verb that is more descriptive of the action.

The girls held their dolls when they jumped over the rocks.

_____

Claire put her purse in the locker just to be safe.

_____

The bee went past my ear. _____

Thunder sounded in the distance. _____

We made beaded jewelry. _____

Brooke loved chocolate candy. _____

Miss Jones said what to study for the test. _____

The children went down the hill like a herd of elephants. _____

_____

Mother put butter on the bread. _____

The skaters skated around the rink. _____

Some adjectives create more vivid pictures than others.

Substitute the adjectives in the sentences below. Rewrite each sentence using
a more descriptive adjective.

The team was happy after they won the tournament.

_____

The big man weighed over 300 pounds.

_____

Everyone was tired after the hike.

_____

The shaking dog hid under the bed during the storm.

_____

We planned a picnic on a nice day.

_____

The kite soared in the good wind.

_____

Name _____

She's a Real Gem!

A metaphor is a comparison between two unlike things. One thing is called the other, although it is not.
My friend is <u>a gem</u>.

Rewrite the sentences below. Change the underlined words to metaphors.

1. The trees formed <u>shade</u> for the forest's floor.

   _____

2. The rain was <u>noisy</u> against the window pane.

   _____

3. <u>Herds</u> were driven into the cattle cars.

   _____

4. The <u>sunset</u> is pretty. _____

5. The kitten is <u>soft</u>. _____

6. A <u>rainbow</u> appeared after the storm.

   _____

7. The sidewalks are <u>so</u> <u>hot</u> from the heat wave.

   _____

8. Although the bed was <u>lumpy</u>, I fell asleep.

   _____

9. <u>Clouds</u> formed before the storm.

   _____

10. Al is <u>an</u> <u>important</u> <u>person</u> on the City Council.

    _____

11. The girl's eyes were <u>shiny</u>. _____

12. The shadow cast a <u>mark</u> on the ground.

    _____

13. The sun's rays are <u>pleasant</u> after days of rain.

    _____

14. The highway was <u>slick</u>. _____

15. The orange house was <u>bright</u> in the neighborhood.

    _____

16. Tammy was <u>silly</u> to eat four candy bars in two minutes.

Name _____

Swimming in Butter

Two writing techniques that catch the attention of the reader and emphasize a point are alliteration and hyperboles. Alliteration is the repetition of the same sound at the beginning of several words in a sentence.

> She says Sally seems silly.

A hyperbole is an exaggeration. It is similar to a metaphor because one thing may be called another or said to perform an act of which it is incapable.

> The basketball player was so tall he touched the top of the Empire State Building.

Write ten sentences using alliteration. At least three words next to each other must begin with the same letter and create a feeling or mental picture.

_____
_____
_____
_____
_____
_____
_____
_____
_____
_____

Complete each sentence by using a hyperbole or an exaggeration.

There is so much snow that

_____

Her nails were so long

_____

While we waited for John to finish

_____

Mike was so mad

_____

Water in the basement rose

_____

Name _____

Parachutes Floating Down

A sentence fragment is a group of words that do not contain both a subject and a predicate.

Some sentence fragments are sentences that are punctuated incorrectly.

Rewrite the sentence fragments and the sentences below making the necessary corrections.

1. Coughed for two hours before falling asleep.

   _____

2. Dolphins are graceful swimmers. In the zoo's show.

   _____

3. To do laundry every night.

   _____

4. The car with a huge dent was hit. From behind by a huge truck.

   _____

5. Overturned the bowl filled with whipping cream.

   _____

6. Behind the closet door very quietly.

   _____

7. The herds of cattle into the corral.

   _____

8. The road to Chicago is under repair. Between South Bend and Gary, Indiana.

   _____

9. The skier broke his own record. At the slalom races in Utah.

   _____

10. After dinner we rode bikes. Up the hill to see the sunset.

    _____

11. The string of beads on the ground.

    _____

12. Promised Cathy and me ice cream for dessert.

    _____

13. Walking along the side of the road.

    _____

Name _____

"Variety Is the Spice of Life"

Writing is more interesting when sentences are written in different ways. Sentences may be short or long, begin with phrases or clauses, change their order or be of different kinds.

Rewrite the paragraphs below. Divide some sentences. Combine others or their subjects and verbs. Vary their beginnings. Use different kinds of sentences.

My sister broke her leg playing soccer. She was playing center. She was in a tournament. She tripped over the ball when she tried to trap the ball and fell to the ground immediately. An ambulance came and an ambulance had on its siren and she went away in the ambulance.

_____
_____
_____
_____
_____

The school year was about to begin. I had to get ready for it. Mother took me to the store. I had to get a notebook. I had to get paper. I had to get pens with blue ink and pencils with erasers. I saw my friends at the store. They were getting ready for school too.

_____
_____
_____
_____

Jamie's mother got a new car. It was a good-looking one. The car was bright red and it had a sun roof and it had a stereo and it could go fast. It had four speeds forward. Jamie could not give anyone a lift there were only two seats. Jamie was not old enough to drive. He sat in the second seat next to his Mom.

_____
_____
_____

Name _____

What's the Idea?

A topic sentence is usually the first sentence in a paragraph. It states the paragraph's main idea.

Tell what the main idea of each paragraph will be from each topic sentence below.

The dog looked skinny and tired. _____

The formal dinner began with soup. _____

Oranges are round and bananas are long. _____

Our word for today is "outrageous." _____

The school day begins at 8:45. _____

I did homework for three hours last night. _____

Jason was elected class president by one vote. _____

America has many national parks in the west. _____

We got Rex from the animal shelter. _____

The ground was covered with forty inches of snow. _____

The farmers are harvesting their crops. _____

Politicians do not always do as they promise. _____

The new boy did not like his new school. _____

The robin built her nest on the windowsill. _____

Write a topic sentence for each main idea below.

homesick _____

_____

polka-dots _____

_____

made in America _____

_____

cats as pets _____

_____

a safe environment _____

_____

pioneering spirit _____

_____

a nightmare _____

_____

late for school _____

_____

Name _____

Eek!

Write some descriptive or sensory words and phrases that:

1) describe a person's feelings. _____

_____

2) describe sounds. _____

_____

3) describe how different foods can taste. _____

4) describe how an object can feel to the touch. _____

5) describe how something can smell. _____

_____

Write sensory words and phrases that describe each of the
following situations.

a new student with no friends _____

_____

stepping barefoot on a piece of calves liver _____

_____

riding a bus in a city during rush hour _____

_____

making popcorn _____

_____

Write a topic sentence for each above situation.

_____

_____

_____

Rewrite one of the topic sentences below. Follow it with support sentences
with sensory details that will help create the feeling or mental picture of the
situation.

_____

_____

_____

Name _____

Mouth-Watering

Sensory images may be expressed in topic sentences. To express the images more clearly, sentences dealing with the senses support the topic sentences.

Example: When I opened the door, I knew Mother had been baking. The aroma of cinnamon drifted toward me. The house was warm from the oven's heat. When I ran to the kitchen, my mouth watered when I saw my favorite cookies cooling on the rack.

Write a topic sentence that creates a sensory image for each of the following situations. Follow it with three support sentences that involve the senses.

Camping by a river

_____
_____
_____
_____

Stuck in an elevator for five hours

_____
_____
_____
_____

Summer in a garden filled with hundreds of flowers

_____
_____
_____
_____

Being present when an earthquake occurred

_____
_____
_____
_____

Name _____

Paragraph Planning

It is best to plan a paragraph before you write it. Go through the steps on this page to write a well-organized paragraph.

Choose a subject.
Select it from the box or use one of your own. Write your choice on the line. _____
_____

A long creature
When I look up
The strange smell
A rainy day

List details about your subject. _____
_____
_____
_____

Write a topic sentence expressing the main idea about your subject. _____
_____
_____

Use the details you have written to write support sentences explaining or supporting the main idea.
_____
_____
_____
_____
_____

Read what you have written. If the paragraph will hold together better with a wrap-up sentence, write one.
_____
_____

Rewrite the sentences above in good paragraph form. Remember to indent the first line of the paragraph. Use correct punctuation.
_____
_____
_____
_____

Name _____

Time to Organize

Organize paragraphs in the following manner.

- Plan a strong opening sentence that introduces the topic you will be discussing in this paragraph.

- Select supporting details that add information to your opening sentence.

- Organize your details so that the most important are included and the least important can be left out. Edit (alone or with a partner) using the checklist at the bottom of the page.

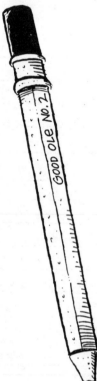

_____
(Title)

_____

_____

_____

_____

_____

_____

_____

_____

_____

Checklist:

Circle the correct answers and then edit if needed.

Does your paragraph have a topic sentence?	Yes	No
Does your paragraph have supporting details?	Yes	No
Did you use the most important details?	Yes	No
Have you checked for run-ons and fragments?	Yes	No
Did you indent the first sentence?	Yes	No
Did you use correct punctuation?	Yes	No

DON'T FORGET TO PUT A DENT IN THAT FIRST SENTENCE!

Name _____

Let Me Persuade You

A persuasive paragraph clearly states an opinion and backs it up with reasons. In a well-organized persuasive paragraph, the topic sentence lists the opinion. Sequence words introduce the sentences that support the opinion. A persuasive paragraph is stronger when the strongest reason is given last.

Write persuasive paragraphs for the topics below. Give four reasons for each.

Why you should look before you leap

_____

_____

_____

_____

_____

Why dog is man's best friend

_____

_____

_____

_____

_____

Why you can't tell a book by its cover

_____

_____

_____

_____

_____

Why he who hesitates is lost

_____

_____

_____

_____

_____

_____

Name _____

The Setting

Write the setting (where and when) for each of the following situations.

The dog wagged his tail as he cleaned the crumbs from under the table.

_____

Sally wrapped herself in another blanket and continued to watch a scary television program alone in the dark. _____

_____

When the clock chimed four times, the seniors started marching into the auditorium to receive their diplomas. _____

_____

Select one of the above settings. Write a paragraph about it. Describe what the place looked like and what sounds could be heard.

_____

_____

_____

_____

_____

Look at the picture below. Describe the setting. Do not describe it with a direct statement such as "The sun is shining." Use words that appeal to the senses.

_____

_____

_____

_____

_____

_____

_____

_____

_____

_____

Name _____

The Plot

The main part of a story is the plot. The plot usually has a problem. The characters in the story interact in the plot to solve the problem.

Listed below are some problems. Write one way each problem might be solved.

On its way home from a field trip, the sixth grade's bus broke down on a highway ten miles from the nearest exit. _____

_____

The new puppy chewed only shoes belonging to Dad, and only left shoes at that. _____

_____

The wind came up suddenly. The crowd on the beach saw the boat Tom and Dick were in capsize. _____

_____

A plot does not go directly from the problem to its solution. It begins with an introduction of the situation or problem and its characters. The middle part develops the situation and tells of the interactions of the characters in their attempts to solve the problem. Near the end of the interactions, the plot becomes most exciting. This is called the climax. It occurs just before the story's end and the solution.

Pick one of the problems from above. Write it. _____

_____

List some characters that could be involved. Briefly describe each one.

_____

_____

List three ways the characters might interact trying to solve the problem. Make the third way the most interesting and exciting.

_____

_____

Write your solution. If the one from above fits, use it. If not, write a new one.

_____

     Daily Learning Drills Grade 6

Name _____

Character Development

An author needs to develop his or her characters so they are believable. In which of the paragraphs below, **A** or **B**, do you have a better image of what Penny is like?____ Why?_____

A. Penny arrived early at the Johnson's because it was her first time to sit for their little girl, Lori. Lori looked at Penny. She was tiny. Her hair was pulled back, and her constant smile made even her freckles sparkle. Lori asked Penny to play dolls with her.

B. Penny was sitting for the Johnson's little girl, Lori, for the first time. Lori looked at Penny. She looked friendly. Lori brought out her dolls and begin to play on the floor next to Penny.

Developing a character does not mean to just tell what he or she looks like, but also to create a feeling of what sort of person the character is. Adjectives are not the only way to describe a person. A picture of a character may be created through his or her actions.

Write words and actions that might be characteristic of the following:

a monster _____

_____

a young neighborhood child _____

_____

an old man_____

_____

a clown _____

_____

Select one of the above people, or one of your own choice. On the lines below, develop the character so that it has a recognizable image and personality.

_____

_____

_____

_____

_____

Name _____

Outlining

One way to get ready to write a report or story is to make an outline. Plan the content of the writing by paragraphs. The heading after each Roman numeral will become the topic sentence. The items after each letter tell something about the topic sentence. Notice the letter of the first word of each item after the Roman numerals and letters is capitalized, and the item is not a sentence itself.

Look at the outline for a paragraph about "Manners."

Manners
I. Behavior at school
  A. In the halls
  B. Lunch time
  C. Addressing staff

What is this paragraph about? _____
What details will be included in the paragraph? _____

Write a topic sentence for this paragraph. _____

Make a one paragraph outline for "The First Thing in the Morning."

The First Thing in the Morning

What will be the main idea of the subject?
I. _____
What should be included in the paragraph to support the main idea?
  A. _____
  B. _____
  C. _____
  D. _____

Use the outline to write a paragraph about "The First Thing in the Morning."

_____
_____
_____
_____
_____

Choose a topic from the list below. Circle your choice.

My Brother   The Neighbor's Dog   Sick on My Birthday
A Good Friend   Chewing Gum   My Last Vacation

Go on to the next page.

Outlining (cont.)

Write the topic you circled on the last page on the title line below. Write an outline for one paragraph about the topic.

_____

I. _____
   A. _____
   B. _____
   C. _____
   D. _____

Take the information from the outline and write a paragraph.

_____
_____
_____
_____
_____

Longer stories and reports are organized the same way. Each paragraph begins with a new Roman numeral.

Basketball

I. History of the game
   A. Inventor of game
   B. Where and when first played
   C. How first played
II. Changes over time
   A. Rules
   B. Equipment
III. Organization now
   A. College basketball
   B. Professional basketball
   C. Leagues

What is the first paragraph in this story going to be about?

_____
_____

The second paragraph?

_____
_____

The third paragraph?

_____
_____

Choose a topic from the list below. Circle it. Write an outline for at least a two or three paragraph story.

| Ghosts in the Attic | Yesterday | Building a Bird House |
| A Broken Arm | The Missing Boy | Computer Magic |

I. _____
   A. _____
   B. _____
   C. _____
II. _____
   A. _____

   B. _____
   C. _____
III. _____
   A. _____
   B. _____
   C. _____

Name _____

Common Proofreading Symbols

The following list of editing symbols may be kept in your writing folders. Refer to it when editing and proofing your writing drafts. Use this page to complete the activities on pages 42 and 43.

Symbol	Meaning	Example
∧	Insert	I heard the church bell ring.
_e_	Delete	She is the most prettiest girl.
stet	Let it stand	Mother has a very beautiful voice. stet
#	Add a space	What a hot day it is!
¶	New paragraph	Potatoes are a vegetable.
⌒	Close to one space	I will pay the bill.
⌣	Close up entirely	To night is my birthday party.
∼ tr	Transpose	Don't take taht book. tr
≡ cap	Capitalize	Labor day is a holiday. cap
/ lc	Make lowercase	My Father is a policeman.
⩘	Add a comma	Tigers, elephants, and whales
⊙	Add a period	Marcia ran for office ⊙
∨	Add an apostrophe	Mary's tapes
⧠ ⧠	Add quotation marks	Run for cover! Jane yelled.

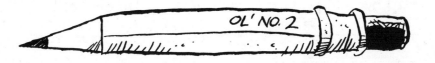

Name _____

Editing Practice

Make the necessary editorial corrections using proofreading symbols. Then copy each sentence correctly.

1. Since tomorrow is a Holiday, will we not have school

_____

2. To day we will see a video on the War Civil.

_____

3. have you checked for run ons and fragments?

_____

4. Pleese pass the   potatoes.

_____

5. Ann and Mary is bestest friends

_____

6. Theboys baseball team won the Middle school Tournament.

_____

7. I knew i shouldn't hvae threwn the base ball to you, said Sam?

_____

_____

Name _____

Be an Editor/Writer

Proofread this paragraph carefully. Make the necessary corrections using proofreading symbols. The first two corrections have been done for you.

u/(cap)/

It was a sunny friday morning at Green valley JuniorHigh. Al though the

first bell hda rang a school was arriving with the lastest bunch of noisey

students. mr. Smith, the french teacher, meet the students at the front

door saying put you're books in your Lockers and goto the

gymnasome. To day we are having a special _____ .

Fill in the blank above and continue the story.

_____

_____

_____

_____

_____

_____

_____

_____

Name _____

No Excuse!

MY HOMEWORK? WELL, UM, LIKE, I HAD IT ALL DONE WHEN THIS UFO LANDED IN MY BACKYARD... YEAH, THAT'S IT... AND MICHAEL JORDAN GOT OUT AND ASKED ME FOR MY BASEBALL GLOVE AND, LIKE, UH... YOU DON'T BELIEVE ME? ASK MY MOM!

No Homework Excuse

Do you remember the time you forgot or misplaced your homework? When you gave your excuse to your teacher, he/she may have said, "Sorry, but that's an *F*." Have you ever thought that perhaps your excuse wasn't creative enough or that you needed to give the explanation in a more believable way? Write a creative homework excuse. Tell it as though it really happened.

_____
(Title)

_____

_____

_____

_____

_____

_____

_____

_____

_____

_____

_____

_____

_____

Name _____

I'll Never Forget . . .

"Elephants never forget" is an old saying. What is it that you'll never forget? Could it be a vacation, or a party? Maybe it was a special gift you received, or the time you broke your arm. Tell about it.

I'LL NEVER FORGET MY 1ST PEANUT!

_____
(Title)

_____
_____
_____
_____
_____
_____
_____
_____
_____
_____
_____
_____
_____
_____
_____
_____

Name _____

Make Me Laugh

Everyone, both young and old, likes to laugh. Cartoons, comic strips, jokes, amusing stories, sitcoms, and funny incidents are some things that can prompt laughter. Describe something that made you laugh.

_____
(Title)

_____

_____

_____

_____

_____

_____

_____

_____

_____

_____

_____

_____

_____

Name _____

Free at Last!

It's Friday, the last day of school before semester break. Your locker is loaded with stuff, such as discarded papers, smelly sneakers, books, sports equipment, coats, and stale crackers.

Give each of the items in your locker a voice. What do they think and feel? How will they feel when you empty out your locker?

_____
(Title)

_____

_____

_____

_____

_____

_____

_____

_____

_____

_____

_____

_____

_____

_____

_____

_____

Name _____

Eight Is Enough!

Can you imagine having eight arms, like an octopus? Write about some sports, school activities, or household chores for which you wished you had the help of eight arms. How would the time you spend doing chores change? Could you do several homework assignments at once? Describe.

EIGHT ARMS TO PLAY EIGHT-BALL, DUDE!

POP

_____
(Title)

_____

_____

_____

_____

_____

_____

_____

_____

_____

_____

Travelin' Around

Name _____

Is there a state that you have always wanted to visit? Identify the state. Describe the attractions you've heard about in the state and tell why you would like to visit there.

_____
(Title)

_____
_____
_____
_____
_____
_____
_____
_____
_____
_____
_____
_____
_____
_____
_____
_____
_____

What's New at the Zoo?

A strange, new, never-before-seen animal
has been discovered. Describe this new
animal and the events surrounding its
capture. On the back of this paper draw
a picture of this animal.

_____
(Title)

_____

_____

_____

_____

_____

_____

_____

_____

_____

_____

_____

_____

Name _____

If Only They Could Talk . . .

From Gibraltar to Plymouth, rocks have an impressive history to relate. Have you ever wondered what incredible and fascinating facts we might learn if only rocks could talk and reveal to us what they've witnessed over the centuries?

Pick a rock! Study it carefully. Try to determine whether it is igneous, metamorphic, or sedimentary. Imagine how it might have gotten to the place where it was found. Then, write a story (myth or legend) from the rock's point of view which you will read to the class. Include the following:

A. Name of rock (personalize it)

B. Characteristics (human qualities)

C. The story of its journey from the past to the present.

Hint: Think about how the Native Americans personalized all things on the earth.

Writer's Guide

	Possible Points (teacher will determine)	Points Earned
The Written Work		
1. Rock origin (igneous, metamorphic, sedimentary) is identified in the opening paragraph.	_____	_____
2. The story (myth/legend) is told from the rock's point of view.	_____	_____
3. The rock has a name and characteristics (human qualities—personification).	_____	_____
4. The rock has a story (history) to tell.	_____	_____
The Presentation		
The reader speaks clearly and distinctly; makes eye contact; voice can be heard in back of room.	_____	_____
Total points possible	_____	_____

Name _____

News Spotlight

Use this page to spotlight a report, novel, story, poem, or news article.

Identify 5 or 6 facts from your story, poem, etc. that fit under the following clues (the 5 W's and 1 H).

Title: _____

_____

_____

_____

Who _____

What _____

When _____

Where _____

Why _____

_____

How _____

_____

_____

Now that you have the basics, write a brief news story. Be sure to include your clues, the 5 W's and 1 H.

Name _____

Work Wanted

_____
_____
_____
_____
_____
_____
_____
_____
_____
_____
_____
_____
_____
_____

Pretend you are an unemployed ghost, witch, or vampire.

You desperately need work! Write your own "Work Wanted" ad. You might mention that you are **hauntingly** dependable; can give well-known references that **date back** **hundreds of years**; are willing to **live in**; don't mind working the **graveyard** shift; and have been considered a **screaming** success in your past employment positions.

Characterization Through Poetry

The cinquain is a five-line poem that sets a mood or a feeling. It can also be used to zero in on a personality or character.

The Cinquain

Model

_____

_____ _____

_____ _____ _____

_____ _____ _____ _____

_____

Line 1: noun (perhaps a name)

Line 2: two words describing the noun

Line 3: three action words

Line 4:   four words about the noun (can be a phrase or sentence)

Line 5: one word referring back to first word (can be a synonym or antonym)

• Select a character of your choice and write a cinquain poem on the lines below.

Example:

Napoleon	Line 1: _____
Powerful, leader	Line 2: _____ _____
Orders, rules, deceives	Line 3: _____ _____ _____
Promised a better Life	Line 4: _____ _____ _____ _____
Pig!	Line 5: _____

The Acrostic

An acrostic poem forms a word that can be read vertically, while the horizontal lines relate more information about the vertical word.

• Select a character of your choice and write an acrostic poem on the lines below.

Example: *From the Adventures of Tom Sawyer*

___ _____

___ _____

Beauty   ___ _____

Exalted   ___ _____

Creates   ___ _____

Kindhearted   ___ _____

Youth   ___ _____

Name _____

Character Silhouette

Use with page 56.

Choose a personality from fiction, history, or contemporary society. Draw a "silhouette outline" of that person's head in the frame below. Then go on to page 56.

Name _____

Character Silhouette

Use with page 55.

On a scrap piece of paper, list some adjectives to describe the personality you chose on page 55. Cut out and/or draw pictures that reflect the adjectives you've chosen. Paste these in place inside the blank silhouette you have drawn on page 55. The

completed collage presents a **visual** characterization.

Then, in the space below, write a physical description of the character you have selected. Limit your writing to no more than 25 to 30 words.

Character's Name:_____

Adjectives:_____

Physical Description:_____

_____

_____

_____

_____

_____

_____

_____

_____

_____

_____

_____

Name _____

"Foot"-notes

Follow the directions to write "foot"-notes for a book review. Write each "foot"-note on enlarged copies of the "foot"-note supplied by your teacher.

"Foot"-note 1: Record your name, class, and teacher.
Write the book title, author, and genre on succeeding lines.

"Foot"-note 2: Choose one of the literary elements below that you believe is significant to your novel. Tell your reader why and how this particular element is important.

Plot	Setting	Characterization
Theme	Symbol	Point of View

"Foot"-note 3: Write an objective (no "I's") review of the novel.
Tell why it would, or would not, be good to read. For example, the book is good to read because it helps the reader better understand a historical event or character, or it is not good to read because it presents an outdated, or biased view of a subject; does not hold interest or does not fully develop characters.

"Foot"-note 4: Write about a subjective insight: relate it to yourself (use "I" messages).
Identify problems, solutions, activities, characters, behaviors, etc., that relate to you and your life.

Example: I can relate to this story because I, too, . . .
have a stepmother.
argue with my _____ .
have _____ without thinking it through first.

"Foot"-note 5: Would you recommend this novel to others?
Briefly explain the rationale behind your answer.

On the back side of "Foot"-note 5, rate your book . . .
✓ ✓ ✓ = Excellent; ✓ ✓ = Good; ✓ = Okay; **X** = Don't recommend

Note to teacher: Supply each student with five enlarged copies of the footnote shown here.

Book Reporting Think Sheet

While reading a mystery book, think like Sherlock.

Title _____ **Author** _____

Identify the mystery. _____
_____
_____

List the facts. _____
_____
_____
_____

List the inferences you can make based on the facts.

Tell why you can make each of these inferences.

_____   _____
_____   _____
_____   _____
_____   _____

List the assumptions you can make based on the facts and inferences.

Tell why these assumptions are possible.

_____   _____
_____   _____
_____   _____

What conclusions can you draw from the information? _____
_____
_____
_____

Name _____

Book Report Interviews
Autobiography/Biography

For this activity you will work in pairs. Each of you are to read a different autobiography or biography. Then, in front of class, one person becomes the interviewer and the other person pretends to be the famous person the book is about. Switch roles when the first interview is complete. Conduct the interview using the following format.

GO AHEAD & TELL 'EM ALL ABOUT THE KING. THANK YOU, THANK YOU VERY MUCH.

- Prepare a list of questions for the interviewer to use when interviewing you as the famous person.

- Questions should cover these areas:
  a. the person's life before achieving greatness

  b. the event or achievement which brought success

  c. what the achievement meant to that person

  d. personal life, future plans, etc.

- The interviewer introduces the famous person with a brief statement. **Example:**

"Today we will be talking with Michael Jordan, former member of the Chicago Bulls basketball team."

or . . .

"Today we will be talking with Sally Ride, the United States' first female astronaut."

- Your list of questions and answers will be turned in to the teacher after the oral interviews have been completed.

- You will be graded on the quality of the questions you prepared for the interview and how well you answered them.

- You will also be graded on your role as an interviewer.

TODAY WE'RE TALKING WITH LARRY DUFFLEBAG, THE ONLY MAN TO EAT 57 PIZZAS IN A ROW!

Name _____

Science Fiction Book Report

Fill in the blanks on this page to write a report on a science fiction book.

1. List the title and author of your book. _____
_____

2. Name two major characters and give a brief description of each. Be sure to include both a physical and personality description. _____
_____
_____

3. Describe briefly how the book's setting differs from today's "real" world. _____
_____
_____

4. What circumstances and/or technology used in this book make it science fiction?
_____
_____

5. Do these circumstances or technology help the fictional world or do they create problems? Explain. _____
_____
_____

6. Is this fictional world a better place than the "real" world? Explain. _____
_____
_____

7. In your judgment, have the people or society of this fictional world truly advanced? Explain. _____
_____
_____

8. Summarize the plot in three sentences. _____
_____
_____
_____

A Delectable Winner!

I nominate _____ for the "Dessert Hall of Fame."
                        (dessert)

Think of your favorite dessert. List five descriptive adjectives that would help your reader see and taste your favorite dessert. Then, write a letter to the **Dessert Hall of Fame** nominating the dessert you believe is worthy to be included there. Check the writer's guide below to see what should be included in your letter.

Writer's Guide:		Points Possible	Points Earned
• Friendly letter format including date, salutation, body, and closing		**10 points**	_____
• Include five descriptive adjectives. Highlight or underline the adjectives.		**10 points**	_____
• Use of correct spelling, punctuation, capitalization, word placement, and legible writing		**5 points**	_____
	Total	**25 points**	_____
• Mouth-watering description and an accompanying visual	**Extra Credit**	**5 points**	_____

Name _____

A Letter Home

Pretend you are one of the historical personalities below, or choose one of your own. Write a letter home describing your situation or experiences. Follow the criteria listed below when writing the letter.

World History

Ulysses' Journey Home from Troy
Roman Legionnaire from Britain
Crew Member on the Niña
Londoner during the Plague

American History

Settler of Roanoke or Plymouth
Soldier at Valley Forge
Prospector during the Gold Rush
Soldier at Fort Sumter

Use the following criteria:

1. Heading—address and date historically accurate.

2. Letter must contain historically accurate information of the writer's experiences.

3. Age letters by staining with tea or weak coffee; use plain white paper, brown paper bag, or craft paper.

4. Fold, roll, seal, and/or stamp to fit the historical time period and writer's status.

5. Letter must be three-fourths to one full page in length.

6. Ballpoint pen **may not be used**. Use fountain pen or Flair™—blue or black ink.

   Pencil may be used in some cases. For example, a prospector during the Gold Rush probably did not have a pen. See your teacher for permission.

Dear Margo, Thar's gold in them thar hills!

Dear Earth, How's the weather?

Name _____

The Art of Cartooning

A picture is worth a thousand words! At least, that's how the saying goes. From the list of proverbs below, select one and cartoon it in your own creative style.

List of Proverbs

1. You can lead a horse to water but you can't make him drink.
2. A bird in the hand is worth two in the bush.
3. Don't count your chickens before they hatch.
4. A stitch in time saves nine.
5. Birds of a feather flock together.
6. The pen is mightier than the sword.
7. A penny saved is a penny earned.
8. The early bird catches the worm.
9. People who live in glass houses shouldn't throw stones.
10. Look before you leap.
11. Don't put all your eggs in one basket.
12. Your choice: _____
_____

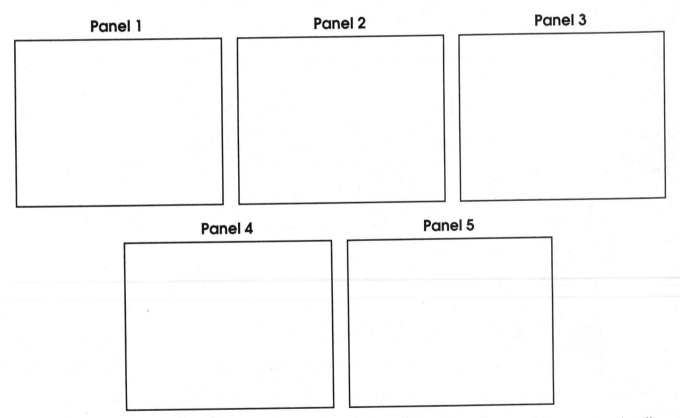

Panel 1

Panel 2

Panel 3

Panel 4

Panel 5

After cartooning a proverb, write a creative story illustrating its concept. You may not write the proverb in the title of the story. Your story should include the idea of the proverb. At the end of your story you may write out the proverb in parentheses.

Optional: Read your story in class and see how many students can correctly name the proverb it is illustrating.

Name _____

Facts and Opinions

Read the following.

Jessica and Suzanne were friends and lived two houses away from each other. They loved to solve mysteries and were members of the Mystery Solvers' Club. One Saturday afternoon, the day of the regular meeting, Suzanne went to her room at 2:00 p.m. to get her notes from the last meeting. She could not find her journal! The journal contained all the secret information about the club and all the notes from each of the cases the club had solved. Suzanne ran to the meeting place behind Jo's house at 505 West Dame Avenue. Suzanne proclaimed, "Someone has taken my journal! You must help me find it!"

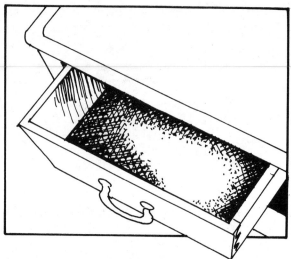

The club members were very concerned because they had not yet solved last week's case. They needed those notes. "Suzanne, tell us everything you know to help determine how the journal might have disappeared," Jessica said.

Suzanne replied, "I keep the journal in the drawer in the small table beside my bed. Last night while I was writing in it, I was also eating a roast beef sandwich. I can't remember much else except that I was very tired. I didn't think about it this morning, and I didn't check to make sure it was in the drawer, but I *almost* always put it there!"

Write down at least 5 facts from this story. Remember: Facts can be proven!

1. _____

2. _____

3. _____

4. _____

5. _____

Now, finish the story any way you want. Remember: The solution must be based on facts!

_____

_____

_____

_____

_____

Name _____

Which "Tells" the Real You?

A fact is a statement that can be proven. An opinion is a person's personal judgment or belief. A good sleuth must differentiate between the facts and opinions, or conjectures, in a case.

❑ My name is _____ .

If you wrote your real name, the one given to you at birth, then that statement is a fact; it is true and can be proven.

❑ I was born on _____ .

If you wrote your birth date as it is written on your birth certificate, then that too is a statement of fact; it is true and can be proven.

❑ _____ is the best month of the year in which to be born.

Whatever month you chose to write in the blank is simply your opinion. There is no way to prove that it is better to be born in one month than in another.

Create a time line of factual events in your life. Ask your parents about important events in your life and the date on which they occurred.

Use this sheet as a worksheet and then create your own time line on another sheet of paper. Include pictures, dates, etc.

_____

_____

_____

_____

_____

_____

_____

_____

_____

_____

_____

_____

_____

Name _____

What a Slithering Mess!

Miss Freed is upset. She and her friend Alice were planning to go to Guam, an island in the Pacific Ocean, for vacation next week. Miss Freed has decided she's not going. She just read that Guam has been overrun by nocturnal brown tree snakes.

Alice tells Miss Freed to relax. She says the snakes will probably disappear soon. But Miss Freed says this isn't so. She says that it is believed that the uninvited guests arrived in Guam as shipboard stowaways after World War II. She also tells Alice that these up-to-ten feet long snakes are mean and slightly poisonous. Alice listens attentively when Miss Freed tells her that the snake has no natural enemies. Alice realizes that if the snake has no enemies, then nothing is killing it. She begins to think she doesn't want to go to Guam either. She's not crazy about snakes.

Miss Freed goes on to tell her that millions of these snakes have decimated Guam wildlife and crawled into homes. That's enough for Alice. Hawaii sounds inviting now. Why didn't they plan to go there in the first place?

The last straw for Alice comes when Miss Freed says that in at least one area of Guam, the density of the snakes has reached about 30,000 per square mile! Alice is definitely not going to Guam. She figures that the approximate 130,000 Guamanians must be terribly outnumbered on their 209-square-mile island. She is not going to join them. Hawaii here they come!

Label.
1. Asia is northwest of Guam, and Australia is southwest of it. Label these on the map.
2. Label the Pacific Ocean.

Write.
Write what you would do to deal with these snakes under the title.

Create.
Create a math word problem using any facts found on this page.

Circle.
Circle the word on this page that means "active at night."

Write.
If you could be a stowaway on a ship, where would you go and why? _____
_____

•SOMETHING EXTRA•
The brown tree snakes have wiped out nine of twelve bird species and subspecies on Guam. Write about the effect this could have on the environment.

Name _____

The First Civilization

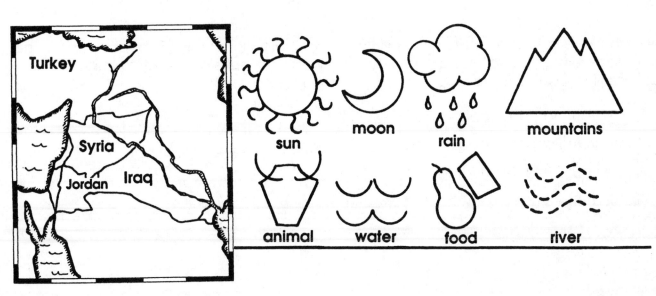

The first civilization developed in southern Mesopotamia in an area that became known as Sumer. The world's first cities were established here around 3500 B.C. This civilization flourished until about 2000 B.C.

1. Next to the title, write the word from the paragraph above that means "fared well."

2. Sumer was located in an area that is now southeastern Iraq. Color this area blue on the map.

3. The Sumerians invented the world's first writing system, which was basically a set of word pictures. Write a story on the back of this page using all of the symbols above.

4. Add three symbols of your own to the key above to represent three nouns in your story. Replace the words with the symbols.

5. Most Sumerians grew crops or raised livestock. On the map, draw one symbol to represent crops and one to represent livestock.

6. Several Sumerian cities grew into independent city-states. Write the definition for city-state under the map.

7. The more powerful Sumerian city-states conquered their neighbors and became small kingdoms. These kingdoms included Kish, Lagash, Umma, Ur, and Uruk. Write these names in the empty space under the symbols above.

8. During the 2300's B.C., Uruk controlled all of Sumer. Circle Uruk in the line above and under it write about how many years ago this occurred.

9. The Persians conquered Sumer in 539 B.C. Persia is another name for a country. Write its other name under the kingdoms.

10. The Sumerians built magnificent palaces and temples. Draw one on a piece of paper. Write about a day you spent in your palace or temple.

Name _____

Read Carefully!

One of the keys to success in life is the ability to follow directions. This is especially true in the area of test-taking. The following exercise is designed to check your ability to follow directions. Read all 12 items carefully before you begin the test.

1. Write your name in capital letters. _____

2. Write your first name backwards. _____

3. Write your middle name three times. _____

4. Look at the clock and write the correct time. _____

5. Draw a small circle within a circle.

6. Write one color your teacher is wearing today. _____

7. Write what type of shoes (sandal, tennis, etc.) you are wearing today. _____

8. Write your correct age. Include months and days. _____

9. Write the age you will be in the year 2000. _____

10. Draw a tulip.

11. Write the name of your favorite song. _____

12. Now that you have read all the directions, check to see if you wrote your name in the space at the top of the page and then write "I followed the directions!" above your name. Do not do any of the 11 other directions.

    Instead, turn this paper over and write directions to tie your shoes. Exchange directions with a friend and see if you can follow each other's directions.

Name _____

Island Adventure

Solving problems involves using prior knowledge or information already known. Gathering new information and asking pertinent questions are two other essential problem-solving techniques. Read the situation below and decide what information would be helpful for survival.

It took two hours for you and three of your friends to reach a group of uninhabited mountain islands off the coast of Lake Michigan. The small outboard rig hit a boulder and sprung a leak about 500 feet from the shore of the nearest island, which stretches half-a-mile wide and one mile long with plenty of lush vegetation. All of you swam ashore leaving behind everything but a plastic bag of sandwiches wrapped in foil. Tired and frightened, you realized you must take stock of the situation. You looked upward toward the clear sky and bright sun and noticed birds circling overhead. One of you spied footprints in the sand.

State some conclusions from the information provided in the paragraph.

1. _____
2. _____
3. _____
4. _____

Ask some questions to obtain more information.

1. _____
2. _____
3. _____
4. _____

What prior knowledge would be helpful in this situation?

1. _____
2. _____
3. _____
4. _____

State some sensible things to do.

1. _____
2. _____
3. _____
4. _____

Challenge!
State some creative things to do to be rescued. _____

_____

_____

Name _____

Atalanta and the Golden Apples

Many legends have come down to us from ancient Greece, but one of the best is about the remarkable Atalanta, a woman who was beautiful, strong, and fleet of foot.

When Atalanta was born, her father was disappointed, for he had wanted a son. So he took his daughter to a mountainside and left her to die. But Atalanta was discovered by a bear who nursed her and raised her. Later, kindly hunters adopted her and taught her the ways of humans.

As Atalanta grew, she became a strong fighter and a fast runner. In fact, she could run faster than any of the young men she met and could out-wrestle them as well. Because she was beautiful and wise, many men wanted to marry Atalanta. But Atalanta liked her life just as it was and did not want to be married. So she thought of a very clever plan. She announced she would marry the first man who could beat her in a foot race. And although her speed was famous throughout the country, many men came to race against her. But all failed to outrun the swift Atalanta.

Finally, a young man named Melanion challenged her. He was not as swift as many of the others, but he was smarter. From the end of the world, he had gotten three apples of pure gold, which no one could resist.

As the race started, Atalanta sprinted into the lead. Then Melanion rolled one of the golden apples ahead of her. Atalanta could not help stopping to pick it up, and by the time she had retrieved the apple, Melanion had caught up to her. The two runners were side by side for a moment. Then Atalanta took the lead again, and Melanion rolled the second apple. Again, Atalanta stopped to pick it up. Melanion used the last of his strength to take the lead. But when Atalanta saw Melanion ahead of her, she sprinted like the wind into the lead. Then Melanion rolled the last of the golden apples, and as Atalanta stooped to pick it up, she saw Melanion cross the finish line just ahead of her. True to her word, Atalanta married the clever Melanion, for she admired his spirit and wisdom.

Think About It
Do you think Atalanta and Melanion were happy together? Why or why not?

Atalanta and the Golden Apples (cont.)

Name _____

Main Idea
1. Choose another title for this story.

_____ The Race

_____ How Melanion Outsmarted Atalanta

_____ The Fastest Runner

Sequencing
2. Number the events below in the order that they happened.

_____ Kindly hunters adopted Atalanta.

_____ Melanion won by dropping the golden apples.

_____ Atalanta's father left her on a mountainside.

_____ Melanion challenged Atalanta to a race.

_____ Atalanta married Melanion.

_____ Atalanta announced she would marry the first man who could beat her in a foot race.

Reading for Details
3. Scan the story to answer these questions.

Who nursed Atalanta and raised her? _____

What plan did Atalanta think of to avoid marriage? _____

_____

Where did Melanion get the three golden apples? _____

When did Atalanta sprint like the wind? _____

Why did Atalanta marry Melanion? _____

Reading for Understanding
4. Check the correct answer(s).
Atalanta became a fast runner because she

_____ didn't weigh much.

_____ was strong.

_____ was raised in the wild.

She avoided marriage because she

_____ was happy with her life.

_____ didn't like men.

_____ was waiting for a bear.

She married Melanion because she

_____ said she would.

_____ liked him.

_____ admired his cleverness.

Name _____

Li Ching and the Rain Makers

According to Chinese legend, dragon-gods made the sky, the earth, and all the people and animals. The dragon-gods lived in splendid homes beyond the sky, where they were responsible for making rain. In this way, the dragon-gods were supposed to take care of the people on earth, but sometimes they needed help.

One day, a great scholar named Li Ching was hunting in the forest when he spotted a deer. Although he chased it for hours, it escaped him, and he found himself in a strange land. Night was coming, and Li Ching was lost. Through the rising mist he saw lights and followed them to a grand palace. His knock on the door was answered by a beautifully dressed woman. She took pity on Li Ching and said he could spend the night.

Li Ching had only been asleep for a few hours when someone woke him up. "You must help me," cried the woman. "My sons are the dragon rain makers. Tonight they were supposed to ride through the sky to make rain, but they cannot return from their travels in time to do so. Our masters will be displeased if there is no rain, for there has been a great drought." She gave Li Ching her sons' magic horse and a small jar. Li Ching was instructed to put one drop of water from the jar on the horse's mane at every cloud.

Li Ching mounted the horse, and it leaped into the air. At every cloud the horse stopped, and Li Ching shook one drop of water onto the horse's mane. The horse tossed its head, and the drop fell to the cloud below. All night they rode, stopping at every cloud, and in the morning they returned to the palace.

The mother of the dragon rain makers was waiting for Li Ching at the gate. "Thank you so much for helping," she said, as she handed him a small silk bag filled with pearls. Then she showed him a path that would lead him back to his village and bid him farewell. As Li Ching looked back, the lady and the palace vanished in the mist.

When Li Ching arrived home, his friends ran to meet him, talking of the great rain that had ended the long drought. Li Ching smiled, but said nothing.

Think About It
Why didn't Li Ching tell his friends what he had done?

Name _____

Li Ching and the Rain Makers (cont.)

Main Idea
1. This story explains

_____ how the dragon rain makers could not make rain.

_____ how Li Ching helped make the rain that ended the long drought.

_____ how Li Ching lost his way.

Sequencing
2. Number the events below in the order that they happened.

_____ Li Ching rode the horse all night long making the rain.

_____ His friends ran to meet him and told him about the great rain.

_____ Li Ching went hunting and got lost.

_____ Li Ching was given a bag of pearls for his help and shown the way home.

_____ He found a grand palace.

Reading for Details
3. Scan the story to answer these questions.

Who tells the legend about the dragon-gods? _____

What did the woman ask Li Ching to do? _____

Where was Li Ching instructed to put the drop of water? _____

_____

When did Li Ching return to the palace? _____

Why didn't the woman's sons make the rain? _____

_____

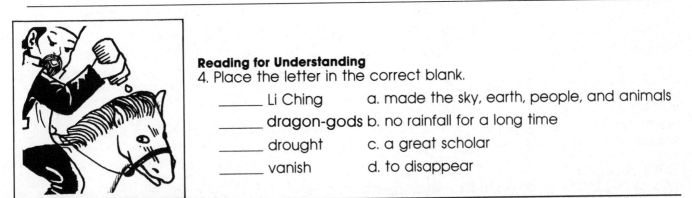

Reading for Understanding
4. Place the letter in the correct blank.

_____ Li Ching   a. made the sky, earth, people, and animals

_____ dragon-gods   b. no rainfall for a long time

_____ drought   c. a great scholar

_____ vanish   d. to disappear

Name _____

Rembrandt

Rembrandt was one of the greatest artists of all time. He was born on July 15, 1606, in Leiden, Holland. Rembrandt began painting at an early age. At the age of fifteen, he traveled to Amsterdam to study art. But he soon returned home to paint on his own.

Rembrandt's first paintings were of subjects from the Bible and from history. He used bright colors and glossy paints. These paintings were very popular, and soon, Rembrandt was well-known in his community.

In 1628, Rembrandt began to teach art. He was a respected teacher with many students.

In 1632, Rembrandt again moved to Amsterdam. He began painting portraits of many well-known people in Amsterdam. He soon became famous in Holland for his beautiful portraits.

In 1634, he married a wealthy and educated girl named Saskia. They moved into a large home where Rembrandt hung many of the paintings that he had collected.

Rembrandt continued to succeed as an artist. But tragedy began to strike his family. Three of his four children died at a very early age. And then in 1642, his wife, Saskia, died.

Rembrandt became very sad. He began to paint with darker colors. But, somehow, his painting grew even more beautiful. He used dark colors around the figures in his paintings. The figures themselves were painted as if a soft light were shining on them.

Rembrandt began to paint more for himself and less for other people. Although his work was brilliant, he was not able to make enough money to keep his house. In 1657, his house and his possessions were auctioned off. Rembrandt was bankrupt.

But until he died on October 4, 1669, Rembrandt continued to paint. His most famous painting was named "The Night Watch."

Rembrandt created over 600 paintings, 300 etchings and 1400 drawings. Some of his most fascinating paintings were the portraits which he painted of himself. The hundred self-portraits leave a remarkable record of his lifetime.

Check.

Rembrandt's first paintings were of subjects from the

☐ legends   ☐ history.
        and from
☐ Bible   ☐ myths.

Name _____

Rembrandt (cont.)

True or False

Rembrandt . . .

_____ was one of the greatest artists of all time.

_____ was born on July 15, 1606, in Florence, Italy.

_____ began painting at an early age.

_____ traveled to Amsterdam at the age of fifteen to study art.

_____ stayed in Amsterdam for thirteen years.

Check and write.

Rembrandt used ☐ soft ☐ bright colors and _____ paints.

Underline.

In 1634, Rembrandt married . . .

a wealthy and educated girl named Saskia.

a poor girl from Amsterdam named Saskia.

Check, write.

Although Rembrandt was successful as an artist,

☐ tragedy ☐ good fortune began to strike his family.

Three of his _____ children died at a very early age.

In 1642, ☐ Rembrandt's father died.

☐ Rembrandt's wife died.

Rembrandt's sadness caused him to use ☐ darker ☐ lighter colors.

Underline.

In 1657 . . .

Rembrandt sold his house and moved to Italy.

Rembrandt's house and possessions were auctioned off.

Check, circle, write.

Rembrandt was ☐ bankrupt. ☐ retired.

Rembrandt died on October 4, 1669. 1700.

Rembrandt's most famous painting was named _____.

Rembrandt's works included:

☐ paintings ☐ drawings

☐ etchings ☐ self-portraits

Name _____

Frederic Chopin

Frederic Chopin was one of the most brilliant composers for piano in history. During his life, Chopin wrote over 200 compositions for piano.

Chopin was born on February 22, 1810, in Warsaw, Poland. He began to take piano lessons at age six. By the time he was eight, he was performing in public. At the age of twelve, he was composing his own music. Chopin was considered to be a child prodigy—a child with an extraordinary talent.

For several years, Chopin traveled through the country performing his music. At one concert, the Czar of Russia was so thrilled with Chopin's music that he gave him a diamond and gold ring. Although Chopin enjoyed performing for large groups, he preferred playing for small groups in the homes of friends.

When Chopin was twenty years old, he left Poland and moved to Paris, France. When he left his home, friends gave him a silver goblet filled with Polish earth. Chopin kept this gift for the rest of his life.

Chopin's music was very popular in Paris. He became a well-known music teacher. It was while living in Paris that Chopin met two very important people in his life. One was Franz Liszt, another famous composer. Liszt and Chopin became friends and

shared their love of music.

It was Liszt who introduced Chopin to a woman named George Sand, a French writer. Sand and Chopin became dear friends. Many of his most famous compositions were inspired by their friendship.

In 1839, Chopin became ill with tuberculosis. Although he traveled to an island near Spain to rest, his condition worsened. Chopin somehow managed to continue to compose and perform his music for several years.

On October 17, 1849, Chopin died at the age of 39. Chopin's own music was played at his funeral. The Polish earth, which Chopin had brought from Poland almost twenty years before, was sprinkled on his grave.

Underline.

Frederic Chopin. . .

was one of the most brilliant composers for violin in history.

was one of the most brilliant composers for piano in history.

Frederic Chopin (cont.)

Circle and write.

Chopin wrote over   500 / 200   compositions for _____.

Chopin was born in   1810 / 1910   in Warsaw, _____.

Write.

Chopin was considered to be a child _____ .

Check.

The term "child prodigy" means:

☐ a child who likes music.

☐ a child with an extraordinary talent.

Write, circle, match.

At the age of twenty, Chopin left _____ and moved to _____ .

Friends gave Chopin a _____ goblet filled with _____ earth.

In Paris, Chopin became well-known as a   lecturer. / music teacher.

In Paris, Chopin met:

Franz Liszt   a French writer

George Sand   a famous composer

Many of Chopin's compositions were inspired by his friendship

with _____ .

Underline the sentence which tells what the Czar of Russia gave Chopin after his performance.

True or False

Chopin . . .

_____ became ill with tuberculosis in 1939.

_____ traveled to an island near Spain to rest.

_____ recovered and remained in good health for years.

_____ continued to compose for several years even though he was ill.

On October 17,   1849, / 1900,   Chopin died at the age of _____ .

Name _____

Arnold's Awful Antics

Arnold was up to his dirty tricks again. This time he really did it! Miss Freed was out sick, and the sixth graders had a substitute teacher, Miss Spencer. Poor unsuspecting Miss Spencer asked for a volunteer to write some information on the board for the class to copy. When Arnold raised his hand, Miss Spencer gave him the information. Arnold, as usual, messed things up for everyone. He wrote all the information on the board, but he wrote it out of order. Then, to be even meaner, he tore up the only copy of the information and threw it away!

Help Miss Spencer and the sixth graders write the information below in correct order so that they can learn about the history of baseball.

Also in the late 1800s, 1876 to be exact, the National League was founded. Ty Cobb, Christy Mathewson, Cy Young, and Babe Ruth were just a few of the many early, outstanding baseball players. About 24 years later, in 1900, the American League was founded. The two major leagues had some great players. Baseball first began in the mid-1800s in the eastern United States. In this modern era, the two major leagues were formed and most baseball rules were the same as today. Current outstanding players are Ozzie Smith and George Brett. Throughout the country, men were playing the game by the late 1800s. It was also in 1900 that the modern era of major league baseball began.

1. _____
2. _____
3. _____
4. _____
5. _____
6. _____
7. _____
8. _____
9. _____

Name _____

Anagrams

Write as many anagrams as you can on the lines below.

Example: peal-leap-plea-pale

1. trace _____
2. pots _____
3. nips _____
4. least _____
5. emits _____
6. scrape _____
7. cast _____
8. miles _____
9. tones _____
10. pets _____
11. ropes _____
12. read _____
13. eats _____
14. lame _____
15. meat _____
16. reteach _____
17. reaps _____

18. wets _____
19. cares _____
20. tries _____
21. hoes _____
22. wane _____
23. stake _____
24. naps _____
25. hams _____
26. dens _____
27. tear _____
28. tens _____
29. sprite _____
30. own _____
31. albs _____
32. dealer _____
33. tar _____
34. reread _____

Name _____

Forming Words Game

Make 30 new words from the letters in **PHYSICAL EDUCATION** and write them on the lines below. Use the scoring table to figure your points for each word and write that number beside the word.

Words	Points
1. _____	_____
2. _____	_____
3. _____	_____
4. _____	_____
5. _____	_____
6. _____	_____
7. _____	_____
8. _____	_____
9. _____	_____
10. _____	_____
11. _____	_____
12. _____	_____
13. _____	_____
14. _____	_____
15. _____	_____
16. _____	_____
17. _____	_____
18. _____	_____
19. _____	_____
20. _____	_____
21. _____	_____
22. _____	_____
23. _____	_____
24. _____	_____
25. _____	_____
26. _____	_____
27. _____	_____
28. _____	_____
29. _____	_____
30. _____	_____

Scoring
3-letter word = 1 point
4-letter word = 2 points
5-letter word = 3 points

Add 1 point for each letter over 5.

Total your points to see how you rate.

How do you rate?
over 120   = Excellent
100-120   = Good
80-99   = Fair
under 80   = Try Again

Your Score _____

Name _____

LANGUAGE ARTS

Word Squares

Word squares spell the same word both down and across. Fill in the word squares with words. Use the letters above each square.

Example:

S	O	W
O	N	E
W	E	T

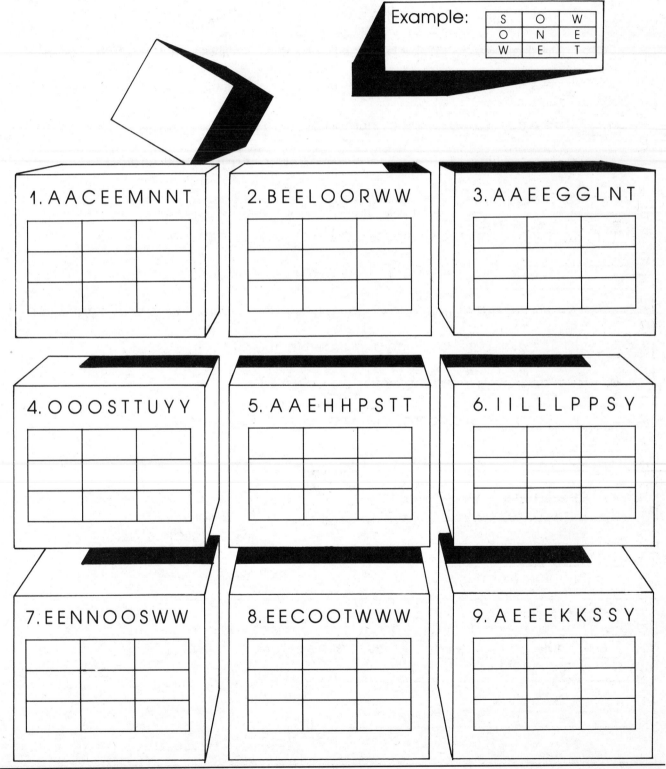

1. A A C E E M N N T

2. B E E L O O R W W

3. A A E E G G L N T

4. O O O S T T U Y Y

5. A A E H H P S T T

6. I I L L L P P S Y

7. E E N N O O S W W

8. E E C O O T W W W

9. A E E E K K S S Y

Name _____

Summer Daze

Write the number of the definition that defines each underlined word.

_____ 1. When Mr. Wong works, he never <u>putters</u> around.

_____ 2. Mabel would <u>cop</u> the prize as the best stickball player in the fifth grade.

_____ 3. The two small girls will <u>stalk</u> the tiger swallowtail very carefully.

_____ 4. The <u>cop</u> smiled as Shirley humbly scurried by.

_____ 5. I would wear gloves if I wished to climb that <u>spruce</u> in the forest.

_____ 6. The <u>putter</u> asked for complete silence as he sighted the ball.

_____ 7. Shirley imagined spiders <u>stalking</u> her in the furnace room.

_____ 8. She never considered that she might <u>cop</u> fruit from the market.

_____ 9. Will the students <u>spruce</u> up the playground before they leave for the summer?

_____ 10. The clan burned <u>spruce</u> and aspen for fuel.

_____ 11. The <u>putter</u> missed the ninth hole by a mile.

_____ 12. Shirley discovered that she liked celery <u>stalks</u> very much.

	Glossary		
stalk	1) a plant stem 2) to stealthily pursue one's prey 3) to walk with a slow, stiff stride	*putter*	1) a golf club used on the green 2) a golfer who putts 3) to work slowly
cop	1) to steal 2) to capture 3) a police officer	*spruce*	1) an evergreen tree 2) the wood from this tree 3) to make neat

Challenge: Make as many 4-, 5- and 6-letter words as you can from the diamond to the right. The letters must be adjacent, but you may return to a letter that you've already used.

```
            P
        S       O
     D     E       C
        L       A
            K
```

Name _____

It's All in the Word

Write a glossary entry for each of the words listed. First, indicate the origin of the word; second, write its definition; third, use the word correctly in an original sentence. Illustrate each glossary entry.

Example:

• *avenue* (Fr.)—a way of approach or departure; a wide roadway; thoroughfare. The avenue was bordered on both sides by tall, leafy oak trees.

1. chapeau _____
_____
_____
_____

2. poncho _____
_____
_____
_____

3. taco _____
_____
_____
_____

4. lariat _____
_____
_____
_____

Name _____

Name That Sleuth

A sleuth can be known by other names as well. Use a dictionary to look up the definitions that tell why a sleuth might be called one of the names below. Remember, find the definition that has something related to sleuth!

1. investigator _____
   _____

2. gumshoe _____

3. scout _____
   _____

4. mouser _____
   _____

5. nose _____
   _____

6. bloodhound _____

7. detective _____
   _____

Choose one of the words from above and make up a name for a sleuth that matches one of the nicknames. (Example: Ked Wriggly—Gumshoe)

_____

What might be his/her investigative specialty? _____

If you were a sleuth, which nickname would you choose for yourself? Why? _____

_____

_____

_____

Name _____

Match Them Up

Write the numbers in the blanks to match the words with their definitions.

_____ gabled   1. to move back and forth between two places

_____ refinery   2. heavy material used to keep a craft steady

_____ galleon   3. ferry boat

_____ leeward   4. a floating structure frequently used with others to support bridges

_____ veerboot   5. having a triangular wall formed where the top ends of a pitched roof meet

_____ pontoon   6. place where crude oil is made into gasoline

_____ ballast   7. the side sheltered from the wind

_____ shuttle   8. large, square-rigged sailing ship of long ago

For each problem below circle the letter of the sentence which uses the underlined word correctly.

1. a. The geese <u>gabled</u> near Fort Amsterdam.
   b. Henrik lived in a <u>gabled</u> blue house three streets away.

2. a. The <u>refinery</u> manufactured fuel for war planes.
   b. Mother could not purchase dresses of <u>refinery</u> on the island.

3. a. A tanker loaded with 40,000 <u>galleons</u> of crude oil was sunk by a German submarine.
   b. Spanish <u>galleons</u> once sailed the waters of the Schottegat.

4. a. My mom gave me a <u>leeward</u> glance when I told her I wouldn't leave Curacao.
   b. We sat on the <u>leeward</u> side of the ship.

5. a. The <u>veerboots</u> carried no cars that morning.
   b. Few ship workers would labor without wearing their waterproof <u>veerboots.</u>

6. a. The <u>pontoons</u> bobbed slightly in the waves as we drove up.
   b. The wood of the <u>pontoon</u> tree makes excellent lumber.

7. a. The <u>ballast</u> was so strong we returned to our cabin.
   b. Barrels of oil were used as the ship's <u>ballast.</u>

8. a. Crude oil was <u>shuttled</u> to Willemstad from the Venezuelan oil fields.
   b. The crew closed our ship's <u>shuttle</u> to prevent water damage.

Get Your Cue from the Clue

Add letters to each given word to make a new word. Use letters from the Letter Bank and the clues to help. The letter(s) may be added anywhere to make the new word.

Example:

clue	word		letter(s)		new word
burn at edges	sing	+	e	=	singe

Clue	Beginning Word	Amount of Letters to Add	New Word
surprise	sound	(2)	_____
a shallow pond connected to a larger body of water	loon	(2)	_____
to enjoy a pleasant feeling	ask	(1)	_____
in a royal manner	really	(1)	_____
to read carefully	ore	(1)	_____
to confuse	found	(3)	_____
carry	toe	(1)	_____
a distinct kind	spies	(2)	_____
tight	at	(2)	_____
document which gives exclusive rights	pen	(3)	_____
self-important	opus	(3)	_____
of a common cultural group	tic	(3)	_____
to rumple	use	(3)	_____
a list of court cases	doe	(3)	_____
illness	lay	(3)	_____
distant	rote	(2)	_____

Letter Bank
A A A A B C C C D E E E G G H K L M M M N N O O O P P T T T T T T U

Name _____

Word Stairs

Begin climbing the stairs with the word on the bottom step. Remove the letter that is on the side of the step and rearrange the remaining letters to form a new word. Keep going until you reach the top.

Example:

Name _____

Tagalong Wordsearch

Find the word in the wordsearch that is a **homonym** of the word in the word list. **Roe-row** has been done for you.

In tagalongs, the last letter of the word just found is the first letter of the word to be found.

Word List

roe	sale	rights	low	knit
wood	leek	seel	ore	two
dew	not	lyre	rale	oar
owe	there	wrap	loots	eery
hue	read	pane	see	you
wares	died	neigh	ale	el
seem	dynes	y'all	lone	
made	sheer			
deer	rain			
ruff	knew			
heal	weighs			
lead	steel			
daze	leech			
stares	herd			
site	doe			
tale	hose			
lode	some			
duel	male			
lien	lei			
knight	you're			
tax	raze			
sine	sew			
know	ode			
won	done			
ate	knave			
threw	air			
horse	rude			
urns	due			

T	A	C	K	S	W	E	A	R	S	E	A	M	A	I	D	L
V	H	G	I	C	E	O	D	L	U	O	~~W~~O~~R~~		E	E	E
E	I	G	H	T	H	R	O	U	G	H	S	Y	A	D	H	E
N	N	L	I	A	S	I	W	H	O	T	B	R	O	U	G	H
O	L	E	A	N	N	E	L	A	A	G	S	Y	A	W	N	Q
S	O	A	U	X	R	O	R	I	L	U	T	E	S	C	E	U
Y	W	K	U	J	A	S	R	A	A	I	E	R	E	I	G	N
A	E	N	Y	D	E	S	I	G	H	T	A	P	A	I	L	R
R	D	O	K	Y	E	Z	H	C	A	E	L	R	R	O	D	S
U	U	T	H	E	I	R	B	E	H	F	A	M	A	A	E	E
O	N	M	T	D	I	N	E	S	A	O	L	N	P	T	I	A
Y	F	A	U	L	L	E	W	E	I	R	E	W	I	A	E	L
A	A	I	V	S	E	O	H	G	U	O	D	R	A	T	I	O
D	I	L	S	E	R	R	O	O	D	E	W	L	O	Y	A	N

Name _____

Where Can I Find . . . ?

A smart sleuth knows that there is too much information in this world to learn everything. A very important skill to learn is how to locate information. The library is one of a sleuth's best friends. Knowing what reference materials are available, where they are located and how to use them are the skills every master sleuth must possess.

Write the best type of reference material you would use in order to answer each question.

telephone book	thesaurus	dictionary
biographical dictionary	encyclopedia	almanac
book of quotations	rhyming dictionary	atlas

1. Who was Sir Arthur Conan Doyle? _____

2. What is the definition of sleuth? _____

3. Was Sherlock Holmes a real person? _____

4. Are there any private investigators in your town? _____

5. Was it Holmes who said, "To be or not to be. That is the question"?

    _____

6. What are some other words for detective? _____

7. What nights of this month would be bright enough to look for clues (full moon)?

    _____

8. What is a good way to travel from London, England, to Dublin, Ireland?

    _____

    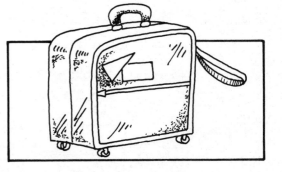

9. What are some words that rhyme with *sleuth*?

    _____

Now, on another paper, use the references you listed to answer the questions. Try another source if you cannot locate the information. Write down the reference used.

Name _____

It's a Record!

Use the *Guinness Book of World Records* to answer the questions below.

1. How many grand slams did Don Mattingly hit in 1987? _____

2. Who has the record for base hits at 4,256? _____

3. What was the most home runs Babe Ruth scored in one season? _____

4. What pitcher has recorded the most no-hitters? _____

   How many no-hitters did he have? _____

5. What is the record attendance for a series in the World Series? _____

   What year was this? _____

6. Which pitcher has the only perfect game in World Series play? _____

   In what year was this perfect game? _____

7. What is Joe DiMaggio's longest hitting streak? _____

8. Who has the most lifetime home runs? _____

9. What Yankee slugger was known as "Mr. October" during the 1977 _____
   World Series?

10. What was the shortest nine-inning major league game? Teams: _____

    Date/Time: _____

11. What major league player had the smallest strike zone? _____

12. What pitcher won the most games in his career? _____

    How many did he win? _____

13. Who struck out the most batters in a single nine-inning game? _____

    How many batters did he strike out? _____

14. Who was the oldest player in major league baseball? _____

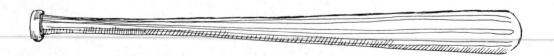

Name _____

Outrageous Outfits

Flaky Frannie the Fashion Consultant has a unique sense of style. Draw lines connecting the equivalent fractions to see the outfits Frannie has coordinated.

MATH

$= \dfrac{3}{7}$

$= \dfrac{15}{18}$

$= \dfrac{3}{10}$

$= \dfrac{35}{42}$

$= \dfrac{3}{8}$

$= \dfrac{10}{40}$

$= \dfrac{1}{4}$

$= \dfrac{17}{68}$

$= \dfrac{12}{32}$

$= \dfrac{21}{70}$

$= \dfrac{12}{28}$

$= \dfrac{35}{45}$

$= \dfrac{28}{36}$

$= \dfrac{7}{9}$

$= \dfrac{18}{42}$

$= \dfrac{18}{48}$

$= \dfrac{9}{30}$

$= \dfrac{5}{6}$

Name _____

Game, Set, Match

Match the improper fractions and the mixed numbers by drawing lines to those that are equivalent.

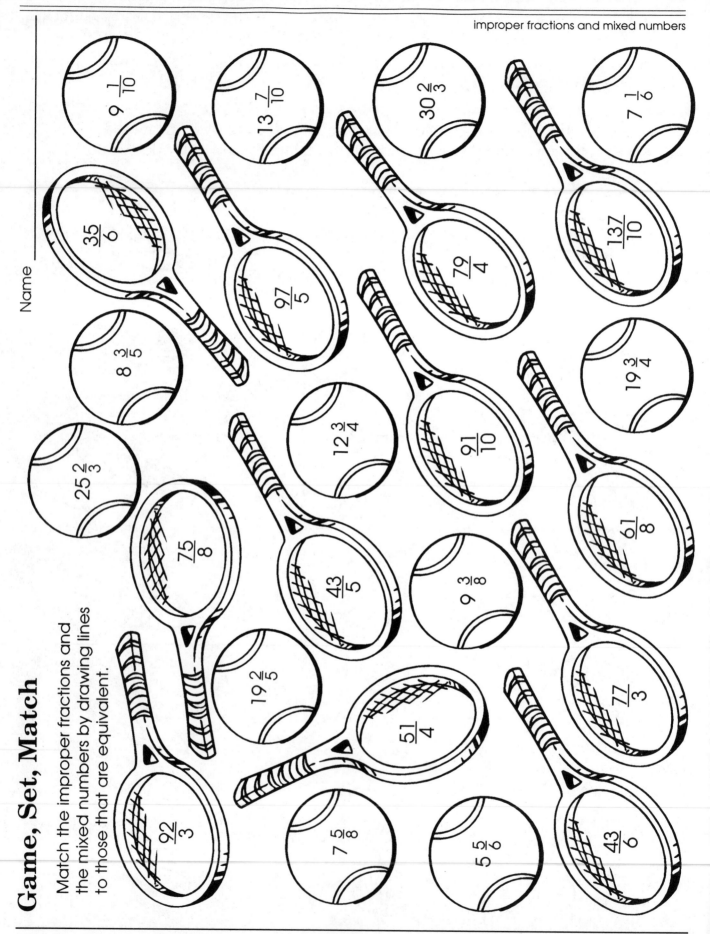

$9\frac{1}{10}$

$13\frac{7}{10}$

$30\frac{2}{3}$

$7\frac{1}{6}$

$\frac{35}{6}$

$\frac{97}{5}$

$\frac{79}{4}$

$\frac{137}{10}$

$8\frac{3}{5}$

$19\frac{3}{4}$

$25\frac{2}{3}$

$12\frac{3}{4}$

$\frac{91}{10}$

$\frac{75}{8}$

$\frac{43}{5}$

$9\frac{3}{8}$

$\frac{61}{8}$

$19\frac{2}{5}$

$\frac{51}{4}$

$77\frac{}{3}$

$\frac{92}{3}$

$7\frac{5}{8}$

$5\frac{5}{6}$

$\frac{43}{6}$

Name

Baby Faces

Draw the correct hair on the babies by finding the decimal for each fraction. Then, draw the correct mouths on the babies by finding the fraction for each decimal.

Name _____

Mountain-Climbing Madge

Help Madge the Mountain Climber find the easiest path to the top of the mountain by finding the LCM of the numbers in the trees and connecting them in order. Write the sum of the LCM's and put it on the line at the top of the mountain.

Name _____

Map Math

What is a mapmaker called? To find out, solve the following addition problems in the map and put the letter above the answer.

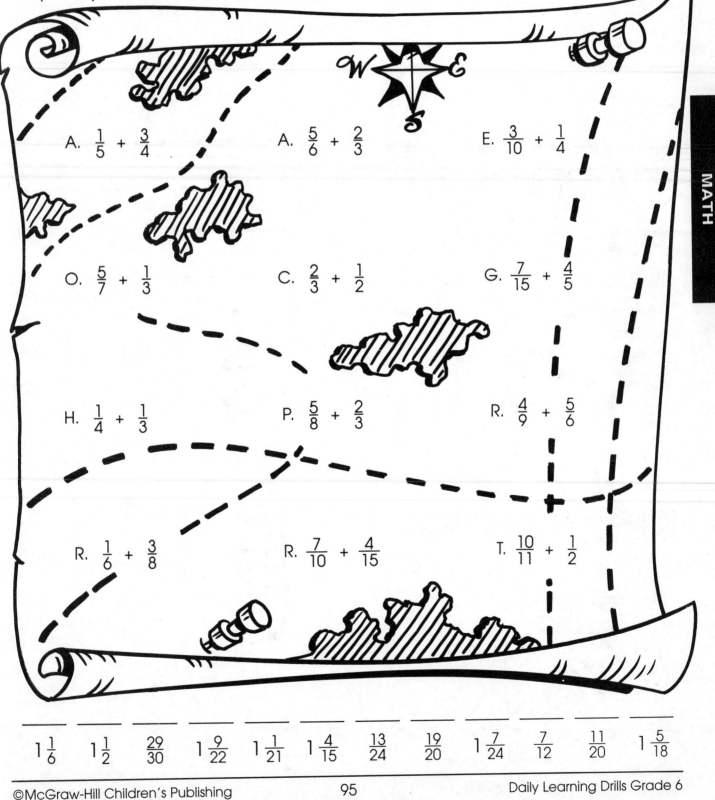

A. $\frac{1}{5} + \frac{3}{4}$ A. $\frac{5}{6} + \frac{2}{3}$ E. $\frac{3}{10} + \frac{1}{4}$

O. $\frac{5}{7} + \frac{1}{3}$ C. $\frac{2}{3} + \frac{1}{2}$ G. $\frac{7}{15} + \frac{4}{5}$

H. $\frac{1}{4} + \frac{1}{3}$ P. $\frac{5}{8} + \frac{2}{3}$ R. $\frac{4}{9} + \frac{5}{6}$

R. $\frac{1}{6} + \frac{3}{8}$ R. $\frac{7}{10} + \frac{4}{15}$ T. $\frac{10}{11} + \frac{1}{2}$

$1\frac{1}{6}$ $1\frac{1}{2}$ $\frac{29}{30}$ $1\frac{9}{22}$ $1\frac{1}{21}$ $1\frac{4}{15}$ $\frac{13}{24}$ $\frac{19}{20}$ $1\frac{7}{24}$ $\frac{7}{12}$ $\frac{11}{20}$ $1\frac{5}{18}$

Number Sentences

Name _____

Examine these number sentences.

$$\frac{9}{10} - \frac{2}{5} =$$

$$\frac{1}{4} - \frac{3}{16} =$$

$$- \frac{1}{8} =$$

$$\frac{1}{2} - \frac{7}{16} = \qquad - \frac{3}{8}$$

$$\frac{1}{6} \qquad \frac{9}{10} - \frac{3}{4} =$$

$$\frac{2}{3} - \frac{5}{12} =$$

Just "Great"

Work the problems. Use the answers to decode and say "great" in . . .

French

$\overline{1\frac{7}{10}}$ $\overline{1\frac{29}{40}}$ $\overline{4\frac{5}{6}}$ $\overline{9\frac{19}{70}}$

$\overline{17\frac{9}{16}}$ $\overline{41\frac{37}{56}}$ $\overline{2\frac{3}{4}}$ $\overline{3\frac{13}{15}}$

Chinese

$\overline{2\frac{9}{10}}$ $\overline{4\frac{3}{8}}$ $\overline{4\frac{9}{20}}$ $\overline{1\frac{5}{8}}$ $\overline{28\frac{7}{9}}$ $\overline{1\frac{1}{2}}$ $\overline{9\frac{3}{8}}$

Japanese

$\overline{2\frac{7}{8}}$ $\overline{5\frac{7}{12}}$ $\overline{4\frac{3}{4}}$ $\overline{1\frac{15}{16}}$ $\overline{7\frac{3}{5}}$ $\overline{3\frac{7}{12}}$ $\overline{11\frac{1}{2}}$ $\overline{3\frac{3}{4}}$ $\overline{35\frac{25}{28}}$ $\overline{4\frac{15}{28}}$

S. $21\frac{7}{10} - 12\frac{3}{7}$

H. $76\frac{4}{9} - 47\frac{2}{3}$

D. $5\frac{1}{5} - 2\frac{3}{10}$

A. $4\frac{1}{8} - 2\frac{3}{16}$

W. $10\frac{1}{8} - \frac{3}{4}$

L. $59\frac{3}{4} - 23\frac{6}{7}$

S. $12\frac{1}{3} - \frac{5}{6}$

E. $6\frac{2}{3} - 1\frac{5}{6}$

I. $5\frac{1}{4} - \frac{7}{8}$

N. $7\frac{2}{3} - 3\frac{4}{5}$

N. $16\frac{7}{10} - 12\frac{1}{4}$

R. $8\frac{3}{5} - 6\frac{7}{8}$

G. $3\frac{1}{2} - 1\frac{7}{8}$

L. $7\frac{2}{7} - 2\frac{3}{4}$

H. $6\frac{1}{2} - 2\frac{3}{4}$

B. $71\frac{5}{16} - 53\frac{3}{4}$

S. $7\frac{1}{4} - 4\frac{3}{8}$

A. $5\frac{1}{4} - 1\frac{2}{3}$

E. $7\frac{1}{4} - 4\frac{1}{2}$

B. $12\frac{1}{2} - 7\frac{3}{4}$

I. $83\frac{2}{7} - 41\frac{5}{8}$

O. $8\frac{1}{3} - 6\frac{5}{6}$

T. $7\frac{3}{10} - 5\frac{3}{5}$

U. $14\frac{1}{3} - 8\frac{3}{4}$

R. $16\frac{1}{10} - 8\frac{1}{2}$

Name _____

Unearthing Answers

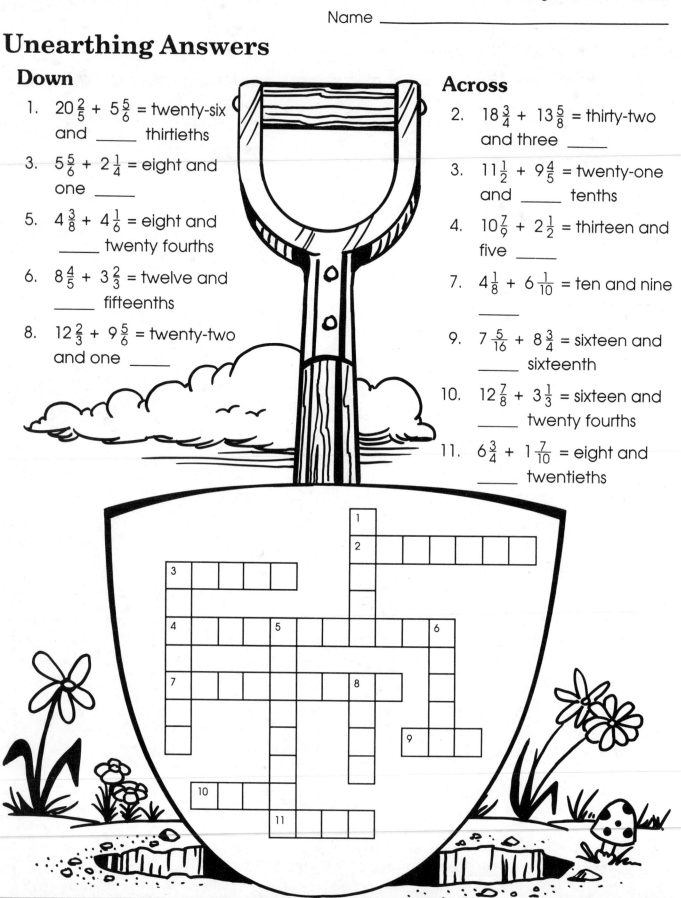

Down

1. $20\frac{2}{5} + 5\frac{5}{6}$ = twenty-six and _____ thirtieths

3. $5\frac{5}{6} + 2\frac{1}{4}$ = eight and one _____

5. $4\frac{3}{8} + 4\frac{1}{6}$ = eight and _____ twenty fourths

6. $8\frac{4}{5} + 3\frac{2}{3}$ = twelve and _____ fifteenths

8. $12\frac{2}{3} + 9\frac{5}{6}$ = twenty-two and one _____

Across

2. $18\frac{3}{4} + 13\frac{5}{8}$ = thirty-two and three _____

3. $11\frac{1}{2} + 9\frac{4}{5}$ = twenty-one and _____ tenths

4. $10\frac{7}{9} + 2\frac{1}{2}$ = thirteen and five _____

7. $4\frac{1}{8} + 6\frac{1}{10}$ = ten and nine _____

9. $7\frac{5}{16} + 8\frac{3}{4}$ = sixteen and _____ sixteenth

10. $12\frac{7}{8} + 3\frac{1}{3}$ = sixteen and _____ twenty fourths

11. $6\frac{3}{4} + 1\frac{7}{10}$ = eight and _____ twentieths

Name _____

Braille Subtraction

Braille is a system of raised dots that can be read by touch by the blind. Use the Braille decoder box to solve the following subtraction problems. Give your answers in Braille.

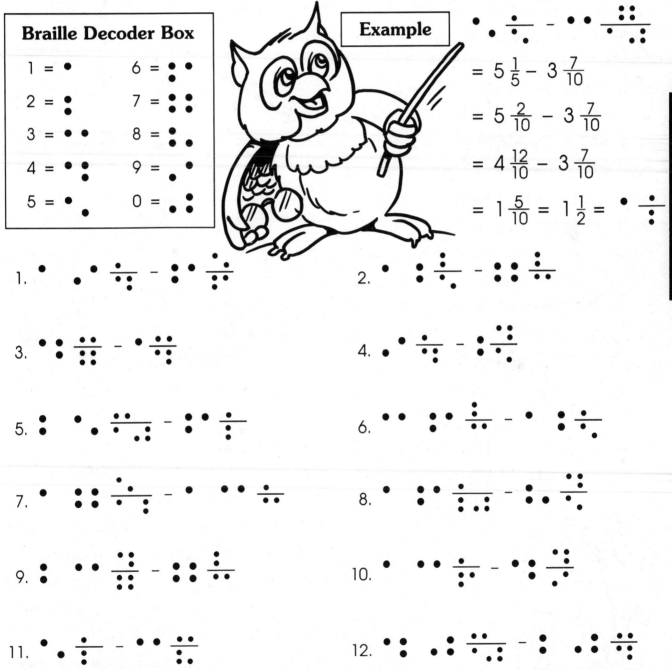

Louis Braille was the French inventor of this raised dot system. He was accidently blinded at the age of 3 and came up with Braille when he was only 15 years old!

Name _____

Fun Facts

The World Trade Center towers are so large and tall that each tower has its own

___ ___ ___   ___ ___ ___ ___ !
  1   2   3   4   5   6   7

To find the answer, follow the directions below.

Put an O above number 5 if the estimated difference between $13\frac{1}{3}$ and $5\frac{3}{7}$ is 8.

Put an A above number 6 if the estimated difference between $21\frac{5}{6}$ and $9\frac{4}{9}$ is 12.

Put an R above number 4 if the estimated difference between $16\frac{9}{20}$ and $13\frac{11}{15}$ is 3.

Put a B above number 1 if the estimated difference between $8\frac{3}{5}$ and $3\frac{7}{12}$ is 6.

Put a C above number 4 if the estimated difference between $25\frac{7}{20}$ and $13\frac{7}{12}$ is 11.

Put an E above number 7 if the estimated difference between $32\frac{7}{15}$ and $14\frac{9}{16}$ is 17.

Put a D above number 3 if the estimated difference between $18\frac{1}{3}$ and $15\frac{4}{13}$ is 2.

Put an I above number 2 if the estimated difference between $19\frac{7}{10}$ and $9\frac{6}{11}$ is 10.

Put a D above number 7 if the estimated difference between $15\frac{9}{20}$ and $2\frac{8}{15}$ is 13.

Put a P above number 3 if the estimated difference between $58\frac{5}{12}$ and $42\frac{3}{10}$ is 16.

Put a D above number 6 if the estimated difference between $30\frac{13}{20}$ and $19\frac{7}{18}$ is 12.

Put an L above number 1 if the estimated difference between $11\frac{5}{7}$ and $5\frac{2}{5}$ is 6.

Put a Z above number 1 if the estimated difference between $16\frac{3}{8}$ and $9\frac{3}{7}$ is 7.

       Daily Learning Drills Grade 6

Name _____

Can Crushers

Do these number sentences.

$\frac{5}{8}$	x	$\frac{4}{15}$	=	
x		x		
$\frac{12}{25}$	x	$\frac{5}{6}$	=	
=		=		
	x		=	
				x
$\frac{7}{12}$	x	$\frac{9}{14}$	=	
x		x		=
$\frac{6}{35}$		$\frac{21}{36}$		
=		=		
	x		=	

Name _____

Willie the Worm

Help Willie the Worm reach the apple by solving the multiplication problems.
Find the path by following the answers from least to greatest.

$14 \times \frac{2}{9} \times \frac{1}{4}$

$11 \times \frac{1}{8} \times \frac{1}{6}$

$5 \times \frac{9}{16} \times \frac{1}{12}$

$\frac{1}{8} \times \frac{1}{4} \times 26$

$2 \times \frac{5}{8} \times \frac{3}{4}$

$2 \times \frac{3}{8} \times \frac{1}{9}$

$\frac{1}{16} \times 15 \times \frac{4}{5}$

$\frac{1}{3} \times \frac{8}{10} \times 4$

$5 \times \frac{3}{8} \times \frac{5}{9}$

$2 \times \frac{5}{6} \times \frac{4}{5}$

$8 \times \frac{3}{8} \times \frac{2}{9}$

$\frac{1}{2} \times 9 \times \frac{3}{7}$

$\frac{6}{7} \times 3 \times \frac{1}{3}$

$2 \times \frac{3}{8} \times \frac{2}{9}$

$66 \times \frac{1}{12} \times \frac{3}{8}$

$\frac{3}{10} \times 32 \times \frac{4}{12}$

$\frac{2}{9} \times \frac{3}{8} \times 41$

$36 \times \frac{3}{8} \times \frac{6}{9}$

Daily Learning Drills Grade 6

Pooch's Products

Draw a line from the multiplication problem to the correct estimated product.

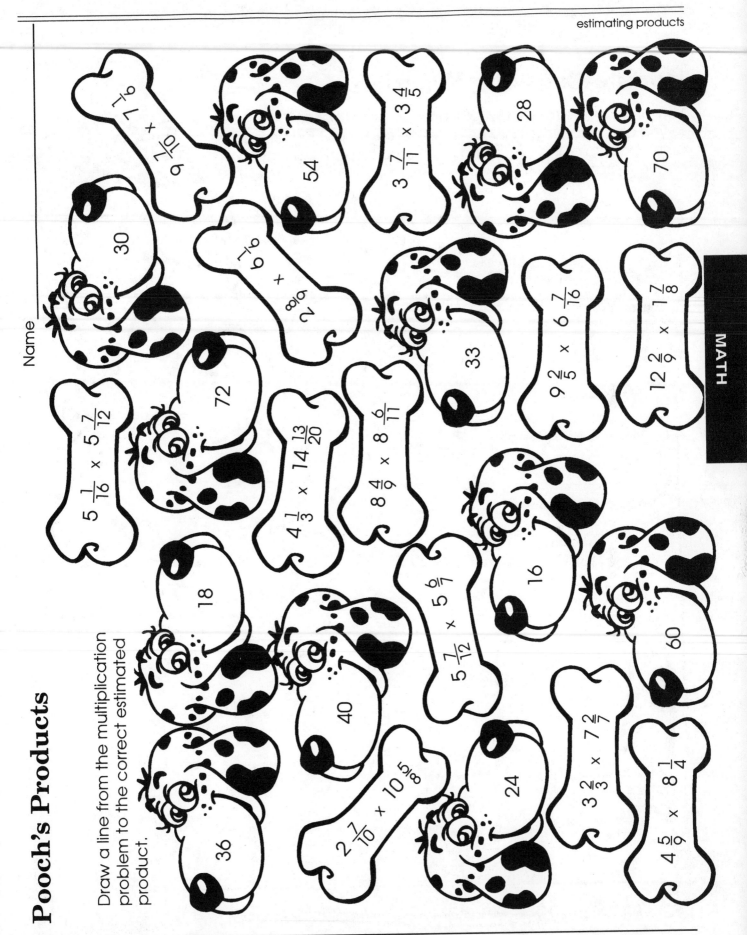

Name _____

Problems shown on bones:
$9\frac{7}{10} \times 7\frac{1}{8}$
$3\frac{7}{11} \times 3\frac{4}{5}$
$2\frac{9}{9} \times 6\frac{1}{8}$
$9\frac{2}{5} \times 6\frac{7}{16}$
$12\frac{2}{9} \times 1\frac{7}{8}$
$5\frac{1}{16} \times 5\frac{7}{12}$
$4\frac{1}{3} \times 14\frac{13}{20}$
$8\frac{4}{9} \times 8\frac{6}{11}$
$5\frac{7}{12} \times 5\frac{6}{7}$
$2\frac{7}{10} \times 10\frac{5}{8}$
$3\frac{2}{3} \times 7\frac{2}{7}$
$4\frac{5}{9} \times 8\frac{1}{4}$

Numbers shown on dogs: 54, 28, 70, 30, 33, 72, 18, 16, 60, 40, 24, 36

Name _____

Double-Crossing Fractions

My name has become a synonym for the word *traitor*. Who am I?
To find out, locate the answers to the following division problems
at the bottom of the page and put the corresponding letter
above the answer.

A. $\dfrac{2}{5} \div \dfrac{3}{10}$

B. $\dfrac{7}{12} \div \dfrac{3}{4}$

C. $\dfrac{9}{16} \div \dfrac{3}{4}$

D. $\dfrac{2}{7} \div \dfrac{4}{5}$

D. $\dfrac{3}{4} \div \dfrac{3}{8}$

E. $\dfrac{8}{9} \div \dfrac{4}{7}$

I. $\dfrac{5}{6} \div \dfrac{2}{3}$

L. $\dfrac{3}{20} \div \dfrac{9}{10}$

N. $\dfrac{8}{9} \div \dfrac{1}{4}$

O. $\dfrac{3}{8} \div \dfrac{3}{4}$

R. $\dfrac{8}{11} \div \dfrac{2}{5}$

E. $\dfrac{5}{6} \div \dfrac{1}{5}$

T. $\dfrac{5}{6} \div \dfrac{5}{18}$

N. $\dfrac{14}{15} \div \dfrac{4}{5}$

$\dfrac{7}{9}$ $4\dfrac{1}{6}$ $3\dfrac{5}{9}$ $1\dfrac{5}{9}$ 2 $1\dfrac{1}{4}$ $\dfrac{3}{4}$ 3 $1\dfrac{1}{3}$ $1\dfrac{9}{11}$ $1\dfrac{1}{6}$ $\dfrac{1}{2}$ $\dfrac{1}{6}$ $\dfrac{5}{14}$

Daily Learning Drills Grade 6

Name _____

Fruity Fractions

Try this fruity crossword!

Down

1. $6\frac{2}{3} \div 2\frac{1}{12}$ = _____ and one fifth

2. $2\frac{5}{8} \div 4\frac{9}{10}$ = _____ twenty eighths

3. $5\frac{5}{6} \div 4\frac{4}{9}$ = one and five _____

4. $15\frac{3}{4} \div 10\frac{1}{8}$ = one and five _____

6. $5\frac{2}{3} \div 25\frac{1}{2}$ = _____ ninths

8. $16\frac{1}{2} \div 6\frac{7}{8}$ = two and two _____

9. $4\frac{5}{6} \div 5\frac{4}{5}$ = five _____

Across

2. $2\frac{1}{10} \div 8\frac{2}{5}$ = one _____

3. $5\frac{2}{5} \div 2\frac{17}{20}$ = one and _____ nineteenths

5. $1\frac{11}{15} \div 1\frac{19}{20}$ = _____ ninths

7. $7\frac{1}{2} \div 5\frac{5}{8}$ = one and one _____

10. $8\frac{3}{4} \div 5\frac{3}{5}$ = one and nine _____

Name _____

Movie Math

What famous movie's name is a city in Morocco? To find out, follow the directions below.

1. Put an A above number 7 if the estimated quotient of $8 \frac{7}{10}$ and $2 \frac{4}{7}$ is 3.

2. Put an S above number 3 if the estimated quotient of $24 \frac{3}{5}$ and $5 \frac{7}{15}$ is 5.

3. Put a B above number 1 if the estimated quotient of $32 \frac{4}{9}$ and $7 \frac{10}{23}$ is 5.

4. Put a C above number 9 if the estimated quotient of $55 \frac{5}{8}$ and $7 \frac{7}{12}$ is 7.

5. Put a T above number 4 if the estimated quotient of $80 \frac{1}{3}$ and $9 \frac{3}{7}$ is 8.

6. Put an N above number 8 if the estimated quotient of $34 \frac{11}{12}$ and $6 \frac{4}{5}$ is 5.

7. Put an A above number 4 if the estimated quotient of $33 \frac{8}{17}$ and $11 \frac{7}{18}$ is 3.

8. Put an L above number 6 if the estimated quotient of $59 \frac{8}{11}$ and $5 \frac{6}{7}$ is 10.

9. Put an O above number 10 if the estimated quotient of $64 \frac{1}{6}$ and $7 \frac{13}{25}$ is 9.

10. Put an A above number 2 if the estimated quotient of $99 \frac{9}{13}$ and $9 \frac{19}{29}$ is 10.

11. Put an A above number 10 if the estimated quotient of $24 \frac{2}{6}$ and $3 \frac{8}{13}$ is 6.

12. Put a B above number 5 if the estimated quotient of $41 \frac{8}{11}$ and $5 \frac{3}{5}$ is 7.

13. Put a C above number 1 if the estimated quotient of $20 \frac{1}{6}$ and $5 \frac{3}{8}$ is 4.

___ ___ ___ ___ ___ ___ ___ ___ ___ ___
 1   2   3   4   5   6   7   8   9   10

Daily Learning Drills Grade 6

Name _____

Marvelous Mentor!

What is another word for teacher? To find out, solve problems 1-9. Then, find the answers in the chalkboard and put the corresponding letter above that question's number. Then, solve the rest of the problems.

O = .0111	U = 17.666	G = 8.04	B = 31.039
U = 6.499	P = .1368	A = 5.614	I = 5.6
T = 26.892	E = 26.98	G = 12.82	E = 17.675
M = .1376	L = 8.043	U = .0049	D = 31.0299

Which decimal is largest?

1. 5.614, 5.6114, 5.6

2. 26.892, 26.98

3. .0049, .0005, .0111

4. 17.675, 17.666

Which decimal is smallest?

5. 8.043, 8.04

6. 31.0349, 31.0299, 31.0329

7. 6.5, 6.499, 6.511

8. .1376, .1369, .1368

9. 12.82, 12.821, 12.9

___ ___ ___ ___ ___ ___ ___ ___ ___
8   4   6   1   9   3   5   7   2

Put in increasing order.

10. 16.198, 16.199, 16.189

11. 102.09, 102.101, 102.011

12. 8.0321, 8.0322, 8.03121

13. .6032, .6132, .6022

Put in decreasing order.

14. .301, .311, .302

15. 12.1212, 12.1221, 12.1222

16. 4.404, 4.414, 4.441

17. .7811, .7812, .7821

Name _____

Itchy Insects

Only which mosquitoes bite? To find out, follow the directions below.

1. Put an E above number 2 if 3.596 rounded to the nearest one is 4.

2. Put an A above number 1 if 23.4512 rounded to the nearest ten is 23.

3. Put an O above number 5 if 649.3 rounded to the nearest hundred is 650.

4. Put an E above number 6 if 2.19 rounded to the nearest tenth is 2.2.

5. Put an M above number 1 if .0388 rounded to the nearest hundredth is .039.

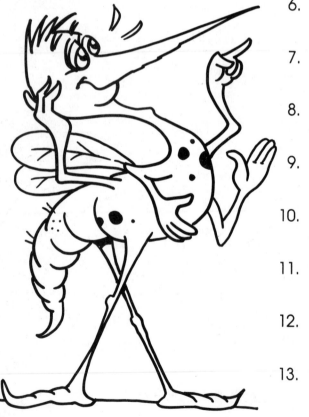

6. Put a C above number 5 if 57.86 rounded to the nearest ten is 58.9.

7. Put a D above number 3 if 4.355 rounded to the nearest hundredth is 4.35.

8. Put an A above number 4 if 14.86 rounded to the nearest one is 15.

9. Put an L above number 5 if .2315 rounded to the nearest thousandth is .232.

10. Put a B above number 2 if 717.1717 rounded to the nearest tenth is 717.17.

11. Put an M above number 3 if 5.066 rounded to the nearest one is 5.

12. Put a D above number 6 if 44.689 rounded to the nearest ten is 44.7.

13. Put an F above number 1 if .86424 rounded to the nearest ten-thousandth is .8642.

___ ___ ___ ___ ___ ___
 1   2   3   4   5   6

Name _____

Wheels Away!

Add center number to number in first circle to find the answer. Next, add all answers on wheel. Then, add all wheel answers to get total of all wheels.

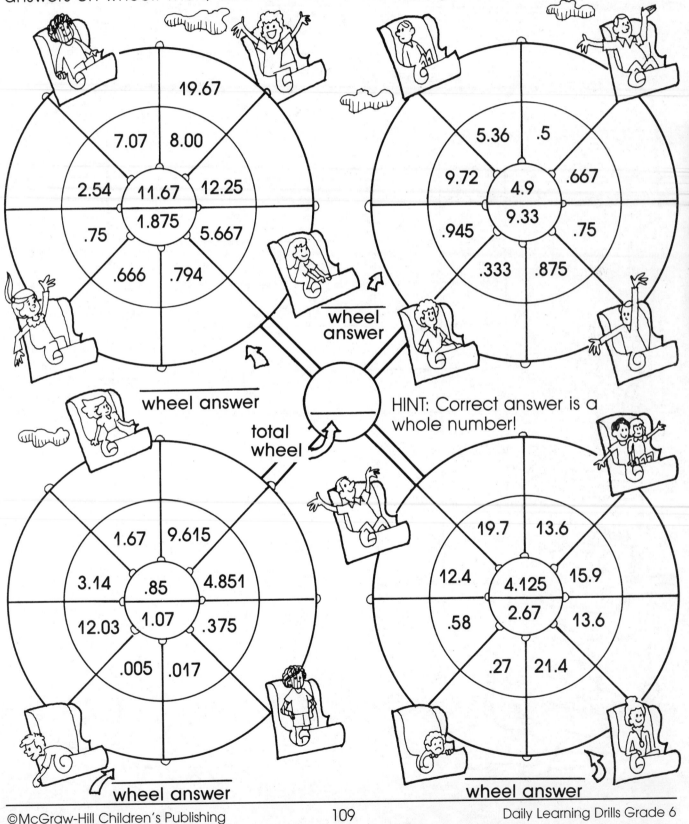

19.67

7.07 | 8.00

2.54 | 11.67 | 12.25

1.875

.75 | 5.667

.666 | .794

5.36 | .5

9.72 | 4.9 | .667

9.33

.945 | .75

.333 | .875

wheel answer

wheel answer

total wheel

HINT: Correct answer is a whole number!

1.67 | 9.615

3.14 | .85 | 4.851

1.07

12.03 | .375

.005 | .017

19.7 | 13.6

12.4 | 4.125 | 15.9

2.67

.58 | 13.6

.27 | 21.4

wheel answer

wheel answer

Name _____

Swiss Sentences

Finish these cheesy number sentences.

1.862	+	.9854	=	
+		+		
.53	+	6.72	=	
=		=		
	+		=	
				+

.9076	+	.995	=	
+		+		=
6.53	+	5.47	=	
=		=		
	+		=	

110

Scoops and Cones

Draw a line from the addition problem to the estimated sum.

Name

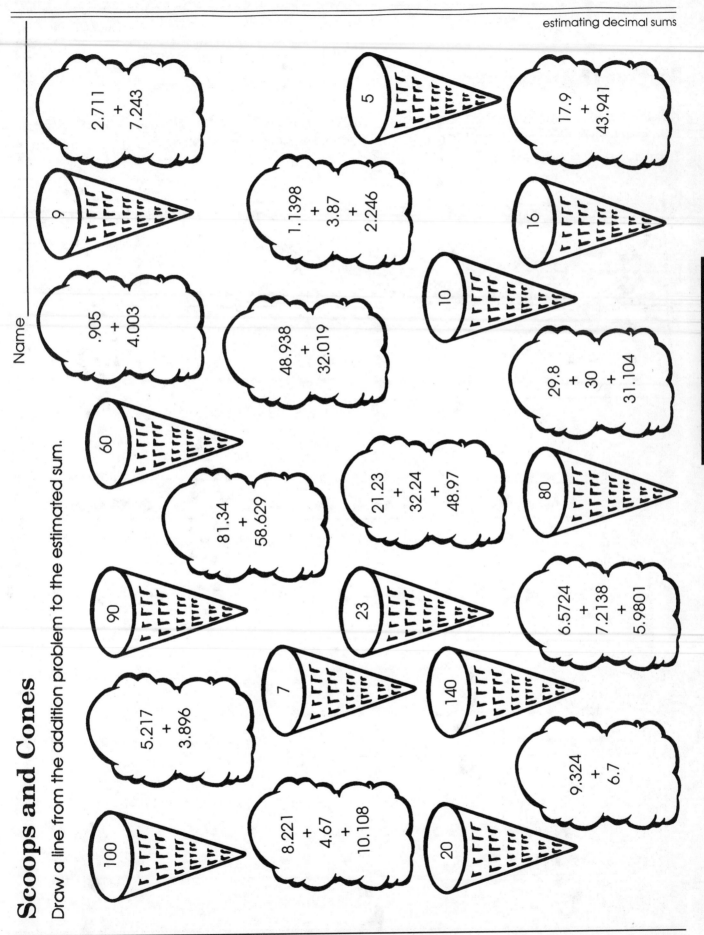

2.711
+
7.243

5

17.9
+
43.941

9

1.1398
+
3.87
+
2.246

16

.905
+
4.003

48.938
+
32.019

10

29.8
+
30
+
31.104

60

81.34
+
58.629

21.23
+
32.24
+
48.97

80

90

23

6.5724
+
7.2138
+
5.9801

5.217
+
3.896

7

140

9.324
+
6.7

100

8.221
+
4.67
+
10.108

20

MATH

Name _____

Tut's Homework

King Tut's teacher left some subtraction problems for him to do on the wall of a pyramid. Use the following hieroglyphic decoder box to decipher the numbers. Then work the problems.

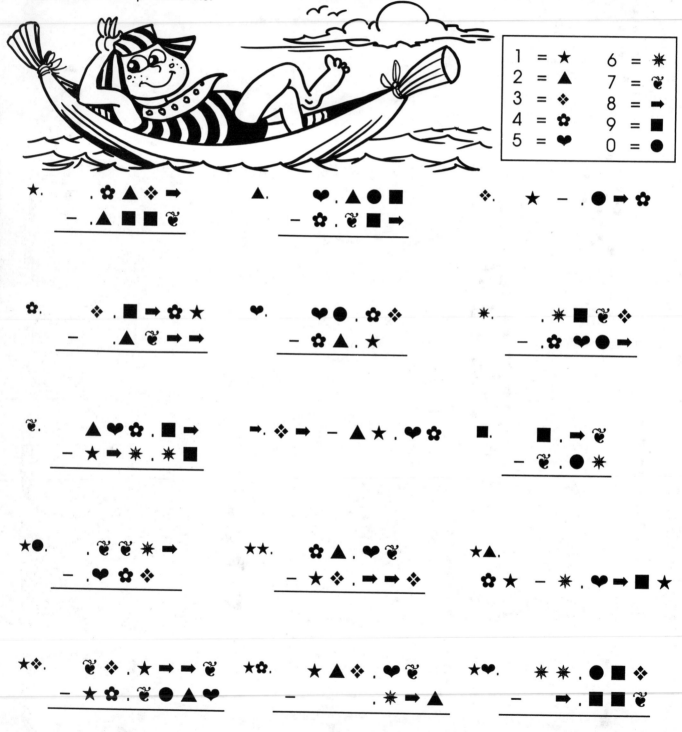

Boxer's Subtraction

Draw a line from the subtraction problem to the estimated difference.

Name _____

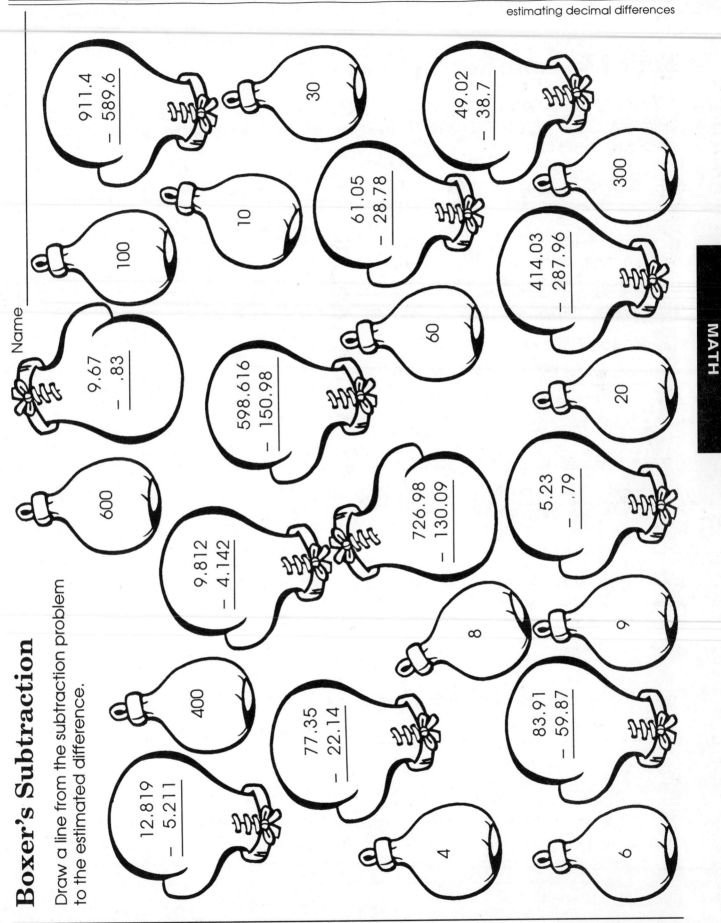

$911.4 - 589.6$

30

$49.02 - 38.7$

100

10

$61.05 - 28.78$

300

$9.67 - .83$

$598.616 - 150.98$

60

$414.03 - 287.96$

600

$9.812 - 4.142$

$726.98 - 130.09$

$5.23 - .79$

20

400

$77.35 - 22.14$

$83.91 - 59.87$

8

9

$12.819 - 5.211$

4

6

Daily Learning Drills Grade 6

MATH

Name _____

Major League Multiplication

What was "Babe" Ruth's real name? To find out, solve the following multiplication problems. Then, find the answers in the mitt. Put the corresponding letter above that problem's number.

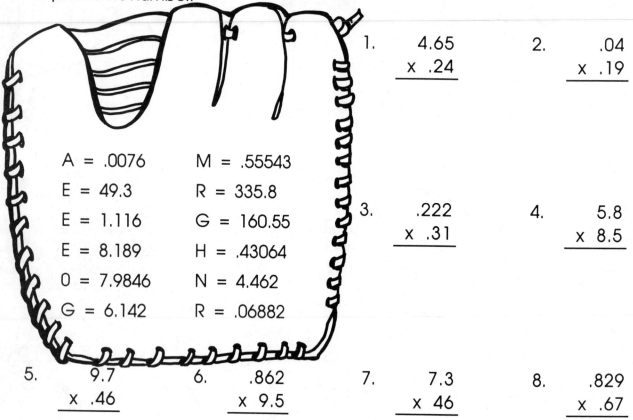

A = .0076   M = .55543

E = 49.3   R = 335.8

E = 1.116   G = 160.55

E = 8.189   H = .43064

O = 7.9846   N = 4.462

G = 6.142   R = .06882

1. 4.65
   x .24

2. .04
   x .19

3. .222
   x .31

4. 5.8
   x 8.5

5. 9.7
   x .46

6. .862
   x 9.5

7. 7.3
   x 46

8. .829
   x .67

9. 9.62 x .83   10. .769 x .56   11. 24.7 x 6.5   12. 8.3 x .74

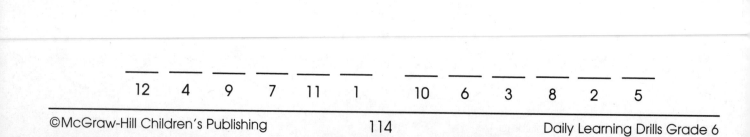

___ ___ ___ ___ ___ ___   ___ ___ ___ ___ ___ ___
12   4   9   7 11   1   10   6   3   8   2   5

Name _____

Solving for Touchdowns

Tackle this cross number! Decimal points
will take up their own squares.

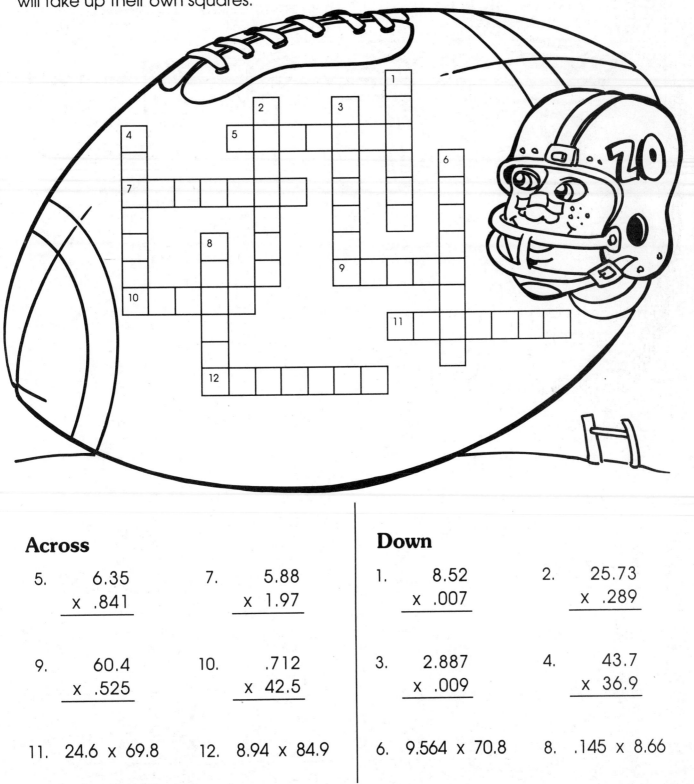

Across

5.　　6.35
　　×　.841

7.　　5.88
　　×　1.97

9.　　60.4
　　×　.525

10.　　.712
　　×　42.5

11.　24.6 × 69.8

12.　8.94 × 84.9

Down

1.　　8.52
　　×　.007

2.　　25.73
　　×　.289

3.　　2.887
　　×　.009

4.　　43.7
　　×　36.9

6.　9.564 × 70.8

8.　.145 × 8.66

Planting Products

Draw a line from the multiplication problem to the estimated product.

Name _____

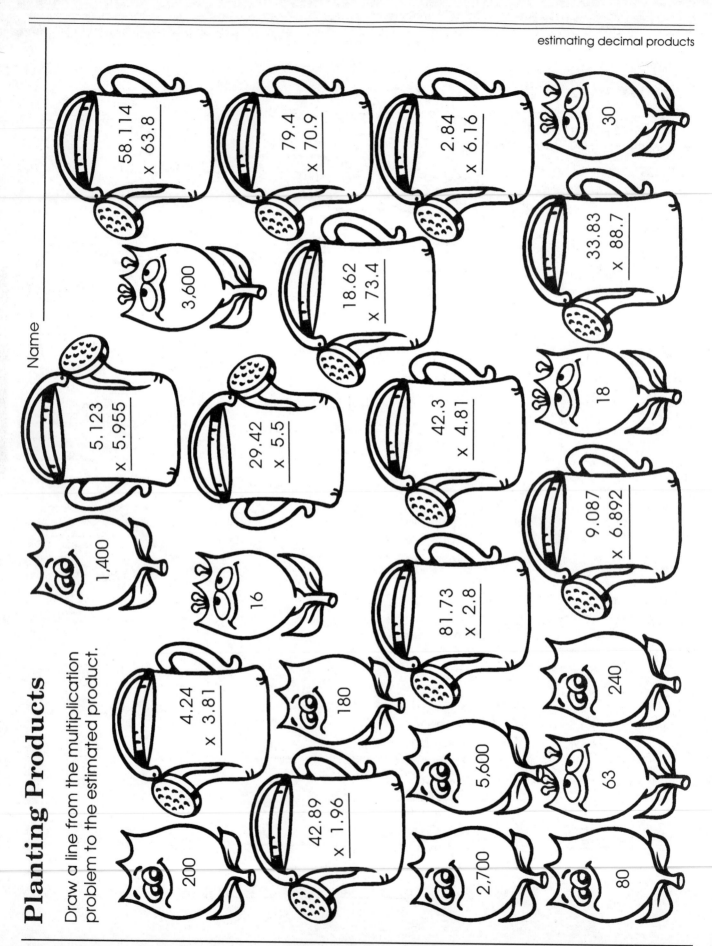

58.114
x 63.8
———

79.4
x 70.9
———

2.84
x 6.16
———

30

3,600

18.62
x 73.4
———

33.83
x 88.7
———

5.123
x 5.955
———

29.42
x 5.5
———

42.3
x 4.81
———

18

1,400

16

81.73
x 2.8
———

9.087
x 6.892
———

4.24
x 3.81
———

180

240

5,600

63

200

42.89
x 1.96
———

2,700

80

Daily Learning Drills Grade 6

Name _____

Decimal Trivia

What is pictured on the back of a $5 bill? To find out, solve the following division problems. Then, find the answers in the $5 bill. Put the corresponding letter above that problem's number.

A = 6.402   L = 98.04

E = .006   L = 43.25

I = 58.3   L = 2.005

I = .884   M = 7.42

O = 3.68   M = .078

O = 33.33   N = .061

C = .084   N = 60.7

R = 1.09

1. $12\overline{)44.16}$

2. $8\overline{).624}$

3. $5\overline{)37.1}$

4. $13\overline{)11.492}$

5. $9\overline{)389.25}$

6. $6\overline{)349.8}$

7. $7\overline{)686.28}$

8. $15\overline{).09}$

9. $22\overline{)1335.4}$

10. $10\overline{)20.05}$

11. $5\overline{)166.65}$

12. $7\overline{).427}$

13. $12\overline{)76.824}$

14. $9\overline{).756}$

15. $13\overline{)14.17}$

___ ___ ___ ___ ___ ___ ___
10   4   9   14   1   7   12

___ ___ ___ ___ ___ ___ ___ ___
3   8   2   11   15   6   13   5

Name _____

Sammie Snail's Shell

Solve the following division problems. Connect the correct answers to assist Sammie Snail in getting into his shell. Write the correct answers to the problems that are wrong.

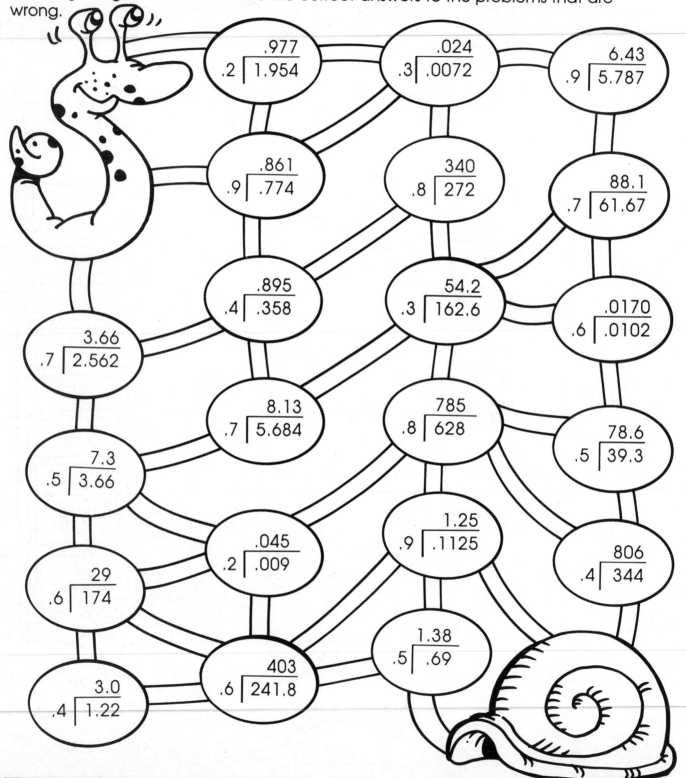

Name _____

Bob Means Business

Does businessman Bob make it up the corporate ladder? Solve the following division problems and shade in the answers on the ladder to find out. If any numbers are not shaded when all the problems have been completed, Bob gets fired. Some answers may not be on the ladder.

1. $.42 \overline{)3.192}$

2. $1.5 \overline{)1.47}$

3. $.22 \overline{)1.936}$

4. $3.6 \overline{)216}$

5. $.53 \overline{)\,.3551}$

6. $.34 \overline{)1.462}$

7. $360 \div 4.5$

8. $.522 \div .18$

9. $2.325 \div 2.5$

10. $1.976 \div .38$

11. $40.32 \div .63$

12. $6.6 \div 1.2$

Ladder:

| 8.8 |
| 60 |
| 5.2 |
| 7.6 |
| 64 |
| 2.9 |
| 5.6 |
| .98 |
| 80 |
| .67 |
| 4.3 |

Does Bob make it or get fired? _____

Name _____

Put Your Best Foot Forward!

Draw a line from the division problem
to the estimated quotient.

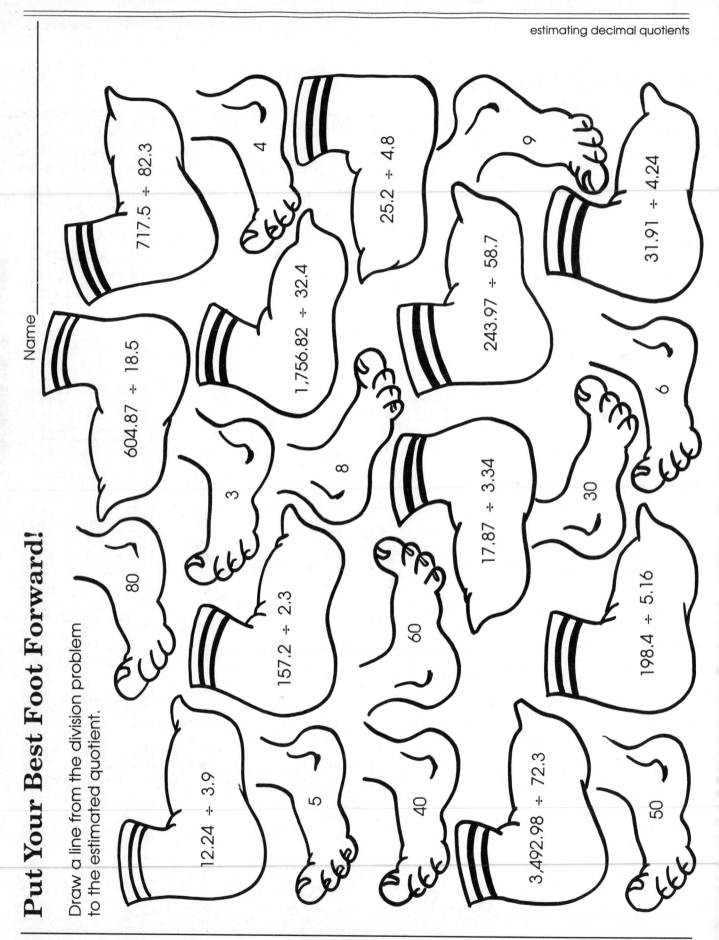

717.5 ÷ 82.3

4

25.2 ÷ 4.8

9

31.91 ÷ 4.24

604.87 ÷ 18.5

1,756.82 ÷ 32.4

243.97 ÷ 58.7

6

80

3

8

17.87 ÷ 3.34

30

157.2 ÷ 2.3

60

198.4 ÷ 5.16

12.24 ÷ 3.9

5

40

3,492.98 ÷ 72.3

50

Name _____

Wheels of Wonder

Find each product or quotient. Multiply or divide each number by the number in the center.

Name _____

Incredible Inventions

What did Samuel Benedict invent? Find out by solving the following problems and finding the answers in the test tube. Put the corresponding letter above that problem's number at the bottom of the page.

Write as a percent.

1. $\dfrac{1}{4}$

2. $\dfrac{5}{8}$

3. $\dfrac{7}{10}$

4. $\dfrac{13}{100}$

5. $\dfrac{3}{5}$

6. $\dfrac{7}{20}$

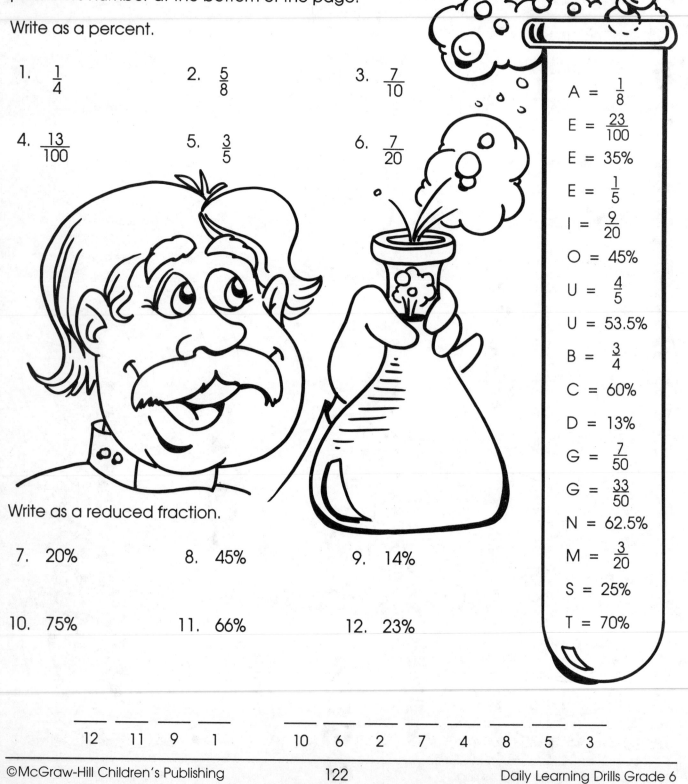

A = $\dfrac{1}{8}$

E = $\dfrac{23}{100}$

E = 35%

E = $\dfrac{1}{5}$

I = $\dfrac{9}{20}$

O = 45%

U = $\dfrac{4}{5}$

U = 53.5%

B = $\dfrac{3}{4}$

C = 60%

D = 13%

G = $\dfrac{7}{50}$

G = $\dfrac{33}{50}$

N = 62.5%

M = $\dfrac{3}{20}$

S = 25%

T = 70%

Write as a reduced fraction.

7. 20%

8. 45%

9. 14%

10. 75%

11. 66%

12. 23%

___ ___ ___ ___   ___ ___ ___ ___ ___ ___ ___ ___
12 11 9 1   10 6 2 7 4 8 5 3

Daily Learning Drills Grade 6

Name _____

Bobby's Bargain Bonanza

Bargain Betty loves to get a good deal and won't buy anything unless it's on sale. So, she decided to go to Bobby's Bargain Basement where everything is on sale.

★ Bobby's Bargain Basement ★

skirts	$26.50	→	40% off	sweaters	$32.40	→	20% off
shirts	$24.00	→	25% off	jeans	$18.50	→	10% off
shoes	$28.60	→	15% off	boots	$30.00	→	12% off
socks	$7.20	→	35% off	dresses	$31.90	→	50% off
pants	$27.40	→	30% off	belts	$12.00	→	8% off
coats	$34.00	→	45% off	robes	$28.20	→	5% off

Answer the following questions using Bobby's price list and find the answers at the bottom of the page. Put that problem's letter above the answer to find a word describing Betty. See if your parents know this word!

A.   What is the discount on shoes?

I.   What is the sale price for a pair of socks?

I.   What is the sale price for a pair of pants?

O.   What is the discount on shirts?

O.   What is the discount on coats?

U.   What is the sale price for a skirt?

M.   What is the discount on boots?

N.   What is the sale price for a robe?

P.   What is the sale price for a sweater?

R.   What is the discount on jeans?

S.   What is the sale price for a belt?

S.   What is the discount on dresses?

____ ____ ____ ____ ____ ____ ____ ____ ____ ____ ____ ____
$25.92 $4.29 $1.85 $11.04 $19.18 $3.60 $6.00 $26.79 $4.68 $15.30 $15.90 $15.95

What Am I?

Name _____

To find the answers to the two riddles below, find the answer that matches each figure and write the figure's corresponding letter above it.

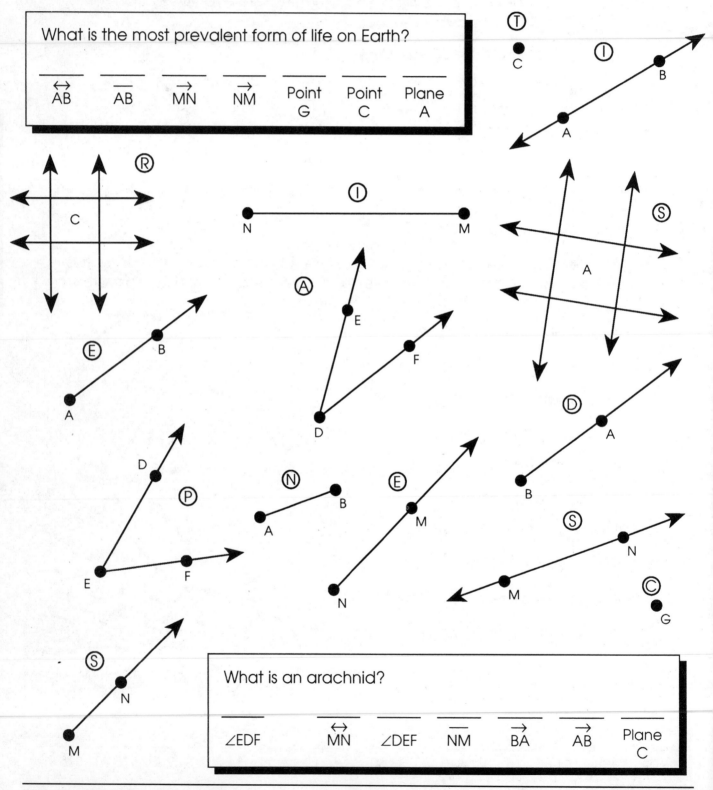

What is the most prevalent form of life on Earth?

| ____ | ____ | ____ | ____ | ____ | ____ | ____ |
| $\overleftrightarrow{AB}$ | $\overline{AB}$ | $\overrightarrow{MN}$ | $\overrightarrow{NM}$ | Point G | Point C | Plane A |

What is an arachnid?

| ____ | ____ | ____ | ____ | ____ | ____ |
| $\angle EDF$ | $\overleftrightarrow{MN}$ | $\angle DEF$ | $\overline{NM}$ | $\overrightarrow{BA}$ | $\overrightarrow{AB}$ | Plane C |

Name _____

I'm Confused!

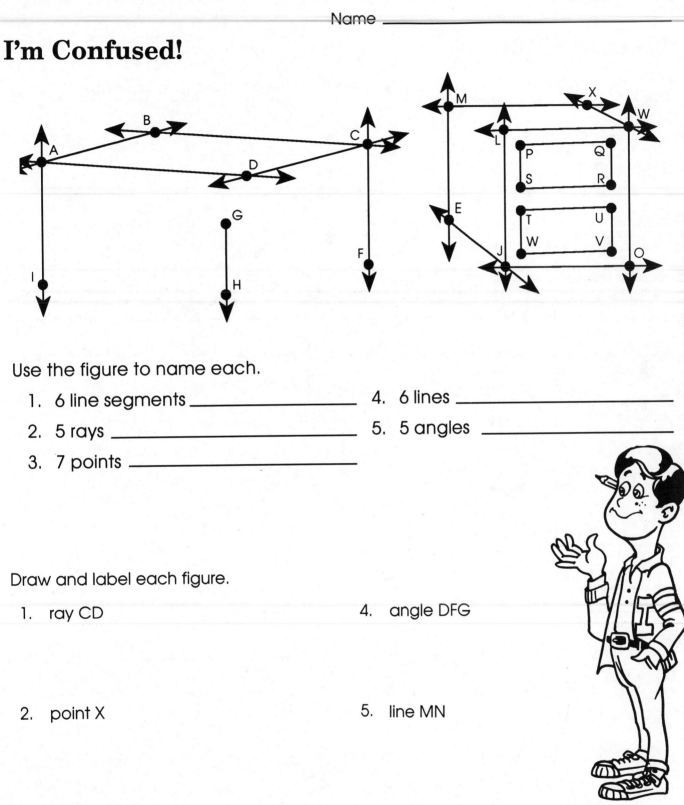

Use the figure to name each.

1. 6 line segments _____   4. 6 lines _____

2. 5 rays _____   5. 5 angles _____

3. 7 points _____

Draw and label each figure.

1. ray CD

2. point X

3. segment AB

4. angle DFG

5. line MN

Name _____

Figure It Out!

Using the figure, list all the ways to name each angle and classify each angle.

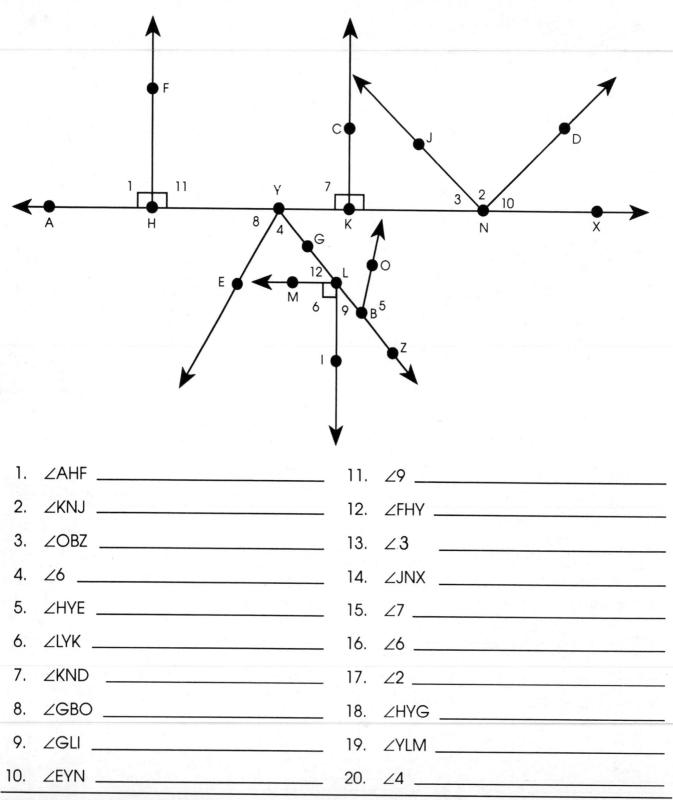

1. ∠AHF _____

2. ∠KNJ _____

3. ∠OBZ _____

4. ∠6 _____

5. ∠HYE _____

6. ∠LYK _____

7. ∠KND _____

8. ∠GBO _____

9. ∠GLI _____

10. ∠EYN _____

11. ∠9 _____

12. ∠FHY _____

13. ∠3 _____

14. ∠JNX _____

15. ∠7 _____

16. ∠6 _____

17. ∠2 _____

18. ∠HYG _____

19. ∠YLM _____

20. ∠4 _____

Daily Learning Drills Grade 6

Name _____

Light the Way

| How long does it take for light from the sun to reach Earth? |

To find out, complete the statements below. Then, write the corresponding letter above its answer at the bottom of the page.

(T) The intersection of the two sides of an angle is called the _____ .

(N) ∠BOE is a _____ angle.

(E) The figure formed by two rays with the same endpoint is an _____ .

(E) Another name for ∠3 is _____ .

(M) A _____ angle measures _____ .

(I) Another name for ∠COE is _____ .

(U) ∠AOD is an _____ angle.

(T) A right angle measures _____ .

(S) ∠BOC is a _____ angle.

(G) Another name for ∠AOD is _____ .

(H) ∠FOC is an _____ angle.

(I) Two rays that form an angle are called the _____ of the angle.

angle	∠2	∠4	acute	vertex		180°	sides	right	obtuse	90°	∠AOF	straight

Name _____

Following Directions

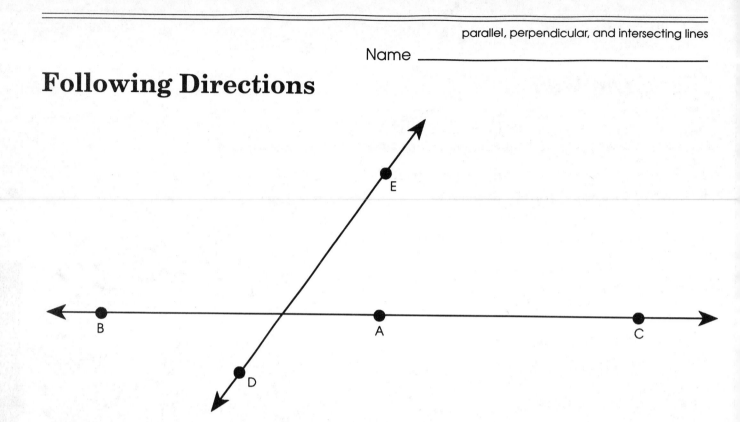

Follow the directions using the figure.

1. Draw a line $\overleftrightarrow{FG}$ parallel to $\overleftrightarrow{DE}$ and intersecting $\overleftrightarrow{BC}$.

2. Draw a ray $\overrightarrow{EH}$ extending from point E and going east. Make it parallel to $\overleftrightarrow{BC}$.

3. Draw a line $\overleftrightarrow{IJ}$ perpendicular to $\overleftrightarrow{AC}$ and intersecting $\overrightarrow{EH}$.

4. Draw a line $\overleftrightarrow{KL}$ intersecting $\overleftrightarrow{BC}$ but not perpendicular or parallel to any line.

5. Draw a line $\overleftrightarrow{MN}$ perpendicular to $\overleftrightarrow{DE}$.

Answer the questions using the figure.

6. What is parallel to $\overleftrightarrow{BA}$? _____

7. What line(s) is perpendicular to $\overleftrightarrow{BA}$? _____

8. What line(s) is parallel to $\overleftrightarrow{DE}$? _____

9. What line(s) is perpendicular to $\overleftrightarrow{DE}$? _____

10. Is $\overleftrightarrow{KL}$ parallel or perpendicular to any lines? _____

Name _____

The Freedom Trail

This map of the Freedom Trail in Boston, Massachusetts, shows several tourist attractions. Use it to answer the questions below.

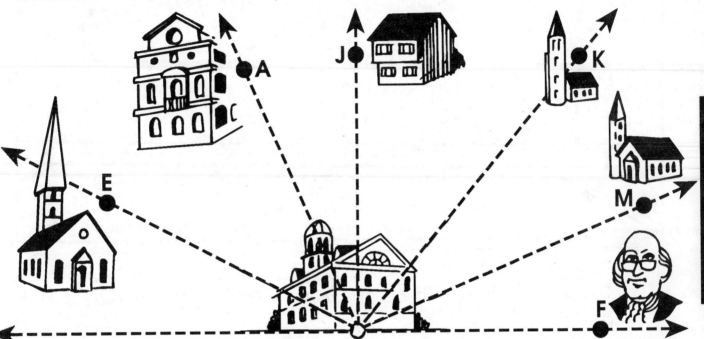

Using a protractor, find the measure (m) of each angle.

1. m∠EOJ = _____
2. m∠JOM = _____
3. m∠AOE = _____
4. m∠KOA = _____
5. m∠FOJ = _____

6. m∠FOA = _____
7. m∠MOK = _____
8. m∠MOE = _____
9. m∠EOF = _____
10. m∠KOE = _____

11. m∠AOJ = _____
12. m∠MOA = _____
13. m∠JOK = _____
14. m∠KOF = _____
15. m∠MOF = _____

Using a protractor, draw the measure of each angle.

16. 28°

17. 180°

18. 115°

19. 95°

20. 63°

21. 125°

Name _____

"Tri" These Angles!

Identify each triangle in the puzzle below by writing in the code letters from the box. Identify only the small triangles, not the ones made from more than one triangle.

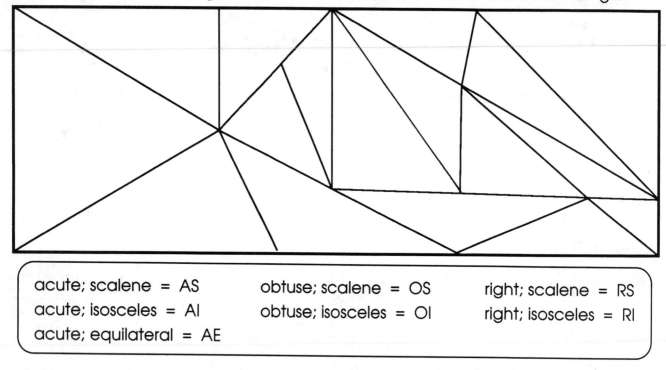

acute; scalene = AS   obtuse; scalene = OS   right; scalene = RS
acute; isosceles = AI   obtuse; isosceles = OI   right; isosceles = RI
acute; equilateral = AE

What part of your body contains a hammer and an anvil?

To find out, find each missing angle measure. Write the angle above its measure at the bottom.

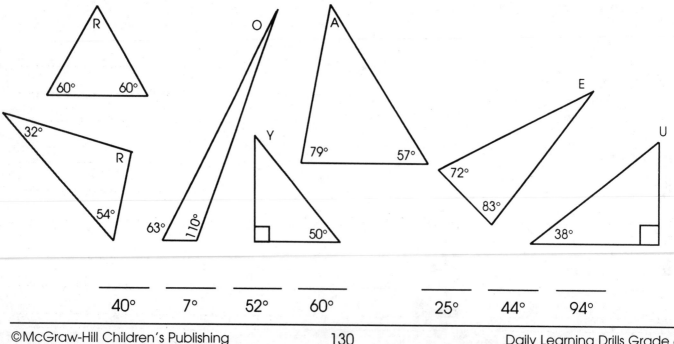

____ ____ ____ ____   ____ ____ ____
40°   7°   52°   60°   25°   44°   94°

Name _____

Super Shapes!

Using the figure, list the line segments that make up each shape. Then, list the angles of each shape. Be careful, there may be more than one of each shape.

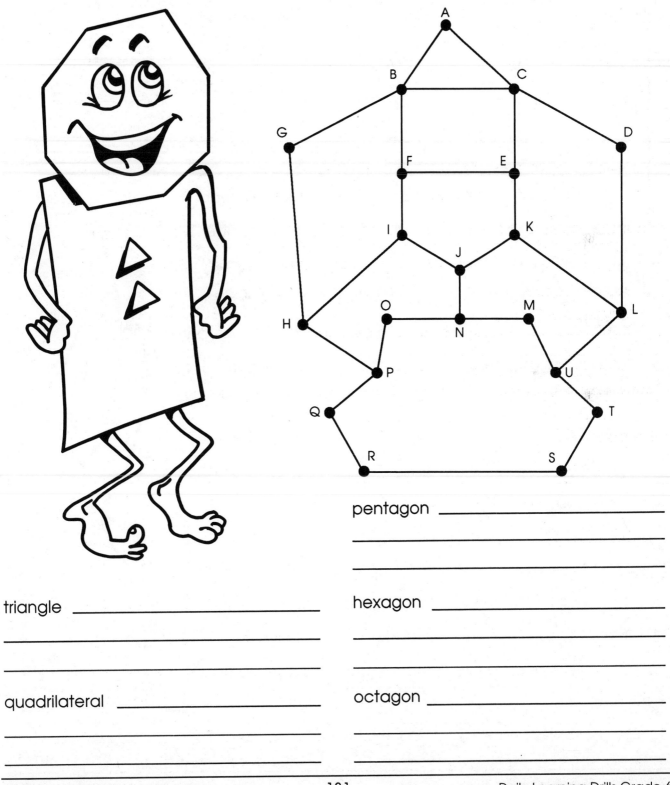

pentagon _____

_____

_____

triangle _____

_____

quadrilateral _____

_____

_____

hexagon _____

_____

octagon _____

_____

Name _____

What a Bill!

What bird's bill may grow as long as its entire body?

To find out, follow the directions below using the following figures.

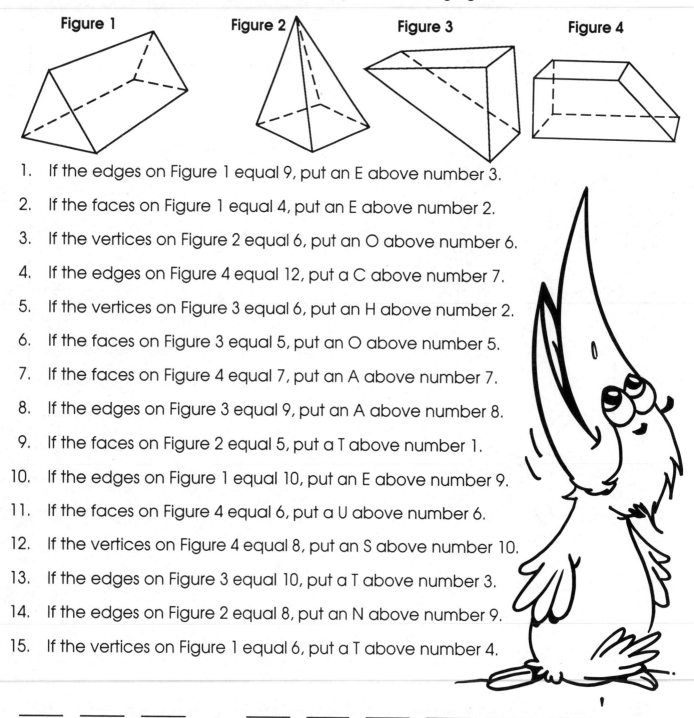

Figure 1 **Figure 2** **Figure 3** **Figure 4**

1. If the edges on Figure 1 equal 9, put an E above number 3.

2. If the faces on Figure 1 equal 4, put an E above number 2.

3. If the vertices on Figure 2 equal 6, put an O above number 6.

4. If the edges on Figure 4 equal 12, put a C above number 7.

5. If the vertices on Figure 3 equal 6, put an H above number 2.

6. If the faces on Figure 3 equal 5, put an O above number 5.

7. If the faces on Figure 4 equal 7, put an A above number 7.

8. If the edges on Figure 3 equal 9, put an A above number 8.

9. If the faces on Figure 2 equal 5, put a T above number 1.

10. If the edges on Figure 1 equal 10, put an E above number 9.

11. If the faces on Figure 4 equal 6, put a U above number 6.

12. If the vertices on Figure 4 equal 8, put an S above number 10.

13. If the edges on Figure 3 equal 10, put a T above number 3.

14. If the edges on Figure 2 equal 8, put an N above number 9.

15. If the vertices on Figure 1 equal 6, put a T above number 4.

___ ___ ___ ___ ___ ___ ___ ___ ___ ___
 1   2   3   4   5   6   7   8   9   10

Name _____

Browser

To find the hidden picture, use a pencil to graph the ordered pairs in each group and connect each point with the next point using a straight line. Do not connect the last point in one group with the first point in another group.

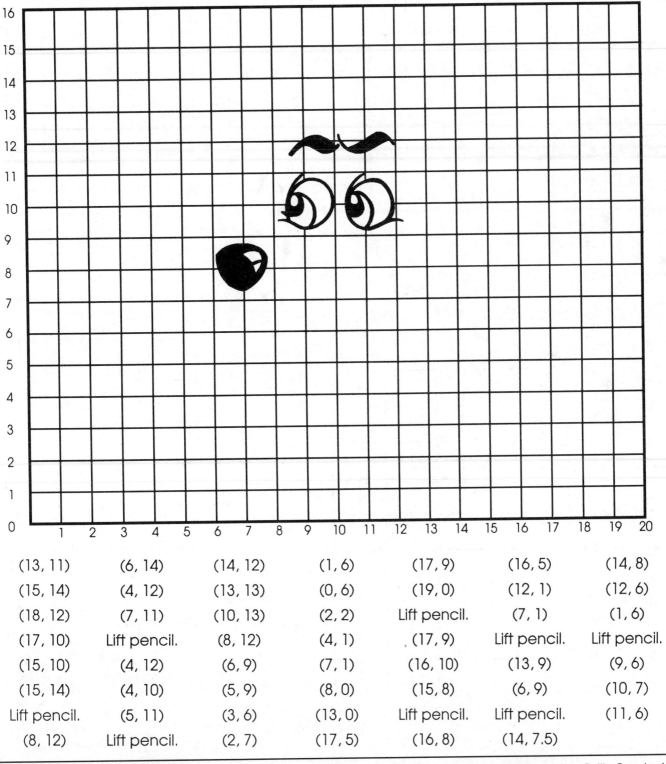

(13, 11)	(6, 14)	(14, 12)	(1, 6)	(17, 9)	(16, 5)	(14, 8)
(15, 14)	(4, 12)	(13, 13)	(0, 6)	(19, 0)	(12, 1)	(12, 6)
(18, 12)	(7, 11)	(10, 13)	(2, 2)	Lift pencil.	(7, 1)	(1, 6)
(17, 10)	Lift pencil.	(8, 12)	(4, 1)	(17, 9)	Lift pencil.	Lift pencil.
(15, 10)	(4, 12)	(6, 9)	(7, 1)	(16, 10)	(13, 9)	(9, 6)
(15, 14)	(4, 10)	(5, 9)	(8, 0)	(15, 8)	(6, 9)	(10, 7)
Lift pencil.	(5, 11)	(3, 6)	(13, 0)	Lift pencil.	Lift pencil.	(11, 6)
(8, 12)	Lift pencil.	(2, 7)	(17, 5)	(16, 8)	(14, 7.5)	

Name _____

What Am I?

Graph the following ordered pairs. Connect the points in order and give the names of the polygons.

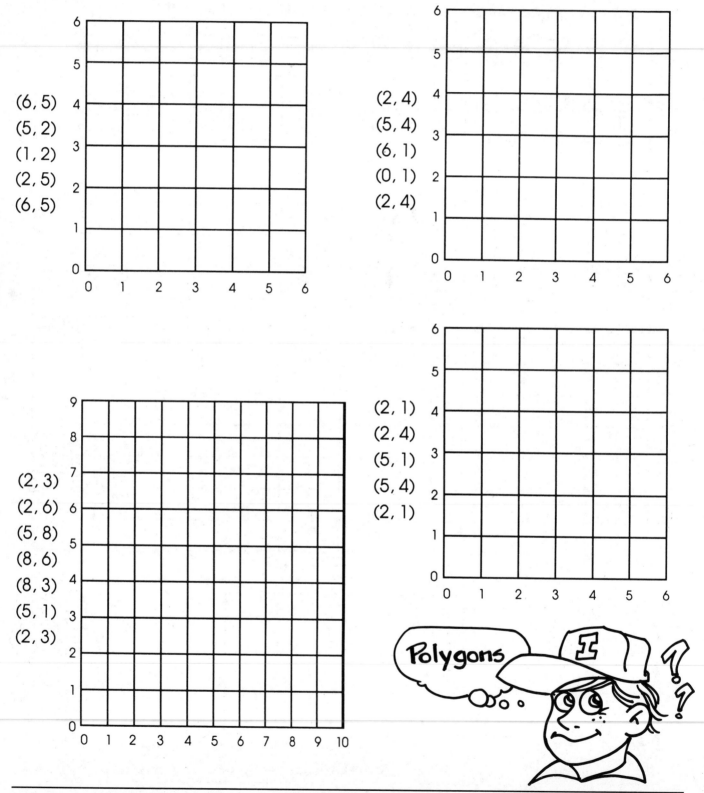

(6, 5)
(5, 2)
(1, 2)
(2, 5)
(6, 5)

(2, 4)
(5, 4)
(6, 1)
(0, 1)
(2, 4)

(2, 3)
(2, 6)
(5, 8)
(8, 6)
(8, 3)
(5, 1)
(2, 3)

(2, 1)
(2, 4)
(5, 1)
(5, 4)
(2, 1)

Polygons

Name _____

Randy the Robot

Find the area of each parallelogram that makes up the robot.

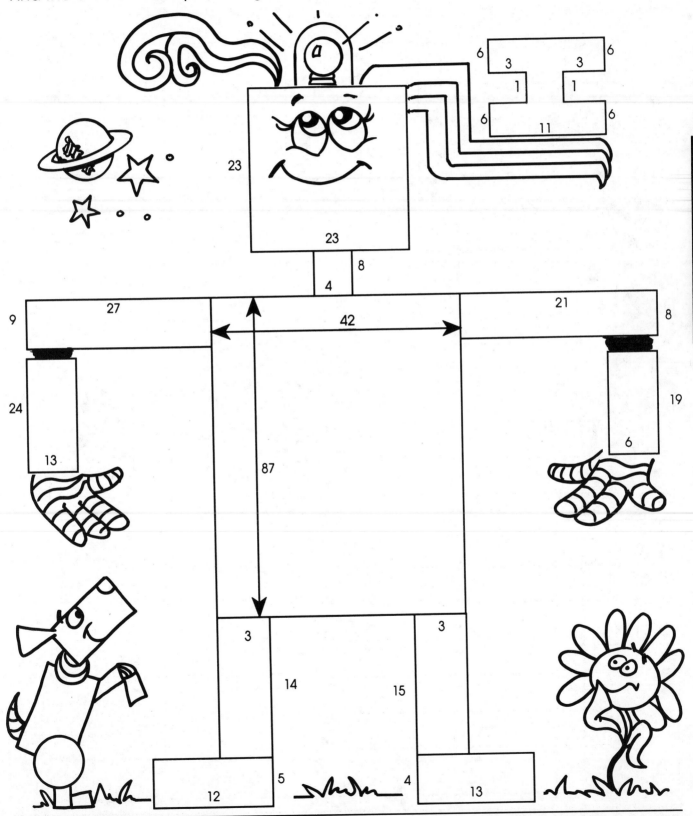

135

Name _____

I'm Hungry!

Help Gerry the Giraffe get to the tree by shading in the path that contains the correct areas. Then, find the correct areas for the ones that are wrong.

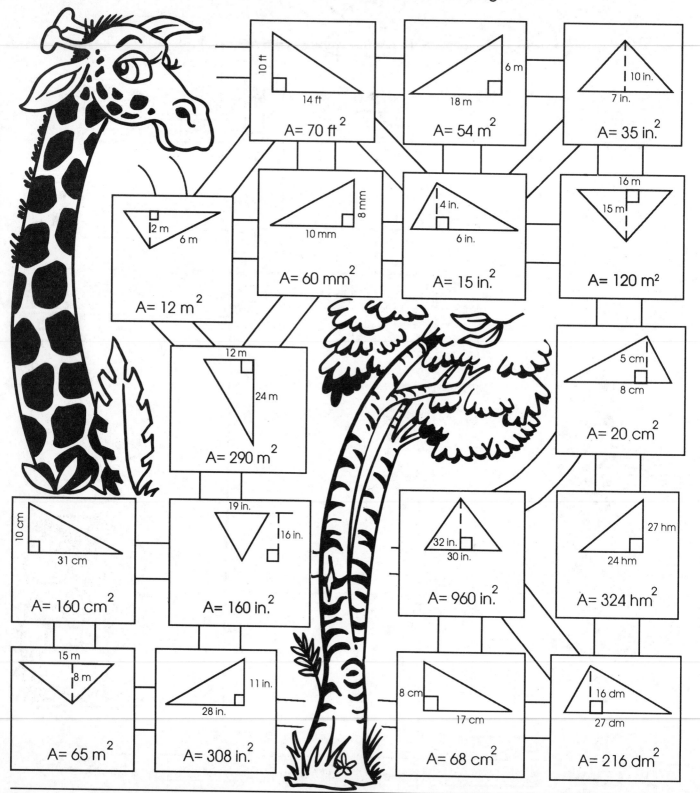

Name _____

Rocky Road

What is the only type of rock that can float?

To find out, find the areas of the following triangles at the bottom of the page and put the corresponding letter above each answer. Some answers may not be given.

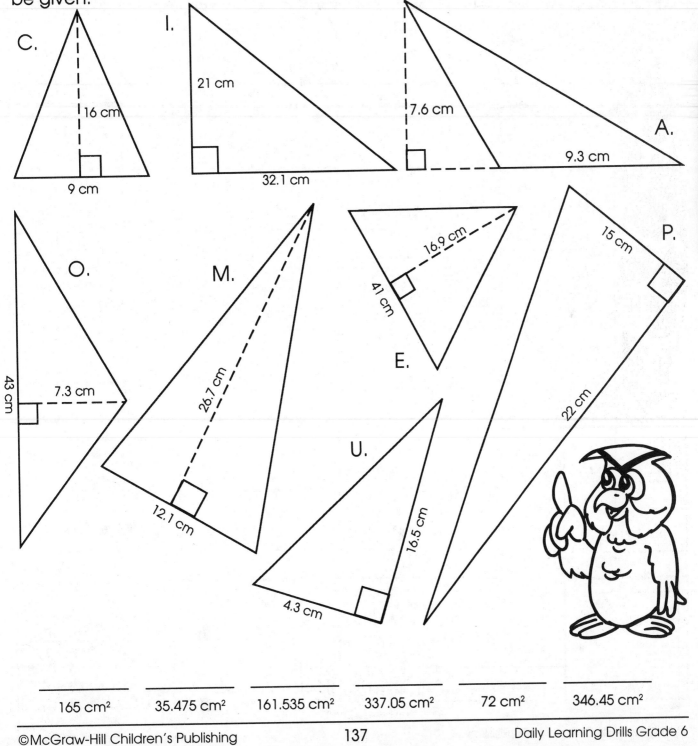

C. 16 cm, 9 cm

I. 21 cm, 32.1 cm

A. 7.6 cm, 9.3 cm

O. 43 cm, 7.3 cm

M. 26.7 cm, 12.1 cm

E. 41 cm, 16.9 cm

P. 15 cm, 22 cm

U. 16.5 cm, 4.3 cm

165 cm²	35.475 cm²	161.535 cm²	337.05 cm²	72 cm²	346.45 cm²

Name _____

Alex the Anteater

Help Alex the Anteater get to his dinner by finding the correct path. Shade in the path of the circumferences that are true. Then, find the correct circumferences for the ones that are wrong.

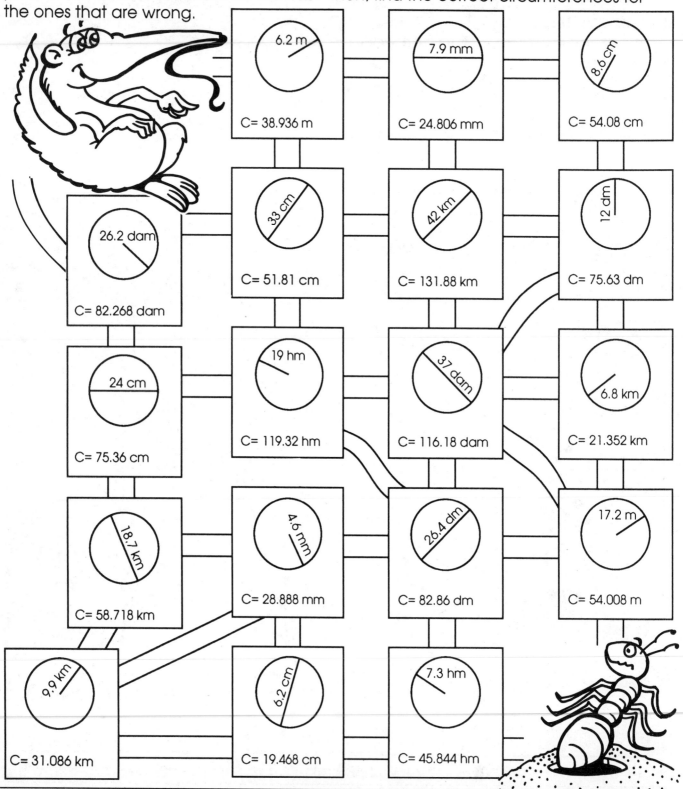

Name _____

No Bones About It!

What part of your body contains one quarter of all of your bones?

To find out, find the area (rounded to the nearest one) of each circle or shaded region below. Then, write the corresponding letter of the problem above the answer at the bottom of the page.

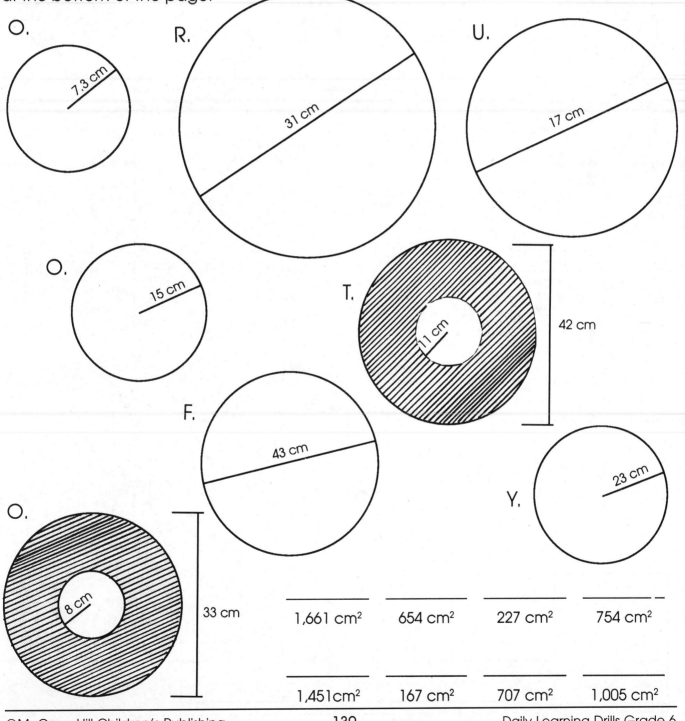

O. 7.3 cm

R. 31 cm

U. 17 cm

O. 15 cm

T. 11 cm 42 cm

F. 43 cm

Y. 23 cm

O. 8 cm 33 cm

1,661 cm²	654 cm²	227 cm²	754 cm²
1,451cm²	167 cm²	707 cm²	1,005 cm²

Name _____

Roberta the Robot

Find each of the perimeters that make up Roberta the Robot.

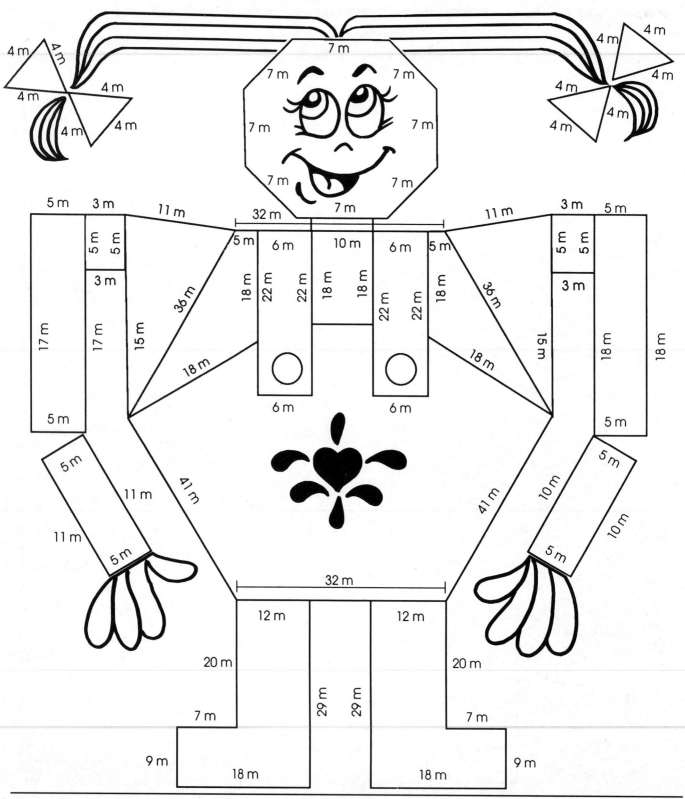

Name _____

Harry the Horse

Help Harry find a way to his hay by shading in the boxes with correct equations.

		11,000 ft = 21 mi	80 ft = 26 yd
		33,500 yd = 19 mi	136 in. = 11 ft
26 ft = 310 in.	5 ft = 60 in.	3 mi = 15,800 ft	18 yd = 55 ft
13 yd = 40 ft	288 in. = 8 yd	10,560 ft = 6 mi	16 mi = 85,000 ft
1,050 in. = 29 yd	33 ft = 11 yd	9 yd = 330 in.	15 mi = 26,000 yd
100 ft = 32 yd	6 mi = 31,680 ft	48 ft = 16 yd	144 in. = 12 ft
32 ft = 386 in.	26 yd = 100 in.	1,000 in. = 28 yd	8 mi = 14,080 yd
52,800 ft = 10 mi	7 yd = 252 in.	504 in. = 14 yd	63,360 ft = 12 mi
720 in. = 20 yd	310 in. = 25 ft	400 in. = 10 yd	11 yd = 40 ft
8 yd = 24 ft	11 mi = 58,000 ft	55 ft = 18 yd	
7,040 yd = 4 mi	18 yd = 648 in.	22 ft = 264 in.	

141

Daily Learning Drills Grade 6

Name _____

Puzzling Lengths

Write the word form of the answers in the puzzle.

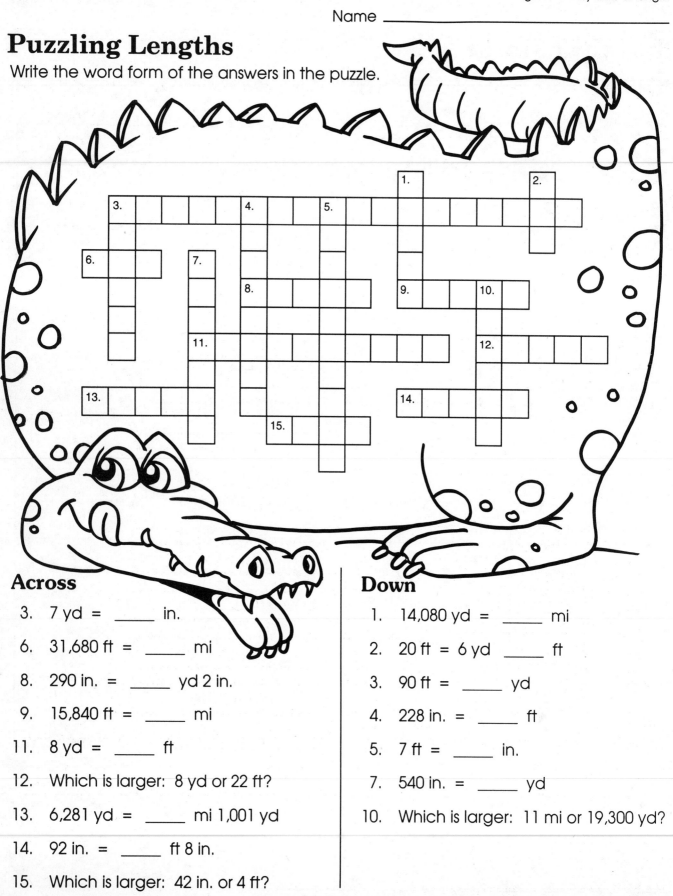

Across

3. 7 yd = _____ in.

6. 31,680 ft = _____ mi

8. 290 in. = _____ yd 2 in.

9. 15,840 ft = _____ mi

11. 8 yd = _____ ft

12. Which is larger: 8 yd or 22 ft?

13. 6,281 yd = _____ mi 1,001 yd

14. 92 in. = _____ ft 8 in.

15. Which is larger: 42 in. or 4 ft?

Down

1. 14,080 yd = _____ mi

2. 20 ft = 6 yd _____ ft

3. 90 ft = _____ yd

4. 228 in. = _____ ft

5. 7 ft = _____ in.

7. 540 in. = _____ yd

10. Which is larger: 11 mi or 19,300 yd?

Name _____

Metric Match Magic

Match the equivalent measurements. Then write the words on the lines below.

100 centimeters (cm) = 1 meter (m)
1,000 meters (m) = 1 kilometer (km)

Match.

1. 2 m •

2. 900 cm •

3. 4,000 m •

4. 700 cm •

5. 3 km •

6. 5,000 m •

7. 6 m •

8. 2 km •

9. 800 cm •

10. 5 m •

11. 2,000 m •

12. 7 km •

• 7 m) of

• 600 cm) draw

• 500 cm) very

• 200 cm) on

• 7,000 m) animal

• 5 km) paper

• 9 m) the

• 2,000 m) a

• 4 km) back

• 3,000 m) this

• 8 m) magician's

• 2 km) favorite

Write the word beside each answer on the line. Then follow the directions.

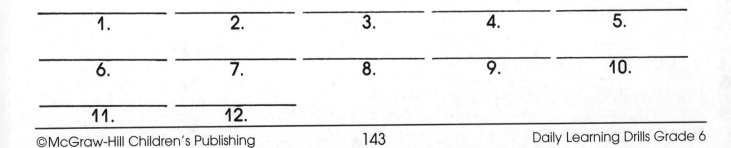

1. _____ 2. _____ 3. _____ 4. _____ 5. _____

6. _____ 7. _____ 8. _____ 9. _____ 10. _____

11. _____ 12. _____

Name _____

An Amazing Animal

> What African animal is born underwater and swims before it walks?

To find out, solve the problems on the left. Draw a straight line connecting the problem to its answer. The line should pass through a letter and a number. Put the letter above the box with the correct answer at the bottom of the page.

41 dL = _____ hL ❑ ⑦

7.2 kg = _____ dg ❑ ⑬

11.01 g = _____ mg ❑

21.6 cL = _____ daL ❑

7 cL = _____ hL ❑

16.013 kg = _____ dag ❑

.062 g = _____ cg ❑

310 hg = _____ g ❑

210 mL = _____ L ❑

.013 cL = _____ hL ❑

21.9 daL = _____ kL ❑

11 L = _____ hL ❑

.121 cg = _____ dag ❑

11.61 hL = _____ dL ❑

29.6 mg = _____ g ❑

Ⓔ Ⓜ Ⓟ Ⓞ ⑩ ③ ⑤ Ⓣ ② Ⓢ Ⓟ ⑨ ⑥ Ⓘ ⑮ ⑫ Ⓐ ① Ⓞ Ⓤ ⑭ Ⓟ ⑧ Ⓗ Ⓣ ⑪ ④ Ⓗ

❑ 1601.3

❑ .11

❑ 72,000

❑ .0216

❑ .0000013

❑ .041

❑ 6.2

❑ 11,610

❑ .21

❑ 11,010

❑ .219

❑ 31,000

❑ .0296

❑ .000121

❑ .007

1	2	3		4	5	6	7	8	9	10	11	12	13	14	15

Name _____

Hhhmm?

What do the four H's stand for in the 4-H Club?

To find out, solve the following ratios. Find the answers at the bottom of the page. Put the corresponding problem letter above the answer. When you have answered the riddle, write each ratio two other ways and find two equivalent ratios for each one.

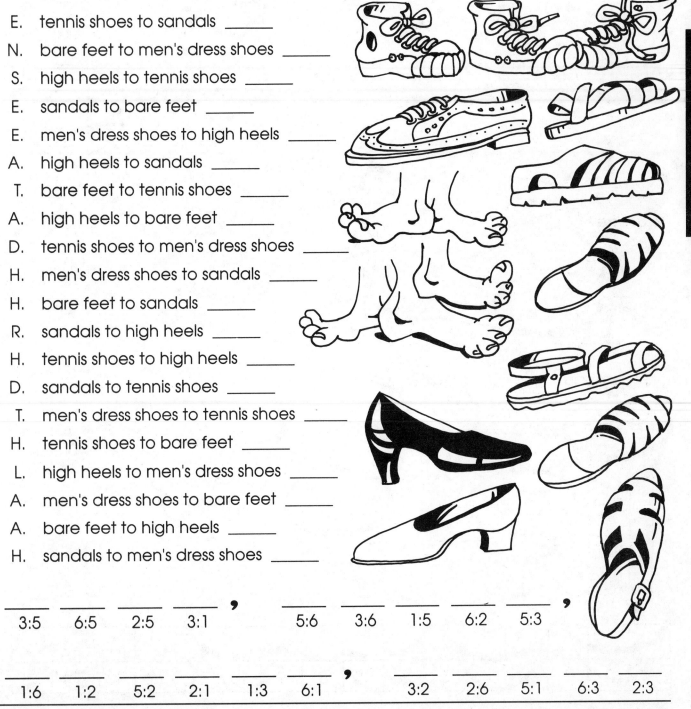

E. tennis shoes to sandals _____

N. bare feet to men's dress shoes _____

S. high heels to tennis shoes _____

E. sandals to bare feet _____

E. men's dress shoes to high heels _____

A. high heels to sandals _____

T. bare feet to tennis shoes _____

A. high heels to bare feet _____

D. tennis shoes to men's dress shoes _____

H. men's dress shoes to sandals _____

H. bare feet to sandals _____

R. sandals to high heels _____

H. tennis shoes to high heels _____

D. sandals to tennis shoes _____

T. men's dress shoes to tennis shoes _____

H. tennis shoes to bare feet _____

L. high heels to men's dress shoes _____

A. men's dress shoes to bare feet _____

A. bare feet to high heels _____

H. sandals to men's dress shoes _____

___ ___ ___ ___ , ___ ___ ___ ___ ___ ___ ,
3:5 6:5 2:5 3:1   5:6 3:6 1:5 6:2 5:3

___ ___ ___ ___ ___ ___ , ___ ___ ___ ___ ___
1:6 1:2 5:2 2:1 1:3 6:1   3:2 2:6 5:1 6:3 2:3

MATH

Name _____

Sam the Squirrel

Help Sam get his acorns to his tree by shading in the path containing the correct proportions.

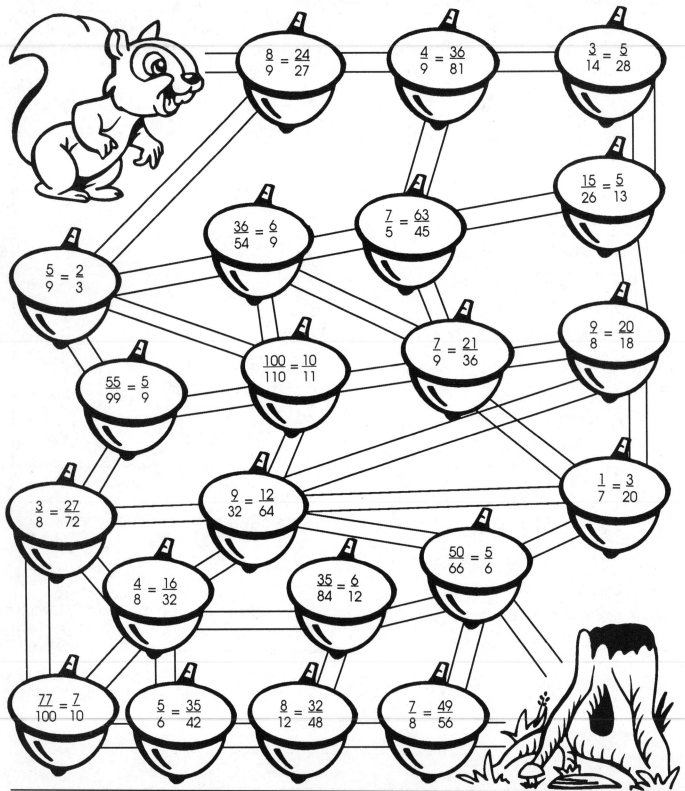

$\frac{8}{9} = \frac{24}{27}$

$\frac{4}{9} = \frac{36}{81}$

$\frac{3}{14} = \frac{5}{28}$

$\frac{15}{26} = \frac{5}{13}$

$\frac{36}{54} = \frac{6}{9}$

$\frac{7}{5} = \frac{63}{45}$

$\frac{5}{9} = \frac{2}{3}$

$\frac{9}{8} = \frac{20}{18}$

$\frac{55}{99} = \frac{5}{9}$

$\frac{100}{110} = \frac{10}{11}$

$\frac{7}{9} = \frac{21}{36}$

$\frac{3}{8} = \frac{27}{72}$

$\frac{9}{32} = \frac{12}{64}$

$\frac{1}{7} = \frac{3}{20}$

$\frac{4}{8} = \frac{16}{32}$

$\frac{35}{84} = \frac{6}{12}$

$\frac{50}{66} = \frac{5}{6}$

$\frac{77}{100} = \frac{7}{10}$

$\frac{5}{6} = \frac{35}{42}$

$\frac{8}{12} = \frac{32}{48}$

$\frac{7}{8} = \frac{49}{56}$

Daily Learning Drills Grade 6

Name _____

Map It Out!

Make your own map using the map scale that is given.

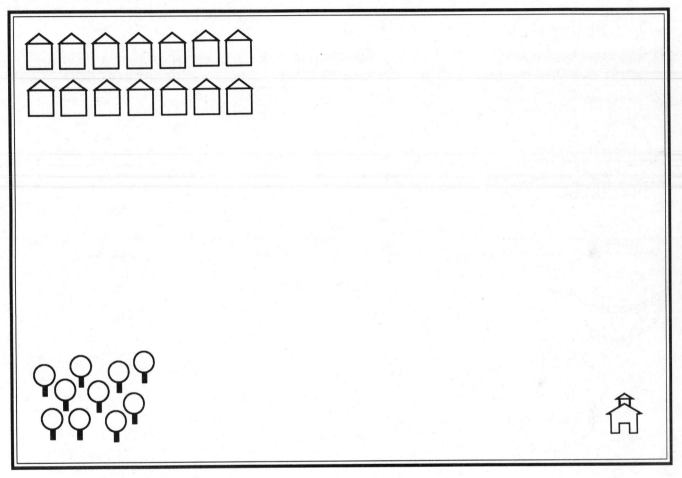

├──┤ 1 cm = 2.5 miles

1. Draw a road 16 miles long going east to west between the park and the neighborhood. Label it Hill Road.

2. Draw a road 21 miles long going north to south starting from the schoolhouse. Label it Schoolhouse Drive.

3. Draw a road 18 miles long perpendicular to and intersecting Hill Road. Make sure it starts by the houses. Label it Neighborhood Road.

4. Draw a public swimming pool 24 miles northeast of the park.

5. Draw a playground 12 miles south of the swimming pool and 20 miles east of the park.

6. Draw a soccer field 27 miles east of the neighborhood.

7. Draw a fountain 11 miles northeast of the pool and 17.5 miles from the schoolhouse.

Name _____

Graphs Galore!

Make each of the following graphs using the information given. Then, refer to the graphs to answer the questions.

__Broken-Line Graph__	__Bar Graph__	__Circle Graph__

TEMPERATURES IN ST. LOUIS FOR ONE WEEK		TOTAL NUMBER OF HITS FOR ONE SEASON		SIXTH GRADERS' FAVORITE CLASS IN SCHOOL	
Saturday	63°	Sally	18	Math	20%
Sunday	65°	Sue	16	History	10%
Monday	61°	Jill	23	Science	30%
Tuesday	63°	Mary	15	Reading	20%
Wednesday	70°	Lee	31	Physical Ed.	10%
Thursday	68°	Janie	23	Music	5%
Friday	66°	Judy	33	Art	5%

1. Who had the most number of hits in one season? _____

2. What day was the warmest? _____

3. What percent of sixth graders like either math or music? _____

4. What day was the coldest? _____

5. What two players had the same number of hits? _____

6. What is the difference between the highest and lowest temperatures? _____

7. What is the sixth graders' favorite class? _____

8. Who had the least number of hits in one season? _____

9. On what two days was the temperature 63°? _____

Name _____

What Time?

Solve the following problems.

1. Mary was out of bed at 6:30 a.m. She had lunch 6 hours later. What time did Mary have lunch?

   6 hours __Ahead__ = _____ p.m.

2. Mary returned from school at 4:00 p.m. Mary had left for school 8½ hours earlier. What time did Mary leave for school?

   8½ hours __Back__ = _____

3. Mary ate breakfast at 7:00 a.m. and ate dinner 11 hours later. What time did she eat dinner?

   11 hours _____ = _____

4. Mary started her homework at 7:30 p.m. and studied for 3½ hours. What time did she stop studying?

   3½ hours _____ = _____

5. On Saturday Mary was baby-sitting a neighbor's child. The parents returned at 3:00 p.m. They had been gone 5 hours. At what time did Mary start baby-sitting?

   5 hours _____ = _____

6. Mary's party started at 8:00 p.m. and was over 2½ hours later. Mary spent 1½ hours cleaning up after the last guest left. What time was Mary through cleaning?

   _____ hours _____ = _____

7. Mary's math class starts at 9:30 a.m. Her music class starts 4½ hours later. What time does Mary's music class start?

   _____ hours _____ = _____

8. School is out at 3:00 p.m. Baseball practice lasts 2 hours, and then the team takes ½ hour to shower and get dressed. What time does the team leave school?

   _____ hours _____ = _____

Name _____

Police Patrol

Solve the following problems.

1. The local police department has 52 members. ¼ of the police are women. ⅔ of the men are over 45 years of age. How many of the men are over 45?

   Step 1: 4 ⟌52   Step 2: 3 x _____ = _____

   Step 3: 3 ⟌⎺⎺   Step 4: 2 x _____ = _____

2. In one week the police investigated 4 times as many auto wrecks and fires combined as burglaries. They were called to 94 wrecks and 82 fires. How many burglaries did they investigate?

3. The police were called to investigate 42 fights where the people fighting were not related. They investigated 25 times that many family arguments. How many fights in all did the police investigate?

4. The police issued 480 parking tickets and 124 speeding tickets. "Driving under the influence" tickets totaled ¼ as many as the number of speeding tickets. How many tickets were issued in all?

5. Last week ¾ of the 124 speeders and ⅓ of the 72 jay walkers caught were second offenders and had to attend safety school. How many people altogether had to attend safety school?

6. The health insurance plan costs the city $27.00 per month for each of the 52 police force members. Life insurance costs ⅓ as much. How much is spent each year on insurance for the police force?

7. The city bought 7 new police cars that cost $16,500.00 each. 7 old police cars brought $3,400.00 each when traded in on new ones. How much was paid for the 7 new cars after the trade-in?

8. The banquet for 2 retiring police officers was attended by 250 local residents. Each resident paid $12.50 for the dinner. $500.00 of the money collected was spent on gifts for the retirees. How much was left to pay for the banquet?

Name _____

Decisions, Decisions!

You have $200 to spend on purchases before you travel west to search for gold. If you wait to buy the items in California, they will cost at least three times as much. Circle the items you will buy and number them in order of importance.

	Item	Cost		Item	Cost
_____	pan for panning gold	$5	_____	boots	$5
_____	change of clothes	$10	_____	dishes (set of four)	$5
_____	book about California	$20	_____	50 lb. bag of flour	$10
_____	washtub	$10	_____	ammunition (50-count)	$5
_____	20 lbs. of cured beef	$20	_____	revolver	$20
_____	three cloth bags (for gold)	$5	_____	pocket watch	$30
_____	matches (100-count)	$5	_____	one pair of mules	$30
_____	one pair of oxen	$40	_____	dozen fishhooks	$5
_____	dress suit	$20	_____	hunting knife	$10
_____	six chickens	$5	_____	two blankets	$5
_____	canvas for tent	$5	_____	cooking pot	$10
_____	sleeping cot	$20	_____	pick	$5
_____	shovel	$5			
_____	ax	$5		**Total Cost** _____	
_____	rifle	$50		**Money Remaining** _____	

Today the average income per worker in our country is more than $15,000 per year. In 1848, the average income of a common laborer was about $288, yet goods in the California territory were terribly expensive.

Directions: To compare the costs of the following items in 1848 with today's costs, take 1848's cost and divide by today's cost. Round to the nearest hundredth and convert your answers from decimals to percents to show the rate of inflation.

Example: jar of pickles $11 (1848's Cost) ÷ $1.59 (Today's Cost) = 6.918 or 692% (inflation rate)

Item	1848 Cost	Today's Cost	Inflation Rate	
one onion	$2.00	$ .15	_____ or _____	%
one egg	$3.00	$ .07	_____	%
1 lb. of potatoes	$1.25	$ .30	_____	%
1 lb. of sugar	$1.00	$ .40	_____	%
box of baking soda	$8.00	$ .35	_____	%
loaf of bread	$2.00	$ 1.19	_____	%
1/2 lb. of cheese	$3.00	$ 1.30	_____	%
barrel of flour	$800.00	$ 20.00	_____	%
one candle	$1.00	$ .60	_____	%
two spools of thread	$7.50	$ 2.00	_____	%

Name _____

Something's Missing

Use this Table of Measures to help solve the problems on this page.

8 fluid ounces = 1 cup	2 pints = 1 quart	8 quarts = 1 peck	16 ounces = 1 pound
2 cups = 1 pint	4 quarts = 1 gallon	4 pecks = 1 bushel	2,000 pounds = 1 ton

1. The 5 pounds of hamburger needed for a cookout cost $5.60. How much does the hamburger cost per ounce?

step 1: 5 ⟌5.60

step 2: **1 pound** = _____ ounces

step 3: **16**⟌‾‾‾

2. A new tractor weighs 1¼ tons. How many pounds does the tractor weigh?

3. A gallon of ice cream sells for $3.20. How much will a 1-cup serving of ice cream cost?

4. 5 quarts of oil are needed for a car's oil change. How many oil changes can a mechanic make from a 50-gallon drum of oil?

5. Martha poured 24 cups of water into a jug. Her mother told her she needed 16 more cups of water to fill the jug. How many quarts will the jug hold?

6. A bushel of apples sells for $5.80. How much would a peck cost?

7. Bill sold a peck of strawberries at 85¢ a quart. How much money did he receive in all?

Name _____

Something Else Is Missing

Use this Table of Measures to help solve the problems on this page.

100 centimeters (cm) = 1 meter (m)   10 decimeters (dm) = 1 meter (m)
1,000 meters (m) = 1 kilometer (km)   1,000 grams (g) = 1 kilogram (kg)

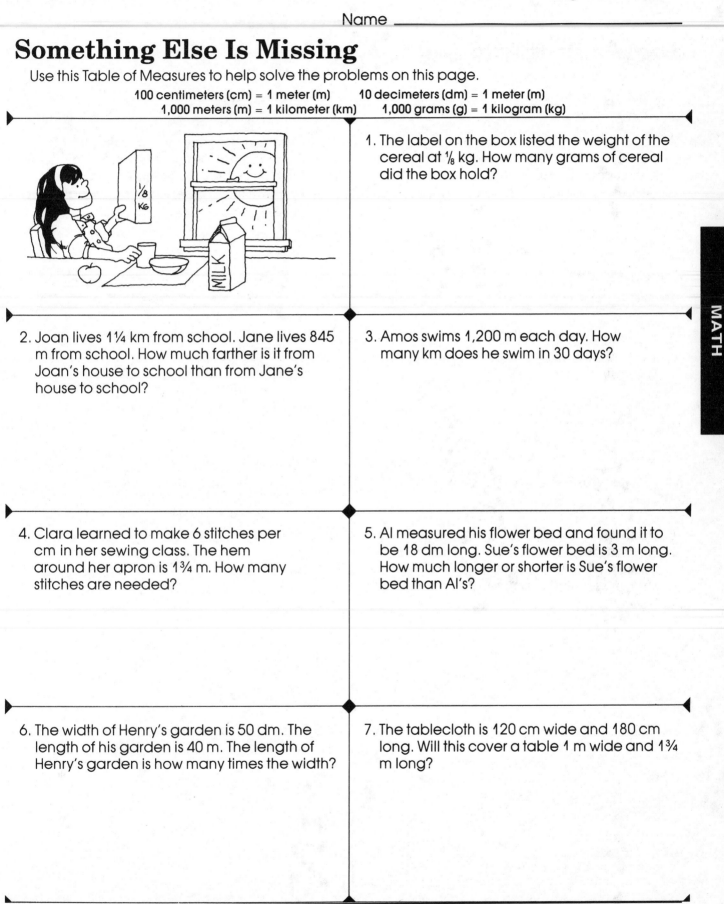

1. The label on the box listed the weight of the cereal at ⅛ kg. How many grams of cereal did the box hold?

2. Joan lives 1¼ km from school. Jane lives 845 m from school. How much farther is it from Joan's house to school than from Jane's house to school?

3. Amos swims 1,200 m each day. How many km does he swim in 30 days?

4. Clara learned to make 6 stitches per cm in her sewing class. The hem around her apron is 1¾ m. How many stitches are needed?

5. Al measured his flower bed and found it to be 18 dm long. Sue's flower bed is 3 m long. How much longer or shorter is Sue's flower bed than Al's?

6. The width of Henry's garden is 50 dm. The length of his garden is 40 m. The length of Henry's garden is how many times the width?

7. The tablecloth is 120 cm wide and 180 cm long. Will this cover a table 1 m wide and 1¾ m long?

Name _____

Too Much Information

Underline the **distractor** (unused fact) in each story and solve the problem.

1. Carl studied math for ¾ hour and then played with his dog for ½ hour before dinner. After dinner he studied 1½ hours for his other classes. How long altogether did Carl study?

2. Mr. Thomas teaches mathematics for 4½ hours each day and then spends 2½ hours each day coaching the basketball team. How much time does he spend on basketball in 5 days?

3. After school Marla spends ⅓ of her time practicing the piano, ¼ of her time on soccer practice and ⅙ of her time on voice lessons. What fraction of her time does Marla spend on music?

4. Mrs. Harper has 64 students in her choir. Of these students, ⅓ are boys. She also conducts the 48-member orchestra. How many music students does Mrs. Harper have in all?

5. In one class of 24 students, 8 are in the band and 12 are involved in athletics. What fraction of the class is in the band?

6. Mr. Wood works for 6 hours cleaning up after each ball game. Altogether, there are 34 ball games. Mr. Wood is paid at the rate of $6.00 per hour. How many hours in all does Mr. Wood spend cleaning up after ball games?

7. A year is 365 days long. Students spend 180 days a year in school. Each school day is 6 hours long. How many hours do students spend in school each year?

Name _____

Too Much or Not Enough?

Each of the following problems contains too much or too little information. If too much information is given, underline the distractor and solve the problem. If not enough information is given, write "NE."

1. Chuck has 6 rows across the garden for every 5 feet of space. How many rows in all are in his garden?

2. Chuck has 3 times as many rows of beans as peas, and he has 4 times as many rows of potatoes as peas. He has 3 rows of peas. How many rows of beans are there in Chuck's garden?

3. Cucumber plants produced an average of 18 cucumbers per hill. 5 of the cucumbers weighed one pound each. There were 12 hills altogether. How many cucumbers were produced in all?

4. Chuck had 49 potato plants. The average potato weighed 1¼ pounds. How much did the potatoes weigh altogether?

5. Chuck paid Bill $3.50 per hour to help him in his garden. Bill dug potatoes for 7 hours and picked beans for 1½ hours. How much did Chuck pay Bill to dig potatoes?

6. Potatoes sell for $2.79 per 10-pound bag. Chuck bagged potatoes for 6 hours. How much money did he make?

7. Chuck sold $4.50 worth of green beans and $2.70 worth of tomatoes. At 30¢ per pound, how many pounds of green beans did Chuck sell?

Name _____

Write Your Own Problem

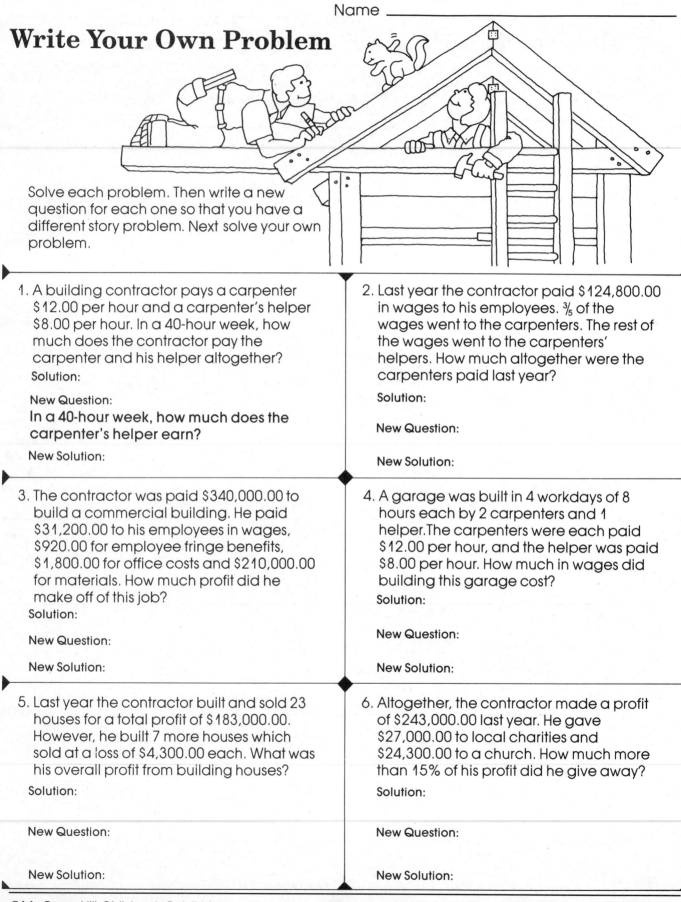

Solve each problem. Then write a new question for each one so that you have a different story problem. Next solve your own problem.

1. A building contractor pays a carpenter $12.00 per hour and a carpenter's helper $8.00 per hour. In a 40-hour week, how much does the contractor pay the carpenter and his helper altogether?

Solution:

New Question:
In a 40-hour week, how much does the carpenter's helper earn?

New Solution:

2. Last year the contractor paid $124,800.00 in wages to his employees. ⅗ of the wages went to the carpenters. The rest of the wages went to the carpenters' helpers. How much altogether were the carpenters paid last year?

Solution:

New Question:

New Solution:

3. The contractor was paid $340,000.00 to build a commercial building. He paid $31,200.00 to his employees in wages, $920.00 for employee fringe benefits, $1,800.00 for office costs and $210,000.00 for materials. How much profit did he make off of this job?

Solution:

New Question:

New Solution:

4. A garage was built in 4 workdays of 8 hours each by 2 carpenters and 1 helper. The carpenters were each paid $12.00 per hour, and the helper was paid $8.00 per hour. How much in wages did building this garage cost?

Solution:

New Question:

New Solution:

5. Last year the contractor built and sold 23 houses for a total profit of $183,000.00. However, he built 7 more houses which sold at a loss of $4,300.00 each. What was his overall profit from building houses?

Solution:

New Question:

New Solution:

6. Altogether, the contractor made a profit of $243,000.00 last year. He gave $27,000.00 to local charities and $24,300.00 to a church. How much more than 15% of his profit did he give away?

Solution:

New Question:

New Solution:

Name _____

You Can Do It!

Solve the following problems.

1. The school is ⅝ mile from Jack's house. How many miles does Jack ride his bike to and from school in 5 days?

2. The library is 2¼ miles farther from Jack's house than the school is. The school is ⅝ mile away. How far does Jack live from the library?

3. The library is 2¼ miles from Jack's house. The ice cream parlor is ½ mile farther down the street. How far has he pedaled his bike if he goes to the library, then to the ice cream parlor, and then back home?

4. Jack lives 12 miles from the ball park. He can pedal his bike 10 miles in 30 minutes. How long will it take Jack to ride his bike to the ball park?

5. It takes 4 trips around the track to make a mile. Jack pedaled his bike around the track 24 times. It took him 30 minutes. How many miles per hour was Jack pedaling?

6. It takes Jack 15 minutes to walk a mile. It takes Jack 4 minutes to ride his bike a mile. How much farther can he ride his bike than he can walk in one hour?

7. Jack rode his bike for 2⅓ hours at a speed of 12 miles per hour. The next 1½ hours his speed dropped to 10 miles per hour. How many miles did he cover altogether?

Name _____

Blast Off!

Study each problem carefully and then find the solution.

1. The 6th grade class has decided to hold a class reunion in space during the year 2010. The first stop will be on the Earth's moon, which is 240,000 miles from Earth. If the trip to the moon takes 3 hours, how many miles per hour will they be traveling?

2. The next stop of the class reunion will be on Mercury, where everyone will wish to be weighed. On Mercury your weight is only ¼ of your weight on Earth. How much would a 256-pound Earthling weigh on Mercury?

3. Earth is 93,000,000 miles from the sun. Mercury is ⅖ as far from the sun as Earth is. How far is Mercury from the sun?

4. On Mars your weight will be 0.38 times your Earth weight. How many pounds will a 200-pound Earthling weigh on Mars?

5. Mars is 1½ times as far from the sun as Earth is. Earth is 93,000,000 miles from the sun. How many miles is it from Mars to the sun?

6. From Mars the group will travel to Jupiter, a distance of 998,000,000 kilometers. In the year 2010, the students' trip to Jupiter will take 40 days. How many kilometers will they be traveling per day?

7. The group probably will not visit Pluto because traveling there would take about 8 months. It is 3,600,000,000 miles from Earth to Pluto. To make the trip in 8 months, the spaceship would have to travel how many miles per month?

8. Isaac Newton was born in 1642. Twenty years later he discovered the law of gravity. In the year 2010, the former 6th graders will discover that Newton's law of gravity is still true. In the year 2010, how many years will it have been since Newton discovered the gravitation law?

Name _____

Booming Business

Pat wants to put "A Pet in Every Home," so he is having a gigantic sale on all of his wonderful pets.

	Work the problems on another paper.	**Answer Space**
1.	Pat has 18 rabbits which he is selling for $2.99 each. How much money will he earn if he sells all 18 rabbits?	
2.	You bought a pet parrot for $2.39 and a myna bird for $8.67. What was your total cost?	
3.	He is selling 12 goldfish for $.84. How much does he receive for each goldfish?	
4.	Your teacher bought a ribbon snake for the classroom. It cost $4.79. How much change did she receive from a $20.00 bill?	
5.	Pat is selling a pet python for $9.99. A pet monkey costs $13.45. What is the difference in their prices?	
6.	Your principal bought 60 guppies for the school carnival for $23.40. How much did each guppy cost?	
7.	Pat is selling hamsters for $1.41 each. How much will he receive for 40 hamsters?	
8.	Pat sold 10 cocker spaniel puppies for $2.99 each. How much did he receive for all 10?	
9.	Your teacher loves rodents. She buys a pair of mice for $2.39 and a pair of hamsters for $3.13. How much does it cost her altogether?	
10.	Pat sold 19 chameleons for a total of $41.04. How much did he charge for each chameleon?	

Name _____

Big Bucks for You

Your book, *The Secret Life of a Teenage Dracula*, earns you a nice bit of money in royalties. You need a checking account to keep the money in while you find ways to spend your new wealth.

Use the information on the next page and compute your payments, deposits, and balance on the checkbook record below.

Problem Number	Transaction	Payment	Deposit	Balance
1	Deposit (Royalty Check)		$1000.00	$1000.00
1	Record Store			

Work the problems on another paper.

1. You receive your first royalty check for $1,000.00 and deposit it in your checking account. You go directly to the record store and spend $234.56 on new records. What is your balance?

2. You naturally treat all your friends to pizzas which costs you $47.76. You pay with a check. What is your balance now?

3. You decide to restock your wardrobe and buy $389.99 worth of new clothes. What is your balance?

4. Your next royalty check arrives, and you deposit $1,712.34. You also treat yourself to a new 15-speed bicycle which costs $667.09. What is your balance?

5. You buy your teacher some perfume for a present. You write a check for $37.89. What is your balance?

6. You need a tennis racket and some other sports equipment. The bill comes to $203.45. What is your new balance?

7. You treat your family to dinner at **Snails in a Pail** where the check comes to $56.17. What is your new balance?

8. You join a health club, and the first payment is $150.90. What is your new balance?

9. You deposit your latest royalty check which amounts to $4,451.01. What is your new balance?

10. To celebrate this good fortune, you take the entire school to a professional football game. The bill comes to $4,339.98. What is your new balance?

11. You need a good radio to boom out your favorite music. You spend $198.79 on a radio that is "state of the art." What is your new balance?

12. Your best friend borrows $500.00 from you. What is your balance?

13. You get a royalty check from your book for $456.78. What is your new balance?

14. You run up a large phone bill which comes to $793.55. What is your new balance?

MATH

Name _____

Something's Fishy at Pat's Pet Shop

Pat has received a gigantic shipment of fish at his
pet shop for his "Love a Fish Sale." Help him
figure out the following problems.

Work the problems on another paper.

Answer Space

1.	Pat has 1,750 guppies which he sells at 10 for $1.00. How much money will he get if he sells all of them?	

2.	Pat has 324 black mollies which he sells at 6 for $3.25. How much could he make on the black mollies?	

3.	Pat has 648 swordtails which he sells at 12 for $1.00. How much will he get if he sells all of them?	

4.	He was sent 371 white cloud fish which are now on sale at 7 for $.99. How much will Pat make if he sells all of the white clouds?	

5.	He has 675 neons which sell at 25 for $2.00. How much could Pat make by selling all of the neons?	

6.	Pat has 1,281 comet goldfish which he sells at 21 for $4.99. How much will he make if he sells all of them?	

7.	Pat sells 25 angelfish for $3.00. How much will he get for 900 angelfish?	

8.	He has 253 tiger barbs which he sells at 11 for $1.99. How much will he get if he sells all of them?	

9.	Pat has 168 head-and-tail-light fish which he is selling at 3 for $2.99. How much will he make if he sells all of them?	

10.	He has 1,452 telescope goldfish which he is selling at 33 for $6.79. If he sells them all, how much money will he receive?	

Hairy Spiders and Mighty Mites

Work the problems on another paper.

Answer Space

1.	A male spitting spider is 4/16 in. long. A female is 3/8 in. long. How much longer is the female?
2.	A forest wolf spider is 1/2 in. long. A female rabid wolf spider is 3/4 in. long. What is the difference in their lengths?
3.	A male trapdoor spider is 11/12 in. long. A violin spider is 1/4 in. long. How much longer is the trapdoor spider?
4.	A female green lynx spider is 5/8 in. long. A male is 1/2 in. long. What is their total length?
5.	A male barn spider is 2/3 in. long. A female is 7/8 in. long. What is their total length?
6.	A male hammock spider is 1/4 in. long. A female is 1/3 in. long. What is their total length?
7.	A velvet mite is 1/8 in. long. A soft tick is 3/12 in. long. What is the difference in their lengths?
8.	A spider mite is only 1/32 in. long. A water mite is 1/8 in. long. How much longer is a water mite?
9.	A female garden spider is 3/4 in. long. A male is 6/12 in. long. How much longer is the female?
10.	A female bola spider is 1/2 in. long. A male bola is 1/12 in. long. What is the total?

Name _____

Eartha Wurm's Pizzas

Eartha Wurm believes that pizzas have become flat, dull, tasteless and boring. She has created new pizza toppings to put some zing back into your taste buds.

Work the problems on another paper.

1.	Eartha Wurm wanted to cut 7 Red Hot Red Worm Pizzas into slices. Each slice would be 1/5 of a pizza. How many slices could she get from the 7 pizzas?	
2.	Each slice of Spicy Caterpillar Pizza is 1/6 of a pizza. How many slices could Eartha get from 15 of these pizzas?	
3.	Eartha gave away 2/7 of a Tasty Angleworm Pizza to each customer until all 12 of these pizzas were gone. How many customers received free pizza?	
4.	Eartha Wurm made 10 Fiery Flatworm Pizzas. She cut them into 1/4 size pieces. How many pieces of Flatworm Pizza did she have?	
5.	Every child under 7 feet tall was given 1/3 of a Chili Roundworm Pizza. Eartha gave away 40 of these pizzas. How many children received free pizza?	
6.	Eartha's Wiggly Worm 'n Horseradish Pizza is so hot that she will sell only 2/9 of a pizza to each customer. How many customers can she serve with 16 of these pizzas?	
7.	Each member of your softball team was treated to 3/7 of a Tangy Earthworm Pizza. It took 6 pizzas to treat all of you. How many members were on your team?	
8.	The entire cast of your school play was rewarded with 3/5 of a Sweet and Sour Night Crawler Pizza. It took 18 pizzas. How many people took part in your school play?	
9.	Eartha Wurm gave 4/9 of a pizza free to every person who came into her restaurant dressed like an earthworm. She gave away 4 pizzas. How many people came dressed up as earthworms?	
10.	Your music teacher treated every member of the school chorus to 5/12 of a pizza. It took 20 pizzas. How many children were in the school chorus?	

Name _____

Sam Sillicook's Secret Recipe!

Sam Sillicook, world-famous pizza maker, has just published his super secret recipe for The Tongue Blaster Pizza. It contains:

1/4 cup of Tabasco sauce   3/8 cup of mustard

1/3 cup of red onions   2/7 cup of chili pepper

2/5 cup of horseradish   2/9 cup of garlic

1/6 cup of cayenne pepper   **Serves 6 hungry people**

Work the problems on another paper.

1.

Your teacher wants to make a smaller serving. She is going to make only 1/3 times as much. How much will she need of each ingredient?

_____ cup of Tabasco sauce

_____ cup of red onions

_____ cup of horseradish

_____ cup of cayenne pepper

_____ cup of mustard

_____ cup of chili pepper

_____ cup of garlic

2.

Your mother is going to serve this recipe to her bridge club. She needs only 1/2 of the recipe. How much of each ingredient will she need?

_____ cup of Tabasco sauce

_____ cup of red onions

_____ cup of horseradish

_____ cup of cayenne pepper

_____ cup of mustard

_____ cup of chili pepper

_____ cup of garlic

3.

The principal decides to bring this treat to the teachers' Christmas party. He is going to make 5/6 times as much as the recipe reads. How much of each ingredient will he need?

_____ cup of Tabasco sauce

_____ cup of red onions

_____ cup of horseradish

_____ cup of cayenne pepper

_____ cup of mustard

_____ cup of chili pepper

_____ cup of garlic

4.

You decide to make 1/4 as much of this recipe for your favorite teacher. How much will you need of each ingredient?

_____ cup of Tabasco sauce

_____ cup of red onions

_____ cup of horseradish

_____ cup of cayenne pepper

_____ cup of mustard

_____ cup of chili pepper

_____ cup of garlic

Daily Learning Drills Grade 6

Name _____

Krab E. Krabby

Krab E. Krabby likes to make unusual things, but he gets very cranky trying to figure out how much material he needs. Give him a hand so he won't be crabby.

Work the problems on another paper.

Answer Space

1.	Krab E. Krabby wants to make a paper clip jump rope 60 inches long. Each paper clip is 1 1/4 in. long. How many paper clips will he need?	
2.	Mr. Krabby wants to make a 39-inch-long belt by stringing string beans together. Each string bean is exactly 3 1/4 in. long. How many string beans will he need?	
3.	Krab E. Krabby hopes to make a 45-inch-high tower using dead batteries. Each battery is 2 1/2 in. tall. How many batteries will he need?	
4.	He is anxious to make a 9-inch-long wristband of seashells for his favorite teacher. He is going to use 1 1/8-inch-long seashells. How many will he need?	
5.	Krab would like to put a 180-inch border around his teacher's desk using pine cones that are 4 1/2 in. long. How many cones will he need?	
6.	Krabby wants to give his sister a 30-inch-long string of beads for her birthday. Each bead is 1 1/2 inches in diameter. How many beads will he need?	
7.	He is going to put together a 13-inch headband decorated with buttons that are 1 5/8 inches in diameter. How many buttons will he need?	
8.	He is going to glue together bottle caps that are 1 7/8 inch in diameter to make a school banner 150 inches long. How many bottle caps will he need?	
9.	Krab is gluing jumbo jellybeans end-to-end to create a jellybean necklace 20 inches long for his girlfriend. Each jellybean is 2 1/2 in. long. How many of them will he need?	
10.	Krabby wants to make an 81-inch border for the science counter using clam shells that are exactly 3 3/8 in. long. How many clam shells will he need?	

         Daily Learning Drills Grade 6

Name _____

The Super Twist

Mr. M.T. Whole has invented a whole new kind of doughnut which he calls the Super Twist. It is filled with whipped cream, jammed with jelly and topped with powdered sugar.

Work the problems on another paper.   Answer Space

1.	M.T. Whole uses 3 1/2 gallons of milk to make a batch of Whole Jelly Twists. He uses 1 3/4 gallons of milk for a batch of Plain Twists. What is the difference?
2.	M.T. Whole needs 10 1/3 gallons of jam for his Super Jam-Filled Doughnut Twists. He needs only 4/5 as much jam for his Regular Jam Doughnuts. How much jam does he need for the latter doughnuts?
3.	Mr. Whole wants to make as many Super Twists as he can with 280 ounces of strawberry jam. Each twist uses 2 4/5 ounces of jam. How many Super Twists can he make?
4.	M.T. is making a huge batch of Creamy Blackberry Twists which requires 198 5/6 ounces of flour. He is also using 134 7/8 ounces of flour for his Plain Twists. What is the total?
5.	His Stuffed Strawberry Twists use 1 1/3 ounces of jam in each twist. How many twists can he fill with 124 ounces of jam?
6.	M.T.'s Chock Full of Chocolate Twists require 3 5/7 ounces of chocolate for each one. How many ounces of chocolate are in 84 Chock Full of Chocolate Twists?
7.	In one week, M.T. uses 114 1/2 gallons of milk and 99 7/9 gallons of cream. How much more milk does he use in a week?
8.	M.T. uses 66 1/2 ounces of grape jelly for his Great Grape Twists. A batch of his Blueberry Twists requires 49 9/10 ounces of jelly. How many more ounces of grape jelly does he use?
9.	Mr. M.T. Whole is especially proud of the Dreamy Creamy Twist, a scrumptious doughnut that uses 2 8/9 ounces of creamy filling. How many ounces of filling are in 84 Dreamy Creamy Twists?
10.	M.T. Whole's Chock Full of Chocolate Twists each require 4 1/3 ounces of flour. How many ounces does he need for 180 of these doughnuts?

Name _____

The Super Sac

McMealworms wants your business. They have just introduced the Super Sac, a triple decker McMealworm Burger that comes with Roasted Roaches and a Cricket Cola.

Work the problems on another paper.

Answer Space

1. You buy a Super Sac for $3.79. How much change do you get from a $20.00 bill?

2. Your best friend buys a Super Sac for $3.79 and an extra order of Roasted Roaches for $.79. What is his total bill?

3. The largest cockroach you can find in your order of Roasted Roaches is 5.1 cm long. The shortest is 3.99 cm long. What is their total length?

4. Your mother spends $14.39 at McMealworms, and your sister spends another $4.99. What is their total cost?

5. The longest mealworm you can find in your Super Sac is 3.19 cm long. The shortest one is 1.7 cm. What is the difference in their lengths?

6. If you buy a triple decker burger, Roasted Roaches and a Cricket Cola separately, it costs $4.27. How much do you save by buying the Super Sac?

7. A regular McMealworm Burger costs $1.69. A triple decker costs $2.59. How much more is the triple decker?

8. You find one cockroach that weighs .321 grams and another that weighs .4 grams. What is their total weight?

9. Your friend finds a mealworm beetle that weighs .41 grams. The heaviest one you can find is .378 grams. How much heavier is your friend's beetle?

10. What is the difference in length between a 3.17 cm long mealworm and a 1.6 cm long mealworm?

Name _____

Kookey's Creations

Professor Kook E. Kookey has invented a
cookie that is shaped like a child's
alphabet block and tastes like a super
sweet candy bar. He also has cubic
cookie candy bars that are crammed
with berries and chunks of chocolate.

Work the problems on another paper.

Answer Space

1.	Professor Kookey's Fudge-Filled Cubic Cookie Candy Bar has 3.7 ounces of fudge. How many ounces are in 35 bars?
2.	Kook E. Kookey's Chock Full of Chocolate Cookie Candy Bar has 5.3 ounces of chocolate. How many ounces are in 68 bars?
3.	Kook's Cubic Munchy Crunchies use 6.78 ounces of peanuts in each one. How many ounces are there in .25 of a bar?
4.	Kookey's Crunchies also use 5.34 ounces of maple sugar. How much maple sugar is in .25 of a bar?
5.	His Chunky Chocolate Cubic Cookie Candy Bars have 12.306 ounces of chocolate in each bar. How many ounces are in 3.5 bars?
6.	Kookey needs 7.5 ounces of cream for each Stuffed Strawberry and Cream Bar. How many ounces does he use for 30.5 bars?
7.	Professor Kookey's Stuffed Strawberry and Cream Bars each need 11.504 ounces of berries. How many ounces of berries are in 40 bars?
8.	Kook E.'s Caramel Raspberry Cubic Cookie Candy Bars use 4.67 ounces of caramel in each bar. How many ounces of caramel are in .33 of a bar?
9.	Professor Kookey uses 5.6 ounces of blueberries for his Blueberry and Banana Bars. How many ounces does he need for 200 bars?
10.	Kook E. Kookey's Lemondrop Lollipop Cubic Cookie Candy Bars each have 2.013 ounces of lemon flavoring. How many ounces are needed for 28 bars?

Name _____

You and Major League Baseball

You have won a national contest sponsored by Olog's Groaty Oaties. The prize is a chance for you to play in the majors. All you have to do is bat over .300 against the majority of the major leaguers.

Reminder: To find your batting average, divide the number of "at bats" into the number of "hits." (4.000 ÷ 10 = .400)

Work the problems on another paper.

		Answer Space
1.	You got 4 hits in 10 at bats against Dizzy Dolan. What was your batting average against Dizzy?	
2.	You faced Herman "The Tank" Sherman and belted out 16 hits in 20 trips to the plate. What was your average against Herman?	
3.	Against the famous pitcher, "Moonbeam" Malone, you smacked 7 hits in 14 trips to the plate. What was your batting average against Moonbeam?	
4.	You smashed 13 hits in 20 at bats against "Bullets" Bascom. What was your batting average against Bullets?	
5.	You faced the fireballing pitcher called Lefty Writey and banged out 9 hits in 12 times at bat. What was your batting average against Lefty?	
6.	You crushed 5 hits in 8 at bats against "Piano Legs" Jones. What was your batting average against Jones?	
7.	"Lightning" Bill Smith gave you a hard time, and you got only 2 hits in 10 at bats. What was your average against Bill?	
8.	You crunched "Knuckles" McBain for 12 hits in 16 at bats. What was your batting average?	
9.	You smashed 17 hits in 20 at bats against Victor "The Vulture" Rollins. What was your batting average against Rollins?	
10.	Altogether you belted out 114 hits in 175 at bats. What was your overall batting average?	

Name _____

Creepy Crawly Critters

	Work the problems on another paper.	Answer Space
1.	A female black widow spider is 9 mm long. An Eastern diamondback rattlesnake is 250 times as long. How long is the snake?	
2.	A male black cockroach is 2.5 cm long. A female is 3.499 cm long. What is the length of both together?	
3.	A baby sidewinder is 20 cm long. An adult is 4.1 times as long. How long is the adult?	
4.	A gila monster is 60.9 cm long. A copperhead snake is 134.6 cm long. How much longer is the snake?	
5.	An American alligator is 5.84 m long. An American crocodile is 4.6 m long. What is the difference?	
6.	A glass lizard is 106.699 cm long. A Southern alligator lizard is 42.8 cm long. What is the difference?	
7.	A male grass spider is 1.5 cm long. A female is 1.334 times as long. How long is the female?	
8.	A male rabid wolf spider is 1.3 cm long. A female is 1.611 times as long. How long is the female?	
9.	A yellow-bellied water snake is 157.50 cm long. You could lay 225 bed bugs in a line that long. How long is each bed bug?	
10.	A green water snake is 185.6 cm long. You could lay 32 elephant stag beetles in a line that long. How long is a stag beetle?	

Name _____

The N.B.A. Wants You!

You have just been named "The Young Basketball Player of the Year." Your reward is a chance to go one-on-one against the superstars of the N.B.A.

Compute your shooting percentage and round it off to the nearest whole percent.

Work the problems on another paper.

Answer Space

1. You hit 13 out of 20 against Sam "Bamm-Bamm" Smith. What was your shooting percentage?

2. "Bamm-Bamm" nailed only 3 shots out of 20 against you. What percentage did he shoot?

3. Against Hye N. Skye you hit 15 baskets in 25 attempts. What was your percentage?

4. Hye N. Skye made only 8 out of 25 shots against you. What was his percentage?

5. You sank 7 of 14 shots against James "Slick Shot" Jones. What was your shooting percentage?

6. "Slick" hit 6 out of 14 shots against you. What did he shoot?

7. You hit 9 out of 12 shots against "Slammin'-Jammin' " Mann. What was your shooting percentage?

8. "Slammin'-Jammin' " sank only 2 of 12 shots while you guarded him. What did he shoot?

9. You hit 15 of 22 shots against "Dunkin" Dolan. What was your shooting percentage?

10. "Dunkin" iced only 4 of 22 against you. What did he shoot?

Name _____

The N.F.L. Wants You!

You were so spectacular in your last school football game that every team in the N.F.L. wanted to draft you as their number 1 quarterback. You ended up with a new team that really needed your help, the **Oki Doki Outlaws.**

Compute your passing percentage against these teams to the nearest whole percent.

Work the problems on another paper.

Answer Space

1.	You completed 25 out of 30 passes against the Nevada Gamblers led by "Lucky Ducky" Tucky. What was your percentage of completions?	
2.	"Brainbasher" Brown and the Boston Bobcats were no match for you. You completed 16 of 24 passes. What was your passing percentage?	
3.	You faced the Kansas Coyotes led by Doc "The Scalpel" Jones and still completed 11 out of 16 attempts. What was your percentage of completions?	
4.	The Missouri Maulers really tried to maul you, but you still connected for 17 passes out of 25 attempts. What was your completion percentage?	
5.	The Arizona Alleycats, led by linebacker "All Bad" Larry Badd, were no match for your perfect passes. You completed 33 out of 36 attempts. What was your passing percentage?	
6.	The Texas Tornadoes, led by linebacker "Bonemuncher" Bolanger, tried to contain you, but you still completed 28 out of 40 passes. What was your percentage?	
7.	The Virginia Vigilantes, with their great linebacker, "The Steel Wheel" Peale, gave you some trouble. You completed 11 out of 34 attempts. What was your passing percentage?	
8.	Ivan "The Intimidator" Evans led the Florida Flyers against you. You were unimpressed and hit 37 of 42 passes. What was your percentage of completions?	
9.	Clarence "Clank" Clunker gave you a hard time, and you hit only 7 of 23 against the Utah Utes. What was your percentage of completions?	
10.	During the season, you completed 234 passes out of 298 attempts. What was your passing percentage for the season?	

MATH

Name _____

Mean Monster Puts a Lock on Wrestling

Mean Monster, a great defensive back in football, decided to take on all the top wrestlers in order to keep in shape during the off-season. He weighed 569 lbs. 7 oz. and stood 7 ft. 3 in. tall.
(Remember: 1 lb. = 16 oz.   1 ft. = 12 in.)

Work the problems on another paper.

Answer Space

1. Mean Monster's first bout was with Harry "The Hammer" Brown who weighed 397 lbs. 4 ounces. How much more did Mean Monster weigh?

2. He did so well in his first round that he faced Marvelous Marvin Morton in the next event. Marvelous Marvin stood 6 ft. 9 in. tall. How much taller was Mean Monster?

3. Awesome Albert Alston was 167 lbs. 11 oz. lighter than Mean Monster. What did Awesome Albert weigh?

4. Irwin "The Icebox" weighed 478 lbs. 14 oz. He and Mean Monster stood together on the scale. What did it read?

5. Dazzling Doug Dugan ate 146 oz. of meat before the match. Mean Monster ate 5 lbs. 9 oz. of meat. How much meat did they eat altogether?

6. Si "Stilts" Stone stood 8 ft. 1 in. tall. How much shorter was Mean Monster?

7. Dreadful Dan "The Mighty Man" weighed 777 lbs. 7 oz. What was his weight in ounces?

8. Ivan the Incredible ate an 18 lb. 8 oz. meal before his bout. Mean Monster had only 188 oz. of food before the match. How much more did Ivan eat?

9. Melvin the Magnificent was a dainty 478 lbs. 15 oz. He stood with Mean Monster and Dreadful Dan on the same scale. What was their total weight?

10. Mean Monster's brother Itty Bitty Monster weighed 134 lbs. 15 oz. less than his big brother. What did Itty Bitty weigh?

Name _____

It's for the Birds

Key Facts:
1 ft. = 12 in.
1 yd. = 3 ft. = 36 in.

Work the problems on another paper.

1.	The black vulture has a wingspan of 60 inches. How many feet is its wingspan?	
2.	A gray hawk has a 3-foot wingspan. How many inches is that?	
3.	The turkey vulture has a 72-inch wingspan. How many yards is that?	
4.	A red-shouldered hawk has a 4-foot wingspan. How many inches can he spread his wings?	
5.	A sparrow hawk has a 24-inch wingspan. How many feet can its wings spread out?	
6.	A California condor has a 114-inch wingspan. How many feet is that? How many inches are left over?	
7.	The golden eagle has a wingspan of 7 ft. 8 in. How many inches is his wingspan?	
8.	The bald eagle has a 96-inch wingspan. What is his wingspan in feet?	
9.	A red-shouldered hawk is 2 feet long. How long is that in inches?	
10.	The red-tailed hawk has a 54-inch wingspan. How many feet is that? How many inches are left over?	

Name _____

The Bear Facts

Key Facts:

1 meter = 100 centimeters = 1000 millimeters
1 centimeter = 10 millimeters

Work the problems on another paper.

Answer Space

1.	A black bear has a tail 190 mm long. How many cm is that?
2.	The hind foot of a grizzly bear is 26 cm long. How many mm is that?
3.	The claws of a grizzly bear are 10 cm long. How many mm is that?
4.	A polar bear is 300 cm long. How many meters is that?
5.	The grizzly bear is 130 cm tall. How tall is that in meters?
6.	The tail of a polar bear is 130 mm long. How many cm is that?
7.	A brown bear is 200 cm long. How many meters is that?
8.	The black bear is 100 cm tall. How many meters tall is that?
9.	A brown bear has a tail that is 70 mm long. How many cm is that?
10.	The black bear is 188 cm long. How many mm long is the black bear?

Daily Learning Drills Grade 6

Name _____

Leapin' Lizards

Key Facts:

1 meter = 100 centimeters = 1000 millimeters
10 millimeters = 1 centimeter

Work the problems on another paper.

Answer Space

1.	A desert iguana is 40.6 cm long. How many mm is this?	
2.	A gila monster is 61 cm long. How many meters is this?	
3.	A jungle runner is 63.5 cm long. A gila whiptail is 30.6 cm long. What is the difference in their lengths?	
4.	A racerunner is 26.7 cm long. How much less than a meter is this?	
5.	A worm lizard is 40.6 cm long. How many cm less than a meter is this?	
6.	A ruin lizard is 25 cm long. A green lizard is 13.7 cm longer than a ruin lizard. How long is the green lizard?	
7.	A leopard lizard is 38.4 cm long. A common iguana is 200 cm long. How much longer is the iguana?	
8.	A common iguana is 200 cm long. How many meters is this?	
9.	A collard lizard is 35.6 cm long. How many mm is this?	
10.	A curly-tailed lizard is 26.6 cm long. A short-tailed lizard is 14.9 cm long. What is the difference in their lengths?	

MATH

Name _____

The Support System

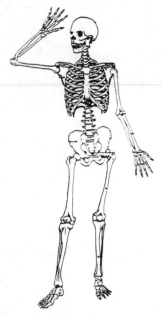

The bones are the body's supportive system. They are usually divided into two major groups — bones of the middle (skull, backbone and ribs) and bones of the arms and legs (including the shoulder and hip bones).

When you were born, your skeleton was made of soft bones called **cartilage**. As you grew, most of that cartilage turned into bone. However, all people still have some cartilage in their bodies. Our noses and our ears are cartilage, and there are pads of cartilage between sections of the backbone that act as cushions.

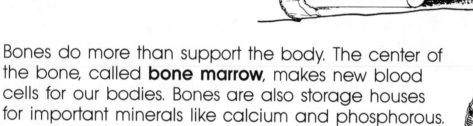

Bones do more than support the body. The center of the bone, called **bone marrow**, makes new blood cells for our bodies. Bones are also storage houses for important minerals like calcium and phosphorous.

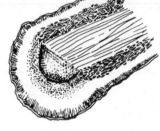

Answer the questions below. You might need your science book or an encyclopedia to help you.

1. What are the main functions of the skeletal system? _____
_____
_____

2. What is the largest bone in your body? _____

3. What is the smallest bone in your body? _____

4. What do bones first develop as? _____

5. What does bone marrow do? _____

6. Do all bones have real bone marrow? _____

7. What is the outer layer of a bone called? _____

8. Where two bones meet is called a _____

Fascinating Fact! Did you know that a giraffe has the same number of vertebrae in its neck as you?

Name _____

A Bag of Bones

The skin is a sack that contains the bones. If the skin and muscle layers were peeled away, the body's bones would be exposed. Some bones are seen only from either the front or back, others are seen from both sides. Use the names in the box below each skeleton. Label the bones as they appear on the front and the back of the body. (On lines going across the center of the page, write the bones that can be seen from the front and back. Although they appear in both boxes, only write the answer once.)

Front   **Back**

SCIENCE

SKULL	CLAVICLE	RIBS	PATELLA
VERTEBRAE	RADIUS	HUMERUS	TIBIA
PUBIS	CARPALS	METACARPALS	ULNA
PHALANGES (hand)		ILIUM	ISCHIUM
FEMUR	FIBULA	STERNUM	TARSALS
METATARSALS		PHALANGES (feet)	

SKULL	SCAPULA	VERTEBRAE	RIBS
ILIUM	ISCHIUM	FEMUR	FIBULA
RADIUS	HUMERUS	PHALANGES (hand)	
TALUS	CALCANEUS	METACARPALS	
	CARPALS	ULNA	TIBIA

Name _____

Meeting Places

Where two bones meet, they form a **joint**. Joints allow us to bend, twist or turn our bodies. The human body has several different types of joints. Each allows a different kind of movement. Look at some of the examples below. Then, write examples of the joints below each description.

Ball-and-Socket Joint

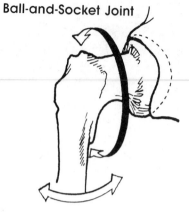

Hinge Joint — These joints can only move in one direction, like a door hinge. One bone works against another. Movement is back and forth on one plane.
Examples: _____

Ball-and-Socket Joint — These joints provide us with swinging and rotating movements. Make a fist with one hand. Cup the fingers of the other. Put your fist inside the cupped hand. You can turn your fist (the ball) in any direction within your cupped hand (the socket).
Examples: _____

Saddle Joint — These joints move in two directions - either back and forth, up and down or in rotation.
Examples: _____

Hinge Joint

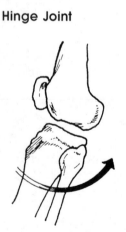

Sliding Joint — In the case of these joints, several bones next to one another bend together in limited, glidinglike movement.
Examples: _____

Pivot Joint — These joints give us a rotating motion.
Examples: _____

Fixed Joint — With these types of joints, bones are fused together and permit no movement.
Examples: _____

Fascinating Fact: What part of your body can move forward, backward, side to side and around on top of a vertical axis and is not one of the above? _____

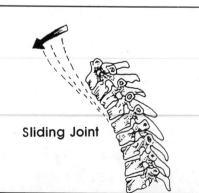

Sliding Joint

Name _____

The Leg Bone's Connected to the Hip Bone

The place where two or more bones meet is called a **joint**. Joints are either movable or immovable. There are four kinds of movable joints: **hinge, pivot, gliding and ball-and-socket.** Label each joint on the skeleton below.

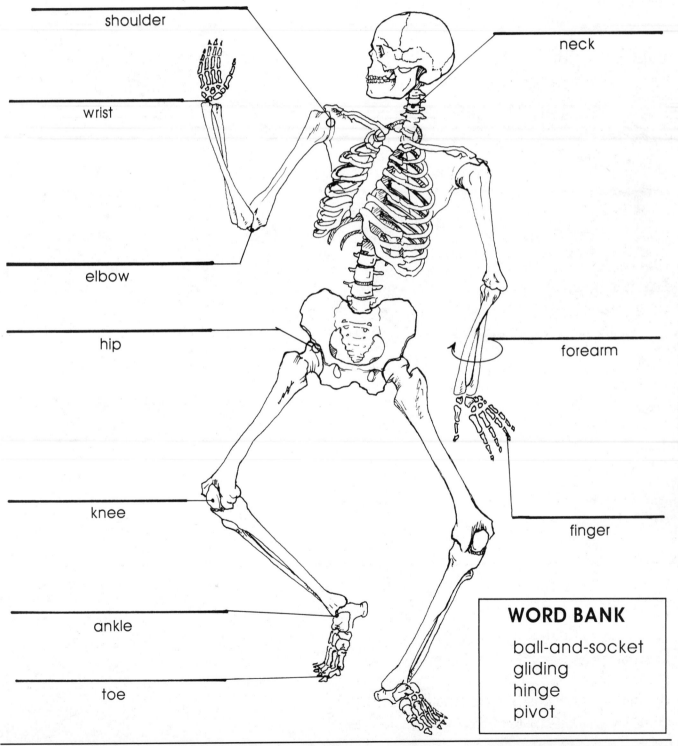

shoulder

neck

wrist

elbow

hip

forearm

knee

finger

ankle

toe

WORD BANK

ball-and-socket
gliding
hinge
pivot

Daily Learning Drills Grade 6

Name _____

Muscle Man

There are hundreds of muscle groups in your body. Label these muscles that appear on the surface of your body.

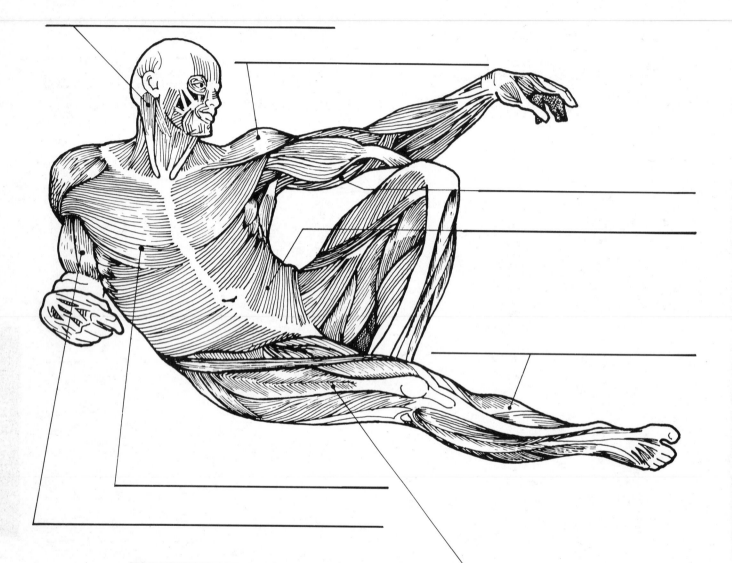

WORD BANK

Common Name (Scientific Name)

chest muscles (pectorals)
calf muscles (gastrocnemius)
biceps
head muscles (sternocleidomastoids)
stomach muscles (inter coastals)

thigh muscles (quadraceps)
shoulder muscles (deltoids)
triceps

Name _____

Muscle Power

Use your science book or another source to help.

Fill in the blanks with words from the word bank.

There are _____ kinds of muscles. Internal organs, such as the intestines, the stomach, and the esophagus are moved by the _____ muscles. The _____ muscles move your skeleton and external body parts. The heartbeat is controlled by the _____ muscle. Muscles which need a special message from your brain in order to work are called _____ muscles. Muscles which move automatically, without conscious thought, are called _____ muscles. The tough cords that connect the skeletal muscles to your bones are called _____.

Word Bank

| involuntary | smooth | skeletal | tendons |
| voluntary | cardiac | three | |

cardiac   smooth   skeletal

hamstring

tendon

finger tendons

Fill in the chart.

Activity	Do I need conscious thought to do it?	Voluntary or Involuntary Action	Kind of Muscle
jumping rope			
heart beating			
waving			
breathing			
swallowing food			
pumping blood			
whistling			
running			
digestion			

Find Out

Who is your Achilles' tendon named for and why?

SCIENCE

Name _____

The Brain

With the help of your science book or an encyclopedia, label the diagram of the brain below. Use the words below the diagram to help you.

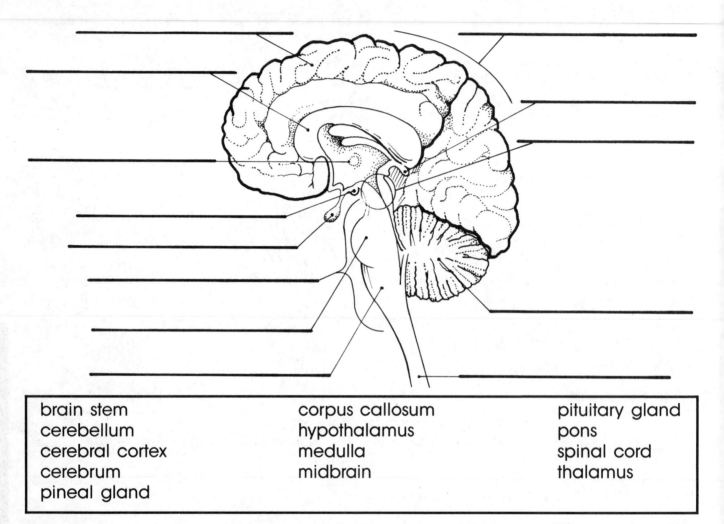

brain stem	corpus callosum	pituitary gland
cerebellum	hypothalamus	pons
cerebral cortex	medulla	spinal cord
cerebrum	midbrain	thalamus
pineal gland		

Using the list of words above, solve the following riddles.

1. I connect the hemispheres of the cerebrum to the spinal cord. What am I? _____

2. I am a gland that produces chemical substances, called hormones, that are distributed to the body through the blood stream. What am I?

_____

3. There are two of us although only one of us is shown in the diagram. We are on each side of the brain. We receive nerve impulses from various parts of the body and route them to the correct place in the cerebral cortex. What are we? _____

Name _____

The Brain (cont.)

4. I regulate body temperature, hunger and other internal conditions. What am I? _____

5. I contain nerve centers which help control eye movements and the size of the pupils. What am I? _____

6. I am the largest nerve fiber that connects the two sides of the brain. What am I? _____

7. I am the gray outer part of the cerebrum. I have many ridges and grooves. What am I? _____

8. I am part of the brain stem. I have nerve centers that control many of the body's vital processes. What am I? _____

Right/Left Brain Dominance

The brain is divided into left and right hemispheres by a large groove called a fissure. Yet, the brain still works as one unit. It is the headquarters for the nervous system.

Each hemisphere controls different functions like motor skills, speech, hearing, sight, etc. However, the left half of the brain controls the right side of the body and vice versa. Most people depend more on the left hemisphere. That is why most people are right-handed.

Do the activity below to test your right/left brain dominance.
With what hand do you write? _____
That is controlled by the _____ side of the brain.
Take a walk. On what foot did you step out first? _____
Hop across the room. What foot did you use? _____
It seems you are _____-footed. Your foot movements are controlled by the _____ hemisphere.

Read the following sentence with only one eye. (Close the other.)
   I am learning about brain dominance.
With what eye did you read? _____ Your reading is controlled by the _____ side (hemisphere) of the brain.
Did the same hemisphere of your brain control all your movements? _____
If yes, it means your _____ hemisphere is dominant.
If no, it means you have a mixed dominance.
What are you? _____

Fascinating Fact! The left half of the brain plays a role in language, logical thinking and mathematics.

Name _____

Think Fast

While riding your bike down the street, a car suddenly pulls out in front of you. Your eyes send a message to your brain. Your brain sends a message to your muscles to apply the brakes. How long did it take you to stop? This time is called your **reaction time.**

Here is a simple experiment to find out your reaction time. The only materials you will need are a 30 cm ruler and a partner.

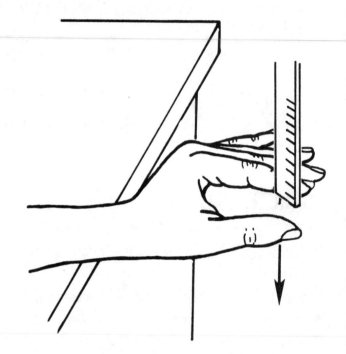

1. Place your left arm on your desk with your hand over the edge.
2. Space your thumb and index finger apart a little more than the thickness of the ruler.
3. Your partner will hold one end of the ruler with the other end level with the top of your index finger.
4. Your partner will say "ready," pause a few seconds, and drop the ruler.
5. Catch the ruler and check the distance by reading the level at the bottom of the index finger.
6. Record your results.
7. Now, try the experiment again with your right hand.

Trial	Left hand	Right hand
1		
2		
3		
4		
5		

Average: _____ _____

Which hand had the fastest reaction

time? _____

Fun Fact

Nerve impulses, or messages, travel at 100 meters per second!

Message Transmissions

Use your science book or another source to help.
Fill in the spaces with words from the Word Bank.

Your body has its own system for sending
messages to your brain. This system of individual
nerves and their pathways is found throughout
the body. It is called the **peripheral nervous system.**
The peripheral nervous system is a pathway to the
brain for your five senses. It also serves your internal
organs and helps you respond to your
environment.

Messages are sent to the brain through a
network of nerve cells called _____.
Neurons have long arms, called _____,
and shorter arms, called _____.

In order for messages to travel along the
pathway, the neurons must connect with each
other. This connection is called a _____.
Messages enter each neuron through the
dendrite. Messages exit the neuron through the
axon.

Word Bank

axons
dendrites
synapse
neurons

Color the parts of
the nervous system.

brain - gray
spinal cord - blue
nerves - red

Color the parts of the neuron.

nucleus - green
axon - orange
dendrite - purple

Fun Fact

Sensory nerves send 100 million messages to the brain every second.

SCIENCE

Name _____

Your Heart

Label the parts of your heart.

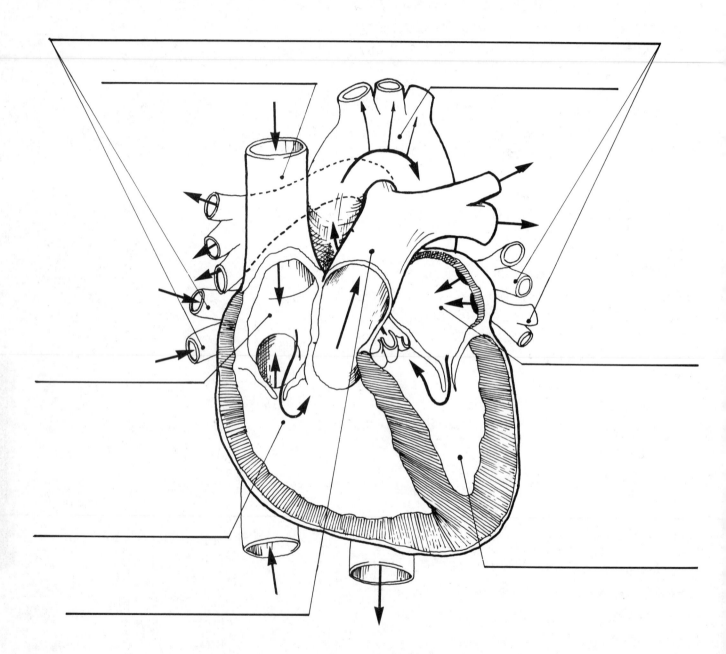

WORD BANK

left atrium	right atrium	vena cava
left ventricle	right ventricle	aorta
pulmonary artery	pulmonary veins	

Name _____

Huff and Puff
(Respiratory System Review)

Use the Word Bank to complete the puzzle.

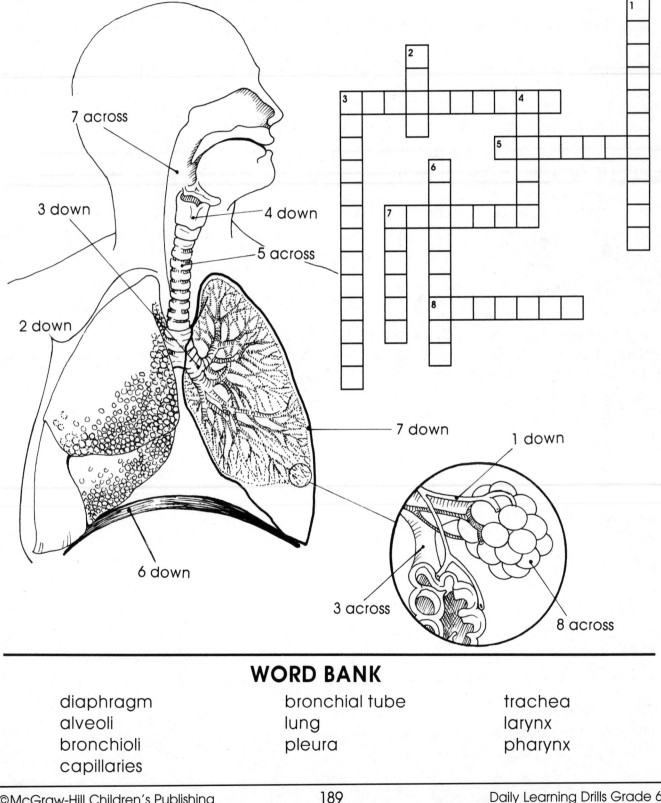

7 across

3 down

4 down

5 across

2 down

7 down

1 down

6 down

3 across

8 across

WORD BANK

diaphragm	bronchial tube	trachea
alveoli	lung	larynx
bronchioli	pleura	pharynx
capillaries		

Name _____

Respiratory Riddles

Your breathing, or respiratory, system is made of many parts. Solve the respiratory riddles using the Word Bank.

1. "I'm the windpipe that brings fresh air to your lungs." _____
2. "There are 600 million of us tiny air sacs in your lungs." _____
3. "Tra-la-la. I'm your voice box." _____
4. "We branch to the left and right from your windpipe." _____
5. "I enter your blood with each breath of fresh air." _____
6. "I help squeeze the air out of your lungs." _____

Label the diagram using the words from the word bank.

During exercise your body needs more oxygen. Your brain signals your lungs to breathe more quickly and take deeper breaths. Look at the results of the experiment below to answer the questions. Complete the chart.

Activity	Air in each breath (volume)	×	Number of breaths per minute	=	Air in lungs each minute
reading	.5 liters	×	16	=	
walking	1 liter	×	25	=	
playing basketball	2 liters	×	60	=	

Word Bank

alveoli
bronchial tubes
diaphragm
larynx
oxygen
trachea

Which activity makes you breathe fastest? _____
Which activity requires the most oxygen? _____
How much more air per minute does walking take than reading? _____

Name _____

Traveling Through the Alimentary Canal

After you take a bite of food, it takes a path through the human body called the **alimentary canal,** or the digestive tract. The canal, as it is shown here, is not how it actually is inside the body. Inside your body, it is folded back and forth so that it fits.

Fill in the missing words in the paragraph below about the path food follows in the alimentary canal. Use the words in the word bank. You might need your science book or an encyclopedia to help you.

Food and water enter the alimentary canal by way of the
_____. Digestion of food begins here where it is
_____ and broken into smaller pieces. Digestive enzymes,
produced by _____ _____, further help to break
down food before it is swallowed and passed through the
_____ into the _____. In the stomach, the food is
further mixed with _____ and digestive juices in a churning
motion. As the food is digested, it changes into a thick liquid called
_____. The chyme passes into the _____
_____ in small amounts. The _____ produces
pancreatic juices, and the _____ produces _____ which
is stored in the _____ _____. These are released
into the small intestine as needed to work with intestinal juices and
contractions made by the intestine's walls to move the chyme along. The
digested food is absorbed by tiny _____ and lymph vessels in the
_____ of the small intestine and carried through the
_____ system to feed the body. Small amounts of water and
minerals are removed from undigested food matter, and this, plus waste food
products are stored in the _____ _____. This waste
becomes a solid, brown material called _____, which is finally
eliminated through the _____.

SCIENCE

Word Bank

salivary glands	enzymes	large intestine	chyme
pancreas	mouth	small intestine	esophagus
bile	rectum	stomach	gall bladder	feces
circulatory	chewed	blood	walls	liver

Fascinating Fact! Did you know that during your lifetime, your digestive system may process between 60,000 and 100,000 pounds of food?

Name _____

Labeling the Digestive System

With the help of reference materials, label and then color the parts of the digestive system as directed.

duodenum - tan
pharynx - yellow
pancreas - green
stomach - white
esophagus - brown

small intestine - black
large intestine - yellow/green
gall bladder - grey
salivary glands - red

rectum - lilac
mouth - blue
teeth - orange
liver - purple

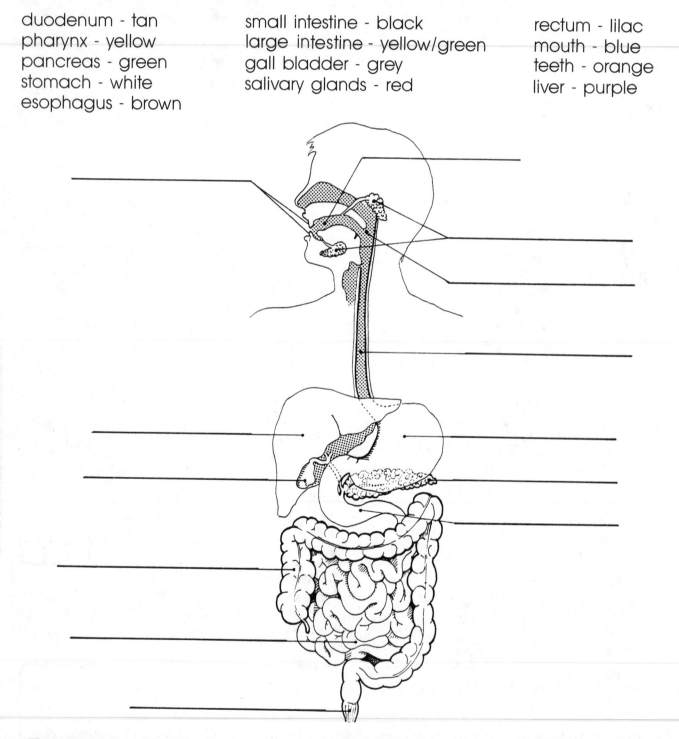

Fascinating Fact! The small intestine is roughly four times longer than the average person is tall!

             Daily Learning Drills Grade 6

Name _____

The Body's Camera

Use your science book or another source to help. Label the parts of the eye with terms from the Word Bank.

Word Bank

lens	pupil
cornea	retina
optic nerve	sclera
iris	vitreous humor

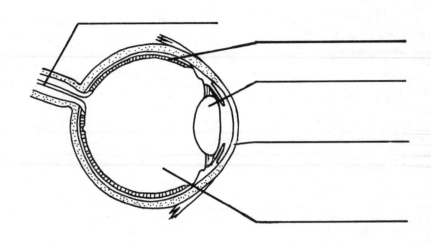

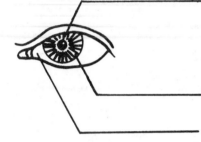

Complete the word puzzle using some of the words from the word bank.

Across
3. Dark area which changes size with the amount of light
5. Colored part of the eye
7. White covering of the eye
8. The clear jelly-like humor in the eye

Down
1. Transparent window of the eye
2. The nerve which sends light stimulus to the brain
4. Focuses light onto the retina
6. Sensitive area containing rods and cones

Something Special

Your retina is made up of light-sensitive cells that can be stimulated by pressure. Close your eyes and very gently press on them. The stars that you are seeing are called pressure flashes.

Name _____

Catching Good Vibes

Use your science book or another source to help. Complete the following sentences using words from the Word Bank.

   The car honks its horn. The sound waves are collected by your _____ and travel down the _____. The sound strikes the _____ causing the tight skin to vibrate. Three tiny bones called the _____, _____, and _____ magnify and send the sound to the inner ear. The sound travels to the _____, a coiled, snail-shaped passage filled with liquid and nerve hairs. The nerve hairs send signals through the _____ to the brain.

Label the parts of the ear using words from the word bank.

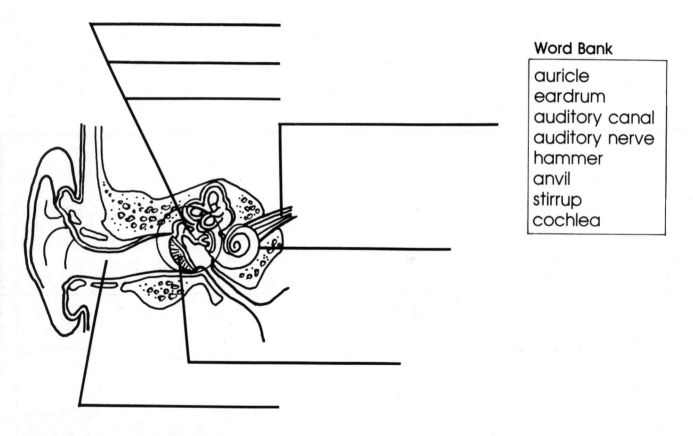

Word Bank

auricle
eardrum
auditory canal
auditory nerve
hammer
anvil
stirrup
cochlea

Something Special

Answer these riddles.
Which part of your ear has the most rhythm?
What pierces your ears without leaving holes?

Organ Systems

Mark an "X" in the correct box to show to which system/systems each organ belongs. One is done for you. You may need to use your science book or another source.

Organs	Digestive	Respiratory	Urinary	Reproductive	Circulatory	Nervous	Endocrine
Systems							
Bladder			X				
Brain							
Heart							
Ovaries							
Liver							
Pancreas							
Kidneys							
Spinal Cord							
Lungs							
Small Intestines							
Diaphragm							
Mouth							
Nerves							
Testes							
Thyroid Gland							
Arteries							
Esophagus							
Cerebellum							

SCIENCE

Name _____

Tree Trivia

Research and find the answers to the questions below. Use an encyclopedia to help you.

1. What is the world's largest living tree? _____
   What kind of tree is this? _____
   Write three more facts about this tree.
   1) _____
   2) _____
   3) _____

2. Write a small paragraph about the Traveler's-Tree.
   _____
   _____
   _____
   _____
   _____

3. Where can the thickest tree trunk be found? _____
   What kind of tree is this? _____

4. In Africa, some people hollow out this tree to store water in it. Its leaves, seeds and roots are used in many ways. What is the name of this tree? _____

5. The largest seeds belong to what tree? _____
   In what form are these seeds and how big are they? _____

6. Where are the tallest trees found and what kind are they? _____
   _____

7. What are coniferous trees? _____
   Name some things made from these trees. _____
   _____

8. Trees protected by very thick bark are only scarred by fire — the wood is not damaged. Name two types of this kind of tree. _____
   _____

Pick a tree that you find interesting and unusual. Pretend you are that tree. Write clues about yourself. Bring in pictures or objects relating to the tree you chose. Present yourself to the class. Give them clues and help them guess what kind of tree you are.

Fascinating Fact! Can trees whistle? Whistling Thorn trees can make eerie music when the wind blows! Ants make holes for homes in some of the hollow balls on their branches. When they move out, the wind blowing across the holes makes the trees "whistle" in the wind.

Name _____

A World of Plants

From the small, one-celled algae to the giant redwood trees, our world is filled with thousands of different kinds of plants. Scientists have a special way of classifying, or grouping, the many kinds of plants. Study the diagram below.

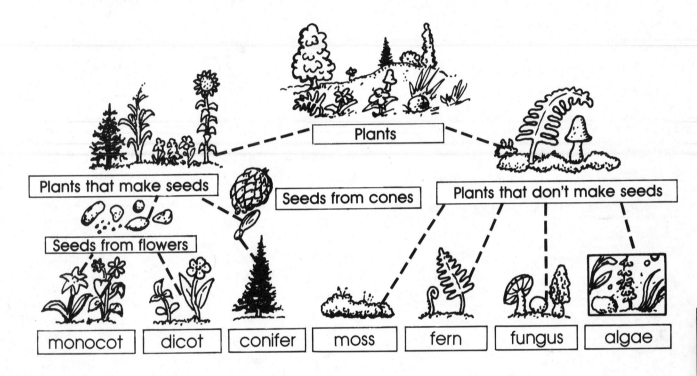

Look carefully at the plant characteristics listed below. Place a (✔) in the column or columns that represent the plant with that characteristic.

	monocot	dicot	conifer	moss	fern	fungus	algae
1. is green							
2. makes seeds							
3. makes seeds in a flower							
4. flower made seed with two seed parts							
5. flower made seed with one seed part							
6. makes seeds in a cone							
7. produces spores							
8. has leaves with veins							
9. has leaves with parallel veins							
10. has leaves with net-like veins							
11. has needle-like leaves							
12. one-celled plant							

Name _____

Plant Pipelines

How does the plant get its food? Thin tubes in the stem carry food from the leaf to the rest of the plant. Other tubes carry water and minerals from the roots to the leaves. Both kinds of tubes are found in bundles in the stem.

The tube bundles are arranged in two ways. A **monocot** stem has bundles scattered throughout the stem. **Dicot** stems have their bundles arranged in a ring around the edge of the stem.

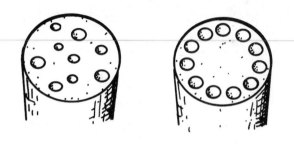

_____   _____

Dicot or monocot stem? Label the two pictures above.

Experiment: Observing Plant Pipelines

Materials:
drinking glass
water
food coloring
eye dropper
knife
stalk of celery

Directions:
Put a few drops of food coloring in a glass of water. Trim off the bottom 2 cm of a stalk of celery. Place the celery in the water. Let stand for 3-4 hours.

Results:

1. Describe what you see. _____

_____

2. Cut the stalk crosswise. Look at the cut ends. What do you see?

_____

3. What carried the water up the stalk? _____

4. What would happen if the stem of a plant were broken? Why?

_____

_____

Something Special

Try the experiment above, but with a new twist. Use a white flower instead of celery; carnations or daisies work great. Watch what happens!

Name _____

Plant Facts

Use encyclopedias or a science book to help you answer the questions below.

1. Explain how trees grow fatter. _____
_____
_____

2. Name the four tissue layers of the tree and their functions.
   1) _____
   2) _____
   3) _____
   4) _____

3. Explain the process of pollination. Include pistil and stamen in your explanation. _____
_____
_____

4. What is the difference between a dicot and a monocot?
_____
_____

5. Name the two kinds of xylem and their functions. _____
_____

6. Name three ways that plants are helpful to people and three ways they are not helpful to people.
   1) _____
   2) _____
   3) _____
   4) _____
   5) _____
   6) _____

7. Name 3 plants found in each of the following regions:
   1) High Mountains: _____
   2) Broadleaf Forest: _____
   3) Tropical Rain Forest: _____
   4) Desert: _____
   5) Grassland: _____

Fascinating Fact! The first plant to flower and produce seeds in the zero gravity of space is called Arabidopsis. It was grown onboard the Soviet Union's Salyut-7 space station in 1982.

SCIENCE

Name _____

Very Interesting Vertebrates

Mr. Fridley, the science teacher, has been teaching Miss Freed's sixth graders about vertebrates. Vertebrates are animals with backbones and a cranium. He asked the students to name as many vertebrates as they could. They came up with frog, chicken, fish, horse, turtle, cow, cat, dog, bird, human, and many others. Mr. Fridley was surprised human was one of their answers, since most people forget that they are vertebrates too.

The students learned about the many characteristics of verte-brates. Mr. Fridley told them that when you say that an animal has a backbone, it does not mean that there is one single bone. Rather, the backbone consists of many bones linked together. He also told them, however, that some vertebrates' backbones, such as the shark, are made of cartilage. Maria said she had read that the backbone is part of the *endoskeleton*—an internal skel-eton. Mr. Fridley was excited that Maria knew this. He continued and said that endoskeletons give vertebrates their shape. They also help protect internal organs. For example, the skull protects the brain and the ribs protect the heart and lungs.

Mr. Fridley also said that most vertebrates have two pairs of limbs. Mr. Fridley said that these limbs could be arms, legs, wings, fins, or flippers. He concluded by telling the students that each endoskeleton has bones that connect limbs to the backbone and that a vertebrate's endoskeleton makes it possible for the animal to move. Miss Freed was happy to learn how interested her vertebrates were in other vertebrates

Check.

Vertebrates . . .

☐ have no backbone.

☐ have the same shape.

☐ have an endoskeleton.

☐ include worms, cats, and mice.

☐ include humans, frogs, and dogs.

☐ have a backbone.

Write.

List ten words from the story relating to the word *vertebrate*. _____

_____

List five vertebrates and the two pairs of limbs each one has. _____

_____

Underline.

An invertebrate is probably an animal with . . .

a vertebrate inside.   a backbone inside.   no backbone.

Name _____

What's an Invertebrate?

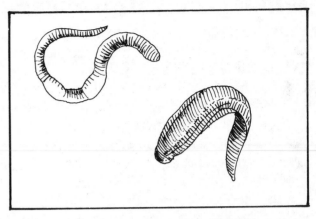

Mr. Fridley arranged for Miss Freed's class to spend a whole morning learning about invertebrates. Miss Freed was very excited for her students.

Off the sixth graders marched to Mr. Fridley's science lab. When they walked in, they were greeted by dozens of pictures of animals hanging from the ceiling, on the walls, and arranged around the room. The students saw pictures of sponges, jellyfish, worms, snails, sea stars, and insects. Mr. Fridley asked the students if they knew what these animals had or didn't have in common. The students thought hard and made lots of guesses. Finally, Kim said, "They don't have a backbone!" She had guessed correctly. Mr. Fridley was proud of her.

Mr. Fridley explained that there are so many invertebrates (more than one million species), and they include so many forms of animals that they have been divided into several major groups. These groups are called phyla. There are nine *phyla*, each with its own characteristics. As an example of a phylum (singular for phyla), Mr. Fridley told them about the phylum *Annelida*, which includes worms with bodies made of segments. The earthworm, sandworm, and leech belong to this group. He then divided the class into eight groups and assigned a phylum for each to research.

Check.

Invertebrates have . . .

- [ ] a backbone.
- [ ] major groups called phyla.
- [ ] a million different species.
- [ ] no backbone.
- [ ] nothing in common.
- [ ] nine phyla called Annelida.

Write.

List five vertebrates and five invertebrates. What physical differences can you see between these

groups of animals? _____

_____

_____

Underline.

There are _____ numbers of invertebrates.

multitudinous   myriad   voluminous   scant

Circle.

The singular and plural group names for invertebrates respectively are . . .

phyla/phylum.   phyla/phylas.   phylum/phylums.   phylum/phyla.

SCIENCE

Name _____

What's the Difference?

One day, David and Donald were discussing alligators. David insisted that alligators and crocodiles were the same animal but that people called them by different names. Donald insisted, however, that the two animals were entirely different reptiles. Kim walked up just in time to save the boys from further squabbling. Kim, who lived in Florida for ten years, could settle this one.

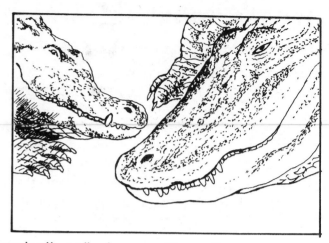

She told David that yes, alligators and crocodiles were indeed separate reptiles. She told them that although they are similar looking and are both called crocodilians, they are very different. Both have a long, low, cigar-shaped body, short legs, and a long, powerful tail to help them swim, but most crocodiles have a pointed snout instead of a round one like the alligator's. She also pointed out that while both have tough hides, long snouts, and sharp teeth to grasp their prey, the crocodile is only about two-thirds as heavy as an American alligator of the same length and can therefore move much more quickly. David and Donald were impressed with Kim's knowledge.

Kim also told the boys of another way to tell the two reptiles apart. She said that both have an extra long lower fourth tooth. This tooth fits into a pit in the alligator's upper jaw, while in the crocodile, it fits into a groove in the side of the upper jaw and shows when the crocodile's mouth is closed. David and Donald thanked Kim for the information, looked at each other sheepishly, and walked away laughing.

Match.

crocodile   fourth tooth shows when mouth is shut

                   fourth tooth is in a pocket in upper jaw

alligator   round snout

                   called crocodilian

                   pointed snout

Write.

Write three ways alligators and crocodiles are alike and three ways they are different.

1. _____   1. _____
2. _____   2. _____
3. _____   3. _____

Underline.

The crocodile . . .

has a long snout.   is called a crocodilian.   is fast.

has long, low legs.   has a round snout.   is a reptile.

         Daily Learning Drills Grade 6

Name _____

Insect Behavior

Insects are interesting creatures to observe. They have successfully adapted to all kinds of environments. And they are both harmful and helpful to humans. Some eat plants and cause great damage. Others pollinate our food plants and are a great help to our agriculture. Have you wondered about insects? How they travel, their speed of travel, preferred environments, etc.?

Today you are going to be working in groups to collect insects and put them in containers. To do this, you can use a net, turn over stones and logs or shake tree branches with a sheet underneath. As you observe your insects, answer the following questions.

Where were the insects found? _____

Do you recognize any of the insects? _____

If so, what are the names you know them by? _____

_____

Those you don't recognize, try to identify by using an insect book.

Take one insect at a time and see how it travels. Record how far it will go in one minute. Then, put an object in its path such as a pencil or a tiny rock to see what happens.

Name or description of insect	Pattern it makes as it travels	How far it travels in 1 minute	Reaction to object in its path
_____	_____	_____	_____
_____	_____	_____	_____
_____	_____	_____	_____
_____	_____	_____	_____

Ahead of time, bring shoe box lids from home. Glue different colors of construction paper in the inside leaving a white box as a starting point. Place your insects one at a time at the starting point. On which color do they travel the most? _____

Do you think insects can see? _____

Why or why not?

_____

_____

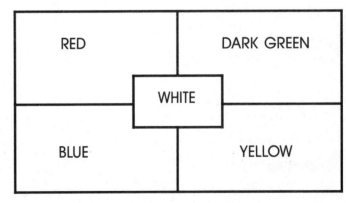

Fascinating Fact! The cockroach is one of the fastest running insects reaching 30 cm per second.

Name _____

Sarah's Sea Stones!

Unscramble the letters in each box to name types of shelled animals, or mollusks. Use the word list at the bottom. Then, using information in the encyclopedia, classify each shell according to the types described below.

Types of Mollusk Shells

1. univalve: one shell
2. bivalve: two matching shells
3. tooth: long, needle-like
4. chitons: eight-plated
5. squids and octopuses: internal or no shell

sumels	tiscuhtlef	wocnr hnocc

_____ _____ _____

grite weroic	stanuliu	malc

_____ _____ _____

leSsertl ohtinc	yotsre	nomo lasin

_____ _____ _____

lopalsc	penteahl skut	flet-ddeanh lewk

_____ _____ _____

scallop	crown conch	nautilus
clam	moon snail	tiger cowrie
cuttlefish	Steller's chiton	oyster
left-handed welk	mussel	elephant tusk

What a Whale Shark!

Miss Freed is surprising her class with a field trip to a sealife exhibit. She knows that her students will be excited because the main attraction at the exhibit is a whale shark. Her sixth graders are fascinated by this monstrous but docile creature. They first learned about the whale shark, the largest fish in the world, when they were studying ocean life. It seemed they couldn't get enough information about it.

Beth and Kim gave a great report on the whale shark. They reported that this up-to-50-foot-long fish eats plankton and small schooling fish. Some whale sharks have even let divers grab on to their dorsal fin and go for a ride.

Jack learned that the whale shark may be found in a band around the equator extending roughly 30° north and 35° south. He reported that they seem to prefer surface-water temperatures in the 70s or low 80s.

Always concerned with protecting animals, Cassie pointed out in her research that the whale shark has much more to fear from humans than humans have to fear from it. These gentle animals are harpooned and eaten near India and in Taiwan. The Japanese, however, don't like to kill the whale shark. It supposedly brings good luck and is named after a patron god of the sea. Miss Freed wonders how they managed to get a fish as large as this in the exhibit. The students are going to love this field trip.

Check.
The whale shark is . . .

☐ a fish.   ☐ a shark.   ☐ gentle.   ☐ huge.   ☐ the largest fish in the world.

Match.
Match the person(s) to the fact he or she reported.

Kim and Beth	The whale shark has a lot to fear from humans.
Cassie	Whale sharks eat plankton and small fish.
Jack	Whale sharks like warmer waters.

Underline.
The Japanese think the whale shark . . .

should be eaten.   brings good luck.   is dangerous.

Write.
Why does the whale shark have more to fear from humans than humans do from whale sharks?

_____

_____

                   Daily Learning Drills Grade 6

SCIENCE

Name _____

Classy Sea Creatures

Nearly every major group of animals is represented in the ocean community. These animals range in size from the over 100-ton blue whale to the microscopic plankton.

A very simple "family tree" of ocean life is illustrated on this page. List examples of various sea organisms that represent each major group.

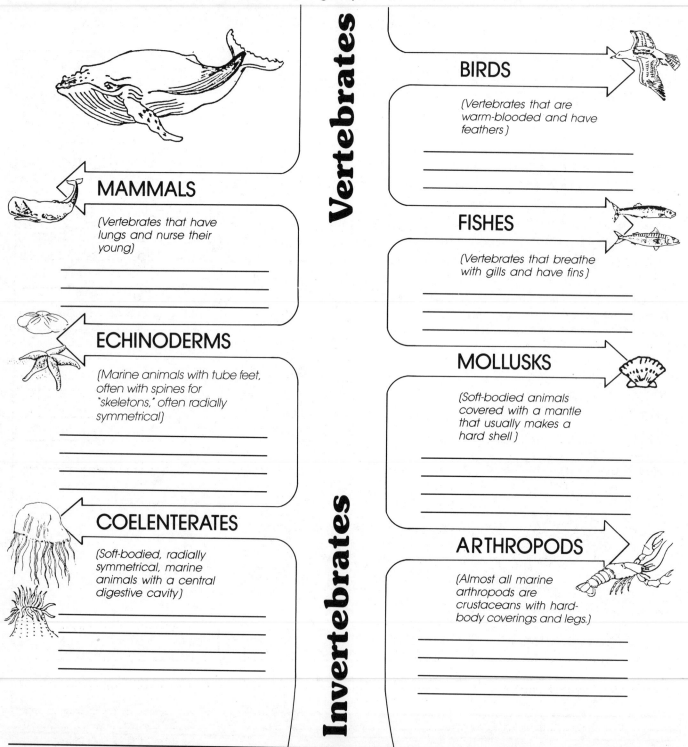

Vertebrates

BIRDS

(Vertebrates that are warm-blooded and have feathers)

_____
_____
_____

MAMMALS

(Vertebrates that have lungs and nurse their young)

_____
_____
_____

FISHES

(Vertebrates that breathe with gills and have fins)

_____
_____
_____

ECHINODERMS

(Marine animals with tube feet, often with spines for "skeletons," often radially symmetrical)

_____
_____
_____

MOLLUSKS

(Soft-bodied animals covered with a mantle that usually makes a hard shell)

_____
_____
_____

Invertebrates

COELENTERATES

(Soft-bodied, radially symmetrical, marine animals with a central digestive cavity)

_____
_____
_____

ARTHROPODS

(Almost all marine arthropods are crustaceans with hard-body coverings and legs.)

_____
_____
_____

Daily Learning Drills Grade 6

Name _____

Endangered Species

Discover the habitat and the reason(s) each animal is endangered.

Whooping Crane
North America
Habitat: _____
_____

Why Endangered: _____
_____
_____
_____
_____

Cassowary
Australia; New Guinea
Habitat: _____
_____

Why Endangered: _____
_____
_____
_____
_____

Nile Crocodile
Africa
Habitat: _____
_____

Why Endangered: _____
_____
_____
_____
_____

Giant Panda
Asia
Habitat: _____
_____

Why Endangered: _____
_____
_____
_____
_____

Giant Armadillo
South America
Habitat: _____
_____

Why Endangered: _____
_____
_____
_____
_____

Name _____
Continent _____
Habitat: _____
_____

Why Endangered: _____
_____
_____
_____

Student's Choice

SCIENCE

Name _____

Meat, Salad, and Casseroles

Animals and plants often get their food from different sources. Plants that make their food from sunlight, air, and water are called **producers.** Animals are **consumers;** they get their food from other sources. Animals that eat only plants are called **herbivores. Carnivores** are animals that eat only meat. **Omnivores** are animals that eat both plants and meat. Which of these are you?

Study the picture below. Then list all the carnivores, herbivores, omnivores, and producers that you can find.

Carnivore	Herbivore	Omnivore	Producer
_____	_____	_____	_____
_____	_____	_____	_____
_____	_____	_____	_____
_____	_____	_____	_____

Something Special

Make a food chain using the organisms found in the picture above. Label each member by writing **C, H, O,** or **P** over each carnivore, herbivore, omnivore, and producer in the chain.

Name _____

Where in the World?

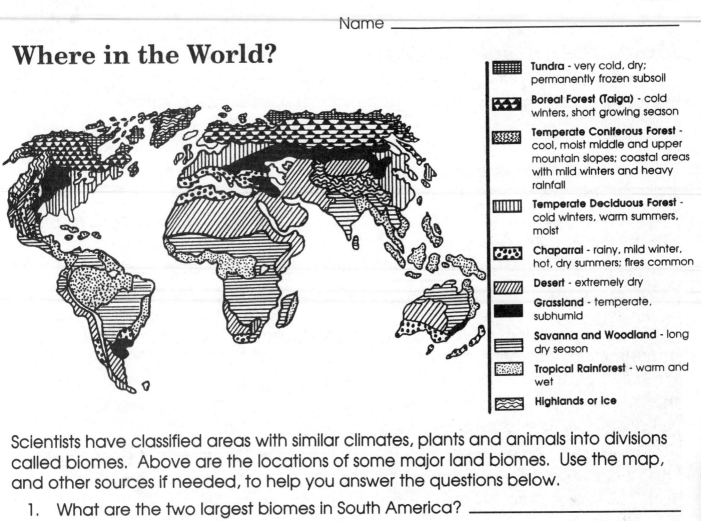

Tundra - very cold, dry; permanently frozen subsoil

Boreal Forest (Taiga) - cold winters, short growing season

Temperate Coniferous Forest - cool, moist middle and upper mountain slopes; coastal areas with mild winters and heavy rainfall

Temperate Deciduous Forest - cold winters, warm summers, moist

Chaparral - rainy, mild winter, hot, dry summers; fires common

Desert - extremely dry

Grassland - temperate, subhumid

Savanna and Woodland - long dry season

Tropical Rainforest - warm and wet

Highlands or Ice

Scientists have classified areas with similar climates, plants and animals into divisions called biomes. Above are the locations of some major land biomes. Use the map, and other sources if needed, to help you answer the questions below.

1. What are the two largest biomes in South America? _____

2. What kinds of biomes are not found in North America? _____
   Why do you think this is so? _____

3. What kinds of biomes are found in Australia? _____

   _____

4. Where can tundra biomes be found? _____
   Why do you think they are not found in Europe? _____

5. Which biome is found only in North America? _____

6. On which continents are chaparral biomes found? _____

   _____

7. Which two continents have the biggest biomes of savanna and woodland?

   _____

8. Which continent has the largest variety of biomes? _____
   Why do you think this is so? _____

   _____

SCIENCE

Name _____

Meteors—Shooting Stars

Use words from the Word Bank to fill in the blanks and complete the crossword puzzle.

Word Bank			
craters	sand	200 million	comets
asteroids	meteor	meteorite(s)	burn
atmosphere	dust	showers	orbit(s)
friction			

A brilliant streak flashes across the sky. What appears to be a "shooting star" or "falling star" is really a meteoroid from outer space that is burning up in Earth's _____. The _____ of Earth's atmosphere makes the meteoroid form a bright streak called a _____. More than _____ meteors enter Earth's atmosphere every day! Most of the meteors that we see are loose _____ particles, no larger than a grain of _____. Meteoroids that reach Earth's surface are called _____. It is estimated that they add about 3,000 pounds to the mass of Earth every day. Most meteorites burn away until very little is left of them, but Earth has been struck by meteors weighing several tons. These large meteorites that strike Earth's surface form large _____. Most of these large meteorites are probably parts of _____ and comets.

It is a spectacular sight when the sky is filled with a swarm of flying sparks called a meteor shower. Some of these swarms of meteoroids have _____ around the sun similar to comets.

Across

2. Meteor _____ fill the sky with streaks of light.
5. Friction of Earth's _____ heats the meteoroids.
6. Some swarms of meteoroids _____ the sun.

Down

1. Large meteorites strike Earth forming large _____.
2. Most meteoroids are no larger than a grain of _____.
3. Large meteorites are pieces of asteroids and _____.
4. Meteoroid that enters Earth's atmosphere
7. Friction makes meteoroids _____ up in Earth's atmosphere.

Name _____

Match Up the Solar System!

Use reference materials to match the following words with the correct definitions or facts. Place the numbers of the words in the spaces by the clues. On another sheet of paper, write a story as if you were an astronaut exploring space. Use as many words from the list on the left as you can.

1. asteroid

2. black hole

3. comet

4. Jupiter

5. meteor

6. Milky Way Galaxy

7. moon

8. Pleiades

9. Pluto

10. quasar

11. skylab

12. solar system

13. space shuttle

14. star

15. sun

16. telescope

17. Triton

18. Uranus

19. Viking spacecraft

20. Voyager 2

____ A group of stars found in the constellation, Leo

____ The name of the planet that spins faster than any other planet

____ The "sideways" planet

____ Ships and stars are affected by its pull.

____ A giant ball of hot, burning gases

____ Astronomers have been unable to prove that it exists.

____ In 1963, Maarten Schmidt proved that it was not a star.

____ Also known as "shooting star"

____ Also known as a "minor planet"

____ Kohoutek, one of its kind, was studied by men in space.

____ It is made of star clusters, dust, gases, planets and stars.

____ An orderly community that centers around one star consisting of thousands of orbiting objects

____ One of its kind is Alpha Centauri.

____ A reusable transport vehicle

____ It went into space on August 20, 1977, but was not popular until 1989.

____ First U.S. manned space laboratory

____ Landed on Mars on July 20, 1976

____ George Ellery Hale made it big and famous.

____ A moon of the planet, Neptune

____ It was discovered by the use of mathematics.

SCIENCE

Name _____

Out in Space

Use the Word Bank and other sources to complete the puzzle.

Across

2. Path of a comet
4. Holes on Earth or moon made by meteorites
5. Another name for asteroid
6. Band (of asteroids)
8. Wind that pushes a comet's tail
9. Comet's gas cloud
12. Meteor _____ fill the night sky.
13. Comet part that can be millions of miles long
14. Asteroids have irregular _____ .
15. A meteor is a _____ star.

Down

1. Resistance that heats meteoroids
3. Famous comet
4. Meteor showers are named after _____ in which they appear to come.
7. Asteroid belt between Jupiter and _____
9. Largest known asteroid
10. Meteor that strikes Earth's surface
14. Gives comets its illumination

Word Bank		
belt		solar
Ceres	Mars	friction
craters	shooting	orbit
Halley's	shape	Sun
showers	planetoid	tail
constellations	meteorite	coma

Name _____

Twenty Questions

Below are 20 clues about a person. After reading the clues, use your science book or other resource and your own logical thinking to guess who the person is. When you are finished, write your own 20 clues about a person, place, or object in the solar system. Give it to a friend.

I am a person.

1. My theory was that Earth was a moving planet.
2. I disagreed with Ptolemy's theory of the universe.
3. I was raised by my uncle, a wealthy bishop.
4. I was born in 1473.
5. I studied medicine at the University of Padua, Italy.
6. Johannes Kepler was influenced by my work.
7. I said the planetary system was heliocentric, or sun-centered.
8. I died only hours after seeing the first complete copy of my famous book.
9. My book showed Earth orbiting the sun.
10. I explained how Earth's motion could be used to explain movements of other heavenly bodies.
11. I believed that Earth traveled through space.
12. I died in 1543.
13. My Polish name is Mikolaj Kopernik.
14. I studied mathematics, astronomy, medicine and theology.
15. I lived around the same time as Columbus and Martin Luther.
16. My studies showed that Earth rotates on its axis.
17. I was born in Poland.
18. Galileo's discoveries with his telescope supported my ideas.
19. I wrote *On the Revolutions of the Celestial Spheres* in 1543.
20. I am the founder of modern astronomy.

I am _____.

I am _____.
1. _____
2. _____
3. _____
4. _____
5. _____
6. _____
7. _____
8. _____
9. _____
10. _____
11. _____
12. _____
13. _____
14. _____
15. _____
16. _____
17. _____
18. _____
19. _____
20. _____
I am _____.

SCIENCE

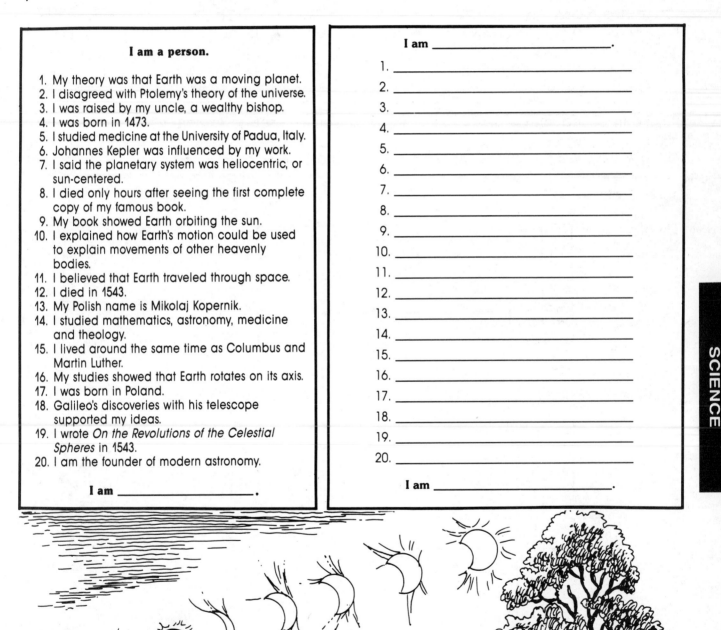

Name _____

The Moon

With the help of your encyclopedia or other sources, solve the crossword puzzle below.

Across

2. Space program that put a man on the moon
5. He did the first "moonwalk."
7. The moon orbits _____ .
9. Shadow cast by one object in space on another
10. The moon cannot be seen from Earth during this phase.
12. A "sea" on the moon
13. Bowl-shaped pits on the moon's surface

Down

1. The moon's changing "shapes" are called _____ .
3. The moon shines by reflected _____ .
4. The moon's path around Earth
6. The moon is Earth's natural _____ .
8. Vehicle used to explore the moon's surface
11. The moon's gravity is 6 times _____ than that on Earth's surface.

Name _____

A Time Line in Space

On October 4, 1957, history was made. Sputnik I, the first artificial satellite to circle Earth, was launched by Russia. Since then, many accomplishments have been made, including the United States having the first man on the moon. Below are some space-age facts. Research to find the date when each event occurred. Make a time line of the events on the back of this page. On another sheet of paper, write a paragraph about what you think space exploration will be like in the future.

Date

1. Pioneer X, first spacecraft to travel beyond all the planets   _____

2. Neil Armstrong, first man on the moon   _____

3. Viking II, landed on Mars   _____

4. Voyager 2, photographed Neptune's rings   _____

5. Yuri Gagarin, first manned space flight   _____

6. Mariner IX, orbited Mars   _____

7. John Glenn, first American to orbit Earth   _____

8. Venera 9, photographed surface of Venus   _____

9. Surveyor 5, landed on Moon   _____

10. John Young and Robert Crippen, astronauts in first space shuttle   _____

11. The last manned landing on the moon   _____

12. Chaffee, White and Grissom, killed in a U.S. spacecraft   _____

13. Alan B. Shepard, Jr., first American in space   _____

14. Apollo 14 mission with the CSM Kitty Hawk   _____

SCIENCE

Fascinating Fact! Did you know that the moon always keeps the same half facing Earth?

Name _____

Land Beneath the Ocean

The land beneath the ocean has features that are very similar to those that you would see if you traveled across North America.

- Study the picture of the ocean floor. First label the picture and then the descriptions below, using the words from the word bank.

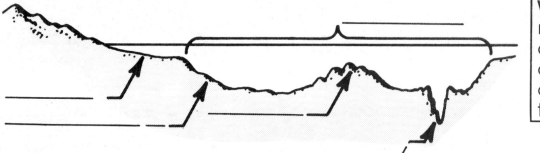

Word Bank
mid-ocean ridge
continental slope
continental shelf
ocean basin
trench

1. _____ A narrow, deep valley in the ocean basin.

2. _____ A steep incline at the edge of the continental shelf.

3. _____ A chain of mountains on the ocean floor.

4. _____ The part of the ocean floor nearest the continents.

5. _____ The deepest part of the ocean which contains valleys, plains, and mountains.

Many mountains on the mid-ocean ridges are almost 7,000 meters high, but still don't reach the surface of the ocean.

6. What is formed when an underwater mountain reaches the ocean's

   surface? _____

7. Give an example for number 6. _____

   _____

8. Most commercial fishermen do not fish beyond the continental shelf. Why do

   you think this is so? _____

   _____

Find Out: The Mariana Trench in the Pacific Ocean is nearly 11,000 meters deep. Mt. Everest is the highest mountain on earth, but is it higher than the Mariana Trench is deep? How does it compare in size?

Name _____

"Ping-Ping"

The depth of the ocean can be measured using a device called an echo sounder. A sound, "ping," is sent from a ship to the ocean floor. The length of time it takes for the "ping" to strike the ocean floor and bounce back to the ship is recorded. Sound travels in water at a speed of 1,500 meters per second. If a ping takes 6 seconds for a round trip, then a one way trip must take 3 seconds. The depth of the ocean at that point must be 4,500 m (3 sec. x 1,500 m/sec. = 4,500 m).

1. Find the various depths of the ocean using the "ping" soundings on this chart.

2. Using the depths you have listed on the chart, graph your results on the chart below. Connect the points to make a profile of the ocean floor.

3. Put a ✱ on the deep ocean trench.

4. Put an **X** on the continental slope.

5. Put an **M** on the undersea mountain.

Sounding	Time (sec.)		Speed (m/sec.)		Depth (m)
1	.4	X	1,500	=	600
2	.4	X	1,500	=	600
3	3	X	1,500	=	
4	2.6	X	1,500	=	3,900
5	3	X	1,500	=	
6	2	X	1,500	=	
7	1	X	1,500	=	
8	2	X	1,500	=	
9	3	X	1,500	=	
10	3.4	X	1,500	=	5,100
11	2	X	1,500	=	
12	7	X	1,500	=	
13	1	X	1,500	=	

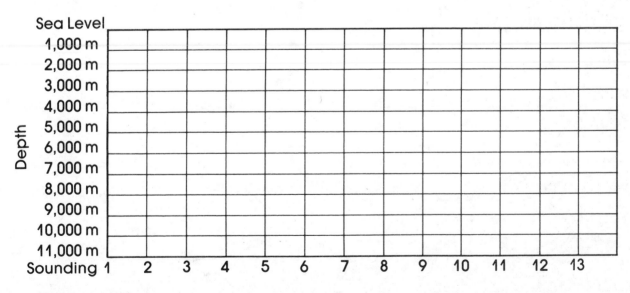

Fun Fact: Only 5% of the world's marine animals live below 1,000 meters, in the sea's eternal darkness where sunlight cannot penetrate.

Name _____

Eruptions

Volcanoes are one of the most destructive forces on Earth. While some eruptions are very quiet, others are very violent. Eruptions can bring great damage to property and can take many lives. Throughout history, there have been many eruptions that will long be remembered.

Use an atlas, encyclopedia and other reference materials to learn about some of the most famous volcanic eruptions. Organize your data by completing the chart below.

Volcano	Location	Type of volcano	Date of eruption	Description of eruption and the damage it caused

On another sheet of paper, write an imaginary story about your feelings if you lived at the foot of a volcano threatening to erupt.

Name _____

The Ring of Fire

Most of the active volcanoes in the world can be found along the edges of the continents. More than half of these volcanoes encircle the Pacific Ocean in an area known as the "Ring of Fire." Many of the others are found in southern Europe, Iceland, and Hawaii.

Use other sources to locate and label the following famous volcanoes. Color the area on the map red to indicate the "Ring of Fire."

Mount Fuji   Krakatoa   Mount Etna   Cotopaxi
Mauna Loa   Mt. St. Helens   El Chichón   Lassen Peak
Paricutín   Vesuvius   Mount Tambora   Mont Pelée

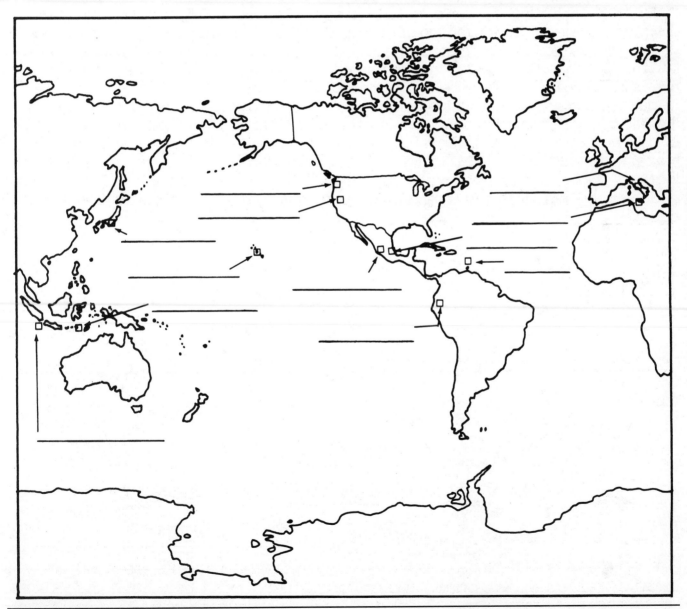

SCIENCE

Name _____

Earthquakes

Suddenly one day while Miss Freed's sixth graders were taking a spelling test, the lights flickered, chalk dropped off the chalkboard, and books fell off the shelves. No one knew what was happening. Then, just as suddenly as the strange occurrence started, it stopped. Dukwilma had experienced a small earthquake. Of course Miss Freed found this to be the perfect time to study earthquakes.

Miss Freed told her students that earthquakes can be explained according to the plate tectonics theory. In this theory, the Earth's surface consists of about 30 rigid plates that move slowly past one another. This motion causes rocks at the plates' edges to be strained and stressed. When the force is too great, the rocks break and shift and an earthquake occurs. Miss Freed also said that most of the breaks, or faults, lie beneath the surface. Others, however, such as the San Andreas Fault in California, are visible.

Jack and Cassie pointed out the damage that can occur in an earthquake. Why, just with the little one they had, all the chalk was broken and books had to be reshelved. Maria quickly reminded them of the recent earthquake in California. Major highways crumbled, houses fell, many fires started, and myriads of other problems occurred. Lee also pointed out that earthquakes can damage water pipes, electric lines, and gas mains. Miss Freed and her students considered themselves very lucky after their study of the damage earthquakes can cause.

Match.

cause of earthquake   Thirty rigid plates move slowly past one another.

effect of earthquake   Rocks break and shift.

                             Fires start, buildings crumble, debris falls.

                             Rocks at plates' edges are strained and stressed.

Check.
Some effects earthquakes can have include:

☐ emotional trauma   ☐ falling bricks   ☐ rocks straining
☐ loss of life   ☐ physical injury   ☐ plates sliding

Write.
In your own words, write what causes an earthquake. _____

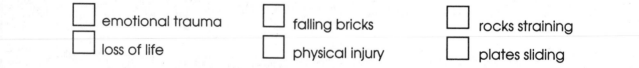

_____

Name _____

Crazy Cameras

Make your own pinhole camera.

Materials:
shoebox wax paper tape aluminum foil
candle or flashlight

Steps:

1. Cut out one end of the box. Fasten the lid securely so your box is sturdy.

2. Cut a small hole (1 to 2 centimeters diameter) in the center of the opposite end of the box.

3. Cover the large opening with wax paper and tape securely so there are no folds or creases.

4. Cover the small hole with aluminum foil and secure with tape. Make a tiny pinhole in the foil.

5. In a darkened room light a candle or use a flashlight. Point the camera's pinhole toward the light source and observe the image which appears on the wax paper.

6. You may look through your camera at other light sources (particularly lamp bulbs) or out a window on a bright day.

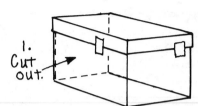

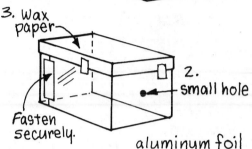

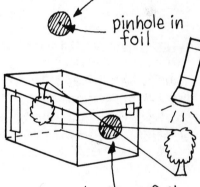

What do you notice about the image on your camera's screen?

_____

_____

_____

Think about it!

What would happen if . . . your pinhole were smaller? . . . larger? . . . you had bright light behind you? Should you line the inside of your box with anything?

Can you think of any ways to improve your camera?

_____

_____

_____

Name _____

Electroscope

Facts to Know

Static electricity does not flow in a current. Friction or rubbing creates static electricity. When insulators, which do not conduct electricity, are rubbed together, static electricity is created. Dry, cool days are the best times to make static electricity.

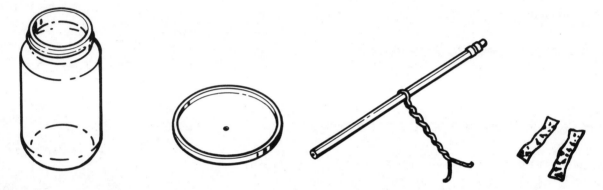

Making an Electroscope

Use a glass jar with a wide mouth and a plastic lid a little larger than the mouth. Poke a small hole in the lid with the point of a compass. Bend a 10-inch piece of bare copper wire in half. Form a loop at the fold by wrapping the wire around a pencil. Twist the wire down to the ends. Take the pencil out and stick the ends of the wire through the hole in the lid. Use clear tape to keep the wire tight against the lid. Bend the bottom ends of the wire up about 1/2 inch away from each other. Cut two pieces of aluminum foil 1/2 inch wide and 1 1/2 inches long. Poke a hole in each foil piece at one end. Hang each piece over one end of the wire. The foil pieces should be about 1/4 to 1/2 inch from each other. Put the lid on the jar with the foil inside the jar.

Using the Electroscope

Run a comb through your hair 30 times. Go in one direction only. Touch the comb to the wire. What happened? _____
Rub a balloon against your hair, on a woolen sweater, on your arm, against a shiny blouse or against another similar object. Rub about 30 times in only one direction. Touch the balloon against the wire. What happened? _____

Name _____

Atomizers

Facts to Know

Air pressure increases as air moves more slowly. Air pressure is reduced as air moves more quickly.

Making an Atomizer

Fill a clear plastic cup 3/4 full with water. Place a straw in the water. The straw must not touch the bottom of the cup. Hold another straw at a 90-degree angle to the first one. Blow hard through the second straw. What happened? _____

_____

Can you make the straw squirt a fine mist like a perfume atomizer? _____ Try blowing with less force and then with more force. Did it still work? _____ How do you think the atomizer works? _____

_____

Testing Hypotheses

If the first straw touched the bottom of the cup, what do you think would happen? _____

_____

_____

If you held the straw at different angles while blowing, what do you think would happen?

_____

_____

Test both of your hypotheses. What happened?

_____

_____

How could you make the atomizer work better?

_____

_____

Draw a picture of this last design for an atomizer on the back of this sheet.

Test the new atomizer. How does it work compared to the first design? _____

_____

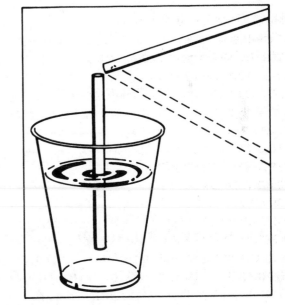

Daily Learning Drills Grade 6

SCIENCE

Name _____

Balloons and Airfoils

Investigate

Blow up two balloons. Tie each one to a piece of fish line. Tie one piece of line to the end of a pencil. Tie the other one so that the balloons hang about 1 inch apart.

What do you think would happen if you blew between the two balloons? _____
_____
_____

Blow between the balloons. What did happen? _____
_____
_____

Use a straw to blow between them. What happened? _____
_____
_____

Why do you think the balloons pull together rather than apart? _____
_____
_____

Blow across the air outside of one balloon.
What happened? _____
_____

Blow on the outside of the balloon on the other side. What happened? _____
_____

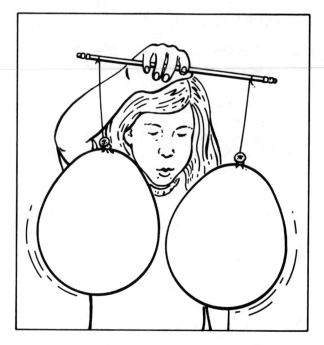

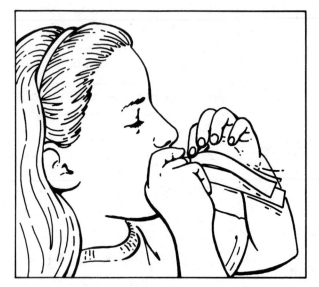

Working With an Airfoil

To create an airfoil, a surface that affects the movement of air, cut out a long rectangular piece of paper. Wrap the paper over a pencil with the edges facing away from you. What do you think will happen when you blow on it as the person is doing in the picture? _____
Blow on the airfoil. What happened? _____
Why do you think the flaps blew apart rather than together? _____

How are the airfoil and the balloons alike? _____

Name _____

Buzzer Telegraph

Use with pages 226 and 227.

Fact to Know

A telegraph is an instrument which uses an electromagnet and a switch to transmit messages.

Materials

A 2-x-6-inch piece of wood, two small paper clips, two large paper clips, one D or other size alkaline battery, two rubber bands, 1 yard of thin, insulated wire, a piece of sandpaper, three large 1/2-inch thumbtacks, a short nail, a pair of scissors

Making the Switch

Bend a large paper clip into the shape shown. Cut the wire into two pieces: one 4-inch piece and one 32-inch piece. Strip the insulation off the ends of both wires by rubbing a piece of sandpaper against the insulation until the end of the wire is bare.

Wrap one bare end of the 4-inch wire around a large thumbtack. Tightly wrap the bent end of the large paper clip around the same thumbtack and press the tack into the wood as far as it will go. Wrap the one bare end of the long wire around another large thumbtack. Line up the tack under the other end of the paper clip and press this thumbtack into the wood as far as it will go also. This is the telegraph switch.

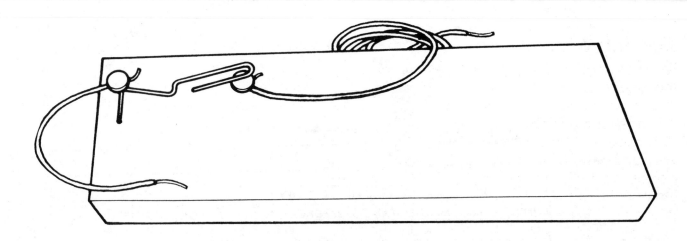

Name _____

Buzzer Telegraph

Use with pages 225 and 227.

Making a Battery Holder

Wind two rubber bands very tightly around the positive and negative poles of the battery. Slip a small paper clip under the rubber band at each pole and bend the clips over. This is your battery holder.

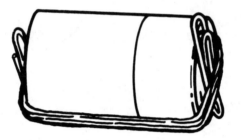

Making the Buzzer

With a hammer or similar tool, tap a short nail into the wood. It should be stuck firmly but not too deeply. To create an electromagnet, wrap the long wire around the nail in neat coils until there is only about 4 inches left. Tightly wrap one end of the other large paper clip around a third thumbtack. Line up the other end of the paper clip above the coils and press the thumbtack into the wood as far as it will go. Connect the end of the long wire to the paper clip at the positive pole (top of the battery). Connect the bare end of the short wire to the paper clip at the negative pole (bottom of the battery). The telegraph is now ready for use.

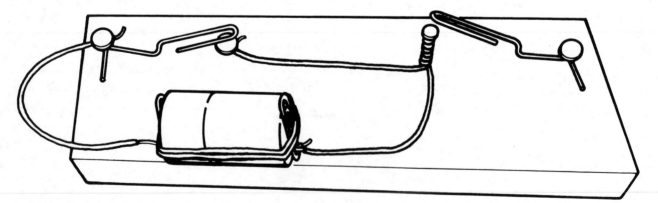

Press the paper clip switch to the thumbtack and the circuit should be complete, making an electromagnet which pulls the paper clip buzzer down with a click. Release the switch and the paper clip buzzer should bounce back up. If it doesn't work, check all connections and the strength of your battery. You may also need to adjust the heights of the paper clips used in the switch and buzzer.

Name _____

Sending Telegraph Messages

Use with pages 225 and 226.

Working with the Morse Code

With the Morse Code, messages are sent by using dots and dashes that represent letters. A dot is made by briefly tapping a telegraph switch. A dash is made by holding the switch down a little longer. Use the Morse Code to send messages to your partner. Start by sending short names or very simple words. Gradually work up to sentences, making sure to pause between words. Take turns sending and receiving messages.

International Morse Code

A ·—	B —···	C —·—·	D —··
E ·	F ··—·	G ——·	H ····
I ··	J ·———	K —·—	L ·—··
M ——	N —·	O ———	P ·——·
Q ——·—	R ·—·	S ···	T —
U ··—	V ···—	W ·——	X —··—
Y —·——	Z ——··		

Sending Messages

Write out your message. Then place the dots and dashes under each letter.

_____

_____

_____

Decoding Messages

Record the dots and dashes as your partner sends a message. Then place the matching letters above the dots and dashes.

_____

_____

_____

_____

SCIENCE

Name _____

Acids and Bases

Facts to Know

Acids and bases are chemical compounds. Some of these compounds are strong and abrasive. Many are used as cleaning agents. Litmus paper is an indicator. Indicators are affected when an acid or base is present in a substance. Blue litmus paper turns red when dipped in an acid. Red litmus paper turns blue when dipped in a base.

Testing for Acids and Bases

Use blue and red litmus paper to test each of the substances on the chart. Record the results by writing the color the paper turns when dipped and whether the substance is an acid or a base. The first one is done for you.

Substance	Blue Litmus	Red Litmus	Acid, Base or Neither
lemon juice	red	red	acid
vinegar			
ammonia			
orange juice			
tea			
milk			
baking soda and water			
cleanser and water			
water			
vinegar and salt			
grapefruit juice			
antacid pills and water			
cola			

Name _____

Testing for Starch

Facts to Know

Starch is found in many foods and plants. Iodine is an indicator of starch. It turns blue-black when placed on a substance containing starch.

Testing for Starch

Safety Note: Iodine can be dangerous. Do not taste, spill or misuse it in any way.
Place a drop of iodine on each of the substances listed on the chart. Record the results. The first one is done for you.

Substance	Color of Iodine	Starch: Yes or No
white bread	blue-black	yes
brown bread		
dry cereal		
brown leaf		
popped popcorn		
oatmeal		
orange peel		
lemon peel		
liquid starch		
newspaper		
paper towel		
tissue		
water		
alcohol		
dish soap		
cloth		

SCIENCE

Name _____

Testing for Calcite

Facts to Know

There are three main types of rock: sedimentary, igneous and metamorphic. Sedimentary rock is formed underwater from layers of sediment. Igneous rock is rock that erupted from a volcano in a liquid form and later became solid. Metamorphic rock is rock that was once sedimentary or igneous but was changed by heat or pressure deep within the earth. One way to identify rocks is to check for calcite or lime in the rock.

Testing for Calcite

Collect a variety of rocks. Carefully wash each one. Number and initial pieces of tape for each so that you can tell them apart. Put the tape pieces on the rocks. Place a few drops of vinegar on the first rock with an eyedropper. Did it fizz?_____
Are there any bubbles? _____
Dip the rock partway into the cup of vinegar. Hold the rock to your ear.
Can you hear it fizz? _____ Are there any bubbles? _____
Rocks which fizz or show the bubbles in this acid have calcite, lime or calcium carbonate in them.

Chart Making

Check your rocks and those of your friends. Record the number and initial of each rock. Tell whether you noted any fizzing or bubbles by writing "yes" or "no" on the chart.

Number/Initial	Fizzing?	Bubbles?	Calcite or Lime Present?
Example: 1TS	yes	no	yes

Drawing Conclusions

Are most rocks which contain calcite or lime sedimentary or igneous? _____
What are your reasons? _____
_____

Name _____

Testing Hardness

Facts to Know

Scientists use many tests to identify and classify rocks. One such test is a hardness scale in which materials are rated from softest to hardest. For example, a material such as talc is rated #1, the softest on the scale. On this scale, diamond is rated #10, the hardest. Use this information to help you in testing the hardness of each of your rocks.

Hardness Scale	Test
#1 and #2	A fingernail can scratch these.
#3	A penny can scratch it.
#4 and #5	A knife can scratch these.
#6 and #7	They can scratch glass.
#8, #9, #10	They can scratch any rock that is lower on the scale.

Testing Rocks for Hardness

Make sure your rocks are clean. Write a different number and your initials on pieces of tape. Put the pieces of tape on each rock and list each number-initial identification in the first column of the chart. Use your fingernail, a penny, a knife and a glass jar to test each rock. Record the results on the chart by writing "yes" or "no" as in the example. Use the information above to help classify each rock's hardness. Work carefully and check your results twice.

Safety Note:
Be very careful not to cut yourself with the knife. You don't have to press too forcefully with the knife. Also, do not press the rock too hard against the jar. Do not break the jar!

Number/Initial	Fingernail Scratch	Penny Scratch	Knife Scratch	Scratches Jar	Scratches Rocks Less Than 8, 9, 10	Hardness Range
Example: 1TS	yes	yes	yes	no	no	#4 – #5

SCIENCE

Name _____

What Do You See in the Ink?

Background:

Chromatography, the separation of the substances of a mixture through the use of an absorbing material, can be used to separate things such as blood or ink from another substance. If something stained is placed in a solvent, that solvent can cause some of the substance to be pulled, or attracted, away. The colors, or pigments, can be used as a comparison to other substances. If colors "bleed" in the same manner, they could be from the same source. When a crime is committed, this test may be used to provide clues for solving it.

Materials Needed:

paper towel strips (1 x 3 inches), water, straws, cups, tape, six black ink pens - each of a different brand

Procedure:

1. Divide class into three groups and give each group two pens and two small strips of paper towels.

2. Use a different pen to draw a line across the center of each of the paper towel strips.

3. Tape the paper towel strips to the center of the straws so that they will hang when the straws are placed crosswise on top of the cups. The cups should contain enough water so that the paper strips will hang into the water, but not touch the bottom of the cup. The ink mark should remain above the water.

Record the Data:

1. What happened when the paper touched the water? _____

_____

_____

2. What is on the paper? _____

_____

_____

You should see various color patterns from the different kinds of ink. These ink color patterns are called chromatograms. Using this technique in investigating crimes, one can determine, by matching the color patterns, if the possibility exists that a specific pen or typewriter might have been used in the perpetration of a crime.

Name _____

The Bill of Rights

Write a bill of rights for your school. _____

_____

_____

_____

_____

_____

_____

_____

_____

_____

Write a personal bill of rights. _____

_____

_____

_____

_____

_____

_____

_____

_____

Write an amendment you would like to see added to the U.S. Constitution. _____

_____

_____

_____

SOCIAL STUDIES

Name _____

Three Branches at Work

Write what you would do as a member of each branch of government in regard to the "law" being proposed.

> **Law under consideration:** The penny would no longer be a coin in the U.S. monetary system. Everything would cost five cents or more.

As a member of Congress: _____

_____

_____

_____

As President: _____

_____

_____

_____

As a judge on the Supreme Court: _____

_____

_____

_____

> **Law under consideration:** Every company with ten or more workers must hire the same number of men and women.

As a member of Congress: _____

_____

_____

_____

As President: _____

_____

_____

_____

As a judge on the Supreme Court: _____

_____

_____

_____

Three Branches at Work (cont.)

Law under consideration: The first Monday of every other month beginning in February 1997 will be a national holiday. No other holidays will be observed.

As a member of Congress: _____

_____

_____

_____

As President: _____

_____

_____

_____

As a judge on the Supreme Court: _____

_____

_____

_____

Law under consideration: All schools in the United States must be open for students' attendance the same number of days. They will open on the first Monday after August 24th and will close the first Friday after June 5th.

As a member of Congress: _____

_____

_____

_____

As President: _____

_____

_____

_____

As a judge on the Supreme Court: _____

_____

_____

_____

SOCIAL STUDIES

Name _____

Getting Involved

Choose a candidate to research. Then complete the following activities.

Create a newspaper advertisement.

Write out what you might say in a telephone call on behalf of a candidate.

Hello. My name is _____

I am calling to ask you to _____

_____

_____

because _____

_____

_____

Please vote next _____

Thank you for your consideration.

Goodbye.

Write a slogan.

_____

Write a letter to the editor expressing your views about a particular candidate and his/her views on a particular issue.

Dear _____ ,

_____

_____

_____

_____

_____

_____

_____

Make a poster, button and flyer on other sheets of paper.

Name _____

Getting Involved (cont.)

Create a commercial endorsing a
candidate on a view or an issue
for TV or radio. Act it out.

With another student, debate both sides
of an issue.

Draw an editorial cartoon featuring
a candidate on a view or an issue.

Write an editorial to go with the cartoon.

_____
_____
_____
_____
_____
_____
_____
_____
_____
_____
_____
_____

Write a speech for your issue or candidate.

_____
_____
_____
_____
_____
_____
_____
_____
_____

SOCIAL STUDIES

Name _____

The President

The President of the U.S. is often considered the most powerful elected official in the world. It makes sense then that not everybody is eligible to hold this important position. Complete the page below to find out the necessary qualifications one must have in order to be President and to find out the important responsibilities that are a part of this position.

1. At least how old does the President have to be? _____

   Why do you think this is so? _____

2. How long does someone have to live in the U.S. before he/she can be President? _____
   _____ Do you agree with this? Why? _____
   _____

3. What is the 3rd legal qualification for a President besides the two listed above? _____
   _____

4. How can someone be nominated for the Presidency? _____
   _____

5. To what political party does our current President belong? _____

6. What is the Electoral College? _____
   _____

7. When is the Presidential Inauguration held? _____
   _____

8. How long is the term of a President? _____

9. Effective in 1951, the 22nd Amendment says a President can serve how many terms? ___

10. What kind of salary does the President receive? _____

11. What happens if a President dies, resigns or is removed from office? _____
    _____

12. What branch of the federal government does the President head? _____

13. What does this branch consist of? _____
    _____

14. Name the seven basic roles of the President. _____
    _____

Something Extra: Pick one of the seven roles of the President. List the responsibilities involved in this role. Make a list of things the current President has done in this role.

Name _____

Birthplaces of Presidents

Did you know that only 19 out of the 50 states have been the birthplaces of Presidents? Did you know that 8 Presidents came from Virginia and 7 came from Ohio? Complete the page below to see if any Presidents have been born in your state.

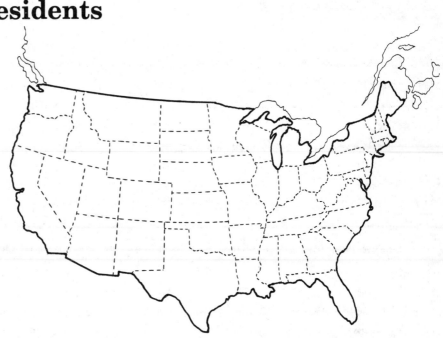

1. Washington, Jefferson, Madison, Monroe, W. H. Harrison, Tyler, Taylor and Wilson were all born in Virginia. Label this state on the map and put the number 8 next to it.

2. Grant, Hayes, Garfield, B. Harrison, McKinley, Taft and Harding were born in Ohio. Label this state and put the number 7 next to it.

3. New York is the birthplace of Van Buren, Fillmore, T. Roosevelt and F. D. Roosevelt. Put a number 4 and the name of this state on the map where it belongs.

4. Four Presidents were also born in Massachusetts - J. Adams, J. Q. Adams, Kennedy and Bush. Label this state and put the number 4 next to it.

5. North Carolina, Texas and Vermont each had 2 Presidents born in them. Polk and A. Johnson were born in North Carolina, Eisenhower and L. B. Johnson claim Texas as their birthplace and Vermont is the birthplace of Arthur and Coolidge. Label these states and put a number 2 next to each of them.

6. The rest of the Presidents were all born in different states. They are listed below. Write the name of the state from which each President came in the state where it belongs.

Arkansas - Clinton	Iowa - Hoover	New Hampshire - Pierce
California - Nixon	Kentucky - Lincoln	New Jersey - Cleveland
Georgia - Carter	Missouri - Truman	Pennsylvania - Buchanan
Illinois - Reagan	Nebraska - Ford	South Carolina - Jackson

7. Label the Atlantic and the Pacific Oceans on the map. Have more Presidents been born near the Atlantic or the Pacific Ocean? _____

8. Label the rest of the states on the map. If no President has been born in your state, tell why you think this is so on the back of this page. If one (or more) has been born in your state, write if you think he was or is a good representative of your state and tell why.

SOCIAL STUDIES

Name _____

Presidential Firsts

There is always a first time for everything! Use the clues below to find out which Presidents were the first to do the things listed. Fill in the blanks using the names in the box and other references to help you.

Abraham Lincoln	John Adams	Franklin Pierce
William Taft	Calvin Coolidge	George Washington
Thomas Jefferson	Woodrow Wilson	Theodore Roosevelt
Andrew Jackson	James Polk	John Tyler
Lyndon Johnson	William Henry Harrison	Gerald Ford

1. He was our first President and the first to be elected unanimously. _____

2. The first President to live in the White House, his son was also President. _____

3. This President was the first to win the Nobel Peace Prize, and he became our nation's youngest President after McKinley's assassination. _____

4. The first President born in the 20th century, he was also President when Martin Luther King, Jr. was assassinated in 1968. _____

5. This President was the first Vice President not elected by the people to become President and was our 38th President. _____

6. The first President born in a log cabin, the first President to be elected by a national convention and the first President to ride on a railroad train, he was President from 1829-1837. _____

7. John Tyler became the first Vice President to become President when this President was the first to die in office. _____

8. He was the first to hold regular press conferences, to speak on the radio and was in office when World War I ended in 1918. _____

9. This President was the only one born on the 4th of July and was the first to be sworn in by a former President. _____

10. He was the first President born after the adoption of the U.S. Constitution, the first President whose wife died while he was in office and the first President to marry while in office. He was our 10th President. _____

11. This President was the first to be born in the 19th century. _____

12. He was the first President to serve as Speaker of the House and was President when gold was discovered in California in 1848. _____

13. The first President to be inaugurated in Washington, D.C., this man died on the 4th of July. _____

14. He was our first President to be assassinated. _____

15. This man was the first to become Chief Justice after serving as President, and the first to open the baseball season in 1910. _____

Something Extra: Have you ever been the first in your class or family to do something? Write about it. Or write about the first time you did something special.

Name _____

Two Presidents

Jack and Beth spent several hours trying to decide which two famous people they wanted to compare. First, they thought they would compare famous athletes. Jack wanted to compare football players, and Beth wanted to compare volleyball players. Famous authors came up, but they could not agree on authors either. Finally, they decided to compare U.S. Presidents. They each picked a number between one and 42. They chose ten and 15. It was decided. They would compare John Tyler, our tenth President, and James Buchanan, our fifteenth.

Jack and Beth were surprised to learn how similar Tyler and Buchanan were. For instance, both went to college and practiced law. They both ran successfully for seats in the U.S. House of Representatives: Tyler in 1816 and Buchanan four years later. Jack learned that Tyler was elected to the U.S. Senate in 1827 and that Buchanan followed him there seven years later. But he also noted that whereas Buchanan went on to become Secretary of State and minister to Great Britain after serving about ten years in the Senate, Tyler went from the Senate to become Vice-President of the United States under William Henry Harrison. Beth then told Jack that Tyler became President only one month after Harrison's inauguration due to Harrison's death. Buchanan, Beth noted, was elected President.

Beth and Jack went on to learn that three new states entered the Union under Buchanan and that under Tyler, China opened its ports to American trade and Florida joined the Union.

When they were done researching for their comparison, Jack and Beth were surprised at the amount of information they had gathered. Now came the hard part of putting it all together!

Fill in.

The following apply to **a.** Tyler, or **b.** Buchanan. Put the appropriate letter in the box.

☐ became President when Harrison died

☐ Secretary of State

☐ three new states entered the Union during his presidency

☐ elected President

☐ Vice-President

☐ Florida joined the Union during his presidency

Write.

List similarities and differences between Tyler and Buchanan.

Similarities	**Differences**
1. _____	1. _____
2. _____	2. _____
3. _____	3. _____
4. _____	4. _____

SOCIAL STUDIES

Name _____

Contributing Factors

Many people have greatly influenced our country. Find out how the people below have contributed, or are contributing, to our country by filling in the chart. Then answer the questions below.

Name	Date Born	Date Died	Number of Years Lived	Contribution(s) to our Society/ Best Known For
Betsy Ross				
Noah Webster				
John Chapman				
Davy Crockett				
Francis Scott Key				
John C. Frémont				
Sitting Bull				
William Tweed				
Harriet B. Stowe				
Carry Nation				
Jesse James				
Wilbur & Orville Wright				
Babe Ruth				
Albert Einstein				
Norman Rockwell				
Walt Disney				
Louis Armstrong				
Rosa Lee Parks				
Betty Friedan				

1. Who do you think has made the most important contribution to society? Why? _____
   _____

2. Who do you feel achieved the greatest results in the shortest amount of time? Defend your answer. _____
   _____

3. Whose achievements can still be seen, felt, witnessed, etc. today? _____

4. Name the people who worked or fought for specific causes or movements. Write the cause or movement after each person's name. _____

Something Extra: Find three people you think have contributed or are contributing to society. Tell the class about your choices.

Name _____

Fantastic Philanthropist

The sixth-grade students in Miss Freed's class have decided to become philanthropists. They have agreed to set apart one day each month on which to hold a bake sale or car wash to raise money for a good cause or to help others in need. Miss Freed has been teaching her students about some of the famous philanthropists in our country. One of them is John Davison Rockefeller. To learn about his life, number the boxes below in the correct order. Cut each one apart and glue it to its own page. Illustrate the pages and put them in order. Then you will have a biography of Rockefeller.

In 1882, Rockefeller organized the Standard Oil Trust. At this time, he controlled almost all U.S. oil refining and distribution and much of the world's oil trade.	Rockefeller's Standard Oil Company controlled the flow of all oil products from producer to consumer.
From 1895 to 1897, Rockefeller gradually retired from business. He had already started his vast philanthropic activities.	John Davison Rockefeller was born in 1839 in New York.
By 1910, he had given about $35 million to the University of Chicago. In all, Rockefeller gave away about $520 million during his lifetime. He died in 1937.	In 1890, Rockefeller helped found the University of Chicago.
The trust was dissolved because of the vastness of Rockefeller's holdings and because of public criticism of his methods.	Rockefeller used the profits from the grain house to enter the oil business in about 1862.
When Rockefeller was 14 years old, his family moved to Cleveland where he started work as a clerk in a small produce firm at age 16.	Fifteen years after he had entered the oil business, Rockefeller achieved his goal of making the oil industry orderly and efficient with the Standard Oil Company.
He formed a partnership in a grain commission house after working as a clerk.	About two years later, in 1892, the Ohio Supreme Court dissolved the Standard Oil Trust.

•SOMETHING EXTRA•

If you had $520 million dollars to give away, who would you give it to?

SOCIAL STUDIES

Name _____

Using Your Resources

Use resources to fill in the chart and learn more about inventive minds.

Name	Invention	Country	Year
John E. Lundstrom		Sweden	
	paper		c.105
Chester Greenwood		U.S.A.	
	ballpoint pen	Hungary	
George de Mestral			1948
	safety pin	U.S.A.	
	oil lubricators for steam engines		1872
	laser	U.S.A.	
	jeans		c.1849
Johannes Gutenberg		Germany	
	Bunsen burner	Germany	
Evangelista Torricelli			1643
	hypodermic syringe		1853
Garrett Morgan			1923
	water clock		400 B.C.
Zacharias Janssen		Netherlands	
Clarence Birdseye			1949

Name _____

Tale of Two Cities

City A is located on a small island in Southeast Asia. This major port city is densely populated with 2.7 million people who live in 221 square miles. City A is a prosperous and bustling center of trade, finance, and industry with clean air and a pollution-free environment. There is little unemployment. Cultural diversity is evident in dress styles, ethnic foods, creative art, and religious beliefs. The literacy rate is 83%, which is high. The government is a republic with a 79-member council that makes the laws which regulate most aspects of the citizens' lives. For example, the government banned the sale of gum after an elevator door was jammed shut with gum. Citizens are not allowed to own guns. Consequently, there is very little crime. People accused of a crime are presumed guilty. Citizens are heavily fined for minor infractions of the law, and serious crimes result in the death penalty.

City B is a large city in the U.S. It is known as one of the world's largest manufacturing centers. City B is a port city on a river that carries more shipping vessels than almost any other river in North America. About 1.2 million people live in its 140 square miles. Slums and air and water pollution are major problems. Racial tension and crime are widespread. Guns and weapons are easily accessible. Drugs have infiltrated the community. The city experiences hardship when production decreases. Schools are overcrowded and the literacy rate is low.

Culturally, City B offers museums and art centers, a symphony orchestra, and a theater that features opera and dramatic art performances. Musical performances are scheduled throughout the year. Spectator sports, including basketball, hockey, football, and baseball are another big part of the city's life.

Name things the two cities have in common.

_____

_____

What would be some reasons why you might like to live in City A?

_____

_____

Why might you not like to live in City A? _____

_____

What would have to take place for City B to be more like City A? _____

_____

Which city has more living space per person? _____

Challenge!

Tell which city you would prefer living in and why. _____

_____

_____

SOCIAL STUDIES

Global Nation

Culture encompasses the ideas, customs, styles of dress, beliefs, and language of a particular group of people. Sometimes religion defines a culture, such as in the Hindu, Jewish, or Amish cultures. Culture is also defined by language and country, such as in Japan and Germany.

Historically, members of a culture group who migrated to the United States located with members of that same culture. Today, people of all cultures often mix together in one community.

The following cultural characteristics provide examples of differences among ethnic groups:
- Some cultures do not celebrate Christmas.
- Some groups will not salute the flag of the United States or say the Pledge of Allegiance.
- Culture groups are known for their food. For instance, Italian Americans are known for their pasta.
- Culture groups have different educational philosophies. For example, Muslims do not seat boys next to girls.
- A crime in one culture may not be a crime or as serious a crime in another culture.

Contact between cultures is causing change in society. People are adopting traits from other cultures. As a result, America is becoming more diversified in its appearance, style of dress, food choices, and customs.

Think about the cultural differences among your classmates, friends, and neighbors. Think of differences in religion, language, habits, art, and customs. Then complete the following.

Why is the title "Global Nation" a good title for this activity? Can you think of another one?

_____

_____

Name two problems in society or school that occur as a result of mixing cultures.

_____

_____

Name two benefits of a multicultural society.

_____

_____

Think of two things you might use or do that have their origins in another culture. Two examples are: fur parka—Eskimo, bowing—Japanese.

_____

Imagine yourself in the year 2020. What do you think newborn Americans will look like?

_____

Name some things that are products of American culture, such as jazz and blue jeans.

_____

_____

Name _____

A Fountain of Faith

Use the Word Bank to fill in the chart below. You will not use every word!

Word Bank				
	church	Koran	Daniel	tabernacle
	c.2000 B.C.	Egypt	Bible	the Five Pillars
	c.610 A.D.	Torah	Canaan	Judea and Galilee
	Abraham	500 B.C.	mosque	Western Saudi Arabia
	synagogue	c.30 A.D.	Jesus	Mohammed

	Judaism	Christianity	Islam
Date Religion Began			
First Leader			
Birthplace of Religion			
Sacred Writings			
Building Where Worship Takes Place			

Challenge! There are five pillars of the Islamic faith. Find out what they are.

SOCIAL STUDIES

Name _____

America at Conflict

Since the Revolutionary War, The U.S. has fought in several other wars. Write the years the United States was involved in these wars and who the President or Presidents were at the time.

War	Entered	Ended	President(s)
War of 1812			
Mexican War			
Civil War			
Spanish American War			
World War I			
World War II			
Korean War			
Vietnam War			
War in the Persian Gulf			

Fill in the name of one of the wars from above after the statement below that tells about it.

1. No states had the right to end the Union. _____

2. The United States failed to achieve its goals. _____

3. Cuba gained its independence from Spain. _____

4. The Treaty of Ghent brought this war to an end. _____

5. The United Nations was formed as a result of this war. _____

6. Nazi war criminals were tried in Nuremberg after this war. _____

7. It was the shortest war in which the United States ever fought. _____

8. England intercepted a note from Germany to Mexico asking Mexico to attack the United States. _____

9. This was the only war fought completely on American soil and in its waters.

   _____

10. The settlement of this war revived arguments over slavery on whether or not the newly acquired territory was free. _____

11. This was the first war in which a world organization (the United Nations) played a military role. _____

12. After this war, each side had to give up all the land it had captured during the war. _____

13. England, France, Russia and the United States (the Allies) fought against the Axis (Germany, Italy and Japan). _____

14. This was the longest war in which the United States was ever involved. _____

Name _____

A Horrible Mess

Several of the parents of Miss Freed's students served in the Vietnam War. These include Jackie and Beth's fathers as well as Lee's mom. These sixth graders don't know much about this war or why it lasted almost 18 years.

Help Miss Freed's students better understand what went on during this time by sorting through the information below and organizing it chronologically on the lines provided. **Hint:** If two lines are provided, two sentences should be written.

One year later, in 1964, the U.S. Congress passed the Tonkin Gulf Resolution. This gave the President the power to take "all necessary measures" and "to prevent further aggression." On January 27, 1973, a cease-fire agreement was signed between the U.S., North and South Vietnam, and the Viet Cong. In 1957, the Communist-trained South Vietnamese rebels, or Viet Cong, began rebelling against the South Vietnamese government headed by President Diem. To begin, Vietnam was divided into Communist-ruled North Vietnam and non-Communist South Vietnam. Some Communist-trained South Vietnamese rebels then decided to join with North Vietnam to overtake South Vietnam. In 1969, President Nixon announced that U.S. troops would start withdrawing from Vietnam. In November of 1963, South Vietnamese generals overthrew the Diem government, and the next day Diem was killed. In 1968, the Viet Cong and North Vietnam launched a major campaign to overtake South Vietnamese cities. The last U.S. ground troops left Vietnam on March 29, 1973. President Lyndon B. Johnson sent U.S. Marines to South Vietnam on March 6, 1965. These were the first U.S. ground troops in the war. South Vietnam surrendered on April 30, 1975.

1. _____

_____

2. _____

3. _____

4. _____

_____

5. _____

_____

6. _____

7. _____

8. _____

9. _____

10. _____

Name _____

Pinpointing North American Cities

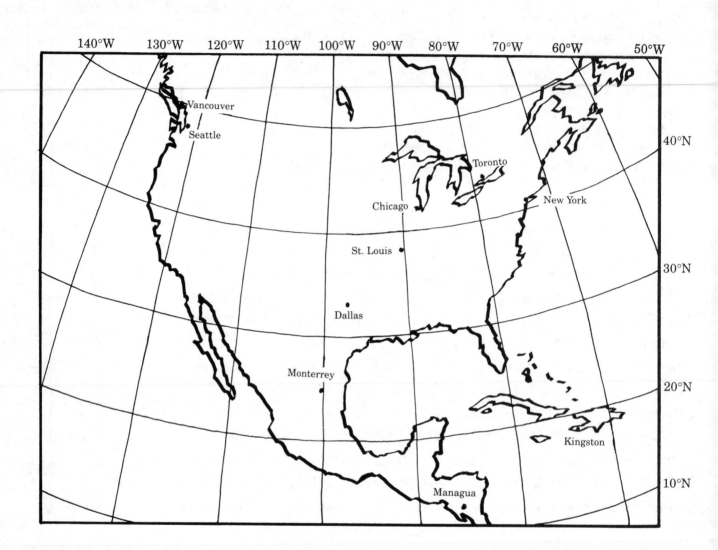

Use the lines of latitude and longitude to determine the approximate coordinates of the North American cities on the map above. Write the coordinates for each city in the blanks.

	Latitude	Longitude			Latitude	Longitude
1. Seattle	_____	_____	6. St. Louis		_____	_____
2. Kingston	_____	_____	7. Toronto		_____	_____
3. Dallas	_____	_____	8. New York		_____	_____
4. Vancouver	_____	_____	9. Monterrey		_____	_____
5. Managua	_____	_____	10. Chicago		_____	_____

Name _____

Plotting North American Cities

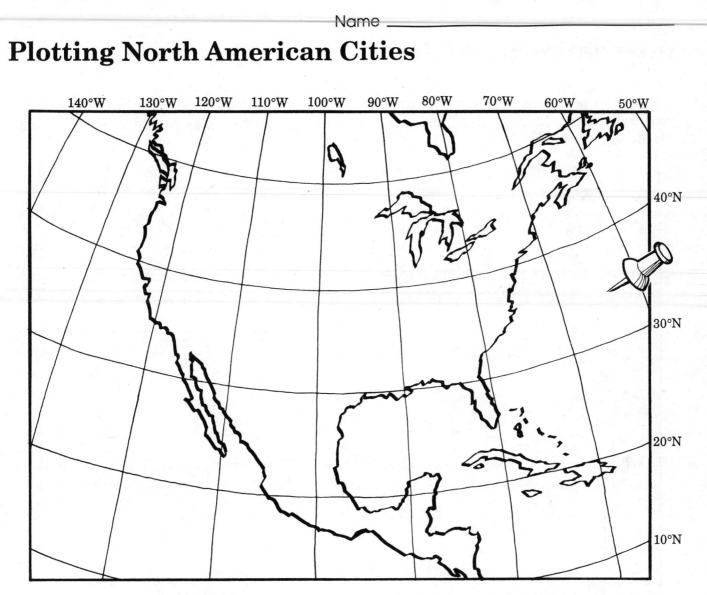

Use a globe or map to identify the city that is located at each set of coordinates. Write the name of the city on the blank and in the correct location on the map. There may be some slight variance in the degrees.

	City	Latitude	Longitude		City	Latitude	Longitude
1.	_____	25°N	80°W	6.	_____	19°N	99°W
2.	_____	39°N	104°W	7.	_____	51°N	114°W
3.	_____	50°N	97°W	8.	_____	33°N	84°W
4.	_____	23°N	82°W	9.	_____	42°N	83°W
5.	_____	37°N	122°W	10.	_____	46°N	71°W

Daily Learning Drills Grade 6

SOCIAL STUDIES

Name _____

International Riddles

The answer to each of these wacky riddles is the name of a country. Use the latitude and longitude clues to help you find the name of each country. (Degrees may vary slightly depending on the source used.)

1. What did Livia's husband tell her to do when it was her turn to throw the bowling ball?

_____
17°S, 65°W

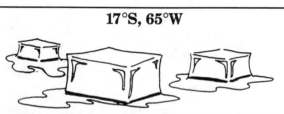

2. This is what I did when six dogs chased me.

_____
32°N, 53°E

3. Where is a great place to visit on a hot summer day?

_____
65°N, 18°W

4. When Occo finished all the food on his plate his mother asked, "Do you want

_____?"
32°N, 5°W

5. Two "guays" equal a . . .

_____
22°N, 58°W

6. What do you need when your wheel squeaks?

_____
39°N, 22°E

7. What did Susan and Daniel decide to name their new little baby?

_____
10° S, 30° W

8. In this land, nobody is a winner or a loser.

_____
15° N, 100° E

Neighbors

Use a map of the United States to locate your state. In the direction boxes write the names of all the states and/or countries surrounding your state/province.

Northwest	North	Northeast
West	**My State**	**East**
	Draw an outline map of your state/province.	
Southwest	**South**	**Southeast**

Name _____

Growing Populations

Every second of every minute, the population of the world increases by almost three people. That is an increase of more than 90 million people each year. A country's population changes for many reasons.

Explain how each of these can affect an increase or decrease in a country's population.

Natural disaster (flood, drought, earthquake, hurricane, etc.) _____

_____

Health care _____

_____

Study the *World Population Growth Map* (page 255). Find two examples for each category below. Use an almanac or other source to find the countries' populations.

Population Growth Group	Countries	Population
Countries with below average population growth	_____ _____	_____ _____
Countries with above average population growth	_____ _____	_____ _____
Countries with very high population growth	_____ _____	_____ _____

Name _____

World Population Growth Map

Use with page 254.

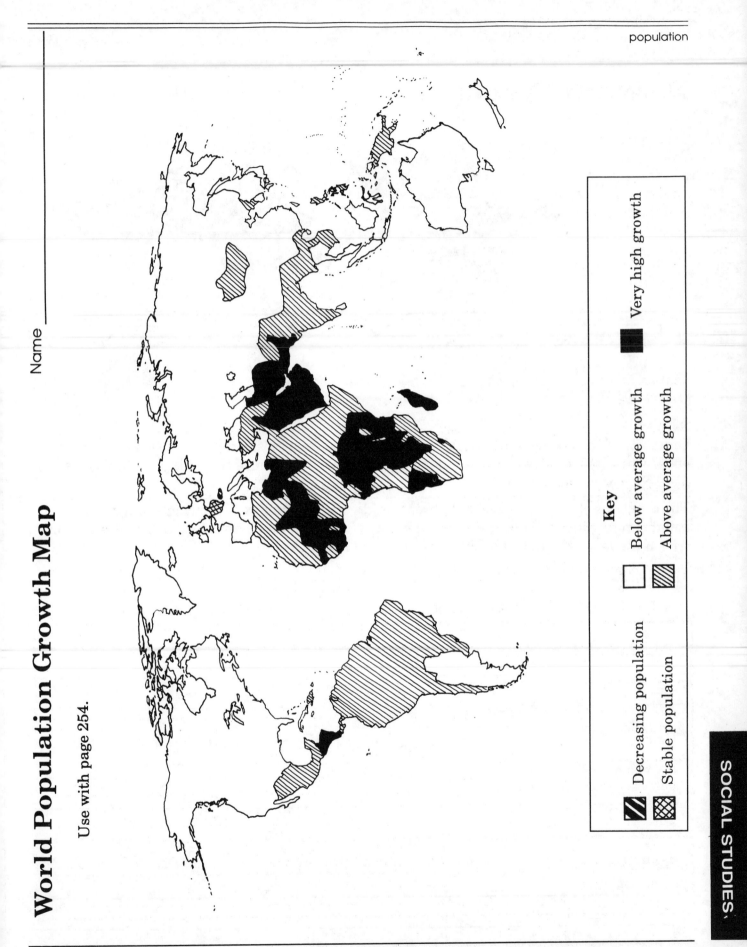

Key

☐ Decreasing population	☐ Below average growth	■ Very high growth	
▨ Stable population	▨ Above average growth		

Name _____

Developing Countries

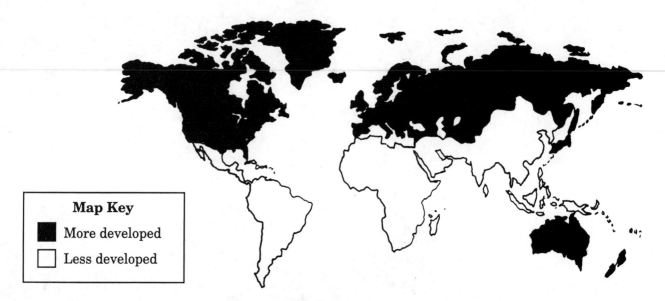

Map Key
■ More developed
□ Less developed

Only 25% of the people in the world live in developed countries. A country is said to be "developed" when its industry continues to increase and the people have the ability to obtain jobs, food, education, and health care.

The countries of the world are at different stages of development. The richer countries are usually highly industrialized and are therefore considered **more developed**. The poorer countries have very little industry and are considered **less developed**.

Study the map above and list three countries in each category below.

More Developed Countries   **Less Developed Countries**

_____   _____

_____   _____

_____   _____

• Choose one of the less developed countries and tell what things you think would help it to

become more developed. _____

_____

_____

• Explain how a poor family often finds it difficult to overcome poverty and disease. _____

_____

_____

Name _____

Which Is Which?

Use the charts to answer the questions.

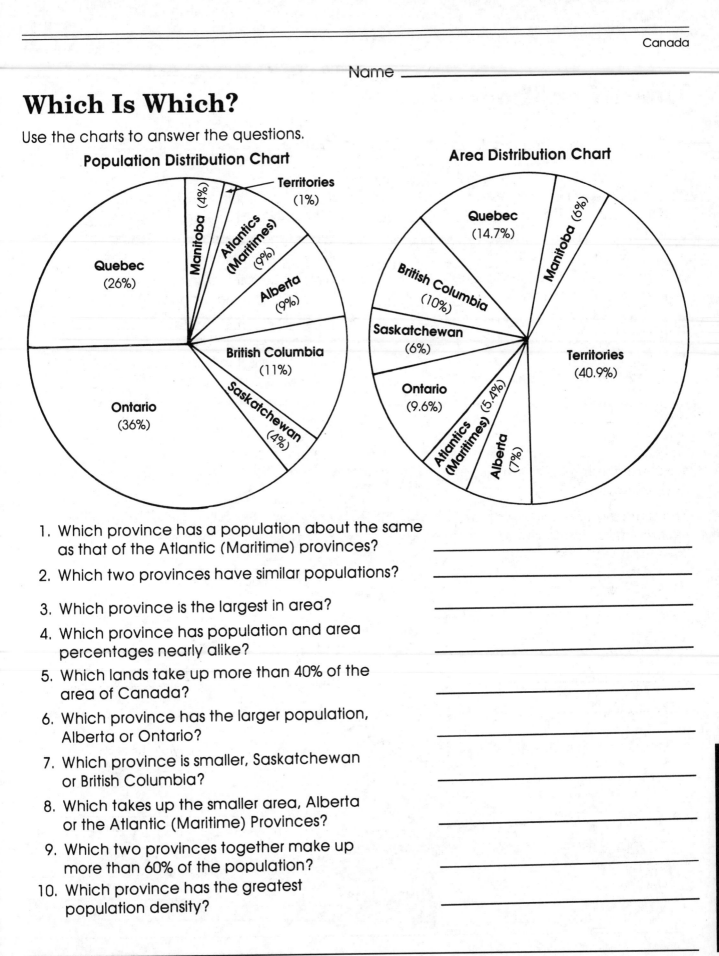

Population Distribution Chart

Quebec (26%)

Manitoba (4%)

Territories (1%)

Atlantics (Maritimes) (9%)

Alberta (9%)

British Columbia (11%)

Ontario (36%)

Saskatchewan (4%)

Area Distribution Chart

Quebec (14.7%)

Manitoba (6%)

British Columbia (10%)

Saskatchewan (6%)

Ontario (9.6%)

Territories (40.9%)

Atlantics (Maritimes) (5.4%)

Alberta (7%)

1. Which province has a population about the same as that of the Atlantic (Maritime) provinces? _____

2. Which two provinces have similar populations? _____

3. Which province is the largest in area? _____

4. Which province has population and area percentages nearly alike? _____

5. Which lands take up more than 40% of the area of Canada? _____

6. Which province has the larger population, Alberta or Ontario? _____

7. Which province is smaller, Saskatchewan or British Columbia? _____

8. Which takes up the smaller area, Alberta or the Atlantic (Maritime) Provinces? _____

9. Which two provinces together make up more than 60% of the population? _____

10. Which province has the greatest population density? _____

SOCIAL STUDIES

Name _____

Time After Time

Use the map to fill in the blanks with the correct times.

1. What time is it in Calgary
   if it is 2 p.m. in Thunder Bay? _____

2. What time is it in Quebec
   if it is 4 a.m. in Victoria? _____

3. What time is it in Whitehorse
   if it is 6 a.m. in Halifax? _____

4. What time is it in St. John's
   if it is 4 p.m. in Saint John? _____

5. What time is it in Toronto
   if it is 11:20 p.m. in Yellowknife? _____

6. What time is it in Inuvik
   if it is 3:42 p.m. in Regina? _____

7. What time is it in Charlottetown
   if it is 8:42 a.m. in Fort Nelson? _____

8. What time is it in Winnipeg
   if it is 5:30 p.m. in Montreal? _____

9. What time is it in Victoria
   if it is 4:16 a.m. in Halifax? _____

10. What time is it in Edmonton
    if it is 8:43 p.m. in Ottawa? _____

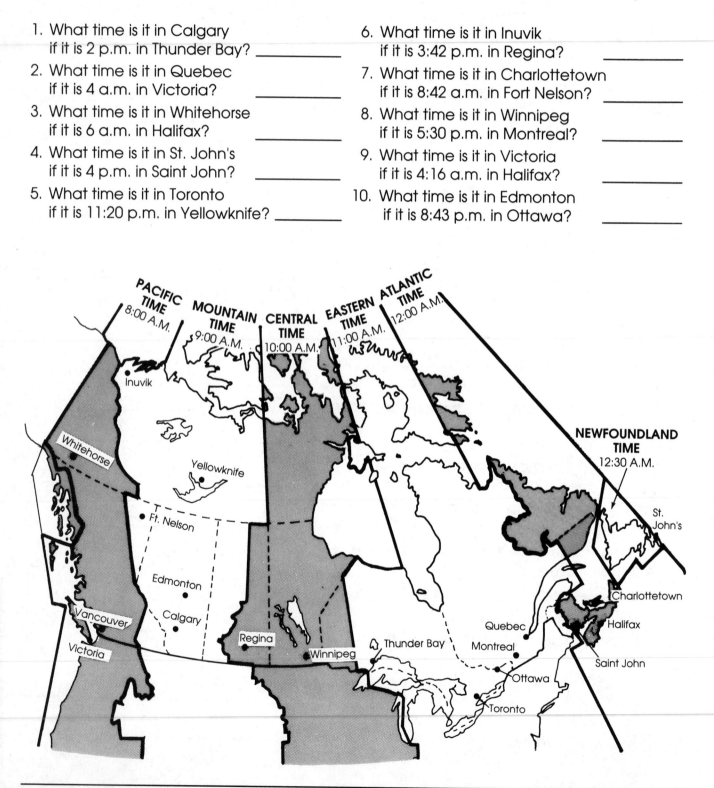

Name _____

Speaking Canadian

Use the Word Bank to complete the puzzle and you will discover the name of a company given the rights to a huge tract of land in northern Canada in 1570.

Word Bank	constable	hydro	mukluk	zed	Klondike
	curling	char	métis	reveillon	
	coureur de bois	loyalists	Lower Canada	wapiti	
	Québécois	Eskimo	Dominion Day	Micmac	

1. a trout-like fish

2. animal-skin boot

3. the letter "z" (for those who haven't watched "Sesame Street")

4. Indian word meaning "eaters of raw meat"

5. Quebec's French-speaking citizens

6. area once famed for its gold

7. police officer

8. French traders not licensed to gather furs

9. name once given to French-speaking Canada

10. colonists loyal to Britain during the American Revolution, many of whom fled to Nova Scotia

11. a game in which heavy stones are slid toward a target

12. _____ electricity

13. descendents of French settlers and their Indian wives

14. elk

15. Indian tribe from Eastern Canada

16. Quebec feast which follows the Christmas Midnight Mass

17. Canada's birthday

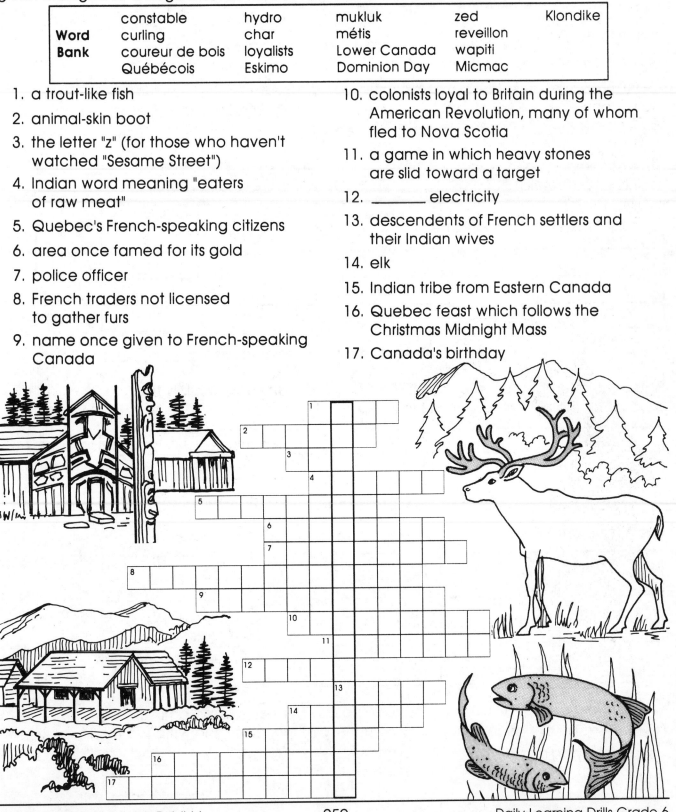

Name _____

And Off We Go!

Using your own or a rented vehicle, carefully plan a two-week trip to one of the Canadian provinces or territories. On another sheet of paper make charts like the ones below for a two-week period and fill in the information.

Planning the Budget

Rental fee, if renting a vehicle: _____

How many miles per gallon does your vehicle get? _____

How many miles will your trip total? _____

What is the average cost for a gallon of fuel? _____

Total costs including one oil change and one new tire: _____

Every night you will need lodging, whether at a campsite or at a motel.

Name and Type of Lodging	Number of Nights	Cost per Night	Total

Total expected lodging costs: _____

Figure the average daily meal costs for your travel party and multiply this amount by the number of days of your trip.

Breakfast	Lunch	Dinner	Snacks	Daily Totals

Total expected food costs: _____

Use a map and travel brochures to help determine your daily itinerary.

Day	Starting Place	Miles	Arrival Time	Destination	Activities and Sites
1	Detroit	240	3:00 p.m.	Toronto	Casa Loma—98-room castle Toronto Blue Jays—Exhibition Stadium
2					

Will you take any tours? Do you plan to go to any museums, zoos, amusement parks, movies, etc.? Plan your expected entertainment costs and write the total.

Total: _____

Total Budget for Trip: _____

Name _____

Best Spot on Earth!

Research a Canadian province or territory and complete the information below.

Province/Territory _____

Capital _____

Population _____

Area _____

Bordering Provinces/Territories/U.S. States _____

_____

Chief Agricultural Products	Major Industries
_____	_____
_____	_____
_____	**Interesting Places to Visit**
Natural Resources	_____
_____	_____
_____	_____
Brief History	**Map of Province or Territory** with rivers, lakes, cities, etc.
_____	
_____	
_____	
_____	
_____	
_____	

SOCIAL STUDIES

Name _____

South America

South America, the fourth-largest continent, has a land surface similar to North America. It has tall mountains in the west, highlands in the east, and plains that cover much of the central area. Let's learn more about the physical features of South America.

You will need:

atlas or physical map of South America
copy of the map of South America (page 263)
colored pencils, markers, or crayons

Directions:

1. Look at the physical features listed under each heading below. Each group contains one feature which does not belong in South America. Consult the physical map or atlas. Cross out the feature which does not belong.

Rivers

Amazon River	Paraná River	Uruguay River
Paraguay River	Orinoco River	Niger River

Bodies of Water

Rio de la Plata	Atlantic Ocean	Pacific Ocean
Baltic Sea	Caribbean Sea	

Mountains and Land Regions

Andes Mountains	Cape Horn	Pampas (farmlands)
Brazilian Highlands	Appalachian Highlands	Rainforest

2. Draw and label all but the crossed-out features on the map on page 263.

South America

Use with page 262.

SOCIAL STUDIES

Name _____

Australia

Australia, the smallest of the seven continents, is the only one that is also a country. Australia is surrounded by water, but it is not considered an island because of its large size. Most of Australia is low and flat with a few mountains along the eastern coast. Let's learn more about the physical features of Australia.

You will need:
atlas or physical map of Australia
copy of the map of *Australia* (page 265)
colored pencils, markers, or crayons

Directions:

1. Look at the physical features listed under each heading below. Each group contains one feature which does not belong in Australia. Consult the physical map or atlas. Cross out the feature which does not belong.

Rivers

Murry River   Mekong River   Darling River

Mountain Ranges

Australian Alps   Mount Kosciusko   Snowy Mountains
MacDonnell Ranges   Musgrave Ranges   Pyrenees
Great Dividing Range

Deserts

Great Sandy Desert   Gobi Desert   Simpson Desert
Great Victoria Desert Gibson Desert

Bodies of Water

Great Barrier Reef   Indian Ocean   Tasman Sea
Coral Sea   Timor Sea   Gulf of Carpentaria
English Channel

2. Draw and label all but the crossed-out features on the map on page 265.

Name _____

Australia

Use with page 264.

SOCIAL STUDIES

Name _____

Europe

Europe, the second-smallest of the seven continents, borders Asia on its eastern side. Because the landmasses of Europe and Asia are not completely separated by water, some people say that Europe is part of a giant continent called Eurasia. Let's learn more about the physical features of Europe.

You will need:
atlas or physical map of Europe
copy of the map of *Europe* (page 267)
colored pencils, markers, or crayons

Directions:

1. Look at the physical features listed under each heading below. Each group contains one feature which does not belong in Europe. Consult the physical map or atlas. Cross out the feature which does not belong.

Rivers

Volga River	Danube River	Rhine River
Thames River	Po River	Elbe River
Ganges River		

Bodies of Water

Mediterranean Sea	Atlantic Ocean	Caspian Sea	Baltic Sea
North Sea	Bay of Biscay	Indian Ocean	Strait of Gibraltar
English Channel	Black Sea		

Mountain Ranges

Alps	Andes Mountains	Pyrenees
Ural Mountains	Caucasus Mountains	Carpathian Mountains

2. Draw and label all but the crossed-out features on the map on page 267.

Europe

Use with page 266.

SOCIAL STUDIES

Name _____

Africa

Africa, the second-largest continent on Earth, is
a huge plateau with scattered mountain ranges.
In some areas it is bordered by a narrow coastal
plain. Africa is the home of the world's largest
desert, the Sahara, and the world's longest river,
the Nile. Let's learn more about the physical
features of Africa.

You will need:
  atlas or physical map of Africa
  copy of the map of *Africa* (page 269)
  colored pencils, markers, or crayons

Directions:

1. Look at the physical features listed under each heading below. Each group contains one
   feature which does not belong in Africa. Consult the physical map or atlas. Cross out the
   feature which does not belong.

Rivers

Nile River	Congo River	Niger River
Rhine River	Limpopo River	Zambezi River

Lakes

Lake Tanganyika   Lake Victoria   Lake Geneva

Other Bodies of Water

Mediterranean Sea	Red Sea	Pacific Ocean
Atlantic Ocean	Indian Ocean	

Landforms

Andes Mountains   Sahara Desert   Atlas Mountains   Kalahari Desert

2. Draw and label all but the crossed-out features on the map on page 269.

Name _____

Africa

Use with page 268.

Name _____

Asia

Asia, the largest of the seven continents in both population and size, covers almost one-third of the world's land area. Asia has a large variety of land features. The world's highest and lowest land elevations are located in Asia. Let's learn more about the physical features of Asia.

You will need:
atlas or physical map of Asia
copy of the map of *Asia* (page 271)
colored pencils, markers, or crayons

Directions:

1. Look at the physical features listed under each heading below. Each group contains one feature which does not belong in Asia. Consult the physical map or atlas. Cross out the feature which does not belong.

Rivers

Huang He River	Yangtze River	Ob River
Mekong River	Indus River	Ganges River
Tigris River	Danube River	Euphrates River

Deserts

Rub al Khali   Gobi Desert   Sahara Desert   Karakum Desert

Mountain Ranges

Himalaya Mountains   Atlas Mountains   Kunlun Mountains

Bodies of Water

Red Sea	Caspian Sea	Arabian Sea
Indian Ocean	Bay of Biscay	Bay of Bengal
Pacific Ocean	South China Sea	Arctic Ocean

2. Draw and label all but the crossed-out features on the map on page 271.

Name _____

Asia

Use with page 270.

SOCIAL STUDIES

Name _____

Antarctica

Antarctica, the fifth-largest continent, is the ice-covered landmass that surrounds the South Pole. There are no countries in Antarctica. It is a giant outdoor laboratory with a few scientific bases and stations. Scientists from around the world come to this area to do research. Let's learn more about the features of Antarctica.

You will need:
atlas or physical map of Antarctica
copy of the map of *Antarctica* (page 273)
colored pencils, markers, or crayons

Directions:

1. Look at the physical features listed under each heading below. Each group contains one feature which does not belong in Antarctica. Consult the physical map or atlas. Cross out the feature which does not belong.

Bodies of Water

Amundsen Sea   Weddell Sea   Pacific Ocean
Mediterranean Sea   Atlantic Ocean   Arctic Ocean
Ross Sea   Indian Ocean

Other Features

Ross Ice Shelf   South Pole
North Pole   Antarctic Peninsula

2. Draw and label all but the crossed-out features on the map on page 273.

Name _____

Antarctica

Use with page 272.

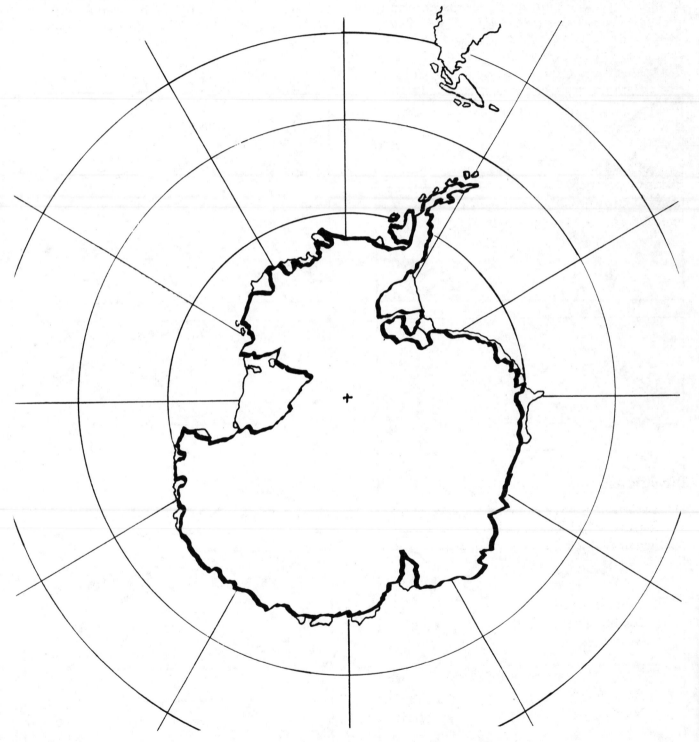

SOCIAL STUDIES

Name _____

Down by the Sea

Connected to the four major oceans are many smaller bodies of water called seas. Use a map, globe, or atlas to locate the places indicated below. Write the name of the sea that lies in each area.

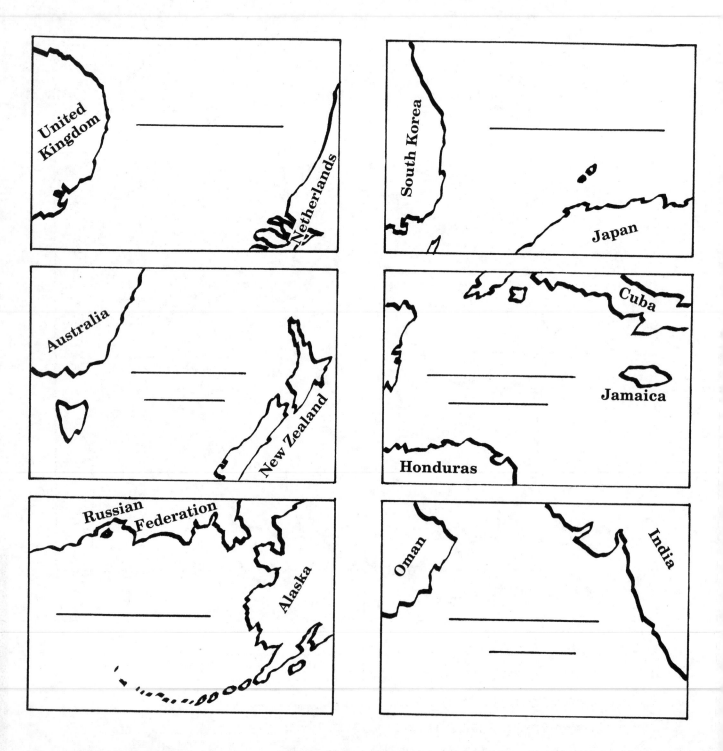

Name _____

Colorful Cartography

Create a special map for this region. Possible types are: climatic, population, physical or agricultural. Identify the type of map. Color code according to type of map. Complete the Map Key to show how to read your map. Label each country and body of water.

_____ **Map**

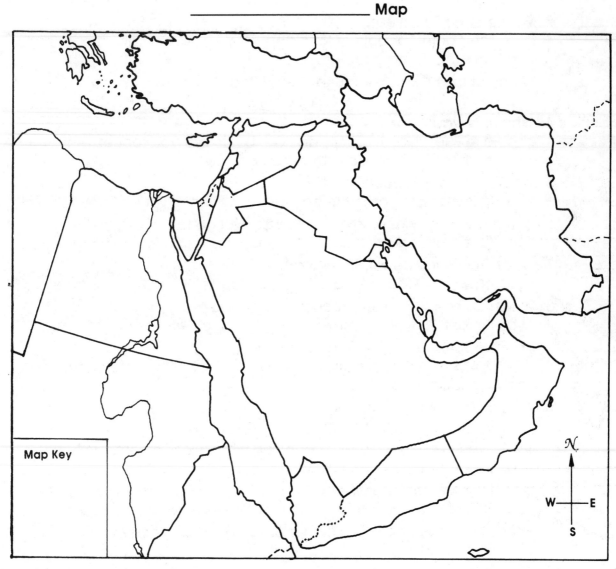

Map Key

Answer the following questions.

1. Which country has the largest area? _____.

2. Which country has the smallest area? _____

3. Which country has the greatest population? _____

4. Which country produces the most oil? _____

5. Which country was invaded by Iraq in August, 1990? _____

6. Which two cultures have been feuding for decades? _____

SOCIAL STUDIES

Name _____

Words in Review

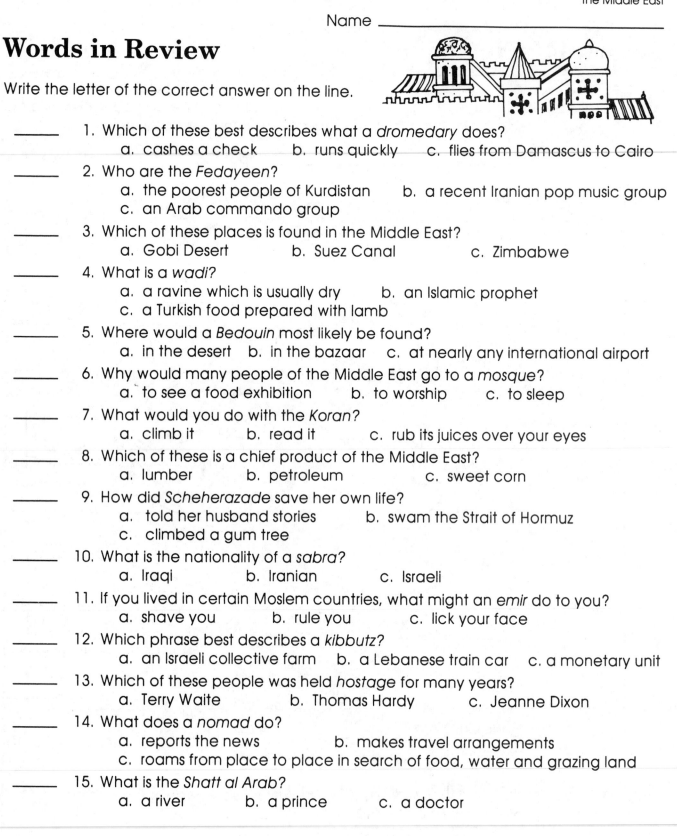

Write the letter of the correct answer on the line.

_____ 1. Which of these best describes what a *dromedary* does?
   a. cashes a check   b. runs quickly   c. flies from Damascus to Cairo

_____ 2. Who are the *Fedayeen*?
   a. the poorest people of Kurdistan   b. a recent Iranian pop music group
   c. an Arab commando group

_____ 3. Which of these places is found in the Middle East?
   a. Gobi Desert   b. Suez Canal   c. Zimbabwe

_____ 4. What is a *wadi*?
   a. a ravine which is usually dry   b. an Islamic prophet
   c. a Turkish food prepared with lamb

_____ 5. Where would a *Bedouin* most likely be found?
   a. in the desert   b. in the bazaar   c. at nearly any international airport

_____ 6. Why would many people of the Middle East go to a *mosque*?
   a. to see a food exhibition   b. to worship   c. to sleep

_____ 7. What would you do with the *Koran*?
   a. climb it   b. read it   c. rub its juices over your eyes

_____ 8. Which of these is a chief product of the Middle East?
   a. lumber   b. petroleum   c. sweet corn

_____ 9. How did *Scheherazade* save her own life?
   a. told her husband stories   b. swam the Strait of Hormuz
   c. climbed a gum tree

_____ 10. What is the nationality of a *sabra*?
   a. Iraqi   b. Iranian   c. Israeli

_____ 11. If you lived in certain Moslem countries, what might an *emir* do to you?
   a. shave you   b. rule you   c. lick your face

_____ 12. Which phrase best describes a *kibbutz*?
   a. an Israeli collective farm   b. a Lebanese train car   c. a monetary unit

_____ 13. Which of these people was held *hostage* for many years?
   a. Terry Waite   b. Thomas Hardy   c. Jeanne Dixon

_____ 14. What does a *nomad* do?
   a. reports the news   b. makes travel arrangements
   c. roams from place to place in search of food, water and grazing land

_____ 15. What is the *Shatt al Arab*?
   a. a river   b. a prince   c. a doctor

Challenge!   On the back of this paper write your own questions for these terms:
Kurds, Tigris, Islam, Zionism, Sunni and Palestinian refugee.

Name _____

Awesome Arabic

Use the original Arabic word and the English definition to find each English word. **Hint:** If necessary, use a dictionary that gives roots and origins. Sources may vary on original spellings. See how many you can do without using a dictionary.

Original	Today's English Meaning	Word in English
suffah	a wide, upholstered seat	__ __ __ __
jamal	a large desert animal with a humped back	__ __ __ __ __
al birquq	a small peach-like fruit	__ __ __ __ __ __ __
qandi	a flavored syrup hardened into small pieces for eating	__ __ __ __ __
attabi	any striped or brindled cat	__ __ __ __ __
shal	a large, broad scarf	__ __ __ __ __
tarifa	taxes placed on imported goods	__ __ __ __ __ __ __
makhzan	a place where things are stored; a periodical filled with articles	__ __ __ __ __ __ __ __
al-manakh	a yearly calendar which forecasts weather and lists many facts	__ __ __ __ __ __ __ __
laymun	a sour, light-yellow fruit	__ __ __ __ __
shaq	a round disk used in certain board games	__ __ __ __ __ __ __
qutn	soft, white plant fibers used to make cloth	__ __ __ __ __ __
al-jabr	type of mathematics which uses letters	__ __ __ __ __ __ __
matrah	a casing of cloth which is filled with soft material and slept upon	__ __ __ __ __ __ __ __
sukkar	a sweet substance made from the cane of a plant	__ __ __ __ __

Daily Learning Drills Grade 6

SOCIAL STUDIES

Name _____

The Dating Game

Fill in the dates and information from the bottom of the page under the correct time period.

Chou Dynasty 1027 - 256 B.C.

1. _____

2. _____

Han Dynasty 202 B.C. - 220 A.D.

1. _____

2. _____

Period of Disunion 263 - 534 A.D.

1. _____

Sui Dynasty 581 - 618 A.D.

1. _____

Sung Dynasty 960 - 1279 A.D.

1. _____

2. _____

3. _____

Ming Dynasty 1368 - 1644 A.D.

1. _____

2. _____

Ch'ing Dynasty (Manchu) 1644 - 1912 A.D.

1. _____

2. _____

Republic of China 1912 A.D.

1. _____

2. _____

People's Republic of China 1949 A.D.

1. _____

2. _____

3. _____

---

610 A.D. Grand Canal is lengthened.

1949 A.D. Chiang Kai-shek moves government of Republic of China to Taiwan.

304-581 A.D. Foreigners rule all or part of northern China.

1972 A.D. President Nixon visits China.

105 A.D. Paper is invented.

C. 1100 A.D. China becomes a major sea power involved in trading.

C. 50 A.D. Buddhism is introduced in China.

C. 1161 A.D. Explosives are used in battle.

400 B.C. Great Wall of China is begun.

1898 A.D. Chinese Nationalists fight Western forces in Boxer Rebellion.

1421 A.D. Peking becomes the capital.

1949 A.D. Mao Zedong heads Communist government.

1946 A.D. Civil War breaks out between the Nationalists and Communists.

1513 A.D. Portuguese sailors arrive at Canton.

1839 A.D. Opium War begins with Britain.

1937 A.D. Japan invades China.

C. 550 B.C. Confucius is born.

1275 A.D. Marco Polo arrives in China.

Name _____

Getting to Know You

Label:

Guangzhou   Mongolia
Chongqing   Mt. Everest
Harbin   Pacific Ocean
Lhasa   Beijing
Yangtze River   Shanghai
Huang He River (Yellow)   Tianjin
Tibet   Ürümqi

Draw the boundaries of, and **label** these former Chinese territories:

North and South Korea

Taiwan

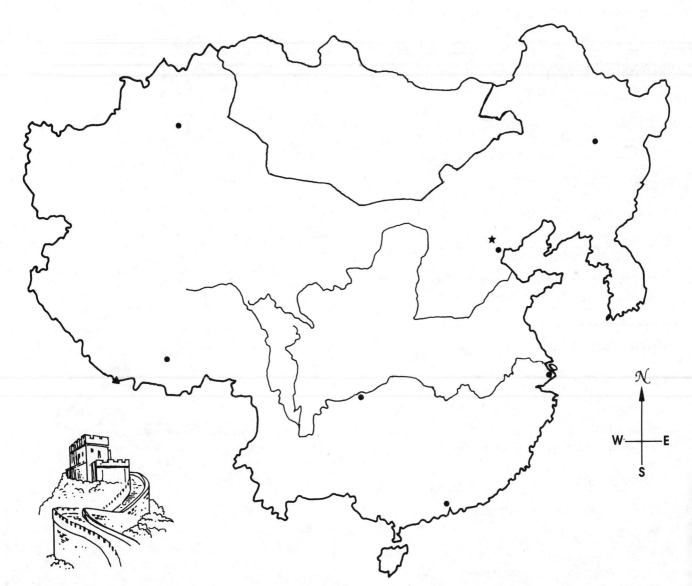

In China there is a man-made structure which can be seen from 200 miles above the earth's surface. The main portion is approximately 2,000 miles long (sources vary) and took over 14 years to construct. What is it?

_____   Draw this structure on your map in green and label it.

SOCIAL STUDIES

Name _____

A Maze of Chinese Terms

Use words from the Word Bank to complete the puzzle.

Across

1. famous twentieth century leader who helped form the Chinese Communist Party

5. flooded field on which rice is grown

6. well-educated man who lived 25 centuries ago and is honored by many as the greatest teacher of all times

8. medical practice of treating illness or reducing pain by inserting needles in particular parts of the body

10. art of fine handwriting

15. powerful government leader who played a major role in the push to modernize China's economy

16. fine earth carried downstream by river currents

17. excellent pottery made from a clay called kaolin

18. beads-and-wire instrument used to compute math problems

Down

2. series of rulers descended from the same ancestor

3. distinctly marked, black-and-white bear-like mammal native to China and Tibet

4. prince from India who taught that people could obtain perfect happiness if they would not be selfish

7. Chinese unit of currency

9. most populous country on Earth

11. three-wheeled vehicle powered by pedal which transports people and baggage

12. third-longest river in the world

13. capital city of China

14. series of daily exercises which help tone the muscles of the body

Word Bank

abacus	acupuncture	
China	calligraphy	Buddha
Beijing	Mao Zedong	paddy
Yangtze	porcelain	dynasty
silt	Confucius	panda
yuan	Deng Xiaoping	pedicab
Tai chi chuan		

Name _____

News About Nippon

Use an encyclopedia and dictionary to research these facts about Japan. Fill the boxes with words or pictures to portray the information.

Money Unit of Japan	Emperor's Name	Number of Large Islands	Flag of Japan

Basic Foods of Japan	Shinto	Highest Mountain – Mount _____

Kimono	Hibachi	The Ginza in Tokyo

Great Buddha	Two Forms of Drama	Favorite Sports

Calligraphy	Sumo	Nippon	Obi

SOCIAL STUDIES

Name _____

Famous Leaders

Use with page 283.

Ivan IV was the first czar of Old Russia. He freed his land of many foreign raiders and gained much territory for Russia. He is often called Ivan the Terrible because he was cruel to those who didn't agree with him. He even went so far as to kill his son with his own hands. He was known for being volatile and extremely paranoid about his power.

Peter I did much to modernize Russia. The Russia of 1700 was weak and backward because of its lack of information and harsh travel conditions. Peter traveled widely, often in disguise, to learn all he could. On an extensive trip to Western Europe, he studied carpentry, shipbuilding, military techniques and other Western crafts. Peter the Great, as he is usually remembered, founded the city of St. Petersburg (for a time known as Leningrad) as his "window to the West."

Catherine the Great was responsible for improving the education of the Russian people by promoting such things as art, science, education and culture. She gained power when her inept husband, Peter III, was removed from the throne and murdered. Sources say Catherine's friends murdered Peter and that she was most likely behind it. During her reign the country won land in wars with Turkey and Poland. To educate her people in modern medical practices, Catherine became the first Russian to be vaccinated against the smallpox virus.

Nicholas II was the last of the Russian czars. By the time he gained the throne, the Russian people were tired of czars. He was blamed for losing Russian territory to the Germans in World War I, and he was forced off the throne in 1917. A year later he was killed with his family.

Vladimir Illich Ulyanov, known as **Lenin**, founded the Communist Party because he was opposed to the government which took over from Czar Nicholas II, in 1917. His party was first called the Bolshe-viks (meaning majority) because he felt the majority of the people would support him. He was right. The Bolsheviks' Red Army fought mightily and drove out the government's White Army which, though aided by Western forces, was disorganized and not unified. Lenin promised the Russian people that the government would provide more food, land and peace. About the same time, the country became known as the Union of Soviet Socialist Republics.

Iosif Djugashvili, known as **Stalin**, became the dictator of the U.S.S.R. when Lenin died. The Communist government took total ownership of all farms and businesses. A "man of steel" as his adopted name implied, Stalin was ruthless in putting down his foes. Those who argued with him could quickly be sent to the Siberian frontier. Others vanished without a trace. Stalin built factories to make the U.S.S.R. independent of the West. His army became formidable in size if not in weaponry. Stalin and Hitler agreed not to fight each other and to share the takeover of Eastern Europe. The U.S.S.R. was double-crossed, however, by Hitler when Germany invaded them. Twenty-million Soviet people lost their lives in the war against Germany.

Mikhail Gorbachev, who became president of the Soviet Union in 1985, promoted change in Commu-nist policy. He gave more rights to the Soviet allies (satellite countries). His open discussions with all the Soviet people whom he visited and conversed with surprised the Western nations. Seeing this they became more friendly with the U.S.S.R. *Glasnost* was a policy initiated by Gorbachev. With it the government publicly declared that it must be more open-minded in discussing the nation's problems.

Name _____

Famous Leaders

Use page 282 to answer these questions.

1. His nickname means "like steel." _____

2. He was the first to call himself *Czar.* _____

3. This ruler was the first Russian vaccinated against the smallpox virus. _____

4. This leader's party thought that they spoke for the majority of Russians. _____

5. He initiated the policy of *Glasnost.* _____

6. He was double-crossed by Hitler during World War II. _____

7. This czar was assassinated with his family in 1918. _____

8. His was more friendly with the West than any other Soviet government during the 20th Century. _____

9. He ordered the founding of St. Petersburg. _____

10. He promised the Russian people that the government would provide more food, land and peace. _____

11. This leader gained land for Russia in wars fought against Turkey and Poland. _____

12. This czar was blamed for losing territory to the Germans in World War I. _____

13. This czar killed his oldest son with his own hands. _____

14. He was leader when his country lost 20-million people in World War II. _____

15. He often put on disguises when he traveled. _____

Research to find out whom the Russian people fought in these wars.

Crimean War _____

World War I _____

Seven Years' War _____

Napoleonic Wars _____

Daily Learning Drills Grade 6

SOCIAL STUDIES

Name _____

Search and Rescue

Use reference materials to complete this puzzle.

Across

1. One- _____ of the earth's land is covered by what was the U.S.S.R.
4. site of world's worst nuclear disaster in 1986
11. first woman in space
17. winner of Olympic women's balance beam and floor exercises in 1972
18. These tribes came from Eastern Europe to the Kiev Rus in the 6th Century.
19. unit of monetary measure
20. original republic closest to Iran and Afghanistan
21. first satellite launched into space
22. This country's Golden Horde attacked early Russians and remained in power for over a century.
23. Peter _____ composed "The Nutcracker" and "Swan Lake."

Down

2. a cold, treeless and often frozen arctic desert
3. author of *Doctor Zhivago* whose government would not permit him to accept the Nobel Prize for literature
5. author of *War and Peace* (Hint: Use an "i" at the end of author's name instead of the more commonly used "y".)
6. capital of Ukraine; known as "the mother of Russian cities"
7. This mountain range separates Asian Russia from European Russia.
8. alphabet used in the former U.S.S.R.
9. largest freshwater lake in Eurasia
10. first human to travel in space
12. Because the U.S.S.R. invaded _____ in 1979, the U.S. boycotted the Moscow Olympic Games in 1980.
13. Czar_____ II freed serfs in 1861.
14. President of Russian Republic during 1991 attempted coup
15. the period of time when the Warsaw Pact nations and NATO nations were adversaries yet did not engage in direct combat
16. number of time zones in the former U.S.S.R.

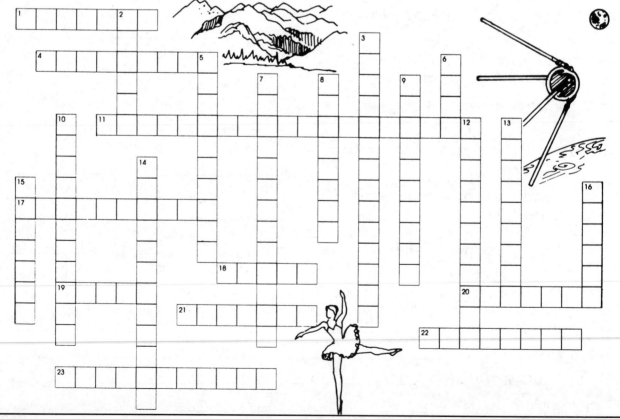

Name _____

Read All About It!

8-18-91 Coup leaders take action; Mikhail Gorbachev is placed under house arrest at his vacation *dacha* in the Crimea.

8-19-91 Gennady Yanayev declares himself acting president and announces a state of emergency.

The mayor of Leningrad, Anatoli Sobchak, declares the coup committee unconstitutional.

Boris Yeltsin declares the coup illegal. Many Soviet troops join him.

Yanayev tells reporters Gorbachev is ill.

Yanayev warns against Yeltsin.

8-20-91 The president of the republic of Kazakhstan resigns from the Politburo and Central Committee to protest the coup.

Ukraine's parliament declares the actions of the coup's leaders null and void.

The coup begins to fall apart; its members quit and fall ill.

Estonia declares its independence.

8-21-91 The Soviet Parliament demands Gorbachev's return to power.

Latvia declares its independence.

Uzbekistan's president outlaws all orders made by coup leaders.

8-22-91 Gorbachev and family return to Moscow.

Lithuania outlaws the Communist Party.

In the republics of Lithuania and Estonia statues of Lenin are torn down.

8-23-91 Moldavia adopts a resolution outlawing Communist Party activities.

Georgia's president calls for a ban of the Communist Party.

Uzbekistan outlaws Communist Party activities.

Gorbachev and Yeltsin purge top officials and appoint proven reformers.

In 1991 you were a reporter assigned to Moscow by *Today's International Press* (TIP). During the coup attempt in the Soviet Union in mid-August you were on the scene. Write your news article for the world!

Include: comments from citizens on the streets, warnings from government officials, the reaction of the people around you, and a "news" photo.

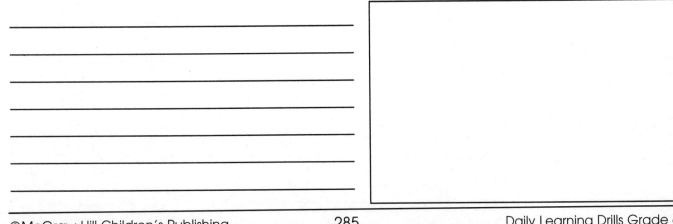

SOCIAL STUDIES

Name _____

Check It Off

Choose a country that takes/took part in the Olympics. Work alone or with others to complete the activities listed here. Check each one off when you have completed it.

_____ 1. Create a flag and make a sign to identify your country.

_____ 2. Design a display which illustrates 10 products (agriculture, industry, animals, etc.) your country is noted for.

_____ 3. Make a crossword puzzle out of at least 15 words which relate to your country.

_____ 4. Make a map of your country which shows and labels: capital city, other major cities, major rivers, lakes and oceans, neighboring countries, mountains and points of interest

_____ 5. Complete the chart of information below and be ready to share it.

_____ 6. Post all team information on the "Olympic Nations in Review" bulletin board.

Country Name: _____

Capital: _____

Population: _____

Shares Border(s) with Countries of: _____

_____

Leader(s) in Government: _____

Major Religion(s): _____

One Important Holiday: _____

One Major Olympic Sport: _____

One Recent Medal Winner: _____

Name _____

Who Am I?

Color each country's flag with the appropriate colors. Then fill in each blank with the letter of the country described in each sentence.

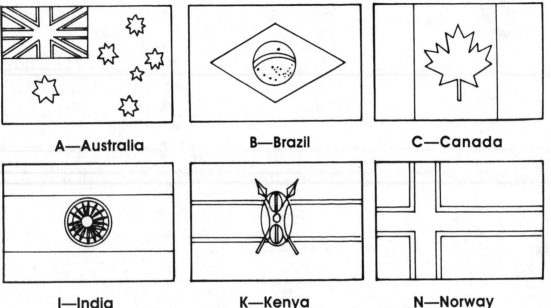

A—Australia   B—Brazil   C—Canada

I—India   K—Kenya   N—Norway

_____ 1. I share a border with the United States.

_____ 2. My capital is Oslo.

_____ 3. I am located just east of Uganda.

_____ 4. I was host to the 1988 Winter Olympics.

_____ 5. The river with the greatest volume of water in the world flows out of my country.

_____ 6. The colors of my flag are black, red and green.

_____ 7. Two animals found only in my country are the bandicoot and the wallaby.

_____ 8. The Hindu people consider my Ganges River to be sacred.

_____ 9. Portuguese is the main language spoken in my country.

_____ 10. One of our modern-day heroes, Mahatma Gandhi, is known worldwide.

_____ 11. I am a country in Europe.

_____ 12. I consist of 10 provinces and 2 territories.

_____ 13. I share a border with Suriname and Colombia, to name a few.

_____ 14. The second-largest freshwater lake in the world, Lake Victoria, can be found partially in my country.

_____ 15. I am located in Asia.

_____ 16. My country is also a continent.

_____ 17. Vikings sailed from my land in ships with square sails.

_____ 18. I am sometimes called the "Land Down Under."

Daily Learning Drills Grade 6

SOCIAL STUDIES

Name _____

Dear Mom, . . .

Imagine you are a contestant in this year's Summer or Winter Olympics. You are far from your family whom you haven't seen in several weeks. Write a letter home telling about your new and exciting adventure.

_____
(Your Country's Team)
Olympic Village

_____
(City/Country)

_____
(Date)

Dear _____ ,

(Describe the city and country in which you are competing.)

_____
_____
_____

_____

(Explain what you like about being here.)

_____
_____
_____

(Discuss your event and how your practice sessions are going.)

_____
_____
_____

(Add your personal comments, complaints, what you miss, best wishes, etc.)

_____
_____
_____

_____

_____

Answer Key

All About Cats . . . and Sentences

Rule All sentences need a punctuation mark at the end.

Exercise Finish each sentence with the correct word(s).

1. A **declarative sentence** ends with a period
2. An **interrogative sentence** ends with a question mark
3. An **exclamatory sentence**, which shows excitement or strong feeling, ends with an exclamation mark
4. An **imperative sentence**, which makes a request or gives a command, ends with a period

Read each sentence and punctuate it correctly. Write what kind of sentence it is on the line: **declarative, interrogative, imperative,** or **exclamatory.**

1. The cat was the most sacred of all Egyptian animals. declarative
2. Amazingly, Egyptians even mummified their cats! exclamatory
3. Long ago, people thought witches could turn into cats. declarative
4. Did you know cats were often burned for this reason? interrogative
5. Incredibly, some people are still frightened of black cats! exclamatory
6. Cats perform a useful service in China and Japan. declarative
7. They protect silkworm cocoons from rats. declarative
8. Are cats really such independent animals? interrogative
9. Domestic cats enjoy the companionship of people. declarative
10. Give your cat a lot of care and attention. imperative
11. Watch the pupils of a cat's eyes contract in bright light. imperative
12. Do cats' eyes reflect light? interrogative
13. I'm amazed that a cat can walk easily on a two-inch-wide surface! exclamatory
14. Look your cat over carefully before buying it. imperative
15. Has your kitten had all the shots it needs? interrogative
16. Pick your cat with care and train it well. imperative

Page 1

A Perfect Gem

Rule A sentence has a **complete subject** and a **complete predicate.** The most important word in the complete subject is the **simple subject.** The most important word or phrase in the complete predicate, the verb, is the **simple predicate.**

Example

complete subject | complete predicate

Exquisitely designed jewelry glittered under the glass.

simple subject — simple predicate

Exercise Put a slash between the **complete subject** and the **complete predicate.** Then circle the **simple subject** and underline the **simple predicate.**

1. People / used stones and gems as a source of protection long ago.
2. People / thought they were protected and helped by these stones.
3. Stones / called birthstones were supposed to bring the wearer good fortune.
4. A stone / is associated with one's birth month / is a birthstone.
5. Different lists of birthstones / are used today.
6. We / are not certain which stones were used by the ancients for which months.
7. The aquamarine / is associated with wisdom.
8. Birthstones / are set in rings or carried in some other way on the person.
9. Both men and women / wear birthstones.
10. Either rings or pins / can be set with these stones.

• Finish the following sentences by adding complete predicates to the complete subjects.

1. The brilliant emerald Sentences will vary.
2. Rubies and garnets
3. The three-carat diamond
4. Her new ring

• Write the simple subjects and the simple predicates here from the sentences you just completed. Simple predicates will vary.

	simple subject	simple predicate		simple subject	simple predicate
1.	emerald		3.	diamond	
2.	Rubies, garnets		4.	ring	

Page 2

Prepare Yourselves

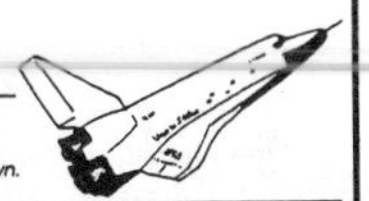

Rule **Reflexive pronouns** reflect the action of the verb back to the subject. **Myself, yourself, herself, himself, itself, ourselves, yourselves,** and **themselves** are reflexive pronouns.

Example

Roger made **himself** *a model of the space shuttle.*

The shuttle landed **itself**, *using only gravity to pull it down.*

Exercise Complete each sentence with the appropriate reflexive pronoun.

1. "You should take yourself to the launch, Cheryl," her parents said.
2. The Davenport children congratulated themselves on the good spot they found.
3. We sure found ourselves a good viewpoint from which to watch the shuttle landing.
4. David imagined himself trying to maneuver in a space shuttle that was hurtling toward earth.
5. "I told myself that I will become a commander someday," Earl said.
6. Deborah settled herself to wait for a glimpse of the space shuttle.
7. David Davenport enjoyed himself at the shuttle launch.
8. "You could train yourselves for space travel if you built a model simulator," Bobbie and David's parents suggested.

• Write the reflexive pronoun from the Word Bank that matches each subject listed below.

1. Peter himself
2. The dog itself
3. Gwen herself
4. Monica and I ourselves
5. Heather and Kimberly themselves
6. You and Carolyn yourselves
7. I myself
8. You yourself

Word Bank: myself, yourself, himself, yourselves, themselves, itself, herself, ourselves

Page 3

Honeybees Buzz

Rule A verb's tenses are formed by its principal parts: the **present**, the **past**, and the **past participle.**

Example

Present: Honeybees **live** *in colonies inside a hive.*

Past: The honeybees **lived** *inside a tree.*

Past Participle: The honeybees **have lived** *in the bee-keeper's hive a long time.*

Exercise Write the tense of the underlined verb: **present, past,** or **past participle.**

1. About 50,000 honeybees followed the scouts to the new location. past
2. The queen lays about 2,000 eggs in one day. present
3. She has produced many fertilized eggs that will become female worker bees. past participle
4. The unfertilized eggs that she has placed in the brood nest will become male drones. past participle
5. Worker bees work very hard during their lifetime of about 6 weeks. present
6. Worker bees dance to tell the others in the hive where the flowers are containing the nectar and pollen they need for food. present
7. Some workers danced in a circle to explain that the food was nearby. past
8. Others have danced in a different direction to let the other workers know where to find the flowers farther away. past participle
9. The youngest worker bees in the hive cleaned the empty cells. past
10. They feed "royal jelly" to the larvae in the hive. present
11. Young worker bees build the honeycomb. present
12. A worker bee guarded the hive. past
13. During the last three weeks of the worker bee's life she has collected much pollen and nectar. past participle
14. Honeybees have helped us by making honey and wax and by fertilizing flowers. past participle

Page 4

Camel Trivia

Rule Verbs that show action are called **action verbs.**

Example *The camels walked across the desert.*

Rule **Linking verbs** do not show action. Instead, they link the subject with a word or words in the predicate that tell something about the subject.

Linking verbs are forms of the verb **be** and verbs such as **seem** and **become.**

Example *Camels are desert animals.*

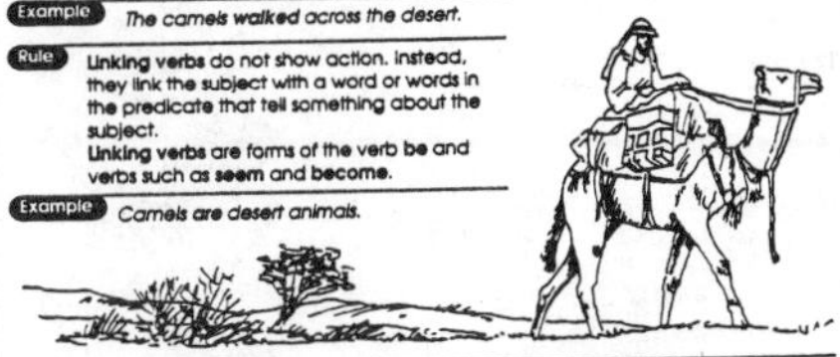

Exercise Underline the verbs or verb phrases. Then write **action** or **linking** in each blank.

1. The Dromedary and Bactrian are two types of camels. linking
2. Camels have transported men and goods across vast areas of sand. action
3. Camels can travel miles without food or water. action
4. The camel carries its own food supply. action
5. This food supply is a hump on the camel's back. linking
6. Camels were a food source to many desert people. linking
7. Fat was melted from the hump to make butter. action
8. People eat the meat of camels. action
9. They make cheese from its milk. action
10. Camels lose their fur each spring. action
11. However, they will grow a new coat again. action
12. Camels have been tamed by man for centuries. action
13. Camels are unfriendly animals, though. linking
14. A camel will bite anything near it. action
15. It has strong teeth. action
16. The camel uses these teeth as weapons. action
17. People drink the camel's milk. action
18. Camels are desert animals. linking
19. A baby camel runs soon after birth. action
20. The baby stays with its mother for about four years. action

Page 5

Action!

Rule A **verb phrase** is made up of a **main verb** and one or more **helping verbs.**

Example *Our class* **is studying** *the Roman Empire.*

Exercise Find the verb phrase. Circle the **main verb** and underline its helpers.

1. The passenger must have (forgotten) his ticket.
2. He had (carried) his luggage to the airport in his trunk.
3. The airplane must have been (delayed) by the severe storm.
4. The travelers were (touring) the country by bus.

Rule **Action verbs** show action. **Linking verbs** link the subject with a word or words in the predicate.

Example *(Action verb)* *Harold ran into the field.* *(Linking verb)* *He was a fast runner.*

Exercise Underline each verb. Then tell if it is an **action verb** or **linking verb.**

1. Today is Tuesday. linking
2. We practiced today. action
3. Jim was late. linking
4. The coach teased him. action
5. Jim was embarrassed. linking
6. Next time he will run. action

Rule Verbs have simple tenses: **past, present,** and **future.**

Exercise Draw a line under each **verb phrase.** Tell if the tense is **past, present,** or **future.**

1. The hockey team will be playing a game in two weeks. future
2. They are practicing every afternoon after school. present
3. They have skated many hours on the practice rink. past
4. Soon the crowd will cheer their teams. future

• Complete this chart.

	Verb	Present/Singular	Past	Past with helpers
Ex.	talk	talks	talked	has talked
	go	goes	went	has gone
	buzz	buzzes	buzzed	has buzzed
	move	moves	moved	has moved
	take	takes	took	has taken
	choose	chooses	chose	has chosen

Page 6

The Staff of Life

Rule A **transitive verb** is followed by a direct object.
An **intransitive verb** is not followed by a direct object.

Exercise Underline the verbs or verb phrases. Circle the direct object if there is one. Identify the kind of verb by writing **transitive** or **intransitive** in the chart below.

1. Bread is often called the (staff) of life.
2. Bread, in different forms, has been eaten for thousands of years.
3. Man has made (bread) longer than any other manufactured food.
4. The earliest breads were made in a hard, flat form.
5. A mixture of ground grain and water formed the (dough).
6. The sun or hot rocks baked the (mixture) into bread.
7. A wide variety of breads are eaten by people around the world.
8. Farmers grow many (kinds) of grains for the various flours.
9. People in other countries may prefer different (kinds) of bread.
10. Asian people eat (bread) made from rice.
11. In Scotland, oatcakes and barley breads are preferred.
12. Central Americans enjoy flat (cakes) of cornmeal dough.
13. The roots of the cassava plant provide (flour) in the West Indies.
14. The first leavened bread was made by the Egyptians.
15. Hard, flat loaves changed into soft, air-filled loaves.
16. The Egyptians built the first (ovens), too.
17. The lighter, leavened bread couldn't be baked on hot rocks.
18. An enclosed, heated area was needed to bake the larger masses of dough.
19. We still use the (principles) of early bread-making today.
20. We all enjoy many (forms) of bread in our daily diets.

Transitive or Intransitive

1.	transitive	8.	transitive	15.	intransitive
2.	intransitive	9.	transitive	16.	transitive
3.	transitive	10.	transitive	17.	intransitive
4.	intransitive	11.	intransitive	18.	intransitive
5.	transitive	12.	transitive	19.	transitive
6.	transitive	13.	transitive	20.	transitive
7.	intransitive	14.	intransitive		

Page 7

Show Time

Rule The past and past participle forms of irregular verbs are not formed by adding **-ed.**

Example ***Present:*** *The talent show* **begins** *at 6:30 p.m.*
Past: *It* **began** *right on time.*
Past Participle: *The show* **has begun** *with a smash hit by Joey on the piano.*

Exercise Complete each sentence with the correct form of the irregular verb in parentheses.

1. Many guests have (ate, eaten) eaten the hors d'oeuvres which were served on trays.
2. Samuel (sang, sung) sang a very funny song accompanied by piano.
3. Joey, dressed in a gorilla suit, (fell, fallen) fell down twice while reciting his poem.
4. Katelyn Dawn (stole, stolen) stole the show when she sang "God Bless America."
5. Mark has (wrote, written) written a song to play on his saxophone.
6. The choir has (chose, chosen) chosen to sing a song that the director arranged.
7. They all (rose, risen) rose together at the director's signal.
8. The audience has (gave, given) given Heather the loudest applause of all.

• Complete the chart below:

Present	Past	Past Participle
1. Bill *chooses*	*chose*	(has, have) *chosen*
2. Alexa *says*	said	(has, have) said
3. Eva *speaks*	spoke	(has, have) spoken
4. David *throws*	threw	(has, have) thrown
5. Monica *teaches*	taught	(has, have) taught
6. Gwen *swims*	swam	(has, have) swum
7. Cheryl *rides*	rode	(has, have) ridden
8. Thomas *writes*	wrote	(has, have) written

Page 8

Hats Off to You

Rule and Example

1. A singular subject takes a singular verb.
   Bill washes the dishes.
2. A plural subject takes a plural verb.
   They watch television.
3. A compound subject connected by **and** takes a plural verb.
   Mary and Bill read books.
4. For a compound subject connected by **either/or** or **neither/nor**, the verb agrees with the subject closer to it.
   Either my aunt or my uncle takes us to games.
   Neither my grandfather nor my grandmothers are over 85 years old.
5. A singular indefinite pronoun as the subject takes a singular verb. (anybody, anyone, everybody, everyone, no one, somebody, someone, something)
   Everyone enjoys games.

Exercise Write the correct present tense form of each verb on the line. Write the number of the rule that was followed after the sentence.

1. Everyone enjoys wearing interesting hats. (enjoy) 5
2. Many people wear hats for various activities. (wear) 2
3. One factory makes only felt hats. (make) 1
4. The coney, rabbit, and hare furnish the fur for felt hats. (furnish) 3
5. Either England or Scotland ships the fur to the U.S. (ship) 4
6. Neither the fur of the squirrel nor the chipmunk makes the best felt hats. (make) 4
7. Either bamboo grass or the leaves of a pine tree make wonderful straw hats. (make) 4
8. Someone prefers to wear straw hats. (prefer) 5
9. Factories produce straw hats, too. (produce) 2
10. Somebody braids the straw material. (braid) 5
11. Either machines or a worker bleaches the braided material. (bleach) 4
12. Chemicals and gelatins stiffen straw hats. (stiffen) 3
13. Ironing finishes the hat-making process. (finish) 1
14. Everybody sometimes sees hats that are interesting. (see) 5

Page 9

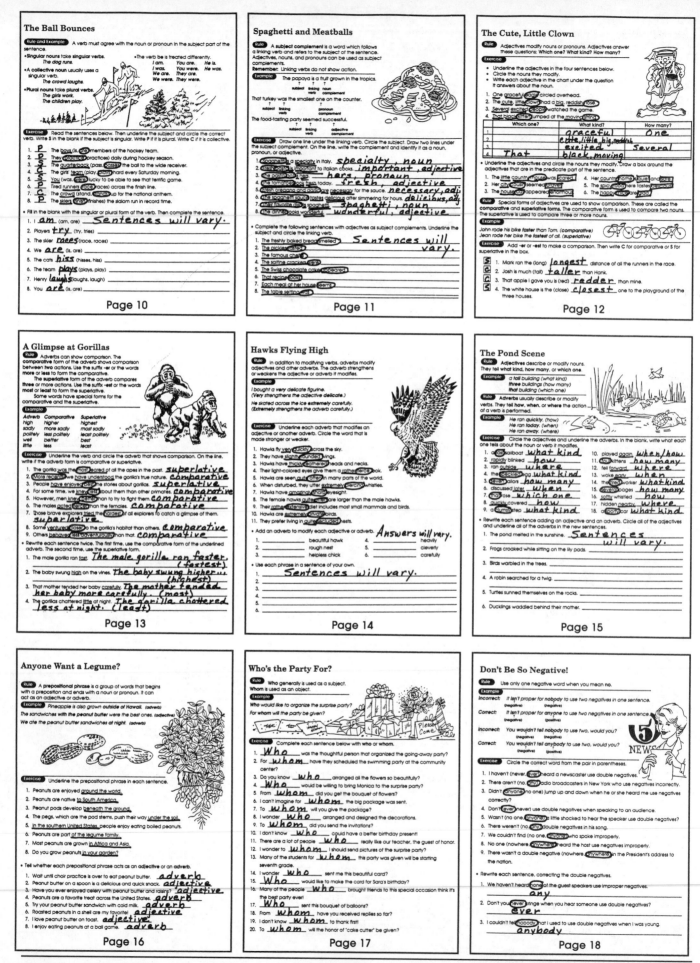

The Ball Bounces

Rule and Example A verb must agree with the noun or pronoun in the subject part of the sentence.

- **Singular nouns** take **singular verbs.**
  The dog runs.
- **A collective noun** usually uses a singular verb.
  The crowd laughs.
- **Plural nouns** take **plural verbs.**
  The girls work.
  The children play.
- The verb **be** is treated differently.

I am.	*You are.*	*He is.*
I was.	*You were.*	*He was.*
We are.	*They are.*	
We were.	*They were.*	

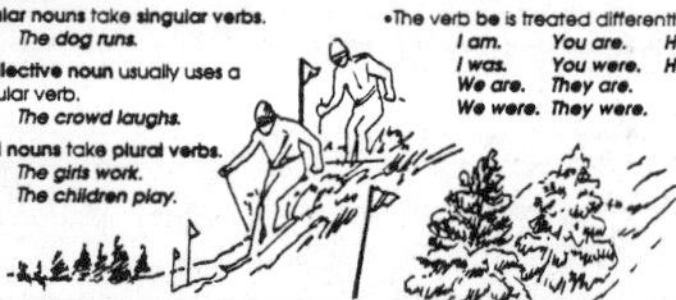

Exercise Read the sentences below. Then underline the subject and circle the correct verb. Write **S** in the blank if the subject is singular. Write **P** if it is plural. Write **C** if it is collective.

1. P The boys (is, are) members of the hockey team.
2. P They (practice, practices) daily during hockey season.
3. S The quarterback (pass, passes) the ball to the wide receiver.
4. C The girls' team (play, plays) hard every Saturday morning.
5. S You (was, were) lucky to be able to see that terrific game.
6. P Tired runners (race, races) across the finish line.
7. C The crowd (stand, stands) up for the national anthem.
8. P The skiers (finish, finishes) the slalom run in record time.

- Fill in the blank with the singular or plural form of the verb. Then complete the sentence.

1. I am (am, are) Sentences will vary.
2. Players try (try, tries)
3. The skier races (race, races)
4. We are (is, are)
5. The cats hiss (hisses, hiss)
6. The team plays (plays, play)
7. Henry laughs (laughs, laugh)
8. You are (is, are)

Page 10

Spaghetti and Meatballs

Rule A **subject complement** is a word which follows a linking verb and refers to the subject of the sentence. Adjectives, nouns, and pronouns can be used as subject complements.
Remember: Linking verbs do not show action.

Example The papaya is a fruit grown in the tropics.
(subject: papaya; linking verb: is; noun complement: fruit)

That turkey was the smallest one on the counter.
(subject: turkey; linking verb: was; pronoun complement: one)

The food-tasting party seemed successful.
(subject: party; linking verb: seemed; adjective complement: successful)

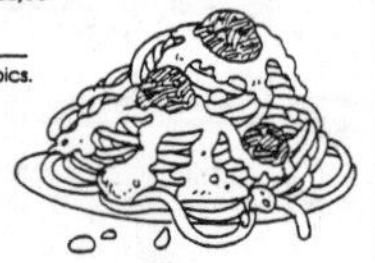

Exercise Draw one line under the linking verb. Circle the subject. Draw two lines under the subject complement. On the line, write the complement and identify it as a noun, pronoun, or adjective.

1. Spaghetti is a specialty in Italy. specialty, noun
2. Fresh pasta is important to Italian cooks. important, adjective
3. The pasta bowl is hers. hers, pronoun
4. The tomatoes look fresh today. fresh, adjective
5. Fresh oregano and garlic are necessary for the sauce. necessary, adj.
6. The spaghetti sauce tastes delicious after simmering for hours. delicious, adj.
7. Their favorite dish is spaghetti. spaghetti, noun
8. The dinner looks wonderful. wonderful, adjective

- Complete the following sentences with adjectives as subject complements. Underline the subject and circle the linking verb.

1. The freshly baked bread smelled Sentences will vary.
2. The pickles tasted
3. The famous chef is
4. The saltine crackers were
5. The Swiss chocolate cake appeared
6. That recipe looks
7. Each meal at her house seems
8. The table setting was

Page 11

The Cute, Little Clown

Rule Adjectives modify nouns or pronouns. Adjectives answer these questions: **Which one? What kind? How many?**

Exercise

- Underline the adjectives in the four sentences below.
- Circle the nouns they modify.
- Write each adjective in the chart under the question it answers about the noun.

1. One graceful eagle circled overhead.
2. The cute, little clown had a big, reddish nose.
3. Several excited people watched the game.
4. That black kitten jumped at the moving string.

	Which one?	What kind?	How many?
1		graceful	One
2		cute, little, big, reddish	
3		excited	Several
4	That	black, moving	

- Underline the adjectives and circle the nouns they modify. Draw a box around the adjectives that are in the predicate part of the sentence.

1. The little country mouse was scared.
2. Her city cousin seemed braver.
3. The house cat appeared enormous.
4. Her country home is quiet and safe.
5. The spicy food here tastes delicious.
6. The happy mice are glad.

Rule Special forms of adjectives are used to show comparison. These are called the **comparative** and **superlative forms.** The comparative form is used to compare two nouns. The superlative is used to compare three or more nouns.

Example
John rode his bike ***faster*** *than Tom.* ***(comparative)***
Jean rode her bike the ***fastest*** *of all.* ***(superlative)***

Exercise Add **-er** or **-est** to make a comparison. Then write **C** for comparative or **S** for superlative in the box.

S 1. Mark ran the (long) longest distance of all the runners in the race.
C 2. Josh is much (tall) taller than Hank.
C 3. That apple I gave you is (red) redder than mine.
S 4. The white house is the (close) closest one to the playground of the three houses.

Page 12

A Glimpse at Gorillas

Rule Adverbs can show comparison. The **comparative** form of the adverb shows comparison between **two** actions. Use the suffix **-er** or the words **more** or **less** to form the comparative.

The **superlative** form of the adverb compares **three** or more actions. Use the suffix **-est** or the words **most** or **least** to form the superlative.

Some words have special forms for the comparative and the superlative.

Example

Adverb	*Comparative*	*Superlative*
high	*higher*	*highest*
sadly	*more sadly*	*most sadly*
politely	*less politely*	*least politely*
well	*better*	*best*
little	*less*	*least*

Exercise Underline the verb and circle the adverb that shows comparison. On the line, write if the adverb form is comparative or superlative.

1. The gorilla was the most feared of all the apes in the past. superlative
2. More recently we have understood the gorilla's true nature. comparative
3. People have enjoyed best the stories about gorillas. superlative
4. For some time, we knew less about them than other primates. comparative
5. However, men knew better than to try to fight them. comparative
6. The males acted fiercer than the females. comparative
7. Those brave explorers tried the hardest of all explorers to catch a glimpse of them. superlative
8. Some ventured closer to the gorilla's habitat than others. comparative
9. Others behaved less adventurously than that. comparative

- Rewrite each sentence twice. The first time, use the comparative form of the underlined adverb. The second time, use the superlative form.

1. The male gorilla ran fast. The male gorilla ran faster. (fastest)
2. The baby swung high on the vines. The baby swung higher... (highest)
3. That mother tended her baby carefully. The mother tended her baby more carefully. (most)
4. The gorillas chattered little at night. The gorilla chattered less at night. (least)

Page 13

Hawks Flying High

Rule In addition to modifying verbs, adverbs modify adjectives and other adverbs. The adverb strengthens or weakens the adjective or adverb it modifies.

Example
I bought a ***very*** *delicate figurine.*
*(****Very*** *strengthens the adjective* ***delicate****.)*
He skated across the ice ***extremely*** *carefully.*
*(****Extremely*** *strengthens the adverb carefully.)*

Exercise Underline each adverb that modifies an adjective or another adverb. Circle the word that is made stronger or weaker.

1. Hawks fly very quickly across the sky.
2. They have slightly rounded wings.
3. Hawks have thickly feathered heads and necks.
4. Their light-colored eyes give them a rather fierce look.
5. Hawks are seen quite often in many parts of the world.
6. When disturbed, they utter extremely piercing whistles.
7. Hawks have amazingly sharp eyesight.
8. The female hawks quite often are larger than the male hawks.
9. Their rather extensive diet includes most small mammals and birds.
10. Hawks are extremely private birds.
11. They prefer living in quite secluded nests.

- Add an adverb to modify each adjective or adverb. Answers will vary.

1. ______	beautiful hawk	4. ______	heavily
2. ______	rough nest	5. ______	cleverly
3. ______	helpless chick	6. ______	carefully

- Use each phrase in a sentence of your own.

1. Sentences will vary.
2.
3.
4.
5.
6.

Page 14

The Pond Scene

Rule **Adjectives** describe or modify nouns. They tell **what kind, how many,** or **which one.**

Example
a ***tall*** *building (what kind)*
three *buildings (how many)*
that *building (which one)*

Rule **Adverbs** usually describe or modify verbs. They tell **how, when,** or **where** the action of a verb is performed.

Example
He ran ***quickly****. (how)*
He ran ***today****. (when)*
He ran ***away****. (where)*

Exercise Circle the adjectives and underline the adverbs. In the blank, write what each one tells about the noun or verb it modifies.

1. a fast sailboat what kind	10. played again when/how
2. rapidly blinked how	11. four kittens how many
3. ran outside where	12. fell forward where
4. the speckled egg what kind	13. woke early when
5. seven sailors how many	14. the tired worker what kind
6. discussed later when	15. several pages how many
7. that rose which one	16. softly whistled how
8. quickly covered how	17. hidden nearby where
9. a clumsy step what kind	18. a sporty car what kind

- Rewrite each sentence adding an adjective and an adverb. Circle all of the adjectives and underline all of the adverbs in the new sentences.

1. The pond melted in the sunshine. Sentences will vary.
2. Frogs croaked while sitting on the lily pads.
3. Birds warbled in the trees.
4. A robin searched for a twig.
5. Turtles sunned themselves on the rocks.
6. Ducklings waddled behind their mother.

Page 15

Anyone Want a Legume?

Rule A **prepositional phrase** is a group of words that begins with a preposition and ends with a noun or pronoun. It can act as an adjective or adverb.

Example *Pineapple is also grown* ***outside of Hawaii****.* ***(adverb)***
The sandwiches ***with the peanut butter*** *were the best ones.* ***(adjective)***
We ate the peanut butter sandwiches ***at night****.* ***(adverb)***

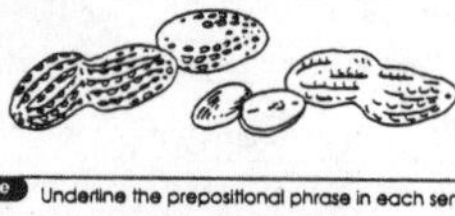

Exercise Underline the prepositional phrase in each sentence.

1. Peanuts are enjoyed around the world.
2. Peanuts are native to South America.
3. Peanut pods develop beneath the ground.
4. The pegs, which are the pod stems, push their way under the soil.
5. In the southern United States, people enjoy eating boiled peanuts.
6. Peanuts are part of the legume family.
7. Most peanuts are grown in Africa and Asia.
8. Do you grow peanuts in your garden?

- Tell whether each prepositional phrase acts as an **adjective** or an **adverb.**

1. Wait until choir practice is over to eat peanut butter. adverb
2. Peanut butter on a spoon is a delicious and quick snack. adjective
3. Have you ever enjoyed celery with peanut butter and raisins? adjective
4. Peanuts are a favorite treat across the United States. adverb
5. Try your peanut butter sandwich with cold milk. adverb
6. Roasted peanuts in a shell are my favorite! adjective
7. I love peanut butter on toast. adjective
8. I enjoy eating peanuts at a ball game. adverb

Page 16

Who's the Party For?

Rule **Who** generally is used as a subject. **Whom** is used as an object.

Example
Who would like to organize the surprise party?
For whom will the party be given?

Exercise Complete each sentence below with **who** or **whom.**

1. Who was the thoughtful person that organized the going-away party?
2. For whom have they scheduled the swimming party at the community center?
3. Do you know who arranged all the flowers so beautifully?
4. Who would be willing to bring Monica to the surprise party?
5. From whom did you get the bouquet of flowers?
6. I can't imagine for whom the big package was sent.
7. To whom will you give the package?
8. I wonder who arranged and designed the decorations.
9. To whom did you send the invitations?
10. I don't know who could have a better birthday present!
11. There are a lot of people who really like our teacher, the guest of honor.
12. I wonder to whom I should send pictures of the surprise party?
13. Many of the students for whom this party was given will be starting seventh grade.
14. I wonder who sent me this beautiful card?
15. Who would like to make the card for Sara's birthday?
16. Many of the people who brought friends to this special occasion think it's the best party ever!
17. Who sent this bouquet of balloons?
18. From whom have you received replies so far?
19. I don't know whom to thank first!
20. To whom will the honor of "cake cutter" be given?

Page 17

Don't Be So Negative!

Rule Use only one negative word when you mean **no.**

Example
Incorrect: *It* ***isn't*** *(negative) proper for* ***nobody*** *(negative) to use two negatives in one sentence.*
Correct: *It* ***isn't*** *(negative) proper for* ***anyone*** *(positive) to use two negatives in one sentence.*
Incorrect: *You* ***wouldn't*** *(negative) tell* ***nobody*** *(negative) to use two, would you?*
Correct: *You* ***wouldn't*** *(negative) tell* ***anybody*** *(positive) to use two, would you?*

Exercise Circle the correct word from the pair in parentheses.

1. I haven't (never, ever) heard a newscaster use double negatives.
2. There aren't (no, any) radio broadcasters in New York who use negatives incorrectly.
3. Didn't (anyone, no one) jump up and down when he or she heard me use negatives correctly?
4. Don't (ever, never) use double negatives when speaking to an audience.
5. Wasn't (no one, anyone) a little shocked to hear the speaker use double negatives?
6. There weren't (no, any) double negatives in his song.
7. We couldn't find (no one, anyone) who spoke improperly.
8. No one (nowhere, anywhere) heard the host use negatives improperly.
9. There wasn't a double negative (nowhere, anywhere) in the President's address to the nation.

- Rewrite each sentence, correcting the double negatives.

1. We haven't heard none of the guest speakers use improper negatives.
any
2. Don't you never cringe when you hear someone use double negatives?
ever
3. I couldn't tell nobody that I used to use double negatives when I was young.
anybody

Page 18

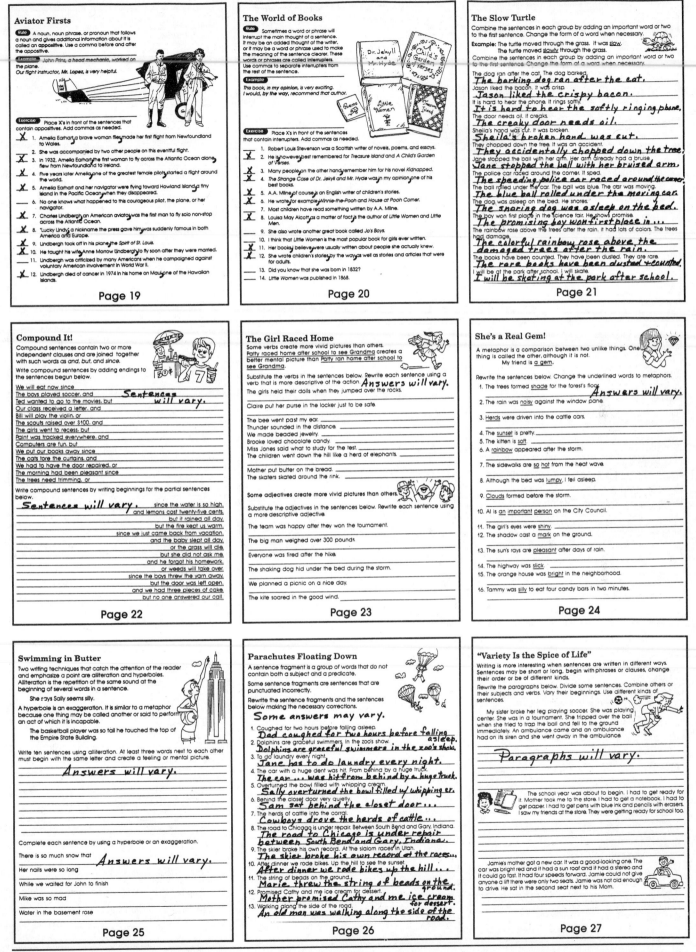

Aviator Firsts

Rule A noun, noun phrase, or pronoun that follows a noun and gives additional information about it is called an **appositive**. Use a comma before and after the appositive.

Example *John Prins, a head mechanic, worked on the plane.*
Our flight instructor, Mr. Lopez, is very helpful.

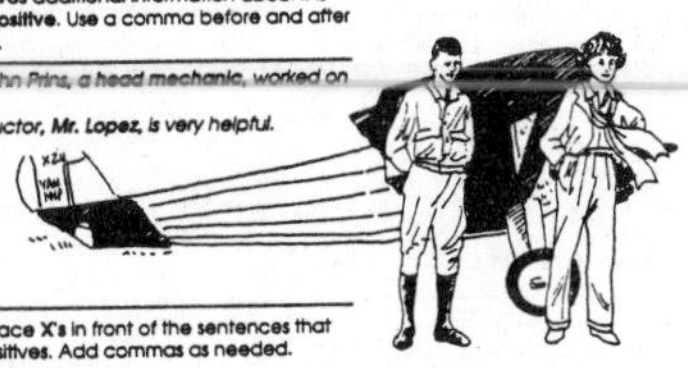

Exercise Place X's in front of the sentences that contain appositives. Add commas as needed.

X 1. Amelia Earhart, a brave woman flier, made her first flight from Newfoundland to Wales.
___ 2. She was accompanied by two other people on this eventful flight.
X 3. In 1932, Amelia Earhart, the first woman to fly across the Atlantic Ocean alone, flew from Newfoundland to Ireland.
X 4. Five years later Amelia, one of the greatest female pilots, started a flight around the world.
X 5. Amelia Earhart and her navigator were flying toward Howland Island, a tiny island in the Pacific Ocean, when they disappeared.
___ 6. No one knows what happened to this courageous pilot, the plane, or her navigator.
X 7. Charles Lindbergh, an American aviator, was the first man to fly solo non-stop across the Atlantic Ocean.
X 8. "Lucky Lindy," a nickname the press gave him, was suddenly famous in both America and Europe.
X 9. Lindbergh took off in his plane, the *Spirit of St. Louis.*
X 10. He taught his wife, Anne Morrow Lindbergh, to fly soon after they were married.
___ 11. Lindbergh was criticized by many Americans when he campaigned against voluntary American involvement in World War II.
X 12. Lindbergh died of cancer in 1974 in his home on Maui, one of the Hawaiian islands.

Page 19

The World of Books

Rule Sometimes a word or phrase will interrupt the main thought of a sentence. It may be an added thought of the writer, or it may be a word or phrase used to make the meaning of the sentence clearer. These words or phrases are called **interrupters**. Use commas to separate interrupters from the rest of the sentence.

Example
This book, in my opinion, is very exciting.
I would, by the way, recommend that author.

Exercise Place X's in front of the sentences that contain interrupters. Add commas as needed.

___ 1. Robert Louis Stevenson was a Scottish writer of novels, poems, and essays.
X 2. He is, however, best remembered for *Treasure Island* and *A Child's Garden of Verses.*
X 3. Many people, on the other hand, remember him for his novel *Kidnapped.*
X 4. *The Strange Case of Dr. Jekyll and Mr. Hyde* was, in my opinion, one of his best books.
X 5. A.A. Milne, of course, is an English writer of children's stories.
X 6. He wrote, for example, *Winnie-the-Pooh* and *House at Pooh Corner.*
___ 7. Most children have read something written by A.A. Milne.
X 8. Louisa May Alcott, as a matter of fact, is the author of *Little Women* and *Little Men.*
___ 9. She also wrote another great book called *Jo's Boys.*
___ 10. I think that *Little Women* is the most popular book for girls ever written.
X 11. Her books, I believe, were usually written about people she actually knew.
X 12. She wrote children's stories, by the way, as well as stories and articles that were for adults.
___ 13. Did you know that she was born in 1832?
___ 14. *Little Women* was published in 1868.

Page 20

The Slow Turtle

Combine the sentences in each group by adding an important word or two to the first sentence. Change the form of a word when necessary.

Example: The turtle moved through the grass. It was slow.
The turtle moved slowly through the grass.

Combine the sentences in each group by adding an important word or two to the first sentence. Change the form of a word when necessary.

The dog ran after the cat. The dog barked.
The barking dog ran after the cat.
Jason liked the bacon. It was crisp.
Jason liked the crispy bacon.
It is hard to hear the phone. It rings softly.
It is hard to hear the softly ringing phone.
The door needs oil. It creaks.
The creaky door needs oil.
Sheila's hand was cut. It was broken.
Sheila's broken hand was cut.
They chopped down the tree. It was an accident.
They accidentally chopped down the tree.
Jane stopped the ball with her arm. Her arm already had a bruise.
Jane stopped the ball with her bruised arm.
The police car raced around the corner. It sped.
The speeding police car raced around the corner.
The ball rolled under the car. The ball was blue. The car was moving.
The blue ball rolled under the moving car.
The dog was asleep on the bed. He snores.
The snoring dog was asleep on the bed.
The boy won first place in the science fair. He shows promise.
The promising boy won first place in . . .
The rainbow rose above the trees after the rain. It had lots of colors. The trees had damage.
The colorful rainbow rose above the damaged trees after the rain.
The books have been counted. They have been dusted. They are rare.
The rare books have been dusted + counted.
I will be at the park after school. I will skate.
I will be skating at the park after school.

Page 21

Compound It!

Compound sentences contain two or more independent clauses and are joined together with such words as *and, but,* and *since.*

Write compound sentences by adding endings to the sentences begun below.

Sentences will vary.

We will eat now since
The boys played soccer, and
Ted wanted to go to the movies, but
Our class received a letter, and
Bill will play the violin, or
The scouts raised over $100, and
The girls went to recess, but
Paint was tracked everywhere, and
Computers are fun, but
We put our books away since
The cats tore the curtains, and
We had to have the door repaired, or
The morning had been pleasant since
The trees need trimming, or

Write compound sentences by writing beginnings for the partial sentences below.

Sentences will vary.

since the water is so high.
and lemons cost twenty-five cents.
but it rained all day.
but the fire kept us warm.
since we just came back from vacation.
and the baby slept all day.
or the grass will die.
but she did not ask me.
and he forgot his homework.
or weeds will take over.
since the boys threw the yarn away.
but the door was left open.
and we had three pieces of cake.
but no one answered our call.

Page 22

The Girl Raced Home

Some verbs create more vivid pictures than others. Patty raced home after school to see Grandma creates a better mental picture than Patty ran home after school to see Grandma.

Substitute the verbs in the sentences below. Rewrite each sentence using a verb that is more descriptive of the action. Answers will vary.

The girls held their dolls when they jumped over the rocks.
Claire put her purse in the locker just to be safe.
The bee went past my ear.
Thunder sounded in the distance.
We made beaded jewelry.
Brooke loved chocolate candy.
Miss Jones said what to study for the test.
The children went down the hill like a herd of elephants.
Mother put butter on the bread.
The skaters skated around the rink.

Some adjectives create more vivid pictures than others.

Substitute the adjectives in the sentences below. Rewrite each sentence using a more descriptive adjective.

The team was happy after they won the tournament.
The big man weighed over 300 pounds.
Everyone was tired after the hike.
The shaking dog hid under the bed during the storm.
We planned a picnic on a nice day.
The kite soared in the good wind.

Page 23

She's a Real Gem!

A metaphor is a comparison between two unlike things. One thing is called the other, although it is not.
My friend is a gem.

Rewrite the sentences below. Change the underlined words to metaphors.

1. The trees formed shade for the forest's floor.
Answers will vary.
2. The rain was noisy against the window pane.
3. Herds were driven into the cattle cars.
4. The sunset is pretty.
5. The kitten is soft.
6. A rainbow appeared after the storm.
7. The sidewalks are so hot from the heat wave.
8. Although the bed was lumpy, I fell asleep.
9. Clouds formed before the storm.
10. Al is an important person on the City Council.
11. The girl's eyes were shiny.
12. The shadow cast a mark on the ground.
13. The sun's rays are pleasant after days of rain.
14. The highway was slick.
15. The orange house was bright in the neighborhood.
16. Tammy was silly to eat four candy bars in two minutes.

Page 24

Swimming in Butter

Two writing techniques that catch the attention of the reader and emphasize a point are alliteration and hyperboles. Alliteration is the repetition of the same sound at the beginning of several words in a sentence.

She says Sally seems silly.

A hyperbole is an exaggeration. It is similar to a metaphor because one thing may be called another or said to perform an act of which it is incapable.

The basketball player was so tall he touched the top of the Empire State Building.

Write ten sentences using alliteration. At least three words next to each other must begin with the same letter and create a feeling or mental picture.

Answers will vary.

Complete each sentence by using a hyperbole or an exaggeration.

There is so much snow that
Answers will vary.
Her nails were so long
While we waited for John to finish
Mike was so mad
Water in the basement rose

Page 25

Parachutes Floating Down

A sentence fragment is a group of words that do not contain both a subject and a predicate.

Some sentence fragments are sentences that are punctuated incorrectly.

Rewrite the sentence fragments and the sentences below making the necessary corrections.

Some answers may vary.

1. Coughed for two hours before falling asleep.
Dad coughed for two hours before falling asleep.
2. Dolphins are graceful swimmers. In the zoo's show.
Dolphins are graceful swimmers in the zoo's show.
3. To do laundry every night.
Jane has to do laundry every night.
4. The car with a huge dent was hit. From behind by a huge truck.
The car . . . was hit from behind by a huge truck.
5. Overturned the bowl filled with whipping cream.
Sally overturned the bowl filled w/ whipping cr.
6. Behind the closet door very quietly.
Sam sat behind the closet door . . .
7. The herds of cattle into the corral.
Cowboys drove the herds of cattle . . .
8. The road to Chicago is under repair. Between South Bend and Gary, Indiana.
The road to Chicago is under repair between South Bend and Gary, Indiana.
9. The skier broke his own record. At the slalom races in Utah.
The skier broke his own record at the races . . .
10. After dinner we rode bikes. Up the hill to see the sunset.
After dinner we rode bikes up the hill . . .
11. The string of beads on the ground.
Marie threw the string of beads on the ground.
12. Promised Cathy and me ice cream for dessert.
Mother promised Cathy and me ice cream for dessert.
13. Walking along the side of the road.
An old man was walking along the side of the road.

Page 26

"Variety Is the Spice of Life"

Writing is more interesting when sentences are written in different ways. Sentences may be short or long, begin with phrases or clauses, change their order or be of different kinds.

Rewrite the paragraphs below. Divide some sentences. Combine others or their subjects and verbs. Vary their beginnings. Use different kinds of sentences.

My sister broke her leg playing soccer. She was playing center. She was in a tournament. She tripped over the ball when she tried to trap the ball and fell to the ground immediately. An ambulance came and an ambulance had on its siren and she went away in the ambulance.

Paragraphs will vary.

The school year was about to begin. I had to get ready for it. Mother took me to the store. I had to get a notebook. I had to get paper. I had to get pens with blue ink and pencils with erasers. I saw my friends at the store. They were getting ready for school too.

Jamie's mother got a new car. It was a good-looking one. The car was bright red and it had a sun roof and it had a stereo and it could go fast. It had four speeds forward. Jamie could not give anyone a lift there were only two seats. Jamie was not old enough to drive. He sat in the second seat next to his Mom.

Page 27

What's the Idea?

A topic sentence is usually the first sentence in a paragraph. It states the paragraph's main idea.

Tell what the main idea of each paragraph will be from each topic sentence below. **Answers may vary.**

The dog looked skinny and tired. *dog's appearance*
The formal dinner began with soup. *dinner menu*
Oranges are round and bananas are long. *comparison of fruit*
Our word for today is "outrageous." *definition*
The school day begins at 8:45. *school day schedule*
I did homework for three hours last night. *what homework was*
Jason was elected class president by one vote. *class election*
America has many national parks in the west. *national parks*
We got Rex from the animal shelter. *about Rex*
The ground was covered with forty inches of snow. *appearance outside*
The farmers are harvesting their crops. *about harvesting*
Politicians do not always do as they promise. *about breaking promises*
The new boy did not like his new school. *new boy at school*
The robin built her nest on the windowsill. *how robin built nest*

Write a topic sentence for each main idea below.

homesick *Answers will vary.*

polka-dots _____

made in America _____

cats as pets _____

a safe environment _____

pioneering spirit _____

a nightmare _____

late for school _____

Page 28

Eek!

Write some descriptive or sensory words and phrases that:

1) describe a person's feelings. *Answers will vary.*

2) describe sounds. _____

3) describe how different foods can taste. _____

4) describe how an object can feel to the touch. _____

5) describe how something can smell. _____

Write sensory words and phrases that describe each of the following situations.
a new student with no friends _____

stepping barefoot on a piece of calves liver _____

riding a bus in a city during rush hour _____

making popcorn _____

Write a topic sentence for each above situation.

Rewrite one of the topic sentences below. Follow it with support sentences with sensory details that will help create the feeling or mental picture of the situation.

Page 29

Mouth-Watering

Sensory images may be expressed in topic sentences. To express the images more clearly, sentences dealing with the senses support the topic sentences.

Example: When I opened the door, I knew Mother had been baking. The aroma of cinnamon drifted toward me. The house was warm from the oven's heat. When I ran to the kitchen, my mouth watered when I saw my favorite cookies cooling on the rack.

Write a topic sentence that creates a sensory image for each of the following situations. Follow it with three support sentences that involve the senses.

Camping by a river

Answers will vary.

Stuck in an elevator for five hours

Summer in a garden filled with hundreds of flowers

Being present when an earthquake occurred

Page 30

Paragraph Planning

It is best to plan a paragraph before you write it. Go through the steps on this page to write a well-organized paragraph.

Choose a subject.
Select it from the box or use one of your own. Write your choice on the line. _____

> A long creature
> When I look up
> The strange smell
> A rainy day

List details about your subject. *Answers will vary.*

Write a topic sentence expressing the main idea about your subject. _____

Use the details you have written to write support sentences explaining or supporting the main idea.

Read what you have written. If the paragraph will hold together better with a wrap-up sentence, write one.

Rewrite the sentences above in good paragraph form. Remember to indent the first line of the paragraph. Use correct punctuation.

Page 31

Time to Organize

Organize paragraphs in the following manner.

- Plan a strong opening sentence that introduces the topic you will be discussing in this paragraph.
- Select supporting details that add information to your opening sentence.
- Organize your details so that the most important are included and the least important can be left out. Edit (alone or with a partner) using the checklist at the bottom of the page.

Answers will vary.
(Title)

Checklist:
Circle the correct answers and then edit if needed.

Does your paragraph have a topic sentence?	Yes	No
Does your paragraph have supporting details?	Yes	No
Did you use the most important details?	Yes	No
Have you checked for run-ons and fragments?	Yes	No
Did you indent the first sentence?	Yes	No
Did you use correct punctuation?	Yes	No

DON'T FORGET TO PUT A DENT IN THAT FIRST SENTENCE!

Page 32

Let Me Persuade You

A persuasive paragraph clearly states an opinion and backs it up with reasons. In a well-organized persuasive paragraph, the topic sentence lists the opinion. Sequence words introduce the sentences that support the opinion. A persuasive paragraph is stronger when the strongest reason is given last.

Write persuasive paragraphs for the topics below. Give four reasons for each.

Why you should look before you leap *Answers will vary.*

Why dog is man's best friend

Why you can't tell a book by its cover

Why he who hesitates is lost

Page 33

The Setting

Write the setting (where and when) for each of the following situations.
The dog wagged his tail as he cleaned the crumbs from under the table. *under a dining table after a meal*
Sally wrapped herself in another blanket and continued to watch a scary television program alone in the dark. *possibly a winter night, at home alone*
When the clock chimed four times, the seniors started marching into the auditorium to receive their diplomas. *afternoon, graduation ceremony*

Select one of the above settings. Write a paragraph about it. Describe what the place looked like and what sounds could be heard.

Paragraphs will vary.

Look at the picture below. Describe the setting. Do not describe the setting. Do not describe a direct statement such as "The sun is shining." Use words that appeal to the senses.

Descriptions will vary.

Page 34

The Plot

The main part of a story is the plot. The plot usually has a problem. The characters in the story interact in the plot to solve the problem. Listed below are some problems. Write one way each problem might be solved.

Answers will vary.

On its way home from a field trip, the sixth grade's bus broke down on a highway ten miles from the nearest exit. _____

The new puppy chewed only shoes belonging to Dad, and only left shoes at that. _____

The wind came up suddenly. The crowd on the beach saw the boat Tom and Dick were in capsize. _____

A plot does not go directly from the problem to its solution. It begins with an introduction of the situation or problem and its characters. The middle part develops the situation and tells of the interactions of the characters in their attempts to solve the problem. Near the end of the interactions, the plot becomes most exciting. This is called the climax. It occurs just before the story's end and the solution.
Pick one of the problems from above. Write it. _____

List some characters that could be involved. Briefly describe each one.

List three ways the characters might interact trying to solve the problem. Make the third way the most interesting and exciting.

Write your solution. If the one from above fits, use it. If not, write a new one.

Page 35

Character Development

An author needs to develop his or her characters so they are believable. In which of the paragraphs below, A or B, do you have a better image of what Penny is like? *A* Why? *She is described physically and seems efficient and friendly.*

A. Penny arrived early at the Johnson's because it was her first time to sit for their little girl. Lori looked at Penny. She was tiny. Her hair was pulled back, and her constant smile made even her freckles sparkle. Lori asked Penny to play dolls with her.

B. Penny was sitting for the Johnson's little girl, Lori, for the first time. Lori looked at Penny. She looked friendly. Lori brought out her dolls and began to play on the floor next to Penny.

Developing a character does not mean to just tell what he or she looks like, but also to create a feeling of what sort of person the character is. Adjectives are not the only way to describe a person. A picture of a character may be created through his or her actions.

Write words and actions that might be characteristic of the following:
a monster *Answers will vary.*

a young neighborhood child _____

an old man _____

a clown _____

Select one of the above people, or one of your own choice. On the lines below, develop the character so that it has a recognizable image and personality.

Page 36

Writing a Story

Before you write a story, you must decide if it is going to be real or make-believe. Then, you must decide where and when it takes place (the setting), who is in it (the characters), and what the problem is, how it develops, and how it is solved (the plot). You are going to write a story. Think about what you are going to write about. Is it real or make-believe?

Answers will vary.

Now, make notes about your story.

The Setting _____

(State the time and place. Remember in the story to create an impression rather than making a direct statement like above.)

The Characters _____

(Beside their names, include a little about how they look, act and feel.)

The Plot's Introduction (present the problem) _____

Develop the Problem (interaction with characters — have it build to an exciting and interesting interaction: the climax) _____

Climax _____

Solution _____

Use your notes. Write your story on lined paper. Remember to use correct paragraph form.

Page 37

Narrative Story

A narrative story is like a narrative paragraph except it is a series of paragraphs. A narrative story tells a sequence of events in order.

Look at the strips of pictures below. They tell a story.

Each picture is a paragraph in the story. Write a story about what is happening. Tell what is happening in each picture. Write about each picture in order. Use a sequence word or phrase at the beginning of each paragraph. Use other sequence words in each paragraph too if you want.

Answers will vary.

Page 38

Outlining

One way to get ready to write a report or story is to make an outline. Plan the content of the writing by paragraphs. The heading after each Roman numeral will become the topic sentence. The items after each letter tell something about the topic sentence. Notice the letter of the first word of each item is capitalized, and the item is not a sentence itself.

Look at the outline for a paragraph about "Manners."

Manners
I. Behavior at school
  A. In the halls
  B. Lunch time
  C. Addressing staff

What is this paragraph about? *Behavior at school*
What details will be included in the paragraph? *Behavior in the halls and at lunch and how to talk to staff*
Write a topic sentence for this paragraph. *Answers will vary.*

Make a one paragraph outline for "The First Thing in the Morning."

The First Thing in the Morning

What will be the main idea of the subject?
I. *Answers will vary.*
What should be included in the paragraph to support the main idea?
  A. _____
  B. _____
  C. _____
  D. _____

Use the outline to write a paragraph about "The First Thing in the Morning."

Answers will vary.

Choose a topic from the list below. Circle your choice.

| My Brother | The Neighbor's Dog | Sick on My Birthday |
| A Good Friend | Chewing Gum | My Last Vacation |

Go on to the next page.

Page 39

Outlining (cont.)

Write the topic you circled on the last page on the title line below. Write an outline for one paragraph about the topic.

I. *Answers will vary.*
  A. _____
  B. _____
  C. _____
  D. _____

Take the information from the outline and write a paragraph.

_____

Longer stories and reports are organized the same way. Each paragraph begins with a new Roman numeral.

Basketball
I. History of the game
  A. Inventor of game
  B. Where and when first played
  C. How first played
II. Changes over time
  A. Rules
  B. Equipment
III. Organization now
  A. College basketball
  B. Professional basketball
  C. Leagues

What is the first paragraph in this story going to be about? _____

The second paragraph? _____

The third paragraph? _____

Choose a topic from the list below. Circle it. Write an outline for at least a two or three paragraph story.

| Ghosts in the Attic | Yesterday | Building a Bird House |
| A Broken Arm | The Missing Boy | Computer Magic |

I. _____
  A. _____
  B. _____
  C. _____
II. _____
  A. _____

III. _____
  A. _____
  B. _____
  C. _____

Page 40

Common Proofreading Symbols

The following list of editing symbols may be kept in your writing folders. Refer to it when editing and proofing your writing drafts. Use this page to complete the activities on pages 42 and 43.

Common Proofreading Symbols

Symbol	Meaning	Example
∧	Insert	I heard the bell ring.
⸺	Delete	She is the most prettiest girl.
stet	Let it stand	Mother has a very beautiful voice.
#	Add a space	What a holiday it is!
¶	New paragraph	Potatoes are a vegetable.
⌢	Close to one space	I will pay the bill.
⌢	Close up entirely	To night is my birthday party.
∼	Transpose	Don't take your book.
≡	Capitalize	Labor day is a holiday.
/	Make lowercase	My Father is a policeman.
∧	Add a comma	Tigers elephants and whales
⊙	Add a period	Marcia ran for office
∨	Add an apostrophe	Marys tapes
∨ ∨	Add quotation marks	Run for cover! Jane yelled.

Page 41

Editing Practice

Make the necessary editorial corrections using proofreading symbols. Then copy each sentence correctly.

1. Since tomorrow is a holiday, will we not have school.
Since tomorrow is a holiday, we will not have school.

2. To day we will see a video on the War Civil...
Today, we will see a video about the Civil War.

3. have you checked for run-ons and fragments?
Have you checked for run-ons and fragments?

4. Please pass the potatoes.
Please, pass the potatoes.

5. Ann and Mary is best friends.
Ann and Mary are best friends.

6. The boys baseball team won the Middle school Tournament.
The boys' baseball team won the Middle School Tournament.

7. I knew I shouldn't have thrown the base ball to you, said Sam.
"I knew I shouldn't have thrown the baseball to you," said Sam.

Page 42

Be an Editor/Writer

Proofread this paragraph carefully. Make the necessary corrections using proofreading symbols. The first two corrections have been done for you.

It was a sunny friday morning at Green valley Junior High. Although the first bell had rung, school was arriving with the lastest bunch of noisey students. mr. Smith, the french teacher, meet the students at the front door saying put your books in your lockers and goto the gymnasium. To day we are having a special _____

Fill in the blank above and continue the story.

Answers will vary.

Page 43

No Excuse!

No Homework Excuse

Do you remember the time you forgot or misplaced your homework? When you gave your excuse to your teacher, he/she may have said, "Sorry, but that's an F." Have you ever thought that perhaps your excuse wasn't creative enough or that you needed to give the explanation in a more believable way? Write a creative homework excuse. Tell it as though it really happened.

Answers will vary.
(Title)

Page 44

I'll Never Forget . . .

"Elephants never forget" is an old saying. What is it that you'll never forget? Could it be a vacation, or a party? Maybe it was a special gift you received, or the time you broke your arm. Tell about it.

Answers will vary.
(Title)

Page 45

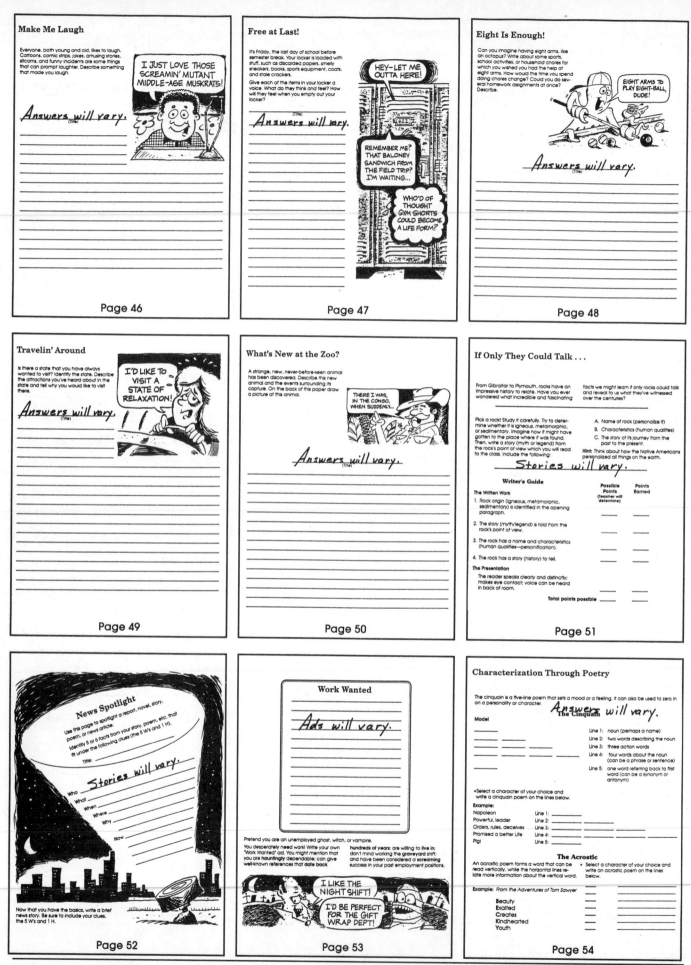

Make Me Laugh

Everyone, both young and old, likes to laugh. Cartoons, comic strips, jokes, amusing stories, sitcoms, and funny incidents are some things that can prompt laughter. Describe something that made you laugh.

Answers will vary.
(Title)

I JUST LOVE THOSE SCREAMIN' MUTANT MIDDLE-AGE MUSKRATS!

Page 46

Free at Last!

It's Friday, the last day of school before semester break. Your locker is loaded with stuff, such as discarded papers, smelly sneakers, books, sports equipment, coats, and stale crackers.

Give each of the items in your locker a voice. What do they think and feel? How will they feel when you empty out your locker?

Answers will vary.
(Title)

HEY—LET ME OUTTA HERE!

REMEMBER ME? THAT BALONEY SANDWICH FROM THE FIELD TRIP? I'M WAITING...

WHO'D OF THOUGHT GYM SHORTS COULD BECOME A LIFE FORM?

Page 47

Eight Is Enough!

Can you imagine having eight arms, like an octopus? Write about some sports, school activities, or household chores for which you wished you had the help of eight arms. How would the time you spend doing chores change? Could you do several homework assignments at once? Describe.

EIGHT ARMS TO PLAY EIGHT-BALL, DUDE!

Answers will vary.
(Title)

Page 48

Travelin' Around

Is there a state that you have always wanted to visit? Identify the state. Describe the attractions you've heard about in the state and tell why you would like to visit there.

I'D LIKE TO VISIT A STATE OF RELAXATION!

Answers will vary.
(Title)

Page 49

What's New at the Zoo?

A strange, new, never-before-seen animal has been discovered. Describe this new animal and the events surrounding its capture. On the back of this paper draw a picture of this animal.

THERE I WAS, IN THE CONGO, WHEN SUDDENLY...

Answers will vary.
(Title)

Page 50

If Only They Could Talk . . .

From Gibraltar to Plymouth, rocks have an impressive history to relate. Have you ever wondered what incredible and fascinating facts we might learn if only rocks could talk and reveal to us what they've witnessed over the centuries?

Pick a rock! Study it carefully. Try to determine whether it is igneous, metamorphic, or sedimentary. Imagine how it might have gotten to the place where it was found. Then, write a story (myth or legend) from the rock's point of view which you will read to the class. Include the following:

A. Name of rock (personalize it)
B. Characteristics (human qualities)
C. The story of its journey from the past to the present.

Hint: Think about how the Native Americans personalized all things on the earth.

Stories will vary.

Writer's Guide

	Possible Points (teacher will determine)	Points Earned
The Written Work		
1. Rock origin (igneous, metamorphic, sedimentary) is identified in the opening paragraph.	___	___
2. The story (myth/legend) is told from the rock's point of view.	___	___
3. The rock has a name and characteristics (human qualities—personification).	___	___
4. The rock has a story (history) to tell.	___	___
The Presentation		
The reader speaks clearly and distinctly; makes eye contact; voice can be heard in back of room.	___	___
Total points possible	___	

Page 51

News Spotlight

Use this page to spotlight a report, novel, story, poem, or news article.

Identify 5 or 6 facts from your story, poem, etc. that fit under the following clues (the 5 W's and 1 H).

Title: ___

Stories will vary.

Who ___
What ___
When ___
Where ___
Why ___
How ___

Now that you have the basics, write a brief news story. Be sure to include your clues, the 5 W's and 1 H.

Page 52

Work Wanted

Ads will vary.

Pretend you are an unemployed ghost, witch, or vampire.

You desperately need work! Write your own "Work Wanted" ad. You might mention that you are hauntingly dependable; can give well-known references that date back hundreds of years; are willing to live in; don't mind working the graveyard shift; and have been considered a screaming success in your past employment positions.

I LIKE THE NIGHT SHIFT!

I'D BE PERFECT FOR THE GIFT WRAP DEPT!

Page 53

Characterization Through Poetry

The cinquain is a five-line poem that sets a mood or a feeling. It can also be used to zero in on a personality or character.

Answers will vary.
The Cinquain

Model

___
___
___
___
___

Line 1: noun (perhaps a name)
Line 2: two words describing the noun
Line 3: three action words
Line 4: four words about the noun (can be a phrase or sentence)
Line 5: one word referring back to first word (can be a synonym or antonym)

•Select a character of your choice and write a cinquain poem on the lines below.

Example:
Napoleon — Line 1: ___
Powerful, leader — Line 2: ___
Orders, rules, deceives — Line 3: ___
Promised a better Life — Line 4: ___
Pig! — Line 5: ___

The Acrostic

An acrostic poem forms a word that can be read vertically, while the horizontal lines relate more information about the vertical word.

• Select a character of your choice and write an acrostic poem on the lines below.

Example: From the Adventures of Tom Sawyer

Beauty
Exalted
Creates
Kindhearted
Youth

Page 54

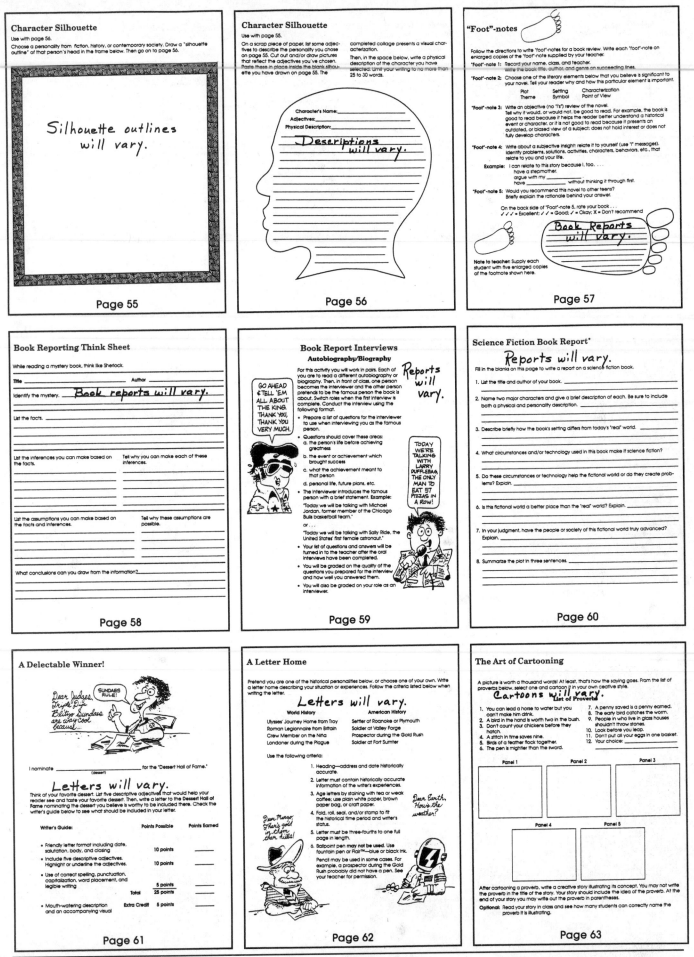

Character Silhouette
Use with page 56.

Choose a personality from fiction, history, or contemporary society. Draw a "silhouette outline" of that person's head in the frame below. Then go on to page 56.

Silhouette outlines will vary.

Page 55

Character Silhouette
Use with page 55.

On a scrap piece of paper, list some adjectives to describe the personality you chose on page 55. Cut out and/or draw pictures that reflect the adjectives you've chosen. Paste these in place inside the blank silhouette you have drawn on page 55. The completed collage presents a visual characterization.

Then, in the space below, write a physical description of the character you have selected. Limit your writing to no more than 25 to 30 words.

Character's Name: _____
Adjectives: _____
Physical Description: _____

Descriptions will vary.

Page 56

"Foot"-notes

Follow the directions to write "foot"-notes for a book review. Write each "foot"-note on enlarged copies of the "foot"-note supplied by your teacher.

"Foot"-note 1: Record your name, class, and teacher. Write the book title, author, and genre on succeeding lines.

"Foot"-note 2: Choose one of the literary elements below that you believe is significant to your novel. Tell your reader why and how this particular element is important.
Plot   Setting   Characterization
Theme   Symbol   Point of View

"Foot"-note 3: Write an adjective (no "I's") review of the novel. Tell why it would, or would not, be good to read. For example, the book is good to read because it helps the reader better understand a historical event or character, or it is not good to read because it presents an outdated, or biased view of a subject; does not hold interest or does not fully develop characters.

"Foot"-note 4: Write about a subjective insight: relate it to yourself (use "I" messages). Identify problems, solutions, activities, characters, behaviors, etc., that relate to you and your life.
Example: I can relate to this story because I, too . . .
have a stepmother.
argue with my _____
have _____ without thinking it through first.

"Foot"-note 5: Would you recommend this novel to other teens? Briefly explain the rationale behind your answer.

On the back side of "Foot"-note 5, rate your book . . .
√√√ = Excellent; √√ = Good; √ = Okay; X = Don't recommend

Book Reports will vary.

Note to teacher: Supply each student with five enlarged copies of the footnote shown here.

Page 57

Book Reporting Think Sheet

While reading a mystery book, think like Sherlock.

Title _____ Author _____

Identify the mystery. Book reports will vary.

List the facts. _____

List the inferences you can make based on the facts. | Tell why you can make each of these inferences.

List the assumptions you can make based on the facts and inferences. | Tell why these assumptions are possible.

What conclusions can you draw from the information? _____

Page 58

Book Report Interviews
Autobiography/Biography

For this activity you will work in pairs. Each of you are to read a different autobiography or biography. Then, in front of class, one person becomes the interviewer and the other person pretends to be the famous person the book is about. Switch roles when the first interview is complete. Conduct the interview using the following format.

Reports will vary.

GO AHEAD & TELL 'EM ALL ABOUT THE KING, THANK YOU, THANK YOU VERY MUCH.

• Prepare a list of questions for the interviewer to use when interviewing you as the famous person.
• Questions should cover these areas:
  a. the person's life before achieving greatness
  b. the event or achievement which brought success
  c. what the achievement meant to that person
  d. personal life, future plans, etc.
• The interviewer introduces the famous person with a brief statement. Example:
  "Today we will be talking with Michael Jordan, former member of the Chicago Bulls basketball team."
  or
  "Today we will be talking with Sally Ride, the United States' first female astronaut."
• Your list of questions and answers will be turned in to the teacher after the oral interviews have been completed.
• You will be graded on the quality of the questions you prepared for the interview and how well you answered them.
• You will also be graded on your role as an interviewer.

TODAY WE'RE TALKING WITH LARRY DUFFLEBAG, THE ONLY MAN TO EAT 57 PIZZAS IN A ROW!

Page 59

Science Fiction Book Report

Reports will vary.

Fill in the blanks on this page to write a report on a science fiction book.

1. List the title and author of your book. _____

2. Name two major characters and give a brief description of each. Be sure to include both a physical and personality description. _____

3. Describe briefly how the book's setting differs from today's "real" world. _____

4. What circumstances and/or technology used in this book make it science fiction? _____

5. Do these circumstances or technology help the fictional world or do they create problems? Explain. _____

6. Is this fictional world a better place than the "real" world? Explain. _____

7. In your judgment, have the people or society of this fictional world truly advanced? Explain. _____

8. Summarize the plot in three sentences. _____

Page 60

A Delectable Winner!

Dear Judges, Triple Dip Blitzo Sundaes are way cool because...

SUNDAES RULE!

I nominate _____ for the "Dessert Hall of Fame."
(dessert)

Letters will vary.

Think of your favorite dessert. List five descriptive adjectives that would help your reader see and taste your favorite dessert. Then, write a letter to the Dessert Hall of Fame nominating the dessert you believe is worthy to be included there. Check the writer's guide below to see what should be included in your letter.

Writer's Guide:	Points Possible	Points Earned
• Friendly letter format including date, salutation, body, and closing	10 points	_____
• Include five descriptive adjectives. Highlight or underline the adjectives.	10 points	_____
• Use of correct spelling, punctuation, capitalization, word placement, and legible writing	5 points	_____
Total	25 points	
• Mouth-watering description and an accompanying visual	Extra Credit 5 points	

Page 61

A Letter Home

Pretend you are one of the historical personalities below, or choose one of your own. Write a letter home describing your situation or experiences. Follow the criteria listed below when writing the letter.

Letters will vary.

World History	American History
Ulysses' Journey Home from Troy	Settler at Roanoke or Plymouth
Roman Legionnaire from Britain	Soldier at Valley Forge
Crew Member on the Niña	Prospector during the Gold Rush
Londoner during the Plague	Soldier at Fort Sumter

Use the following criteria:

1. Heading—address and date historically accurate.
2. Letter must contain historically accurate information of the writer's experiences.
3. Age letters by staining with tea or weak coffee; use plain white paper, brown paper bag, or craft paper.
4. Fold, roll, seal, and/or stamp to fit the historical time period and writer's status.
5. Letter must be three-fourths to one full page in length.
6. Ballpoint pen may not be used. Use fountain pen or Flair™—blue or black ink.
   Pencil may be used in some cases. For example, a prospector during the Gold Rush probably did not have a pen. See your teacher for permission.

Dear Margo, They're gold in them thar hills!

Dear Earth, How's the weather?

Page 62

The Art of Cartooning

A picture is worth a thousand words! At least, that's how the saying goes. From the list of proverbs below, select one and cartoon it in your own creative style.

Cartoons will vary.

List of Proverbs
1. You can lead a horse to water but you can't make him drink.
2. A bird in the hand is worth two in the bush.
3. Don't count your chickens before they hatch.
4. A stitch in time saves nine.
5. Birds of a feather flock together.
6. The pen is mightier than the sword.
7. A penny saved is a penny earned.
8. The early bird catches the worm.
9. People in who live in glass houses shouldn't throw stones.
10. Look before you leap.
11. Don't put all your eggs in one basket.
12. Your choice: _____

Panel 1   Panel 2   Panel 3

Panel 4   Panel 5

After cartooning a proverb, write a creative story illustrating its concept. You may not write the proverb in the title of the story. Your story should include the idea of the proverb. At the end of your story you may write out the proverb in parentheses.

Optional: Read your story in class and see how many students can correctly name the proverb it is illustrating.

Page 63

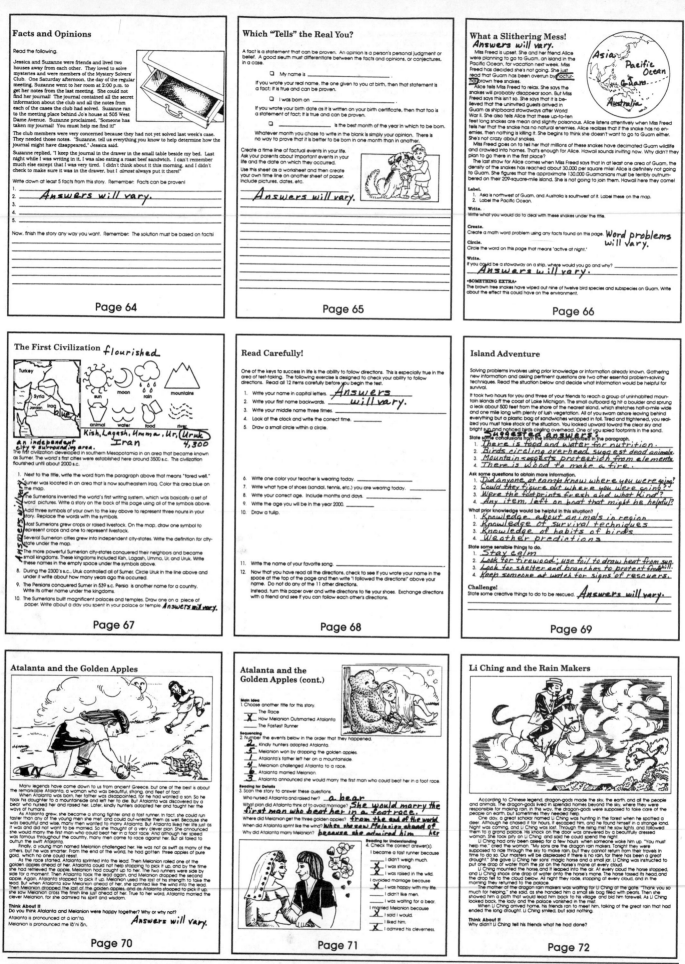

Facts and Opinions

Read the following.

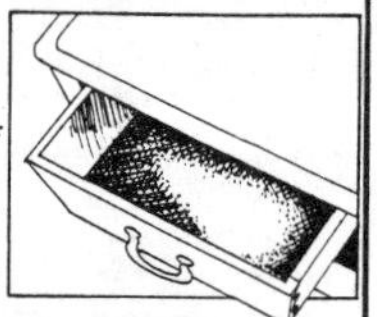

Jessica and Suzanne were friends and lived two houses away from each other. They loved to solve mysteries and were members of the Mystery Solvers' Club. One Saturday afternoon, the day of the regular meeting, Suzanne went to her room at 2:00 p.m. to get her notes from the last meeting. She could not find her journal! The journal contained all the secret information about the club and all the notes from each of the cases the club had solved. Suzanne ran to the meeting place behind Jo's house at 505 West Dame Avenue. Suzanne proclaimed, "Someone has taken my journal! You must help me find it!"

The club members were very concerned because they had not yet solved last week's case. They needed those notes. "Suzanne, tell us everything you know to help determine how the journal might have disappeared," Jessica said.

Suzanne replied, "I keep the journal in the drawer in the small table beside my bed. Last night while I was writing in it, I was also eating a roast beef sandwich. I can't remember much else except that I was very tired. I didn't think about it this morning, and I didn't check to make sure it was in the drawer, but I *almost* always put it there!"

Write down at least 5 facts from this story. Remember: Facts can be proven!

1. ______
2. Answers will vary.
3. ______
4. ______
5. ______

Now, finish the story any way you want. Remember: The solution must be based on facts!

Page 64

Which "Tells" the Real You?

A fact is a statement that can be proven. An opinion is a person's personal judgment or belief. A good sleuth must differentiate between the facts and opinions, or conjectures, in a case.

❑ My name is ______.

If you wrote your real name, the one given to you at birth, then that statement is a fact; it is true and can be proven.

❑ I was born on ______.

If you wrote your birth date as it is written on your birth certificate, then that too is a statement of fact; it is true and can be proven.

❑ ______ is the best month of the year in which to be born.

Whatever month you chose to write in the blank is simply your opinion. There is no way to prove that it is better to be born in one month than in another.

Create a time line of factual events in your life. Ask your parents about important events in your life and the date on which they occurred.

Use this sheet as a worksheet and then create your own time line on another sheet of paper. Include pictures, dates, etc.

Answers will vary.

Page 65

What a Slithering Mess!

Answers will vary.

Asia
Pacific Ocean
Guam
Australia

Miss Freed is upset. She and her friend Alice were planning to go to Guam, an island in the Pacific Ocean, for vacation next week. Miss Freed has decided she's not going. She just read that Guam has been overrun by nocturnal brown tree snakes.

Alice tells Miss Freed to relax. She says the snakes will probably disappear soon. But Miss Freed says this isn't so. She says that it is believed that the uninvited guests arrived in Guam as shipboard stowaways after World War II. She also tells Alice that these up-to-ten feet long snakes are mean and slightly poisonous. Alice listens attentively when Miss Freed tells her that the snake has no natural enemies. Alice realizes that if the snake has no enemies, then nothing is killing it. She begins to think she doesn't want to go to Guam either. She's not crazy about snakes.

Miss Freed goes on to tell her that millions of these snakes have decimated Guam wildlife and crawled into homes. That's enough for Alice. Hawaii sounds inviting now. Why didn't they plan to go there in the first place?

The last straw for Alice comes when Miss Freed says that in at least one area of Guam, the density of the snakes has reached about 30,000 per square mile! Alice is definitely not going to Guam. She figures that the approximate 130,000 Guamanians must be terribly outnumbered on their 209-square-mile island. She is not going to join them. Hawaii here they come!

Label.
1. Asia is northwest of Guam, and Australia is southwest of it. Label these on the map.
2. Label the Pacific Ocean.

Write.
Write what you would do to deal with these snakes under the title.

Create.
Create a math word problem using any facts found on this page. Word problems will vary.

Circle.
Circle the word on this page that means "active at night."

Write.
If you could be a stowaway on a ship, where would you go and why? ______
Answers will vary.

•SOMETHING EXTRA•
The brown tree snakes have wiped out nine of twelve bird species and subspecies on Guam. Write about the effect this could have on the environment.

Page 66

The First Civilization flourished

Turkey
Syria
Jordan
Iraq
blue

sun
moon
rain
mountains
animal
water
food
river

Kish, Lagash, Umma, Ur, Uruk
Iran
4,300

an independent city + surrounding area.

The first civilization developed in southern Mesopotamia in an area that became known as Sumer. The world's first cities were established here around 3500 B.C. This civilization flourished until about 2000 B.C.

1. Next to the title, write the word from the paragraph above that means "fared well."
2. Sumer was located in an area that is now southeastern Iraq. Color this area blue on the map.
3. The Sumerians invented the world's first writing system, which was basically a set of word pictures. Write a story on the back of this page using all of the symbols above.
4. Add three symbols of your own to the key above to represent three nouns in your story. Replace the words with the symbols.
5. Most Sumerians grew crops or raised livestock. On the map, draw one symbol to represent crops and one to represent livestock.
6. Several Sumerian cities grew into independent city-states. Write the definition for city-state under the map.
7. The more powerful Sumerian city-states conquered their neighbors and became small kingdoms. These kingdoms included Kish, Lagash, Umma, Ur, and Uruk. Write these names in the empty space under the symbols above.
8. During the 2300's B.C., Uruk controlled all of Sumer. Circle Uruk in the line above and under it write about how many years ago this occurred.
9. The Persians conquered Sumer in 539 B.C. Persia is another name for a country. Write its other name under the kingdoms.
10. The Sumerians built magnificent palaces and temples. Draw one on a piece of paper. Write about a day you spent in your palace or temple. Answers will vary.

Answers will vary.

Page 67

Read Carefully!

One of the keys to success in life is the ability to follow directions. This is especially true in the area of test-taking. The following exercise is designed to check your ability to follow directions. Read all 12 items carefully before you begin the test.

1. Write your name in capital letters. Answers
2. Write your first name backwards. will vary.
3. Write your middle name three times. ______
4. Look at the clock and write the correct time. ______
5. Draw a small circle within a circle.
6. Write one color your teacher is wearing today. ______
7. Write what type of shoes (sandal, tennis, etc.) you are wearing today. ______
8. Write your correct age. Include months and days. ______
9. Write the age you will be in the year 2000. ______
10. Draw a tulip.
11. Write the name of your favorite song. ______
12. Now that you have read all the directions, check to see if you wrote your name in the space at the top of the page and then write "I followed the directions!" above your name. Do not do any of the 11 other directions.

Instead, turn this paper over and write directions to tie your shoes. Exchange directions with a friend and see if you can follow each other's directions.

Page 68

Island Adventure

Solving problems involves using prior knowledge or information already known. Gathering new information and asking pertinent questions are two other essential problem-solving techniques. Read the situation below and decide what information would be helpful for survival.

It took two hours for you and three of your friends to reach a group of uninhabited mountain islands off the coast of Lake Michigan. The small outboard rig hit a boulder and sprung a leak about 500 feet from the shore of the nearest island, which stretches half-a-mile wide and one mile long with plenty of lush vegetation. All of you swam ashore leaving behind everything but a plastic bag of sandwiches wrapped in foil. Tired and frightened, you realized you must take stock of the situation. You looked upward toward the clear sky and bright sun and noticed birds circling overhead. One of you spied footprints in the sand.

Suggested answers:

State some conclusions from the information provided in the paragraph.
1. There is food and water for nutrition.
2. Birds circling overhead suggest dead animals.
3. Mountain suggests protection from elements.
4. There is wood to make a fire.

Ask some questions to obtain more information.
1. Did anyone at camp know where you were going?
2. Could they figure out where you were going?
3. Were the footprints fresh and what kind?
4. Any item left on boat that might be helpful?

What prior knowledge would be helpful in this situation?
1. Knowledge about animals in region
2. Knowledge of survival techniques
3. Knowledge of habits of birds
4. Weather predictions

State some sensible things to do.
1. Stay calm
2. Look for firewood; use foil to draw heat from sun.
3. Look for shelter and branches to protect from chill.
4. Keep someone at watch for signs of rescuers.

Challenge!
State some creative things to do to be rescued. Answers will vary.

Page 69

Atalanta and the Golden Apples

Many legends have come down to us from ancient Greece, but one of the best is about the remarkable Atalanta, a woman who was beautiful, strong, and fleet of foot.

When Atalanta was born, her father was disappointed, for he had wanted a son. So he took his daughter to a mountainside and left her to die. But Atalanta was discovered by a bear who nursed her and raised her. Later, kindly hunters adopted her and taught her the ways of humans.

As Atalanta grew, she became a strong fighter and a fast runner. In fact, she could run faster than any of the young men she met and could out-wrestle them as well. Because she was beautiful and wise, many men wanted to marry Atalanta. But Atalanta liked her life just as it was and did not want to be married. So she thought of a very clever plan. She announced she would marry the first man who could beat her in a foot race. And although her speed was famous throughout the country, many men came to race against her. But all failed to outrun the swift Atalanta.

Finally, a young man named Melanion challenged her. He was not as swift as many of the others, but he was smarter. From the end of the world, he had gotten three apples of pure gold, which no one could resist.

As the race started, Atalanta sprinted into the lead. Then Melanion rolled one of the golden apples ahead of her. Atalanta could not help stopping to pick it up, and by the time she had retrieved the apple, Melanion had caught up to her. The two runners were side by side for a moment. Then Atalanta took the lead again, and Melanion dropped the second apple. Again, Atalanta stopped to pick it up. Melanion used the last of his strength to take the lead. But when Atalanta saw Melanion ahead of her, she sprinted like the wind into the lead. Then Melanion dropped the last of the golden apples, and as Atalanta stooped to pick it up, she saw Melanion cross the finish line just ahead of her. True to her word, Atalanta married the clever Melanion, for she admired his spirit and wisdom.

Think About It
Do you think Atalanta and Melanion were happy together? Why or why not?

Atalanta is pronounced at a lan'tă.
Melanion is pronounced me lā'ni ăn.

Answers will vary.

Page 70

Atalanta and the Golden Apples (cont.)

Main Idea
1. Choose another title for this story.
___ The Race
_X_ How Melanion Outsmarted Atalanta
___ The Fastest Runner

Sequencing
2. Number the events below in the order that they happened.
_2_ Kindly hunters adopted Atalanta.
_5_ Melanion won by dropping the golden apples.
_1_ Atalanta's father left her on a mountainside.
_4_ Melanion challenged Atalanta to a race.
_6_ Atalanta married Melanion.
_3_ Atalanta announced she would marry the first man who could beat her in a foot race.

Reading for Details
3. Scan the story to answer these questions.
Who nursed Atalanta and raised her? a bear
What plan did Atalanta think of to avoid marriage? She would marry the first man who beat her in a foot race.
Where did Melanion get the three golden apples? from the end of the world
When did Atalanta sprint like the wind? when she saw Melanion ahead of her
Why did Atalanta marry Melanion? because she admired him

Reading for Understanding
4. Check the correct answer(s).
I became a fast runner because
___ I didn't weigh much.
_X_ I was strong.
_X_ I was raised in the wild.
I avoided marriage because
_X_ I was happy with my life.
___ I didn't like men.
___ I was waiting for a bear.
I married Melanion because
_X_ I said I would.
___ I liked him.
_X_ I admired his cleverness.

Page 71

Li Ching and the Rain Makers

According to Chinese legend, dragon-gods made the sky, the earth, and all the people and animals. The dragon-gods lived in splendid homes beyond the sky, where they were responsible for making rain. In this way, the dragon-gods were supposed to take care of the people on earth, but sometimes they needed help.

One day, a great scholar named Li Ching was hunting in the forest when he spotted a deer. Although he chased it for hours, it escaped him, and he found himself in a strange land. Night was coming, and Li Ching was lost. Through the rising mist he saw lights and followed them to a grand palace. His knock on the door was answered by a beautifully dressed woman. She took pity on Li Ching and said he could spend the night.

Li Ching had only been asleep for a few hours when someone woke him up. "You must help me," cried the woman. "My sons are the dragon rain makers. Tonight they were supposed to ride through the sky to make rain, but they cannot return from their travels in time to do so. Our masters will be displeased if there is no rain, for there has been a great drought." She gave Li Ching her sons' magic horse and a small jar. Li Ching was instructed to put one drop of water from the jar on the horse's mane at every cloud.

Li Ching mounted the horse, and it leaped into the air. At every cloud the horse stopped, and Li Ching shook one drop of water onto the horse's mane. The horse tossed its head, and the drop fell to the cloud below. All night they rode, stopping at every cloud, and in the morning they returned to the palace.

The mother of the dragon rain makers was waiting for Li Ching at the gate. "Thank you so much for helping," she said, as she handed him a small silk bag filled with pearls. Then she showed him a path that would lead him back to his village and bid him farewell. As Li Ching looked back, the lady and the palace vanished in the mist.

When Li Ching arrived home, his friends ran to meet him, talking of the great rain that had ended the long drought. Li Ching smiled, but said nothing.

Think About It
Why didn't Li Ching tell his friends what he had done?

Page 72

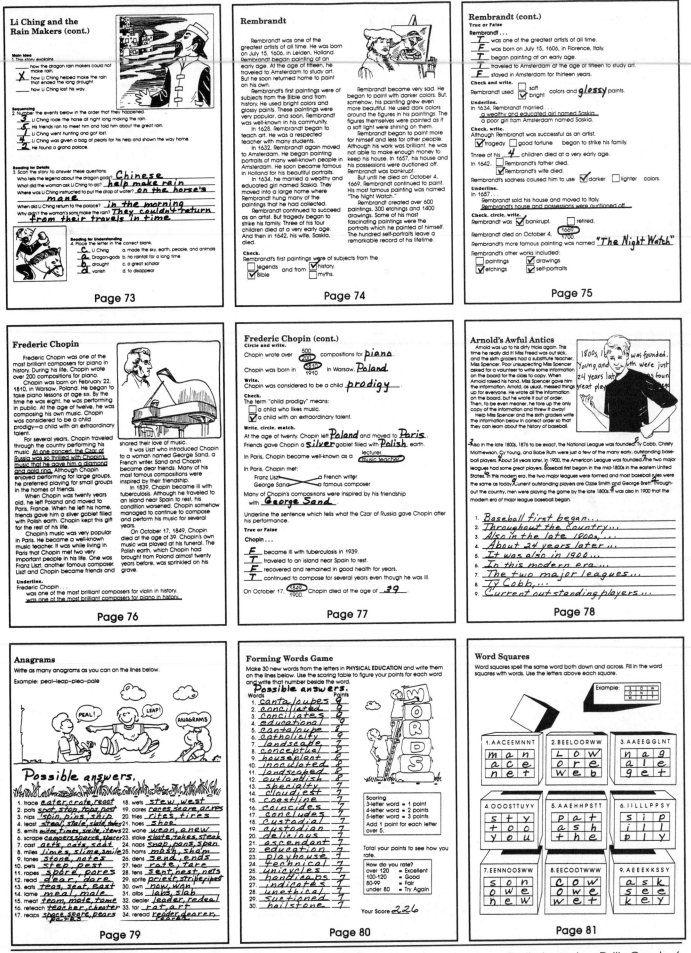

Li Ching and the Rain Makers (cont.)

Main Idea
1. This story explains

____ how the dragon rain makers could not make rain.
X how Li Ching helped make the rain that ended the long drought.
____ how Li Ching lost his way.

Sequencing
2. Number the events below in the order that they happened.

3 Li Ching rode the horse all night long making the rain.
5 His friends ran to meet him and told him about the great rain.
1 Li Ching went hunting and got lost.
4 Li Ching was given a bag of pearls for his help and shown the way home.
2 He found a grand palace.

Reading for Details
3. Scan the story to answer these questions.

Who tells the legend about the dragon gods? Chinese
What did the woman ask Li Ching to do? help make rain
Where was Li Ching instructed to put the drop of water? on the horse's mane
When did Li Ching return to the palace? in the morning
Why didn't the woman's sons make the rain? They couldn't return from their travels in time

Reading for Understanding
4. Place the letter in the correct blank.

c Li Ching — a. made the sky, earth, people, and animals
a Dragon-gods — b. no rainfall for a long time
b drought — c. a great scholar
d vanish — d. to disappear

Page 73

Rembrandt

Rembrandt was one of the greatest artists of all time. He was born on July 15, 1606, in Leiden, Holland. Rembrandt began painting at an early age. At the age of fifteen, he traveled to Amsterdam to study art. But he soon returned home to paint on his own.

Rembrandt's first paintings were of subjects from the Bible and from history. He used bright colors and glossy paints. These paintings were very popular, and soon, Rembrandt was well-known in his community.

In 1628, Rembrandt began to teach art. He was a respected teacher with many students.

In 1632, Rembrandt again moved to Amsterdam. He began painting portraits of many well-known people in Amsterdam. He soon became famous in Holland for his beautiful portraits.

In 1634, he married a wealthy and educated girl named Saskia. They moved into a large home where Rembrandt hung many of the paintings that he had collected.

Rembrandt continued to succeed as an artist. But tragedy began to strike his family. Three of his four children died at a very early age. And then in 1642, his wife, Saskia, died.

Rembrandt became very sad. He began to paint with darker colors. But, somehow, his painting grew even more beautiful. He used dark colors around the figures in his paintings. The figures themselves were painted as if a soft light were shining on them.

Rembrandt began to paint more for himself and less for other people. Although his work was brilliant, he was not able to make enough money to keep his house. In 1657, his house and his possessions were auctioned off. Rembrandt was bankrupt.

But until he died on October 4, 1669, Rembrandt continued to paint. His most famous painting was named "The Night Watch."

Rembrandt created over 600 paintings, 300 etchings and 1400 drawings. Some of his most fascinating paintings were the portraits which he painted of himself. The hundred self-portraits leave a remarkable record of his lifetime.

Check.
Rembrandt's first paintings were of subjects from the
☐ legends ☑ Bible and from ☑ history. ☐ myths.

Page 74

Rembrandt (cont.)

True or False
Rembrandt . . .

T was one of the greatest artists of all time.
F was born on July 15, 1606, in Florence, Italy.
T began painting at an early age.
T traveled to Amsterdam at the age of fifteen to study art.
F stayed in Amsterdam for thirteen years.

Check and write.
Rembrandt used ☐ soft ☑ bright colors and glossy paints.

Underline.
In 1634, Rembrandt married . . .
a wealthy and educated girl named Saskia.
a poor girl from Amsterdam named Saskia.

Check, write.
Although Rembrandt was successful as an artist,
☑ tragedy ☐ good fortune began to strike his family.
Three of his 4 children died at a very early age.
In 1642, ☐ Rembrandt's father died. ☑ Rembrandt's wife died.
Rembrandt's sadness caused him to use ☑ darker ☐ lighter colors.

Underline.
In 1657 . . .
Rembrandt sold his house and moved to Italy.
Rembrandt's house and possessions were auctioned off.

Check, circle, write.
Rembrandt was ☑ bankrupt. ☐ retired.
Rembrandt died on October 4, (1669) 1700.
Rembrandt's more famous painting was named "The Night Watch".
Rembrandt's other works included:
☐ paintings ☑ drawings ☑ etchings ☑ self-portraits

Page 75

Frederic Chopin

Frederic Chopin was one of the most brilliant composers for piano in history. During his life, Chopin wrote over 200 compositions for piano.

Chopin was born on February 22, 1810, in Warsaw, Poland. He began to take piano lessons at age six. By the time he was eight, he was performing in public. At the age of twelve, he was composing his own music. Chopin was considered to be a child prodigy—a child with an extraordinary talent.

For several years, Chopin traveled through the country performing his music. At one concert, the Czar of Russia was so thrilled with Chopin's music that he gave him a diamond and gold ring. Although Chopin enjoyed performing for large groups, he preferred playing for small groups in the homes of friends.

When Chopin was twenty years old, he left Poland and moved to Paris, France. When he left his home, friends gave him a silver goblet filled with Polish earth. Chopin kept this gift for the rest of his life.

Chopin's music was very popular in Paris. He became a well-known music teacher. It was while living in Paris that Chopin met two very important people in his life. One was Franz Liszt, another famous composer. Liszt and Chopin became friends and shared their love of music.

It was Liszt who introduced Chopin to a woman named George Sand, a French writer. Sand and Chopin became dear friends. Many of his most famous compositions were inspired by their friendship.

In 1839, Chopin became ill with tuberculosis. Although he traveled to an island near Spain to rest, his condition worsened. Chopin somehow managed to continue to compose and perform his music for several years.

On October 17, 1849, Chopin died at the age of 39. Chopin's own music was played at his funeral. The Polish earth, which Chopin had brought from Poland almost twenty years before, was sprinkled on his grave.

Underline.
Frederic Chopin . . .
was one of the most brilliant composers for violin in history.
was one of the most brilliant composers for piano in history.

Page 76

Frederic Chopin (cont.)

Circle and write.
Chopin wrote over 500 (200) compositions for piano.
Chopin was born in (1810) 1910 in Warsaw, Poland.

Write.
Chopin was considered to be a child prodigy.

Check.
The term "child prodigy" means:
☐ a child who likes music.
☑ a child with an extraordinary talent.

Write, circle, match.
At the age of twenty, Chopin left Poland and moved to Paris.
Friends gave Chopin a silver goblet filled with Polish earth.
In Paris, Chopin became well-known as a lecturer. (music teacher)
In Paris, Chopin met:
Franz Liszt — famous composer
George Sand — French writer
Many of Chopin's compositions were inspired by his friendship with George Sand.
Underline the sentence which tells what the Czar of Russia gave Chopin after his performance.

True or False
Chopin . . .

F became ill with tuberculosis in 1939.
T traveled to an island near Spain to rest.
F recovered and remained in good health for years.
T continued to compose for several years even though he was ill.

On October 17, (1849) 1900, Chopin died at the age of 39.

Page 77

Arnold's Awful Antics

Arnold was up to his dirty tricks again. This time he really did it! Miss Freed was out sick, and the sixth graders had a substitute teacher, Miss Spencer. Poor unsuspecting Miss Spencer asked for a volunteer to write some information on the board for the class to copy. When Arnold raised his hand, Miss Spencer gave him the information. Arnold, as usual, messed things up for everyone. He wrote all the information on the board, but he wrote it out of order. Then, to be even meaner, he tore up the only copy of the information and threw it away! Help Miss Spencer and the sixth graders write the information below in correct order so that they can learn about the history of baseball.

3 Also in the late 1800s, 1876 to be exact, the National League was founded. 8 Ty Cobb, Christy Mathewson, Cy Young, and Babe Ruth were just a few of the many early, outstanding baseball players. 4 About 24 years later, in 1900, the American League was founded. 7 The two major leagues had some great players. 1 Baseball first began in the mid-1800s in the eastern United States. 6 In this modern era, the two major leagues were formed and most baseball rules were the same as today. 9 Current outstanding players are Ozzie Smith and George Brett. 2 Throughout the country, men were playing the game by the late 1800s. 5 It was also in 1900 that the modern era of major league baseball began.

1. Baseball first began...
2. Throughout the country...
3. Also in the late 1800s,...
4. About 24 years later...
5. It was also in 1900...
6. In this modern era...
7. The two major leagues...
8. Ty Cobb,...
9. Current outstanding players...

Page 78

Anagrams

Write as many anagrams as you can on the lines below.

Example: peal-leap-plea-pale

Possible answers.

1. trace eater, crate, react
2. pots spot, stop, tops, post
3. nips spin, pins, snip
4. least steal, stale, slate, tales
5. emits mites, times, smite, items
6. scrape capers, sparce, spacer
7. cast acts, cats, scat
8. miles limes, slime, smile
9. tones stone, notes
10. pets step, pest
11. ropes spore, pores
12. read dear, dare
13. eats teas, seat, east
14. lame meal, male
15. meat team, mate, tame
16. reteach teacher, cheater
17. reaps space, spare, pears, pares
18. wets stew, west
19. cares races, score, acres
20. tries rites, tires
21. hoes shoe
22. wane wean, anew
23. stake skate, takes, steak
24. naps snap, pans, span
25. hams mash, sham
26. dens send, ends
27. tear rate, tare
28. tens sent, nest, nets
29. sprite priest, stripe, ripest
30. own now, won
31. albs labs, slab
32. dealer leader, redeal
33. tar rat, art
34. reread reader, dearer, reared

Page 79

Forming Words Game

Make 30 new words from the letters in **PHYSICAL EDUCATION** and write them on the lines below. Use the scoring table to figure your points for each word and write that number beside the word.

Possible answers.

Words	Points
1. cantaloupes	9
2. conciliated	9
3. conciliates	9
4. educational	9
5. cantaloupe	8
6. catholicity	9
7. landscape	7
8. conceptual	7
9. houseplant	8
10. inoculated	8
11. landscaped	8
12. outlandish	8
13. specialty	7
14. cloudiest	7
15. coastline	7
16. coincides	7
17. concludes	7
18. custodial	7
19. custodian	7
20. delicious	7
21. ascendant	7
22. education	7
23. playhouse	7
24. technical	7
25. unicycles	7
26. handicaps	7
27. indicates	7
28. unethical	7
29. suctioned	7
30. hailstone	7

Scoring
3-letter word = 1 point
4-letter word = 2 points
5-letter word = 3 points
Add 1 point for each letter over 5.

Total your points to see how you rate.

How do you rate?
over 120 = Excellent
100-120 = Good
80-99 = Fair
under 80 = Try Again

Your Score 226

Page 80

Word Squares

Word squares spell the same word both down and across. Fill in the word squares with words. Use the letters above each square.

Example:

S	O	W
O	N	E
W	E	T

1. AACEEMNNT

m	a	n
a	c	e
n	e	t

2. BEELOORWW

L	O	W
O	r	e
W	e	b

3. AAEEGGLNT

n	a	g
a	l	e
g	e	t

4. OOOSTTUYY

s	t	y
t	o	o
y	o	u

5. AAEHHPSTT

p	a	t
a	s	h
t	h	e

6. IILLLPPSY

s	i	p
i	l	l
p	l	y

7. EENNOOSWW

s	o	n
o	w	e
n	e	w

8. EECOOTWWW

c	o	w
o	w	e
w	e	t

9. AEEEKKSSY

a	s	k
s	e	e
k	e	y

Page 81

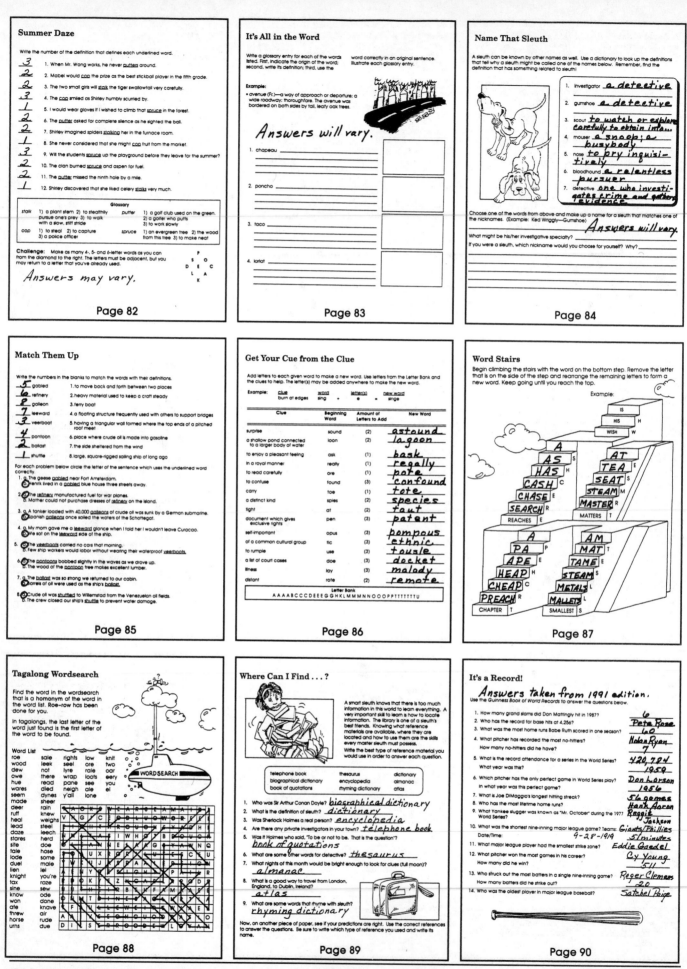

Summer Daze

Write the number of the definition that defines each underlined word.

_3_ 1. When Mr. Wong works, he never *putters* around.
_2_ 2. Mabel would *cop* the prize as the best stickball player in the fifth grade.
_2_ 3. The two small girls will *stalk* the tiger swallowtail very carefully.
_3_ 4. The *cop* smiled as Shirley humbly scurried by.
_1_ 5. I would wear gloves if I wished to climb that *spruce* in the forest.
_2_ 6. The *putter* asked for complete silence as he sighted the ball.
_2_ 7. Shirley imagined spiders *stalking* her in the furnace room.
_1_ 8. She never considered that she might *cop* fruit from the market.
_3_ 9. Will the students *spruce* up the playground before they leave for the summer?
_2_ 10. The clan burned *spruce* and aspen for heat.
_2_ 11. The *putter* missed the ninth hole by a mile.
_1_ 12. Shirley discovered that she liked celery *stalks* very much.

Glossary

stalk 1) a plant stem 2) to stealthily pursue one's prey 3) to walk with a slow, stiff stride
putter 1) a golf club used on the green. 2) a golfer who putts 3) to work slowly
cop 1) to steal 2) to capture 3) a police officer
spruce 1) an evergreen tree 2) the wood from this tree 3) to make neat

Challenge: Make as many 4-, 5- and 6-letter words as you can from the diamond to the right. The letters must be adjacent, but you may return to a letter that you've already used.

P
S O
D E C
L K

Answers may vary.

Page 82

It's All in the Word

Write a glossary entry for each of the words listed. First, indicate the origin of the word; second, write its definition; third, use the word correctly in an original sentence. Illustrate each glossary entry.

Example:
• avenue (Fr.)—a way of approach or departure; a wide roadway; thoroughfare. The avenue was bordered on both sides by tall, leafy oak trees.

Answers will vary.

1. chapeau _____

2. poncho _____

3. taco _____

4. lariat _____

Page 83

Name That Sleuth

A sleuth can be known by other names as well. Use a dictionary to look up the definitions that tell why a sleuth might be called one of the names below. Remember, find the definition that has something related to sleuth!

1. investigator _a detective_
2. gumshoe _a detective_
3. scout _to watch or explore carefully to obtain info..._
4. mouser _a snoop; a busybody_
5. nose _to pry inquisitively_
6. bloodhound _a relentless pursuer_
7. detective _one who investigates crime and gathers evidence_

Choose one of the words from above and make up a name for a sleuth that matches one of the nicknames. (Example: Ked Wriggly—Gumshoe) _Answers will vary._

What might be his/her investigative specialty? _____
If you were a sleuth, which nickname would you choose for yourself? Why? _____

Page 84

Match Them Up

Write the numbers in the blanks to match the words with their definitions.

_5_ gabled
_6_ refinery
_8_ galleon
_7_ leeward
_3_ veerboot
_4_ pontoon
_2_ ballast
_1_ shuttle

1. to move back and forth between two places
2. heavy material used to keep a craft steady
3. ferry boat
4. a floating structure frequently used with others to support bridges
5. having a triangular wall formed where the top ends of a pitched roof meet
6. place where crude oil is made into gasoline
7. the side sheltered from the wind
8. large, square-rigged sailing ship of long ago

For each problem below circle the letter of the sentence which uses the underlined word correctly.

1. a. The geese *gabled* near Fort Amsterdam.
   (b). Henrik lived in a *gabled* blue house three streets away.
2. (a). The *refinery* manufactured fuel for war planes.
   b. Mother could not purchase dresses of *refinery* on the island.
3. a. A tanker loaded with 40,000 *galleons* of crude oil was sunk by a German submarine.
   (b). Spanish *galleons* once sailed the waters of the Schottegat.
4. a. My mom gave me a *leeward* glance when I told her I wouldn't leave Curacao.
   (b). We sat on the *leeward* side of the ship.
5. (a). The *veerboots* carried no cars that morning.
   b. Few ship workers would labor without wearing their waterproof *veerboots*.
6. (a). The *pontoons* bobbed slightly in the waves as we drove up.
   b. The wood of the *pontoon* tree makes excellent lumber.
7. a. The *ballast* was so strong we returned to our cabin.
   (b). Barrels of oil were used as the ship's *ballast*.
8. a. Crude oil was *shuttled* to Willemstad from the Venezuelan oil fields.
   (b). The crew closed our ship's *shuttle* to prevent water damage.

Page 85

Get Your Cue from the Clue

Add letters to each given word to make a new word. Use letters from the Letter Bank and the clues to help. The letter(s) may be added anywhere to make the new word.

Example:
clue: burn at edges | word: sing | + letter(s): e | new word: singe

Clue	Beginning Word	Amount of Letters to Add	New Word
surprise	sound	(2)	astound
a shallow pond connected to a larger body of water	loon	(2)	lagoon
to enjoy a pleasant feeling	ask	(1)	bask
in a royal manner	really	(1)	regally
to read carefully	ore	(1)	pore
to confuse	found	(3)	confound
carry	toe	(1)	tote
a distinct kind	spies	(2)	species
tight	at	(2)	taut
document which gives exclusive rights	pen	(3)	patent
self-important	opus	(3)	pompous
of a common cultural group	tic	(3)	ethnic
to rumple	use	(3)	tousle
a list of court cases	doe	(3)	docket
illness	lay	(3)	malady
distant	rote	(2)	remote

Letter Bank
A A A B C C C D E E E G G H K L M M M N N O O O P P T T T T T T U

Page 86

Word Stairs

Begin climbing the stairs with the word on the bottom step. Remove the letter that is on the side of the step and rearrange the remaining letters to form a new word. Keep going until you reach the top.

Example:
IS
HIS H
WISH W

A
AS S
HAS H
CASH C
CHASE E
SEARCH R
REACHES E

AT
TEA E
SEAT S
STEAM M
MASTER R
MATTERS S

A
PA P
APE E
HEAP H
CHEAP C
PREACH R
CHAPTER T

AM
MAT T
TAME E
STEAM S
METALS L
MALLETS L
SMALLEST S

Page 87

Tagalong Wordsearch

Find the word in the wordsearch that is a homonym of the word in the word list. Roe-row has been done for you.

In tagalongs, the last letter of the word just found is the first letter of the word to be found.

Word List
roe, wood, dew, owe, hue, wares, seem, made, deer, ruff, heal, lead, daze, stares, site, tale, lode, duel, lien, knight, tax, sine, know, won, ate, threw, horse, urns

sale, leek, not, there, read, died, dynes, sheer, rain, knew, weighs, steel, leech, herd, doe, hose, some, male, lei, you're, raze, sew, ode, done, knave, air, rude, due

rights, seel, lyre, wrap, pane, neigh, y'all,

low, ore, rale, loots, see, some,

knit, two, oar, eery, you, el

Page 88

Where Can I Find . . . ?

A smart sleuth knows that there is too much information in this world to learn everything. A very important skill to learn is how to locate information. The library is one of a sleuth's best friends. Knowing what reference materials are available, where they are located and how to use them are the skills every master sleuth must possess.

Write the best type of reference material you would use in order to answer each question.

telephone book | thesaurus | dictionary
biographical dictionary | encyclopedia | almanac
book of quotations | rhyming dictionary | atlas

1. Who was Sir Arthur Conan Doyle? _biographical dictionary_
2. What is the definition of sleuth? _dictionary_
3. Was Sherlock Holmes a real person? _encyclopedia_
4. Are there any private investigators in your town? _telephone book_
5. Was it Holmes who said, 'To be or not to be. That is the question'? _book of quotations_
6. What are some other words for detective? _thesaurus_
7. What nights of this month would be bright enough to look for clues (full moon)? _almanac_
8. What is a good way to travel from London, England, to Dublin, Ireland? _atlas_
9. What are some words that rhyme with sleuth? _rhyming dictionary_

Now, on another piece of paper, see if your predictions are right. Use the correct references to answer the questions. Be sure to write which type of reference you used and write its name.

Page 89

It's a Record!

Answers taken from 1991 edition.
Use the Guinness Book of World Records to answer the questions below.

1. How many grand slams did Don Mattingly hit in 1987? _6_
2. Who has the record for base hits at 4,256? _Pete Rose_
3. What was the most home runs Babe Ruth scored in one season? _60_
4. What pitcher has recorded the most no-hitters? _Nolan Ryan_
   How many no-hitters did he have? _7_
5. What is the record attendance for a series in the World Series? _420,784_
   What year was this? _1959_
6. Which pitcher has the only perfect game in World Series play? _Don Larsen_
   In what year was this perfect game? _1956_
7. What is Joe DiMaggio's longest hitting streak? _56 games_
8. Who has the most lifetime home runs? _Hank Aaron_
9. What Yankee slugger was known as "Mr. October" during the 1977 World Series? _Reggie Jackson_
10. What teams were the shortest nine-inning major league game? _Giants/Phillies_
    Date/Time: _9-28-1919_ _51 minutes_
11. What major league player had the smallest strike zone? _Eddie Gaedel_
12. What pitcher won the most games in his career? _Cy Young_
    How many did he win? _511_
13. Who struck out the most batters in a single nine-inning game? _Roger Clemens_
    How many batters did he strike out? _20_
14. Who was the oldest player in major league baseball? _Satchel Paige_

Page 90

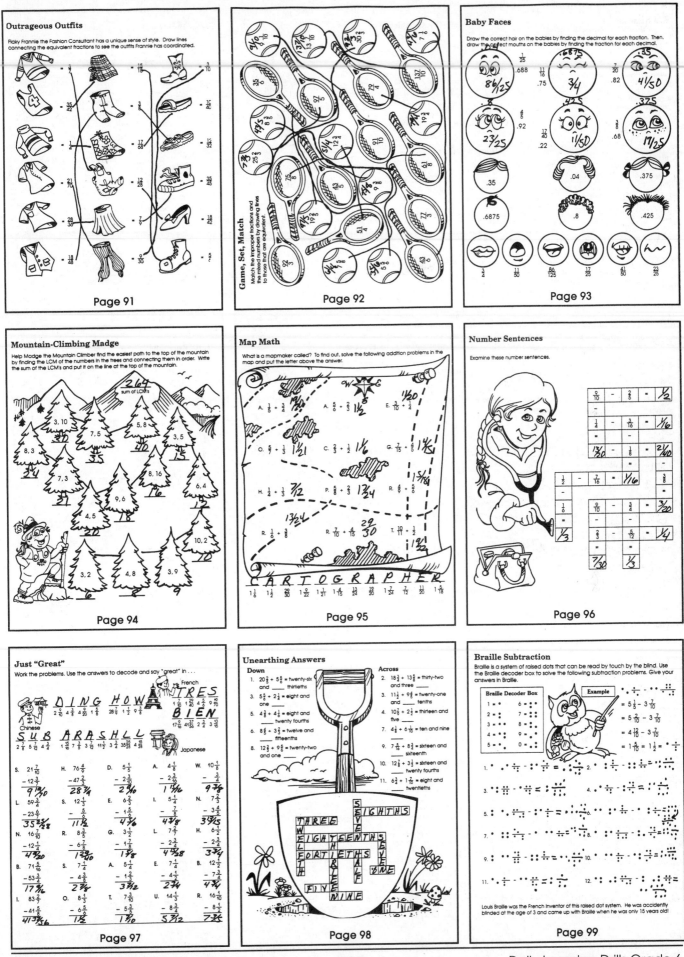

Daily Learning Drills Grade 6

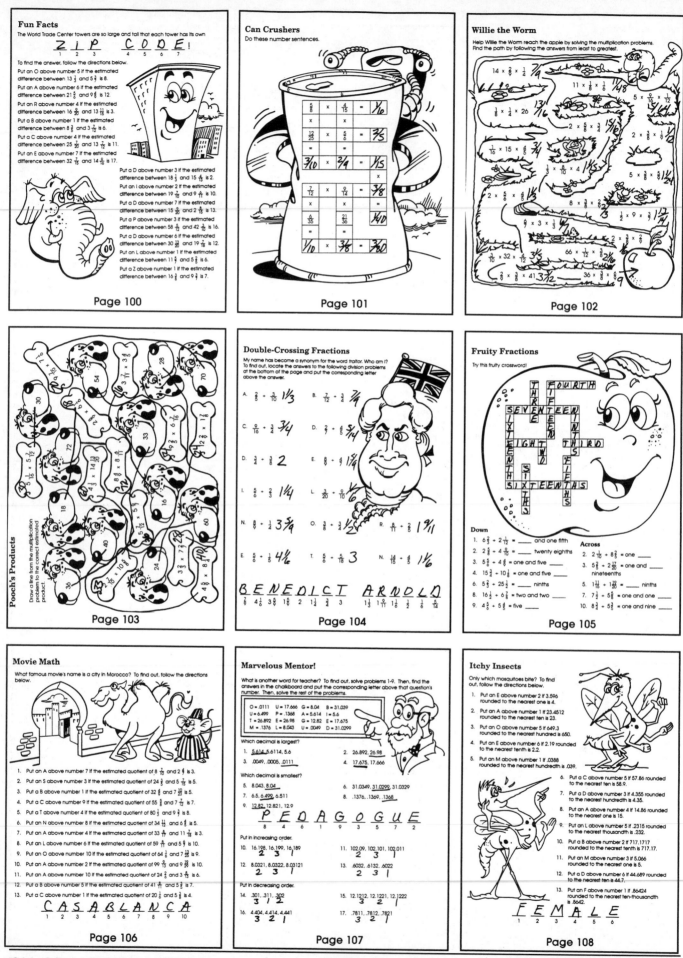

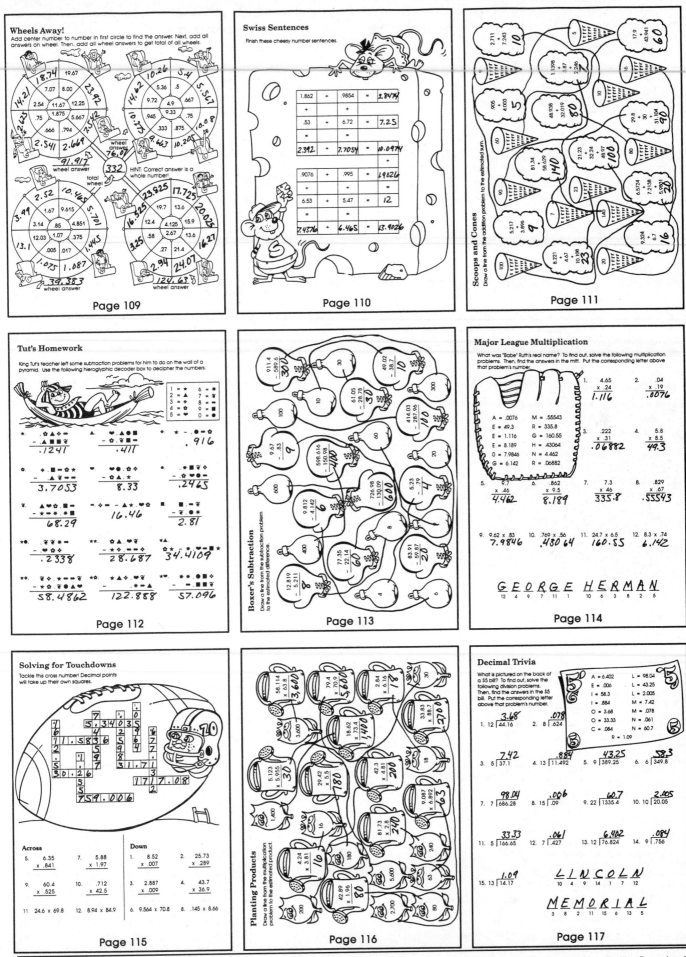

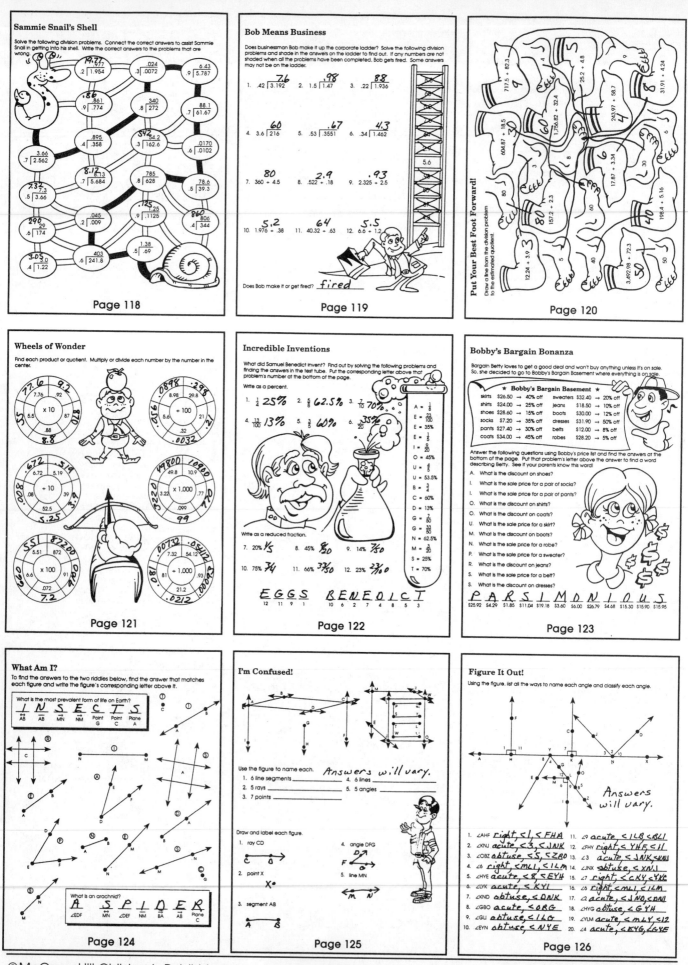

Page 118 — Sammie Snail's Shell

Page 119 — Bob Means Business

Page 120 — Put Your Best Foot Forward!

Page 121 — Wheels of Wonder

Page 122 — Incredible Inventions

Page 123 — Bobby's Bargain Bonanza

Page 124 — What Am I?

Page 125 — I'm Confused!

Page 126 — Figure It Out!

Daily Learning Drills Grade 6

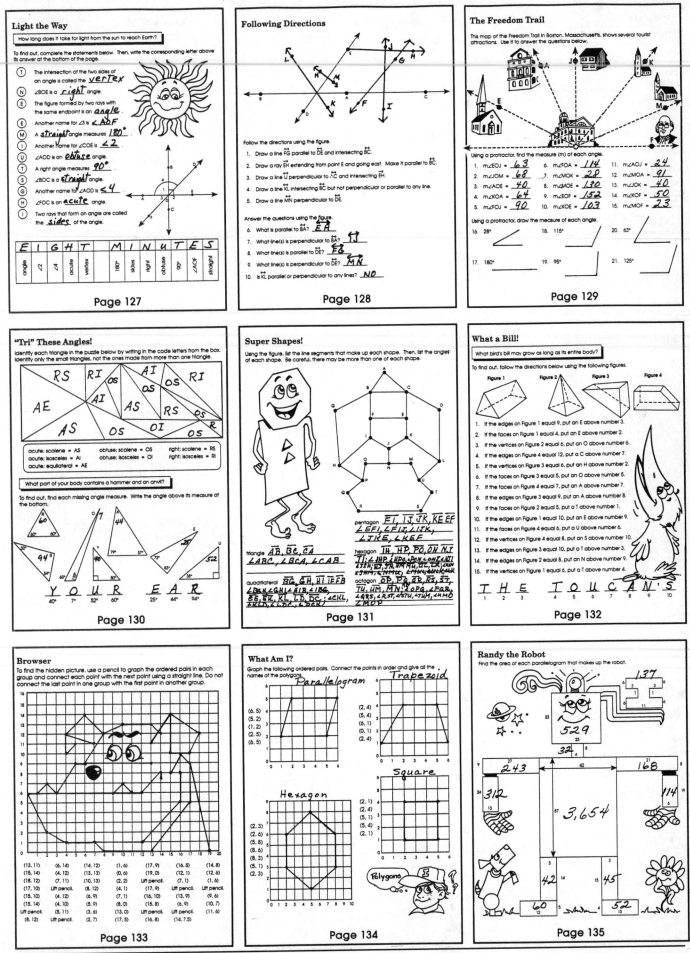

Light the Way

How long does it take for light from the sun to reach Earth?

To find out, complete the statements below. Then, write the corresponding letter above its answer at the bottom of the page.

(T) The intersection of the two sides of an angle is called the **vertex**.
(N) ∠BOE is a **right** angle.
(E) The figure formed by two rays with the same endpoint is an **angle**.
(E) Another name for ∠3 is **∠AOF**.
(M) A **straight** angle measures **180°**.
(I) Another name for ∠COE is **∠2**.
(U) ∠AOD is an **obtuse** angle.
(T) A right angle measures **90°**.
(S) ∠BOC is a **straight** angle.
(G) Another name for ∠AOD is **∠4**.
(H) ∠FOC is an **acute** angle.
(I) Two rays that form an angle are called the **sides** of the angle.

E	I	G	H	T		M	I	N	U	T	E	S
angle	∠2	∠4	acute	vertex		180°	sides	right	obtuse	90°	∠AOF	straight

Page 127

Following Directions

Follow the directions using the figure.

1. Draw a line FG parallel to DE and intersecting BC.
2. Draw a ray EH extending from point E and going east. Make it parallel to BC.
3. Draw a line U perpendicular to AC and intersecting EH.
4. Draw a line KL intersecting BC but not perpendicular or parallel to any line.
5. Draw a line MN perpendicular to DE.

Answer the questions using the figure.

6. What is parallel to BA? **EH**
7. What line(s) is perpendicular to BA? **H**
8. What line(s) is parallel to DE? **FG**
9. What line(s) is perpendicular to DE? **MN**
10. Is KL parallel or perpendicular to any lines? **NO**

Page 128

The Freedom Trail

This map of the Freedom Trail in Boston, Massachusetts, shows several tourist attractions. Use it to answer the questions below.

Using a protractor, find the measure (m) of each angle.

1. m∠EOJ = **63**
2. m∠JOM = **68**
3. m∠AOE = **40**
4. m∠FOJ = **90**
5. (blank)
6. m∠FOA = **114**
7. m∠MOK = **28**
8. m∠MOE = **130**
9. m∠EOF = **152**
10. m∠KOE = **103**
11. m∠AOJ = **24**
12. m∠MOA = **91**
13. m∠JOK = **40**
14. m∠KOF = **50**
15. m∠MOF = **23**

Using a protractor, draw the measure of each angle.

16. 28°   18. 115°   20. 63°
17. 180°   19. 95°   21. 125°

Page 129

"Tri" These Angles!

Identify each triangle in the puzzle below by writing in the code letters from the box. Identify only the small triangles, not the ones made from more than one triangle.

acute; scalene = AS   obtuse; scalene = OS   right; scalene = RS
acute; isosceles = AI   obtuse; isosceles = OI   right; isosceles = RI
acute; equilateral = AE

What part of your body contains a hammer and an anvil?

To find out, find each missing angle measure. Write the angle above its measure at the bottom.

Y	O	U	R		E	A	R
40°	7°	52°	60°		25°	44°	94°

Page 130

Super Shapes!

Using the figure, list the line segments that make up each shape. Then, list the angles of each shape. Be careful, there may be more than one of each shape.

pentagon: EI, IJ, JK, KE EF
∠EFI, ∠FIJ, ∠IJK,
∠JKE, ∠KEF

triangle: AB, BC, CA
∠ABC, ∠BCA, ∠CAB

quadrilateral: BG, GH, HI EFB
∠BGH, ∠GHI, ∠HIB, ∠IBG
EE, EH, KL, LD, DC ∠CKL
∠KLD, ∠LDC, ∠DCK

hexagon: IH, HP, PO, ON NJ
JI ∠IHP ∠HPO ∠PON ∠ONJ
∠NJI, JN, NM MU, UL, LK, KM
∠JNM,∠NMU,∠MUL,∠ULK,∠LKJ

octagon: OP, PQ, QR, RS, ST,
TU, UM, MN ∠OPQ, ∠PQR,
∠QRS, ∠RST, ∠STU, ∠TUM, ∠UMO
∠MOP

Page 131

What a Bill!

What bird's bill may grow as long as its entire body?

To find out, follow the directions below using the following figures.

Figure 1   Figure 2   Figure 3   Figure 4

1. If the edges on Figure 1 equal 9, put an E above number 3.
2. If the edges on Figure 1 equal 4, put an E above number 2.
3. If the vertices on Figure 2 equal 6, put an O above number 6.
4. If the edges on Figure 4 equal 12, put a C above number 7.
5. If the vertices on Figure 3 equal 6, put an H above number 2.
6. If the faces on Figure 3 equal 5, put an O above number 4.
7. If the faces on Figure 4 equal 7, put an A above number 7.
8. If the edges on Figure 3 equal 9, put an A above number 8.
9. If the faces on Figure 2 equal 5, put a T above number 1.
10. If the faces on Figure 1 equal 10, put an E above number 9.
11. If the faces on Figure 4 equal 6, put a U above number 6.
12. If the vertices on Figure 4 equal 8, put an S above number 10.
13. If the edges on Figure 3 equal 10, put a T above number 3.
14. If the edges on Figure 2 equal 8, put an N above number 4.
15. If the vertices on Figure 1 equal 6, put a T above number 4.

T	H	E		T	O	U	C	A	N	'S
1	2	3		4	5	6	7	8	9	10

Page 132

Browser

To find the hidden picture, use a pencil to graph the ordered pairs in each group and connect each point with the next point using a straight line. Do not connect the last point in one group with the first point in another group.

(13, 11) (6, 14) (14, 12) (1, 6) (17, 9) (16, 5) (14, 8)
(15, 14) (4, 12) (13, 13) (0, 6) (19, 0) (12, 1) (12, 6)
(18, 12) (7, 11) (10, 13) (2, 4) Lift pencil. (7, 1) (1, 6)
(17, 10) Lift pencil. (8, 12) (4, 1) (17, 9) Lift pencil. Lift pencil.
(15, 10) (4, 12) (6, 9) (7, 1) (13, 9) (9, 6)
(15, 14) (4, 10) (5, 9) (8, 0) (15, 8) (6, 9) (10, 7)
Lift pencil. (5, 11) (3, 6) (13, 0) Lift pencil. Lift pencil. (11, 6)
(8, 12) Lift pencil. (2, 7) (17, 5) (16, 8) (14, 7.5)

Page 133

What Am I?

Graph the following ordered pairs. Connect the points in order and give all the names of the polygons.

Parallelogram
(6, 5)
(5, 2)
(1, 2)
(2, 5)
(6, 5)

Trapezoid
(2, 4)
(5, 4)
(6, 1)
(0, 1)
(2, 4)

Hexagon
(2, 3)
(2, 6)
(5, 8)
(8, 6)
(8, 3)
(5, 1)
(2, 3)

Square
(2, 1)
(2, 4)
(5, 4)
(5, 1)
(2, 1)

Polygons

Page 134

Randy the Robot

Find the area of each parallelogram that makes up the robot.

Page 135

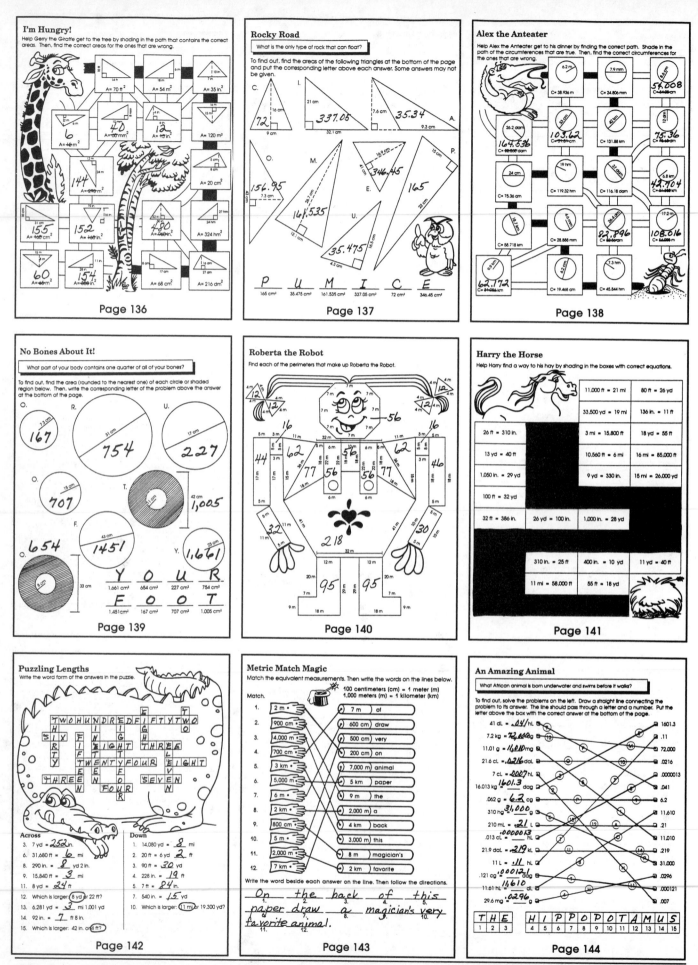

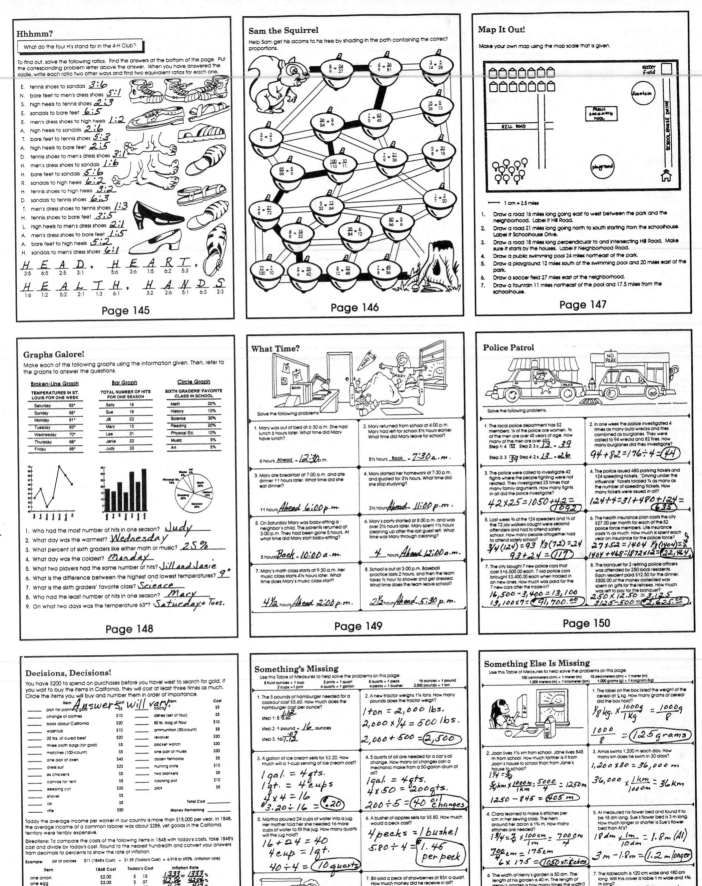

Page 145

Page 146

Page 147

Page 148

Page 149

Page 150

Page 151

Page 152

Page 153

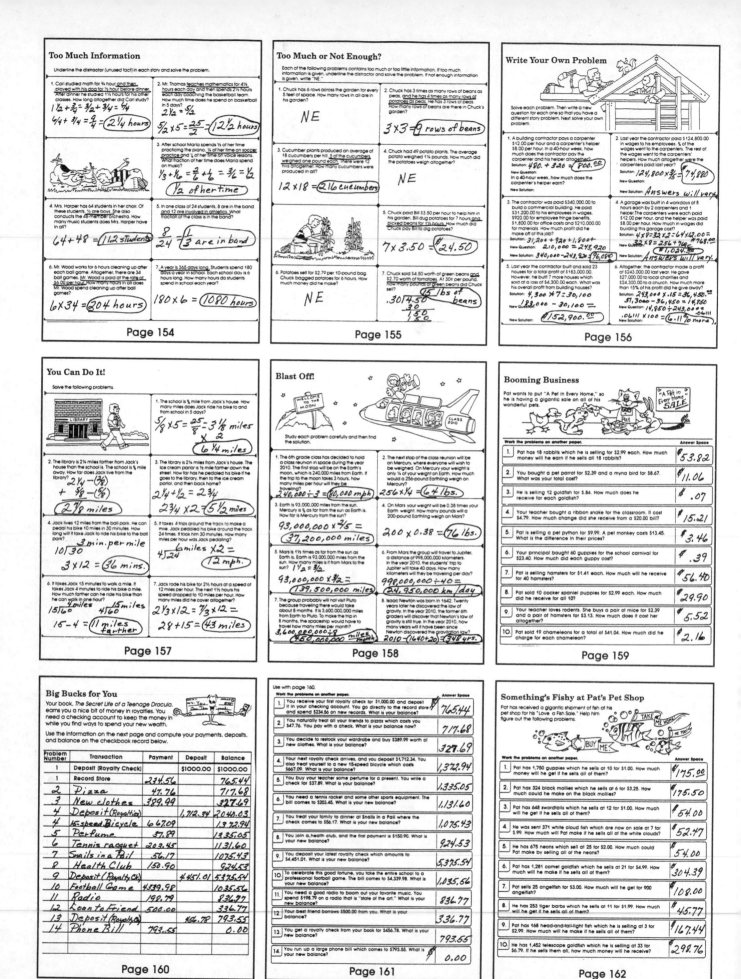

Too Much Information

Underline the distractor (unused fact) in each story and solve the problem.

1. Carl studied math for ¾ hour and then played with his dog for ½ hour before dinner. After dinner he studied 1½ hours for his other classes. How long altogether did Carl study?
   $1\frac{1}{2}+\frac{3}{4}=\frac{3}{2}+\frac{3}{4}=\frac{6}{4}$
   $\frac{6}{4}+\frac{3}{4}=\frac{9}{4}=$ (2¼ hours)

2. Mr. Thomas teaches mathematics for 4½ hours each day and then spends 2½ hours each day coaching the basketball team. How much time does he spend on basketball in 5 days?
   $2\frac{1}{2}=\frac{5}{2}$
   $\frac{5}{2}\times 5=\frac{25}{2}=$ (12½ hours)

3. After school Maria spends ⅓ of her time practicing the piano, ¼ of her time on soccer practice and ⅙ of her time on voice lessons. What fraction of her time does Maria spend on music?
   $\frac{1}{3}+\frac{1}{6}=\frac{2}{6}+\frac{1}{6}=\frac{3}{6}=\frac{1}{2}$
   (½ of her time)

4. Mrs. Harper has 64 students in her choir. Of these students, ⅓ are boys. She also conducts the 48-member orchestra. How many music students does Mrs. Harper have in all?
   64 + 48 = (112 students)

5. In one class of 24 students, 8 are in the band and 12 are involved in athletics. What fraction of the class is in the band?
   $\frac{8}{24}=$ ($\frac{1}{3}$ are in band)

6. Mr. Wood works for 6 hours cleaning up after each ball game. Altogether, there are 34 ball games. Mr. Wood is paid at the rate of $6.00 per hour. How many hours in all does Mr. Wood spend cleaning up after ball games?
   6 × 34 = (204 hours)

7. A year is 365 days long. Students spend 180 days a year in school. Each school day is 6 hours long. How many hours do students spend in school each year?
   180 × 6 = (1080 hours)

Page 154

Too Much or Not Enough?

Each of the following problems contains too much or too little information. If too much information is given, underline the distractor and solve the problem. If not enough information is given, write "NE."

1. Chuck has 6 rows across the garden for every 5 feet of space. How many rows in all are in his garden?
   NE

2. Chuck has 3 times as many rows of beans as peas, and he has 4 times as many rows of potatoes as peas. He has 3 rows of peas. How many rows of beans are there in Chuck's garden?
   3 × 3 = (9 rows of beans)

3. Cucumber plants produced an average of 18 cucumbers per hill. 5 of the cucumbers weighed one pound each. There were 12 hills altogether. How many cucumbers were produced in all?
   12 × 18 = (216 cucumbers)

4. Chuck had 49 potato plants. The average potato weighed 1¼ pounds. How much did the potatoes weigh altogether?
   NE

5. Chuck paid Bill $3.50 per hour to help him in his garden. Bill dug potatoes for 7 hours and picked beans for 1½ hours. How much did Chuck pay Bill to dig potatoes?
   7 × 3.50 = ($24.50)

6. Potatoes sell for $2.79 per 10-pound bag. Chuck bagged potatoes for 6 hours. How much money did he make?
   NE

7. Chuck sold $4.50 worth of green beans and $2.70 worth of tomatoes. At 30¢ per pound, how many pounds of green beans did Chuck sell?
   .30 ⟌ 4.50 = (15 lbs of beans)
   30
   150
   150

Page 155

Write Your Own Problem

Solve each problem. Then write a new question for each one so that you have a different story problem. Next solve your own problem.

1. A building contractor pays a carpenter $12.00 per hour and a carpenter's helper $8.00 per hour. In a 40-hour week, how much does the contractor pay the carpenter and his helper altogether?
   Solution: 480. + 320 = (800.00)
   New Question:
   In a 40-hour week, how much does the carpenter's helper earn?
   New Solution:

2. Last year the contractor paid $124,800.00 in wages to his employees. ⅗ of the wages went to the carpenters. The rest of the wages went to the carpenters' helpers. How much altogether were the carpenters paid last year?
   Solution: 124,800 × ⅗ = (74,880)
   New Question:
   New Solution: Answers will vary.

3. The contractor was paid $340,000.00 to build a commercial building. He paid $31,200.00 to his employees in wages, $920.00 for employee fringe benefits, $1,800.00 for office costs and $210,000.00 for materials. How much profit did he make off of this job?
   Solution: 31,200 + 920 + 1,800 +
   New Question: 210,000 = 243,920
   New Solution: 340,000 − 243,920 = (96,080)

4. A garage was built in 4 workdays of 8 hours each by 2 carpenters and 1 helper. The carpenters were each paid $12.00 per hour, and the helper was paid $8.00 per hour. How much in wages did building this garage cost?
   Solution: 4 × 8 = 32 × 2 = 64 × 12.00 = $768.00
   New Question: 32 × 8 = 256 + 768 = ($1,024.00)
   New Solution: Answers will vary.

5. Last year the contractor built and sold 23 houses for a total profit of $183,000.00. However, he built 7 more houses which sold at a loss of $4,300.00 each. What was his overall profit from building houses?
   Solution: 4,300 × 7 = 30,100
   New Question: 183,000 − 30,100 =
   New Solution: ($152,900.00)

6. Altogether, the contractor made a profit of $243,000.00 last year. He gave $27,000.00 to local charities and $24,300.00 to a church. How much more than 15% of his profit did he give away?
   Solution: 243,000 × .15 = 36,450.00
   51,300 − 36,450 = 14,850
   New Question: 14,850 ÷ 243,000 = .06111
   New Solution: .06111 × 100 = (6.11% more)

Page 156

You Can Do It!

Solve the following problems.

1. The school is ⅝ mile from Jack's house. How many miles does Jack ride his bike to and from school in 5 days?
   $\frac{5}{8}\times 5=\frac{25}{8}=3\frac{1}{8}$ miles
   × 2
   (6¼ miles)

2. The library is 2¼ miles farther from Jack's house than the school is. The school is ⅝ mile away. How far does Jack live from the library?
   2¼ − (2⅜)
   + ⅝ − (⅝)
   (2⅞ miles)

3. The library is 2¼ miles from Jack's house. The ice cream parlor is ½ mile farther down the street. How far has he pedaled his bike if he goes to the library, then to the ice cream parlor, and then back home?
   2¼ + ½ = 2¾
   2¾ × 2 = (5½ miles)

4. Jack lives 12 miles from the ball park. He can pedal his bike 10 miles in 30 minutes. How long will it take Jack to ride his bike to the ball park?
   10 ⟌ 30 = 3 min. per mile
   3 × 12 = (36 mins.)

5. It takes 4 trips around the track to make a mile. Jack pedaled his bike around the track 24 times. It took him 30 minutes. How many miles per hour was Jack pedaling?
   4 ⟌ 24 = 6 miles × 2 =
   (12 mph.)

6. It takes Jack 15 minutes to walk a mile. It takes Jack 4 minutes to ride his bike a mile. How much farther can he ride his bike than he can walk in one hour?
   15 ⟌ 60 = 4 miles 4 ⟌ 60 = 15 miles
   15 − 4 = (11 miles farther)

7. Jack rode his bike for 2⅓ hours at a speed of 12 miles per hour. The next 1½ hours his speed dropped to 10 miles per hour. How many miles did he cover altogether?
   $2\frac{1}{3}\times 12=\frac{7}{3}\times 12=$
   28 + 15 = (43 miles)

Page 157

Blast Off!

Study each problem carefully and then find the solution.

1. The 6th grade class has decided to hold a class reunion in space during the year 2010. The first stop will be on the Earth's moon, which is 240,000 miles from Earth. If the trip to the moon takes 3 hours, how many miles per hour will they be traveling?
   240,000 ÷ 3 = (80,000 mph)

2. The next stop of the class reunion will be on Mercury, where everyone will wish to be weighed. On Mercury your weight is only ¼ of your weight on Earth. How much would a 256-pound Earthling weigh on Mercury?
   256 × ¼ = (64 lbs.)

3. Earth is 93,000,000 miles from the sun. Mercury is ⅖ as far from the sun as Earth is. How far is Mercury from the sun?
   93,000,000 × ⅖ =
   (37,200,000 miles)

4. On Mars your weight will be 0.38 times your Earth weight. How many pounds will a 200-pound Earthling weigh on Mars?
   200 × 0.38 = (76 lbs.)

5. Mars is 1½ times as far from the sun as Earth is. Earth is 93,000,000 miles from the sun. How many miles is it from Mars to the sun? 1½ = 3/2
   93,000,000 × 3/2 =
   (139,500,000 miles)

6. From Mars the group will travel to Jupiter, a distance of 998,000,000 kilometers. In the year 2010, the students' trip to Jupiter will take 40 days. How many kilometers will they be traveling per day?
   998,000,000 ÷ 40 =
   (24,950,000 km/day)

7. The group probably will not visit Pluto because traveling there would take about 8 months. It is 3,600,000,000 miles from Earth to Pluto. To make the trip in 8 months, the spaceship would have to travel how many miles per month?
   3,600,000,000 ÷ 8
   (450,000,000 miles/month)

8. Isaac Newton was born in 1642. Twenty years later he discovered the law of gravity. In the year 2010, the former 6th graders will discover that Newton's law of gravity is still true. In the year 2010, how many years will it have been since Newton discovered the gravitation law?
   2010 − (1640 + 20) = (348 yrs.)

Page 158

Booming Business

Pat wants to put "A Pet in Every Home," so he is having a gigantic sale on all of his wonderful pets.

Work the problems on another paper.

		Answer Space
1.	Pat has 18 rabbits which he is selling for $2.99 each. How much money will he earn if he sells all 18 rabbits?	$53.82
2.	You bought a pet parrot for $2.39 and a myna bird for $8.67. What was your total cost?	$11.06
3.	He is selling 12 goldfish for $.84. How much does he receive for each goldfish?	$ .07
4.	Your teacher bought a ribbon snake for the classroom. It cost $4.79. How much change did she receive from a $20.00 bill?	$15.21
5.	Pat is selling a pet python for $9.99. A pet monkey costs $13.45. What is the difference in their prices?	$3.46
6.	Your principal bought 60 guppies for the school carnival for $23.40. How much did each guppy cost?	$ .39
7.	Pat is selling hamsters for $1.41 each. How much will he receive for 40 hamsters?	$56.40
8.	Pat sold 10 cocker spaniel puppies for $2.99 each. How much did he receive for all 10?	$29.90
9.	Your teacher loves rodents. She buys a pair of mice for $2.39 and a pair of hamsters for $3.13. How much does it cost her altogether?	$5.52
10.	Pat sold 19 chameleons for a total of $41.04. How much did he charge for each chameleon?	$2.16

Page 159

Big Bucks for You

Your book, *The Secret Life of a Teenage Dracula*, earns you a nice bit of money in royalties. You need a checking account to keep the money in while you find ways to spend your new wealth.

Use the information on the next page and compute your payments, deposits, and balance on the checkbook record below.

Problem Number	Transaction	Payment	Deposit	Balance
1	Deposit (Royalty Check)		$1000.00	$1000.00
1	Record Store	234.56		765.44
2	Pizza	47.76		717.68
3	New clothes	389.99		327.69
4	Deposit (Royalties)		1,712.34	2040.03
4	15-speed Bicycle	667.09		1372.94
5	Perfume	37.89		1335.05
6	Tennis racquet	203.45		1131.60
7	Snails in a Pail	56.17		1075.43
8	Health Club	150.90		924.53
9	Deposit (Royalty Ck.)		4451.01	5375.54
10	Football Game	4339.98		1035.56
11	Radio	198.79		836.77
12	Loan to Friend	500.00		336.77
13	Deposit (Royalty Ck.)		456.78	793.55
14	Phone Bill	793.55		0.00

Page 160

Use with page 160.

Work the problems on another paper.

		Answer Space
1.	You receive your first royalty check for $1,000.00 and deposit it in your checking account. You go directly to the record store and spend $234.56 on new records. What is your balance?	$765.44
2.	You naturally treat all your friends to pizzas which costs you $47.76. You pay with a check. What is your balance now?	717.68
3.	You decide to restock your wardrobe and buy $389.99 worth of new clothes. What is your balance?	327.69
4.	Your next royalty check arrives, and you deposit $1,712.34. You also treat yourself to a new 15-speed bicycle which costs $667.09. What is your balance?	1,372.94
5.	You buy your teacher some perfume for a present. You write a check for $37.89. What is your balance?	1,335.05
6.	You need a tennis racket and some other sports equipment. The bill comes to $203.45. What is your new balance?	1,131.60
7.	You treat your family to dinner at Snails in a Pail where the check comes to $56.17. What is your new balance?	1,075.43
8.	You join a health club, and the first payment is $150.90. What is your new balance?	924.53
9.	You deposit your latest royalty check which amounts to $4,451.01. What is your new balance?	5,375.54
10.	To celebrate this good fortune, you take the entire school to a professional football game. The bill comes to $4,339.98. What is your new balance?	1,035.56
11.	You need a good radio to boom out your favorite music. You spend $198.79 on a radio that is "state of the art." What is your new balance?	836.77
12.	Your best friend borrows $500.00 from you. What is your balance?	336.77
13.	You get a royalty check from your book for $456.78. What is your new balance?	793.55
14.	You run up a large phone bill which comes to $793.55. What is your new balance?	$ 0.00

Page 161

Something's Fishy at Pat's Pet Shop

Pat has received a gigantic shipment of fish at his pet shop for his "Love a Fish Sale." Help him figure out the following problems.

Work the problems on another paper.

		Answer Space
1.	Pat has 1,750 guppies which he sells at 10 for $1.00. How much money will he get if he sells all of them?	$175.00
2.	Pat has 324 black mollies which he sells at 6 for $3.25. How much could he make on the black mollies?	$175.50
3.	Pat has 648 swordtails which he sells at 12 for $1.00. How much will he get if he sells all of them?	$54.00
4.	He was sent 371 white cloud fish which are now on sale at 7 for $.99. How much will Pat make if he sells all of the white clouds?	$52.47
5.	He has 675 neons which sell at 25 for $2.00. How much could Pat make by selling all of the neons?	$54.00
6.	Pat has 1,281 comet goldfish which he sells at 21 for $4.99. How much will he make if he sells all of them?	$304.39
7.	Pat sells 25 angelfish for $3.00. How much will he get for 900 angelfish?	$108.00
8.	He has 253 tiger barbs which he sells at 11 for $1.99. How much will he get if he sells all of them?	$45.77
9.	Pat has 168 head-and-tail-light fish which he is selling at 3 for $2.99. How much will he make if he sells all of them?	$167.44
10.	He has 1,452 telescope goldfish which he is selling at 33 for $6.79. If he sells them all, how much money will he receive?	$298.76

Page 162

306 Daily Learning Drills Grade 6

Hairy Spiders and Mighty Mites

Work the problems on another paper.

		Answer Space
1.	A male spitting spider is 4/16 in. long. A female is 3/8 in. long. How much longer is the female?	1/8 in.
2.	A forest wolf spider is 1/2 in. long. A female rabid wolf spider is 3/4 in. long. What is the difference in their lengths?	1/4 in.
3.	A male trapdoor spider is 11/12 in. long. A violin spider is 1/4 in. long. How much longer is the trapdoor spider?	2/3 in.
4.	A female green lynx spider is 5/8 in. long. A male is 1/2 in. long. What is their total length?	1 1/8 in.
5.	A male barn spider is 2/3 in. long. A female is 7/8 in. long. What is their total length?	1 13/24 in.
6.	A male hammock spider is 1/4 in. long. A female is 1/3 in. long. What is their total length?	7/12 in.
7.	A velvet mite is 1/8 in. long. A soft tick is 3/12 in. long. What is the difference in their lengths?	1/8 in.
8.	A spider mite is only 1/32 in. long. A water mite is 1/8 in. long. How much longer is a water mite?	3/32 in.
9.	A female garden spider is 3/4 in. long. A male is 6/12 in. long. How much longer is the female?	1/4 in.
10.	A female bola spider is 1/2 in. long. A male bola is 1/12 in. long. What is the total?	7/12 in.

Page 163

Eartha Wurm's Pizzas

Eartha Wurm believes that pizzas have become flat, dull, tasteless and boring. She has created new pizza toppings to put some zing back into your taste buds.

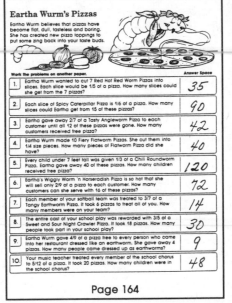

Work the problems on another paper.

		Answer Space
1.	Eartha Wurm wanted to cut 7 Red Hot Red Worm Pizzas into slices. Each slice would be 1/5 of a pizza. How many slices could she get from the 7 pizzas?	35
2.	Each slice of Spicy Caterpillar Pizza is 1/6 of a pizza. How many slices could Eartha get from 15 of these pizzas?	90
3.	Eartha gave away 2/7 of a Tasty Angleworm Pizza to each customer until all 12 of these pizzas were gone. How many customers received free pizza?	42
4.	Eartha Wurm made 10 Fiery Flatworm Pizzas. She cut them into 1/4 size pieces. How many pieces of Flatworm Pizza did she have?	40
5.	Every child under 7 feet tall was given 1/3 of a Chili Roundworm Pizza. Eartha gave away 40 of these pizzas. How many children received free pizza?	120
6.	Eartha's Wiggly Worm 'n Horseradish Pizza is so hot that she will sell only 2/9 of a pizza to each customer. How many customers can she serve with 16 of these pizzas?	72
7.	Each member of your softball team was treated to 3/7 of a Tangy Earthworm Pizza. It took 6 pizzas to treat all of you. How many members were on your team?	14
8.	The entire cast of your school play was rewarded with 3/5 of a Sweet and Sour Night Crawler Pizza. It took 18 pizzas. How many people took part in your school play?	30
9.	Eartha Wurm gave 4/9 of a pizza free to every person who came into her restaurant dressed like an earthworm. She gave away 4 pizzas. How many people came dressed up as earthworms?	9
10.	Your music teacher treated every member of the school chorus to 5/12 of a pizza. It took 20 pizzas. How many children were in the school chorus?	48

Page 164

Sam Sillicook's Secret Recipe!

Sam Sillicook, world-famous pizza maker, has just published his super secret recipe for The Tongue Blaster Pizza. It contains:

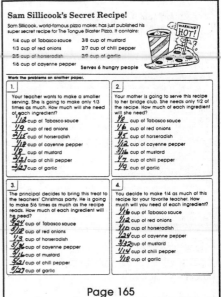

1/4 cup of Tabasco sauce	3/8 cup of mustard
1/3 cup of red onions	2/7 cup of chili pepper
2/5 cup of horseradish	2/9 cup of garlic
1/6 cup of cayenne pepper	Serves 6 hungry people

Work the problems on another paper.

1. Your teacher wants to make a smaller serving. She is going to make only 1/3 times as much. How much will she need of each ingredient?
   - 1/12 cup of Tabasco sauce
   - 1/9 cup of red onions
   - 2/15 cup of horseradish
   - 1/18 cup of cayenne pepper
   - 1/8 cup of mustard
   - 2/21 cup of chili pepper
   - 2/27 cup of garlic

2. Your mother is going to serve this recipe to her bridge club. She needs only 1/2 of the recipe. How much of each ingredient will she need?
   - 1/8 cup of Tabasco sauce
   - 1/6 cup of red onions
   - 1/5 cup of horseradish
   - 1/12 cup of cayenne pepper
   - 3/16 cup of mustard
   - 1/7 cup of chili pepper
   - 1/9 cup of garlic

3. The principal decides to bring this treat to the teachers' Christmas party. He is going to make 5/6 times as much as the recipe reads. How much of each ingredient will he need?
   - 5/24 cup of Tabasco sauce
   - 5/18 cup of red onions
   - 1/3 cup of horseradish
   - 5/36 cup of cayenne pepper
   - 5/16 cup of mustard
   - 5/21 cup of chili pepper
   - 5/27 cup of garlic

4. You decide to make 1/4 as much of this recipe for your favorite teacher. How much will you need of each ingredient?
   - 1/16 cup of Tabasco sauce
   - 1/12 cup of red onions
   - 1/10 cup of horseradish
   - 1/24 cup of cayenne pepper
   - 3/32 cup of mustard
   - 1/14 cup of chili pepper
   - 1/18 cup of garlic

Page 165

Krab E. Krabby

Krab E. Krabby likes to make unusual things, but he gets very cranky trying to figure out how much material he needs. Give him a hand so he won't be crabby.

Work the problems on another paper.

		Answer Space
1.	Krab E. Krabby wants to make a paper clip jump rope 60 inches long. Each paper clip is 1 1/4 in. long. How many paper clips will he need?	48
2.	Mr. Krabby wants to make a 39-inch-long belt by stringing string beans together. Each string bean is exactly 3 1/4 in. long. How many string beans will he need?	12
3.	Krab E. Krabby hopes to make a 45-inch-high tower using dead batteries. Each battery is 2 1/2 in. tall. How many batteries will he need?	18
4.	He is anxious to make a 9-inch-long wristband of seashells for his favorite teacher. He is going to use 1 1/8-inch-long seashells. How many will he need?	8
5.	Krab would like to put a 180-inch border around his teacher's desk using pine cones that are 4 1/2 in. long. How many cones will he need?	40
6.	Krabby wants to give his sister a 30-inch-long string of beads for her birthday. Each bead is 1 1/2 inches in diameter. How many beads will he need?	20
7.	He is going to put together a 13-inch headband decorated with buttons that are 1 5/8 inches in diameter. How many buttons will he need?	8
8.	He is going to glue together bottle caps that are 1 7/8 inch in diameter to make a school banner 150 inches long. How many bottle caps will he need?	80
9.	Krab is gluing jumbo jellybeans end-to-end to create a jellybean necklace 20 inches long for his girlfriend. Each jellybean is 2 1/2 in. long. How many of them will he need?	8
10.	Krabby wants to make an 81-inch border for the science counter using clam shells that are exactly 3 3/8 in. long. How many clam shells will he need?	24

Page 166

The Super Twist

Mr. M.T. Whole has invented a whole new kind of doughnut which he calls the Super Twist. It is filled with whipped cream, jammed with jelly and topped with powdered sugar.

Work the problems on another paper.

		Answer Space
1.	M.T. Whole uses 3 1/2 gallons of milk to make a batch of Whole Jelly Twists. He uses 1 3/4 gallons of milk for a batch of Plain Twists. What is the difference?	1 3/4 gal.
2.	M.T. Whole needs 10 1/3 gallons of jam a week for his Super Jam-Filled Doughnut Twists. He needs only 4/5 as much jam for his Regular Jam Doughnuts. How much does he need for them?	8 4/15 gal.
3.	Mr. Whole wants to make as many Super Twists as he can with 280 ounces of strawberry jam. Each twist uses 2 4/5 ounces of jam. How many Super Twists can he make?	100
4.	M.T. is making a huge batch of Creamy Blackberry Twists which requires 198 5/6 ounces of flour. He is also using 134 7/8 ounces of flour for his Plain Twists. What is the total?	333 17/24
5.	His Stuffed Strawberry Twists use 1 1/3 ounces of jam in each twist. How many twists can he fill with 124 ounces of jam?	93
6.	M.T.'s Chock Full of Chocolate Twists require 3 5/7 ounces of chocolate for each one. How many ounces of chocolate are in 84 Chock Full of Chocolate Twists?	312
7.	In one week, M.T. uses 114 1/2 gallons of milk and 99 7/9 gallons of cream. How much more milk does he use in a week?	14 13/18
8.	M.T. uses 66 1/2 ounces of grape jelly for his Great Grape Twists. A batch of his Blueberry Twists requires 49 9/10 ounces of jelly. How many more ounces of grape jelly does he use?	16 3/5
9.	Mr. M.T. Whole is especially proud of the Dreamy Creamy Twist, a scrumptious doughnut that uses 2 8/9 ounces of creamy filling. How many ounces of filling are in 84 Dreamy Creamy Twists?	242 2/3
10.	M.T. Whole's Chock Full of Chocolate Twists each require 4 1/3 ounces of flour. How many ounces does he need for 180 of these doughnuts?	1170 oz.

Page 167

The Super Sac

McMealworms wants your business. They have just introduced the Super Sac, a triple decker McMealworm Burger that comes with Roasted Roaches and a Cricket Cola.

Work the problems on another paper.

		Answer Space
1.	You buy a Super Sac for $3.79. How much change do you get from a $20.00 bill?	$16.21
2.	Your best friend buys a Super Sac for $3.79 and an extra order of Roasted Roaches for $.79. What is his total bill?	$4.58
3.	The largest cockroach you can find in your order of Roasted Roaches is 5.1 cm long. The shortest is 3.99 cm long. What is their total length?	9.09 cm
4.	Your mother spends $14.39 at McMealworms, and your sister spends another $4.99. What is their total cost?	$19.38
5.	The longest mealworm you can find in your Super Sac is 3.19 cm long. The shortest one is 1.7 cm. What is the difference in their lengths?	1.49 cm
6.	If you buy a triple decker burger, Roasted Roaches and a Cricket Cola separately, it costs $4.27. How much do you save by buying the Super Sac?	$.48
7.	A regular McMealworm Burger costs $1.69. A triple decker costs $2.59. How much more is the triple decker?	$.90
8.	You find one cockroach that weighs .321 grams and another that weighs .4 grams. What is their total weight?	.721 g
9.	Your friend finds a mealworm beetle that weighs .41 grams. The heaviest one you can find is .378 grams. How much heavier is your friend's beetle?	.032 g
10.	What is the difference in length between a 3.17 cm long mealworm and a 1.6 cm long mealworm?	1.57 cm

Page 168

Kookey's Creations

Professor Kook E. Kookey has invented a cookie that is shaped like a child's alphabet block and tastes like a super sweet candy bar. He also has cubic cookie candy bars that are crammed with berries and chunks of chocolate.

Work the problems on another paper.

		Answer Space
1.	Professor Kookey's Fudge-Filled Cubic Cookie Candy Bar has 3.7 ounces of fudge. How many ounces are in 35 bars?	129.5 oz.
2.	Kook E. Kookey's Chock Full of Chocolate Cookie Candy Bar has 5.3 ounces of chocolate. How many ounces are in 68 bars?	360.4 oz.
3.	Kook's Cubic Munchy Crunchies use 6.78 ounces of peanuts in each one. How many ounces are there in .25 of a bar?	1.695 oz.
4.	Kookey's Crunchies also use 5.34 ounces of maple sugar. How much maple sugar is in .25 of a bar?	1.335 oz.
5.	His Chunky Chocolate Cubic Cookie Candy Bars have 12.306 ounces of chocolate in each bar. How many ounces are in 3.5 bars?	43.071 oz.
6.	Kookey needs 7.5 ounces of cream for each Stuffed Strawberry and Cream Bar. How many ounces does he use for 30.5 bars?	228.75 oz.
7.	Professor Kookey's Stuffed Strawberry and Cream Bars each need 11.504 ounces of berries. How many ounces of berries are in 40 bars?	460.16
8.	Kook E.'s Caramel Raspberry Cubic Cookie Candy Bars use 4.67 ounces of caramel in each bar. How many ounces of caramel are in .33 of a bar?	1.5411
9.	Professor Kookey uses 5.6 ounces of blueberries for his Blueberry and Banana Bars. How many ounces does he need for 200 bars?	1120
10.	Kook E. Kookey's Lemondrop Lollipop Cubic Cookie Candy Bars each have 2.013 ounces of lemon flavoring. How many ounces are needed for 28 bars?	56.364

Page 169

You and Major League Baseball

You have won a national contest sponsored by Olog's Groaty Oaties. The prize is a chance for you to play in the majors. All you have to do is bat over .300 against the majority of the major leaguers.

Reminder: To find your batting average, divide the number of "at bats" into the number of "hits." (4.000 ÷ 10 = .400)

Work the problems on another paper.

		Answer Space
1.	You got 4 hits in 10 at bats against Dizzy Dolan. What was your batting average against Dizzy?	.400
2.	You faced Herman "The Tank" Sherman and belted out 16 hits in 20 trips to the plate. What was your average against Herman?	.800
3.	Against the famous pitcher, "Moonbeam" Malone, you smacked 7 hits in 14 trips to the plate. What was your batting average against Moonbeam?	.500
4.	You smashed 13 hits in 20 at bats against "Bullets" Bascom. What was your batting average against Bullets?	.650
5.	You faced the fireballing pitcher called Lefty Writey and banged out 9 hits in 12 times at bat. What was your batting average against Lefty?	.750
6.	You crushed 5 hits in 8 at bats against "Piano Legs" Jones. What was your batting average against Jones?	.625
7.	"Lightning" Bill Smith gave you a hard time, and you got only 2 hits in 10 at bats. What was your average against Bill?	.200
8.	You crunched "Knuckles" McBain for 12 hits in 16 at bats. What was your batting average?	.750
9.	You smashed 17 hits in 20 at bats against Victor "The Vulture" Rollins. What was your batting average against Rollins?	.850
10.	Altogether you belted out 114 hits in 175 at bats. What was your overall batting average?	.651

Page 170

Creepy Crawly Critters

Work the problems on another paper.

		Answer Space
1.	A female black widow spider is 9 mm long. An Eastern diamondback rattlesnake is 250 times as long. How long is the snake?	2.25 m
2.	A male black cockroach is 2.5 cm long. A female is 3.499 cm long. What is the length of both together?	5.999 cm
3.	A baby sidewinder is 20 cm long. An adult is 4.1 times as long. How long is the adult?	82 cm
4.	A gila monster is 60.9 cm long. A copperhead snake is 134.6 cm long. How much longer is the snake?	73.7 cm
5.	An American alligator is 5.84 m long. An American crocodile is 4.6 m long. What is the difference?	1.24 m
6.	A glass lizard is 106.699 cm long. A Southern alligator lizard is 42.8 cm long. What is the difference?	63.899 cm
7.	A male grass spider is 1.5 cm long. A female is 1.334 times as long. How long is the female?	2.001 cm
8.	A male rabid wolf spider is 1.3 cm long. A female is 1.611 times as long. How long is the female?	2.0943 cm
9.	A yellow-bellied water snake is 157.50 cm long. You could lay 225 bed bugs in a line that long. How long is each bed bug?	.7 cm
10.	A green water snake is 185.6 cm long. You could lay 32 elephant stag beetles in a line that long. How long is a stag beetle?	5.8 cm

Page 171

The N.B.A. Wants You!

You have just been named "The Young Basketball Player of the Year." Your reward is a chance to go one-on-one against the superstars of the N.B.A.

Compute your shooting percentage and round it off to the nearest whole percent.

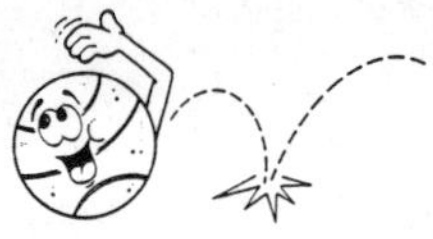

Work the problems on another paper.

		Answer Space
1.	You hit 13 out of 20 against Sam "Bamm-Bamm" Smith. What was your shooting percentage?	65%
2.	"Bamm-Bamm" nailed only 3 shots out of 20 against you. What percentage did he shoot?	15%
3.	Against Hye N. Skye you hit 15 baskets in 25 attempts. What was your percentage?	60%
4.	Hye N. Skye made only 8 out of 25 shots against you. What was his percentage?	32%
5.	You sank 7 of 14 shots against James "Slick Shot" Jones. What was your shooting percentage?	50%
6.	"Slick" hit 6 out of 14 shots against you. What did he shoot?	43%
7.	You hit 9 out of 12 shots against "Slammin'-Jammin' " Mann. What was your shooting percentage?	75%
8.	"Slammin'-Jammin' " sank only 2 of 12 shots while you guarded him. What did he shoot?	17%
9.	You hit 15 of 22 shots against "Dunkin" Dolan. What was your shooting percentage?	68%
10.	"Dunkin" iced only 4 of 22 against you. What did he shoot?	18%

Page 172

The N.F.L. Wants You!

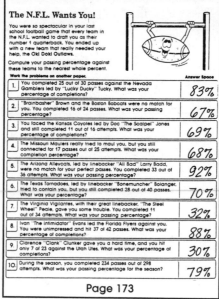

You were so spectacular in your last school football game that every team in the N.F.L. wanted to draft you as their number 1 quarterback. You ended up with a new team that really needed your help, the Oki Doki Outlaws.

Compute your passing percentage against these teams to the nearest whole percent.

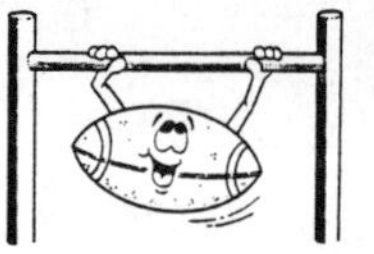

Work the problems on another paper.

		Answer Space
1.	You completed 25 out of 30 passes against the Nevada Gamblers led by "Lucky Ducky" Tucky. What was your percentage of completions?	83%
2.	"Brainbasher" Brown and the Boston Bobcats were no match for you. You completed 16 of 24 passes. What was your passing percentage?	67%
3.	You faced the Kansas Coyotes led by Doc "The Scalpel" Jones and still completed 11 out of 16 attempts. What was your percentage of completions?	69%
4.	The Missouri Maulers really tried to maul you, but you still connected for 17 passes out of 25 attempts. What was your completion percentage?	68%
5.	The Arizona Alleycats, led by linebacker "All Bad" Larry Badd, were no match for your perfect passes. You completed 33 out of 36 attempts. What was your passing percentage?	92%
6.	The Texas Tornadoes, led by linebacker "Bonemuncher" Bolanger, tried to contain you, but you still completed 28 out of 40 passes. What was your percentage?	70%
7.	The Virginia Vigilantes, with their great linebacker, "The Steel Wheel" Peale, gave you some trouble. You completed 11 out of 34 attempts. What was your passing percentage?	32%
8.	Ivan "The Intimidator" Evans led the Florida Flyers against you. You were unimpressed and hit 37 of 42 passes. What was your percentage of completions?	88%
9.	Clarence "Clank" Clunker gave you a hard time, and you hit only 7 of 23 against the Utah Utes. What was your percentage of completions?	30%
10.	During the season, you completed 234 passes out of 298 attempts. What was your passing percentage for the season?	79%

Page 173

Mean Monster Puts a Lock on Wrestling

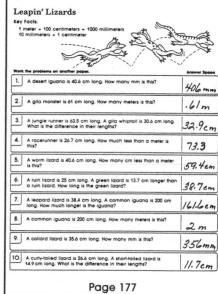

Mean Monster, a great defensive back in football, decided to take on all the top wrestlers in order to keep in shape during the off-season. He weighed 569 lbs. 7 oz. and stood 7 ft. 3 in. tall.
(Remember: 1 lb. = 16 oz. 1 ft. = 12 in.)

Work the problems on another paper.

		Answer Space
1.	Mean Monster's first bout was with Harry "The Hammer" Brown who weighed 397 lbs. 4 ounces. How much more did Mean Monster weigh?	172 lbs. 3 oz.
2.	He did so well in his first round that he faced Marvelous Marvin Morton in the next event. Marvelous Marvin stood 6 ft. 9 in. tall. How much taller was Mean Monster?	6 in.
3.	Awesome Albert Alston was 167 lbs. 11 oz. lighter than Mean Monster. What did Awesome Albert weigh?	401 lbs. 12 oz.
4.	Irwin "The Icebox" weighed 478 lbs. 14 oz. He and Mean Monster stood together on the scale. What did it read?	1,048 lbs. 5 oz.
5.	Dazzling Doug Dugan ate 146 oz. of meat before the match. Mean Monster ate 5 lbs. 9 oz. of meat. How much meat did they eat altogether?	235 oz. or 14 lbs. 11 oz.
6.	Si "Stilts" Stone stood 8 ft. 1 in. tall. How much shorter was Mean Monster?	10 in.
7.	Dreadful Dan "The Mighty Man" weighed 777 lbs. 7 oz. What was his weight in ounces?	12,439 oz.
8.	Ivan the Incredible ate an 18 lb. 8 oz. meal before his bout. Mean Monster had only 188 oz. of food before the match. How much more did Ivan eat?	6 lbs. 12 oz. or 108 oz.
9.	Melvin the Magnificent was a dainty 478 lbs. 15 oz. He stood with Mean Monster and Dreadful Dan on the same scale. What was their total weight?	1,825 lbs. 13 oz.
10.	Mean Monster's brother Itty Bitty Monster weighed 134 lbs. 15 oz. less than his big brother. What did Itty Bitty weigh?	434 lbs. 8 oz.

Page 174

It's for the Birds

Key Facts:
1 ft. = 12 in.
1 yd. = 3 ft. = 36 in.

Work the problems on another paper.

		Answer Space
1.	The black vulture has a wingspan of 60 inches. How many feet is its wingspan?	5 ft.
2.	A gray hawk has a 3-foot wingspan. How many inches is that?	36 ins.
3.	The turkey vulture has a 72-inch wingspan. How many yards is that?	2 yds.
4.	A red-shouldered hawk has a 4-foot wingspan. How many inches can he spread his wings?	48 ins.
5.	A sparrow hawk has a 24-inch wingspan. How many feet can its wings spread out?	2 ft.
6.	A California condor has a 114-inch wingspan. How many feet is that? How many inches are left over?	9 ft. 6 ins.
7.	The golden eagle has a wingspan of 7 ft. 8 in. How many inches is his wingspan?	92 ins.
8.	The bald eagle has a 96-inch wingspan. What is his wingspan in feet?	8 ft.
9.	A red-shouldered hawk is 2 feet long. How long is that in inches?	24 ins.
10.	The red-tailed hawk has a 54-inch wingspan. How many feet is that? How many inches are left over?	4 ft. 6 ins.

Page 175

The Bear Facts

Key Facts:
1 meter = 100 centimeters = 1000 millimeters
1 centimeter = 10 millimeters

Work the problems on another paper.

		Answer Space
1.	A black bear has a tail 190 mm long. How many cm is that?	19 cm
2.	The hind foot of a grizzly bear is 26 cm long. How many mm is that?	260 mm
3.	The claws of a grizzly bear are 10 cm long. How many mm is that?	100 mm
4.	A polar bear is 300 cm long. How many meters is that?	3 m
5.	The grizzly bear is 130 cm tall. How tall is that in meters?	1.3 m
6.	The tail of a polar bear is 130 mm long. How many cm is that?	13 cm
7.	A brown bear is 200 cm long. How many meters is that?	2 m
8.	The black bear is 100 cm tall. How many meters tall is that?	1 m
9.	A brown bear has a tail that is 70 mm long. How many cm is that?	7 cm
10.	The black bear is 188 cm long. How many mm long is the black bear?	1880 mm

Page 176

Leapin' Lizards

Key Facts:
1 meter = 100 centimeters = 1000 millimeters
10 millimeters = 1 centimeter

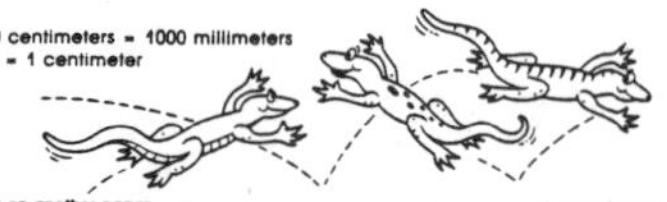

Work the problems on another paper.

		Answer Space
1.	A desert iguana is 40.6 cm long. How many mm is this?	406 mm
2.	A gila monster is 61 cm long. How many meters is this?	.61 m
3.	A jungle runner is 63.5 cm long. A gila whiptail is 30.6 cm long. What is the difference in their lengths?	32.9 cm
4.	A racerunner is 26.7 cm long. How much less than a meter is this?	73.3
5.	A worm lizard is 40.6 cm long. How many cm less than a meter is this?	59.4 cm
6.	A ruin lizard is 25 cm long. A green lizard is 13.7 cm longer than a ruin lizard. How long is the green lizard?	38.7 cm
7.	A leopard lizard is 38.4 cm long. A common iguana is 200 cm long. How much longer is the iguana?	161.6 cm
8.	A common iguana is 200 cm long. How many meters is this?	2 m
9.	A collard lizard is 35.6 cm long. How many mm is this?	356 mm
10.	A curly-tailed lizard is 26.6 cm long. A short-tailed lizard is 14.9 cm long. What is the difference in their lengths?	11.7 cm

Page 177

The Support System

The bones are the body's supportive system. They are usually divided into two major groups — bones of the middle (skull, backbone and ribs) and bones of the arms and legs (including the shoulder and hip bones).

When you were born, your skeleton was made of soft bones called **cartilage**. As you grew, most of that cartilage turned into bone. However, all people still have some cartilage in their bodies. Our noses and our ears are cartilage, and there are pads of cartilage between sections of the backbone that act as cushions.

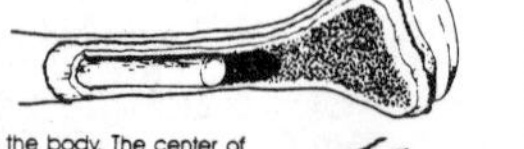

Bones do more than support the body. The center of the bone, called **bone marrow**, makes new blood cells for our bodies. Bones are also storage houses for important minerals like calcium and phosphorous.

Answer the questions below. You might need your science book or an encyclopedia to help you.

1. What are the main functions of the skeletal system? 1) shapes, supports body 2) protects soft body 3) makes blood cells 4) stores minerals 5) assists in movement
2. What is the largest bone in your body? femur (thighbone)
3. What is the smallest bone in your body? middle ear bone.
4. What do bones first develop as? cartilage
5. What does bone marrow do? makes new red blood cells
6. Do all bones have real bone marrow? No
7. What is the outer layer of a bone called? compact
8. Where two bones meet is called a joint

Fascinating Fact! Did you know that a giraffe has the same number of vertebrae in its neck as you?

Page 178

A Bag of Bones

The skin is a sack that contains the bones. If the skin and muscle layers were peeled away, the body's bones would be exposed. Some bones are seen only from either the front or back, others are seen from both sides. Use the names in the box below each skeleton. Label the bones as they appear on the front and the back of the body. (On lines going across the center of the page, write the bones that can be seen from the front and back. Although they appear in both boxes, only write the answer once.)

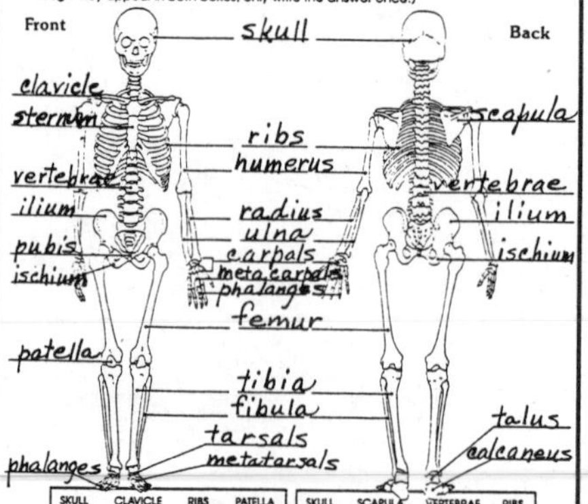

SKULL CLAVICLE RIBS PATELLA VERTEBRAE RADIUS HUMERUS TIBIA PUBIS CARPALS METACARPALS ULNA PHALANGES (hand) ILIUM ISCHIUM FEMUR FIBULA STERNUM TARSALS METATARSALS PHALANGES (feet)

SKULL SCAPULA VERTEBRAE RIBS ILIUM ISCHIUM FEMUR FIBULA RADIUS HUMERUS PHALANGES (hand) TALUS CALCANEUS METACARPALS CARPALS ULNA TIBIA

Page 179

Meeting Places

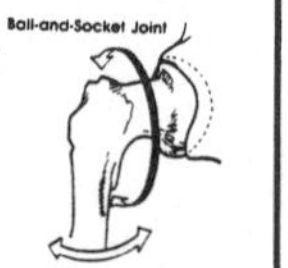

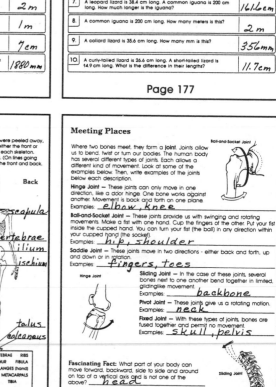

Where two bones meet, they form a **joint**. Joints allow us to bend, twist or turn our bodies. The human body has several different types of joints. Each allows a different kind of movement. Look at some of the examples below. Then, write examples of the joints below each description.

Hinge Joint — These joints can only move in one direction, like a door hinge. One bone works against another. Movement is back and forth on one plane.
Examples: elbow, knee

Ball-and-Socket Joint — These joints provide us with swinging and rotating movements. Make a fist with one hand. Cup the fingers of the other. Put your fist inside the cupped hand. You can turn your fist (the ball) in any direction within your cupped hand (the socket).
Examples: hip, shoulder

Saddle Joint — These joints move in two directions - either back and forth, up and down or in rotation.
Examples: fingers, toes

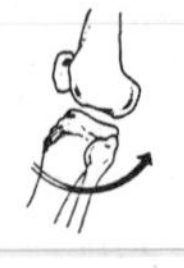

Sliding Joint — In the case of these joints, several bones next to one another bend together in limited, glidinglike movement.
Examples: backbone

Pivot Joint — These joints give us a rotating motion.
Examples: neck

Fixed Joint — With these types of joints, bones are fused together and permit no movement.
Examples: skull, pelvis

Fascinating Fact: What part of your body can move forward, backward, side to side and around on top of a vertical axis and is not one of the above? head

Page 180

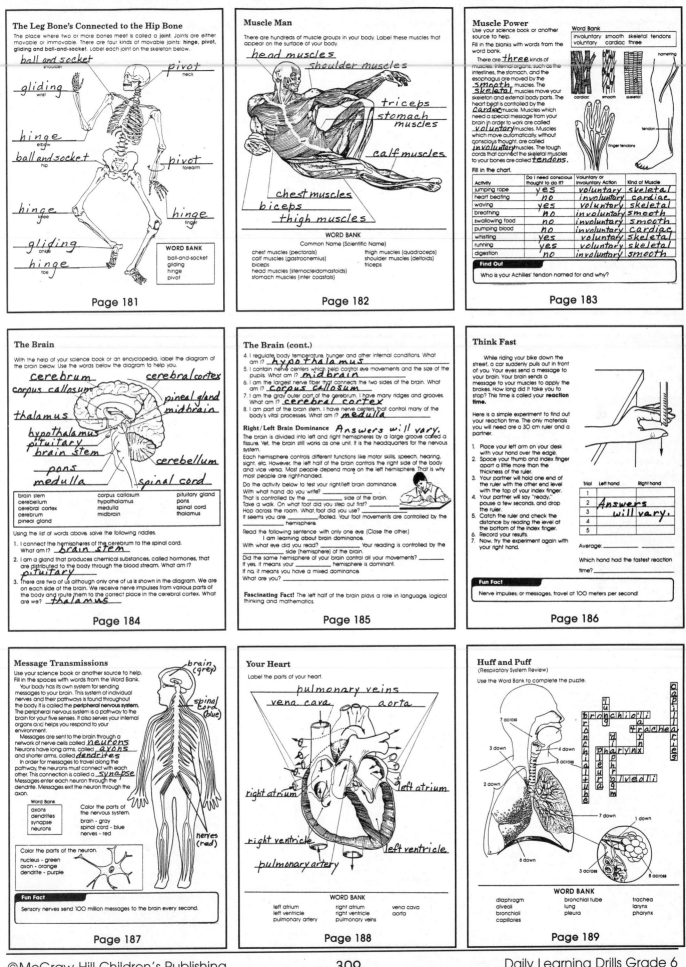

The Leg Bone's Connected to the Hip Bone

The place where two or more bones meet is called a **joint**. Joints are either movable or immovable. There are four kinds of movable joints: **hinge, pivot, gliding** and **ball-and-socket**. Label each joint on the skeleton below.

ball and socket (shoulder)
pivot (neck)
gliding (wrist)
hinge (elbow)
ball and socket (hip)
pivot (forearm)
hinge (knee)
hinge (finger)
gliding (ankle)
hinge (toe)

WORD BANK
ball-and-socket
gliding
hinge
pivot

Page 181

Muscle Man

There are hundreds of muscle groups in your body. Label these muscles that appear on the surface of your body.

head muscles
shoulder muscles
triceps
stomach muscles
calf muscles
chest muscles
biceps
thigh muscles

WORD BANK
Common Name (Scientific Name)

chest muscles (pectorals)
calf muscles (gastrocnemius)
biceps
head muscles (sternocleidomastoids)
stomach muscles (inter costals)
thigh muscles (quadraceps)
shoulder muscles (deltoids)
triceps

Page 182

Muscle Power

Use your science book or another source to help.

Fill in the blanks with words from the word bank.

There are **three** kinds of muscles. Internal organs, such as the intestines, the stomach, and the esophagus are moved by the **smooth** muscles. The **skeletal** muscles move your skeleton and external body parts. The heart beat is controlled by the **cardiac** muscle. Muscles which need a special message from your brain in order to work are called **voluntary** muscles. Muscles which move automatically, without conscious thought, are called **involuntary** muscles. The tough cords that connect the skeletal muscles to your bones are called **tendons**.

Word Bank
involuntary smooth skeletal tendons
voluntary cardiac three

Fill in the chart.

Activity	Do I need conscious thought to do it?	Voluntary or involuntary Action	Kind of Muscle
jumping rope	yes	voluntary	skeletal
heart beating	no	involuntary	cardiac
waving	yes	voluntary	skeletal
breathing	no	involuntary	smooth
swallowing food	no	involuntary	smooth
pumping blood	no	involuntary	cardiac
whistling	yes	voluntary	skeletal
running	yes	voluntary	skeletal
digestion	no	involuntary	smooth

Find Out

Who is your Achilles' tendon named for and why?

Page 183

The Brain

With the help of your science book or an encyclopedia, label the diagram of the brain below. Use the words below the diagram to help you.

cerebrum
cerebral cortex
corpus callosum
pineal gland
thalamus
midbrain
hypothalamus
pituitary
brain stem
cerebellum
pons
medulla
spinal cord

brain stem	corpus callosum	pituitary gland
cerebellum	hypothalamus	pons
cerebral cortex	medulla	spinal cord
cerebrum	midbrain	thalamus
pineal gland		

Using the list of words above, solve the following riddles.

1. I connect the hemispheres of the cerebrum to the spinal cord. What am I? *brain stem*

2. I am a gland that produces chemical substances, called hormones, that are distributed to the body through the blood stream. What am I? *pituitary*

3. There are two of us although only one of us is shown in the diagram. We are on each side of the brain. We receive nerve impulses from various parts of the body and route them to the correct place in the cerebral cortex. What are we? *thalamus*

Page 184

The Brain (cont.)

4. I regulate body temperature, hunger and other internal conditions. What am I? *hypothalamus*
5. I contain nerve centers which help control eye movements and the size of the pupils. What am I? *midbrain*
6. I am the largest nerve fiber that connects the two sides of the brain. What am I? *corpus callosum*
7. I am the gray outer part of the cerebrum. I have many ridges and grooves. What am I? *cerebral cortex*
8. I am part of the brain stem. I have nerve centers that control many of the body's vital processes. What am I? *medulla*

Right/Left Brain Dominance *Answers will vary.*
The brain is divided into left and right hemispheres by a large groove called a fissure. Yet, the brain still works as one unit. It is the headquarters for the nervous system.
Each hemisphere controls different functions like motor skills, speech, hearing, sight, etc. However, the left half of the brain controls the right side of the body and vice versa. Most people depend more on the left hemisphere. That is why most people are right-handed.
Do the activity below to test your right/left brain dominance.
With what hand do you write? _____
That is controlled by the _____ side of the brain.
Take a walk. On what foot did you step out first? _____
Hop across the room. What foot did you use? _____
It seems you are a _____-footed. Your foot movements are controlled by the _____ hemisphere.
Read the following sentence with only one eye. (Close the other.)
I am learning about brain dominance.
With what eye did you read? _____ Your reading is controlled by the _____ side (hemisphere) of the brain.
Did the same hemisphere of your brain control all your movements? _____
If yes, it means your _____ hemisphere is dominant.
If no, it means you have a mixed dominance.
What are you? _____

Fascinating Fact! The left half of the brain plays a role in language, logical thinking and mathematics.

Page 185

Think Fast

While riding your bike down the street, a car suddenly pulls out in front of you. Your eyes send a message to your brain. Your brain sends a message to your muscles to apply the brakes. How long did it take you to stop? This time is called your **reaction time.**

Here is a simple experiment to find out your reaction time. The only materials you will need are a 30 cm ruler and a partner.

1. Place your left arm on your desk with your hand over the edge.
2. Space your thumb and index finger apart a little more than the thickness of the ruler.
3. Your partner will hold one end of the ruler with the other end level with the top of your index finger.
4. Your partner will say "ready," pause a few seconds, and drop the ruler.
5. Catch the ruler and check the distance by reading the level at the bottom of the index finger.
6. Record your results.
7. Now, try the experiment again with your right hand.

Trial	Left hand	Right hand
1		
2	Answers	
3	will	vary.
4		
5		

Average: _____

Which hand had the fastest reaction time? _____

Fun Fact

Nerve impulses, or messages, travel at 100 meters per second!

Page 186

Message Transmissions

Use your science book or another source to help. Fill in the spaces with words from the Word Bank.
Your body has its own system for sending messages to your brain. This system of individual nerves and their pathways is found throughout the body. It is called the **peripheral nervous system.** The peripheral nervous system is a pathway to the brain for your five senses. It also serves your internal organs and helps you respond to your environment.
Messages are sent to the brain through a network of nerve cells called **neurons.** Neurons have long arms, called **axons** and shorter arms, called **dendrites.**
In order for messages to travel along the pathway, the neurons must connect with each other. This connection is called a **synapse.** Messages enter each neuron through the dendrite. Messages exit the neuron through the axon.

brain (grey)
spinal cord (blue)
nerves (red)

Word Bank
axons
dendrites
synapse
neurons

Color the parts of the nervous system.
brain - gray
spinal cord - blue
nerves - red

Color the parts of the neuron.
nucleus - green
axon - orange
dendrite - purple

Fun Fact

Sensory nerves send 100 million messages to the brain every second.

Page 187

Your Heart

Label the parts of your heart.

pulmonary veins
vena cava
aorta
right atrium
left atrium
right ventricle
left ventricle
pulmonary artery

WORD BANK

left atrium
left ventricle
pulmonary artery
right atrium
right ventricle
pulmonary veins
vena cava
aorta

Page 188

Huff and Puff
(Respiratory System Review)

Use the Word Bank to complete the puzzle.

7 across, 3 down, 4 down, 5 across, 2 down, 6 down, 3 across, 7 down, 1 down, 8 across

bronchioli, capillaries, trachea, larynx, pharynx, pleura, alveoli, lung, bronchial tube

WORD BANK

diaphragm
alveoli
bronchioli
capillaries
bronchial tube
lung
pleura
trachea
larynx
pharynx

Page 189

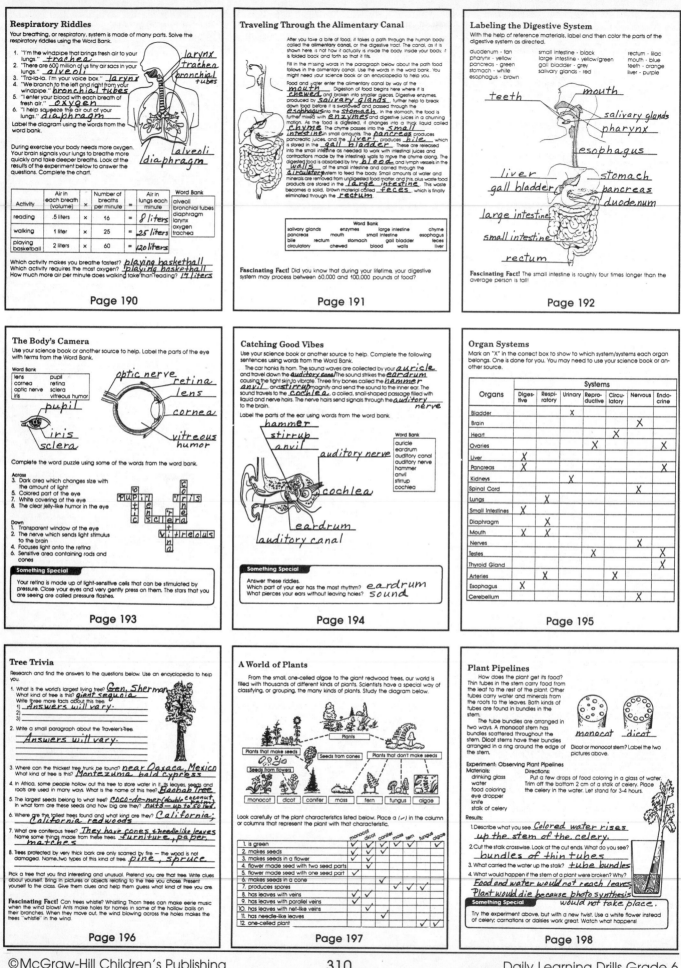

Respiratory Riddles

Your breathing, or respiratory, system is made of many parts. Solve the respiratory riddles using the Word Bank.

1. "I'm the windpipe that brings fresh air to your lungs." *trachea*
2. "There are 600 million of us tiny air sacs in your lungs." *alveoli*
3. "Tra-la-la. I'm your voice box." *larynx*
4. "We branch to the left and right from your windpipe." *bronchial tubes*
5. "I enter your blood with each breath of fresh air." *oxygen*
6. "I help squeeze the air out of your lungs." *diaphragm*

Label the diagram using the words from the word bank.

larynx
trachea
bronchial tubes
alveoli
diaphragm

During exercise your body needs more oxygen. Your brain signals your lungs to breathe more quickly and take deeper breaths. Look at the results of the experiment below to answer the questions. Complete the chart.

Activity	Air in each breath (volume)	×	Number of breaths per minute	=	Air in lungs each minute	Word Bank
reading	.5 liters	×	16	=	8 liters	alveoli
walking	1 liter	×	25	=	25 liters	bronchial tubes, diaphragm, larynx, oxygen, trachea
playing basketball	2 liters	×	60	=	120 liters	

Which activity makes you breathe fastest? *playing basketball*
Which activity requires the most oxygen? *playing basketball*
How much more air per minute does walking take than reading? *17 liters*

Page 190

Traveling Through the Alimentary Canal

After you take a bite of food, it takes a path through the human body called the alimentary canal, or the digestive tract. The canal, as it is shown here, is not how it actually is inside the body. Inside your body, it is folded back and forth until it fits.

Fill in the missing words in the paragraph below about the path food follows in the alimentary canal. Use the words in the word bank. You might need your science book or an encyclopedia to help you.

Food and water enter the alimentary canal by way of the *mouth*. Digestion of food begins here where it is *chewed*, and broken into smaller pieces. Digestive enzymes, produced by *salivary glands*, further help to break down food before it is swallowed and passed through the *esophagus* into the *stomach*. In the stomach, the food is further mixed with *enzymes* and digestive juices in a churning motion. As the food is digested, it changes into a thick liquid called *chyme*. The chyme passes into the *small intestine* in small amounts. The *pancreas* produces pancreatic juices, and the *liver* produces *bile*, which is stored in the *gall bladder*. These are released into the small intestine as needed to work with intestinal juices and contractions made by the intestine's walls to move the chyme along. The digested food is absorbed by tiny *blood* and lymph vessels in the *walls* of the small intestine and carried through the *circulatory* system to feed the body. Small amounts of water and minerals are removed from undigested food matter and this, plus waste food products are stored in the *large intestine*. This waste becomes a solid, brown material called *feces*, which is finally eliminated through the *rectum*.

Word Bank
salivary glands · enzymes · large intestine · chyme
pancreas · mouth · small intestine · esophagus
bile · rectum · stomach · gall bladder · feces
circulatory · chewed · blood · walls · liver

Fascinating Fact! Did you know that during your lifetime, your digestive system may process between 60,000 and 100,000 pounds of food?

Page 191

Labeling the Digestive System

With the help of reference materials, label and then color the parts of the digestive system as directed.

duodenum - tan
pharynx - yellow
pancreas - green
stomach - white
esophagus - brown
small intestine - black
large intestine - yellow/green
gall bladder - grey
salivary glands - red
rectum - lilac
mouth - blue
teeth - orange
liver - purple

teeth
mouth
salivary glands
pharynx
esophagus
liver
gall bladder
large intestine
small intestine
rectum
stomach
pancreas
duodenum

Fascinating Fact! The small intestine is roughly four times longer than the average person is tall!

Page 192

The Body's Camera

Use your science book or another source to help. Label the parts of the eye with terms from the Word Bank.

Word Bank
lens · pupil
cornea · retina
optic nerve · sclera
iris · vitreous humor

optic nerve
retina
lens
cornea
vitreous humor
pupil
iris
sclera

Complete the word puzzle using some of the words from the word bank.

Across
3. Dark area which changes size with the amount of light
7. Colored part of the eye
7. White covering of the eye
8. The clear jelly-like humor in the eye

Down
1. Transparent window of the eye
2. The nerve which sends light stimulus to the brain
4. Focuses light onto the retina
6. Sensitive area containing rods and cones

(crossword) pupil · iris · lens · cornea · sclera · retina · vitreous

Something Special
Your retina is made up of light-sensitive cells that can be stimulated by pressure. Close your eyes and very gently press on them. The stars that you are seeing are called pressure flashes.

Page 193

Catching Good Vibes

Use your science book or another source to help. Complete the following sentences using words from the Word Bank.

The car honks its horn. The sound waves are collected by your *auricle* and travel down the *auditory canal*. The sound strikes the *eardrum* causing the tight skin to vibrate. Three tiny bones called the *hammer*, *anvil*, and *stirrup* magnify and send the sound to the inner ear. The sound travels to the *cochlea*, a coiled, snail-shaped passage filled with liquid and nerve hairs. The nerve hairs send signals through the *auditory nerve* to the brain.

Label the parts of the ear using words from the word bank.

hammer
stirrup
anvil
auditory nerve
cochlea
eardrum
auditory canal

Word Bank
auricle
eardrum
auditory canal
auditory nerve
hammer
anvil
stirrup
cochlea

Something Special
Answer these riddles.
Which part of your ear has the most rhythm? *eardrum*
What pierces your ears without leaving holes? *sound*

Page 194

Organ Systems

Mark an "X" in the correct box to show to which system/systems each organ belongs. One is done for you. You may need to use your science book or another source.

Organs	Digestive	Respiratory	Urinary	Reproductive	Circulatory	Nervous	Endocrine
Bladder			X				
Brain						X	
Heart					X		
Ovaries				X			X
Liver	X						
Pancreas	X						X
Kidneys			X				
Spinal Cord						X	
Lungs		X					
Small Intestines	X						
Diaphragm		X					
Mouth	X	X					
Nerves						X	
Testes				X			X
Thyroid Gland							X
Arteries					X		
Esophagus	X						
Cerebellum						X	

Page 195

Tree Trivia

Research and find the answers to the questions below. Use an encyclopedia to help you.

1. What is the world's largest living tree? *Gen. Sherman*
   What kind of tree is this? *giant sequoia*
   Write three more facts about this tree.
   1) *Answers will vary.*
   2)
   3)
2. Write a small paragraph about the Traveler's-Tree.
   Answers will vary.

3. Where can the thickest tree trunk be found? *near Oaxaca, Mexico*
   What kind of tree is this? *Montezuma bald cypress*
4. In Africa, some people hollow out this tree to store water in its leaves, seeds and roots are used in many ways. What is the name of this tree? *Baobab Tree*
5. The largest seeds belong to what tree? *coco-de-mer (double coconut)*
   In what form are these seeds and how big are they? *nuts — up to 50 lbs.*
6. Where are the tallest trees found and what kind are they? *California; California redwoods*
7. What are conifers? *They have cones & needlelike leaves*
   Name some things made from these trees. *furniture, paper, matches*
8. Trees protected by very thick bark are only scarred by fire — the wood is not damaged. Name two types of this kind of tree. *pine, spruce*

Pick a tree that you find interesting and unusual. Pretend you are that tree. Write clues about yourself in pictures or objects relating to the tree you chose. Present yourself to the class. Give them clues and help them guess what kind of tree you are.

Fascinating Fact! Can trees whistle? Whistling Thorn trees can make eerie music when the wind blows! Ants make holes for homes in some of the hollow balls on their branches. When they move out, the wind blowing across the holes makes the trees "whistle" in the wind.

Page 196

A World of Plants

From the small, one-celled algae to the giant redwood trees, our world is filled with thousands of different kinds of plants. Scientists have a special way of classifying, or grouping, the many kinds of plants. Study the diagram below.

Plants
Plants that make seeds
Seeds from cones
Plants that don't make seeds
Seeds from flowers
monocot · dicot · conifer · moss · fern · fungus · algae

Look carefully at the plant characteristics listed below. Place a (✓) in the column or columns that represent the plant with that characteristic.

	monocot	dicot	conifer	moss	fern	fungus	algae
1. is green	✓	✓	✓	✓	✓		✓
2. makes seeds	✓	✓	✓				
3. makes seeds in a flower	✓	✓					
4. flower made seed with two seed parts		✓					
5. flower made seed with one seed part	✓						
6. makes seeds in a cone			✓				
7. produces spores				✓	✓	✓	
8. has leaves with veins	✓	✓	✓		✓		
9. has leaves with parallel veins	✓						
10. has leaves with net-like veins		✓					
11. has needle-like leaves			✓				
12. one-celled plant						✓	✓

Page 197

Plant Pipelines

How does the plant get its food? Thin tubes in the stem carry food from the leaf to the rest of the plant. Other tubes carry water and minerals from the roots to the leaves. Both kinds of tubes are found in bundles in the stem.

The tube bundles are arranged in two ways. A monocot stem has bundles scattered throughout the stem. Dicot stems have their bundles arranged in a ring around the edge of the stem.

monocot · dicot

Dicot or monocot stem? Label the two pictures above.

Experiment: Observing Plant Pipelines

Materials:
drinking glass
water
food coloring
eye dropper
knife
stalk of celery

Directions:
Put a few drops of food coloring in a glass of water. Trim off the bottom 2 cm of a stalk of celery. Place the celery in the water. Let stand for 3-4 hours.

Results:
1. Describe what you see. *Colored water rises up the stem of the celery.*
2. Cut the stalk crosswise. Look at the cut ends. What do you see? *bundles of thin tubes*
3. What carried the water up the stalk? *tube bundles*
4. What would happen if the stem of a plant were broken? Why? *Food and water would not reach leaves. Plant would die because photosynthesis would not take place.*

Something Special
Try the experiment above, but with a new twist. Use a white flower instead of celery; carnations or daisies work great. Watch what happens!

Page 198

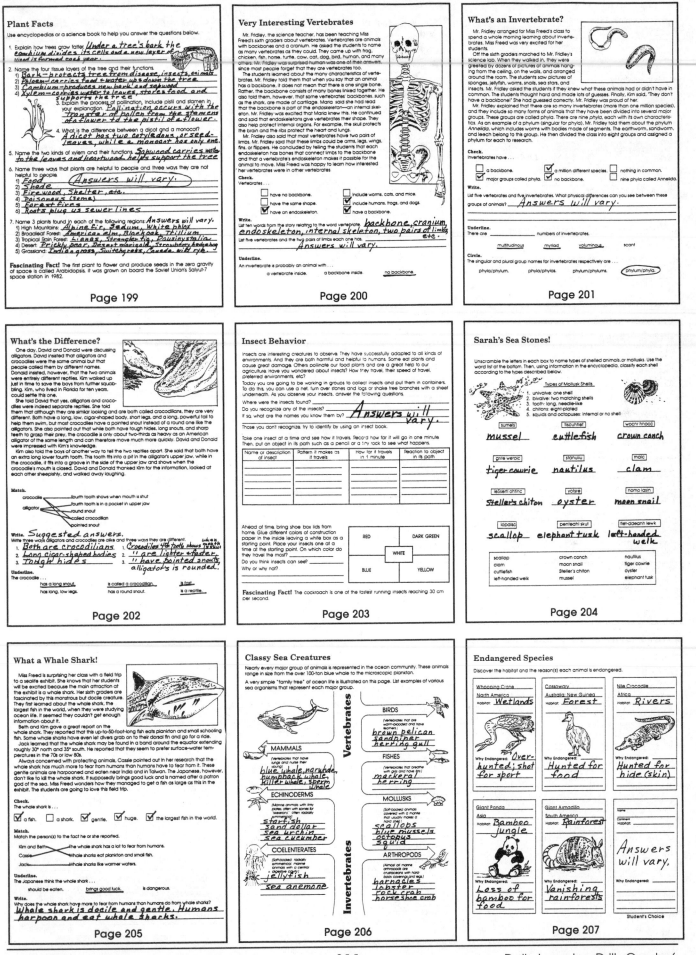

Plant Facts

Use encyclopedias or a science book to help you answer the questions below.

1. Explain how trees grow fatter. *Under a tree's bark the cambium divides its cells and a new layer of wood is formed each year.*

2. Name the four tissue layers of the tree and their functions.
   1) *Bark - protects tree from disease, insects, animals*
   2) *Phloem - carries food & water up & down the tree*
   3) *Cambium - produces new leaves, stores food and supports the tree*
   4) *Xylem - carries water to leaves*

3. Explain the process of pollination. Include pistil and stamen in your explanation. *Pollination occurs with the transfer of pollen from the stamens of a flower to the pistil of a flower.*

4. What is the difference between a dicot and a monocot? *A dicot has two cotyledons, or seed-leaves, while a monocot has only one.*

5. Name the two kinds of xylem and their functions. *Sapwood carries water to the leaves and heartwood helps support the tree.*

6. Name three ways that plants are helpful to people and three ways they are not helpful to people. *Answers will vary.*
   1) *Food*
   2) *Shade*
   3) *Firewood, Shelter, etc.*
   4) *Poisonous (stems)*
   5) *Forest Fires*
   6) *Roots plug up sewer lines*

7. Name 3 plants found in each of the following regions: *Answers will vary.*
   1) High Mountains: *Alpine fir, Sedum, White phlox*
   2) Broadleaf Forest: *American elm, Blackoak, Trillium*
   3) Tropical Rain Forest: *Lianas, Strangler fig, Pausinystalia*
   4) Desert: *Prickly pear, Desert marigold, Strawberry hedgehog*
   5) Grassland: *India grass, Switchgrass, Canada wild rye*

Fascinating Fact! The first plant to flower and produce seeds in the zero gravity of space is called Arabidopsis. It was grown on board the Soviet Union's Salyut-7 space station in 1982.

Page 199

Very Interesting Vertebrates

Mr. Fridley, the science teacher, has been teaching Miss Freed's sixth graders about vertebrates. Vertebrates are animals with backbones and a cranium. He asked the students to name as many vertebrates as they could. They came up with fish, chicken, fish, horse, turtle, cow, cat, dog, bird, human, and many others. Mr. Fridley was surprised human was one of their answers, since most people forget that they are vertebrates too.

The students learned about the many characteristics of vertebrates. Mr. Fridley told them that when you say that an animal has a backbone, it does not mean that there is one single bone. Rather, the backbone consists of many bones linked together. He also told them, however, that some vertebrates backbones, such as the shark, are made of cartilage. Maria said she had read that the backbone is part of the endoskeleton—an internal skeleton. Mr. Fridley was excited that Maria knew this. He continued and said that endoskeletons give vertebrates their shape. They also help protect internal organs. For example, the skull protects the brain and the ribs protect the heart and lungs.

Mr. Fridley also said that most vertebrates have two pairs of limbs. Mr. Fridley said that these limbs could be arms, legs, wings, fins, or flippers. He concluded by telling the students that each endoskeleton has bones that connect limbs to the backbone and that a vertebrate's endoskeleton makes it possible for the animal to move. Miss Freed was happy to learn how interested her vertebrates were in other vertebrates.

Check.
Vertebrates . . .

- [ ] have no backbone.
- [ ] have the same shape.
- [x] have an endoskeleton.
- [ ] include worms, cats, and mice.
- [x] include humans, frogs, and dogs.
- [x] have a backbone.

Write.
List ten words from the story relating to the word vertebrate: *backbone, cranium, endoskeleton, internal skeleton, two pairs of limbs etc.*

List five vertebrates and the two pairs of limbs each one has. *Answers will vary.*

Underline.
An invertebrate is probably an animal with . . .

a vertebrate inside.   a backbone inside.   <u>no backbone</u>

Page 200

What's an Invertebrate?

Mr. Fridley arranged for Miss Freed's class to spend a whole morning learning about invertebrates. Miss Freed was very excited for her students.

Off the sixth graders marched to Mr. Fridley's science lab. When they walked in, they were greeted by dozens of pictures of animals hanging from the ceiling, on the walls, and arranged around the room. The students saw pictures of sponges, jellyfish, worms, snails, sea stars, and insects. Mr. Fridley asked the students if they knew what these animals had or didn't have in common. The students thought hard and made lots of guesses. Finally, Kim said, "They don't have a backbone!" She had guessed correctly. Mr. Fridley was proud of her.

Mr. Fridley explained that so many invertebrates (more than one million species), and they include so many forms of animals that they have been divided into several major groups. These groups are called phyla. There are nine phyla, each with its own characteristics. As an example of a phylum (singular for phyla), Mr. Fridley told them about the phylum Annelida, which includes worms with bodies made of segments. The earthworm, sandworm, and leech belong to this group. He then divided the class into eight groups and assigned a phylum for each to research.

Check.
Invertebrates have . . .

- [x] a backbone.
- [x] a million different species.
- [ ] nothing in common.
- [x] major groups called phyla.
- [x] no backbone.
- [ ] nine phyla called Annelida.

Write.
List five vertebrates and five invertebrates. What physical differences can you see between these groups of animals? *Answers will vary.*

Underline.
There are _____ numbers of invertebrates.

multitudinous   myriad   voluminous   scant

Circle.
The singular and plural group names for invertebrates respectively are . . .

phyla/phylum   phyla/phylas   phylum/phylums   (phylum/phyla)

Page 201

What's the Difference?

One day, David and Donald were discussing alligators. David insisted that alligators and crocodiles were the same animal but that people called them by different names. Donald insisted, however, that the two animals were entirely different reptiles. Kim walked up just in time to save the boys from further squabbling. Kim, who lived in Florida for ten years, could settle this one.

She told David that yes, alligators and crocodiles were indeed separate reptiles. She told them that although they are similar looking and are both called crocodilians, they are very different. Both have a long, low, cigar-shaped body, short legs, and a tail to help them swim, but most crocodiles have a pointed snout instead of a round one like the alligator. She also pointed out that while both have tough hides, long snouts, and sharp teeth to grasp their prey, the crocodile is only about two-thirds as heavy as an American alligator of the same length and can therefore move much more quickly. David and Donald were impressed with Kim's knowledge.

Kim also told the boys of another way to tell the two reptiles apart. She said that both have an extra long lower fourth tooth. This tooth fits into a pit in the alligator's upper jaw, while in the crocodile, it fits into a groove in the side of the upper jaw and shows when the crocodile's mouth is closed. David and Donald thanked Kim for the information, looked at each other sheepishly, and walked away laughing.

Match.
crocodile — fourth tooth shows when mouth is shut
alligator — fourth tooth is in a pocket in upper jaw
— round snout
— called crocodilian
— pointed snout

Write. *Suggested answers.*
Write three ways alligators and crocodiles are alike and three ways they are different.
1. *Both are crocodilians* — 1. *Crocodiles 4th tooth shows when mouth is shut*
2. *Long cigar-shaped bodies* — 2. *" are lighter + faster.*
3. *Tough hides* — 3. *" have pointed snouts; alligator's is rounded.*

Underline.
The crocodile . . .

has a long snout.   is called a crocodilian.   <u>is fast.</u>
has long, low legs.   has a round snout.   is a reptile.

Page 202

Insect Behavior

Insects are interesting creatures to observe. They have successfully adapted to all kinds of environments. And they are both harmful and helpful to humans. Some eat plants and cause great damage. Others pollinate our food plants and are a great help to our agriculture. Have you wondered about insects? How they travel, their speed of travel, preferred environments, etc?

Today we are going to be working in groups to collect insects and put them in containers. To do this, as you use a net, turn over stones and logs or shake tree branches with a sheet underneath. As you observe your insects, answer the following questions.

Where were the insects found?
Do you recognize any of the insects?
If so, what are the names you know them by? *Answers will vary.*

Those you don't recognize, try to identify by using an insect book.

Take one insect at a time and see how it travels. Record how far it will go in one minute. Then, put an object in its path such as a pencil or a tiny rock to see what happens.

Name or description of insect	Pattern it makes as it travels	How far it travels in 1 minute	Reaction to object in its path

Ahead of time, bring shoe box lids from home. Glue different colors of construction paper in the inside leaving a white box as a starting point. Place your insects one at a time at the starting point. On which color do they travel the most?

RED		DARK GREEN
	WHITE	
BLUE		YELLOW

Do you think insects can see?
Why or why not?

Fascinating Fact! The cockroach is one of the fastest running insects reaching 30 cm per second.

Page 203

Sarah's Sea Stones!

Unscramble the letters in each box to name types of shelled animals, or mollusks. Use the word list at the bottom. Then, using information in the encyclopedia, classify each shell according to the types described below.

Types of Mollusk Shells
1. univalve: one shell
2. bivalve: two matching shells
3. tooth: long, needle-like
4. chitons: eight-plated
5. squids and octopuses: internal or no shell

sumels	tiscutfief	wocnr hhocc
mussel	*cuttlefish*	*crown conch*

grite weroic	stanuliu	maic
tiger cowrie	*nautilus*	*clam*

leSsertl ohtinc	yotsre	nomo lasin
Steller's chiton	*oyster*	*moon snail*

lopalsc	penteahl skut	fiet-ddeanh lewk
scallop	*elephant tusk*	*left-handed welk*

scallop	crown conch	nautilus
clam	moon snail	tiger cowrie
cuttlefish	Steller's chiton	oyster
left-handed welk	mussel	elephant tusk

Page 204

What a Whale Shark!

Miss Freed is surprising her class with a field trip to a sealife exhibit. She knows that her students will be so excited because the main attraction at the exhibit is a whale shark. Her sixth graders are fascinated by this monstrous but docile creature. They first learned about the whale shark, the largest fish in the world, when they were studying ocean life. It seemed they couldn't get enough information about it.

Beth and Kim gave a great report on the whale shark. They reported that this up-to-50-foot-long fish eats plankton and small schooling fish. Some whale sharks have even let divers grab on to their dorsal fin and go for a ride.

Jack learned that the whale shark may be found in a band around the equator extending roughly 30° north and 35° south. He reported that they seem to prefer surface-water temperatures in the 70s or low 80s.

Always concerned with protecting animals, Cassie pointed out in her research that the whale shark has much more to fear from humans than humans have to fear from it. These gentle giants are harpooned and eaten near India and in Taiwan. The Japanese, however, don't like to kill the whale shark. It supposedly brings good luck and is named after a patron god of the sea. Miss Freed wonders how they managed to get a fish as large as this in the exhibit. The students are going to love this field trip.

Check.
The whale shark is . . .

- [x] a fish.
- [ ] a shark.
- [x] gentle.
- [x] huge.
- [x] the largest fish in the world.

Match.
Match the person(s) to the fact he or she reported.
Kim and Beth — the whale shark has a lot to fear from humans
Cassie — Whale sharks eat plankton and small fish.
Jack — Whale sharks like warmer waters.

Underline.
The Japanese think the whale shark . . .

should be eaten.   <u>brings good luck.</u>   is dangerous.

Write.
Why does the whale shark have more to fear from humans than humans do from whale sharks? *Whale shark is docile and gentle. Humans harpoon and eat whale sharks.*

Page 205

Classy Sea Creatures

Nearly every major group of animals is represented in the ocean community. These animals range in size from the over 100-ton blue whale to the microscopic plankton.

A very simple "family tree" of ocean life is illustrated on this page. List examples of various sea organisms that represent each major group.

Vertebrates

BIRDS
(Vertebrates that are warm-blooded and have feathers.)
brown pelican
sandpiper
herring gull

MAMMALS
(Vertebrates that have lungs and nurse their young.)
blue whale, narwhale, humpback whale, killer whale, sperm whale

FISHES
(Vertebrates that breathe with gills and have fins.)
mackerel
herring

ECHINODERMS
(Marine animals with spiny plates, often with spines for protection.)
starfish
sand dollar
sea urchin
sea cucumber

MOLLUSKS
(Soft-bodied animals covered with a mantle that usually makes a shell.)
scallops
blue mussels
octopus
squid

COELENTERATES
(Soft-bodied radially symmetrical animals with a central digestive cavity.)
jellyfish
sea anemone

ARTHROPODS
(Almost all marine arthropods are crustaceans with hard body coverings and legs.)
barnacles
lobster
rock crab
horseshoe crab

Invertebrates

Page 206

Endangered Species

Discover the habitat and the reason(s) each animal is endangered.

Whooping Crane	Cassowary	Nile Crocodile
North America	Australia: New Guinea	Africa
Habitat: *Wetlands*	Habitat: *Forest*	Habitat: *Rivers*
Why Endangered: *Over-hunted; shot for sport*	Why Endangered: *Hunted for food*	Why Endangered: *Hunted for hide (skin)*

Giant Panda	Giant Armadillo	
Asia	South America	
Habitat: *Bamboo Jungle*	Habitat: *Rainforest*	Habitat:
		Answers will vary.
Why Endangered: *Loss of bamboo for food*	Why Endangered: *Vanishing rainforests*	Why Endangered:
		Student's Choice

Page 207

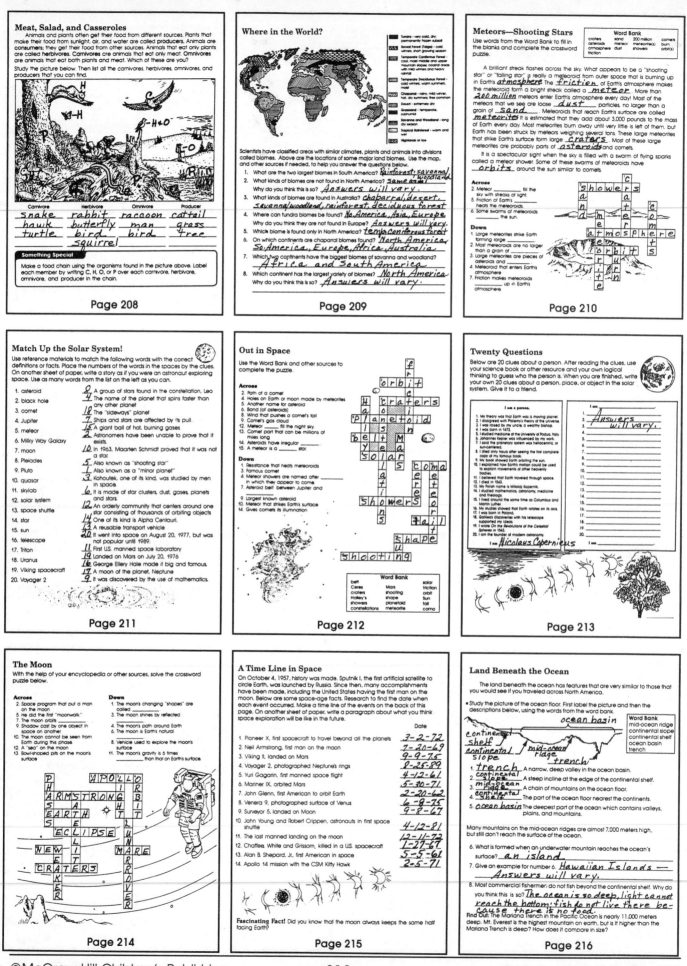

Meat, Salad, and Casseroles

Animals and plants often get their food from different sources. Plants that make their food from sunlight, air, and water are called producers. Animals are consumers; they get their food from other sources. Animals that eat only plants are called herbivores. Carnivores are animals that eat only meat. Omnivores are animals that eat both plants and meat. Which of these are you?

Study the picture below. Then list all the carnivores, herbivores, omnivores, and producers that you can find.

Carnivore	Herbivore	Omnivore	Producer
snake	rabbit	racoon	cattail
hawk	butterfly	man	grass
turtle	bird	bird	tree
	squirrel		

Something Special

Make a food chain using the organisms found in the picture above. Label each member by writing C, H, O, or P over each carnivore, herbivore, omnivore, and producer in the chain.

Page 208

Where in the World?

Scientists have classified areas with similar climates, plants and animals into divisions called biomes. Above are the locations of some major land biomes. Use the map, and other sources if needed, to help you answer the questions below.

1. What are the two largest biomes in South America? _rainforest; savanna/ woodland_
2. What kinds of biomes are not found in North America? _Same as will vary._ Why do you think this is so? _Answers will vary._
3. What kinds of biomes are found in Australia? _chabarral, desert, savanna/woodland, rainforest, deciduous forest_
4. Where can tundra biomes be found? _No. America, Asia, Europe_ Why do you think they are not found in Europe? _Answers will vary._
5. Which biome is found only in North America? _Temp. coniferous forest_
6. On which continents are chaparral biomes found? _North America, So. America, Europe, Africa, Australia_
7. Which two continents have the biggest biomes of savanna and woodland? _Africa and South America_
8. Which continent has the largest variety of biomes? _North America_ Why do you think this is so? _Answers will vary._

Page 209

Meteors—Shooting Stars

Use words from the Word Bank to fill in the blanks and complete the crossword puzzle.

Word Bank
craters · sand · 200 million · comets · asteroids · meteor · meteorite(s) · burn · atmosphere · dust · showers · orbit(s) · friction

A brilliant streak flashes across the sky. What appears to be a "shooting star" or "falling star" is really a meteoroid from outer space that is burning up in Earth's _atmosphere_. The _friction_ of Earth's atmosphere makes the meteoroid form a bright streak called a _meteor_. More than _200 million_ meteors enter Earth's atmosphere every day! Most of the meteors we see are loose _dust_ particles, no larger than a grain of _sand_. Meteoroids that reach Earth's surface are called _meteorites_. It is estimated that they add about 3,000 pounds to the mass of Earth every day. Most meteorites burn away until very little is left of them, but Earth has been struck by meteors weighing several tons. These large meteorites that strike Earth's surface form large _craters_. Most of these large meteorites are probably parts of _asteroids_ and comets.

It is a spectacular sight when the sky is filled with a swarm of flying sparks called a meteor shower. Some of these swarms of meteoroids have _orbits_ around the sun similar to comets.

Across
2. Meteor _____ fill the sky with streaks of light.
3. Friction of Earth's _____ heats the meteoroids.
6. Some swarms of meteoroids _____ the sun.

Down
1. Large meteorites strike Earth forming large _____
2. Most meteorites are no larger than a grain of _____
3. Large meteorites are pieces of asteroids and _____
4. Meteoroid that enters Earth's atmosphere
5. Friction makes meteoroids _____ up in Earth's atmosphere

Page 210

Match Up the Solar System!

Use reference materials to match the following words with the correct definitions or facts. Place the numbers of the words in the spaces by the clues. On another sheet of paper, write a story as if you were an astronaut exploring space. Use as many words from the list on the left as you can.

1. asteroid
2. black hole
3. comet
4. Jupiter
5. meteor
6. Milky Way Galaxy
7. moon
8. Pleiades
9. Pluto
10. quasar
11. skylab
12. solar system
13. space shuttle
14. sun
15. sun
16. telescope
17. Triton
18. Uranus
19. Viking spacecraft
20. Voyager 2

_8_ A group of stars found in the constellation, Leo
_4_ The name of the planet that spins faster than any other planet
_18_ The "sideways" planet
_7_ Ships and stars are affected by its pull.
_15_ A giant ball of hot, burning gases
_2_ Astronomers have been unable to prove that it exists.
_10_ In 1963, Maarten Schmidt proved that it was not a star.
_5_ Also known as "shooting star"
_1_ Also known as "minor planet"
_3_ Kohoutek, one of its kind, was studied by men in space.
_6_ It is made of star clusters, dust, gases, planets and stars.
_12_ An orderly community that centers around one star consisting of thousands of orbiting objects
_14_ One of its kind is Alpha Centauri.
_13_ A reusable transport vehicle
_20_ It went into space on August 20, 1977, but was not popular until 1989.
_11_ First U.S. manned space laboratory
_19_ Landed on Mars on July 20, 1976
_16_ George Ellery Hale made it big and famous.
_17_ A moon of the planet, Neptune
_9_ It was discovered by the use of mathematics.

Page 211

Out in Space

Use the Word Bank and other sources to complete the puzzle.

Across
2. Path of a comet
4. Holes in Earth or moon made by meteorites
5. Another name for asteroid
6. Band (of asteroids)
8. Wind that pushes a comet's tail
9. Comet's gas cloud
12. Meteor _____ fill the night sky.
13. Comet part that can be millions of miles long
14. Asteroids have irregular _____.
15. A meteor is a _____ star.

Down
1. Resistance that heats meteoroids
3. Famous comet
4. Meteor showers are named after _____ in which they appear to come.
7. Asteroid belt _____ between Jupiter and Mars
9. Largest known asteroid
10. Meteor that strikes Earth's surface
14. Gives comets its illumination

Word Bank
belt · Ceres · craters · Halley's · showers · constellations · Mars · shooting · shape · planetoid · meteorite · solar · friction · orbit · Sun · tail · coma

Page 212

Twenty Questions

Below are 20 clues about a person. After reading the clues, use your science book or other resource and your own logical thinking to guess who the person is. When you are finished, write your own 20 clues about a person, place, or object in the solar system. Give it to a friend.

I am a person.
1. My theory was that Earth was a moving planet.
2. I disagreed with Ptolemy's theory of the universe.
3. I was raised by my uncle, a wealthy bishop.
4. I was born in 1473.
5. I studied medicine at the University of Padua, Italy.
6. Johannes Kepler was influenced by my work.
7. I said the planetary system was heliocentric, or sun-centered.
8. I died only hours after seeing the first complete copy of my famous book.
9. My book showed Earth orbiting the sun.
10. I explained how Earth's motion could be used to explain movements of other heavenly bodies.
11. I believed that Earth traveled through space.
12. I died in 1543.
13. My Polish name is Mikolaj Kopernik.
14. I studied mathematics, astronomy, medicine and theology.
15. I lived around the same time as Columbus and Martin Luther.
16. My studies showed that Earth rotates on its axis.
17. I was born in Poland.
18. Galileo's discoveries with his telescope supported my ideas.
19. I wrote On the Revolutions of the Celestial Spheres in 1543.
20. I am the founder of modern astronomy.

I am _Nicolaus Copernicus_

I am
1.
2. _Answers will vary._
...

Page 213

The Moon

With the help of your encyclopedia or other sources, solve the crossword puzzle below.

Across
2. Space program that put a man on the moon
6. He did the first "moonwalk."
7. The moon orbits
9. Shadow cast by one object in space on another
10. The moon cannot be seen from Earth during this phase
12. A "sea" on the moon
13. Bowl-shaped pits on the moon's surface

Down
1. The moon's changing "shapes" are called
3. The moon shines by reflected _____
4. The moon's path around Earth
6. The moon is Earth's natural _____
9. Vehicle used to explore the moon's surface
11. The moon's gravity is 6 times _____ than on Earth's surface

Page 214

A Time Line in Space

On October 4, 1957, history was made. Sputnik I, the first artificial satellite to circle Earth, was launched by Russia. Since then, many accomplishments have been made, including the United States having the first man on the moon. Below are some space-age facts. Research to find the date when each event occurred. Make a time line of the events on the back of this page. On another sheet of paper, write a paragraph about what you think space exploration will be like in the future.

	Date
1. Pioneer X, first spacecraft to travel beyond all the planets	3-2-72
2. Neil Armstrong, first man on the moon	7-20-69
3. Viking II, landed on Mars	9-9-75
4. Voyager 2, photographed Neptune's rings	8-25-89
5. Yuri Gagarin, first manned space flight	4-12-61
6. Mariner IX, orbited Mars	5-30-71
7. John Glenn, first American to orbit Earth	2-20-62
8. Venera 9, photographed surface of Venus	6-8-75
9. Surveyor 5, landed on Moon	9-8-67
10. John Young and Robert Crippen, astronauts in first space shuttle	4-12-81
11. The last manned landing on the moon	12-11-72
12. Chaffee, White and Grissom, killed in a U.S. spacecraft	1-27-67
13. Alan B. Shepard, Jr., first American in space	5-5-61
14. Apollo 14 mission with the CSM Kitty Hawk	2-5-71

Fascinating Fact! Did you know that the moon always keeps the same half facing Earth?

Page 215

Land Beneath the Ocean

The land beneath the ocean has features that are very similar to those that you would see if you traveled across North America.

- Study the picture of the ocean floor. First label the picture and then the descriptions below, using the words from the word bank.

Word Bank
mid-ocean ridge · continental slope · continental shelf · ocean basin · trench

trench A narrow, deep valley in the ocean basin.
continental slope A steep incline at the edge of the continental shelf.
mid-ocean ridge A chain of mountains on the ocean floor.
continental shelf The part of the ocean floor nearest the continents.
ocean basin The deepest part of the ocean which contains valleys, plains, and mountains.

Many mountains on the mid-ocean ridges are almost 7,000 meters high, but still don't reach the surface of the ocean.

6. What is formed when an underwater mountain reaches the ocean's surface? _an island_
7. Give an example for number 6. _Hawaiian Islands — Answers will vary._
8. Most commercial fishermen do not fish beyond the continental shelf. Why do you think this is so? _The ocean is so deep, light cannot reach the bottom; fish do not live there because there is no food._

Find Out: The Mariana Trench in the Pacific Ocean is nearly 11,000 meters deep. Mt. Everest is the highest mountain on earth, but is it higher than the Mariana Trench is deep? How does it compare in size?

Page 216

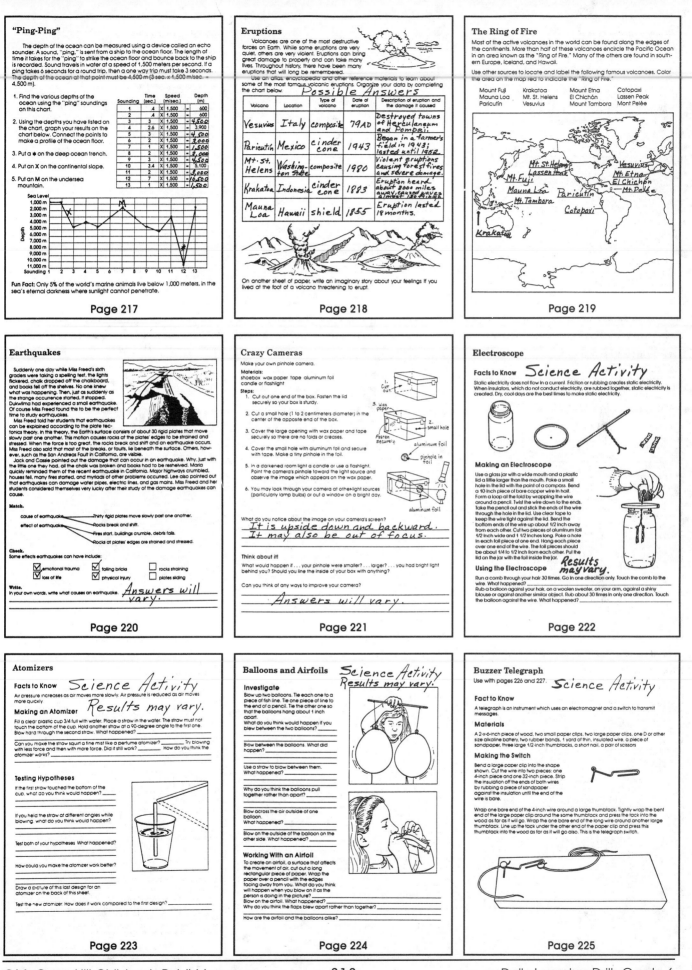

"Ping-Ping"

The depth of the ocean can be measured using a device called an echo sounder. A sound, "ping," is sent from a ship to the ocean floor. The length of time it takes for the "ping" to strike the ocean floor and bounce back to the ship is recorded. Sound travels in water at a speed of 1,500 meters per second. If a ping takes 6 seconds for a round trip, then a one way trip must take 3 seconds. The depth of the ocean at that point must be 4,500 m (3 sec. x 1,500 m/sec. = 4,500 m).

1. Find the various depths of the ocean using the "ping" soundings on this chart.

2. Using the depths you have listed on the chart, graph your results on the chart below. Connect the points to make a profile of the ocean floor.

3. Put a ✱ on the deep ocean trench.

4. Put an X on the continental slope.

5. Put an M on the undersea mountain.

Sounding	Time (sec.)	Speed (m/sec.)	Depth (m)
1	.4	X 1,500	= 600
2	.4	X 1,500	= 600
3	3	X 1,500	= 4,500
4	2.6	X 1,500	= 3,900
5	3	X 1,500	= 4,500
6	2	X 1,500	= 3,000
7	1	X 1,500	= 1,500
8	2	X 1,500	= 3,000
9	3	X 1,500	= 4,500
10	3.4	X 1,500	= 5,100
11	2	X 1,500	= 3,000
12	7	X 1,500	= 10,500
13	1	X 1,500	= 1,500

Fun Fact: Only 5% of the world's marine animals live below 1,000 meters, in the sea's eternal darkness where sunlight cannot penetrate.

Page 217

Eruptions

Volcanoes are one of the most destructive forces on Earth. While some eruptions are very quiet, others are very violent. Eruptions can bring great damage to property and can take many lives. Throughout history, there have been many eruptions that will long be remembered.

Use an atlas, encyclopedia and other reference materials to learn about some of the most famous volcanic eruptions. Organize your data by completing the chart below. *Possible Answers*

Volcano	Location	Type of volcano	Date of eruption	Description of eruption and the damage it caused
Vesuvius	Italy	composite	79 AD	Destroyed towns of Herculaneum and Pompeii
Parícutin	Mexico	cinder cone	1943	Began in a farmer's field in 1943; lasted until 1952
Mt. St. Helens	Washington State	composite	1980	Violent eruptions causing forest fires and severe damage.
Krakatoa	Indonesia	cinder cone	1883	Eruption heard about 3000 miles away; caused waves almost 130 feet high
Mauna Loa	Hawaii	shield	1855	Eruption lasted 18 months.

On another sheet of paper, write an imaginary story about your feelings if you lived at the foot of a volcano threatening to erupt.

Page 218

The Ring of Fire

Most of the active volcanoes in the world can be found along the edges of the continents. More than half of these volcanoes encircle the Pacific Ocean in an area known as the "Ring of Fire." Many of the others are found in southern Europe, Iceland, and Hawaii.

Use other sources to locate and label the following famous volcanoes. Color the area on the map red to indicate the "Ring of Fire."

Mount Fuji   Krakatoa   Mount Etna   Cotopaxi
Mauna Loa   Mt. St. Helens   El Chichón   Lassen Peak
Parícutin   Vesuvius   Mount Tambora   Mont Pelée

Page 219

Earthquakes

Suddenly one day while Miss Freed's sixth graders were taking a spelling test, the lights flickered, chalk dropped off the chalkboard, and books fell off the shelves. No one knew what was happening. Then, just as suddenly as the strange occurrence started, it stopped. Dukwilma had experienced a small earthquake. Of course Miss Freed found this to be the perfect time to study earthquakes.

Miss Freed told her students that earthquakes can be explained according to the plate tectonics theory. In this theory, the Earth's surface consists of about 30 rigid plates that move slowly past one another. This motion causes rocks at the plates' edges to be strained and stressed. When the force is too great, the rocks break and shift and an earthquake occurs. Miss Freed also said that most of the breaks, or faults, lie beneath the surface. Others, however, such as the San Andreas Fault in California, are visible.

Jack and Cassie pointed out the damage that can occur in an earthquake. Why, just with the little one they had, all the chalk was broken and books had to be reshelved. Maria quickly reminded them of the recent earthquake in California. Major highways crumbled, houses fell, many fires started, and myriads of other problems occurred. Lee also pointed out that earthquakes can damage water pipes, electric lines, and gas mains. Miss Freed and her students considered themselves very lucky after their study of the damage earthquakes can cause.

Match.

cause of earthquake — Thirty rigid plates move slowly past one another.
— Rocks break and shift.
effect of earthquake — Fires start, buildings crumble, debris falls.
— Rocks at plates' edges are strained and stressed.

Check.
Some effects earthquakes can have include:
☑ emotional trauma   ☑ falling bricks   ☐ rocks straining
☑ loss of life   ☑ physical injury   ☐ plates sliding

Write.
In your own words, write what causes an earthquake. *Answers will vary.*

Page 220

Crazy Cameras

Make your own pinhole camera.

Materials:
shoebox   wax paper   tape   aluminum foil   candle or flashlight

Steps:
1. Cut out one end of the box. Fasten the lid securely so your box is sturdy.
2. Cut a small hole (1 to 2 centimeters diameter) in the center of the opposite end of the box.
3. Cover the large opening with wax paper and tape securely so there are no folds or creases.
4. Cover the small hole with aluminum foil and secure with tape. Make a tiny pinhole in the foil.
5. In a darkened room light a candle or use a flashlight. Point the camera's pinhole toward the light source and observe the image which appears on the wax paper.
6. You may look through your camera at other light sources (particularly lamp bulbs) or out a window on a bright day.

What do you notice about the image on your camera's screen?
It is upside down and backward. It may also be out of focus.

Think about it!
What would happen if . . . your pinhole were smaller? . . . larger? . . . you had bright light behind you? Should you line the inside of your box with anything?

Can you think of any ways to improve your camera?
Answers will vary.

Page 221

Electroscope

Facts to Know   *Science Activity*

Static electricity does not flow in a current. Friction or rubbing creates static electricity. When insulators, which do not conduct electricity, are rubbed together, static electricity is created. Dry, cool days are the best times to make static electricity.

Making an Electroscope

Use a glass jar with a wide mouth and a plastic lid a little larger than the mouth. Poke a small hole in the lid with the point of a compass. Bend a 10-inch piece of bare copper wire in half. Form a loop at the fold by wrapping the wire around a pencil. Twist the wire down to the ends. Take the pencil out and stick the ends of the wire through the hole in the lid. Use clear tape to keep the wire tight against the lid. Bend the bottom ends of the wire up 1/2 inch away from each other. Cut two pieces of aluminum foil 1/2 inch wide and 1 1/2 inches long. Poke a hole in each foil piece at one end. Hang each piece over one end of the wire. The foil pieces should be about 1/4 to 1/2 inch from each other. Put the lid on the jar with the foil inside the jar.

Using the Electroscope   *Results may vary.*

Run a comb through your hair 30 times. Go in one direction only. Touch the comb to the wire. What happened? _____
Rub a balloon against your hair, on a woolen sweater, on your arm, against a shiny blouse or against another similar object. Rub about 30 times in only one direction. Touch the balloon against the wire. What happened? _____

Page 222

Atomizers

Facts to Know   *Science Activity*   *Results may vary.*

Air pressure increases as air moves more slowly. Air pressure is reduced as air moves more quickly.

Making an Atomizer

Fill a clear plastic cup 3/4 full with water. Place a straw in the water. The straw must not touch the bottom of the cup. Hold another straw at a 90-degree angle to the first one. Blow hard through the second straw. What happened? _____

Can you make the straw squirt a fine mist like a perfume atomizer? _____ Try blowing with less force and then with more force. Did it still work? _____ How do you think the atomizer works? _____

Testing Hypotheses

If the first straw touched the bottom of the cup, what do you think would happen? _____

If you held the straw at different angles while blowing, what do you think would happen? _____

Test both of your hypotheses. What happened? _____

How could you make the atomizer work better? _____

Draw a picture of this last design for an atomizer on the back of this sheet.

Test the new atomizer. How does it work compared to the first design? _____

Page 223

Balloons and Airfoils

Science Activity   *Results may vary!*

Investigate

Blow up two balloons. Tie each one to a piece of fish line. Tie one piece of line to the end of a pencil. Tie the other one so that the balloons hang about 1 inch apart.
What do you think would happen if you blew between the two balloons? _____

Blow between the balloons. What did happen? _____

Use a straw to blow between them. What happened? _____

Why do you think the balloons pull together rather than apart? _____

Blow across the air outside of one balloon. What happened? _____

Blow on the outside of the balloon on the other side. What happened? _____

Working With an Airfoil

To create an airfoil, a surface that affects the movement of air, cut out a long rectangular piece of paper. Wrap the paper over a pencil with the edges facing away from you. What do you think will happen when you blow on it as the person is doing in the picture?
Blow on the airfoil. What happened? _____
Why do you think the flaps blew apart rather than together? _____

How are the airfoil and the balloons alike? _____

Page 224

Buzzer Telegraph

Use with pages 226 and 227.   *Science Activity*

Fact to Know

A telegraph is an instrument which uses an electromagnet and a switch to transmit messages.

Materials

A 2-x-6-inch piece of wood, two small paper clips, two large paper clips, one D or other size alkaline battery, two rubber bands, 1 yard of thin, insulated wire, a piece of sandpaper, three large 1/2-inch thumbtacks, a short nail, a pair of scissors

Making the Switch

Bend a large paper clip into the shape shown. Cut the wire into two pieces: one 4-inch piece and one 32-inch piece. Strip the insulation off the ends of both wires by rubbing a piece of sandpaper against the insulation until the end of the wire is bare.

Wrap one bare end of the 4-inch wire around a large thumbtack. Tightly wrap the bent end of the large paper clip around the same thumbtack and press the tack into the wood as far as it will go. Wrap the one bare end of the long wire around another large thumbtack. Line up the tack under the other end of the paper clip and press this thumbtack into the wood as far as it will go also. This is the telegraph switch.

Page 225

Buzzer Telegraph

Use with pages 225 and 227. *Science Activity*

Making a Battery Holder

Wind two rubber bands very tightly around the positive and negative poles of the battery. Slip a small paper clip under the rubber band at each pole and bend the clips over. This is your battery holder.

Making the Buzzer

With a hammer or similar tool, tap a short nail into the wood. It should be stuck firmly but not too deeply. To create an electromagnet, wrap the long wire around the nail in neat coils until there is only about 4 inches left. Tightly wrap one end of the other large paper clip around a third thumbtack. Line up the other end of the paper clip above the coils and press the thumbtack into the wood as far as it will go. Connect the end of the long wire to the paper clip at the positive pole (top of the battery). Connect the bare end of the short wire to the paper clip at the (negative pole (bottom of the battery). The telegraph is now ready for use.

Press the paper clip switch to the thumbtack and the circuit should be complete, making an electromagnet which pulls the paper clip buzzer down with a click. Release the switch and the paper clip buzzer should bounce back up. If it doesn't work, check all connections and the strength of your battery. You may also need to adjust the heights of the paper clips used in the switch and buzzer.

Page 226

Sending Telegraph Messages

Use with pages 225 and 226.

Working with the Morse Code

With the Morse Code, messages are sent by using dots and dashes that represent letters. A dot is made by briefly tapping a telegraph switch. A dash is made by holding the switch down a little longer. Use the Morse Code to send messages to your partner. Start by sending short names or very simple words. Gradually work up to sentences, making sure to pause between words. Take turns sending and receiving messages.

International Morse Code

A	B	C	D
E	F	G	H
I	J	K	L
M	N	O	P
Q	R	S	T
U	V	W	X
Y	Z		

Sending Messages *Answers will vary*

Write out your message. Then place the dots and dashes under each letter.

Decoding Messages

Record the dots and dashes as your partner sends a message. Then place the matching letters above the dots and dashes.

Page 227

Acids and Bases

Facts to Know

Acids and bases are chemical compounds. Some of these compounds are strong and abrasive. Many are used as cleaning agents. Litmus paper is an indicator. Indicators are affected when an acid or base is present in a substance. Blue litmus paper turns red when dipped in an acid. Red litmus paper turns blue when dipped in a base.

Testing for Acids and Bases

Use blue and red litmus paper to test each of the substances on the chart. Record the results by writing the color the paper turns when dipped and whether the substance is an acid or a base. The first one is done for you.

Science Activity

Substance	Blue Litmus	Red Litmus	Acid, Base or Neither
lemon juice	red	red	acid
vinegar			
ammonia			
orange juice			
tea			
milk			
baking soda and water			
cleanser and water			
water			
vinegar and salt			
grapefruit juice			
antacid pills and water			
cola			

Page 228

Testing for Starch

Facts to Know

Starch is found in many foods and plants. Iodine is an indicator of starch. It turns blue-black when placed on a substance containing starch.

Testing for Starch

Safety Note: Iodine can be dangerous. Do not taste, spill or misuse it in any way. Place a drop of iodine on each of the substances listed on the chart. Record the results. The first one is done for you.

Science Activity

Substance	Color of Iodine	Starch: Yes or No
white bread	blue-black	yes
brown bread		
dry cereal		
brown leaf		
popped popcorn		
oatmeal		
orange peel		
lemon peel		
liquid starch		
newspaper		
paper towel		
tissue		
water		
alcohol		
dish soap		
cloth		

Page 229

Testing for Calcite

Facts to Know

There are three main types of rock: sedimentary, igneous and metamorphic. Sedimentary rock is formed underwater from layers of sediment. Igneous rock is rock that erupted from a volcano in a liquid form and later became solid. Metamorphic rock is rock that was once sedimentary or igneous but was changed by heat or pressure deep within the earth. One way to identify rocks is to check for calcite or lime in the rock.

Testing for Calcite *Science Activity*

Collect a variety of rocks. Carefully wash each one. Number and initial pieces of tape for each so that you can tell them apart. Put the tape pieces on the rocks. Place a few drops of vinegar on the first rock with an eyedropper. Did it fizz? _____ Are there any bubbles? _____
Dip the rock partway into the cup of vinegar. Hold the rock to your ear. Can you hear it fizz? _____ Are there any bubbles? _____
Rocks which fizz or show the bubbles in this acid have calcite, lime or calcium carbonate in them.

Chart Making

Check your rocks and those of your friends. Record the number and initial of each rock. Tell whether you noted any fizzing or bubbles by writing "yes" or "no" on the chart.

Number/Initial	Fizzing?	Bubbles?	Calcite or Lime Present?
Example: 1TS	yes	no	yes

Drawing Conclusions

Are most rocks which contain calcite or lime sedimentary or igneous? _____
What are your reasons? _____

Page 230

Testing Hardness

Facts to Know *Science Activity*

Scientists use many tests to identify and classify rocks. One such test is a hardness scale in which materials are rated from softest to hardest. For example, a material such as talc is rated #1, the softest on the scale. On this scale, diamond is rated #10, the hardest. Use this information to help you in testing the hardness of each of your rocks.

Hardness Scale	Test
#1 and #2	A fingernail can scratch these.
#3	A penny can scratch it.
#4 and #5	A knife can scratch these.
#6 and #7	They can scratch glass.
#8, #9, #10	They can scratch any rock that is lower on the scale.

Testing Rocks for Hardness

Make sure your rocks are clean. Write a different number and your initials on pieces of tape. Put the pieces of tape on each rock and list each number-initial identification in the first column of the chart. Use your fingernail, a penny, a knife and a glass jar to test each rock. Record the results on the chart by writing "yes" or "no" as in the example. Use the information above to help classify each rock's hardness. Work carefully and check your results twice.

Safety Note:
Be very careful not to cut yourself with the knife. You don't have to press too forcefully with the knife. Also, do not press the rock too hard against the jar. Do not break the jar!

Number/Initial	Fingernail Scratch	Penny Scratch	Knife Scratch	Scratches Jar	Scratches Rocks Less Than 8,9,10	Hardness Range
Example: 1TS	yes	yes	yes	no	no	#4 – #5

Page 231

What Do You See in the Ink?

Background:

Chromatography, the separation of the substances of a mixture through the use of an absorbing material, can be used to separate things such as blood or ink from another substance. If something stained is placed in a solvent, that solvent can cause some of the substance to be pulled, or attracted, away. The colors, or pigments, can be used as a comparison to other substances. If colors "bleed" in the same manner, they could be from the same source. When a crime is committed, this test may be used to provide clues for solving it.

Materials Needed:

paper towel strips (1 x 3 inches), water, straws, cups, tape, six black ink pens - each of a different brand

Procedure:

1. Divide class into three groups and give each group two pens and two small strips of paper towels.
2. Use a different pen to draw a line across the center of each of the paper towel strips.
3. Tape the paper towel strips to the center of the straws so that they will hang when the straws are placed crosswise on top of the cups. The cups should contain enough water so that the paper strips will hang into the water, but not touch the bottom of the cup. The ink mark should remain above the water.

Record the Data: *Results may vary.*

1. What happened when the paper touched the water? _____
2. What is on the paper? _____

You should see various color patterns from the different kinds of ink. These ink color patterns are called chromatograms. Using this technique in investigating crimes, one can determine, by matching the color patterns, if the possibility exists that a specific pen or typewriter might have been used in the perpetration of a crime.

Page 232

The Bill of Rights

Write a bill of rights for your school. *Answers will vary.*

_____

Write a personal bill of rights.

_____

Write an amendment you would like to see added to the U.S. Constitution.

_____

Page 233

Three Branches at Work

Write what you would do as a member of each branch of government in regard to the "law" being proposed.

> Law under consideration: The penny would no longer be a coin in the U.S. monetary system. Everything would cost five cents or more.

As a member of Congress: *Answers will vary.*
_____

As President: _____

As a judge on the Supreme Court: _____

> Law under consideration: Every company with ten or more workers must hire the same number of men and women.

As a member of Congress: *Answers will vary.*
_____

As President: _____

As a judge on the Supreme Court: _____

Page 234

Three Branches at Work (cont.)

Law under consideration: The first Monday of every other month beginning in February 1997 will be a national holiday. No other holidays will be observed.

As a member of Congress: Answers will vary.

As President:

As a judge on the Supreme Court:

Law under consideration: All schools in the United States must be open for students' attendance the same number of days. They will open on the first Monday after August 24th and will close the first Friday after June 5th.

As a member of Congress: Answers will vary.

As President:

As a judge on the Supreme Court:

Page 235

Getting Involved

Choose a candidate to research. Then complete the following activities.

Create a newspaper advertisement. Answers will vary.

Write out what you might say in a telephone call on behalf of a candidate.

Hello. My name is ______
I am calling to ask you to ______

because ______

Please vote next ______
Thank you for your consideration.
Goodbye.

Write a slogan.

Write a letter to the editor expressing your views about a particular candidate and his/her views on a particular issue.

Dear ______ ,

Make a poster, button and flyer on other sheets of paper.

Page 236

Getting Involved (cont.)

Create a commercial endorsing a candidate on a view or an issue for TV or radio. Act it out.

With another student, debate both sides of an issue.

Draw an editorial cartoon featuring a candidate on a view or an issue.

Write an editorial to go with the cartoon. Answers will vary.

Write a speech for your issue or candidate.

Page 237

The President

The President of the U.S. is often considered the most powerful elected official in the world. It makes sense then that not everybody is eligible to hold this important position. Complete the page below to find out the necessary qualifications one must have in order to be President and to find out the important responsibilities that are a part of this position.

1. At least how old does the President have to be? 35 years old
   Why do you think this is so? Answers will vary.
2. How long does someone have to live in the U.S. before he/she can be President? 14 years Do you agree with this? Why? Answers will vary.
3. What is the 3rd legal qualification for a President besides the two listed above? natural-born citizen
4. How can someone be nominated for the Presidency? by a national political party convention
5. To what political party does our current President belong? Subject to change
6. What is the Electoral College? Electors chosen by voters in each state & D.C. to officially elect the President
7. When is the Presidential Inauguration held? noon on January 20. If the 20th is a Sunday, it takes place on 21st.
8. How long is the term of a President? 4 years
9. Effective in 1951, the 22nd Amendment says a President can serve how many terms? 2
10. What kind of salary does the President receive? $200,000.00
11. What happens if a President dies, resigns or is removed from office? Vice President assumes the office.
12. What branch of the federal government does the President head? Executive
13. What does this branch consist of? Office of the President, President's cabinet, plus exec. agencies
14. Name the seven basic roles of the President. chief exec., commander in chief, foreign policy director, legislative leader, political party head, popular leader, chief of state

Something Extra: Pick one of the seven roles of the President. List the responsibilities involved in this role. Make a list of things the current President has done in this role. Answers will vary.

Page 238

Birthplaces of Presidents

Did you know that only 18 out of the 50 states have been the birthplaces of Presidents? Did you know that 8 Presidents came from Virginia and 7 came from Ohio? Complete the page below to see if any Presidents have been born in your state.

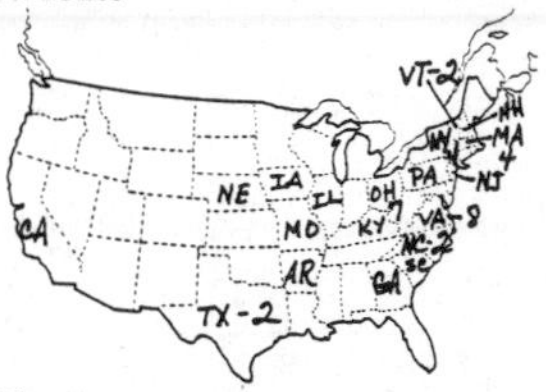

1. Washington, Jefferson, Madison, Monroe, W. H. Harrison, Tyler, Taylor and Wilson were all born in Virginia. Label this state on the map and put the number 8 next to it.
2. Grant, Hayes, Garfield, B. Harrison, McKinley, Taft and Harding were born in Ohio. Label this state and put the number 7 next to it.
3. New York is the birthplace of Van Buren, Fillmore, T. Roosevelt and F. D. Roosevelt. Put a number 4 and the name of this state on the map where it belongs.
4. Four Presidents were also born in Massachusetts - J. Adams, J. Q. Adams, Kennedy and Bush. Label this state and put the number 4 next to it.
5. North Carolina, Texas and Vermont each had 2 Presidents born in them. Polk and A. Johnson were born in North Carolina. Eisenhower and L. B. Johnson claim Texas as their birthplace and Vermont is the birthplace of Arthur and Coolidge. Label these states and put a number 2 next to each of them.
6. The rest of the Presidents were all born in different states. They are listed below. Write the name of the state from which each President came in the state where it belongs.

Arkansas - Clinton	Iowa - Hoover	New Hampshire - Pierce
California - Nixon	Kentucky - Lincoln	New Jersey - Cleveland
Georgia - Carter	Missouri - Truman	Pennsylvania - Buchanan
Illinois - Reagan	Nebraska - Ford	South Carolina - Jackson

7. Label the Atlantic and the Pacific Oceans on the map. Have more Presidents been born near the Atlantic or the Pacific Ocean? Atlantic
8. Label the rest of the states on the map. If no President has been born in your state, tell why you think this is so on the back of this page. If one (or more) has been born in your state, write if you think he was or is a good representative of your state and tell why.

Answers will vary

Page 239

Presidential Firsts

There is always a first time for everything! Use the clues below to find out which Presidents were the first to do the things listed. Fill in the blanks using the names in the box and other references to help you.

Abraham Lincoln	John Adams	Franklin Pierce
William Taft	Calvin Coolidge	George Washington
Thomas Jefferson	Woodrow Wilson	Theodore Roosevelt
Andrew Jackson	James Polk	John Tyler
Lyndon Johnson	William Henry Harrison	Gerald Ford

1. He was our first President and the first to be elected unanimously. Washington
2. The first President to live in the White House, his son was also President. J. Adams
3. This President was the first to win the Nobel Peace Prize, and he became our nation's youngest President after McKinley's assassination. T. Roosevelt
4. The first President born in the 20th century, he was also President when Martin Luther King, Jr. was assassinated in 1968. L. Johnson
5. This President was the first Vice President not elected by the people to become President and was our 38th President. Gerald Ford
6. The first President born in a log cabin, the first President to be elected by a national convention and the first President to ride on a railroad train, he was President from 1829-1837. A. Jackson
7. John Tyler became the first Vice President to become President when this President was the first to die in office. W. H. Harrison
8. He was the first to hold regular press conferences, to speak on the radio and was in office when World War I ended in 1918. W. Wilson
9. This President was the only one born on the 4th of July and was the first to be sworn in by a former President. Coolidge
10. He was the first President born after the adoption of the U.S. Constitution, the first President whose wife died while he was in office and the first President to marry while in office. He was our 10th President. Tyler
11. This President was the first to be born in the 19th century. Pierce
12. He was the first President to serve as Speaker of the House and was President when gold was discovered in California in 1848. Polk
13. The first President to be inaugurated in Washington, D.C., this man died on the 4th of July. Jefferson
14. He was our first President to be assassinated. Lincoln
15. This man was the first to become Chief Justice after serving as President, and the first to open the baseball season in 1910. Taft

Something Extra: Have you ever been the first in your class or family to do something? Write about it. Or write about the first time you did something special.

Page 240

Two Presidents

Jack and Beth spent several hours trying to decide which two famous people they wanted to compare. First, they thought they would compare famous athletes. Jack wanted to compare football players, and Beth wanted to compare volleyball players. Famous authors came up, but they could not agree on authors either. Finally, they decided to compare U.S. Presidents. They each picked a number between one and 42. They chose ten and 15. It was decided. They would compare John Tyler, our tenth President, and James Buchanan, our fifteenth.

Jack and Beth were surprised to learn how similar Tyler and Buchanan were. For instance, both went to college and practiced law. They both ran successfully for seats in the U.S. House of Representatives: Tyler in 1816 and Buchanan four years later. Jack learned that Tyler was elected to the U.S. Senate in 1827 and that Buchanan followed him there seven years later. But he also noted that whereas Buchanan went on to become Secretary of State and minister to Great Britain after serving about ten years in the Senate, Tyler went from the Senate to become Vice-President of the United States under William Henry Harrison. Beth then told Jack that Tyler became President only one month after Harrison's inauguration due to Harrison's death. Buchanan, Beth noted, was elected President.

Beth and Jack went on to learn that three new states entered the Union under Buchanan and that under Tyler, China opened its ports to American trade and Florida joined the Union.

When they were done researching for their comparison, Jack and Beth were surprised at the amount of information they had gathered. Now came the hard part of putting it all together!

Fill in.
The following apply to a. Tyler, or b. Buchanan. Put the appropriate letter in the box.

- a became President when Harrison died
- b elected President
- b Secretary of State
- a Vice-President
- a three new states entered the Union during his presidency
- a Florida joined the Union during his presidency

Write.
List similarities and differences between Tyler and Buchanan. Possible answers.

Similarities	Differences
1. Went to college	1. Buchanan-minister to Britain
2. Were lawyers	2. Buchanan elected pres.
3. Were senators & reps.	3. Tyler elected vice-pres.
4. Were presidents	4. Tyler, 10th Pres. Buchanan - 15th Pres.

Page 241

Contributing Factors

Many people have greatly influenced our country. Find out how the people below have contributed, or are contributing, to our country by filling in the chart. Then answer the questions below.

Name	Date Born	Date Died	Number of Years Lived	Contribution(s) to our Society/ Best Known For
Betsy Ross	1752	1836	84	1st Am. flag w/stars & stripes
Noah Webster	1758	1843	85	Webster's Dictionary
John Chapman	1774	1845	71	planted apple trees on frontier
Davy Crockett	1786	1836	50	died fighting for TX independence
Francis Scott Key	1779	1843	64	wrote "The Star-Spangled Banner"
John C. Frémont	1813	1890	77	explored area of Rocky Mt. & Pacific
Sitting Bull	1834	1890	56	led fights to keep Indian lands
William Tweed	1823	1878	55	organized corrupt Tweed Ring
Harriet B. Stowe	1811	1896	85	wrote Uncle Tom's Cabin
Carry Nation	1846	1911	65	temperance crusade leader
Jesse James	1847	1882	35	bank and train robber
Wilbur & Orville Wright	1867 / 1871	1912 / 1948	45/77	invented 1st successful airplane
Babe Ruth	1895	1948	53	great home run hitter baseball
Albert Einstein	1879	1955	76	discovered theory of relativity
Norman Rockwell	1894	1978	84	painter of "everyday" people
Walt Disney	1901	1966	65	creator of Mickey Mouse
Louis Armstrong	? 1901	1971	70 (?)	great American trumpeter
Rosa Lee Parks	1913		Ans. vary	helped start civil rights movement
Betty Friedan	1921		Ans. vary	helped form Nat'l. Women's Political Caucus

1. Who do you think has made the most important contribution to society? Why? Answers will vary.
2. Who do you feel achieved the greatest results in the shortest amount of time? Defend your answer.
3. Whose achievements can still be seen, felt, witnessed, etc. today?
4. Name the people who worked or fought for specific causes or movements. Write the cause or movement after each person's name.

Something Extra: Find three people you think have contributed or are contributing to society. Tell the class about your choices.

Page 242

Fantastic Philanthropist

The sixth-grade students in Miss Freed's class have decided to become philanthropists. They have agreed to set apart one day each month on which to hold a bake sale or car wash to raise money for a good cause or to help others in need. Miss Freed has been teaching her students about some of the famous philanthropists in our country. One of them is John Davison Rockefeller. To learn about his life, number the boxes below in the correct order. Cut each one apart and glue it to its own page. Illustrate the pages and put them in order. Then you will have a biography of Rockefeller.

7 In 1882, Rockefeller organized the Standard Oil Trust. At this time, he controlled almost all U.S. oil refining and distribution and much of the world's oil trade.	6 Rockefeller's Standard Oil Company controlled the flow of all oil products from producer to consumer.
11 From 1895 to 1897, Rockefeller gradually retired from business. He had already started his vast philanthropic activities.	1 John Davison Rockefeller was born in 1839 in New York.
12 By 1910, he had given about $35 million to the University of Chicago. In all, Rockefeller gave away about $520 million during his lifetime. He died in 1937.	8 In 1890, Rockefeller helped found the University of Chicago.
10 The trust was dissolved because of the vastness of Rockefeller's holdings and because of public criticism of his methods.	4 Rockefeller used the profits from the grain house to enter the oil business in about 1862.
2 When Rockefeller was 14 years old, his family moved to Cleveland where he started work as a clerk in a small produce firm at age 16.	5 Fifteen years after he had entered the oil business, Rockefeller achieved his goal of making the oil industry orderly and efficient with the Standard Oil Company.
3 He formed a partnership in a grain commission house after working as a clerk.	9 About two years later, in 1892, the Ohio Supreme Court dissolved the Standard Oil Trust.

•SOMETHING EXTRA•
If you had $520 million dollars to give away, who would you give it to?

Page 243

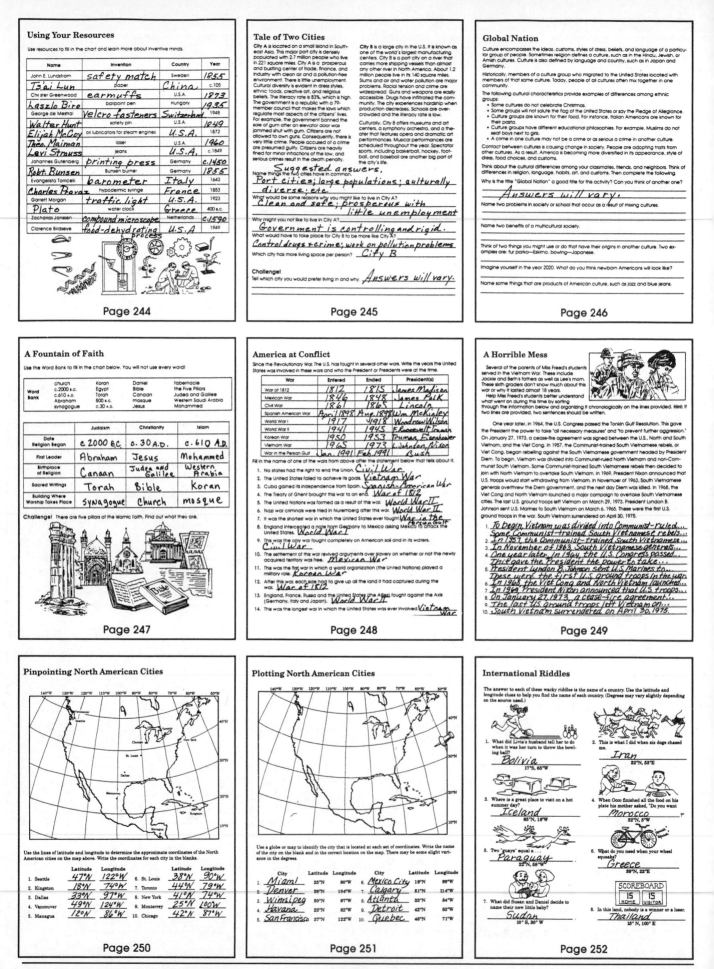

Using Your Resources

Use resources to fill in the chart and learn more about inventive minds.

Name	Invention	Country	Year
John E. Lundstrom	safety match	Sweden	1855
Ts'ai Lun	paper	China	c.105
Chester Greenwood	earmuffs	U.S.A.	1873
Laszlo Biro	ballpoint pen	Hungary	1935
George de Mestral	Velcro fasteners	Switzerland	1948
Walter Hunt	safety pin	U.S.A.	1849
Elijah McCoy	oil lubricators for steam engines	U.S.A.	1872
Theo. Maiman	laser	U.S.A.	1960
Levi Strauss	jeans	U.S.A.	c.1849
Johannes Gutenberg	printing press	Germany	c.1450
Robt. Bunsen	Bunsen burner	Germany	1855
Evangelista Torricelli	barometer	Italy	1643
Charles Pravaz	hypodermic syringe	France	1853
Garrett Morgan	traffic light	U.S.A.	1923
Plato	water clock	Greece	400 B.C.
Zacharias Janssen	compound microscope	Netherlands	c.1590
Clarence Birdseye	food-dehydrating process	U.S.A	1949

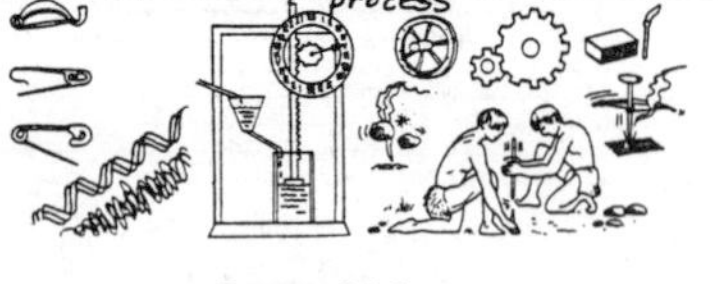

Page 244

Tale of Two Cities

City A is located on a small island in Southeast Asia. This major port city is densely populated with 2.7 million people who live in 221 square miles. City A is a prosperous and bustling center of trade, finance, and industry with clean air and a pollution-free environment. There is little unemployment. Cultural diversity is evident in dress styles, ethnic foods, creative art, and religious beliefs. The literacy rate is 83%, which is high. The government is a republic with a 79-member council that makes the laws which regulate most aspects of the citizens' lives. For example, the government banned the sale of gum after an elevator door was jammed shut with gum. Citizens are not allowed to own guns. Consequently, there is very little crime. People accused of a crime are presumed guilty. Citizens are heavily fined for minor infractions of the law, and serious crimes result in the death penalty.

City B is a large city in the U.S. It is known as one of the world's largest manufacturing centers. City B is a port city on a river that carries more shipping vessels than almost any other river in North America. About 1.2 million people live in its 140 square miles. Slums and air and water pollution are major problems. Racial tension and crime are widespread. Guns and weapons are easily accessible. Drugs have infiltrated the community. The city experiences hardship when production decreases. Schools are overcrowded and the literacy rate is low.

Culturally, City B offers museums and art centers, a symphony orchestra, and a theater that features opera and dramatic art performances. Musical performances are scheduled throughout the year. Spectator sports, including basketball, hockey, football, and baseball are another big part of the city's life.

Suggested answers.

Name things the two cities have in common.
Port cities; large populations; culturally diverse; etc.

What would be some reasons why you might like to live in City A?
Clean and safe; prosperous with little unemployment

Why might you not like to live in City A?
Government is controlling and rigid.

What would have to take place for City B to be more like City A?
Control drugs + crime; work on pollution problems

Which city has more living space per person? City B

Challenge!
Tell which city you would prefer living in and why. Answers will vary.

Page 245

Global Nation

Culture encompasses the ideas, customs, styles of dress, beliefs, and language of a particular group of people. Sometimes religion defines a culture, such as in the Hindu, Jewish, or Amish cultures. Culture is also defined by language and country, such as in Japan and Germany.

Historically, members of a culture group who migrated to the United States located with members of that same culture. Today, people of all cultures often mix together in one community.

The following cultural characteristics provide examples of differences among ethnic groups:

- Some cultures do not celebrate Christmas.
- Some groups will not salute the flag of the United States or say the Pledge of Allegiance.
- Culture groups are known for their food. For instance, Italian Americans are known for their pasta.
- Culture groups have different educational philosophies. For example, Muslims do not seat boys next to girls.
- A crime in one culture may not be a crime or as serious a crime in another culture.

Contact between cultures is causing change in society. People are adopting traits from other cultures. As a result, America is becoming more diversified in its appearance, style of dress, food choices, and customs.

Think about the cultural differences among your classmates, friends, and neighbors. Think of differences in religion, language, habits, art, and customs. Then complete the following.

Why is the title "Global Nation" a good title for this activity? Can you think of another one?
Answers will vary.

Name two problems in society or school that occur as a result of mixing cultures.

Name two benefits of a multicultural society.

Think of two things you might use or do that have their origins in another culture. Two examples are: fur parka—Eskimo, bowing—Japanese.

Imagine yourself in the year 2020. What do you think newborn Americans will look like?

Name some things that are products of American culture, such as jazz and blue jeans.

Page 246

A Fountain of Faith

Use the Word Bank to fill in the chart below. You will not use every word!

Word Bank				
	church	Koran	Daniel	tabernacle
	c.2000 B.C.	Egypt	Bible	the Five Pillars
	c.610 A.D.	Torah	Canaan	Judea and Galilee
	Abraham	500 B.C.	mosque	Western Saudi Arabia
	synagogue	c.30 A.D.	Jesus	Mohammed

	Judaism	Christianity	Islam
Date Religion Began	c 2000 B.C.	c. 30 A.D.	c. 610 A.D.
First Leader	Abraham	Jesus	Mohammed
Birthplace of Religion	Canaan	Judea and Galilee	Western Arabia
Sacred Writings	Torah	Bible	Koran
Building Where Worship Takes Place	synagogue	church	mosque

Challenge! There are five pillars of the Islamic faith. Find out what they are.

Page 247

America at Conflict

Since the Revolutionary War, The U.S. has fought in several other wars. Write the years the United States was involved in these wars and who the President or Presidents were at the time.

War	Entered	Ended	President(s)
War of 1812	1812	1815	James Madison
Mexican War	1846	1848	James Polk
Civil War	1861	1865	Lincoln
Spanish American War	April 1898	Aug. 1898	Wm McKinley
World War I	1917	1918	Woodrow Wilson
World War II	1941	1945	F. Roosevelt, Truman
Korean War	1950	1953	Truman, Eisenhower
Vietnam War	1965	1973	L. Johnson, Nixon
War in the Persian Gulf	Jan. 1991	Feb. 1991	Bush

Fill in the name of one of the wars from above after the statement below that tells about it.

1. No states had the right to end the Union. Civil War
2. The United States failed to achieve its goals. Vietnam War
3. Cuba gained its independence from Spain. Spanish-American War
4. The Treaty of Ghent brought this war to an end. War of 1812
5. The United Nations was formed as a result of this war. World War II
6. Nazi war criminals were tried in Nuremberg after this war. World War II
7. It was the shortest war in which the United States ever fought. War in the Persian Gulf
8. England intercepted a note from Germany to Mexico asking Mexico to attack the United States. World War I
9. This was the only war fought completely on American soil and in its waters. Civil War
10. The settlement of this war revived arguments over slavery on whether or not the newly acquired territory was free. Mexican War
11. This was the first war in which a world organization (the United Nations) played a military role. Korean War
12. After this war, each side had to give up all the land it had captured during the war. War of 1812
13. England, France, Russia and the United States (the Allies) fought against the Axis (Germany, Italy and Japan). World War II
14. This was the longest war in which the United States was ever involved. Vietnam War

Page 248

A Horrible Mess

Several of the parents of Miss Freed's students served in the Vietnam War. These include Jackie and Beth's fathers as well as Lee's mom. These sixth graders don't know much about this war or why it lasted almost 18 years.

Help Miss Freed's students better understand what went on during this time by sorting through the information below and organizing it chronologically on the lines provided. **Hint:** If two lines are provided, two sentences should be written.

One year later, in 1964, the U.S. Congress passed the Tonkin Gulf Resolution. This gave the President the power to take "all necessary measures" and "to prevent further aggression." On January 27, 1973, a cease-fire agreement was signed between the U.S., North and South Vietnam, and the Viet Cong. In 1957, the Communist-trained South Vietnamese rebels, or Viet Cong, began rebelling against the South Vietnamese government headed by President Diem. To begin, Vietnam was divided into Communist-ruled North Vietnam and non-Communist South Vietnam. Some Communist-trained South Vietnamese rebels then decided to join with North Vietnam to overtake South Vietnam. In 1969, President Nixon announced that U.S. troops would start withdrawing from Vietnam. In November of 1963, South Vietnamese generals overthrew the Diem government, and the next day Diem was killed. In 1968, the Viet Cong and North Vietnam launched a major campaign to overtake South Vietnamese cities. The last U.S. ground troops left Vietnam on March 29, 1973. President Lyndon B. Johnson sent U.S. Marines to South Vietnam on March 6, 1965. These were the first U.S. ground troops in the war. South Vietnam surrendered on April 30, 1975.

1. To begin, Vietnam was divided into Communist-ruled... Some Communist-trained South Vietnamese rebels...
2. In 1957, the Communist-trained South Vietnamese...
3. In November of 1963, South Vietnamese generals...
4. One year later, in 1964, the U.S. Congress passed... This gave the President the power to take...
5. President Lyndon B. Johnson sent U.S. Marines to... These were the first U.S. ground troops in the war
6. In 1968, the Viet Cong and North Vietnam launched...
7. In 1969 President Nixon announced that U.S. troops...
8. On January 27, 1973, a cease-fire agreement...
9. The last U.S. ground troops left Vietnam on...
10. South Vietnam surrendered on April 30, 1975.

Page 249

Pinpointing North American Cities

Use the lines of latitude and longitude to determine the approximate coordinates of the North American cities on the map above. Write the coordinates for each city in the blanks.

	Latitude	Longitude		Latitude	Longitude
1. Seattle	47°N	122°W	6. St. Louis	38°N	90°W
2. Kingston	18°N	74°W	7. Toronto	44°N	79°W
3. Dallas	33°N	97°W	8. New York	41°N	74°W
4. Vancouver	49°N	124°W	9. Monterrey	25°N	100°W
5. Managua	12°N	86°W	10. Chicago	42°N	87°W

Page 250

Plotting North American Cities

Use a globe or map to identify the city that is located at each set of coordinates. Write the name of the city on the blank and in the correct location on the map. There may be some slight variance in the degrees.

City	Latitude	Longitude	City	Latitude	Longitude
1. Miami	25°N	80°W	6. Mexico City	19°N	99°W
2. Denver	39°N	104°W	7. Calgary	51°N	114°W
3. Winnipeg	50°N	97°W	8. Atlanta	33°N	84°W
4. Havana	23°N	82°W	9. Detroit	42°N	83°W
5. San Francisco	37°N	122°W	10. Quebec	46°N	71°W

Page 251

International Riddles

The answer to each of these wacky riddles is the name of a country. Use the latitude and longitude clues to help you find the name of each country. (Degrees may vary slightly depending on the source used.)

1. What did Livia's husband tell her to do when it was her turn to throw the bowling ball?
Bolivia
17°S, 65°W

2. This is what I did when six dogs chased me.
Iran
32°N, 53°E

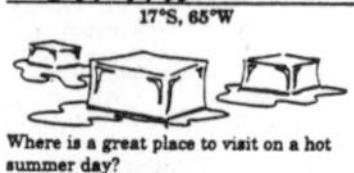

3. Where is a great place to visit on a hot summer day?
Iceland
65°N, 18°W

4. When Occo finished all the food on his plate his mother asked, "Do you want Morocco?"
32°N, 5°W

5. Two "guays" equal a . . . Paraguay.
22°N, 58°W

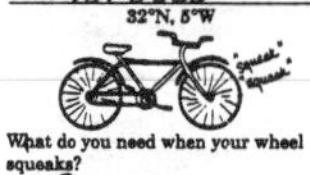

6. What do you need when your wheel squeaks?
Greece
39°N, 22°E

7. What did Susan and Daniel decide to name their new little baby?
Sudan.
10° S, 30° W

8. In this land, nobody is a winner or a loser.
Thailand
15° N, 100° E

Page 252

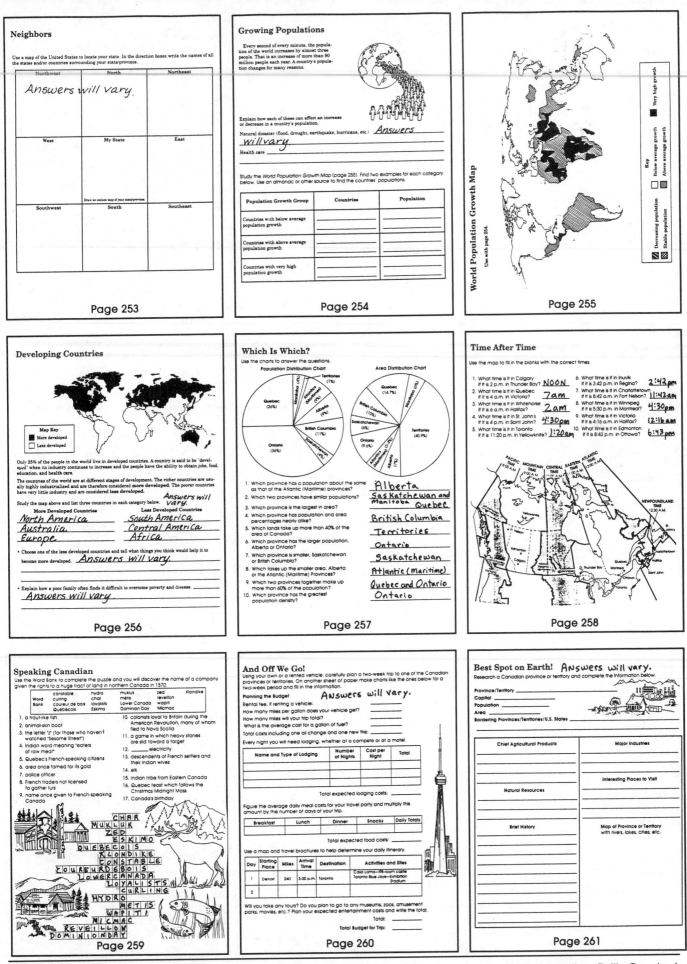

Neighbors

Use a map of the United States to locate your state. In the direction boxes write the names of all the states and/or countries surrounding your state/province.

Northwest	North	Northeast
Answers will vary.		
West	My State	East
	Draw an outline map of your state/province.	
Southwest	South	Southeast

Page 253

Growing Populations

Every second of every minute, the population of the world increases by almost three people. That is an increase of more than 90 million people each year. A country's population changes for many reasons.

Explain how each of these can affect an increase or decrease in a country's population.

Natural disaster (flood, drought, earthquake, hurricane, etc.) *Answers will vary*

Health care _____

Study the *World Population Growth Map* (page 255). Find two examples for each category below. Use an almanac or other source to find the countries' populations.

Population Growth Group	Countries	Population
Countries with below average population growth		
Countries with above average population growth		
Countries with very high population growth		

Page 254

World Population Growth Map

Use with page 254.

Key
- Very high growth
- Below average growth
- Above average growth
- Decreasing population
- Stable population

Page 255

Developing Countries

Map Key
- More developed
- Less developed

Only 25% of the people in the world live in developed countries. A country is said to be "developed" when its industry continues to increase and the people have the ability to obtain jobs, food, education, and health care.

The countries of the world are at different stages of development. The richer countries are usually highly industrialized and are therefore considered more developed. The poorer countries have very little industry and are considered less developed.

Study the map above and list three countries in each category below. *Answers will vary*

More Developed Countries	Less Developed Countries
North America	South America
Australia	Central America
Europe	Africa

- Choose one of the less developed countries and tell what things you think would help it to become more developed. *Answers will vary*

- Explain how a poor family often finds it difficult to overcome poverty and disease. *Answers will vary*

Page 256

Which Is Which?

Use the charts to answer the questions.

Population Distribution Chart
- Territories (1%)
- Manitoba (4%)
- Quebec (26%)
- Alberta (9%)
- British Columbia (11%)
- Saskatchewan (3%)
- Ontario (36%)

Area Distribution Chart
- Quebec (14.7%)
- Manitoba (6%)
- British Columbia (10%)
- Saskatchewan (6%)
- Ontario (9.6%)
- Alberta (7%)
- Territories (40.9%)

1. Which province has a population about the same as that of the Atlantic (Maritime) provinces? **Alberta**
2. Which two provinces have similar populations? **Saskatchewan and Manitoba**
3. Which province is the largest in area? **Quebec**
4. Which province has population and area percentages nearly alike? **British Columbia**
5. Which lands take up more than 40% of the area of Canada? **Territories**
6. Which province has the larger population, Alberta or Ontario? **Ontario**
7. Which province is smaller, Saskatchewan or British Columbia? **Saskatchewan**
8. Which takes up the smaller area, Alberta or the Atlantic (Maritime) Provinces? **Atlantic (Maritime)**
9. Which two provinces together make up more than 60% of the population? **Quebec and Ontario**
10. Which province has the greatest population density? **Ontario**

Page 257

Time After Time

Use the map to fill in the blanks with the correct times.

1. What time is it in Calgary if it is 2 p.m. in Thunder Bay? **NOON**
2. What time is it in Quebec if it is 4 a.m. in Victoria? **7am**
3. What time is it in Whitehorse if it is 6 a.m. in Halifax? **2am**
4. What time is it in St. John's if it is 4 p.m. in Saint John? **4:30pm**
5. What time is it in Toronto if it is 11:20 p.m. in Yellowknife? **1:20am**
6. What time is it in Inuvik if it is 3:42 p.m. in Regina? **2:42pm**
7. What time is it in Charlottetown if it is 8:42 a.m. in Fort Nelson? **11:42am**
8. What time is it in Winnipeg if it is 5:30 p.m. in Montreal? **4:30pm**
9. What time is it in Victoria if it is 4:16 a.m. in Halifax? **12:16am**
10. What time is it in Edmonton if it is 8:43 p.m. in Ottawa? **6:43pm**

Page 258

Speaking Canadian

Use the Word Bank to complete the puzzle and you will discover the name of a company given the rights to a huge tract of land in northern Canada in 1570.

Word Bank				
constable	hydro	mukluk	zed	Klondike
curling	char	métis	réveillon	
coureur de bois	loyalists	Lower Canada	wapiti	
Québécois	Eskimo	Dominion Day	Micmac	

1. a trout-like fish
2. animal-skin boot
3. the letter 'z' (for those who haven't watched "Sesame Street")
4. Indian word meaning "eaters of raw meat"
5. Quebec's French-speaking citizens
6. area once famed for its gold
7. police officer
8. French traders not licensed to gather furs
9. name once given to French-speaking Canada
10. colonists loyal to Britain during the American Revolution, many of whom fled to Nova Scotia
11. a game in which heavy stones are slid toward a target
12. _____ electricity
13. descendants of French settlers and their Indian wives
14. elk
15. Indian tribe from Eastern Canada
16. Quebec feast which follows the Christmas Midnight Mass
17. Canada's birthday

CHAR
MUKLUK
ZED
ESKIMO
QUEBECOIS
KLONDIKE
CONSTABLE
COUREURDEBOIS
LOWERCANADA
LOYALISTS
CURLING
HYDRO
METIS
WAPITI
MICMAC
REVEILLON
DOMINIONDAY

Page 259

And Off We Go!

Using your own or a rented vehicle, carefully plan a two-week trip to one of the Canadian provinces or territories. On another sheet of paper make charts like the ones below for a two-week period and fill in the information.

Planning the Budget *Answers will vary.*

Rental fee, if renting a vehicle: _____
How many miles per gallon does your vehicle get? _____
How many miles will your trip total? _____
What is the average cost for a gallon of fuel? _____
Total costs including one oil change and one new tire: _____

Every night you will need lodging, whether at a campsite or at a motel.

Name and Type of Lodging	Number of Nights	Cost per Night	Total

Total expected lodging costs: _____

Figure the average daily meal costs for your travel party and multiply this amount by the number of days of your trip.

Breakfast	Lunch	Dinner	Snacks	Daily Totals

Total expected food costs: _____

Use a map and travel brochures to help determine your daily itinerary.

Day	Starting Place	Miles	Arrival Time	Destination	Activities and Sites
1	Detroit	240	3:00 p.m.	Toronto	Casa Loma—98-room castle, Toronto Blue Jays—Exhibition Stadium
2					

Will you take any tours? Do you plan to go to any museums, zoos, amusement parks, movies, etc.? Plan your expected entertainment costs and write the total.

Total: _____

Total Budget for Trip: _____

Page 260

Best Spot on Earth! *Answers will vary.*

Research a Canadian province or territory and complete the information below.

Province/Territory _____
Capital _____
Population _____
Area _____
Bordering Provinces/Territories/U.S. States _____

Chief Agricultural Products	Major Industries
Natural Resources	Interesting Places to Visit
Brief History	Map of Province or Territory with rivers, lakes, cities, etc.

Page 261

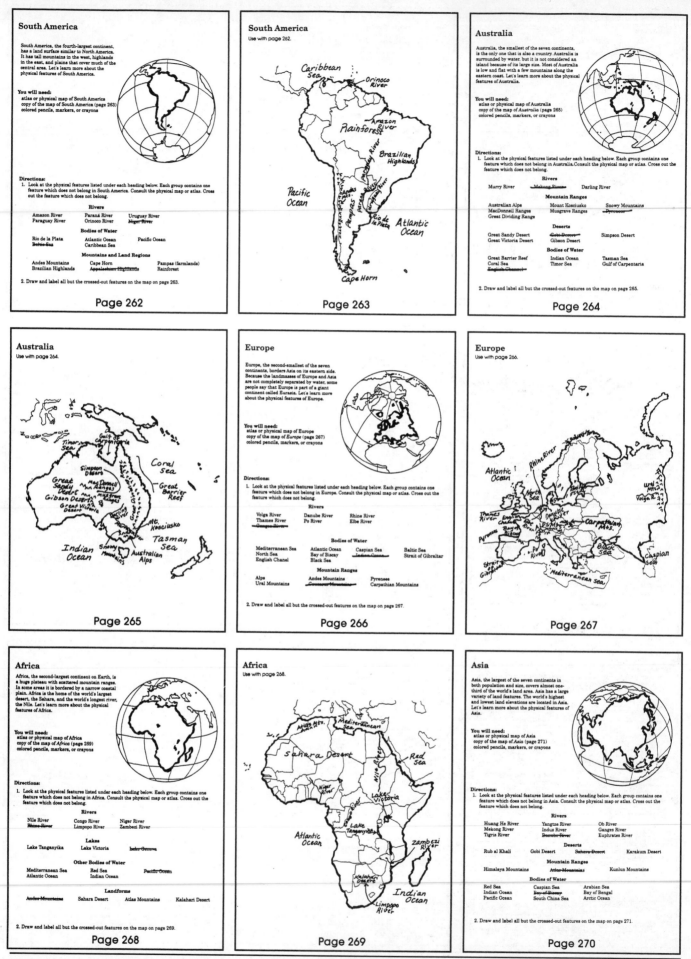

South America — Page 262

South America, the fourth-largest continent, has a land surface similar to North America. It has tall mountains in the west, highlands in the east, and plains that cover much of the central area. Let's learn more about the physical features of South America.

You will need:
atlas or physical map of South America
copy of the map of South America (page 263)
colored pencils, markers, or crayons

Directions:
1. Look at the physical features listed under each heading below. Each group contains one feature which does not belong in South America. Consult the physical map or atlas. Cross out the feature which does not belong.

Rivers
Amazon River   Paraná River   Uruguay River
Paraguay River   Orinoco River   ~~Niger River~~

Bodies of Water
Rio de la Plata   Atlantic Ocean   Pacific Ocean
~~Baltic Sea~~   Caribbean Sea

Mountains and Land Regions
Andes Mountains   Cape Horn   Pampas (farmlands)
Brazilian Highlands   ~~Appalachian Highlands~~   Rainforest

2. Draw and label all but the crossed-out features on the map on page 263.

Page 262

South America — Page 263

Use with page 262.

(Map labels: Caribbean Sea, Orinoco River, Amazon River, Rainforest, Brazilian Highlands, Pacific Ocean, Andes, Paraguay River, Rio de la Plata, Atlantic Ocean, Cape Horn)

Page 263

Australia — Page 264

Australia, the smallest of the seven continents, is the only one that is also a country. Australia is surrounded by water, but it is not considered an island because of its large size. Most of Australia is low and flat with a few mountains along the eastern coast. Let's learn more about the physical features of Australia.

You will need:
atlas or physical map of Australia
copy of the map of Australia (page 265)
colored pencils, markers, or crayons

Directions:
1. Look at the physical features listed under each heading below. Each group contains one feature which does not belong in Australia. Consult the physical map or atlas. Cross out the feature which does not belong.

Rivers
Murry River   ~~Mekong River~~   Darling River

Mountain Ranges
Australian Alps   Mount Kosciusko   Snowy Mountains
MacDonnell Ranges   Musgrave Ranges   ~~Pyrenees~~
Great Dividing Range

Deserts
Great Sandy Desert   ~~Gobi Desert~~   Simpson Desert
Great Victoria Desert   Gibson Desert

Bodies of Water
Great Barrier Reef   Indian Ocean   Tasman Sea
Coral Sea   Timor Sea   Gulf of Carpentaria
~~English Channel~~

2. Draw and label all but the crossed-out features on the map on page 265.

Page 264

Australia — Page 265

Use with page 264.

(Map labels: Timor Sea, Gulf of Carpentaria, Coral Sea, Great Barrier Reef, Simpson Desert, MacDonnell Ranges, Musgrave Ranges, Great Sandy Desert, Gibson Desert, Great Victoria Desert, Mt. Kosciusko, Tasman Sea, Indian Ocean, Snowy Mountains, Australian Alps)

Page 265

Europe — Page 266

Europe, the second-smallest of the seven continents, borders Asia on its eastern side. Because the landmasses of Europe and Asia are not completely separated by water, some people say that Europe is part of a giant continent called Eurasia. Let's learn more about the physical features of Europe.

You will need:
atlas or physical map of Europe
copy of the map of Europe (page 267)
colored pencils, markers, or crayons

Directions:
1. Look at the physical features listed under each heading below. Each group contains one feature which does not belong in Europe. Consult the physical map or atlas. Cross out the feature which does not belong.

Rivers
Volga River   Danube River   Rhine River
Thames River   Po River   Elbe River
~~Congo River~~

Bodies of Water
Mediterranean Sea   Atlantic Ocean   Caspian Sea   Baltic Sea
North Sea   Bay of Biscay   ~~Indian Ocean~~   Strait of Gibraltar
English Chanel   Black Sea

Mountain Ranges
Alps   Andes Mountains   Pyrenees
Ural Mountains   ~~Caucasus Mountains~~   Carpathian Mountains

2. Draw and label all but the crossed-out features on the map on page 267.

Page 266

Europe — Page 267

Use with page 266.

(Map labels: Atlantic Ocean, Rhine River, Thames River, English Channel, North Sea, Po River, Danube River, Alps, Pyrenees, Strait of Gibraltar, Ural Mts., Volga River, Carpathian Mts., Black Sea, Caspian Sea, Mediterranean Sea)

Page 267

Africa — Page 268

Africa, the second-largest continent on Earth, is a huge plateau with scattered mountain ranges. In some areas it is bordered by a narrow coastal plain. Africa is the home of the world's largest desert, the Sahara, and the world's longest river, the Nile. Let's learn more about the physical features of Africa.

You will need:
atlas or physical map of Africa
copy of the map of Africa (page 269)
colored pencils, markers, or crayons

Directions:
1. Look at the physical features listed under each heading below. Each group contains one feature which does not belong in Africa. Consult the physical map or atlas. Cross out the feature which does not belong.

Rivers
Nile River   Congo River   Niger River
~~Rhine River~~   Limpopo River   Zambezi River

Lakes
Lake Tanganyika   Lake Victoria   ~~Lake Geneva~~

Other Bodies of Water
Mediterranean Sea   Red Sea   ~~Pacific Ocean~~
Atlantic Ocean   Indian Ocean

Landforms
~~Andes Mountains~~   Sahara Desert   Atlas Mountains   Kalahari Desert

2. Draw and label all but the crossed-out features on the map on page 269.

Page 268

Africa — Page 269

Use with page 268.

(Map labels: Atlas Mts., Mediterranean Sea, Sahara Desert, Red Sea, Niger River, Nile River, Lake Victoria, Lake Tanganyika, Atlantic Ocean, Zambezi River, Kalahari Desert, Indian Ocean, Limpopo River)

Page 269

Asia — Page 270

Asia, the largest of the seven continents in both population and size, covers almost one-third of the world's land area. Asia has a large variety of land features. The world's highest and lowest land elevations are located in Asia. Let's learn more about the physical features of Asia.

You will need:
atlas or physical map of Asia
copy of the map of Asia (page 271)
colored pencils, markers, or crayons

Directions:
1. Look at the physical features listed under each heading below. Each group contains one feature which does not belong in Asia. Consult the physical map or atlas. Cross out the feature which does not belong.

Rivers
Huang He River   Yangtze River   Ob River
Mekong River   Indus River   Ganges River
Tigris River   ~~Danube River~~   Euphrates River

Deserts
Rub al Khali   Gobi Desert   ~~Sahara Desert~~   Karakum Desert

Mountain Ranges
Himalaya Mountains   ~~Atlas Mountains~~   Kunlun Mountains

Bodies of Water
Red Sea   Caspian Sea   Arabian Sea
Indian Ocean   ~~Bay of Biscay~~   Bay of Bengal
Pacific Ocean   South China Sea   Arctic Ocean

2. Draw and label all but the crossed-out features on the map on page 271.

Page 270

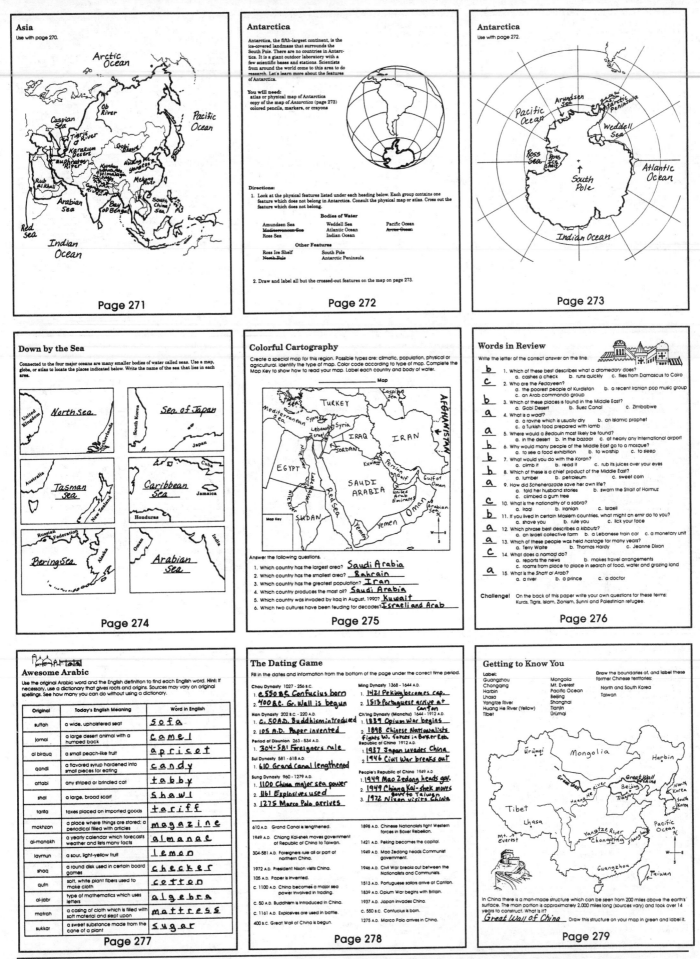

Asia
Use with page 270.

Page 271

Arctic Ocean, Pacific Ocean, Indian Ocean, Red Sea, Arabian Sea, Bay of Bengal, South China Sea, Caspian Sea, Tigris River, Karakum Desert, Gobi Desert, Euphrates River, Rub al Khali, Himalayas

Antarctica

Antarctica, the fifth-largest continent, is the ice-covered landmass that surrounds the South Pole. There are no countries in Antarctica. It is a giant outdoor laboratory with a few scientific bases and stations. Scientists from around the world come to this area to do research. Let's learn more about the features of Antarctica.

You will need:
atlas or physical map of Antarctica
copy of the map of Antarctica (page 273)
colored pencils, markers, or crayons

Directions:
1. Look at the physical features listed under each heading below. Each group contains one feature which does not belong in Antarctica. Consult the physical map or atlas. Cross out the feature which does not belong.

Bodies of Water

Amundsen Sea	Weddell Sea	~~Pacific Ocean~~
~~Mediterranean Sea~~	Atlantic Ocean	~~Arctic Ocean~~
Ross Sea	Indian Ocean	

Other Features

Ross Ice Shelf   South Pole
~~North Pole~~   Antarctic Peninsula

2. Draw and label all but the crossed-out features on the map on page 273.

Page 272

Antarctica
Use with page 272.

Pacific Ocean, Amundsen Sea, Antarctic Peninsula, Weddell Sea, Ross Sea, Ross Ice Shelf, South Pole, Atlantic Ocean, Indian Ocean

Page 273

Down by the Sea

Connected to the four major oceans are many smaller bodies of water called seas. Use a map, globe, or atlas to locate the places indicated below. Write the name of the sea that lies in each area.

North Sea
Sea of Japan
Tasman Sea
Caribbean Sea
Bering Sea
Arabian Sea

Page 274

Colorful Cartography

Create a special map for this region. Possible types are: climatic, population, physical or agricultural. Identify the type of map. Color code according to type of map. Complete the Map Key to show how to read your map. Label each country and body of water.

Answer the following questions.

1. Which country has the largest area? **Saudi Arabia**
2. Which country has the smallest area? **Bahrain**
3. Which country has the greatest population? **Iran**
4. Which country produces the most oil? **Saudi Arabia**
5. Which country was invaded by Iraq in August, 1990? **Kuwait**
6. Which two cultures have been feuding for decades? **Israeli and Arab**

Page 275

Words in Review

Write the letter of the correct answer on the line.

b   1. Which of these best describes what a dromedary does?
      a. cashes a check   b. runs quickly   c. flies from Damascus to Cairo
c   2. Who are the Fedayeen?
      a. the poorest people of Kurdistan   b. a recent Iranian pop music group
      c. an Arab commando group
b   3. Which of these places is found in the Middle East?
      a. Gobi Desert   b. Suez Canal   c. Zimbabwe
a   4. What is a wadi?
      a. a ravine which is usually dry   b. an Islamic prophet
      c. a Turkish food prepared with lamb
a   5. Where would a Bedouin most likely be found?
      a. in the desert   b. in the bazaar   c. at nearly any international airport
b   6. Why would many people of the Middle East go to a mosque?
      a. to see a food exhibition   b. to worship   c. to sleep
b   7. What would you do with the Koran?
      a. climb it   b. read it   c. rub its juices over your eyes
b   8. Which of these is a chief product of the Middle East?
      a. lumber   b. petroleum   c. sweet corn
a   9. How did Scheherazade save her own life?
      a. told her husband stories   b. swam the Strait of Hormuz
      c. climbed a gum tree
c   10. What is the nationality of a sabra?
      a. Iraqi   b. Iranian   c. Israeli
b   11. If you lived in certain Moslem countries, what might an emir do to you?
      a. shave you   b. rule you   c. lick your face
a   12. Which phrase best describes a kibbutz?
      a. an Israeli collective farm   b. a Lebanese train car   c. a monetary unit
a   13. Which of these people was held hostage for many years?
      a. Terry Waite   b. Thomas Hardy   c. Jeanne Dixon
c   14. What does a nomad do?
      a. reports the news   b. makes travel arrangements
      c. roams from place to place in search of food, water and grazing land
a   15. What is the Shatt al Arab?
      a. a river   b. a prince   c. a doctor

Challenge! On the back of this paper write your own questions for these terms: Kurds, Tigris, Islam, Zionism, Sunni and Palestinian refugee.

Page 276

Awesome Arabic

Use the original Arabic word and the English definition to find each English word. Hint: If necessary, use a dictionary that gives roots and origins. Sources may vary on original spellings. See how many you can do without using a dictionary.

Original	Today's English Meaning	Word in English
suffah	a wide, upholstered seat	sofa
jamal	a large desert animal with a humped back	camel
al birqua	a small peach-like fruit	apricot
qandi	a flavored syrup hardened into small pieces for eating	candy
attabi	any striped or brindled cat	tabby
shal	a large, broad scarf	shawl
tarifa	taxes placed on imported goods	tariff
makhzan	a place where things are stored; a periodical filled with articles	magazine
al-manakh	a yearly calendar which forecasts weather and lists many facts	almanac
laymun	a sour, light-yellow fruit	lemon
shaq	a round disk used in certain board games	checker
qutn	soft, white plant fibers used to make cloth	cotton
al-jabr	type of mathematics which uses letters	algebra
matrah	a casing of cloth which is filled with soft material and slept upon	mattress
sukkar	a sweet substance made from the cane of a plant	sugar

Page 277

The Dating Game

Fill in the dates and information from the bottom of the page under the correct time period.

Chou Dynasty 1027 - 256 B.C.
1. c. 550 B.C. Confucius born
2. 400 B.C. Gr. Wall is begun

Han Dynasty 202 B.C. - 220 A.D.
1. c. 50 A.D. Buddhism introduced
2. 105 A.D. Paper invented

Period of Disunion 263 - 534 A.D.
1. 304-581 Foreigners rule

Sui Dynasty 581 - 618 A.D.
1. 610 Grand Canal lengthened

Sung Dynasty 960 - 1279 A.D.
1. 1100 China major sea power
2. 1161 Explosives used
3. 1275 Marco Polo arrives

Ming Dynasty 1368 - 1644 A.D.
1. 1421 Peking becomes cap.
2. 1513 Portuguese arrive at Canton

Ch'ing Dynasty (Manchu) 1644 - 1912 A.D.
1. 1839 Opium War begins
2. 1898 Chinese Nationalists fights W. forces in Boxer Reb.

Republic of China 1912 A.D.
1. 1937 Japan invades China
2. 1946 Civil War breaks out

People's Republic of China 1949 A.D.
1. 1949 Mao Zedong heads gov.
2. 1949 Chiang Kai-shek moves govt to Taiwan
3. 1972 Nixon visits China

610 A.D.   Grand Canal is lengthened.
1949 A.D. Chiang Kai-shek moves government of Republic of China to Taiwan.
304-581 A.D. Foreigners rule all or part of northern China.
1972 A.D. President Nixon visits China.
105 A.D.   Paper is invented.
c. 1100 A.D. China becomes a major sea power involved in trading.
c. 50 A.D. Buddhism is introduced in China.
c.1161 A.D. Explosives are used in battle.
400 B.C.   Great Wall of China is begun.

1898 A.D. Chinese Nationalists fight Western forces in Boxer Rebellion.
1421 A.D. Peking becomes the capital.
1949 A.D. Mao Zedong heads Communist government.
1946 A.D. Civil War breaks out between the Nationalists and Communists.
1513 A.D. Portuguese sailors arrive at Canton.
1839 A.D. Opium War begins with Britain.
1937 A.D. Japan invades China.
c. 550 B.C. Confucius is born.
1275 A.D. Marco Polo arrives in China.

Page 278

Getting to Know You

Label:
Guangzhou
Changqing
Harbin
Lhasa
Yangtze River
Huang He River (Yellow)
Tibet
Mongolia
Mt. Everest
Pacific Ocean
Beijing
Shanghai
Tianjin
Ürümqi

Draw the boundaries of, and label these former Chinese territories:
North and South Korea
Taiwan

In China there is a man-made structure which can be seen from 200 miles above the earth's surface. The main portion is approximately 2,000 miles long (sources vary) and took over 14 years to construct. What is it? **Great Wall of China** Draw this structure on your map in green and label it.

Page 279

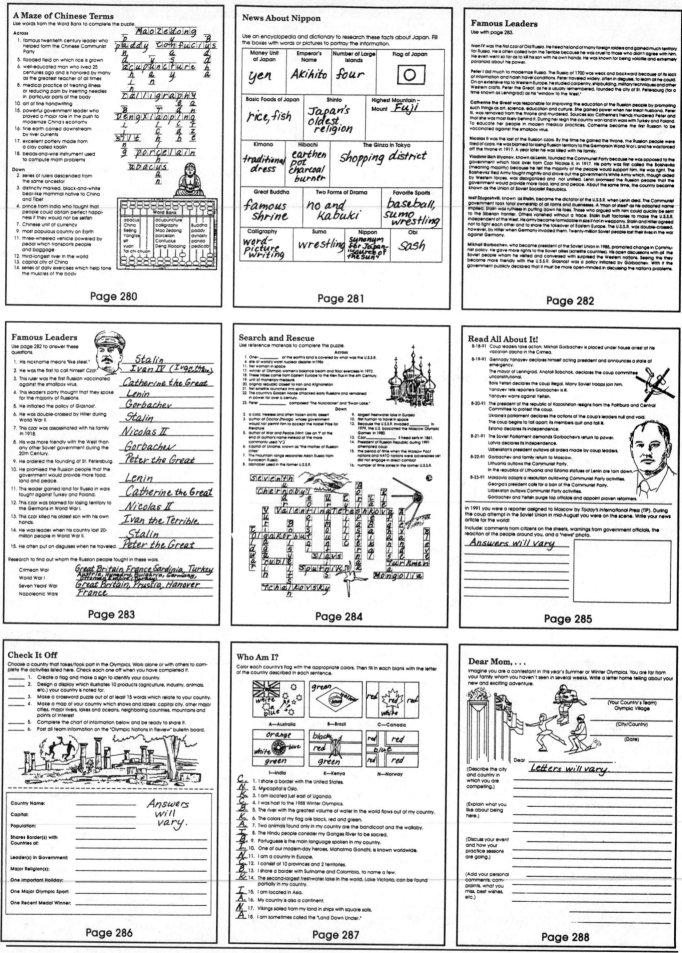

A Maze of Chinese Terms

Use words from the Word Bank to complete the puzzle.

Across

1. famous twentieth century leader who helped form the Chinese Communist Party
5. flooded field on which rice is grown
6. well-educated man who lived 25 centuries ago and is honored by many as the greatest teacher of all times
8. medical practice of treating illness or reducing pain by inserting needles in particular parts of the body
10. art of fine handwriting
15. powerful government leader who played a major role in the push to modernize China's economy
16. fine earth carried downstream by river currents
17. excellent pottery made from a clay called kaolin
18. beads-and-wire instrument used to compute math problems

Down

2. series of rulers descended from the same ancestor
3. distinctly marked, black-and-white bear-like mammal native to China and Tibet
4. prince from India who taught that people could obtain perfect happiness if they would not be selfish
7. Chinese unit of currency
9. most populous country on Earth
11. three-wheeled vehicle powered by pedal which transports people and baggage
12. third-longest river in the world
13. capital city of China
14. series of daily exercises which help tone the muscles of the body

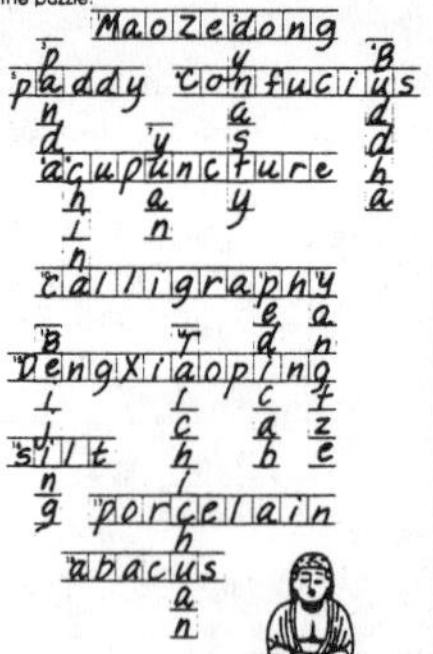

Mao Zedong
paddy
Confucius
acupuncture
calligraphy
Deng Xiaoping
silt
porcelain
abacus
dynasty
panda
Buddha
yuan
China
pedicab
Yangtze
Beijing
Tai chi chuan

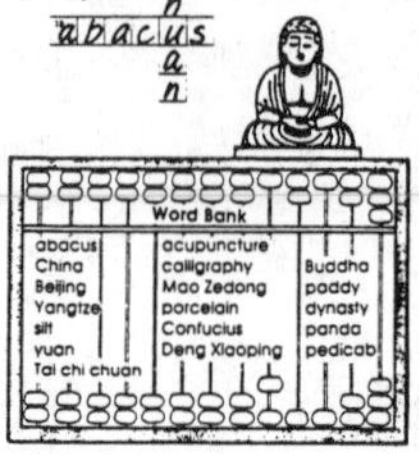

Word Bank
abacus
China
Beijing
Yangtze
silt
yuan
Tai chi chuan
acupuncture
calligraphy
Mao Zedong
porcelain
Confucius
Deng Xiaoping
Buddha
paddy
dynasty
panda
pedicab

Page 280

News About Nippon

Use an encyclopedia and dictionary to research these facts about Japan. Fill the boxes with words or pictures to portray the information.

Money Unit of Japan	Emperor's Name	Number of Large Islands	Flag of Japan
yen	Akihito	four	◯

Basic Foods of Japan	Shinto	Highest Mountain – Mount
rice, fish	Japan's oldest religion	Fuji

Kimono	Hibachi	The Ginza in Tokyo
traditional dress	earthen pot charcoal burner	shopping district

Great Buddha	Two Forms of Drama	Favorite Sports
famous shrine	no and Kabuki	baseball, sumo wrestling

Calligraphy	Sumo	Nippon	Obi
word-picture writing	wrestling	synonym for Japan- "source of the sun"	sash

Page 281

Famous Leaders

Use with page 283.

Ivan IV was the first czar of Old Russia. He freed his land of many foreign raiders and gained much territory for Russia. He is often called Ivan the Terrible because he was cruel to those who didn't agree with him. He even went so far as to kill his son with his own hands. He was known for being volatile and extremely paranoid about his power.

Peter I did much to modernize Russia. The Russia of 1700 was weak and backward because of its lack of information and harsh travel conditions. Peter traveled widely, often in disguise, to learn all he could. On an extensive trip to Western Europe, he studied carpentry, shipbuilding, military techniques and other Western crafts. Peter the Great, as he is usually remembered, founded the city of St. Petersburg (for a time known as Leningrad) as his "window to the West."

Catherine the Great was responsible for improving the education of the Russian people by promoting such things as art, science, education and culture. She gained power when her inept husband, Peter III, was removed from the throne and murdered. Sources say Catherine's friends murdered Peter and that she was most likely behind it. During her reign the country won land in wars with Turkey and Poland. To educate her people in modern medical practices, Catherine became the first Russian to be vaccinated against the smallpox virus.

Nicolas II was the last of the Russian czars. By the time he gained the throne, the Russian people were tired of czars. He was blamed for losing Russian territory to the Germans in World War I, and he was forced off the throne in 1917. A year later he was killed with his family.

Vladimir Ilich Ulyanov, known as **Lenin**, founded the Communist Party because he was opposed to the government which took over from Czar Nicolas II, in 1917. His party was first called the Bolsheviks (meaning majority) because he felt the majority of the people would support him. He was right. The Bolsheviks' Red Army fought mightily and drove out the government's White Army which, though aided by Western forces, was disorganized and not unified. Lenin promised the Russian people that the government would provide more food, land and peace. About the same time, the country became known as the Union of Soviet Socialist Republics.

Iosif Djugashvili, known as **Stalin**, became the dictator of the U.S.S.R. when Lenin died. The Communist government took total ownership of all farms and businesses. A "man of steel" as his adopted name implied, Stalin was ruthless in putting down his foes. Those who argued with him could quickly be sent to the Siberian frontier. Others vanished without a trace. Stalin built factories to make the U.S.S.R. independent of the West. His army became formidable in size if not in weaponry. Stalin and Hitler agreed not to fight each other and to share the takeover of Eastern Europe. The U.S.S.R. was double-crossed, however, by Hitler when Germany invaded them. Twenty-million Soviet people lost their lives in the war against Germany.

Mikhail Gorbachev, who became president of the Soviet Union in 1985, promoted change in Communist policy. He gave more rights to the Soviet allies (satellite countries). His open discussions with all the Soviet people whom he visited and conversed with surprised the Western nations. Seeing this they became more friendly with the U.S.S.R. *Glasnost* was a policy initiated by Gorbachev. With it the government publicly declared that it must be more open-minded in discussing the nation's problems.

Page 282

Famous Leaders

Use page 282 to answer these questions.

1. His nickname means "like steel." Stalin
2. He was the first to call himself Czar. Ivan IV (Ivan the Terrible)
3. This ruler was the first Russian vaccinated against the smallpox virus. Catherine the Great
4. This leader's party thought that they spoke for the majority of Russians. Lenin
5. He initiated the policy of *Glasnost*. Gorbachev
6. He was double-crossed by Hitler during World War II. Stalin
7. This czar was assassinated with his family in 1918. Nicolas II
8. His was more friendly with the West than any other Soviet government during the 20th Century. Gorbachev
9. He ordered the founding of St. Petersburg. Peter the Great
10. He promised the Russian people that the government would provide more food, land and peace. Lenin
11. This leader gained land for Russia in wars fought against Turkey and Poland. Catherine the Great
12. This czar was blamed for losing territory to the Germans in World War I. Nicolas II
13. This czar killed his oldest son with his own hands. Ivan the Terrible.
14. He was leader when his country lost 20-million people in World War II. Stalin
15. He often put on disguises when he traveled. Peter the Great

Research to find out whom the Russian people fought in these wars.

Crimean War: Great Britain, France, Sardinia, Turkey
World War I: Austria, Hungary, Bulgaria, Germany, Ottoman Empire (Turkey)
Seven Years' War: Great Britain, Prussia, Hanover
Napoleonic Wars: France

Page 283

Search and Rescue

Use reference materials to complete this puzzle.

Across

1. One-________ of the earth's land is covered by what was the U.S.S.R.
4. site of world's worst nuclear disaster in 1986
11. first woman in space
17. winner of Olympic women's balance beam and floor exercises in 1972
18. These tribes came from Eastern Europe to the Kiev Rus in the 6th Century.
19. unit of monetary measure
20. original republic closest to Iran and Afghanistan
21. first satellite launched into space
22. This country's Golden Horde attacked early Russians and remained in power for over a century.
23. Peter ____________ composed "The Nutcracker" and "Swan Lake."

Down

2. a cold, treeless and often frozen arctic desert
3. author of *Doctor Zhivago* whose government would not permit him to accept the Nobel Prize for literature
5. author of *War and Peace* (Hint: Use an "i" at the end of author's name instead of the more commonly used "y".)
6. capital of Ukraine; known as "the mother of Russian cities"
7. This mountain range separates Asian Russia from European Russia.
8. alphabet used in the former U.S.S.R.
9. largest freshwater lake in Eurasia
10. first human to travel in space
12. Because the U.S.S.R. invaded ________ in 1979, the U.S. boycotted the Moscow Olympic Games in 1980.
13. Czar____________ II freed serfs in 1861.
14. President of Russian Republic during 1991 attempted coup
15. the period of time when the Warsaw Pact nations and NATO nations were adversaries yet did not engage in direct combat
16. number of time zones in the former U.S.S.R.

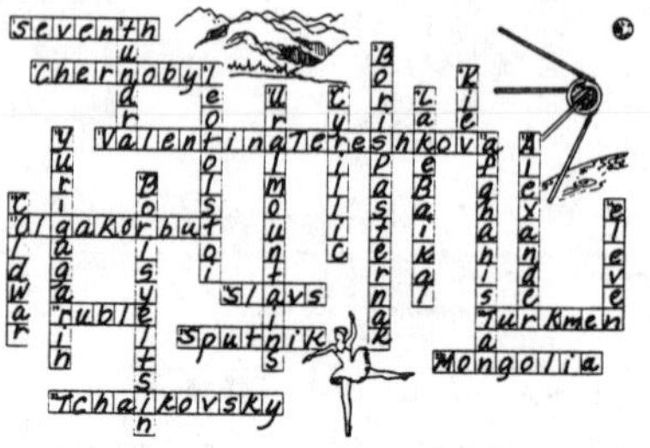

Seventh
Chernobyl
Valentina Tereshkova
Olga Korbut
Slavs
ruble
Turkmen
Sputnik
Mongolia
Tchaikovsky
tundra
Leo Tolstoi
Ural Mountains
Cyrillic
Boris Pasternak
Lake Baikal
Kiev
Yuri Gagarin
Boris Yeltsin
Afghanistan
Alexander
Cold War
eleven

Page 284

Read All About It!

8-18-91 Coup leaders take action; Mikhail Gorbachev is placed under house arrest at his vacation *dacha* in the Crimea.

8-19-91 Gennady Yanayev declares himself acting president and announces a state of emergency.
The mayor of Leningrad, Anatoli Sobchak, declares the coup committee unconstitutional.
Boris Yeltsin declares the coup illegal. Many Soviet troops join him.
Yanayev tells reporters Gorbachev is ill.
Yanayev warns against Yeltsin.

8-20-91 The president of the republic of Kazakhstan resigns from the Politburo and Central Committee to protest the coup.
Ukraine's parliament declares the actions of the coup's leaders null and void.
The coup begins to fall apart; its members quit and fall ill.
Estonia declares its independence.

8-21-91 The Soviet Parliament demands Gorbachev's return to power.
Latvia declares its independence.
Uzbekistan's president outlaws all orders made by coup leaders.

8-22-91 Gorbachev and family return to Moscow.
Lithuania outlaws the Communist Party.
In the republics of Lithuania and Estonia statues of Lenin are torn down.

8-23-91 Moldavia adopts a resolution outlawing Communist Party activities.
Georgia's president calls for a ban of the Communist Party.
Uzbekistan outlaws Communist Party activities.
Gorbachev and Yeltsin purge top officials and appoint proven reformers.

In 1991 you were a reporter assigned to Moscow by *Today's International Press* (TIP). During the coup attempt in the Soviet Union in mid-August you were on the scene. Write your news article for the world!

Include: comments from citizens on the streets, warnings from government officials, the reaction of the people around you, and a "news" photo.

Answers will vary

Page 285

Check It Off

Choose a country that takes/took part in the Olympics. Work alone or with others to complete the activities listed here. Check each one off when you have completed it.

_____ 1. Create a flag and make a sign to identify your country.
_____ 2. Design a display which illustrates 10 products (agriculture, industry, animals, etc.) your country is noted for.
_____ 3. Make a crossword puzzle out of at least 15 words which relate to your country.
_____ 4. Make a map of your country which shows and labels: capital city, other major cities, major rivers, lakes and oceans, neighboring countries, mountains and points of interest
_____ 5. Complete the chart of information below and be ready to share it.
_____ 6. Post all team information on the "Olympic Nations in Review" bulletin board.

Country Name: ____________ Answers will vary.
Capital: ____________
Population: ____________
Shares Border(s) with Countries of: ____________
Leader(s) in Government: ____________
Major Religion(s): ____________
One Important Holiday: ____________
One Major Olympic Sport: ____________
One Recent Medal Winner: ____________

Page 286

Who Am I?

Color each country's flag with the appropriate colors. Then fill in each blank with the letter of the country described in each sentence.

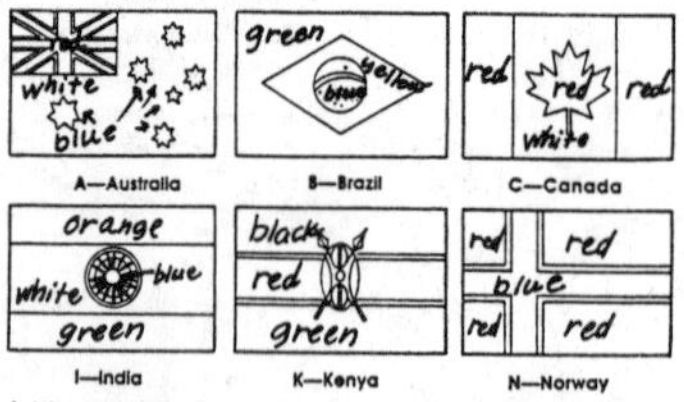

white
blue
green
yellow
blue
red
red
red
white
orange
white
blue
green
black
red
green
red
red
blue
red
red

A—Australia B—Brazil C—Canada
I—India K—Kenya N—Norway

C. 1. I share a border with the United States.
N. 2. My capital is Oslo.
K. 3. I am located just east of Uganda.
C. 4. I was host to the 1988 Winter Olympics.
B. 5. The river with the greatest volume of water in the world flows out of my country.
K. 6. The colors of my flag are black, red and green.
A. 7. Two animals found only in my country are the bandicoot and the wallaby.
I. 8. The Hindu people consider my Ganges River to be sacred.
B. 9. Portuguese is the main language spoken in my country.
I. 10. One of our modern-day heroes, Mahatma Gandhi, is known worldwide.
N. 11. I am a country in Europe.
C. 12. I consist of 10 provinces and 2 territories.
B. 13. I share a border with Suriname and Colombia, to name a few.
K. 14. The second-largest freshwater lake in the world, Lake Victoria, can be found partially in my country.
I. 15. I am located in Asia.
A. 16. My country is also a continent.
N. 17. Vikings sailed from my land in ships with square sails.
A. 18. I am sometimes called the "Land Down Under."

Page 287

Dear Mom, . . .

Imagine you are a contestant in this year's Summer or Winter Olympics. You are far from your family whom you haven't seen in several weeks. Write a letter home telling about your new and exciting adventure.

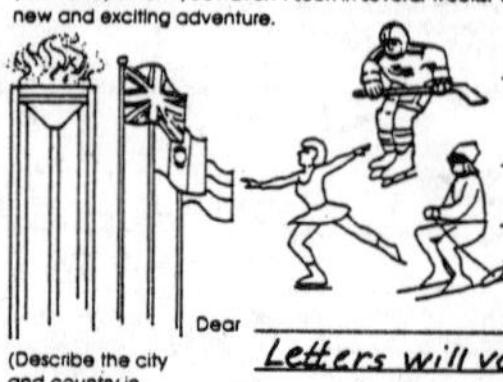

____________ (Your Country's Team) Olympic Village
____________ (City/Country)
____________ (Date)

Dear ____________,

Letters will vary.

(Describe the city and country in which you are competing.)

(Explain what you like about being here.)

(Discuss your event and how your practice sessions are going.)

(Add your personal comments, complaints, what you miss, best wishes, etc.)

Page 288

Name _____

Which Kind Is It?

A **declarative** sentence tells something. It ends with a period. (.)
An **interrogative** sentence asks something. It ends with a question mark. (?)
An **imperative** sentence gives an order. It ends with a period. (.)
An **exclamatory** sentence shows strong feeling. It ends with an exclamation mark. (!)

Read each sentence in this dialog. Write an abbreviation to tell what kind of sentence it is:
        D—declarative   *Int*—interrogative   *Imp*—imperative   *E*—exclamatory
Then write the missing punctuation mark.

Imp   **Mr. Chen:** Class, listen up .

D   For math today, we are going outside to play games .

_____   **Class:** Yay

_____   **Maria:** What are we going to play

_____   **Mr. Chen:** I don't know—you will be making up the games

_____   **Kevin:** How do we do that

_____   **Mr. Chen:** I am giving every group a box with materials and directions

_____   Meet with your group now

_____   **Kevin:** Maria, Yu-Chih, and Julie, do you want to work at the table in the back

_____   **Julie:** That sounds good

_____   **Maria:** I'll go get our box

_____   **Yu-Chih:** What's in the box, Maria

_____   **Maria:** There's a measuring tape, a whistle, and 10 empty two-liter bottles

_____   **Julie:** Look and see if there is anything else

_____   **Yu-Chih:** Here are the directions

_____   **Kevin:** Read them aloud for us, Yu-Chih

_____   **Yu-Chih:** Use these materials to make up a metric measurement relay game

_____   **Maria:** Hey, this'll be fun

_____   **Julie:** Does anybody have an idea

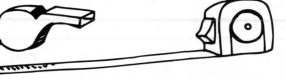

Name _____

Ancient China

A **complete sentence** has both a subject and a predicate.
• The **subject** is the part of a sentence that tells whom or what the sentence is about.
• The **predicate** is the part of a sentence that tells what the subject is or does.

A **fragment** is not a complete sentence. It may be missing the subject or the predicate.

Read these exercises. Label each **CS** if it is a complete sentence or **F** if it is a fragment. Then choose one of the fragments. Rewrite it as a complete sentence on the back of this page. *Underline the subject. Circle the predicate.*

_____ 1. We are studying Ancient China.

_____ 2. The world's oldest continuous civilization.

_____ 3. For thousands of years, China was ruled by different dynasties.

_____ 4. A dynasty is a series of rulers from the same family.

_____ 5. During the reign of the First Emperor, much of the Great Wall of China was built.

_____ 6. The longest structure in the world.

_____ 7. The Chinese were the first to make paper.

_____ 8. Silk rags and fibrous materials, such as bamboo and hemp.

_____ 9. The *Diamond Sutra* is the earliest known printed book.

_____ 10. Was made in A.D. 868.

_____ 11. Several forms of weaponry were invented in China.

_____ 12. Gunpowder, fireworks, rockets, and bombs.

_____ 13. Among the other Chinese inventions were the magnetic compass, the wheelbarrow, kites, umbrellas, paper money, porcelain, and silk.

_____ 14. The arts of calligraphy, poetry, and painting.

_____ 15. Calligraphy is the art of fine handwriting.

_____ 16. It was an important part of many Chinese paintings.

_____ 17. Created beautiful porcelain pottery.

_____ 18. The Chinese made exquisite blue-and-white pottery during the Ming Dynasty.

Name _____

Boring Verb + Adverb < Vivid Verb

A **verb** is an action word. A vivid, or descriptive, verb is stronger than a boring verb used with an adverb or adverb phrase.

Read these verbs and adverbs. Write a vivid verb for each that has about the same meaning. You may want to look up some of the verbs in a thesaurus to get ideas.

run quickly   <   _____bolt_____

1. say quietly   <   _____

2. pull hard   <   _____

3. secretly watch   <   _____

4. win by a lot   <   _____

5. go away completely   <   _____

6. strongly dislike   <   _____

7. like a lot   <   _____

8. move leisurely   <   _____

9. tell loudly   <   _____

10. cry passionately   <   _____

11. think carefully   <   _____

12. look closely   <   _____

13. try hard   <   _____

14. walk slowly   <   _____

15. cut a little   <   _____

16. cut a lot   <   _____

17. really want   <   _____

18. eat a lot   <   _____

19. act meanly   <   _____

20. deliberately trick   <   _____

Name _____

Peppy Prepositions

A **preposition** is a word (or words) that shows the relationship between a noun or pronoun and another word in a sentence. A preposition is always part of a phrase: _with_ a pair of scissors, _from_ me, _instead of_ chicken.

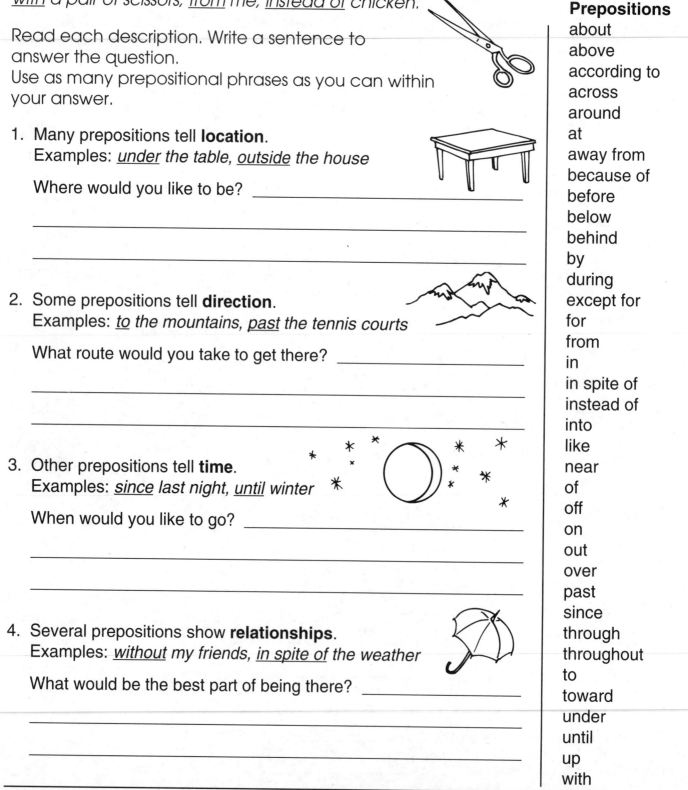

Read each description. Write a sentence to answer the question.
Use as many prepositional phrases as you can within your answer.

1. Many prepositions tell **location**.
   Examples: _under_ the table, _outside_ the house

   Where would you like to be? _____

   _____

   _____

2. Some prepositions tell **direction**.
   Examples: _to_ the mountains, _past_ the tennis courts

   What route would you take to get there? _____

   _____

   _____

3. Other prepositions tell **time**.
   Examples: _since_ last night, _until_ winter

   When would you like to go? _____

   _____

   _____

4. Several prepositions show **relationships**.
   Examples: _without_ my friends, _in spite of_ the weather

   What would be the best part of being there? _____

   _____

   _____

Prepositions

about
above
according to
across
around
at
away from
because of
before
below
behind
by
during
except for
for
from
in
in spite of
instead of
into
like
near
of
off
on
out
over
past
since
through
throughout
to
toward
under
until
up
with

Name _____

Fill in for a Laugh

On the lines, write an antonym or homophone for each word in parentheses.
When you are finished, you will have a complete joke.

A man was bitten by a dog. _____ a _____, he became very
                              (Before)   **(weak)**

_____. He decided to see a doctor. The doctor examined
(well)

_____ and said, "_____ have been bitten
(hymn)   **(Ewe)**

_____ a _____ dog. Now you have rabies."
(buy)   **(glad)**

The man _____ _____ a pencil and paper. Then he spent an
          (answered)   **(four)**

_____ thinking and _____. The doctor finally broke the
(our)   **(righting)**

_____. "You are certainly making a _____ will."
(noise)   **(short)**

"Oh, I'm _____ writing my will," the man said. "I'm making a list of people
          (knot)

I'm going to bite."

Name _____

Animal Expressions

Expressions that use the names of animals are often used. Match each expression to its definition. If you get stuck, use your dictionary.

1. _____ bear hug

2. _____ beeline

3. _____ birdbrain

4. _____ bird's-eye-view

5. _____ bookworm

6. _____ bullheaded

7. _____ busy bee

8. _____ charley horse

9. _____ chicken feed

10. _____ crocodile tears

11. _____ crow's-feet

12. _____ dog-eared

13. _____ firebug

14. _____ fish story

15. _____ frogman

16. _____ henpecked

17. _____ horse sense

18. _____ lionhearted

19. _____ lion's share

20. _____ loan shark

21. _____ piggyback

22. _____ pigtails

23. _____ road hog

24. _____ scapegoat

25. _____ swan song

26. _____ wolf in sheep's clothing

a. a driver who takes up the whole road

b. a person who reads a lot

c. a moneylender who charges high interest

d. a tight embrace

e. an arsonist: a person who burns down buildings

f. a person blamed for something he or she didn't do

g. dangerous person pretending to be harmless

h. underwater swimmer with mask, flippers, and air supply

i. wrinkles at the corner of the eyes

j. brave

k. a straight, direct path or course

l. stupid person

m. up on someone's back and shoulders

n. false weeping

o. stubborn; headstrong

p. a very active person

q. the largest portion of something

r. shabby; worn (as pages of a book)

s. final act or farewell performance

t. seen from above

u. braids of hair

v. small amount of money

w. muscle strain in the leg

x. common sense

y. husband who is nagged

z. doubtful or suspicious story

Name _____

Reading Ads

Can you spot techniques ad writers use to persuade you to buy their products? Read the ads on this page. Then answer the questions by writing the name of the correct product.

Winner's Circle

"A better brand of running shoes."

These shoes are so comfortable, people wear them for every occasion. At these prices, they're good for much more than just sports . . . Butter-soft, yet rugged . . . imported from Spain . . . a quality shoe in a class by itself.

Super Treds

Everyone wears Super Treds. So join the team. Buy Super Treds while supplies last. Come in and have a fit!

Champion Stock

Flo Jo, famous Olympic track star, wears Champion Stock. Why don't you wear the shoes of champions? In the long run, you'll be better off.

Panther

There's no tiptoeing around in Panther running shoes. They're made for real tough cats. So put bounce in your every move and stay clear of the pack. Beat your opponents with the ease of a panther!

1. Which ad suggests you buy the product because everybody does?

   _____

2. Which ad suggests you buy the product because a famous person does? _____

   _____

3. Which ad has a "snob" appeal? _____

4. Which ad tries to create a powerful image? _____

5. Which ad appealed to you most? _____

   Why? _____

Name _____

Outlining

When you write a report, you collect a lot of information about a subject. Sometimes it's hard to organize all the facts into good paragraphs. When you outline, write all your facts under headings. Then you can use the headings and facts to write paragraphs.

Below is an outline for a report on Wolfgang Amadeus Mozart. Use the outline to write a short report about him.

Wolfgang Amadeus Mozart (1756–1791)

I. Childhood

   A. Born in Salzburg, Austria

   B. Father wrote music for the arch bishop; was his teacher

   C. Showed talent early

      1. wrote music at age 5

         a. played harpsichord at age 4

      2. performed with his older sister on tours throughout Europe

II. Adulthood

   A. Lived in Vienna, Austria

   B. Composed music and performed

      1. yet unable to support family

   C. Died poor at age 36

III. Achievements

   A. Wrote more than 600 compositions and 22 operas

   B. Music withstood test of time

      1. His music is played around the world today.

      2. Summer music festivals honor him.

The title of my report will be _____.

Tricky Names and Titles

Do capitalize
- names and initials of people
    Fatima   Lawrence   Alvin Ailey   S.E. Hinton
- family members when the words are used as names or when the words are followed by the person's name
    Grandma   Dad   Mother   my Uncle Bill   Grandpa Rogers
- titles or abbreviations used with names
    President Lincoln   Queen Victoria   Mrs. Lopez   Dr. Martin Luther King Jr.
- a title used without a person's name when you are talking <u>to</u> the person
    Good afternoon, Senator.   Great game, Coach.

Do not capitalize
- family members used with a possessive noun or pronoun, but not the person's name
    my aunt   their great-grandfather   his mom   Brigitte's papa
- a title used without a person's name when you are talking <u>about</u> the person
    our president   the professor

Read the sentences. Find the 30 names, initials, or titles that should be capitalized. Underline those letters three times. The first word has been done for you.

1. Have you seen my backpack, <u>d</u>ad?

2. I am going to visit my grandparents and my aunt eleanor.

3. Did you know that dr. matthews, my dentist, is danny's mom?

4. The United States has a president rather than a king or queen.

5. Jenny wrote her report on president james madison.

6. During the Civil War, general robert e. lee was the leader of the Southern troops.

7. Some people believe he was America's finest general ever.

8. ms. andrews read us an article about chief joseph, leader of the Nez Perce Indians.

9. We invited rev. johnson, fr. donally, and rabbi bronstein to speak to our class.

10. It is a pleasure to meet you, governor.

11. The first female Supreme Court judge was justice sandra day o'Connor.

12. My favorite character in the game Clue is professor plum.

Name _____

Proofread a Bibliography

A **bibliography** is a listing of resources you used in a report. Bibliography styles vary.

General guidelines:

1. Resources are listed in alphabetical order by the last name of the author. If you do not know the author, begin with the title.

2. Titles of books, encyclopedias, and CD-ROMs should be underlined or in *italics*. Titles of encyclopedia articles should be in "quotation marks."

3. For books, give the place of publication, publisher, and publication date. For encyclopedias, give the publication date and volume. For CD-ROM encyclopedias, give the format, publisher, and publication date.

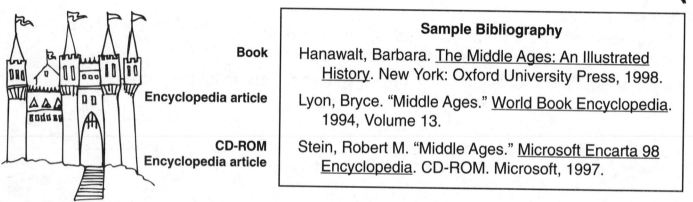

Book

Encyclopedia article

CD-ROM
Encyclopedia article

Sample Bibliography

Hanawalt, Barbara. The Middle Ages: An Illustrated History. New York: Oxford University Press, 1998.

Lyon, Bryce. "Middle Ages." World Book Encyclopedia. 1994, Volume 13.

Stein, Robert M. "Middle Ages." Microsoft Encarta 98 Encyclopedia. CD-ROM. Microsoft, 1997.

Proofread this bibliography. Add the missing underlining and punctuation marks (commas, periods, quotation marks, and colons).

Proofread the bibliography. Add the missing underlining and punctuation marks (commas, periods, quotation marks, and colons).

Bibliography

Aliki   A Medieval Feast   New York   Crowell   1983

Caselli Giovanni   The Middle Ages   New York   Peter Bedrick Books   1988

Gravett Christopher   Knight   New York   Knopf   1993

Macaulay David   Cathedral   Boston   Houghton Mifflin   1973

Middle Ages   Compton's Encyclopedia   1992   Volume 15

Rosenthal Joel T   Knights and Knighthood   World Book Encyclopedia   1994   Volume 11

Soergel Philip M   Chivalry   Microsoft Encarta 98 Encyclopedia   CD-ROM   Microsoft 1997

Steele Philip   Castles   New York   Kingfisher   1998

Name _____

What Do You Think?

An **essay** is a type of writing in which you express your opinion. To write a really good essay, you have to back up your opinion with details and examples. Think of a topic you feel strongly about or choose one from the list below. Use the form on this page as a practice model for writing.

> *Why School Should (or Shouldn't) Be Year-Round*
>
> *Why We Should (or Shouldn't) Save the Rain Forest*
>
> *What Courses Should Be Offered in Middle School*
>
> *Why Grades Should (or Shouldn't) Be Eliminated*
>
> *Why It Is (or Isn't) Important to Know More Than One Language*

Something I believe strongly about is _____

_____

_____

One reason I believe this is _____

_____

_____

Another reason is _____

_____

_____

An example that proves this point is _____

_____

_____

I strongly feel that _____

_____

_____

In closing, let me say that _____

_____

_____

Name _____

Mysterious Mother Goose

Ask any of your friends who Mother Goose was, and you will be told that she was the woman who wrote all those classic nursery rhymes. You may even get a description of the famous author as an old lady with a crooked nose who took to riding atop an enormous goose. If your friend is really up on preschool prattle, he may even be able to rattle off a long list of Mother Goose nursery rhyme titles or recite entire rhymes by heart. Yet even if your friend is a children's literature scholar, he will not be able to give you a definitive full name for the strange old bird, nor birth and death dates for the woman. The true identity of Mother Goose has been disputed for centuries. The earliest sighting of her name appeared in a 1650 French poem which

included the line, ". . . like a tale from Mother Goose." Forty-seven years later, her name was attached to a Charles Perrault book of retold fairy tales including "Cinderella" and "Sleeping Beauty." The book, entitled *Stories and Tales of Times Past, with Morals,* was subtitled *Tales of My Mother the Goose*. Then in the early 1700s, the English book publisher John Newbery titled a collection of nursery rhymes *Mother Goose's Melody*. Other nursery rhyme collections that followed also credited Mother Goose with authorship.

So who was the Mother Goose to which the seventeenth- and eighteenth-century collectors of fairy tales and nursery rhymes referred? Theories abound. A common story among Americans suggests that Mother Goose was really Elizabeth Goose (or Vertigoose) from colonial Boston. Elizabeth Goose was the mother-in-law of a man named Thomas Fleet. Thomas Fleet is said to have collected the tales Elizabeth told her grandchildren into a published book entitled *Songs for the Nursery*. Most historians discredit the Elizabeth Goose theory, however, for several reasons: the book that was said to have held her tales has never been located; dates in the Elizabeth Goose theory do not ring true; and the earliest appearances of references to Mother Goose all come out of Europe.

Others theorize a much older original Mother Goose. Some swear that she was a witch during Medieval times, responsible for birthing babies, nursing the sick, and raising the young. Others claim that she was the eighth-century mother of Charlemagne, Queen Bertha, who is said to have been known as Queen Goose-foot in her day. Some allege that the term was a reference to Fru Gosen of German folklore. Still others maintain that the Mother Goose to which the old European stories refer was the biblical Queen of Sheba. Perhaps the most convincing theory holds that Mother Goose was no single woman, and that the rhymes ascribed to her name have come from many sources both written and passed along orally throughout the centuries of human history.

Name

Name That Rhyme

Match the one-sentence summaries below with the classic rhymes they describe.

_____ 1. This rhyme refers to a boy who jumps over a candlestick.

_____ 2. This rhyme expresses a wish for sunshine.

_____ 3. This rhyme honors the mother of all rhymes.

_____ 4. This rhyme advertises a pastry.

_____ 5. This rhyme refers to a young man who has gone to sea.

_____ 6. This rhyme tells the story of a boy who runs through a village in his pajamas.

_____ 7. This rhyme talks about a mouse that runs up a clock.

_____ 8. This rhyme describes a boy who has gone to bed with his trousers on.

_____ 9. This rhyme describes baking a cake for a baby.

_____ 10. This rhyme tells of a boy who has fallen asleep on the job.

_____ 11. This rhyme tells about a boy who wants to purchase a pie without any money.

_____ 12. This rhyme tells of a boy and girl who climb a hill to fetch water from a well.

_____ 13. The teller of this rhyme is singing to a sheep.

_____ 14. This rhyme tells the tale of a girl who owns a pet lamb.

_____ 15. This rhyme tells the tale of a girl who has lost her sheep.

A. "Mary Had a Little Lamb"

B. "Rain, Rain, Go Away"

C. "Hickory, Dickory, Dock"

D. "Little Boy Blue"

E. "Diddle, Diddle, Dumpling"

F. "Simple Simon"

G. "Little Bo Peep"

H. "Jack Be Nimble"

I. "Pat-a-Cake"

J. "Bobby Shaftoe"

K. "Baa, Baa, Black Sheep"

L. "Old Mother Goose"

M. "Jack and Jill"

N. "Wee Willie Winkie"

O. "Hot Cross Buns"

Name _____

Contemporary Choreographers

Read about four contemporary
choreographers below. Then, answer the
questions that follow in complete sentences.

Mark Morris: Morris began dancing as a child and
was already choreographing pieces by his teenage
years. Touring in Asia in the 1970s, he learned
indigenous dance styles. His own dances mix elements
of classic and modern ballet and Eastern and Western
styles. He has created works for everything from
classical music to punk rock. In 1980, Morris founded
his own dance troupe, which tours internationally and
is scheduled to open its own permanent headquarters in New York. In 1990, Morris collaborated
with Mikhail Baryshnikov on the White Oak Dance Project, which showcased his creativity.

Ann Reinking: Reinking danced and choreographed with Bob Fosse before his death. Following
his death, she worked with Chet Walker to create a musical tribute to her colleague, *Fosse.* She
has worked on such classic Broadway shows as *Chicago, Bye-Bye Birdie,* and *Applause.* She has
worked on four films, including *All That Jazz* and *Annie.* In 1994, she became the founder and
artistic director of the Broadway Theatre Project.

Peter Martins: Martins is a Danish dancer and choreographer who began his career with the
Royal Danish Ballet in 1964. He accepted a position as principal dancer with the New York City
Ballet under the direction of George Balanchine six years later. Balanchine encouraged Martin's
choreographic skills, and in 1981, he became the New York City Ballet's ballet master. His
choreographic pieces include *Calcium Light Night.*

Gerald Arpino: Arpino established the Joffrey Ballet in Chicago along with Robert Joffrey in
1956. When Joffrey died, Arpino succeeded him as artistic director. He has served as the Joffrey
Ballet's resident choreographer since 1961. He creates about one third of the company's works.
Arpino has completed such diverse commissions as a rock ballet set to the music of Prince and a
classic ballet in honor of the American presidency. He holds numerous honors and awards for his
choreographic genius. He serves on various advisory councils and supports the arts in society.

1. Which choreographer likely does the most traveling?_____
2. Which choreographer produces works you would be most interested in seeing?
   _____ Why? _____
3. Which choreographer works for a well-established ballet?_____
4. Which choreographer completes a great deal of work on Broadway?_____
5. Which choreographer might still be a dancer if not for the encouragement of Balanchine?

_____

Letter Fun

In **anagrams**, different words are spelled with the same letters. Take the letters A, B, S, T, for example. They spell three different words in the poem below.

Complete the anagram poems below. The letters that spell the missing words are given in parentheses.

> **The Sports Store Clerks**
>
> They try to keep the baseball BATS.
>
> Lined up beside the baseball hats.
>
> They glue on TABS that name each price.
>
> And each takes a STAB at being nice.

1. **(O, N, W) The Big Winner**

   One time, he _____ a TV set,
   Then lost it in another bet.
   He's wiser _____, for life has shown
   That gamblers can lose all they
   _____.

2. **(A, E, M, T) The Old Gray Mare**

   She is friendly, mild, and _____,
   But since the dog-food makers came
   And thought of her as only
   _____,
   She will no longer drink or eat.

3. **(E, S, T, W) The Cook**

   As the sun sets in the _____
   He makes the table look its best,
   But that won't help his lumpy
   _____.
   It _____ your mouth but
   tastes like glue.

4. **(A, D, E, R) Love Letter**

   Her letter makes him float on air,
   But he can't _____ it.
   Does he _____
   To have it read where all can hear
   His first love letter from his
   _____?

5. **(E, H, O, S) The Awkward Gardener**

   In her yard, she weeds and
   _____.
   And trips upon the garden
   _____.
   She keeps from falling, it is true,
   But rips the heel right off her
   _____.

6. **(E, I, L, V) The Nasty Neighbor**

   That _____ man is never kind.
   He's always plotting in his mind
   To pull some _____ and nasty
   trick.
   All who _____ near him fear
   he's sick.

7. **(A, C, E, R) The Fast Farmer**

   To win an _____ in good
   lands
   She ran a _____ upon her
   hands.
   She didn't _____ just who
   might frown
   Because she knew she'd win hands
   down.

Name _____

Many Meanings

RIDDLE: What has 18 legs and catches flies?
ANSWER: A baseball team.
Flies are certain insects. They are also certain hits in baseball.
The riddle is funny because it uses both meanings.

Each joke below uses a word in two ways. Beneath each joke,
there are three or more meanings of the word presented.
Circle the numbers of the two meanings used in the joke.

1. *Lou:* Why was the actor happy about breaking his leg?
   Sue: He finally got into a cast.

   cast: (1) a hard covering formed by molding; (2) to throw; (3) performers in a play

2. *Tim:* I'll see you when you return. Will you be long?
   Kim: Same as always. About 5' 4".

   long: (1) to wish for; (2) much time; (3) tall or high

3. *Jane:* Is this a rare piece of art?
   Blaine: It certainly isn't well done.

   rare: (1) thin and not dense; (2) cooked for a short time; (3) unlike others of its kind

4. *Bill:* How is an umpire like an orchestra leader?
   Phil: Both have to know the score.

   score: (1) to win; (2) something owed to someone else; (3) a record of points made in a game; (4) a written copy of music

5. *Flo:* Why do you think your pet pig will write you?
   Joe: It has a pen.

   pen: (1) something used for writing; (2) a fenced-in place for animals; (3) slang for prison

6. *Mary:* Why are you buying gloves for your dog?
   Tommy: It is a boxer.

   boxer: (1) a kind of dog; (2) someone who packs boxes; (3) a prizefighter

7. *Ron:* Do you file your nails?
   Don: No. I just cut them off and then throw them away.

   file: (1) to rub smooth with a piece of metal; (2) a line of people or things; (3) to arrange things in a certain order

8. *Customer:* I'd like a steak, and please make it lean.
   Waiter: In which direction?

   lean: (1) to rely on; (2) having little or no fat; (3) to tilt or bend

My Word!

Words come from a variety of places—from people's names, from places, from other languages, etc. Some words are even formed by combining two words. For example, the word *motel* comes from combining *motor* and *hotel*. The word *smog* comes from *smoke* and *fog*. The brand name *Swatch* is a combination of *Swiss* and *watch*.

Can you figure out what two words were put together to create the word *brunch*?

_____

You can make up a new word by combining two others. Feel like having a "jonut"? That's short for *jelly donut*. Or how about a "smug" from a sweetheart? (That's a combination of *smooch* and *hug*.)

Get silly. Get serious. Get your pencil and get ready to make up ten new words. Share your words with the class. Who knows? You may decide to publish a "*sictionary*" (that's a silly dictionary!).

1. _____

2. _____

3. _____

4. _____

5. _____

6. _____

7. _____

8. _____

9. _____

10. _____

Name _____

Lovely Literature

Literature can take many forms and is full of many intriguing components. Use the words in the word box relating to literature to fill in the blanks.

rhythm	alliteration	rhyme	assonance	metaphor	onomatopoeia
stanza	symbol	simile	personification	diction	figurative language

_____ 1. the giving of human qualities to an object, animal, or idea

_____ 2. a direct comparison between two unlike things

_____ 3. the repetition of sounds at the beginning of words

_____ 4. a group of lines that form a unit, like a paragraph

_____ 5. the pattern of stressed and unstressed syllables that may create a beat

_____ 6. a person, place, or object that stands for something beyond itself

_____ 7. a comparison using *like* or *as*

_____ 8. repetition of vowel sounds in stressed syllables

_____ 9. repetition of ending sounds at the end of words

_____ 10. the use of words to imitate sounds

_____ 11. language that communicates ideas beyond the literal meanings of the word

_____ 12. the choices of words in speech or writing

Name _____

Words From the Government

The government of the United States is a very interesting and complex institution. Learn about some words relating to it by filling in the crossword puzzle below. Use the terms from the word box for your answers.

Across

2. to call back or change back

3. a closed meeting of a group of people belonging to the same political party

6. the branch of government that makes laws

9. a formal written request made to an official body or person

Word Box

caucus
referendum
repeal
resolution
legislative
amendment
executive
petition
delegate
judicial

Down

1. the branch of government that carries out the laws

2. a vote on a measure proposed by a legislative body

4. a formal expression of opinion voted on by an official body

5. a person acting for another; a representative in the House of Representatives

7. a change or modification by a constitutional procedure

8. the branch of government that judges and administers justice

Name _____

All the World is a Stage

Theater is an art form in which a series of events, often a written play, is acted out by authors who pretend to be the characters. Learn more about theater and acting by filling in the blanks using words from the word box. Write them next to their correct definitions.

| choreography | soliloquy | callback | audition | cue |
| monologue | protagonist | antagonist | aside | thespian |

_____ o _____   **1.** a dramatic scene performed by one actor

_____ n   **2.** to give a trial performance; to test for a theatrical part

_____ t _____   **3.** the principle character or leading actor

_____ h _____   **4.** relating to drama; actor

_____ e   **5.** an actor's comments heard by the audience, but supposedly not by the characters

s _____   **6.** the act of talking to oneself, presumably alone on the stage

_____ t _____   **7.** the one that opposes the main character or lead actor

_____ a _____   **8.** a second or additional audition for a theatrical part

_____ g _____   **9.** the composition and arrangement of dance and movement upon the stage

_____ e   **10.** a written signal to the performer to begin a specific speech or action

Name _____

Check it Out!

Use the schedule on this page as a guide for writing a research paper or giving a school report. Estimate how long it will take you to do each job. Then check off each task you complete it.

Paper Due Date: _____

PART 1: Gathering Information

Task	Estimated Time	Start Date	Completed
Choose topic.	_____	_____	_____
Go to library.	_____	_____	_____
Begin research.	_____	_____	_____
List sources found.	_____	_____	_____
Take notes on each source.	_____	_____	_____
Write a bibliography.	_____	_____	_____
Sum up the main idea of paper.	_____	_____	_____

PART 2: Organizing Your Research

Task	Estimated Time	Start Date	Completed
Read notes and decide which information to keep or leave out.	_____	_____	_____
Arrange notes in a logical order.	_____	_____	_____
Write an outline based on notes.	_____	_____	_____

PART 3: Writing Your Paper

Task	Estimated Time	Start Date	Completed
Write a rough draft.	_____	_____	_____
Revise, edit, polish.	_____	_____	_____
Rewrite rough draft into final copy.	_____	_____	_____
Proofread and hand in on due date.	_____	_____	_____

Name _____

Look it Up!

References are books and other materials you refer to for information. Reference books cannot be taken out of the library. They have Ref or R on their spines. Some of the most common references are listed below.

Dictionary: The most common dictionary gives spellings, meanings, and pronunciation for words. There are also biographical dictionaries that give facts about famous people. A thesaurus is a special dictionary consisting of just synonyms and antonyms.

Atlas: a book of maps

Almanac: a book of up-to-date information on many subjects, such as population, government, sports, entertainment; A new edition is published each year

Readers' Guide to Periodical Literature: an index of articles that have been published in magazines

Current News on File: an index of newspaper articles

Encyclopedia: a set of books with facts on many subjects

Write the reference(s) you would look in to answer the questions below.

1. In what year was Beethoven born? _____

2. What is another word that means *stout*? _____

3. How far is San Diego from Los Angeles? _____

4. How do you pronounce the word *crochet*? _____

5. Where are the Rocky Mountains? _____

6. Who won the Academy Award for Best Actor last year? _____

7. How are alligators and crocodiles different? _____

8. Which magazines had articles about baseball card collecting? _____

_____

9. Is Mark Twain a fictional character? _____

10. What recent news articles reported on the space shuttle? _____

_____

Designer Fractions

Use the code to color equivalent fractions.

$\frac{1}{2}$ = red $\frac{1}{4}$ = blue $\frac{2}{5}$ = green $\frac{1}{3}$ = yellow $\frac{2}{3}$ = orange

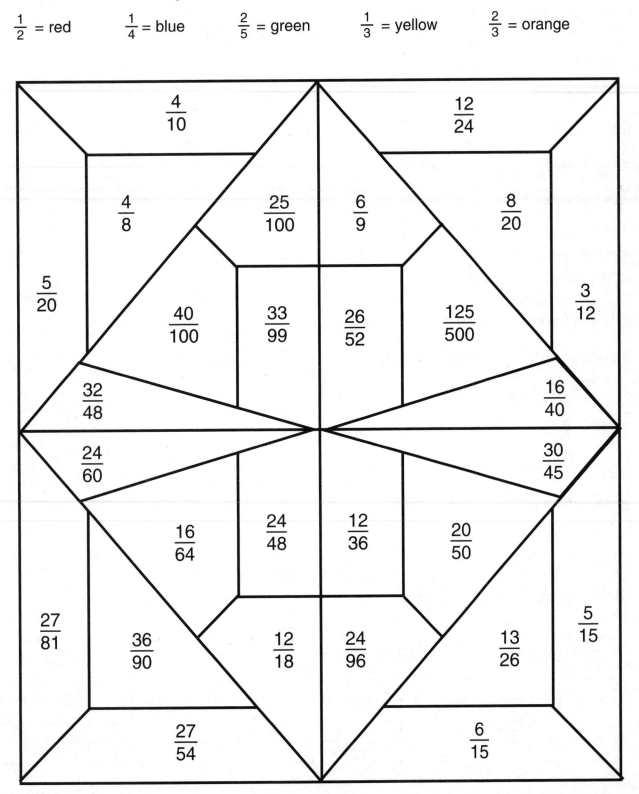

Name _____

Shade-In Message

Find the least common multiple or least common denominator. Shade in one section in the box below that matches each answer. When you are finished, you will discover what to use when adding fractions with unlike denominators.

Least Common Multiple

1. 2 and 8

2. 6 and 4

3. 6 and 3

4. 4 and 10

5. 6 and 9

6. 5 and 10

7. 3 and 5

8. 8 and 12

9. 8 and 10

10. 6 and 8

11. 6 and 10

12. 4 and 7

13. 5 and 6

14. 5 and 12

15. 6 and 12

Least Common Denominator

16. $\frac{5}{6}$ and $\frac{8}{9}$

17. $\frac{1}{2}$ and $\frac{3}{4}$

18. $\frac{9}{10}$ and $\frac{1}{2}$

19. $\frac{2}{5}$ and $\frac{7}{10}$

20. $\frac{2}{3}$ and $\frac{3}{5}$

21. $\frac{2}{3}$ and $\frac{3}{4}$

22. $\frac{2}{3}$ and $\frac{7}{9}$

23. $\frac{5}{16}$ and $\frac{1}{4}$

24. $\frac{4}{7}$ and $\frac{3}{28}$

25. $\frac{1}{2}$ and $\frac{3}{5}$

26. $\frac{5}{6}$ and $\frac{1}{4}$

27. $\frac{5}{6}$ and $\frac{1}{12}$

28. $\frac{7}{8}$ and $\frac{2}{3}$

29. $\frac{3}{10}$ and $\frac{3}{4}$

30. $\frac{2}{9}$ and $\frac{3}{15}$

3	8	13	3	11	12	18	24	60	19	6	15	10	31
5	12	7	5	7	30	17	43	37	3	45	19	23	15
37	24	11	7	23	10	31	29	5	19	12	37	29	12
17	28	37	29	41	28	19	7	37	41	10	13	29	9
13	10	30	20	17	40	4	24	12	17	20	16	18	3

Name _____

Riddle Me This

Multiply.

A. $\frac{1}{4} \times \frac{1}{2} =$ _____

B. $\frac{5}{6} \times 3 =$ _____

C. $2\frac{5}{8} \times 6 =$ _____

D. $3 \times \frac{3}{5} =$ _____

E. $\frac{2}{5} \times \frac{8}{16} =$ _____

F. $12 \times \frac{3}{4} =$ _____

G. $\frac{9}{10} \times \frac{5}{6} =$ _____

H. $3\frac{2}{3} \times \frac{3}{10} =$ _____

I. $\frac{1}{6} \times \frac{9}{10} =$ _____

J. $\frac{4}{5} \times 3\frac{1}{3} =$ _____

K. $\frac{7}{10} \times \frac{5}{15} =$ _____

L. $\frac{3}{10} \times \frac{7}{10} =$ _____

M. $\frac{4}{5} \times \frac{7}{8} =$ _____

N. $7\frac{1}{2} \times 1\frac{7}{10} =$ _____

O. $5\frac{1}{8} \times 9\frac{3}{4} =$ _____

P. $2\frac{1}{4} \times \frac{3}{4} =$ _____

Q. $\frac{5}{8} \times \frac{18}{100} =$ _____

R. $\frac{3}{15} \times \frac{5}{9} =$ _____

S. $\frac{1}{4} \times \frac{1}{5} =$ _____

T. $9\frac{1}{5} \times 6\frac{2}{3} =$ _____

U. $\frac{5}{6} \times \frac{2}{3} =$ _____

V. $\frac{1}{3} \times \frac{2}{3} =$ _____

W. $\frac{11}{12} \times \frac{2}{3} =$ _____

X. $4 \times 6\frac{3}{10} =$ _____

Y. $\frac{1}{2} \times 6\frac{3}{4} =$ _____

Z. $8\frac{1}{2} \times 6\frac{2}{3} =$ _____

Use the answers and letters above to answer the riddle.

What kind of table has no legs?

$\frac{1}{8}$ $\frac{7}{10}$ $\frac{5}{9}$ $\frac{21}{100}$ $61\frac{1}{3}$ $\frac{3}{20}$ $1\frac{11}{16}$ $\frac{21}{100}$ $\frac{3}{20}$ $15\frac{3}{4}$ $\frac{1}{8}$ $61\frac{1}{3}$ $\frac{3}{20}$ $49\frac{31}{32}$ $12\frac{3}{4}$

$61\frac{1}{3}$ $\frac{1}{8}$ $2\frac{1}{2}$ $\frac{21}{100}$ $\frac{1}{5}$

Name _____

Let's Divide

Divide. Write the answers in lowest terms, if necessary.

A. $1\frac{1}{4} \div \frac{1}{4} =$ _____ $2\frac{1}{2} \div \frac{1}{2} =$ _____ $\frac{3}{8} \div \frac{1}{4} =$ _____

B. $3\frac{1}{2} \div \frac{7}{8} =$ _____ $2\frac{1}{4} \div \frac{3}{4} =$ _____ $6 \div \frac{1}{3} =$ _____

C. $2\frac{1}{4} \div \frac{3}{8} =$ _____ $1\frac{1}{2} \div \frac{3}{8} =$ _____ $3\frac{1}{2} \div 1\frac{5}{6} =$ _____

D. $\frac{3}{4} \div \frac{1}{8} =$ _____ $2 \div \frac{1}{4} =$ _____ $\frac{4}{7} \div \frac{2}{3} =$ _____

E. $\frac{1}{2} \div \frac{1}{4} =$ _____ $2\frac{1}{2} \div \frac{1}{2} =$ _____ $\frac{1}{4} \div \frac{1}{8} =$ _____

F. $2\frac{5}{8} \div \frac{1}{8} =$ _____ $\frac{5}{6} \div \frac{3}{18} =$ _____ $1\frac{3}{4} \div \frac{1}{16} =$ _____

G. $1\frac{1}{4} \div \frac{5}{8} =$ _____ $\frac{7}{12} \div \frac{2}{3} =$ _____

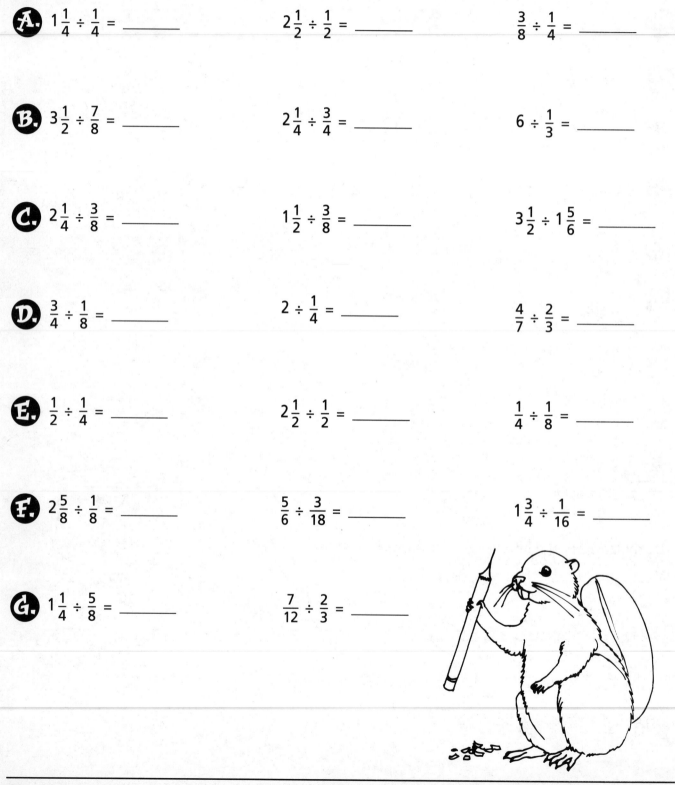

Name _____

In the Sky

Complete each number to make the expression true.

A. 0.30____9 < 0.3019   0.____45 > 0.29   34.3____ > 35.37

B. 16.788 < 16.7____8   8.42____ > 8.427   ____.067 < 1.0671

C. 3.416 > ____.416   28.____47 < 28.147   0.03243 < 0.03____2

D. 5.345 > 5.____45   0.06____83 < 0.06184   178.____71 > 178.789

E. 3.99____ < 3.999   2.527 > 2.____48   17.098 > 1____.908

F. 2.0____3 > 1.999   17.6 > 1.____06   2____7.095 < 217.099

Write the decimals in order from least to greatest.

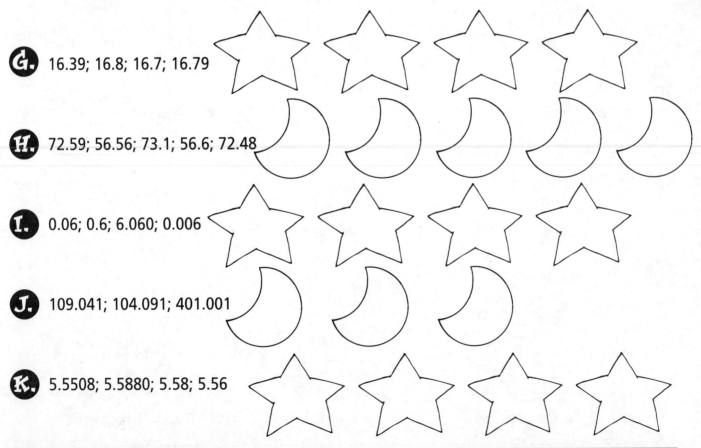

G. 16.39; 16.8; 16.7; 16.79

H. 72.59; 56.56; 73.1; 56.6; 72.48

I. 0.06; 0.6; 6.060; 0.006

J. 109.041; 104.091; 401.001

K. 5.5508; 5.5880; 5.58; 5.56

Name _____

Order, Please!

Frank worked for his sister at the school snack shop. In one hour, he took orders for 20 items. He had to keep track of prices in his head, so he decided to round the prices. Help Frank round each price. Write the number on the price tag.

A. Round to the nearest dollar.

$1.44
hamburger

$1.63
ham sandwich

$2.37
jumbo french fries

B. Round to the nearest tenth.

$2.46
apple pie

$0.34
peach

$1.19
strawberries

C. Round to the nearest whole number.

$6.35
special deal meal

$12.59
value meal

$5.99
hot dog meal

D. Round to the nearest whole number.

$1.29
jumbo popcorn

$2.54
giant cookie

$0.62
brownie

Name _____

Make an Equation

Use the numbers in each circle to create a multiplication equation with two factors and a product. Do the multiplication to check your answer.

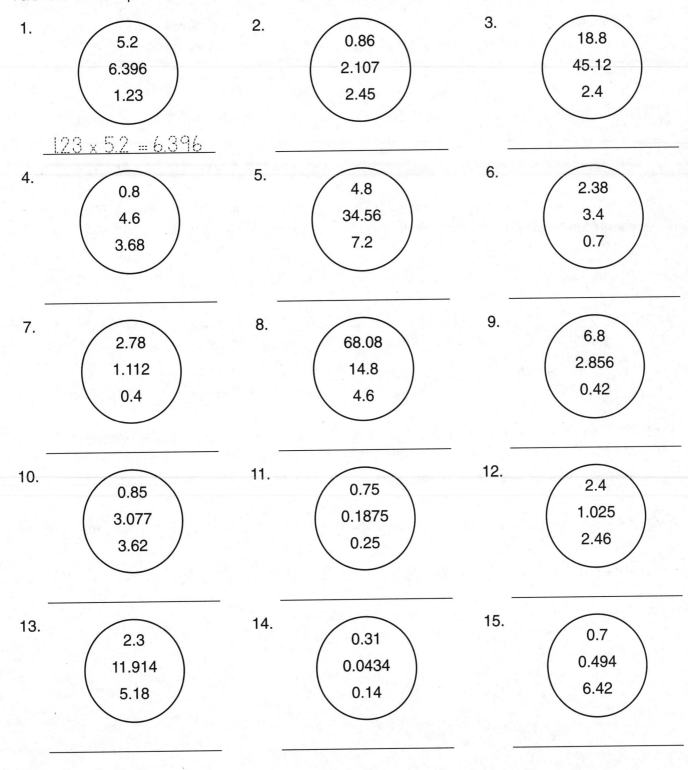

1.

5.2
6.396
1.23

1.23 × 5.2 = 6.396

2.

0.86
2.107
2.45

3.

18.8
45.12
2.4

4.

0.8
4.6
3.68

5.

4.8
34.56
7.2

6.

2.38
3.4
0.7

7.

2.78
1.112
0.4

8.

68.08
14.8
4.6

9.

6.8
2.856
0.42

10.

0.85
3.077
3.62

11.

0.75
0.1875
0.25

12.

2.4
1.025
2.46

13.

2.3
11.914
5.18

14.

0.31
0.0434
0.14

15.

0.7
0.494
6.42

MATH REVIEW

Name _____

Pig Tales

Mack and Sandy raise pigs. Estimate and underline the answer.

A. On Wednesday, Mack and Sandy needed to move 100 pigs from one part of the farm to another. If they can walk .96 miles an hour, how far can they go in 6.42 hours?

About 10 miles   About 4 miles   About 6 miles   About 2 miles

B. Mack and Sandy own 1,021 pigs. Each pen has enough room for 78.7 pigs. About how many pens do they need?

About 13 pens   About 10 pens   About 8 pens   About 5 pens

C. Sandy and Mack need to buy food for the piglets. Each bag of food weighs 58.32 pounds. If each piglet eats about 2.10 pounds every day, about how long will it take one piglet to eat a whole bag of feed?

About 15 days   About 30 days   About 150 days   About 60 days

D. They put the pigs in trucks when they go to the market. The biggest truck on the farm can carry about 4,989.92 pounds. If each pig weighs about 204.23 pounds, about how many pigs can they put in one truck?

About 20 pigs   About 15 pigs   About 12 pigs   About 25 pigs

E. On Thursday, the kids washed out the pig pens. They worked for about 4.85 hours. Each hour they used 1,026 gallons of water. About how much water did they use in all?

About 5,000 gallons   About 100 gallons   About 102 gallons   About 6,000 gallons

F. If each sow can be expected to have about 9.83 piglets each year, about how many piglets will be born in 3 years?

About 1,000 piglets   Not enough information   About 9,000 piglets   About 5,000 piglets

Surfing with Decimals

Divide.

A. $5\overline{)4.85}$ $3\overline{)13.65}$

B. $84\overline{)264.6}$ $4\overline{)16.68}$ $5\overline{)95.5}$ $32\overline{)258.24}$

C. $11\overline{)2.464}$ $13\overline{)35.49}$ $9\overline{)58.5}$ $6\overline{)144.54}$

D. $52\overline{)431.08}$ $19\overline{)2,331.3}$ $12\overline{)494.4}$ $4\overline{)337.8}$

Name _____

Flocking Together

In Australia, huge trees are filled with birds at sunset. Although it can be hard to see these birds at first, you can always hear them! Write a decimal and a percent for each fraction.

 A. Of the parrots in the tree, ⁸/₁₂ were green. Round to the nearest hundredth.

_____

 B. Four-twelfths of the parrots in the tree were blue.

_____

 C. Five flocks of cockatoos landed in the tree just as the sun set. Four-fifths of these birds were white with yellow crests on their heads.

_____

 D. Three-fifths of the pink cockatoos were less than two years old.

_____

 E. Of the black cockatoos in the tree, ¾ sat at the top of the tree.

_____

 F. Five twenty-fifths of the black cockatoos watch the skies for danger.

_____

G. When the sun rises, ²/₅ of the birds in the tree fly away looking for food.

_____

         Daily Learning Drills Grade 6

Name _____

Delightful Daisies

On the flowers in each vase, write the fractions and decimals that are equivalent to the percent shown.

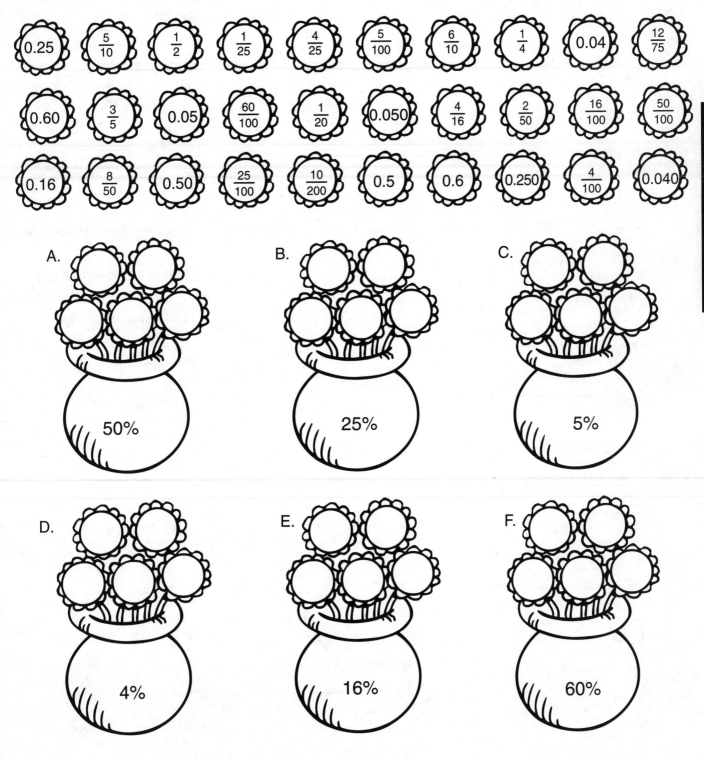

Name _____

Geometry Glossary

Match each picture to its name.

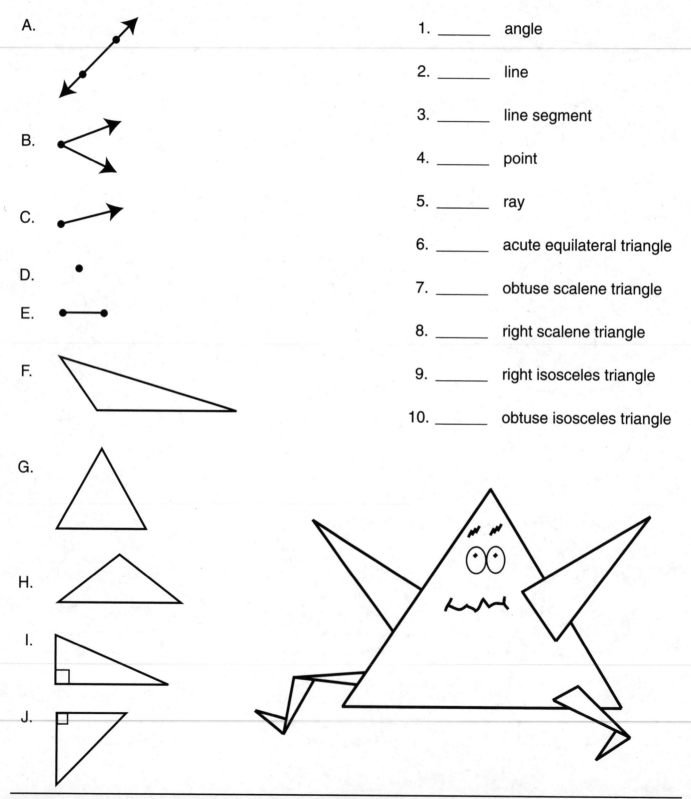

A.

B.

C.

D.

E.

F.

G.

H.

I.

J.

1. _____ angle

2. _____ line

3. _____ line segment

4. _____ point

5. _____ ray

6. _____ acute equilateral triangle

7. _____ obtuse scalene triangle

8. _____ right scalene triangle

9. _____ right isosceles triangle

10. _____ obtuse isosceles triangle

Daily Learning Drills Grade 6

Crazy Compass Art

Use a compass to draw circles around the line segments. Use the line segments as radii and these points as centers for the circles:

Point A   Point C   Point E   Point H
Point I   Point K   Point M

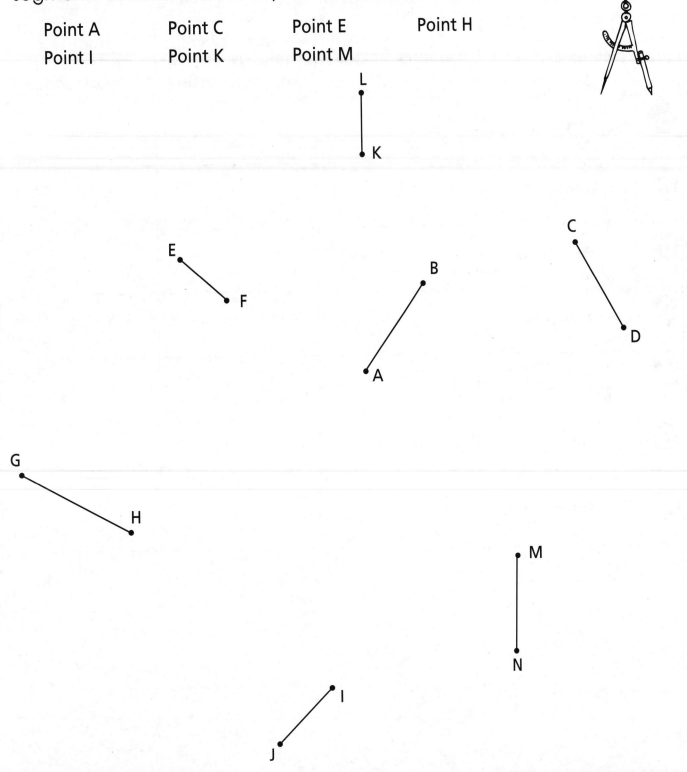

Name _____

Digging for Diagonals

Complete the table below using the pictures at the bottom of the page.
Watch for a pattern and use it to complete problem G.

	Name of figure	Number of sides	Number of diagonals without any intersecting	Number of angles formed by diagonals
A.	Triangle			
B.	Rectangle			
C.	Pentagon			
D.	Hexagon			
E.	Octagon			
F.	Decagon			
G.	20-Sided Figure			

Name _____

An A-Peel-ing Riddle

What shapes are made from banana peels?

To find out, find the area of each shape. Use the formulas to help you. Then use your answers to break the code at the bottom of the page.

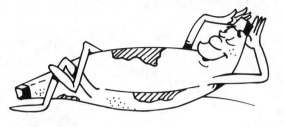

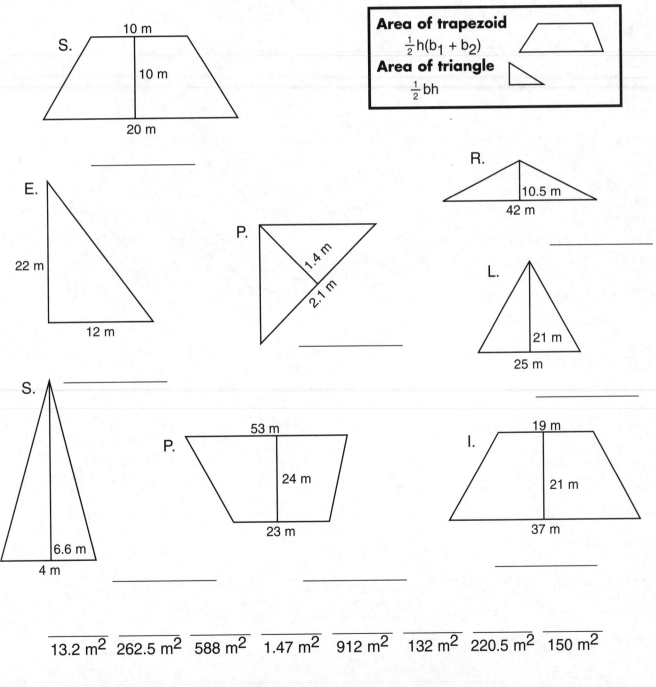

Area of trapezoid
$\frac{1}{2}h(b_1 + b_2)$
Area of triangle
$\frac{1}{2}bh$

S. 10 m / 10 m / 20 m

E. 22 m / 12 m

P. 1.4 m / 2.1 m

R. 10.5 m / 42 m

L. 21 m / 25 m

S. 6.6 m / 4 m

P. 53 m / 24 m / 23 m

I. 19 m / 21 m / 37 m

‾‾13.2 m² ‾‾262.5 m² ‾‾588 m² ‾‾1.47 m² ‾‾912 m² ‾‾132 m² ‾‾220.5 m² ‾‾150 m²

Name _____

Dartboard

Use the dartboard to answer the questions below. (Use 3.14 for p.)

1. Find the area of:

a) the entire circle A. _____

b) the entire circle B. _____

c) the entire circle C. _____

d) the entire circle D. _____

e) the entire circle E. _____

f) the #1 section. _____

g) the #2 section. _____

h) the #3 section. _____

i) the #4 section. _____

2. List the section amounts in order from least to greatest in area.

_____ _____ _____ _____

3. Using area as a guide, which section are you most likely to hit on the dartboard?

_____

Name _____

Symbols and Numbers Together

When metric measurements are labeled, they have two parts: the physical quantity number and the metric label. quantity number → 43 g ← metric label

Because physical quantities can be large or small, the amounts can be changed by simply multiplying or dividing the number by a power of 10. For example, 43 g can also be written as 43,000 mg (1 gram = 1,000 milligrams).

Use the information in the chart below to learn the prefixes and the quantities they represent.

SI PREFIX TERM	kilo	hecto	deka	root	deci	centi	milli
SYMBOL	k	h	dk		d	c	m
VALUE	1 000	100	10	1	0.1	0.01	0.001

Write the appropriate prefix for the numerical amount or the appropriate numerical amount for the prefix.

1. 100 ooooooooooooooooooo

2. d ooooooooooooooooooo

3. m ooooooooooooooooooo

4. 10 ooooooooooooooooooo

5. 1 000 ooooooooooooooooo

6. dk ooooooooooooooooooo

7. h ooooooooooooooooooo

8. 0.01 ooooooooooooooooo

9. 1 oooooooooooooooooooo

10. c ooooooooooooooooooo

11. k ooooooooooooooooooo

12. 0.001 ooooooooooooooo

Write the metric amounts with the correct prefix. (Remember: Root quantities are g = grams, m = meters, L = liters, m² = square meters, m³ = cubic meters.)

13. kilogram ooooooooooooo

14. centimeter ooooooooooo

15. milliliter ooooooooooo

16. cubic meters oooooooooo

17. dekagram ooooooooooooo

18. hectoliter oooooooooooo

19. kilometer oooooooooooo

20. decigram ooooooooooooo

Circle the larger unit in each pair.

21. kilo   deci

22. milli   centi

23. meter   deci

24. deci   deka

25. deka   hecto

26. milli   meter

27. centi   deci

28. hecto   kilo

Name _____

It's a Tie

Look at each group of ratios. Circle the group that is equal to the given ratio. Hint: reduce each ratio to its lowest terms.

A. $\frac{1}{4}$ $\frac{4}{8}, \frac{6}{12}, \frac{5}{10}$ $\frac{25}{100}, \frac{3}{12}, \frac{5}{20}$ $\frac{50}{100}, \frac{6}{12}, \frac{10}{20}$

B. $\frac{5}{6}$ $\frac{30}{40}, \frac{9}{12}, \frac{15}{35}$ $\frac{10}{12}, \frac{25}{30}, \frac{15}{35}$ $\frac{25}{30}, \frac{10}{12}, \frac{20}{24}$

C. $\frac{4}{7}$ $\frac{20}{35}, \frac{12}{14}, \frac{16}{28}$ $\frac{16}{28}, \frac{12}{21}, \frac{20}{35}$ $\frac{12}{21}, \frac{24}{35}, \frac{8}{42}$

D. $\frac{2}{3}$ $\frac{6}{9}, \frac{10}{15}, \frac{18}{27}$ $\frac{15}{15}, \frac{18}{27}, \frac{4}{9}$ $\frac{5}{15}, \frac{3}{9}, \frac{4}{6}$

E. $\frac{1}{6}$ $\frac{7}{42}, \frac{2}{14}, \frac{3}{21}$ $\frac{5}{30}, \frac{6}{36}, \frac{7}{42}$ $\frac{5}{25}, \frac{6}{36}, \frac{7}{42}$

F. $\frac{2}{5}$ $\frac{8}{20}, \frac{6}{15}, \frac{4}{10}$ $\frac{4}{10}, \frac{8}{20}, \frac{9}{30}$ $\frac{4}{10}, \frac{6}{12}, \frac{8}{20}$

G. $\frac{3}{4}$ $\frac{9}{12}, \frac{12}{16}, \frac{15}{24}$ $\frac{6}{8}, \frac{5}{25}, \frac{12}{16}$ $\frac{6}{8}, \frac{9}{12}, \frac{12}{16}$

H. $\frac{1}{8}$ $\frac{2}{16}, \frac{4}{32}, \frac{7}{64}$ $\frac{2}{16}, \frac{6}{48}, \frac{9}{56}$ $\frac{4}{32}, \frac{6}{48}, \frac{2}{16}$

I. $\frac{3}{5}$ $\frac{9}{15}, \frac{6}{12}, \frac{7}{14}$ $\frac{15}{25}, \frac{12}{20}, \frac{9}{15}$ $\frac{21}{30}, \frac{15}{25}, \frac{9}{15}$

J. $\frac{5}{7}$ $\frac{20}{28}, \frac{15}{21}, \frac{10}{14}$ $\frac{10}{14}, \frac{15}{21}, \frac{25}{42}$ $\frac{15}{21}, \frac{20}{28}, \frac{30}{56}$

Name _____

Cooking for a Crowd

Roland is making spaghetti and meat sauce for a party. Below is a list of ingredients he has.

Old Fashioned Tomato
    Meat Sauce
  (serves 12)

48 ounces whole tomatoes

8 ounces tomato paste

16 ounces tomato sauce

1 ½ pounds ground meat

⅛ pound parsley

2 tablespoons minced garlic

1 ¼ teaspoons oregano

1. How would you rewrite the recipe so that it will serve 8 people or 30 people?

_____

_____

2. Rewrite the recipe for each number of guests shown below.

Serve 6   **Serve 36**

_____   _____

_____   _____

_____   _____

_____   _____

_____   _____

_____   _____

Name _____

Staying in Line

A **line graph** is used to plot information with dots. By connecting the dots, you can see trends in the data collected.

Casey practices skating each day. Her mom made a line graph to show how far she skated each day for one week.

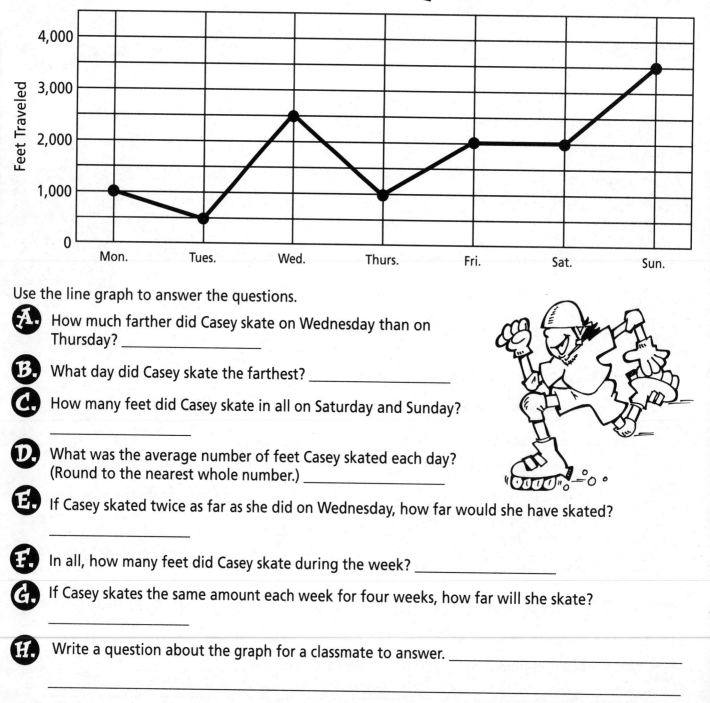

How Far Casey Skated

Use the line graph to answer the questions.

A. How much farther did Casey skate on Wednesday than on Thursday? _____

B. What day did Casey skate the farthest? _____

C. How many feet did Casey skate in all on Saturday and Sunday?

_____

D. What was the average number of feet Casey skated each day? (Round to the nearest whole number.) _____

E. If Casey skated twice as far as she did on Wednesday, how far would she have skated?

_____

F. In all, how many feet did Casey skate during the week? _____

G. If Casey skates the same amount each week for four weeks, how far will she skate?

_____

H. Write a question about the graph for a classmate to answer. _____

_____

Scream for Ice Cream

At the end of the year, 108 sixth graders had an ice-cream party. This circle graph shows how much of the different flavors of ice cream was served and the number of students who chose each flavor.

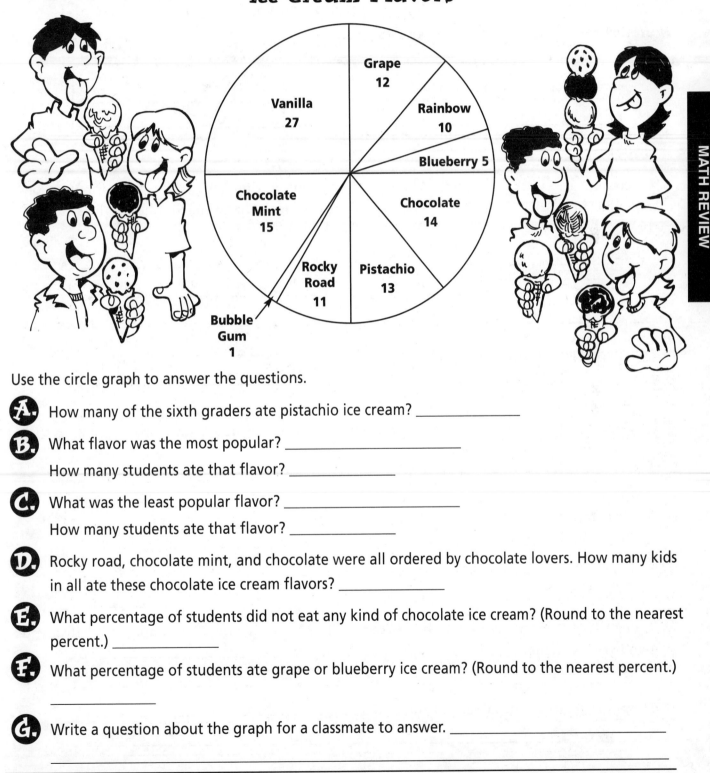

Ice Cream Flavors

Use the circle graph to answer the questions.

A. How many of the sixth graders ate pistachio ice cream? _____

B. What flavor was the most popular? _____
How many students ate that flavor? _____

C. What was the least popular flavor? _____
How many students ate that flavor? _____

D. Rocky road, chocolate mint, and chocolate were all ordered by chocolate lovers. How many kids in all ate these chocolate ice cream flavors? _____

E. What percentage of students did not eat any kind of chocolate ice cream? (Round to the nearest percent.) _____

F. What percentage of students ate grape or blueberry ice cream? (Round to the nearest percent.) _____

G. Write a question about the graph for a classmate to answer. _____

Name _____

Muscle Mania

Muscles are tough elastic tissues that enable body parts to move. Changes in temperature can affect the muscles. To find out how, try the experiment below at home, and share your results with your class members the next day.

Materials: a bowl large enough to place your hand in

ice cubes   water   warm water   pencil   paper

towels   watch or clock with a secondhand

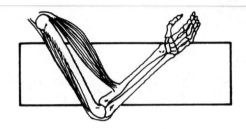

1. Write or print your name 10 times on the back of a separate piece of paper.

2. Place some ice cubes and water in the bowl. Hold your writing hand in the water for 30 seconds. Dry your hand quickly with a paper towel. Write or print your name 10 times in the spaces below.

   _____   _____

   _____   _____

   _____   _____

   _____   _____

3. Replace the ice water with warm water. Place your writing hand in the warm water for 30 seconds. Dry your hand quickly with a paper towel. Write or print your name 10 times in the spaces below.

   _____   _____

   _____   _____

   _____   _____

   _____   _____

4. Compare the appearance of your handwriting. How did the changes in temperature affect your handwriting samples?_____

   _____

5. How does temperature affect your muscles? _____

   _____

Name _____

Parts of a Flower

Most flowers have four main parts. Each of these parts consists of elements. These parts and elements are listed below. In this activity, you will display some of the parts of a real flower.

Materials: one of the following kinds of flowers: daffodils, roses, lilies, tulips, irises, and phlox make good samples; sharp cutting tool (adult supervision and help is required); paper towels; heavy books or bricks; construction paper or posterboard; glue; black marker

1. After you have collected a good flower sample, have an adult help you make a cross-section of the flower. This can be done by carefully slicing the flower using a sharp cutting tool.

2. Place the cross-section between several sheets of paper towels and press for several days with heavy books or bricks.

3. Carefully remove the paper towel. Attach the pressed flower to a sheet of construction paper or posterboard.

4. Cut out the labels to the right. Attach them to the construction paper or posterboard. Use a black marker to draw lines from the labels to the parts of the flower.

PETALS	ANTHER
POLLEN GRAINS	STIGMA
STYLE	STAMENS
FILAMENT	COROLLA
SEPALS	CALYX
OVARY	OVULE
PISTILS	

Daily Learning Drills Grade 6

SCIENCE REVIEW

Name _____

Roots and Shoots

Plants develop from seeds. In this activity, you will measure the length of the roots and shoots of a plant as it develops from its seeds.

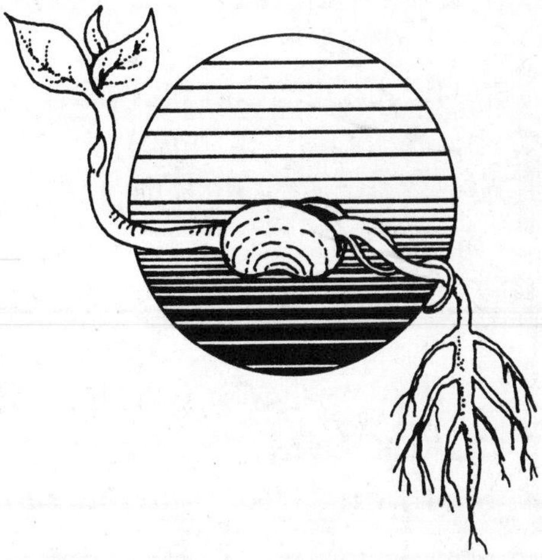

Materials: dried lima beans, paper towels, water, shallow pans, metric ruler, jar, plastic food wrap

DIRECTIONS:

1. Soak some dried lima beans in a jar of water overnight.

2. Place some wet paper towels in the bottom of a shallow pan or dish.

3. Arrange five of the soaked lima beans across the middle of the pan.

4. Cover with several thicknesses of wet paper towels.

5. Wrap the pan with plastic food wrap to prevent rapid evaporation of the water.

6. Each day, carefully uncover the beans and observe any growth of roots or shoots. Once growth begins, measure the lengths of the roots and shoots in centimeters.

7. Keep a record of your measurements and observations in the chart below.

DAY	OBSERVATIONS	LENGTH OF ROOTS (CM)	LENGTH OF SHOOTS (CM)
1			
2			
3			
4			
5			
6			
7			

SCIENCE REVIEW

Name _____

A Special Group of Animals

Some animals have backbones, and some do not. Unscramble the letters to spell the names of some animals that have backbones. Print the answers in the spaces to the right. The circled letters will then identify what animals that have backbones are called. Print those letters at the bottom of the page.

1. A V E R N   _ _ ◯ _ _

2. P E N A T E L H   _ ◯ _ _ _ _ _ _

3. E P R A L O D   _ _ _ _ _ ◯ _

4. R A G A N O N U T   _ _ _ _ _ _ ◯ _ _

5. L E R U V U T   _ _ _ _ ◯ _ _

6. A C O B B T   _ ◯ _ _ _ _

7. N I R A P R E T   _ _ _ ◯ _ _ _ _

8. R U O A C I B   ◯ _ _ _ _ _ _

9. H E H A C E T   _ _ _ ◯ _ _ _

10. N O K Y M E   _ _ _ ◯ _ _

11. R I H S O T C   ◯ _ _ _ _ _ _

What type of animal are you and the rest of the animals listed above?

_ _ _ _ _ _ _ _ _ _ _

What is the meaning of this word? _____

_____

Name _____

Can You Identify These Arthropods?

Arthropods are animals with segmented appendages. They are invertebrates as they have no backbones. Three of the classes of arthropods are arachnids, insects, and crustaceans. Identify the animals below by placing **A** in front of the arachnids, **I** in front of the insects, and **C** in front of the crustaceans.

_____	1. grasshopper	_____	24. silver fish
_____	2. mite	_____	25. louse
_____	3. brine shrimp	_____	26. black widow spider
_____	4. wasp	_____	27. brown recluse spider
_____	5. bumblebee	_____	28. copepod
_____	6. scorpion	_____	29. wood louse
_____	7. tick	_____	30. fiddler crab
_____	8. spider crab	_____	31. walking stick
_____	9. crayfish	_____	32. damsel fly
_____	10. butterfly	_____	33. cat flea
_____	11. hornet	_____	34. roach
_____	12. cockroach	_____	35. tarantula
_____	13. lobster	_____	36. wolf spider
_____	14. water bug	_____	37. cricket
_____	15. hermit crab	_____	38. cicada
_____	16. barnacle	_____	39. aphid
_____	17. earwig	_____	40. trap-door spider
_____	18. beetle	_____	41. orb weaver
_____	19. mole cricket	_____	42. locust
_____	20. stinkbug	_____	43. katydid
_____	21. termite	_____	44. bedbug
_____	22. dragonfly	_____	45. orange garden spider
_____	23. ant	_____	46. blue crab

Name _____

Descriptive Animals

The world is filled with a lot of awesome animals.
Read the clues below to identify the name of each animal.

1. I live in a high place.   _____ gorilla

2. I have a head-covering like a king.   _____ crane

3. I react to funny jokes.   _____ hyena

4. I have lost my hair.   _____ eagle

5. I am very large in size.   _____ panda

6. My head could be a tool.   _____ shark

7. My head is the color of a penny.   _____ snake

8. My tail is like a baby's toy.   _____ snake

9. I live in open spaces out west.   _____ dog

10. My color is the same as that on a stop sign.   _____ fox

11. I do not quack with my bill.   _____ platypus

12. I soar like a glider.   _____ squirrel

13. I have a royal name.   _____ butterfly

14. My shape looks like something that is seen
    in the night sky.   _____ fish

15. I taste good with peanut butter and bread.   _____ fish

16. I appear in the sky as an arc after rain.   _____ trout

17. I live in tropical waters.   _____ horse

18. I live in the cold Arctic.   _____ bear

19. I live in tiny grains of rocks in the sea.   _____ dollar

20. I cover a lawn.   _____ hopper

21. I have a hot flame.   _____ fly

22. I could be a member of the Armed Services.   _____ ant

23. I live on our planet.   _____ worm

24. I like to live alone.   _____ crab

Name _____

Animal Adaptations and Behavior

Animals of all kinds have a lot of interesting ways in which they adapt to their environment and in which they behave. To learn about some of these adaptations and behaviors, match the animals and adaptations or behaviors below.

COLUMN I

1. _____ blue jay
2. _____ bobcat
3. _____ woodpecker
4. _____ crow
5. _____ tree frog
6. _____ heron
7. _____ hornet
8. _____ eagle
9. _____ turkey
10. _____ screech owl
11. _____ robin
12. _____ cicada
13. _____ opossum
14. _____ gray fox
15. _____ big brown bat

COLUMN II

A. A bird that builds a nest called an aerie

B. A large game bird that rests in trees at night

C. A blue-colored bird that squawks loudly when disturbed

D. This bird drills holes in trees in search of insects for food.

E. A fox that prefers to live in woodlands and often climbs trees

F. The males of this type of insect make loud sounds on warm summer evenings.

G. A large-eyed bird that searches for food at night

H. A marsupial that sometimes avoids danger by "playing dead"

I. An amphibian that has sticky pads on its feet to help it climb trees

J. An all-black bird that caws

K. A wild cat that catches its prey by pouncing on small animals

L. A furry mammal that has a wingspan of about 12 inches

M. A long-legged wading bird that nests in flocks

N. A stinging insect that builds a paper nest

O. A red-breasted bird whose arrival signals the beginning of spring

Name _____

Learned Behavior

Read about Ivan Pavlov's famous stimulus-response experiments he did with dogs in Russia in the early 1900s. The reaction of the dogs was a learned behavior. Swimming, riding a bicycle, or driving a car are learned behaviors.

In the chart, list some learned behaviors the animals do.

ANIMALS	LEARNED BEHAVIORS
dogs	
cats	
horses	
birds	
circus animals	
dolphins	
elephants	
chimpanzees	
cows	
humans	

Name _____

The World's Living Things

The chart below is an environmental box score for the world's endangered or threatened animals and plants. Among the endangered species are the cheetah, bald eagle, American crocodile, floating sorrel, and snakeroot. Use library resources to track down the names and ranges (names of locations where species are found) of 10 endangered or threatened species. (Include 5 animals and 5 plants, but be sure you don't include any of the species named above.)

GROUP	ENDANGERED U.S.	FOREIGN	THREATENED U.S.	FOREIGN	TOTAL LISTINGS
Mammals	55	252	9	19	335
Birds	74	178	16	6	274
Reptiles	14	65	19	14	112
Amphibians	7	8	5	1	21
Fishes	65	11	40	0	116
Snails	15	1	7	0	23
Clams	51	2	6	0	59
Crustaceans	14	0	3	0	17
Insects	20	4	9	0	33
Arachnids	5	0	0	0	5
Animal Subtotal	**320**	**521**	**114**	**40**	**995**
Flowering Plants	406	1	90	0	497
Conifers	2	0	0	2	4
Ferns and Others	26	0	2	0	28
Plant Subtotal	**434**	**1**	**92**	**2**	**529**
Grand Total	**754**	**522**	**206**	**42**	**1,524**

Five Endangered/Threatened
Animals   Range

Five Endangered/Threatened
Plants   Range

To save endangered and threatened species, it is vital to protect their habitats and to understand the role of each species within Earth's ecosystems. On a sheet of paper, describe the habitat and ecosystem of one endangered or threatened species.

Name _____

Where Animals Live

Fascinating animals live all over the world! Learn about the places where some of them make their homes. Use your research skills to locate the continent on which each of the animals listed below lives. Match the animals listed on the left with their continents on the right.

Animal

1. _____ vicuña
2. _____ zebra
3. _____ snow leopard
4. _____ Rocky Mountain goat
5. _____ kangaroo
6. _____ red deer
7. _____ platypus
8. _____ emperor penguin
9. _____ saiga
10. _____ koala
11. _____ woolly monkey
12. _____ gorilla
13. _____ moose
14. _____ giant panda
15. _____ dingo
16. _____ roadrunner
17. _____ ostrich
18. _____ coati
19. _____ orangutan
20. _____ prairie dog

Continent

A. Africa

B. North America

C. Asia

D. Europe

E. Australia

F. Antarctica

G. South America

Name _____

Environmental Patterns

Use a climate map in an atlas to locate the world's major rain forests. Then, using a pencil, shade in the shape of the major rain forest areas on the map below. What patterns do the shaded areas show? Use the completed map and an atlas to answer the questions.

1. Where are the three major rain forest areas located? _____,
_____, and _____

2. Use the map's scale in an atlas to measure the approximate distance between each major rain forest area and your community. Write the distances. _____
_____

3. In what kind of climate are rain forests found? _____
_____

4. Compare and contrast your community's climate and the climate of the rain forests.
_____
_____

5. How is climate related to the distribution of rain forests worldwide? _____
_____

     Daily Learning Drills Grade 6

SCIENCE REVIEW

Name _____

Animals and Plants Living in Biomes

Plants and animals of the world live in many different kinds of biomes. A **biome** is a community of plants and animals that lives in a large geographical area that has a similar climate. Identify the biome of each of the animals and plants listed below. Use the following letters for the identifications:

D	desert	**G**	grassland	**R**	tropical rain forest
T	taiga	**TU**	tundra	**F**	temperate forest

1. _____ low shrubs

2. _____ aardvark

3. _____ cactus

4. _____ sagebrush

5. _____ moose

6. _____ grasses

7. _____ oak

8. _____ arctic fox

9. _____ rattlesnake

10. _____ lichens

11. _____ parrot

12. _____ prairie dog

13. _____ snowshoe hare

14. _____ maple

15. _____ kapok tree

16. _____ gibbon

17. _____ caribou

18. _____ conifers

19. _____ pronghorn

20. _____ roadrunner

21. _____ tree ferns

22. _____ elm

23. _____ lemming

24. _____ kangaroo rat

25. _____ brown bear

26. _____ Gila monster

27. _____ sloth

28. _____ jaguar

29. _____ polar bear

30. _____ salamander

31. _____ zebra

32. _____ scorpion

33. _____ monkey

34. _____ African elephant

35. _____ dingo

36. _____ jack rabbit

37. _____ skunk

38. _____ ostrich

39. _____ Indian elephant

40. _____ mahogany

41. _____ squirrel

42. _____ reindeer

43. _____ spruce tree

44. _____ giraffe

45. _____ raccoon

46. _____ fir tree

Name _____

July 20, 1969

On July 20, 1969, the first person stepped onto the surface of the moon. He said, " . . . one small step for a man, one giant leap for mankind." Identify this person by solving the clues and writing the words in the spaces. The circled letters will then spell out the person's name.

1. Latin word for *moon*   ___ ___ ___ ◯ ___

2. Our moon is a _____ of Earth.   ___ ___ ___ ◯ ___ ___ ___ ___

3. During a lunar _____, the moon becomes dark when it passes through the shadow of Earth.   ___ ___ ___ ◯ ___ ___ ___

4. The space mission to the moon was called _____.   ___ ___ ___ ◯ ___ ___

5. Letters that stand for the organization that conducts research into problems of flight within and beyond Earth's atmosphere   ___ ◯ ___ ___

6. American space scientists and explorers are called _____.   ___ ___ ___ ◯ ___ ___ ___ ___ ___ ___

7. The moon's average distance from Earth is about 240,000 _____.   ◯ ___ ___ ___ ◯ ___

8. The moon's surface is pitted with _____.   ___ ___ ___ ◯ ___ ___

9. The circling of the spacecraft around the moon is called its _____.   ___ ___ ◯ ___ ___ ___

10. During a _____ eclipse, the moon comes between the sun and Earth.   ___ ___ ◯ ___ ___

11. A _____ rocket carried the first astronauts to the moon.   ___ ___ ___ ___ ___ ◯

12. The moon's _____ is about one-sixth that of Earth's.   ◯ ___ ___ ___ ___ ___

The first person to step upon the moon was

___ ___ ___ ___   ___ ___ ___ ___ ___ ___ ___ ___ .

SCIENCE REVIEW

Name _____

A Magic Square of Weather

Below are words relating to weather. Write the number of the word which fits a clue in a box on the grid. If you have matched the correct numbers in all 16 squares, the sums of the rows, columns, and diagonals will be the same. This is called a magic square.

1. atmosphere	5. jet streams	9. wind	13. land breeze
2. troposphere	6. stratosphere	10. greenhouse effect	14. doldrums
3. ionosphere	7. mesosphere	11. convection	15. trade winds
4. ozone	8. exosphere	12. sea breeze	16. front

mass of air that surrounds Earth _____	air that rushes in from the north and south to warm the air along the equator _____	calm areas of Earth where there is little wind _____	a gas in the upper part of Earth's atmosphere _____
cold air from the ocean that moves into the warmer land _____	the zone of the atmosphere above the troposphere _____	the zone of the atmosphere above the stratosphere _____	a movement of air close to Earth's surface _____
the outer zone of Earth's atmosphere _____	air above Earth that is warmed by the reflection of the sun's rays and is prevented from easily passing back into space _____	transfer of heat by currents of air or water _____	strong, steady winds high in the atmosphere; used by pilots _____
cold air from land that moves out to warmer air over oceans _____	zone of the atmosphere which affects the transmission of radio waves _____	the zone of the atmosphere which is closest to the surface of Earth _____	the line along which air masses meet _____

What is the magic number for this puzzle? _____

Can you discover other number combinations in the puzzle which give you the same answer?

_____

Name _____

Glaciers

Glaciers are thick masses of ice created by the accumulation and crystallization of snow. Match the clues about glaciers with the terms below.

1. _____ VALLEY GLACIER

2. _____ CIRQUE

3. _____ CONTINENTAL GLACIER

4. _____ CREVASSE

5. _____ DRUMLIN

6. _____ END MORAINE

7. _____ ESKER

8. _____ FIORD

9. _____ KETTLE

10. _____ PLUCKING

11. _____ ROCK FLOUR

12. _____ SURGE

13. _____ TARN

14. _____ TILL

A. material deposited directly by a glacier

B. glacier generally confined to mountain valleys

C. a crack in the glacier caused by movement

D. rapid movement of a glacier

E. the process whereby a glacier loosens and lifts rocks into the ice

F. pulverized rock caused by a glacier's abrasion

G. a bowl-shaped depression at the head of a glacial valley

H. a small lake formed after a glacier has melted away

I. a U-shaped depression formed by a glacier below sea level in a river valley that is flooded by the ocean

J. massive accumulations of ice that cover a large portion of a landmass

K. a hilly ridge of material formed at the end of a valley glacier

L. an oval-shaped hill consisting of rock debris

M. a depression left in part of a glacier formed by the melting of a block of ice

N. ridges of sand and gravel deposited by flowing rivers of melted ice through a glacier

Daily Learning Drills Grade 6

Name _____

The Science of Earthquakes

An earthquake is a sudden shock of Earth's surface. Identify the name of the study of earthquakes by reading the clues below and writing the answers. The circled letters will spell out the name of this science. Print the name at the bottom of the page.

1. large ocean waves created by an earthquake __ Ⓞ __ __ __ __ __

2. These waves, created by the earthquake, are the strongest at the epicenter. __ Ⓞ __ __ __ __ __

3. the area on the surface of Earth directly above the occurrence of the earthquake __ __ Ⓞ __ __ __ __ __ __

4. famous earthquake fault in California Ⓞ __ __ __ __ __ __ __ __

5. the instrument used to record earthquake waves __ __ __ Ⓞ __ __ __ __ __ __

6. the origin of an earthquake under the surface of Earth __ Ⓞ __ __ __

7. a breaking point in layers of Earth __ __ __ Ⓞ

8. the vibrational tremors sent out from an earthquake __ __ Ⓞ __ __ __ __

9. the name given to the area around the Pacific Ocean in which many earthquakes occur __ __ __ Ⓞ __ __ __ __ __

10. the fastest waves from an earthquake; also called push waves __ __ __ __ __ __ Ⓞ

The science of the study of earthquakes is __ __ __ __ __ __ __ __ __ __ __ .

An Electrical Message

By selecting the correct answers and darkening certain letters as described below in the grid, the remaining letters will spell out a message concerning electrical energy.

1. A safety device for circuits with a piece of wire that melts to break the circuit is a(n) _____ .
   switch—Mark out all the letter **A's** in the grid.
   terminal—Mark out all the letter **O's** in the grid.
   fuse—Mark out all the letter **B's** in the grid.
   ammeter—Mark out all the letter **L's** in the grid.

2. The path followed by an electric current is called a(n) _____ .
   voltage—Mark out all the letter **C's** in the grid.
   resistance—Mark out all the letter **E's** in the grid.
   amperage—Mark out all the letter **G's** in the grid.
   circuit—Mark out all the letter **D's** in the grid.

3. An instrument that detects an electric current is a(n) _____ .
   ammeter—Mark out all the letter **K's** in the grid.
   anemometer—Mark out all the letter **H's** in the grid.
   psychrometer—Mark out all the letter **M's** in the grid.
   barometer—Mark out all the letter **R's** in the grid.

4. A device that controls the flow of current by making or breaking a circuit is a(n) _____ .
   terminal—Mark out all the letter **N's** in the grid.
   switch—Mark out all the letter **P's** in the grid.
   resistor—Mark out all the letter **S's** in the grid.
   ammeter—Mark out all the letter **T's** in the grid.

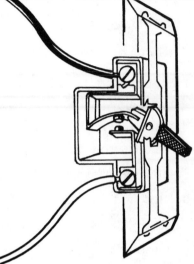

B	D	K	A	P	B	D	V	O	K	D	L	P	B	T	A	P	K	I	C	D	B
C	P	E	B	L	D	L	K	D	C	H	P	A	D	N	P	B	G	K	D	E	S
D	B	P	C	K	H	E	D	B	M	I	P	D	C	K	B	A	K	P	B	L	D
E	P	D	B	N	K	D	B	P	K	E	B	P	K	D	R	K	P	G	D	B	Y
B	T	K	D	O	P	B	P	E	D	B	K	L	E	P	C	B	T	D	R	I	C
D	B	E	P	B	N	D	E	K	B	P	R	D	K	G	B	K	P	Y	P	B	D

Message: ___ ___ ___ ___ ___ ___ ___ ___ ___ ___ ___ ___

___ ___ ___ ___ ___ ___ ___ ___ ___ ___

___ ___ ___ ___ ___ ___ ___ ___ ___ ___ .

Name _____

Energy From Many Sources

Energy comes from a lot of sources. To find out what some sources are, match the terms below with their definitions to complete the crossword puzzle about energy sources.

AMPERE	ENERGY	KILOWATT	TURBINE
ATOM	GENERATOR	NUCLEAR	URANIUM
BIOMASS	GEOTHERMAL	RENEWABLE	VOLT
COAL	HYDROELECTRIC	SOLAR	WATT

Across

2. the capacity for action or to do work

4. the unit of measurement of electric power

7. 1000 watts

10. electric power that is generated by moving water

12. a radioactive element used to produce fuel in nuclear plants

13. capable of being replaced or restored by natural ecological practices or good management practices

14. waste material that is converted to methane gas for fuel

16. the unit of electric pressure

Down

1. the smallest unit of an element that can exist alone

3. underground hot water or steam used to produce electricity

5. unit of electric measure that indicates the flow of electric current

6. a machine in which mechanical energy is converted to electricity

8. an engine in which curved blades are turned by water, steam, or gas

9. relating to the nucleus of an atom

11. solid, black or brown fossil fuel

15. relating to the sun's energy

Name _____

Testing Your Knowledge of Acids and Bases

Acid is any of a group of compounds with certain similar properties. **Base** is any substance that can react with an acid to decrease or neutralize its acidic properties. Use reference materials to help you test your knowledge of acids and bases. Write a **T** before each true statement and an **F** before each false statement.

_____ 1. Acids will not conduct an electric current.

_____ 2. Bases will conduct an electric current.

_____ 3. Acids will turn litmus solution red.

_____ 4. Acids taste bitter.

_____ 5. Acids neutralize bases.

_____ 6. Bases taste sour.

_____ 7. Bases feel slippery.

_____ 8. Bases neutralize acids.

_____ 9. Bases will turn litmus solution red.

_____ 10. Acids react with some metals to produce hydrogen gas.

_____ 11. Acids will turn phenolphthalein indicator pink.

_____ 12. Citrus fruits contain acids.

_____ 13. Vinegar contains bases.

_____ 14. Soaps contain acids.

_____ 15. Ammonia water contains bases.

_____ 16. Red cabbage juice can be used as an acid-base indicator.

_____ 17. An indicator is a substance which changes colors in acids and bases.

_____ 18. Vinegar is acetic acid.

_____ 19. Acetic acid has no color and smells awful.

_____ 20. Phenolphthalein indicator remains clear in an acid.

_____ 21. Some medicinal compounds help neutralize stomach acid.

_____ 22. Acids dissolve many metals.

_____ 23. Sour milk is an acid.

_____ 24. Sink drain cleaners contain strong bases.

Name _____

The Mohs Hardness Scale for Minerals

In 1822, Friedrich Mohs, a German mineralogist, designed a hardness scale for minerals. Ten minerals are used for comparisons in the hardness of other minerals.

Unscramble the letters below to identify the 10 minerals in the scale. Print the words in the spaces.

1. L C T A   ___ ___ ___ ___

2. S P Y M U G   ___ ___ ___ ___ ___ ___

3. T I L E C A C   ___ ___ ___ ___ ___ ___ ___

4. T I R E L U F O   ___ ___ ___ ___ ___ ___ ___ ___

5. T A P I T E A   ___ ___ ___ ___ ___ ___ ___

6. D P A S F E R L   ___ ___ ___ ___ ___ ___ ___ ___

7. Z A R Q U T   ___ ___ ___ ___ ___ ___

8. P O Z A T   ___ ___ ___ ___ ___

9. D O C R U M U N   ___ ___ ___ ___ ___ ___ ___ ___

10. M I N D A D O   ___ ___ ___ ___ ___ ___ ___

After you have identified the 10 minerals, use reference materials to describe some of the physical properties of each mineral.

1. _____
2. _____
3. _____
4. _____
5. _____
6. _____
7. _____
8. _____
9. _____
10. _____

Name _____

The Bill of Rights

The 10 original amendments to the Constitution of the United States are called the Bill of Rights. The Bill of Rights explains the fundamental liberties of the American people. Fin the U.S. Constitution in an encyclopedia or an almanac and write the amendments in the appropriate boxes. Then, for each of the events or situations described below, indicate which amendment applies.

Amendment I	Amendment VI

Amendment II	Amendment VII

Amendment III	Amendment VIII

Amendment IV	Amendment IX

Amendment V	Amendment X

Event/Situation   **Amendment Number**

1. A convicted criminal complains that his or her jail sentence is too long. _____

2. A citizen writes a letter to an editor of a newspaper. _____

3. An accused person at a trial refuses to testify. _____

4. A hunter owns three shotguns. _____

5. A group demands the right to hold a meeting in a public park. _____

6. An accused person is awaiting a trial set for next week. _____

7. A search warrant is issued to the police. _____

SOCIAL STUDIES REVIEW

Name _____

How a Bill Becomes a Law

Passing a law is a multi-step process. Both houses of the U.S. Congress, the Senate and the House of Representatives, have to approve a bill before it can become a law. Many bills are subjected to considerable debate, and a bill can be amended or rejected at many points throughout the process. If a bill is approved by Congress, it goes to the president who can either approve or reject it. The basic steps of a bill becoming a law are listed in random order below. Your task is to place the steps in correct order by putting the letter next to the step inside the correct circle on the line along the bottom of the page. For this activity, assume that the bill started in the U.S. House of Representatives.

A. The bill back to the floor of the Senate for consideration.

B. Once passed by both houses, the bill goes to the president who hopefully signs it into law.

C. The Senate committee revises the bill and then approves it.

D. The vice president of the United States, the presiding officer of the Senate, assigns the proposed bill to one of its standing committees to be studied.

E. A representative introduces a bill in the House.

F. The bill is now introduced to the Senate.

G. The Senate votes on the bill and passes it.

H. The House committee recommends to the House that the bill be passed.

I. The House of Representatives passes the bill with a simple majority.

J. Once passed by the Senate, a conference committee, comprised of members from both houses of Congress, works out any differences concerning the bill.

K. The revised bill is sent back to both houses for final approval.

L. The bill is assigned to one of about 20 standing House committees to be studied.

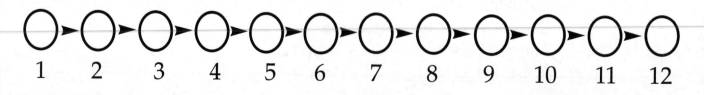

Name _____

Election Results

Maryville County elections were held today! Since closing the polls at 7:00 P.M., the election committee has been busy tallying the votes. As of 8:15, 90% of all votes had been counted. Here are the results at the present time.

Candidate	Office	Political Party	# of Votes
K. Foran	County Clerk	Democrat	245
H. Lietz	County Clerk	Republican	559
B. Warren	County Clerk	Independent	42
C. Aircheson	Family Court Judge	Democrat	341
K. Bennet	Family Court Judge	Republican	505
G. Alle	Council Member	Democrat	180
S. Vitale	Council Member	Republican	333
C. Howard	Council Member	Independent	333
S. Callahan	Selectman	Democrat	291
A. McEarlene	Selectman	Republican	555
H. Kaplan	Dogcatcher	Republican	18
N. Ross	Dogcatcher	Independent	828

Complete the following.

1. Which political party seems to be most popular in Maryville County?

   _____

2. List the candidates who will probably be throwing celebration parties. _____

   _____

3. If C. Howard were informed of the results so far, how would he or she feel?

   _____

4. How will B. Warren feel tomorrow? _____
   How do you know? _____

6. How will the dogs in Maryville County respond to N. Ross? _____

   _____

Name _____

Harlem Renaissance

New York in the 1920s and 1930s saw not only the rise of Ella Fitzgerald and jazz music, but a burst of creativity in all areas of art. A myriad of blacks had recently migrated to northern cities, the economy was "roarin'," and the cultural atmosphere was ripe for change. As a result, Harlem became the place for black artists to write, paint, sing, dance, and act in the early decades of the twentieth century.

Choose one of the early twentieth-century black artists below to study in depth. Write a brief biography of the artist of your choice. Then list works by the artist and include an illustration either of your own creation or copied from another source.

Actors
Paul Robeson
Charles Gilpin
Florence Mills

Painters
Hale Woodruff
Lois Maïlou Jones
William H. Johnson
Palmer Hayden

Poets
Jean Toomer
Zora Neale Hurston
Langston Hughes
Countee Cullen
Claude McKay

Musicians
Dizzy Gillespie
Louis Armstrong
Chick Webb
Jelly Roll Morton

Brief Biographical Sketch:

_____

_____

_____

_____

_____

_____

Works by _____

_____

_____

_____

Illustration of _____

Name _____

Describe a Culture

Anthropologists often try to answer the following question: What are some typical (and predictable) characteristics of a particular society? Based upon your own observations of an experience in American society, describe the probable behavior of Americans in the situations below.

Situations	Probable Behavior
1. Crowd's response when the national anthem is played before start of a football game	1. _____
2. An audience's response to an entertainer's excellent performance	2. _____
3. A student wants to answer a teacher's question.	3. _____
4. Two adults greet one another.	4. _____
5. A person receives a gift from another person.	5. _____
6. A baseball player strikes out.	6. _____
7. A car is driven on the left side of a two-lane road.	7. _____
8. Children attend a birthday party.	8. _____

Daily Learning Drills Grade 6

SOCIAL STUDIES REVIEW

Name _____

Ethnic Concentrations

Americans can trace their ethnic roots back to countries all over the world. Ethnic groups are not equally distributed across the United States. Instead, they are concentrated or clustered in particular areas. The map below shows ethnic group concentrations in four regions of the United States as determined by the U.S. Census Bureau. In order for a particular ethnic group to be considered a "concentration," it had to consist of 100,000 or more population with at least 35% in the region. The percent of each group is in parentheses on the map. Answer the questions.

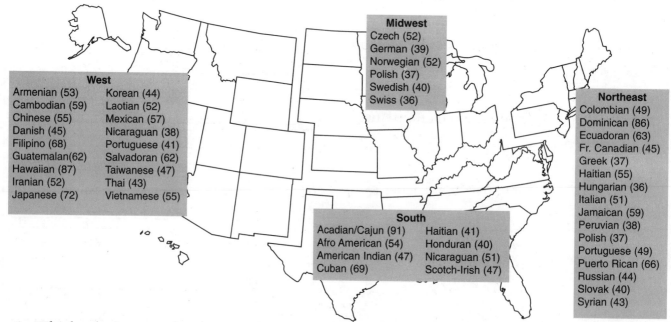

Midwest
Czech (52)
German (39)
Norwegian (52)
Polish (37)
Swedish (40)
Swiss (36)

West
Armenian (53)   Korean (44)
Cambodian (59)   Laotian (52)
Chinese (55)   Mexican (57)
Danish (45)   Nicaraguan (38)
Filipino (68)   Portuguese (41)
Guatemalan(62)   Salvadoran (62)
Hawaiian (87)   Taiwanese (47)
Iranian (52)   Thai (43)
Japanese (72)   Vietnamese (55)

Northeast
Colombian (49)
Dominican (86)
Ecuadoran (63)
Fr. Canadian (45)
Greek (37)
Haitian (55)
Hungarian (36)
Italian (51)
Jamaican (59)
Peruvian (38)
Polish (37)
Portuguese (49)
Puerto Rican (66)
Russian (44)
Slovak (40)
Syrian (43)

South
Acadian/Cajun (91)   Haitian (41)
Afro American (54)   Honduran (40)
American Indian (47) Nicaraguan (51)
Cuban (69)   Scotch-Irish (47)

1. Which ethnic group has 91 percent of 100,000 or more of its members concentrated in the South?_____

2. In which region is there a Norwegian concentration? _____

3. Which region has the most ethnic concentrations?_____

4. From where do all of the Midwest's ethnic concentrations originate? _____

5. Four of the eight ethnic concentrations in the South originate from the same area. What is the area? _____

6. In which region is there a Chinese concentration? _____

7. Which ethnic groups have concentrations in more than one region? _____

_____

8. How many different ethnic groups are listed on the map? _____

Name _____

Searching for Facts

Listed in the box are the names of 10 different cultural groups. Choose one of the groups to research. Then use an encyclopedia to answer the questions about the group's traditional way of life.

Cultural Groups	
Dayak or Dyak	Sioux
Zulu	Eskimo
Asante or Ashanti	Berbers
Maoris	Wampanoag
Basques	Aborigines

Questions

1. What cultural group did you investigate?_____

2. Where does the cultural group live? _____

3. What is the climate like? _____

4. How does the group get food? _____

5. What kinds of work do the people do?_____

6. What are some common plants and animals in the area? _____

7. What are the major geographic features of the area (such as mountains, desert, seashore, forest, river, valley, etc.)?_____

   _____

8. What is the major form of transportation of the people? _____

9. What are some of the typical foods they eat? _____

10. What type of shelter(s) do the people live in? _____

11. What kinds of clothing fo the people wear?_____

   _____

SOCIAL STUDIES REVIEW

Name _____

The Religion of Islam

Islam is one of the world's largest religions. The followers of Islam are called Muslims, and there are over one billion of them worldwide. Muslims believe that God's teachings were revealed to the Prophet Mohammed, a seventh-century Arab. These teachings were written down in the Koran, Islam's holy book. Listed below are some of the countries in which many Muslims live. Use an atlas to find the countries. Label the countries (using the numbers found next to them) and shade them in on the map below.

1. Pakistan	7. Iran	13. Morocco	19. Kuwait	25. Lebanon
2. Afghanistan	8. Egypt	14. Niger	20. Senegal	26. Malaysia
3. Iraq	9. Sudan	15. Chad	21. Yemen	27. Indonesia
4. Syria	10. Libya	16. Mali	22. Oman	28. Burkina Faso
5. Turkey	11. Tunisia	17. Mauritania	23. Saudi Arabia	29. Bangladesh
6. Albania	12. Algeria	18. Somalia	24. Jordan	30. Kazakhstan

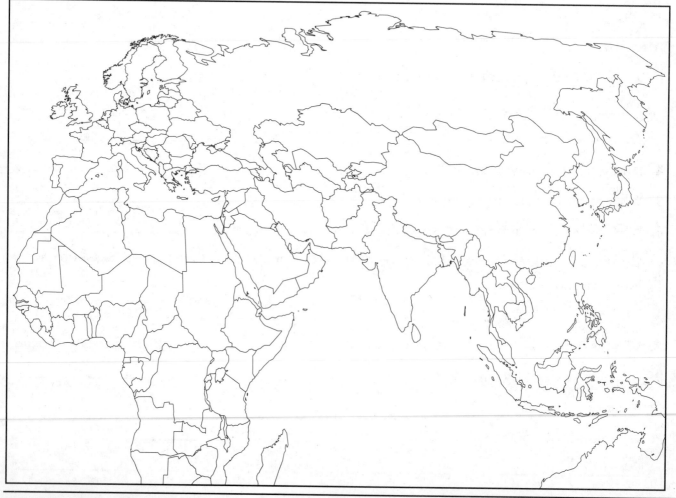

Name _____

Revolutionary War

Many of the important events related to the American Revolution occurred in Massachusetts, New York, Pennsylvania, New Jersey, and Virginia. Some of these important events are listed below. Match the events with the places where they occurred by writing the correct letter of each event on the line that points to its place on the map. Use classroom and library resources to check your answers.

A. War begins at Lexington and Concord.

B. War ends at Battle of Yorktown.

C. British defeated at Battle of Saratoga—a turning point of the war

D. Continental Congress adopts Declaration of Independence in Philadelphia.

E. The Boston Tea Party protests hated tea tax.

F. Colonial Army winters at Valley Forge.

G. Americans route the British at Battle of Princeton.

H. General Washington and his troops cross the Delaware River.

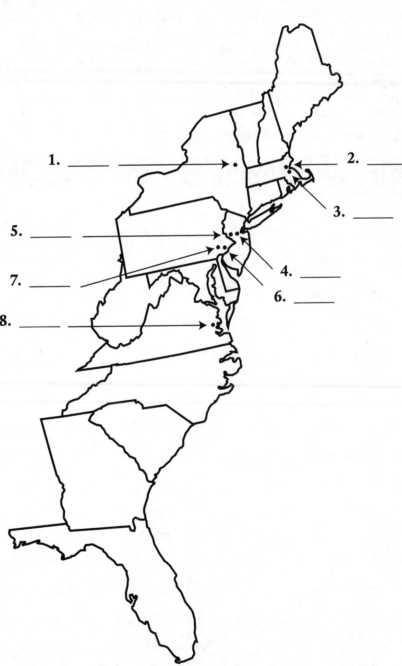

1. _____   2. _____

3. _____

5. _____

7. _____   4. _____

6. _____

8. _____

SOCIAL STUDIES REVIEW

Name _____

Using Latitude and Longitude

Locations on Earth's surface are measured using imaginary lines. that run north and south along Earth's surface are called longitude, and lines that run parallel to the equator are called latitude. Intersecting lines of latitude and longitude form a grid on Earth's surface and help us locate places.

Latitude is the distance in degrees north or south from Earth's equator (0 degrees) as measured through 90 degrees. Longitude is the distance in degrees or time east or west from the prime meridian (0 degrees) as measured through 180 degrees. Each and every place on Earth's surface has an "address" that consists of intersecting lines of latitude and longitude.

Using a globe or an atlas, find the intersecting lines of latitude and longitude below. On the lines provided, write the name of the country in which each intersection is located.

	Latitude	Longitude	Country
1.	52° north	0°	_____
2.	30° south	30° east	_____
3.	52° north	21° east	_____
4.	40° north	100° west	_____
5.	10° north	70° west	_____
6.	20° south	140° east	_____
7.	30° north	110° east	_____
8.	30° north	40° east	_____
9.	60° north	90° east	_____
10.	10° north	30° east	_____
11.	30° south	60° west	_____
12.	10° south	50° west	_____
13.	0°	110° east	_____
14.	40° north	140° east	_____
15.	10° south	20° east	_____
16.	50° north	10° east	_____
17.	30° north	110° west	_____
18.	60° north	10° east	_____

Name _____

Graphing the World's Population

The world's population was estimated to be 5.8 billion in 1996, and it is projected to increase by about 75 million people each year for the next 25 years. Fill in the bar graph to show the world's population projections at five-year increments. The bar for 1996 is already done.

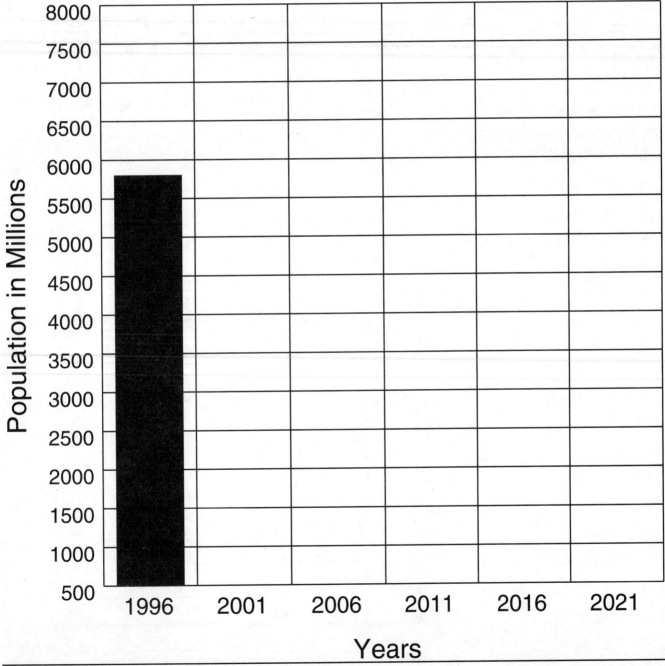

Name _____

The Shape of States

Like a piece of jigsaw puzzle, each of the 50 states in the U.S. has its own unique shape and particular location. What kind of mental picture do you have of the states? Write the names of the states that border each of the states below. Use a map of of the United States to help you.

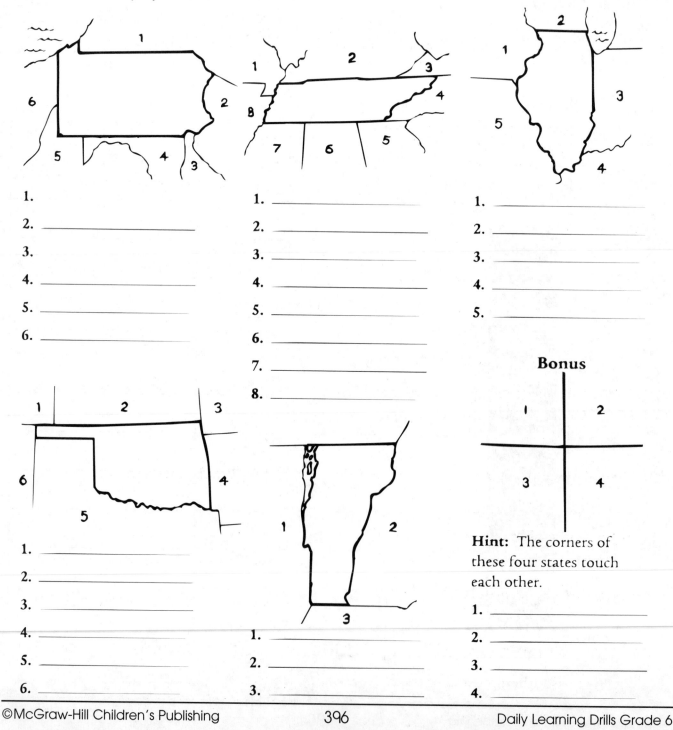

1. _____
2. _____
3. _____
4. _____
5. _____
6. _____

1. _____
2. _____
3. _____
4. _____
5. _____
6. _____
7. _____
8. _____

1. _____
2. _____
3. _____
4. _____
5. _____

1. _____
2. _____
3. _____
4. _____
5. _____
6. _____

1. _____
2. _____
3. _____

Bonus

Hint: The corners of these four states touch each other.

1. _____
2. _____
3. _____
4. _____

Name _____

You Find It!

There are so many fascinating places in the world. Use reference maps from an atlas or encyclopedias to learn about different places and where they are located below.

1. On a boat cruise from New York City to San Francisco, in which direction would you travel on the Panama Canal? _____

2. Which body of water separates Russia and Alaska? _____

3. Which three countries in South America are on the equator? _____

    _____

4. Which three countries border Mexico? _____

    _____

5. Which six countries extend north of the Arctic Circle? _____

    _____

    _____

6. Which 14 African countries are landlocked, or entirely surrounded by other countries?

    _____

    _____

    _____

7. Which large island is located directly east of Mozambique? _____

8. Which continents are completely in the Southern Hemisphere? _____

    _____

9. What are the four main islands of Japan? _____

    _____

10. Which mountain range separates India and Nepal from China? _____

11. On a nonstop jet flight from Anchorage, Alaska, to Moscow, Russia, in which direction(s) (north, south, east, west) would you travel if you took the shortest route? _____

12. Which bodies of water border the continental United States? _____

    _____

13. What is the southernmost country in the Eastern Hemisphere? _____

Name _____

Mapping Latin America

Write the name of each country on the lines below.

1. _____
2. _____
3. _____
4. _____
5. _____
6. _____
7. _____
8. _____
9. _____
10. _____

Name _____

Mapping Europe

Write the name of each country on the lines below.

1. _____   6. _____

2. _____   7. _____

3. _____   8. _____

4. _____   9. _____

5. _____   10. _____

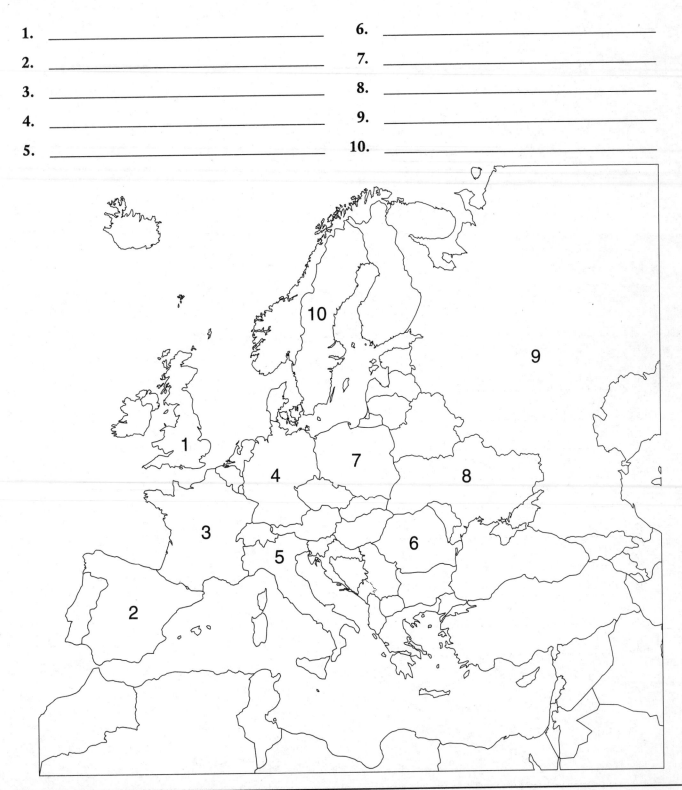

Name _____

Mapping Africa

Write the name of each country on the lines below.

1. _____   6. _____
2. _____   7. _____
3. _____   8. _____
4. _____   9. _____
5. _____   10. _____

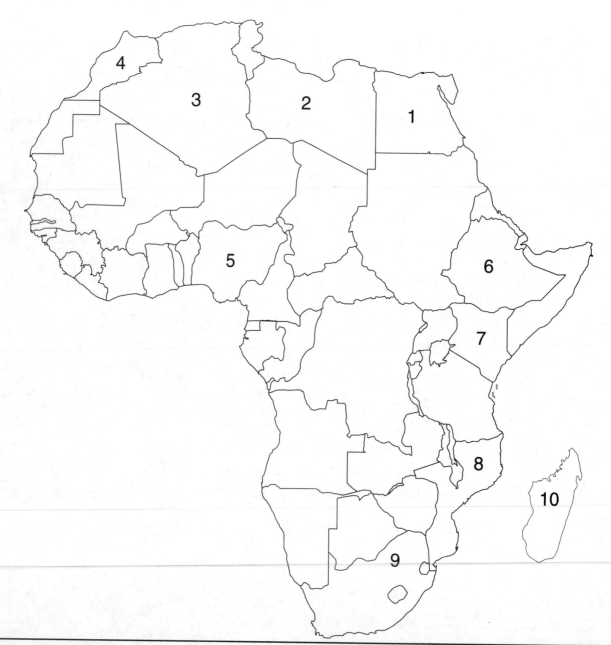

Name _____

Mapping Asia

Write the name of each country on the lines below.

1. _____   6. _____

2. _____   7. _____

3. _____   8. _____

4. _____   9. _____

5. _____   10. _____

Daily Learning Drills Grade 6

SOCIAL STUDIES REVIEW

Name _____

Marvels of the World

Some of the world's most splendid natural and man-made landmarks are listed below. Your task is to use maps and other references to locate each landmark and gather information about its importance. Briefly describe an important characteristic of each landmark in the spaces provided.

1. The Great Sphinx

_____

_____

2. The Great Wall

_____

_____

3. The Matterhorn

_____

_____

4. The Taj Mahal

_____

_____

5. The Eiffel Tower

_____

_____

6. Mount Fuji

_____

_____

7. Victoria Falls

_____

_____

8. The Grand Canyon

_____

_____

9. Kilimanjaro

_____

_____

10. The Colosseum

_____

_____

11. The Alhambra Palace

_____

_____

12. The Parthenon

_____

_____

13. Buckingham Palace

_____

_____

14. Ayers Rock

_____

_____

15. Leaning Tower of Pisa

_____

_____

16. St. Basil's Church

_____

_____

17. Mount Everest

_____

_____

18. Machu Picchu

_____

_____

19. Tikal

_____

_____

20. fiords

_____

_____

Name _____

Flags Around the World

Each country's flag has features that make it unique. Key features of some national flags are listed below. Use your information-gathering skills to correctly match the features with the countries. Write the names of the countries in the spaces. Then identify the countries by using the numbers on the map.

_____ **1.** red maple leaf

_____ **2.** the union jack in one corner; a larger, seven-pointed star and five smaller stars on a blue field

_____ **3.** white cross on a red field

_____ **4.** three vertical bands of equal width—blue nearest the staff, white in the middle, and red on the outside

_____ **5.** three horizontal bands—black on top, red in the middle, and green on the bottom; a shield and spears in the center

_____ **6.** red circle on a white field

_____ **7.** two horizontal bands—red on the top and white on the bottom; a crescent moon and five small stars in the top left corner

_____ **8.** one diagonal black stripe on a red field

_____ **9.** blue Shield or Star of David on a white field

_____ **10.** blue with six small yellow stars and one large yellow star

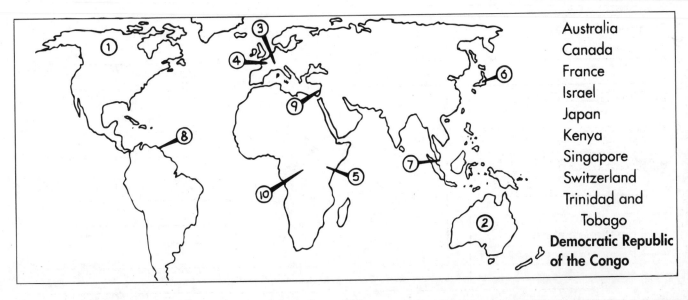

Australia
Canada
France
Israel
Japan
Kenya
Singapore
Switzerland
Trinidad and
  Tobago
**Democratic Republic
of the Congo**

SOCIAL STUDIES REVIEW

Review Answer Key

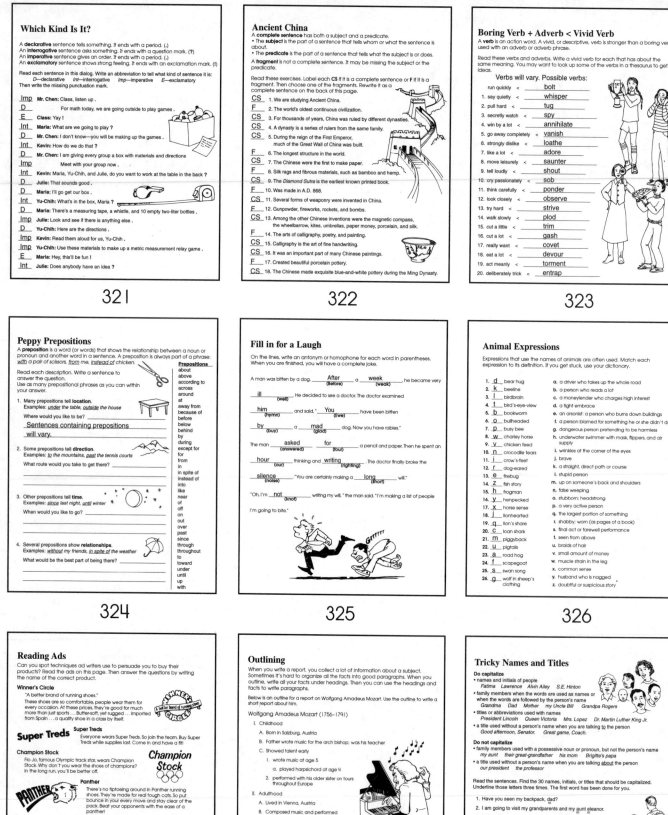

Which Kind Is It?

A **declarative** sentence tells something. It ends with a period. (.)
An **interrogative** sentence asks something. It ends with a question mark. (?)
An **imperative** sentence gives an order. It ends with a period. (.)
An **exclamatory** sentence shows strong feeling. It ends with an exclamation mark. (!)

Read each sentence in this dialog. Write an abbreviation to tell what kind of sentence it is:
D—declarative *Int*—interrogative *Imp*—imperative *E*—exclamatory
Then write the missing punctuation mark.

Imp **Mr. Chen:** Class, listen up .
D For math today, we are going outside to play games .
E **Class:** Yay !
Int **Maria:** What are we going to play ?
D **Mr. Chen:** I don't know—you will be making up the games .
Int **Kevin:** How do we do that ?
D **Mr. Chen:** I am giving every group a box with materials and directions
Imp Meet with your group now .
Int **Kevin:** Maria, Yu-Chih, and Julie, do you want to work at the table in the back ?
D **Julie:** That sounds good .
D **Maria:** I'll go get our box .
Int **Yu-Chih:** What's in the box, Maria ?
D **Maria:** There's a measuring tape, a whistle, and 10 empty two-liter bottles .
Imp **Julie:** Look and see if there is anything else .
D **Yu-Chih:** Here are the directions .
Imp **Kevin:** Read them aloud for us, Yu-Chih .
Imp **Yu-Chih:** Use these materials to make up a metric measurement relay game .
E **Maria:** Hey, this'll be fun !
Int **Julie:** Does anybody have an idea ?

321

Ancient China

A **complete sentence** has both a subject and a predicate.
• The **subject** is the part of a sentence that tells whom or what the sentence is about.
• The **predicate** is the part of a sentence that tells what the subject is or does.

A **fragment** is not a complete sentence. It may be missing the subject or the predicate.

Read these exercises. Label each **CS** if it is a complete sentence or **F** if it is a fragment. Then choose one of the fragments. Rewrite it as a complete sentence on the back of this page.

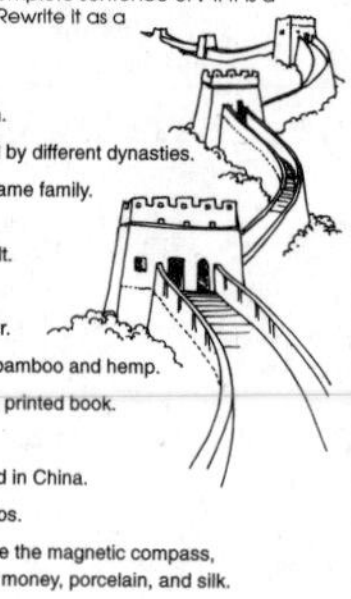

CS 1. We are studying Ancient China.
F 2. The world's oldest continuous civilization.
CS 3. For thousands of years, China was ruled by different dynasties.
CS 4. A dynasty is a series of rulers from the same family.
CS 5. During the reign of the First Emperor, much of the Great Wall of China was built.
F 6. The longest structure in the world.
CS 7. The Chinese were the first to make paper.
F 8. Silk rags and fibrous materials, such as bamboo and hemp.
CS 9. The *Diamond Sutra* is the earliest known printed book.
F 10. Was made in A.D. 868.
CS 11. Several forms of weaponry were invented in China.
F 12. Gunpowder, fireworks, rockets, and bombs.
CS 13. Among the other Chinese inventions were the magnetic compass, the wheelbarrow, kites, umbrellas, paper money, porcelain, and silk.
F 14. The arts of calligraphy, poetry, and painting.
CS 15. Calligraphy is the art of fine handwriting.
CS 16. It was an important part of many Chinese paintings.
F 17. Created beautiful porcelain pottery.
CS 18. The Chinese made exquisite blue-and-white pottery during the Ming Dynasty.

322

Boring Verb + Adverb < Vivid Verb

A **verb** is an action word. A vivid, or descriptive, verb is stronger than a boring verb used with an adverb or adverb phrase.

Read these verbs and adverbs. Write a vivid verb for each that has about the same meaning. You may want to look up some of the verbs in a thesaurus to get ideas.

Verbs will vary. Possible verbs:

run quickly < bolt
1. say quietly < whisper
2. pull hard < tug
3. secretly watch < spy
4. win by a lot < annihilate
5. go away completely < vanish
6. strongly dislike < loathe
7. like a lot < adore
8. move leisurely < saunter
9. tell loudly < shout
10. cry passionately < sob
11. think carefully < ponder
12. look closely < observe
13. try hard < strive
14. walk slowly < plod
15. cut a little < trim
16. cut a lot < gash
17. really want < covet
18. eat a lot < devour
19. act meanly < torment
20. deliberately trick < entrap

323

Peppy Prepositions

A **preposition** is a word (or words) that shows the relationship between a noun or pronoun and another word in a sentence. A preposition is always part of a phrase: *with a pair of scissors, from me, instead of chicken.*

Read each description. Write a sentence to answer the question. Use as many prepositional phrases as you can within your answer.

1. Many prepositions tell **location**. Examples: *under the table, outside the house*
   Where would you like to be?
   Sentences containing prepositions will vary.
2. Some prepositions tell **direction**. Examples: *to the mountains, past the tennis courts*
   What route would you take to get there?
3. Other prepositions tell **time**. Examples: *since last night, until winter*
   When would you like to go?
4. Several prepositions show **relationships**. Examples: *without my friends, in spite of the weather*
   What would be the best part of being there?

Prepositions
about, above, according to, across, around, at, away from, because of, before, below, behind, by, during, except for, for, from, in, in spite of, instead of, into, like, near, of, off, on, out, over, past, since, through, throughout, to, toward, under, until, up, with

324

Fill in for a Laugh

On the lines, write an antonym or homophone for each word in parentheses. When you are finished, you will have a complete joke.

A man was bitten by a dog. After (Before) a week (weak), he became very ill (well). He decided to see a doctor. The doctor examined him (hymn) and said, "You (Ewe) have been bitten by (buy) a mad (glad) dog. Now you have rabies."

The man asked (answered) for (four) a pencil and paper. Then he spent an hour (our) thinking and writing (righting). The doctor finally broke the silence (noise). "You are certainly making a long (short) will."

"Oh, I'm not (knot) writing my will," the man said. "I'm making a list of people I'm going to bite."

325

Animal Expressions

Expressions that use the names of animals are often used. Match each expression to its definition. If you get stuck, use your dictionary.

1. d bear hug
2. k beeline
3. l birdbrain
4. t bird's-eye-view
5. b bookworm
6. o bullheaded
7. p busy bee
8. w charley horse
9. v chicken feed
10. n crocodile tears
11. i crow's-feet
12. r dog-eared
13. e firebug
14. z fish story
15. h frogman
16. y henpecked
17. x horse sense
18. j lionhearted
19. q lion's share
20. c loan shark
21. m piggyback
22. u pigtails
23. a road hog
24. f scapegoat
25. s swan song
26. g wolf in sheep's clothing

a. a driver who takes up the whole road
b. a person who reads a lot
c. a moneylender who charges high interest
d. a tight embrace
e. an arsonist: a person who burns down buildings
f. a person blamed for something he or she didn't do
g. dangerous person pretending to be harmless
h. underwater swimmer with mask, flippers, and air supply
i. wrinkles at the corner of the eyes
j. brave
k. a straight, direct path or course
l. stupid person
m. up on someone's back and shoulders
n. false weeping
o. stubborn; headstrong
p. a very active person
q. the largest portion of something
r. shabby; worn (as pages of a book)
s. final act or farewell performance
t. seen from above
u. braids of hair
v. small amount of money
w. muscle strain in the leg
x. common sense
y. husband who is nagged
z. doubtful or suspicious story

326

Reading Ads

Can you spot techniques ad writers use to persuade you to buy their products? Read the ads on this page. Then answer the questions by writing the name of the correct product.

Winner's Circle
"A better brand of running shoes."
These shoes are so comfortable, people wear them for every occasion. At these prices, they're good for much more than just sports . . . Butter-soft, yet rugged . . . imported from Spain . . . a quality shoe in a class by itself.

Super Treds
Everyone wears Super Treds. So join the team. Buy Super Treds while supplies last. Come in and have a fit!

Champion Stock
Flo Jo, famous Olympic track star, wears Champion Stock. Why don't you wear the shoes of champions? In the long run, you'll be better off.

Panther
There's no tiptoeing around in Panther running shoes. They're made for real tough cats. So put bounce in your every move and stay clear of the pack. Beat your opponents with the ease of a panther!

1. Which ad suggests you buy the product because everybody does? Super Treds
2. Which ad suggests you buy the product because a famous person does? Champion Stock
3. Which ad has a "snob" appeal? Winner's Circle
4. Which ad tries to create a powerful image? Panther
5. Which ad appealed to you most? Answers will
   Why? vary.

327

Outlining

When you write a report, you collect a lot of information about a subject. Sometimes it's hard to organize all the facts into good paragraphs. When you outline, write all your facts under headings. Then you can use the headings and facts to write paragraphs.

Below is an outline for a report on Wolfgang Amadeus Mozart. Use the outline to write a short report about him.

Wolfgang Amadeus Mozart (1756–1791)

I. Childhood
   A. Born in Salzburg, Austria
   B. Father wrote music for the arch bishop; was his teacher
   C. Showed talent early
      1. wrote music at age 5
         a. played harpsichord at age 4
      2. performed with his older sister on tours throughout Europe
II. Adulthood
   A. Lived in Vienna, Austria
   B. Composed music and performed
      1. yet unable to support family
   C. Died poor at age 36
III. Achievements
   A. Wrote more than 600 compositions and 22 operas
   B. Music withstood test of time
      1. His music is played around the world today.
      2. Summer music festivals honor him.

The title of my report will be Answers will vary.

328

Tricky Names and Titles

Do capitalize
• names and initials of people
Fatima Lawrence Alvin Ailey S.E. Hinton
• family members when the words are used as names or when the words are followed by the person's name
Grandma Dad Mother my Uncle Bill Grandpa Rogers
• titles or abbreviations used with names
President Lincoln Queen Victoria Mrs. Lopez Dr. Martin Luther King Jr.
• a title used without a person's name when you are talking to the person
Good afternoon, Senator. Great game, Coach.

Do not capitalize
• family members used with a possessive noun or pronoun, but not the person's name
my aunt their great-grandfather his mom Brigitte's papa
• a title used without a person's name when you are talking about the person
our president the professor

Read the sentences. Find the 30 names, initials, or titles that should be capitalized. Underline those letters three times. The first word has been done for you.

1. Have you seen my backpack, dad?
2. I am going to visit my grandparents and my aunt eleanor.
3. Did you know that dr. matthews, my dentist, is danny's mom?
4. The United States has a president rather than a king or queen.
5. Jenny wrote her report on president james madison.
6. During the Civil War, general robert e. lee was the leader of the Southern troops.
7. Some people believe he was America's finest general ever.
8. ms. andrews read us an article about chief joseph, leader of the Nez Perce Indians.
9. We invited rev. johnson, fr. donally, and rabbi bronstein to speak to our class.
10. It is a pleasure to meet you, governor.
11. The first female Supreme Court judge was justice sandra day o'Connor.
12. My favorite character in the game Clue is professor plum.

329

Proofread a Bibliography

A **bibliography** is a listing of resources you used in a report. Bibliography styles vary.

General guidelines:

1. Resources are listed in alphabetical order by the last name of the author. If you do not know the author, begin with the title.
2. Titles of books, encyclopedias, and CD-ROMs should be underlined or in *italics*. Titles of encyclopedia articles should be in "quotation marks."
3. For books, give the place of publication, publication date. For encyclopedias, give the publication date and volume. For CD-ROM encyclopedias, give the format, publisher, and publication date.

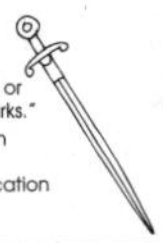

Sample Bibliography

Book	Hanawalt, Barbara. The Middle Ages: An Illustrated History. New York: Oxford University Press, 1998.
Encyclopedia article	Lyon, Bryce. "Middle Ages." World Book Encyclopedia. 1994, Volume 13.
CD-ROM Encyclopedia article	Stein, Robert M. "Middle Ages." Microsoft Encarta 98 Encyclopedia. CD-ROM. Microsoft, 1997.

Proofread this bibliography. Add the missing underlining and punctuation marks (commas, periods, quotation marks, and colons).

Bibliography

Aliki. A Medieval Feast. New York: Crowell, 1983.

Caselli, Giovanni. The Middle Ages. New York: Peter Bedrick Books, 1988.

Gravett, Christopher. Knight. New York: Knopf, 1993.

Macaulay, David. Cathedral. Boston: Houghton Mifflin, 1973.

"Middle Ages." Compton's Encyclopedia. 1992, Volume 15.

Rosenthal, Joel T. "Knights and Knighthood." World Book Encyclopedia. 1994, Volume 11.

Soergel, Philip M. "Chivalry." Microsoft Encarta 98 Encyclopedia. CD-ROM. Microsoft, 1997.

Steele, Philip. Castles. New York: Kingfisher, 1998.

330

What Do You Think?

An **essay** is a type of writing in which you express your opinion. To write a really good essay, you have to back up your opinion with details and examples. Think of a topic you feel strongly about or choose one from the list below. Use the form on this page as a practice model for writing.

Why School Should (or Shouldn't) Be Year-Round
Why We Should (or Shouldn't) Save the Rain Forest
What Courses Should Be Offered in Middle School
Why Grades Should (or Shouldn't) Be Eliminated
Why It Is (or Isn't) Important to Know More Than One Language

Something I believe strongly about is Answers will vary.

One reason I believe this is ______

Another reason is ______

An example that proves this point is ______

I strongly feel that ______

In closing, let me say that ______

331

Name That Rhyme

Match the one-sentence summaries below with the classic rhymes they describe.

H 1. This rhyme refers to a boy who jumps over a candlestick.
B 2. This rhyme expresses a wish for sunshine.
L 3. This rhyme honors the mother of all rhymes.
O 4. This rhyme advertises a pastry.
J 5. This rhyme refers to a young man who has gone to sea.
N 6. This rhyme tells the story of a boy who runs through a village in his pajamas.
C 7. This rhyme talks about a mouse that runs up a clock.
E 8. This rhyme describes a boy who has gone to bed with his trousers on.
I 9. This rhyme describes baking a cake for a baby.
D 10. This rhyme tells of a boy who has fallen asleep on the job.
F 11. This rhyme tells about a boy who wants to purchase a pie without any money.
M 12. This rhyme tells of a boy and girl who climb a hill to fetch water from a well.
K 13. The teller of this rhyme is singing to a sheep.
A 14. This rhyme tells the tale of a girl who owns a pet lamb.
G 15. This rhyme tells the tale of a girl who has lost her sheep.

A. "Mary Had a Little Lamb"
B. "Rain, Rain, Go Away"
C. "Hickory, Dickory, Dock"
D. "Little Boy Blue"
E. "Diddle, Diddle, Dumpling"
F. "Simple Simon"
G. "Little Bo Peep"
H. "Jack Be Nimble"
I. "Pat-a-Cake"
J. "Bobby Shaftoe"
K. "Baa, Baa, Black Sheep"
L. "Old Mother Goose"
M. "Jack and Jill"
N. "Wee Willie Winkie"
O. "Hot Cross Buns"

333

Contemporary Choreographers

Read about four contemporary choreographers below. Then, answer the questions that follow in complete sentences.

Mark Morris: Morris began dancing as a child and was already choreographing pieces by his teenage years. Touring in Asia in the 1970s, he learned indigenous dance styles. His own dances mix elements of classic and modern ballet and Eastern and Western styles. He has created works for everything from classical music to punk rock. In 1980, Morris founded his own dance troupe, which tours internationally and is scheduled to open its own permanent headquarters in New York. In 1990, Morris collaborated with Mikhail Baryshnikov on the White Oak Dance Project, which showcased his creativity.

Ann Reinking: Reinking danced and choreographed with Bob Fosse before his death. Following his death, she worked with Chet Walker to create a musical tribute to her colleague, *Fosse*. She has worked on such classic Broadway shows as *Chicago*, *Bye-Bye Birdie*, and *Applause*. She has worked on four films, including *All That Jazz* and *Annie*. In 1994, she became the founder and artistic director of the Broadway Theatre Project.

Peter Martins: Martins is a Danish dancer and choreographer who began his career with the Royal Danish Ballet in 1964. He accepted a position as principal dancer with the New York City Ballet under the direction of George Balanchine six years later. Balanchine encouraged Martin's choreographic skills, and in 1981, he became the New York City Ballet's ballet master. His choreographic pieces include *Calcium Light Night*.

Gerald Arpino: Arpino established the Joffrey Ballet in Chicago along with Robert Joffrey in 1956. When Joffrey died, Arpino succeeded him as artistic director. He has served as the Joffrey Ballet's resident choreographer since 1961. He creates about one third of the company's works. Arpino has completed such diverse commissions as a rock ballet set to the music of Prince and a classic ballet in honor of the American presidency. He holds numerous honors and awards for his choreographic genius. He serves on various advisory councils and supports the arts in society.

1. Which choreographer likely does the most traveling? Mark Morris
2. Which choreographer produces works you would be most interested in seeing? ______ Why? Personal opinion
3. Which choreographer works for a well-established ballet? Gerald Arpino
4. Which choreographer completes a great deal of work on Broadway? Ann Reinking
5. Which choreographer might still be a dancer if not for the encouragement of Balanchine? Peter Martins

334

Letter Fun

In **anagrams**, different words are spelled with the same letters. Take the letters A, B, S, T, for example. They spell three different words in the poem below.

Complete the anagram poems below. The letters that spell the missing words are given in parentheses.

The Sports Store Clerks
They try to keep the baseball BATS
Lined up beside the baseball hats.
They glue on TABS that name each price.
And each takes a STAB at being nice.

1. **(O, N, W) The Big Winner**
One time, he won a TV set,
Then lost it in another bet.
He's wiser now, for life has shown
That gamblers can lose all they own.

2. **(A, E, M, T) The Old Gray Mare**
She is friendly, mild, and tame,
But since the dog-food makers came
And thought of her as only meat,
She will no longer drink or eat.

3. **(E, S, T, W) The Cook**
As the sun sets in the west
He makes the table look its best,
But that won't help his lumpy stew.
It wets your mouth but tastes like glue.

4. **(A, D, E, R) Love Letter**
Her letter makes him float on air,
But he can't read it.
Does he dare
To have it read where all can hear
His first love letter from his dear?

5. **(E, H, O, S) The Awkward Gardener**
In her yard, she weeds and hoes.
And trips upon the garden hose.
She keeps from falling, it is true,
But rips the heel right off her shoe.

6. **(E, I, L, V) The Nasty Neighbor**
That evil man is never kind.
He's always plotting in his mind
To pull some vile and nasty trick.
All who live near him fear he's sick.

7. **(A, C, E, R) The Fast Farmer**
To win an acre in good lands
She ran a race upon her hands.
She didn't care just who might frown
Because she knew she'd win hands down.

335

Many Meanings

RIDDLE: What has 18 legs and catches flies?
ANSWER: A baseball team
Flies are certain insects. They are also certain hits in baseball. The riddle is funny because it uses both meanings.

Each joke below uses a word in two ways. Beneath each joke, there are three or more meanings of the word presented. Circle the numbers of the two meanings used in the joke.

1. *Lou:* Why was the actor happy about breaking his leg?
Sue: He finally got into a cast.
cast: (1) a hard covering formed by molding; (2) to throw; (3) performers in a play
2. *Tim:* I'll see you when you return. Will you be long?
Kim: Same as always. About 5' 4".
long: (1) to wish for; (2) much time; (3) tall or high
3. *Jane:* Is this a rare piece of art?
Blaine: It certainly isn't well done.
rare: (1) thin and not dense; (2) cooked for a short time; (3) unlike others of its kind
4. *Bill:* How is an umpire like an orchestra leader?
Phil: Both have to know the score.
score: (1) to win; (2) something owed to someone else; (3) a record of points made in a game; (4) a written copy of music
5. *Flo:* Why do you think your pet pig will write you?
Joe: It has a pen.
pen: (1) something used for writing; (2) a fenced-in place for animals; (3) slang for prison
6. *Mary:* Why are you buying gloves for your dog?
Tommy: It is a boxer.
boxer: (1) a kind of dog; (2) someone who packs boxes; (3) a prizefighter
7. *Ron:* Do you file your nails?
Don: No. I just cut them off and then throw them away.
file: (1) to rub smooth with a piece of metal; (2) a line of people or things; (3) to arrange things in a certain order
8. *Customer:* I'd like a steak, and please make it lean.
Waiter: In which direction?
lean: (1) to rely on; (2) having little or no fat; (3) to tilt or bend

336

My Word!

Words come from a variety of places—from people's names, from places, from other languages, etc. Some words are even formed by combining two words. For example, the word ***motel*** comes from combining ***motor*** and ***hotel***. The word ***smog*** comes from ***smoke*** and ***fog***. The brand name ***Swatch*** is a combination of ***Swiss*** and ***watch***.

Can you figure out what two words were put together to create the word *brunch*?

You can make up a new word by combining two others. Feel like having a "jonut"? That's short for *jelly donut*. Or how about a "smug" from a sweetheart? (That's a combination of *smooch* and *hug*.)

Get silly. Get serious. Get your pencil and get ready to make up ten new words. Share your words with the class. Who knows? You may decide to publish a "*sictionary*" (that's a silly dictionary!).

1. Answers will vary.
2.
3.
4.
5.
6.
7.
8.
9.
10.

337

Lovely Literature

Literature can take many forms and is full of many intriguing components. Use the words in the word box relating to literature to fill in the blanks.

rhythm	alliteration	rhyme	assonance	metaphor	onomatopoeia
stanza	symbol	simile	personification	diction	figurative language

personification 1. the giving of human qualities to an object, animal, or idea
metaphor 2. a direct comparison between two unlike things
alliteration 3. the repetition of sounds at the beginning of words
stanza 4. a group of lines that form a unit, like a paragraph
rhythm 5. the pattern of stressed and unstressed syllables that may create a beat
symbol 6. a person, place, or object that stands for something beyond itself
simile 7. a comparison using *like* or *as*
assonance 8. repetition of vowel sounds in stressed syllables
rhyme 9. repetition of ending sounds at the end of words
onomatopoeia 10. the use of words to imitate sounds
figurative language 11. language that communicates ideas beyond the literal meanings of the word
diction 12. the choices of words in speech or writing

338

Words From the Government

The government of the United States is a very interesting and complex institution. Learn about some words relating to it by filling in the crossword puzzle below. Use the terms from the word box for your answers.

Word Box
caucus
referendum
repeal
resolution
legislative
amendment
executive
petition
delegate
judicial

Across

2. to call back or change back
3. a closed meeting of a group of people belonging to the same political party
6. the branch of government that makes laws
9. a formal written request made to an official body or person

Down

1. the branch of government that carries out the laws
2. a vote on a measure proposed by a legislative body
4. a formal expression of opinion voted on by an official body
5. a person acting for another; a representative in the House of Representatives
7. a change or modification by a constitutional procedure
8. the branch of government that judges and administers justice

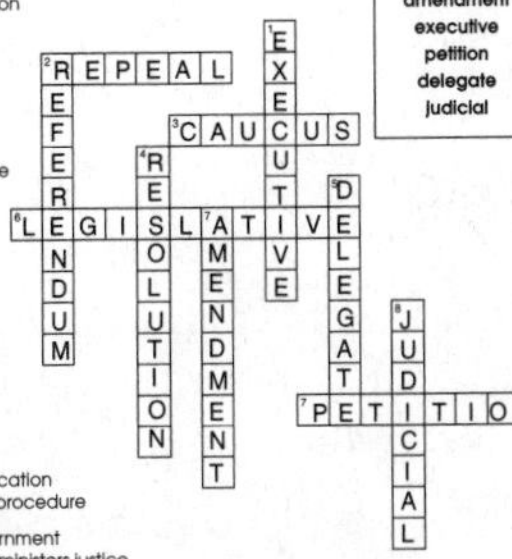

339

405 Daily Learning Drills Grade 6

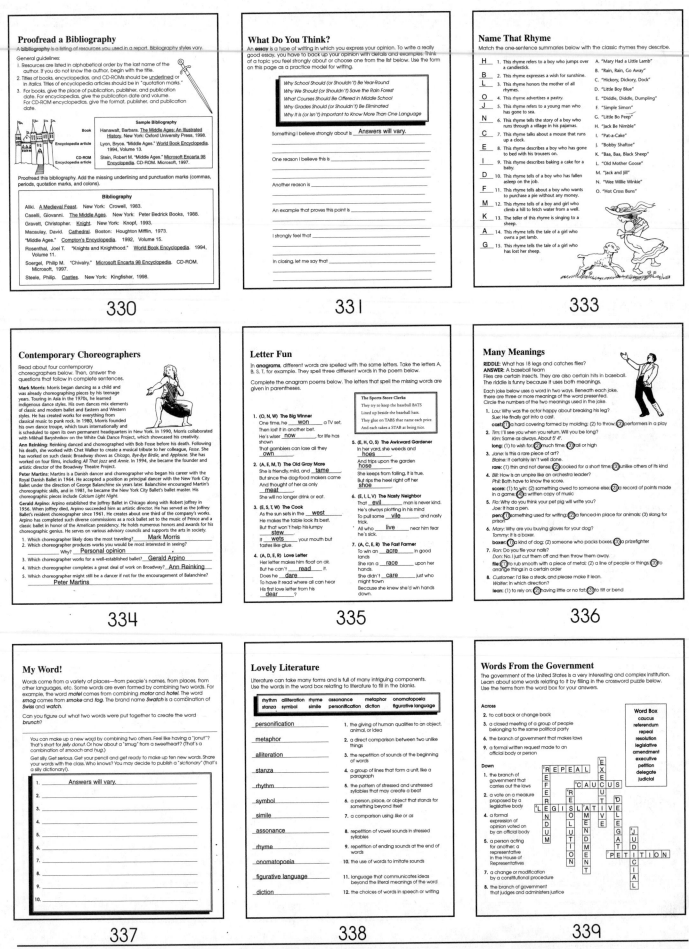

340

All the World is a Stage

Theater is an art form in which a series of events, often a written play, is acted out by authors who pretend to be the characters. Learn more about theater and acting by filling in the blanks using words from the word box. Write them next to their correct definitions.

choreography	soliloquy	callback	audition	cue
monologue	protagonist	antagonist	aside	thespian

mon**ol**o**gue** — 1. a dramatic scene performed by one actor

audition — 2. to give a trial performance; to test for a theatrical part

pro**t**agonist — 3. the principle character or leading actor

t**h**espian — 4. relating to drama; actor

asid**e** — 5. an actor's comments heard by the audience, but supposedly not by the characters

s**ol**iloquy — 6. the act of talking to oneself, presumably alone on the stage

an**t**agonist — 7. the one that opposes the main character or lead actor

c**a**llback — 8. a second or additional audition for a theatrical part

choreo**g**raphy — 9. the composition and arrangement of dance and movement upon the stage

cu**e** — 10. a written signal to the performer to begin a specific speech or action

341

Check it Out!

Use the schedule on this page as a guide for writing a research paper or giving a school report. Estimate how long it will take you to do each job. Then check off each task you complete it.

Paper Due Date: _____

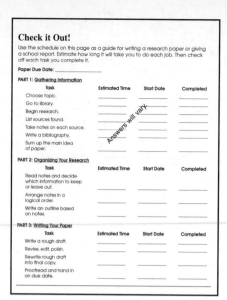

PART 1: Gathering Information

Task	Estimated Time	Start Date	Completed
Choose topic.			
Go to library.			
Begin research.			
List sources found.			
Take notes on each source.			
Write a bibliography.			
Sum up the main idea of paper.			

PART 2: Organizing Your Research

Task	Estimated Time	Start Date	Completed
Read notes and decide which information to keep or leave out.			
Arrange notes in a logical order.			
Write an outline based on notes.			

PART 3: Writing Your Paper

Task	Estimated Time	Start Date	Completed
Write a rough draft.			
Revise, edit, polish.			
Rewrite rough draft into final copy.			
Proofread and hand in on due date.			

Answers will vary.

342

Look it Up!

References are books and other materials you refer to for information. Reference books cannot be taken out of the library. They have Ref or R on their spines. Some of the most common references are listed below.

Dictionary: The most common dictionary gives spellings, meanings, and pronunciation for words. There are also biographical dictionaries that give facts about famous people. A thesaurus is a special dictionary consisting of just synonyms and antonyms.

Atlas: a book of maps

Almanac: a book of up-to-date information on many subjects, such as population, government, sports, entertainment; A new edition is published each year

Readers' Guide to Periodical Literature: an index of articles that have been published in magazines

Current News on File: an index of newspaper articles

Encyclopedia: a set of books with facts on many subjects

Write the reference(s) you would look in to answer the questions below.

1. In what year was Beethoven born? __encyclopedia, biographical dictionary__
2. What is another word that means *stout*? __thesaurus, dictionary__
3. How far is San Diego from Los Angeles? __atlas__
4. How do you pronounce the word *crocher*? __dictionary__
5. Where are the Rocky Mountains? __atlas__
6. Who won the Academy Award for Best Actor last year? __almanac__
7. How are alligators and crocodiles different? __encyclopedia__
8. Which magazines had articles about baseball card collecting? __Reader's Guide to Periodical Literature__
9. Is Mark Twain a fictional character? __biographical dictionary__
10. What recent news articles reported on the space shuttle? __Current News on File__

343

Designer Fractions

Use the code to color equivalent fractions.

$\frac{1}{2}$ = red $\frac{1}{4}$ = blue $\frac{2}{5}$ = green $\frac{1}{3}$ = yellow $\frac{2}{3}$ = orange

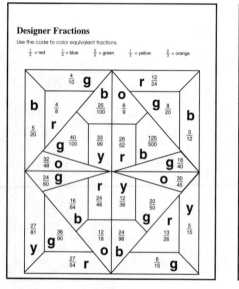

344

Shade-In Message

Find the least common multiple or least common denominator. Shade in one section in the box below that matches each answer. When you are finished, you will discover what to use when adding fractions with unlike denominators.

Least Common Multiple

1. 2 and ⑧
2. 4 and 6 — 12
3. ⑥ and 3
4. 4 and 10 — 20
5. 6 and 9 — 18
6. 5 and ⑩
7. 3 and 5 — 15
8. 8 and 12 — 24
9. 8 and 10 — 40
10. 6 and 8 — 24
11. 6 and 10 — 30
12. 4 and 7 — 28
13. 5 and 6 — 30
14. 5 and 12 — 60
15. 6 and ⑫

Least Common Denominator

16. $\frac{5}{6}$ and $\frac{8}{9}$ — 18
17. $\frac{1}{4}$ and $\frac{3}{4}$ — 4
18. $\frac{9}{10}$ and $\frac{1}{2}$ — 10
19. $\frac{4}{5}$ and $\frac{7}{10}$ — 10
20. $\frac{4}{5}$ and $\frac{2}{3}$ — 15
21. $\frac{5}{6}$ and $\frac{3}{4}$ — 12
22. $\frac{2}{3}$ and $\frac{7}{9}$ — 9
23. $\frac{5}{8}$ and $\frac{1}{4}$ — 16
24. $\frac{4}{7}$ and $\frac{3}{28}$ — 28
25. $\frac{7}{10}$ and $\frac{3}{5}$ — 10
26. $\frac{5}{6}$ and $\frac{1}{12}$ — 12
27. $\frac{4}{13}$ and $\frac{7}{12}$ — 12
28. $\frac{7}{8}$ and $\frac{2}{3}$ — 24
29. $\frac{3}{10}$ and $\frac{3}{4}$ — 20
30. $\frac{2}{9}$ and $\frac{3}{15}$ — 45

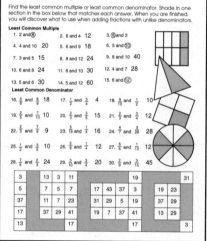

3		13	3	11			19					31
	5	7	5	7		17	43	37	3		19	23
37		11	7	23		31	29	3	19		23	29
17		37	29	41		19	7	37	41		13	29
13			17				17					3

345

Riddle Me This

Multiply.

A. $\frac{1}{4} \times \frac{1}{2} = \frac{1}{8}$

B. $\frac{5}{6} \times 3 = 2\frac{1}{2}$

C. $2\frac{5}{8} \times 6 = 15\frac{3}{4}$

D. $3 \times \frac{3}{16} = \frac{9}{16}$

E. $\frac{2}{5} \times \frac{3}{16} = \frac{1}{?}$

F. $12 \times \frac{3}{4} = 9$

G. $\frac{9}{10} \times \frac{5}{6} = \frac{3}{4}$

H. $3\frac{2}{3} \times \frac{3}{10} = 1\frac{1}{10}$

I. $\frac{1}{6} \times \frac{5}{9} = \frac{5}{54}$

J. $\frac{4}{5} \times 3\frac{1}{3} = 2\frac{2}{3}$

K. $\frac{7}{10} \times \frac{5}{21} = \frac{1}{?}$

L. $\frac{3}{5} \times 7 = \frac{21}{100}$

M. $\frac{4}{5} \times \frac{7}{8} = \frac{7}{10}$

N. $7\frac{1}{2} \times 1\frac{7}{10} = 12\frac{3}{4}$

O. $5\frac{1}{8} \times 9\frac{3}{4} = 49\frac{31}{32}$

P. $2\frac{1}{4} \times \frac{?}{?} = 1\frac{11}{16}$

Q. $\frac{5}{8} \times \frac{18}{?} = \frac{9}{80}$

R. $\frac{3}{15} \times \frac{5}{9} = \frac{1}{9}$

S. $\frac{3}{4} \times \frac{?}{?} = \frac{1}{2}$

T. $9\frac{1}{2} \times 6\frac{2}{3} = 61\frac{11}{?}$

U. $\frac{5}{6} \times \frac{?}{?} = \frac{5}{9}$

V. $\frac{1}{2} \times \frac{1}{2} = \frac{1}{?}$

W. $11\frac{1}{2} \times \frac{?}{?} = \frac{11}{?}$

X. $4 \times 6\frac{3}{10} = 25\frac{1}{5}$

Y. $\frac{1}{2} \times 6\frac{3}{4} = 3\frac{3}{8}$

Z. $8\frac{1}{2} \times 6\frac{2}{3} = 56\frac{2}{3}$

Use the answers and letters above to answer the riddle.
What kind of table has no legs?

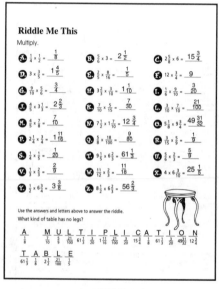

A   M U L T I P L I C A T I O N
$\frac{1}{8}$ $2\frac{1}{2}$ $\frac{21}{100}$ $6\frac{2}{3}$ $1\frac{1}{10}$ $\frac{9}{16}$ $\frac{21}{100}$ $\frac{7}{10}$ $15\frac{3}{4}$ $1\frac{1}{9}$ $6\frac{2}{3}$ $\frac{9}{20}$ $49\frac{31}{32}$ $\frac{5}{9}$

T A B L E
$61\frac{1}{3}$ $\frac{1}{4}$ $2\frac{2}{3}$ $\frac{21}{100}$ $\frac{1}{5}$

346

Let's Divide

Divide. Write the answers in lowest terms, if necessary.

A. $1\frac{1}{4} \div \frac{1}{4} = 5$ $2\frac{1}{2} \div \frac{1}{2} = 5$ $\frac{3}{8} \div \frac{1}{4} = 1\frac{1}{2}$

B. $3\frac{1}{2} \div \frac{7}{8} = 4$ $2\frac{1}{4} \div \frac{3}{4} = 3$ $6 \div \frac{1}{3} = 18$

C. $2\frac{1}{4} \div \frac{3}{8} = 6$ $1\frac{1}{3} \div \frac{1}{3} = 4$ $3\frac{1}{3} \div \frac{5}{6} = 1\frac{10}{11}$

D. $\frac{3}{4} \div \frac{1}{8} = 6$ $2 \div \frac{1}{4} = 8$ $\frac{4}{7} \div \frac{2}{3} = \frac{6}{7}$

E. $\frac{1}{2} \div \frac{1}{4} = 2$ $2\frac{1}{2} \div \frac{1}{2} = 5$ $\frac{1}{4} \div \frac{1}{8} = 2$

F. $2\frac{5}{8} \div \frac{1}{8} = 21$ $5 \div \frac{3}{18} = 5$ $1\frac{3}{4} \div \frac{1}{16} = 28$

G. $1\frac{1}{4} \div \frac{5}{8} = 2$ $\frac{7}{12} \div \frac{1}{2} = \frac{7}{8}$

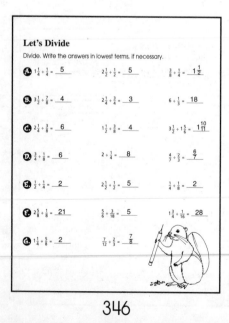

347

In the Sky

Complete each number to make the expression true.

A. $0.30 \_ > 0.3019$ $0.\_\_45 > 0.29$ $34.3\_ > 35.37$

B. $16.788 < 16.7\_8$ $8.42\_ > 8.427$ $\_\_.067 < 1.0671$

C. $3.416 > \_\_.416$ $\_28\_\_47 < 28.147$ $0.03243 < 0.03\_\_2$

D. $5.345 > 5.\_45$ $0.06\_\_83 < 0.06184$ $178.\_\_71 > 178.789$

E. $3.99\_ < 3.999$ $2.527 > 2.\_\_48$ $17.098 > 1\_\_.908$

F. $2.0\_\_3 > 1.999$ $17.6 > 1\_\_.06$ $2\_\_7.095 < 217.099$

Answers will vary.

Write the decimals in order from least to greatest.

G. 16.39; 16.8; 16.7; 16.79   16.39   16.7   16.79   16.8

H. 72.59; 56.56; 73.1; 56.6; 72.48   56.56   56.6   72.48   72.59   73.1

I. 0.06; 0.6; 6.060; 0.006   0.006   0.06   0.6   6.060

J. 109.041; 104.091; 401.001   104.091   109.041   401.001

K. 5.5508; 5.5880; 5.58; 5.56   5.5508   5.56   5.58   5.5880

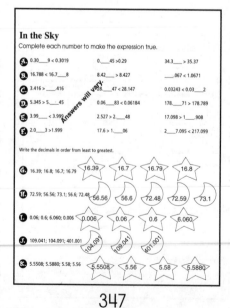

348

Order, Please!

Frank worked for his sister at the school snack shop. In one hour, he took orders for 20 items. He had to keep track of prices in his head, so he decided to round the prices. Help Frank round each price. Write the number on the price tag.

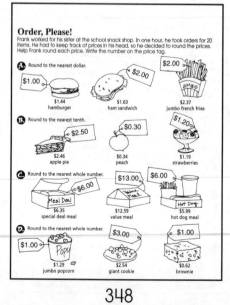

A. Round to the nearest dollar.

$1.00 — hamburger ($1.44)
$2.00 — ham sandwich ($1.63)
$2.00 — jumbo french fries ($2.37)

B. Round to the nearest tenth.

$2.50 — apple pie ($2.46)
$0.30 — peach ($0.34)
$1.20 — strawberries ($1.19)

C. Round to the nearest whole number.

$6.00 — special deal meal ($6.35)
$13.00 — value meal ($12.59)
$6.00 — hot dog meal ($5.99)

D. Round to the nearest whole number.

$1.00 — jumbo popcorn ($1.29)
$3.00 — giant cookie ($2.54)
$1.00 — brownie ($0.62)

Make an Equation

Use the numbers in each circle to create a multiplication equation with two factors and a product. Do the multiplication to check your answer.

1. 5.2 / 6.396 / 1.23
1.23 x 52 = 6.396

2. 0.86 / 2.107 / 2.45
2.45 x .86 = 2.107

3. 18.8 / 45.12 / 2.4
18.8 x 2.4 = 45.12

4. 0.8 / 4.6 / 3.68
4.6 x 0.8 = 3.68

5. 4.8 / 34.56 / 7.2
4.8 x 7.2 = 34.56

6. 2.38 / 3.4 / 0.7
3.4 x 0.7 = 2.38

7. 2.78 / 1.112 / 0.4
2.78 x 0.4 = 1.112

8. 68.08 / 14.8 / 4.6
14.8 x 4.6 = 68.08

9. 6.8 / 2.856 / 0.42
6.8 x 0.42 = 2.856

10. 0.85 / 3.077 / 3.62
3.62 x 0.85 = 3.077

11. 0.75 / 0.1875 / 0.25
0.25 x 0.75 = 0.1875

12. 2.4 / 1.025 / 2.46
2.4 x 1.025 = 2.46

13. 2.3 / 11.914 / 5.18
5.18 x 2.3 = 11.914

14. 0.31 / 0.0434 / 0.14
0.31 x 0.14 = 0.0434

15. 0.7 / 0.494 / 6.42
6.42 x 0.7 = 0.494

349

Pig Tales

Mack and Sandy raise pigs. Estimate and underline the answer.

A. On Wednesday, Mack and Sandy needed to move 100 pigs from one part of the farm to another. If they can walk .96 miles an hour, how far can they go in 6.42 hours?
About 10 miles   About 4 miles   <u>About 6 miles</u>   About 2 miles

B. Mack and Sandy own 1,021 pigs. Each pen has enough room for 78.7 pigs. About how many pens do they need?
<u>About 13 pens</u>   About 10 pens   About 8 pens   About 5 pens

C. Sandy and Mack need to buy food for the piglets. Each bag of food weighs 58.32 pounds. If each piglet eats about 2.10 pounds every day, about how long will it take one piglet to eat a whole bag of feed?
About 15 days   <u>About 30 days</u>   About 150 days   About 60 days

D. They put the pigs in trucks when they go to the market. The biggest truck on the farm can carry about 4,989.92 pounds. If each pig weighs about 204.23 pounds, about how many pigs can they put in one truck?
About 20 pigs   About 15 pigs   About 12 pigs   <u>About 25 pigs</u>

E. On Thursday, the kids washed out the pig pens. They worked for about 4.85 hours. Each hour they used 1,026 gallons of water. About how much water did they use in all?
<u>About 5,000 gallons</u>   About 100 gallons   About 102 gallons   About 6,000 gallons

F. If each sow can be expected to have about 9.83 piglets each year, about how many piglets will be born in 3 years?
About 1,000 piglets   <u>Not enough information</u>   About 9,000 piglets   About 5,000 piglets

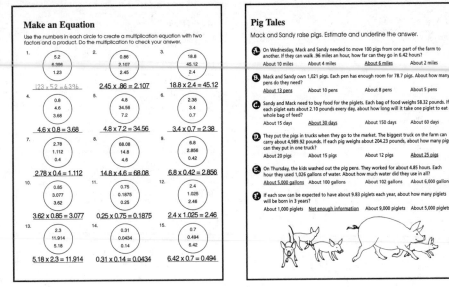

350

Surfing with Decimals

Divide.

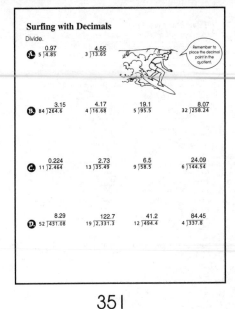

Remember to place the decimal point in the quotient.

A. 0.97 / 5)4.85   4.55 / 3)13.65

B. 3.15 / 84)264.6   4.17 / 4)16.68   19.1 / 5)95.5   8.07 / 32)258.24

C. 0.224 / 11)2.464   2.73 / 13)35.49   6.5 / 9)58.5   24.09 / 6)144.54

D. 8.29 / 52)431.08   122.7 / 19)2,331.3   41.2 / 12)494.4   84.45 / 4)337.8

351

Flocking Together

In Australia, huge trees are filled with birds at sunset. Although it can be hard to see these birds at first, you can always hear them! Write a decimal and a percent for each fraction.

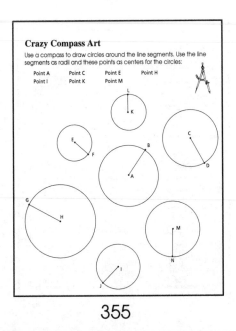

A. Of the parrots in the tree, 9/12 were green. Round to the nearest hundredth.
.67; 67%

B. Four-twelfths of the parrots in the tree were blue.
.33; 33%

C. Five flocks of cockatoos landed in the tree just as the sun set. Four-fifths of these birds were white with yellow crests on their heads.
0.8; 80%

D. Three-fifths of the pink cockatoos were less than two years old.
0.6; 60%

E. Of the black cockatoos in the tree, ¾ sat at the top of the tree.
.75; 75%

F. Five twenty-fifths of the black cockatoos watch the skies for danger.
0.2; 20%

G. When the sun rises, ⅖ of the birds in the tree fly away looking for food.
0.4; 40%

352

Delightful Daisies

On the flowers in each vase, write the fractions and decimals that are equivalent to the percent shown.

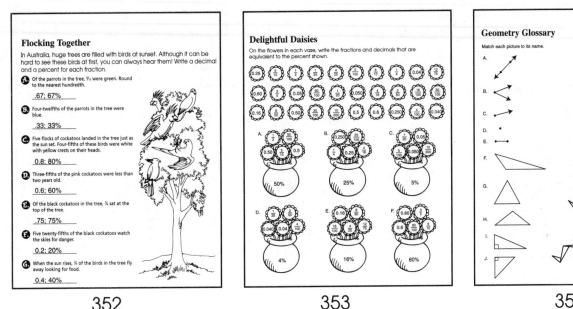

353

Geometry Glossary

Match each picture to its name.

1. B angle
2. A line
3. E line segment
4. D point
5. C ray
6. G acute equilateral triangle
7. F obtuse scalene triangle
8. I right scalene triangle
9. J right isosceles triangle
10. H obtuse isosceles triangle

A. B. C. D. E. F. G. H. I. J.

354

Crazy Compass Art

Use a compass to draw circles around the line segments. Use the line segments as radii and these points as centers for the circles:

Point A   Point C   Point E   Point H
Point I   Point K   Point M

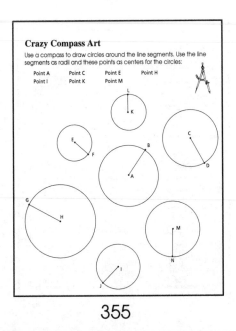

355

Digging for Diagonals

Complete the table below using the pictures at the bottom of the page. Watch for a pattern and use it to complete problem G.

	Name of figure	Number of sides	Number of diagonals without any intersecting	Number of angles formed by diagonals
A	Triangle	3	0	3
B	Rectangle	4	1	6
C	Pentagon	5	2	9
D	Hexagon	6	3	12
E	Octagon	8	5	18
F	Decagon	10	7	24
G	20-Sided Figure	20	17	57

356

An A-Peel-ing Riddle

What shapes are made from banana peels?

To find out, find the area of each shape. Use the formulas to help you. Then use your answers to break the code at the bottom of the page.

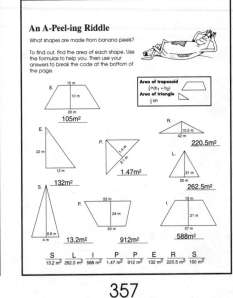

Area of trapezoid
½h(b₁ + b₂)
Area of triangle
½bh

S. 10 m / 10 m / 20 m → 105m²

E. 22 m / 12 m → 132m²

R. 10.5 m / 42 m → 220.5m²

P. 1.4 m / 2.1 m → 1.47m²

L. 25 m / 21 m → 262.5m²

S. 6.6 m / 4 m → 13.2m²

P. 53 m / 24 m / 23 m → 912m²

I. 19 m / 37 m / 21 m → 588m²

S   L   I   P   P   E   R   S
13.2 m² 262.5 m² 588 m² 1.47 m² 912 m² 132 m² 220.5 m² 150 m²

357

Daily Learning Drills Grade 6

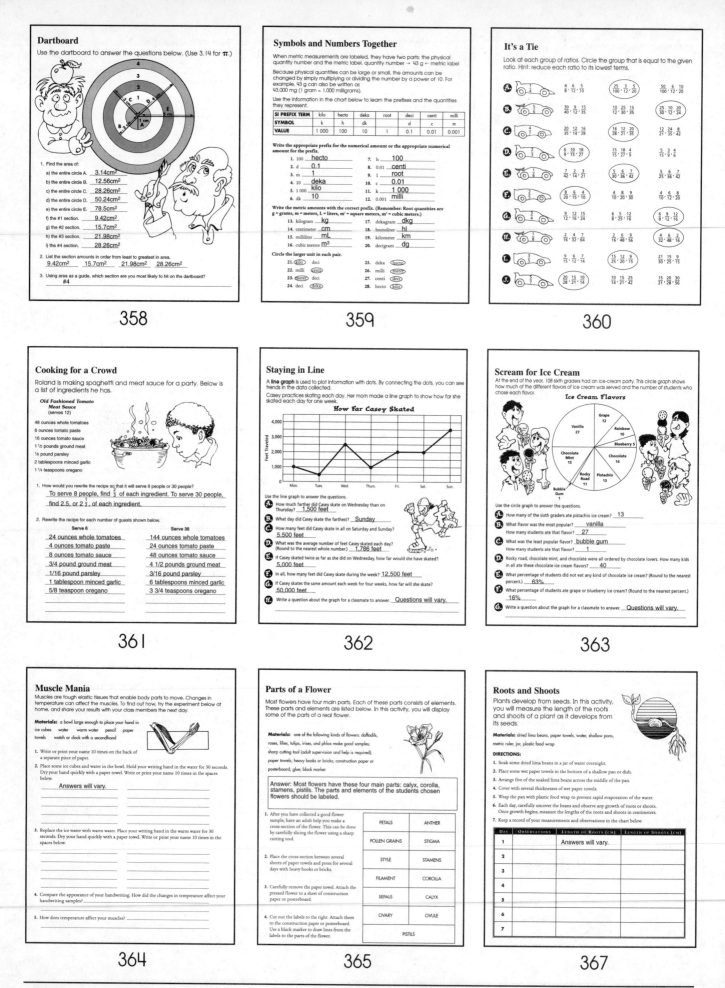

Dartboard

Use the dartboard to answer the questions below. (Use 3.14 for π.)

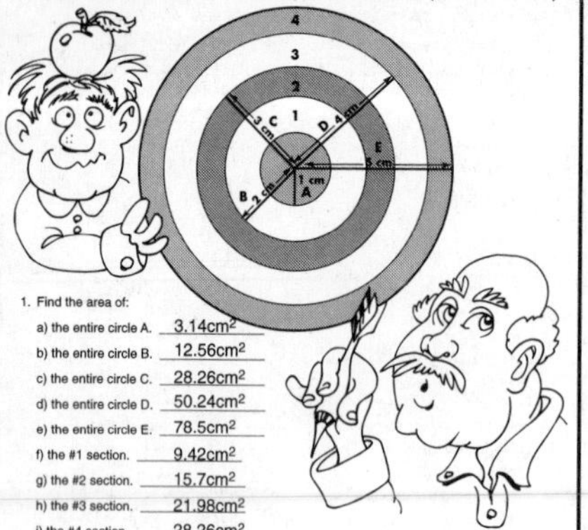
4
3
2
1
A
B
C
D
E
1 cm
2 cm
3 cm
4 cm
5 cm

1. Find the area of:
   - a) the entire circle A. 3.14cm²
   - b) the entire circle B. 12.56cm²
   - c) the entire circle C. 28.26cm²
   - d) the entire circle D. 50.24cm²
   - e) the entire circle E. 78.5cm²
   - f) the #1 section. 9.42cm²
   - g) the #2 section. 15.7cm²
   - h) the #3 section. 21.98cm²
   - i) the #4 section. 28.26cm²
2. List the section amounts in order from least to greatest in area.
   9.42cm² 15.7cm² 21.98cm² 28.26cm²
3. Using area as a guide, which section are you most likely to hit on the dartboard?
   #4

358

Symbols and Numbers Together

When metric measurements are labeled, they have two parts: the physical quantity number and the metric label. quantity number → 43 g ← metric label

Because physical quantities can be large or small, the amounts can be changed by simply multiplying or dividing the number by a power of 10. For example, 43 g can also be written as 43,000 mg (1 gram = 1,000 milligrams).

Use the information in the chart below to learn the prefixes and the quantities they represent.

SI PREFIX TERM	kilo	hecto	deka	root	deci	centi	milli
SYMBOL	k	h	dk		d	c	m
VALUE	1 000	100	10	1	0.1	0.01	0.001

Write the appropriate prefix for the numerical amount or the appropriate numerical amount for the prefix.

1. 100 hecto
2. d 0.1
3. m 1
4. 10 deka
5. 1 000 kilo
6. dk 10
7. h 100
8. 0.01 centi
9. 1 root
10. c 0.01
11. k 1 000
12. 0.001 milli

Write the metric amounts with the correct prefix. (Remember: Root quantities are g = grams, m = meters, L = liters, m² = square meters, m³ = cubic meters.)

13. kilogram kg
14. centimeter cm
15. milliliter mL
16. cubic meters m³
17. dekagram dkg
18. hectoliter hl
19. kilometer km
20. decigram dg

Circle the larger unit in each pair.

21. (kilo) deci
22. milli (centi)
23. (meter) deci
24. deci (deka)
25. deka (hecto)
26. milli (meter)
27. centi (deci)
28. hecto (kilo)

359

It's a Tie

Look at each group of ratios. Circle the group that is equal to the given ratio. Hint: reduce each ratio to its lowest terms.

	Ratio			
A.	1/4	4/8, 6/12, 5/10	(25/100, 3/12, 5/20)	50/100, 6/12, 10/20
B.	5/6	30/40, 9/12, 15/35	10/12, 25/30, 15/35	(25/30, 10/12, 20/24)
C.	4/7	20/35, 12/14, 16/28	(16/28, 12/21, 20/35)	12/21, 24/35, 8/42
D.	2/3	(6/9, 10/15, 18/27)	15/15, 18/27, 4/9	5/15, 3/9, 4/6
E.	1/6	7/42, 2/14, 3/21	(5/30, 6/36, 7/42)	5/25, 6/36, 7/42
F.	2/5	(8/20, 6/15, 4/10)	4/10, 8/20, 9/30	4/10, 6/12, 8/20
G.	3/4	9/12, 12/16, 15/24	6/8, 5/25, 12/16	(6/8, 9/12, 12/16)
H.	1/8	2/16, 4/32, 7/64	2/16, 6/48, 9/56	(4/32, 6/48, 2/16)
I.	3/5	9/15, 6/12, 7/14	(15/25, 12/20, 9/15)	21/30, 15/25, 9/15
J.	5/7	(20/28, 15/21, 10/14)	10/14, 15/21, 25/42	15/21, 20/28, 30/56

360

Cooking for a Crowd

Roland is making spaghetti and meat sauce for a party. Below is a list of ingredients he has.

Old Fashioned Tomato Meat Sauce
(serves 12)

48 ounces whole tomatoes
8 ounces tomato paste
16 ounces tomato sauce
1 ½ pounds ground meat
⅛ pound parsley
2 tablespoons minced garlic
1 ¼ teaspoons oregano

1. How would you rewrite the recipe so that it will serve 8 people or 30 people?
   To serve 8 people, find $\frac{2}{3}$ of each ingredient. To serve 30 people, find 2.5, or $2\frac{1}{2}$, of each ingredient.
2. Rewrite the recipe for each number of guests shown below.

Serve 6	Serve 36
24 ounces whole tomatoes	144 ounces whole tomatoes
4 ounces tomato paste	24 ounces tomato paste
8 ounces tomato sauce	48 ounces tomato sauce
3/4 pound ground meat	4 1/2 pounds ground meat
1/16 pound parsley	3/16 pound parsley
1 tablespoon minced garlic	6 tablespoons minced garlic
5/8 teaspoon oregano	3 3/4 teaspoons oregano

361

Staying in Line

A **line graph** is used to plot information with dots. By connecting the dots, you can see trends in the data collected.

Casey practices skating each day. Her mom made a line graph to show how far she skated each day for one week.

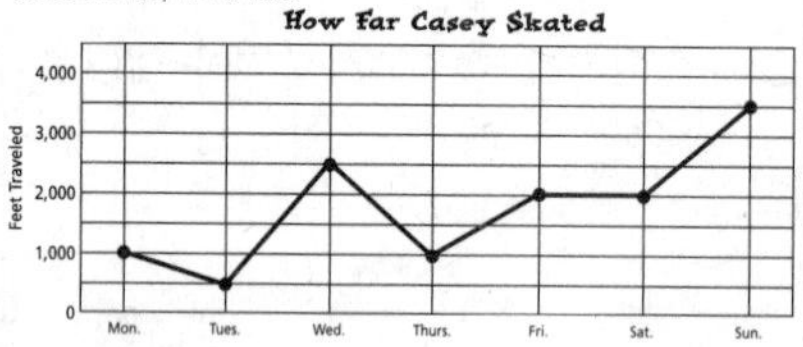
How Far Casey Skated
Feet Traveled
4,000
3,000
2,000
1,000
0
Mon.
Tues.
Wed.
Thurs.
Fri.
Sat.
Sun.

Use the line graph to answer the questions.

- A. How much farther did Casey skate on Wednesday than on Thursday? 1,500 feet
- B. What day did Casey skate the farthest? Sunday
- C. How many feet did Casey skate in all on Saturday and Sunday? 5,500 feet
- D. What was the average number of feet Casey skated each day? (Round to the nearest whole number.) 1,786 feet
- E. If Casey skated twice as far as she did on Wednesday, how far would she have skated? 5,000 feet
- F. In all, how many feet did Casey skate during the week? 12,500 feet
- G. If Casey skates the same amount each week for four weeks, how far will she skate? 50,000 feet
- H. Write a question about the graph for a classmate to answer. Questions will vary.

362

Scream for Ice Cream

At the end of the year, 108 sixth graders had an ice-cream party. This circle graph shows how much of the different flavors of ice cream was served and the number of students who chose each flavor.

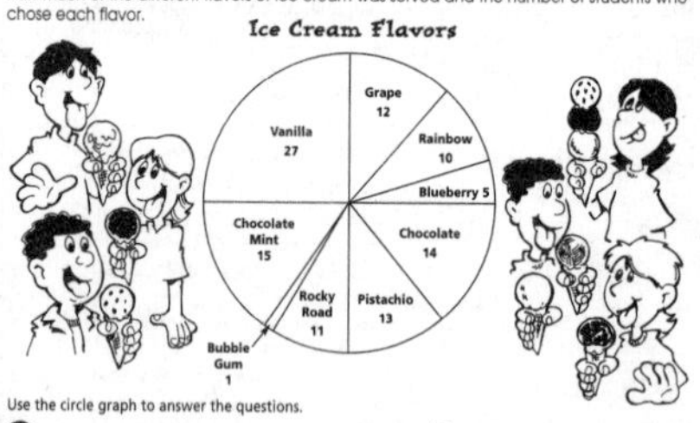
Ice Cream Flavors
Grape 12
Rainbow 10
Blueberry 5
Chocolate 14
Pistachio 13
Rocky Road 11
Bubble Gum 1
Chocolate Mint 15
Vanilla 27

Use the circle graph to answer the questions.

- A. How many of the sixth graders ate pistachio ice cream? 13
- B. What flavor was the most popular? vanilla
  How many students ate that flavor? 27
- C. What was the least popular flavor? bubble gum
  How many students ate that flavor? 1
- D. Rocky road, chocolate mint, and chocolate were all ordered by chocolate lovers. How many kids in all ate these chocolate ice cream flavors? 40
- E. What percentage of students did not eat any kind of chocolate ice cream? (Round to the nearest percent.) 63%
- F. What percentage of students ate grape or blueberry ice cream? (Round to the nearest percent.) 16%
- G. Write a question about the graph for a classmate to answer. Questions will vary.

363

Muscle Mania

Muscles are tough elastic tissues that enable body parts to move. Changes in temperature can affect the muscles. To find out how, try the experiment below at home, and share your results with your class members the next day.

Materials: a bowl large enough to place your hand in ice cubes water warm water pencil paper towels watch or clock with a secondhand

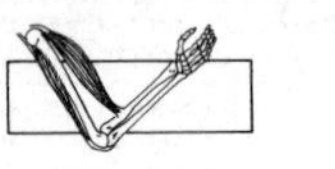

1. Write or print your name 10 times on the back of a separate piece of paper.
2. Place some ice cubes and water in the bowl. Hold your writing hand in the water for 30 seconds. Dry your hand quickly with a paper towel. Write or print your name 10 times in the spaces below.
   Answers will vary.
3. Replace the ice water with warm water. Place your writing hand in the warm water for 30 seconds. Dry your hand quickly with a paper towel. Write or print your name 10 times in the spaces below.
4. Compare the appearance of your handwriting. How did the changes in temperature affect your handwriting samples?
5. How does temperature affect your muscles?

364

Parts of a Flower

Most flowers have four main parts. Each of these parts consists of elements. These parts and elements are listed below. In this activity, you will display some of the parts of a real flower.

Materials: one of the following kinds of flowers: daffodils, roses, lilies, tulips, irises, and phlox make good samples; sharp cutting tool (adult supervision and help is required); paper towels; heavy books or bricks; construction paper or posterboard; glue; black marker

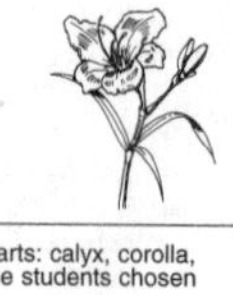

Answer: Most flowers have these four main parts: calyx, corolla, stamens, pistils. The parts and elements of the students chosen flowers should be labeled.

1. After you have collected a good flower sample, have an adult help you make a cross-section of the flower. This can be done by carefully slicing the flower using a sharp cutting tool.
2. Place the cross-section between several sheets of paper towels and press for several days with heavy books or bricks.
3. Carefully remove the paper towel. Attach the pressed flower to a sheet of construction paper or posterboard.
4. Cut out the labels to the right. Attach them to the construction paper or posterboard. Use a black marker to draw lines from the labels to the parts of the flower.

PETALS	ANTHER
POLLEN GRAINS	STIGMA
STYLE	STAMENS
FILAMENT	COROLLA
SEPALS	CALYX
OVARY	OVULE
PISTILS	

365

Roots and Shoots

Plants develop from seeds. In this activity, you will measure the length of the roots and shoots of a plant as it develops from its seeds.

Materials: dried lima beans, paper towels, water, shallow pans, metric ruler, jar, plastic food wrap

DIRECTIONS:

1. Soak some dried lima beans in a jar of water overnight.
2. Place some wet paper towels in the bottom of a shallow pan or dish.
3. Arrange five of the soaked lima beans across the middle of the pan.
4. Cover with several thicknesses of wet paper towels.
5. Wrap the pan with plastic food wrap to prevent rapid evaporation of the water.
6. Each day, carefully uncover the beans and observe any growth of roots or shoots. Once growth begins, measure the lengths of the roots and shoots in centimeters.
7. Keep a record of your measurements and observations in the chart below.

Day	Observations	Length of Roots (cm)	Length of Shoots (cm)
1		Answers will vary.	
2			
3			
4			
5			
6			
7			

367

A Special Group of Animals

Some animals have backbones, and some do not. Unscramble the letters to spell the names of some animals that have backbones. Print the answers in the spaces to the right. The circled letters will then identify what animals that have backbones are called. Print those letters at the bottom of the page.

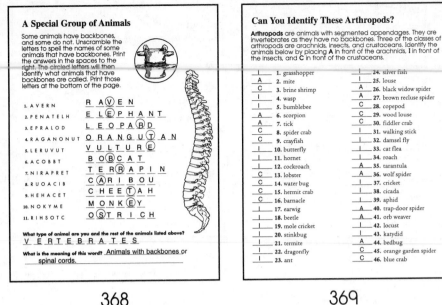

1. A V E R N — R A V E N
2. P E N A T E L H — E L E P H A N T
3. E P R A L O D — L E O P A R D
4. R A G A N O N U T — O R A N G U T A N
5. L E R U V U T — V U L T U R E
6. A C O B B T — B O B C A T
7. N I R A P R E T — T E R R A P I N
8. R U O A C I B — C A R I B O U
9. H E H A C E T — C H E E T A H
10. N O K Y M E — M O N K E Y
11. R I H S O T C — O S T R I C H

What type of animal are you and the rest of the animals listed above?
V E R T E B R A T E S

What is the meaning of this word? Animals with backbones or spinal cords.

368

Can You Identify These Arthropods?

Arthropods are animals with segmented appendages. They are invertebrates as they have no backbone. Three of the classes of arthropods are arachnids, insects, and crustaceans. Identify the animals below by placing **A** in front of the arachnids, **I** in front of the insects, and **C** in front of the crustaceans.

I 1. grasshopper	I 24. silver fish
A 2. mite	I 25. louse
C 3. brine shrimp	A 26. black widow spider
I 4. wasp	A 27. brown recluse spider
I 5. bumblebee	C 28. copepod
A 6. scorpion	C 29. wood louse
A 7. tick	C 30. fiddler crab
C 8. spider crab	I 31. walking stick
C 9. crayfish	I 32. damsel fly
I 10. butterfly	I 33. cat flea
I 11. hornet	I 34. roach
I 12. cockroach	A 35. tarantula
C 13. lobster	A 36. wolf spider
C 14. water bug	I 37. cricket
C 15. hermit crab	I 38. cicada
C 16. barnacle	I 39. aphid
I 17. earwig	A 40. trap-door spider
I 18. beetle	A 41. orb weaver
I 19. mole cricket	I 42. locust
I 20. stinkbug	I 43. katydid
I 21. termite	I 44. bedbug
I 22. dragonfly	C 45. orange garden spider
I 23. ant	C 46. blue crab

369

Descriptive Animals

The world is filled with a lot of awesome animals. Read the clues below to identify the name of each animal.

1. I live in a high place. — mountain / gorilla
2. I have a head-covering like a king. — crowned / crane
3. I react to funny jokes. — laughing / hyena
4. I have lost my hair. — bald / eagle
5. I am very large in size. — giant / panda
6. My head could be a tool. — hammerhead / shark
7. My head is the color of a penny. — copperhead / snake
8. My tail is like a baby's toy. — rattle / snake
9. I live in open spaces out west. — prairie / dog
10. My color is the same as that on a stop sign. — red / fox
11. I do not quack with my bill. — duckbill / platypus
12. I soar like a glider. — flying / squirrel
13. I have a royal name. — monarch / butterfly
14. My shape looks like something that is seen in the night sky. — star / fish
15. I taste good with peanut butter and bread. — jelly / fish
16. I appear in the sky as an arc after rain. — rainbow / trout
17. I live in tropical waters. — sea / horse
18. I live in the cold Arctic. — polar / bear
19. I live in tiny grains of rocks in the sea. — sand / dollar
20. I cover a lawn. — grass / hopper
21. I have a hot flame. — fire / fly
22. I could be a member of the Armed Services. — army / ant
23. I live on our planet. — earth / worm
24. I like to live alone. — hermit

370

Animal Adaptations and Behavior

Animals of all kinds have a lot of interesting ways in which they adapt to their environment and in which they behave. To learn about some of these adaptations and behaviors, match the animals and adaptations or behaviors below.

COLUMN I

1. C blue jay
2. K bobcat
3. D woodpecker
4. J crow
5. I tree frog
6. M heron
7. N hornet
8. A eagle
9. B turkey
10. G screech owl
11. O robin
12. F cicada
13. H opossum
14. E gray fox
15. L big brown bat

COLUMN II

A. A bird that builds a nest called an aerie
B. A large game bird that rests in trees at night
C. A blue-colored bird that squawks loudly when disturbed
D. This bird drills holes in trees in search of insects for food.
E. A fox that prefers to live in woodlands and often climbs trees
F. The males of this type of insect make loud sounds on warm summer evenings.
G. A large-eyed bird that searches for food at night
H. A marsupial that sometimes avoids danger by "playing dead"
I. An amphibian that has sticky pads on its feet to help it climb trees
J. An all-black bird that caws
K. A wild cat that catches its prey by pouncing on small animals
L. A furry mammal that has a wingspan of about 12 inches
M. A long-legged wading bird that nests in flocks
N. A stinging insect that builds a paper nest
O. A red-breasted bird whose arrival signals the beginning of spring

371

Learned Behavior

Read about Ivan Pavlov's famous stimulus-response experiments he did with dogs in Russia in the early 1900s. The reaction of the dogs was a learned behavior. Swimming, riding a bicycle, or driving a car are learned behaviors.

In the chart, list some learned behaviors the animals do.

ANIMALS	LEARNED BEHAVIORS
dogs	Answers will vary.
cats	
horses	
birds	
circus animals	
dolphins	
elephants	
chimpanzees	
cows	
humans	

372

The World's Living Things

The chart below is an environmental box score for the world's endangered or threatened animals and plants. Among the endangered species are the cheetah, bald eagle, American crocodile, floating sorrel, and snakeroot. Use library resources to track down the names and ranges (names of locations where species are found) of 10 endangered or threatened species. (Include 5 animals and 5 plants, but be sure you don't include any of the species named above.)

GROUP	ENDANGERED U.S.	ENDANGERED FOREIGN	THREATENED U.S.	THREATENED FOREIGN	TOTAL LISTINGS
Mammals	55	252	9	19	335
Birds	74	178	16	6	274
Reptiles	14	65	19	14	112
Amphibians	7	8	5	1	21
Fishes	65	11	40	0	116
Snails	15	1	7	0	23
Clams	51	2	6	0	59
Crustaceans	14	0	3	0	17
Insects	20	4	9	0	33
Arachnids	5	0	0	0	5
Animal Subtotal	**320**	**521**	**114**	**40**	**995**
Flowering Plants	406	1	90	0	497
Conifers	2	0	0	2	4
Ferns and Others	26	0	2	0	28
Plant Subtotal	**434**	**1**	**92**	**2**	**529**
Grand Total	**754**	**522**	**206**	**42**	**1,524**

Five Endangered/Threatened
Animals — Range
Plants — Range

Answers will vary.

To save endangered and threatened species, it is vital to protect their habitats and to understand the role of each species within Earth's ecosystems. On a sheet of paper, describe the habitat and ecosystem of one endangered or threatened species.

373

Where Animals Live

Fascinating animals live all over the world! Learn about the places where some of them make their homes. Use your research skills to locate the continent on which each of the animals listed below lives. Match the animals listed on the left with their continents on the right.

Animal

1. G vicuña
2. A zebra
3. C snow leopard
4. B Rocky Mountain goat
5. C kangaroo
6. D red deer
7. E platypus
8. C emperor penguin
9. C saiga
10. E koala
11. C woolly monkey
12. A gorilla
13. B moose
14. C giant panda
15. C dingo
16. B roadrunner
17. A ostrich
18. G coati
19. C orangutan
20. B prairie dog

Continent

A. Africa
B. North America
C. Asia
D. Europe
E. Australia
F. Antarctica
G. South America

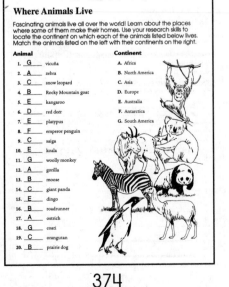

374

Environmental Patterns

Use a climate map in an atlas to locate the world's major rain forests. Then, using a pencil, shade in the shape of the major rain forest areas on the map below. What patterns do the shaded areas show? Use the completed map and an atlas to answer the questions.

1. Where are the three major rain forest areas located? Brazil, Indonesia, and West Central Africa

2. Use the map's scale in an atlas to measure the approximate distance between each major rain forest area and your community. Write the distances. Answers will vary.

3. In what kind of climate are rain forests found? tropical

4. Compare and contrast your community's climate and the climate of the rain forests. Answers will vary.

5. How is climate related to the distribution of rain forests worldwide? Rain forests need constant hot/warm temperatures and high precipitation, which are conditions found at or near the equator.

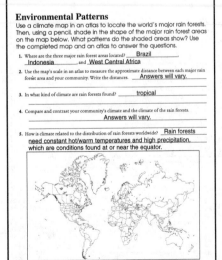

375

Animals and Plants Living in Biomes

Plants and animals of the world live in many different kinds of biomes. A **biome** is a community of plants and animals that lives in a large geographical area that has a similar climate. Identify the biome of each of the animals and plants listed below. Use the following letters for the identifications:

D desert	G grassland	R tropical rain forest	
T taiga	TU tundra	F temperate forest	

1. TU low shrubs
2. G aardvark
3. D cactus
4. G sagebrush
5. T mule
6. G grasses
7. F oak
8. TU arctic fox
9. D rattlesnake
10. TU lichens
11. R parrot
12. G prairie dog
13. TU snowshoe hare
14. F maple
15. R kapok tree
16. R gibbon
17. TU caribou
18. T conifers
19. G pronghorn
20. D roadrunner
21. F tree ferns
22. F elm
23. TU lemming
24. D kangaroo rat
25. F brown bear
26. D Gila monster
27. R sloth
28. R jaguar
29. TU polar bear
30. F salamander
31. G zebra
32. D scorpion
33. R monkey
34. G African elephant
35. D dingo
36. F jack rabbit
37. F skunk
38. G ostrich
39. R Indian elephant
40. R mahogany
41. G squirrel
42. TU reindeer
43. T spruce tree
44. G giraffe
45. R raccoon
46. T fir tree

376

377 — July 20, 1969

On July 20, 1969, the first person stepped onto the surface of the moon. He said, ". . . one small step for a man, one giant leap for mankind." Identify this person by solving the clues and writing the words in the spaces. The circled letters will then spell out the person's name.

1. Latin word for *moon* — l u n a
2. Our moon is a _____ of Earth. — s a t e l l i t e
3. During a lunar _____, the moon becomes dark when it passes through the shadow of Earth. — e c l i p s e
4. The space mission to the moon was called _____. — A p o l l o
5. Letters that stand for the organization that conducts research into problems of flight within and beyond Earth's atmosphere. — N A S A
6. American space scientists and explorers are called _____. — a s t r o n a u t s
7. The moon's average distance from Earth is about 240,000 _____. — m i l e s
8. The moon's surface is pitted with _____. — c r a t e r s
9. The circling of the spacecraft around the moon is called its _____. — o r b i t
10. During a _____ eclipse, the moon comes between the sun and Earth. — s o l a r
11. A _____ rocket carried the first astronauts to the moon. — S a t u r n
12. The moon's _____ is about one-sixth that of Earth's. — g r a v i t y

The first person to step upon the moon was
N e i l A r m s t r o n g

378 — A Magic Square of Weather

Below are words relating to weather. Write the number of the word which fits a clue in a box on the grid. If you have matched the correct numbers in all 16 squares, the sums of the rows, columns, and diagonals will be the same. This is called a magic square.

1. atmosphere
2. troposphere
3. ionosphere
4. ozone
5. jet streams
6. stratosphere
7. mesosphere
8. exosphere
9. wind
10. greenhouse effect
11. convection
12. sea breeze
13. land breeze
14. doldrums
15. trade winds
16. front

mass of air that surrounds earth	air that rushes in from the north and south to warm the air along the equator	calm areas of Earth where there is little wind	a gas in the upper part of Earth's atmosphere
1	15	14	4
cold air from the ocean that moves into the warmer land	the zone of the atmosphere above the troposphere	the zone of the atmosphere above the stratosphere	a movement of air close to Earth's surface
12	6	7	9
the outer zone of Earth's atmosphere	air above Earth that is warmed by the reflection of the sun's rays and is prevented from easily passing back into space	transfer of heat by currents of air or water	strong, steady winds high in the atmosphere; used by pilots
8	10	11	5
cold air from land that moves out to warmer air over oceans	the zone of the atmosphere which affects the transmission of radio waves	the zone of the atmosphere which is closest to the surface of Earth	the line along which air masses meet
13	3	2	16

What is the magic number for this puzzle? 34

Can you discover other number combinations in the puzzle which give you the same answer?
4 squares in each corner, 4 squares in the center

379 — Glaciers

Glaciers are thick masses of ice created by the accumulation and crystallization of snow. Match the clues about glaciers with the terms below.

1. B VALLEY GLACIER
2. G CIRQUE
3. J CONTINENTAL GLACIER
4. C CREVASSE
5. L DRUMLIN
6. K END MORAINE
7. N ESKER
8. I FIORD
9. M KETTLE
10. E PLUCKING
11. F ROCK FLOUR
12. D SURGE
13. H TARN
14. A TILL

A. material deposited directly by a glacier
B. glacier generally confined to mountain valleys
C. a crack in the glacier caused by movement
D. rapid movement of a glacier
E. the process whereby a glacier loosens and lifts rocks into the ice
F. pulverized rock caused by a glacier's abrasion
G. a bowl-shaped depression at the head of a glacial valley
H. a small lake formed after a glacier has melted away
I. a U-shaped depression formed by a glacier below sea level in a river valley that is flooded by the ocean
J. massive accumulations of ice that cover a large portion of a landmass
K. a hilly ridge of material formed at the end of a valley glacier
L. an oval-shaped hill consisting of rock debris
M. a depression left in part of a glacier formed by the melting of a block of ice
N. ridges of sand and gravel deposited by flowing rivers of melted ice through a glacier

380 — The Science of Earthquakes

An earthquake is a sudden shock of Earth's surface. Identify the name of the study of earthquakes by reading the clues below and writing the answers. The circled letters will spell out the name of this science. Print the name at the bottom of the page.

1. large ocean waves created by an earthquake — t s u n a m i
2. These waves, created by the earthquake, are the strongest at the epicenter. — s e i s m i c
3. the area on the surface of Earth directly above the occurrence of the earthquake — e p i c e n t e r
4. famous earthquake fault in California — S a n A n d r e a s
5. the instrument used to record earthquake waves — s e i s m o g r a p h
6. the origin of an earthquake under the surface of Earth — f o c u s
7. a breaking point in layers of Earth — f a u l t
8. the vibrational tremors sent out from an earthquake — s h o c k w a v e s
9. the name given to the area around the Pacific Ocean in which many earthquakes occur — R i n g o f F i r e
10. the fastest waves from an earthquake; also called push waves — p r i m a r y

The science of the study of earthquakes is s e i s m o l o g y

381 — An Electrical Message

By selecting the correct answers and darkening certain letters as described below in the grid, the remaining letters will spell out a message concerning electrical energy.

1. A safety device for circuits with a piece of wire that melts to break the circuit is a(n) _____.
   switch—Mark out all the letter **A's** in the grid.
   terminal—Mark out all the letter **O's** in the grid.
   fuse—Mark out all the letter **B's** in the grid.
   ammeter—Mark out all the letter **L's** in the grid.
2. The path followed by an electric current is called a(n) circuit.
   voltage—Mark out all the letter **C's** in the grid.
   resistance—Mark out all the letter **F's** in the grid.
   amperage—Mark out all the letter **G's** in the grid.
   circuit—Mark out all the letter **D's** in the grid.
3. An instrument that detects an electric current is a(n) ammeter
   ammeter—Mark out all the letter **K's** in the grid.
   anemometer—Mark out all the letter **H's** in the grid.
   psychrometer—Mark out all the letter **M's** in the grid.
   barometer—Mark out all the letter **R's** in the grid.
4. A device that controls the flow of current by making or breaking a circuit is a(n) switch
   terminal—Mark out all the letter **N's** in the grid.
   switch—Mark out all the letter **P's** in the grid.
   resistor—Mark out all the letter **S's** in the grid.
   transistor—Mark out all the letter **T's** in the grid.

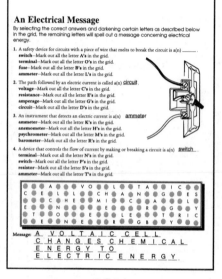

Message: A V O L T A I C C E L L
C H A N G E S C H E M I C A L
E N E R G Y T O
E L E C T R I C E N E R G Y.

382 — Energy From Many Sources

Energy comes from a lot of sources. To find out what some sources are, match the terms below with their definitions to complete the crossword puzzle about energy sources.

AMPERE, ATOM, BIOMASS, COAL, ENERGY, GENERATOR, GEOTHERMAL, HYDROELECTRIC, KILOWATT, NUCLEAR, RENEWABLE, SOLAR, TURBINE, URANIUM, VOLT, WATT

Across
2. the capacity for action or to do work
4. the unit of measurement of electric power
7. 1000 watts
10. electric power that is generated by moving water
12. a radioactive element used to produce fuel in nuclear plants
13. capable of being replaced or restored by natural ecological practices or good management practices
14. waste material that is converted to methane gas for fuel
16. the unit of electric pressure

Down
1. the smallest unit of an element that can exist alone
3. underground hot water or steam used to produce electricity
5. unit of electric measure that indicates the flow of electric current
6. a machine in which mechanical energy is converted to electricity
8. an engine in which curved blades are turned by water, steam, or gas
9. relating to the nucleus of an atom
11. solid, black or brown fossil fuel
15. relating to the sun's energy

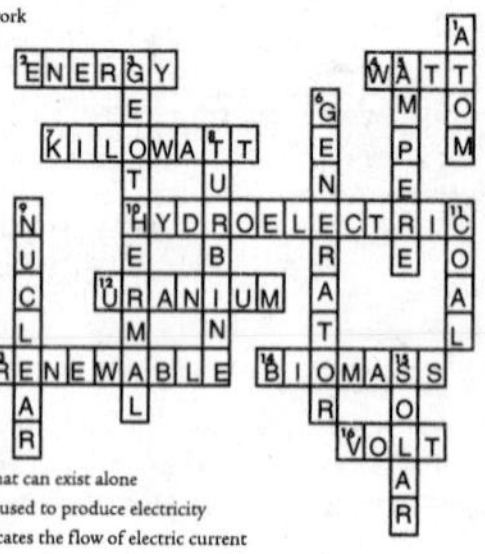

(Crossword answers shown: ENERGY, WATT, ATOM, KILOWATT, GENERATOR, AMPERE, HYDROELECTRIC, NUCLEAR, URANIUM, COAL, RENEWABLE, BIOMASS, TURBINE, SOLAR, VOLT)

383 — Testing Your Knowledge of Acids and Bases

Acid is any of a group of compounds with certain similar properties. **Base** is any substance that can react with an acid to decrease or neutralize its acidic properties. Use reference materials to help you test your knowledge of acids and bases. Write a **T** before each true statement and an **F** before each false statement.

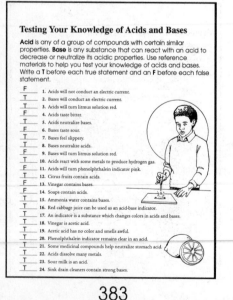

F 1. Acids will not conduct an electric current.
T 2. Bases will conduct an electric current.
T 3. Acids will turn litmus solution red.
F 4. Acids taste bitter.
T 5. Acids neutralize bases.
T 6. Bases taste sour.
T 7. Bases feel slippery.
T 8. Bases neutralize acids.
F 9. Bases will turn litmus solution red.
T 10. Acids react with some metals to produce hydrogen gas.
T 11. Acids will turn phenolphthalein indicator pink.
T 12. Citrus fruits contain acids.
T 13. Vinegar contains bases.
F 14. Soaps contain acids.
T 15. Ammonia water contains bases.
T 16. Red cabbage juice can be used as an acid-base indicator.
T 17. An indicator is a substance which changes colors in acids and bases.
T 18. Vinegar is acetic acid.
T 19. Acetic acid has no color and smells awful.
T 20. Phenolphthalein indicator remains clear in an acid.
T 21. Some medicinal compounds help neutralize stomach acid.
T 22. Acids dissolve many metals.
T 23. Sour milk is an acid.
T 24. Sink drain cleaners contain strong bases.

384 — The Mohs Hardness Scale for Minerals

In 1822, Friedrich Mohs, a German mineralogist, designed a hardness scale for minerals. Ten minerals are used for comparisons in the hardness of other minerals.

Unscramble the letters below to identify the 10 minerals in the scale. Print the words in the spaces.

1. LCTA — T A L C
2. SPYMUG — G Y P S U M
3. TILECAC — C A L C I T E
4. TIRELUFO — F L U O R I T E
5. TAPITEA — A P A T I T E
6. DPASFERL — F E L D S P A R
7. ZARQUT — Q U A R T Z
8. POZAT — T O P A Z
9. DOCRUMUN — C O R U N D U M
10. MINDADO — D I A M O N D

After you have identified the 10 minerals, use reference materials to describe some of the physical properties of each mineral.

Answers will vary.

1. _____
2. _____
3. _____
4. _____
5. _____
6. _____
7. _____
8. _____
9. _____
10. _____

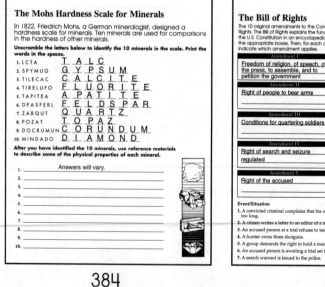

385 — The Bill of Rights

The 10 original amendments to the Constitution of the United States are called the Bill of Rights. The Bill of Rights explains the fundamental liberties of the American people. Find the U.S. Constitution in an encyclopedia or an almanac and write the amendments in the appropriate boxes. Then, for each of the events or situations described below, indicate which amendment applies.

Amendment I
Freedom of religion, of speech, of the press, to assemble, and to petition the government

Amendment II
Right of people to bear arms

Amendment III
Conditions for quartering soldiers

Amendment IV
Right of search and seizure regulated

Amendment V
Right of the accused

Amendment VI
Right to a speedy and public trial

Amendment VII
Right of trial by jury

Amendment VIII
Limits excessive bail or fines and cruel punishment

Amendment IX
Rights kept by the people

Amendment X
Powers of the states and people

Event/Situation	Amendment Number
1. A convicted criminal complains that his or her jail sentence is too long.	VIII
2. A citizen writes a letter to an editor of a newspaper.	I
3. An accused person at a trial refuses to testify.	V
4. A hunter owns three shotguns.	II
5. A group demands the right to hold a meeting in a public park.	I
6. An accused person is awaiting a trial set for next week.	VI
7. A search warrant is issued to the police.	IV

Daily Learning Drills Grade 6

How a Bill Becomes a Law

Passing a law is a multi-step process. Both houses of the U.S. Congress, the Senate and the House of Representatives, have to approve a bill before it can become a law. Many bills are subjected to considerable debate, and a bill can be amended or rejected at many points throughout the process. If a bill is approved by Congress, it goes to the president who can either approve or reject it. The basic steps of a bill becoming a law are listed in random order below. Your task is to place the steps in correct order by putting the letter next to the step inside the correct circle on the line along the bottom of the page. For this activity, assume that the bill started in the U.S. House of Representatives.

A. The bill back to the floor of the Senate for consideration.

B. Once passed by both houses, the bill goes to the president who hopefully signs it into law.

C. The Senate committee revises the bill and then approves it.

D. The vice president of the United States, the presiding officer of the Senate, assigns the proposed bill to one of its standing committees to be studied.

E. A representative introduces a bill in the House.

F. The bill is now introduced to the Senate.

G. The Senate votes on the bill and passes it.

H. The House committee recommends to the House that the bill be passed.

I. The House of Representatives passes the bill with a simple majority.

J. Once passed by the Senate, a conference committee, comprised of members from both houses of Congress, works out any differences concerning the bill.

K. The revised bill is sent back to both houses for final approval.

L. The bill is assigned to one of about 20 standing House committees to be studied.

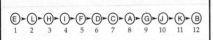

ⓔ	ⓛ	ⓗ	ⓘ	ⓕ	ⓓ	ⓒ	ⓐ	ⓖ	ⓙ	ⓚ	ⓑ
1	2	3	4	5	6	7	8	9	10	11	12

386

Election Results

Maryville County elections were held today! Since closing the polls at 7:00 P.M., the election committee has been busy tallying the votes. As of 8:15, 90% of all votes had been counted. Here are the results at the present time.

Candidate	Office	Political Party	# of Votes
K. Foran	County Clerk	Democrat	245
H. Lietz	County Clerk	Republican	559
B. Warren	County Clerk	Independent	42
C. Aircheson	Family Court Judge	Democrat	341
K. Bennet	Family Court Judge	Republican	505
G. Alle	Council Member	Democrat	180
S. Vitale	Council Member	Republican	333
C. Howard	Council Member	Independent	333
S. Callahan	Selectman	Democrat	291
A. McEarlene	Selectman	Republican	555
H. Kaplan	Dogcatcher	Republican	18
N. Ross	Dogcatcher	Independent	828

Complete the following.
1. Which political party seems to be most popular in Maryville County? **Republican**
2. List the candidates who will probably be throwing celebration parties. **H. Lietz, K. Bennet, A. McEarlene, N. Ross**
3. If C. Howard were informed of the results so far, how would he or she feel? **impatient, nervous, anxious**
4. How will B. Warren feel tomorrow? **disappointed** How do you know? **He lost the election.**
5.
6. How will the dogs in Maryville County respond to N. Ross? **They won't like him/her; they will run away.**

387

Harlem Renaissance

New York in the 1920s and 1930s saw not only the rise of Ella Fitzgerald and jazz music, but a burst of creativity in all areas of art. A myriad of blacks had recently migrated to northern cities, the economy was "soarin'," and the cultural atmosphere was ripe for change. As a result, Harlem became the place for black artists to write, paint, sing, dance, and act in the early decades of the twentieth century.

Choose one of the early twentieth-century black artists below to study in depth. Write a brief biography of the artist of your choice. Then list works by the artist and include an illustration either of your own creation or copied from another source.

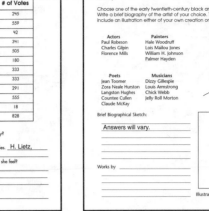

Actors	Painters
Paul Robeson	Hale Woodruff
Charles Gilpin	Lois Mailou Jones
Florence Mills	William H. Johnson
	Palmer Hayden

Poets	Musicians
Jean Toomer	Dizzy Gillespie
Zora Neale Hurston	Louis Armstrong
Langston Hughes	Chick Webb
Countee Cullen	Jelly Roll Morton
Claude McKay	

Brief Biographical Sketch:

Answers will vary.

Works by _____

Illustration of _____

388

Ethnic Concentrations

Americans can trace their ethnic roots back to countries all over the world. Ethnic groups are not equally distributed across the United States. Instead, they are concentrated or clustered in particular areas. The map below shows ethnic group concentrations in four regions of the United States as determined by the U.S. Census Bureau. In order for a particular ethnic group to be considered a "concentration," it had to consist of 100,000 or more population with at least 35% in the region. The percent of each group is in parentheses on the map. Answer the questions.

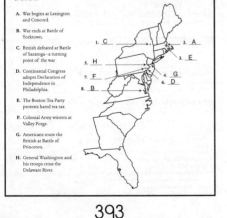

1. Which ethnic group has 91 percent of 100,000 or more of its members concentrated in the South? **Acadian/Cajun**
2. In which region is there a Norwegian concentration? **Midwest**
3. Which region has the most ethnic concentrations? **West**
4. From where do all of the Midwest's ethnic concentrations originate? **Europe**
5. Four of the eight ethnic concentrations in the South originate from the same area. What is the area? **Latin America**
6. In which region is there a Chinese concentration? **West**
7. Which ethnic groups have concentrations in more than one region? **Haitian, Polish, Portuguese, Nicaraguan**
8. How many different ethnic groups are listed on the map? **44**

390

Searching for Facts

Listed in the box are the names of 10 different cultural groups. Choose one of the groups to research. Then use an encyclopedia to answer the questions about the group's traditional way of life.

Cultural Groups	
Dayak or Dyak	Sioux
Zulu	Eskimo
Asante or Ashanti	Berbers
Maoris	Wampanoag
Basques	Aborigines

Questions
1. What cultural group did you investigate? **Answers will vary.**
2. Where does the cultural group live? _____
3. What is the climate like? _____
4. How does the group get food? _____
5. What kinds of work do the people do? _____
6. What are some common plants and animals in the area? _____
7. What are the major geographic features of the area (such as mountains, desert, seashore, forest, river, valley, etc.)? _____
8. What is the major form of transportation of the people? _____
9. What are some of the typical foods they eat? _____
10. What type of shelter(s) do the people live in? _____
11. What kinds of clothing fo the people wear? _____

391

The Religion of Islam

Islam is one of the world's largest religions. The followers of Islam are called Muslims, and there are over one billion of them worldwide. Muslims believe that God's teachings were revealed to the Prophet Mohammed, a seventh-century Arab. These teachings were written down in the Koran, Islam's holy book. Listed below are some of the countries in which many Muslims live. Use an atlas to find the countries. Label the countries (using the numbers found next to them) and shade them in on the map below.

1. Pakistan
2. Afghanistan
3. Iraq
4. Syria
5. Turkey
6. Albania
7. Iran
8. Egypt
9. Sudan
10. Libya
11. Tunisia
12. Algeria
13. Morocco
14. Niger
15. Chad
16. Mali
17. Mauritania
18. Somalia
19. Kuwait
20. Senegal
21. Yemen
22. Oman
23. Saudi Arabia
24. Jordan
25. Lebanon
26. Malaysia
27. Indonesia
28. Burkina Faso
29. Bangladesh
30. Kazakhstan

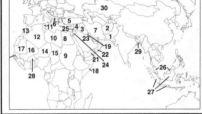

392

Revolutionary War

Many of the important events related to the American Revolution occurred in Massachusetts, New York, Pennsylvania, New Jersey, and Virginia. Some of these important events are listed below. Match the events with the places where they occurred by writing the correct letter of each event on the line that points to its place on the map. Use classroom and library resources to check your answers.

A. War begins at Lexington and Concord.

B. War ends at Battle of Yorktown.

C. British defeated at Battle of Saratoga—a turning point of the war.

D. Continental Congress adopts Declaration of Independence in Philadelphia.

E. The Boston Tea Party protests hated tea tax.

F. Colonial Army winters at Valley Forge.

G. Americans route the British at Battle of Princeton.

H. General Washington and his troops cross the Delaware River.

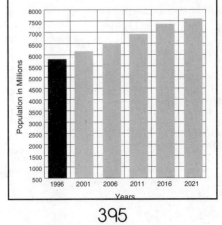

393

Using Latitude and Longitude

Locations on Earth's surface are measured using imaginary lines. that run north and south along Earth's surface are called longitude, and lines that run parallel to the equator are called latitude. Intersecting lines of latitude and longitude form a grid on Earth's surface and help us locate places.

Latitude is the distance in degrees north or south from Earth's equator (0 degrees) as measured through 90 degrees. Longitude is the distance in degrees or time east or west from the prime meridian (0 degrees) as measured through 180 degrees. Each and every place on Earth's surface has an "address" that consists of intersecting lines of latitude and longitude.

Using a globe or an atlas, find the intersecting lines of latitude and longitude below. On the lines provided, write the name of the country in which each intersection is located.

	Latitude	Longitude	Country
1.	52° north	0°	Great Britain
2.	30° north	30° east	South Africa
3.	52° north	21° east	Poland
4.	40° north	100° west	United States
5.	10° north	70° west	Venezuela
6.	20° south	140° east	Australia
7.	30° north	110° east	China
8.	30° north	40° east	Saudi Arabia
9.	60° north	90° east	Russia
10.	10° north	30° east	Sudan
11.	30° south	60° west	Argentina
12.	10° south	50° west	Brazil
13.	0°	110° east	Indonesia
14.	40° north	140° east	Japan
15.	10° south	20° east	Angola
16.	50° north	10° east	Germany
17.	30° north	110° west	Mexico
18.	60° north	10° east	Norway

394

Graphing the World's Population

The world's population was estimated to be 5.8 billion in 1996, and it is projected to increase by about 75 million people each year for the next 25 years. Fill in the bar graph to show the world's population projections at five-year increments. The bar for 1996 is already done.

Population in Millions (y-axis: 500 to 8000)
Years (x-axis): 1996, 2001, 2006, 2011, 2016, 2021

395

The Shape of States

Like a piece of jigsaw puzzle, each of the 50 states in the U.S. has its own unique shape and particular location. What kind of mental picture do you have of the states? Write the names of the states that border each of the states below. Use a map of of the United States to help you.

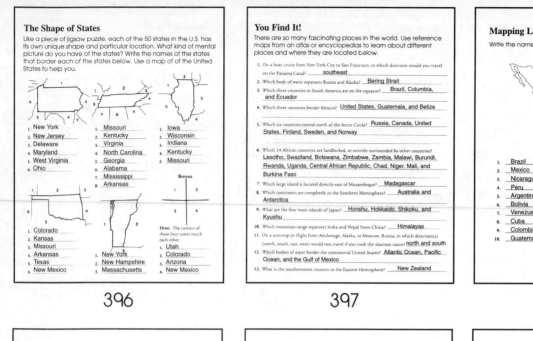

1. New York
2. New Jersey
3. Delaware
4. Maryland
5. West Virginia
6. Ohio

1. Missouri
2. Kentucky
3. Virginia
4. North Carolina
5. Georgia
6. Alabama
7. Mississippi
8. Arkansas

1. Iowa
2. Wisconsin
3. Indiana
4. Kentucky
5. Missouri

1. Colorado
2. Kansas
3. Missouri
4. Arkansas
5. Texas
6. New Mexico

1. New York
2. New Hampshire
3. Massachusetts

Bonus

Hint: The corners of these four states touch each other.

1. Utah
2. Colorado
3. Arizona
4. New Mexico

396

You Find It!

There are so many fascinating places in the world. Use reference maps from an atlas or encyclopedias to learn about different places and where they are located below.

1. On a boat cruise from New York City to San Francisco, in which direction would you travel on the Panama Canal? __southeast__
2. Which body of water separates Russia and Alaska? __Bering Strait__
3. Which three countries in South America are on the equator? __Brazil, Columbia, and Ecuador__
4. Which three countries border Mexico? __United States, Guatemala, and Belize__
5. Which six countries extend north of the Arctic Circle? __Russia, Canada, United States, Finland, Sweden, and Norway__
6. Which 14 African countries are landlocked, or entirely surrounded by other countries? __Lesotho, Swaziland, Botswana, Zimbabwe, Zambia, Malawi, Burundi, Rwanda, Uganda, Central African Republic, Chad, Niger, Mali, and Burkina Faso__
7. Which large island is located directly east of Mozambique? __Madagascar__
8. Which continents are completely in the Southern Hemisphere? __Australia and Antarctica__
9. What are the four main islands of Japan? __Honshu, Hokkaido, Shikoku, and Kyushu__
10. Which mountain range separates India and Nepal from China? __Himalayas__
11. On a nonstop jet flight from Anchorage, Alaska, to Moscow, Russia, in which direction(s) (north, south, east, west) would you travel if you took the shortest route? __north and south__
12. Which bodies of water border the continental United States? __Atlantic Ocean, Pacific Ocean, and the Gulf of Mexico__
13. What is the southernmost country in the Eastern Hemisphere? __New Zealand__

397

Mapping Latin America

Write the name of each country on the lines below.

1. Brazil
2. Mexico
3. Nicaragua
4. Peru
5. Argentina
6. Bolivia
7. Venezuela
8. Cuba
9. Colombia
10. Guatemala

398

Mapping Europe

Write the name of each country on the lines below.

1. United Kingdom
2. Spain
3. France
4. Germany
5. Italy
6. Romania
7. Poland
8. Ukraine
9. Russia
10. Sweden

399

Mapping Africa

Write the name of each country on the lines below.

1. Egypt
2. Lybia
3. Algeria
4. Morocco
5. Nigeria
6. Ethiopia
7. Kenya
8. Mozambique
9. South Africa
10. Madagascar

400

Mapping Asia

Write the name of each country on the lines below.

1. Japan
2. China
3. Mongolia
4. Kazakhstan
5. Afghanistan
6. India
7. Indonesia
8. Philippines
9. South Korea
10. Thailand

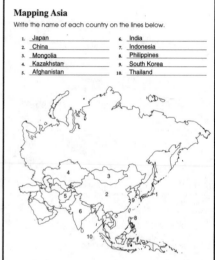

401

Marvels of the World

Some of the world's most splendid natural and man-made landmarks are listed below. Your task is to use maps and other references to locate each landmark and gather information about its importance. Briefly describe an important characteristic of each landmark in the spaces provided.

1. The Great Sphinx
   Egypt (giant stone statue of lion with a human face)
2. The Great Wall
   China (nearly 4,000 miles, the longest structure ever built)
3. The Matterhorn
   between Switzerland and Italy (a steep-sided mountain noted for its distinct shape)
4. The Taj Mahal
   India (a tomb for a ruler's wife; considered to be the most beautiful building)
5. The Eiffel Tower
   France (admired for its distinct shape; tallest structure in Paris)
6. Mount Fuji
   Japan (sacred and beautiful mountain; Japan's highest)
7. Victoria Falls
   between Zambia and Zimbabwe (spectacular waterfall)
8. The Grand Canyon
   United States (awesome mile-deep canyon)
9. Kilimanjaro
   between Tanzania and Kenya (coffee is grown on lower slopes of this mountain)
10. The Colosseum
   Italy (arena where Romans watched gladiators fight)
11. The Alhambra Palace
   Spain (grand example of Moorish architecture)
12. The Parthenon
   Greece (temple where ancient Greeks gathered)
13. Buckingham Palace
   Britain (residence of the royal family)
14. Ayers Rock
   Australia (giant, solitary rock that rises spectacularly from the ground)
15. Leaning Tower of Pisa
   Pisa, Italy (a famous, leaning bell tower)
16. St. Basil's Church
   Russia (famous church in Moscow)
17. Mount Everest
   between Nepal and Tibet (world's highest mountain)
18. Machu Picchu
   Peru (ancient Inca ruins)
19. Tikal
   Guatemala (ancient Maya ruins)
20. fiords
   Norway (steep, rock-walled sea inlets)

402

Flags Around the World

Each country's flag has features that make it unique. Key features of some national flags are listed below. Use your information-gathering skills to correctly match the features with the countries. Write the names of the countries in the spaces. Then identify the countries by using the numbers on the map.

Canada
Australia
Switzerland
France
Kenya
Japan
Singapore
Trinidad and Tobago
Israel
Democratic Republic of the Congo

1. red maple leaf
2. the union jack in one corner; a larger, seven-pointed star and five smaller stars on a blue field
3. white cross on a red field
4. three vertical bands of equal width—blue nearest the staff, white in the middle, and red on the outside
5. three horizontal bands—black on top, red in the middle, and green on the bottom; a shield and spears in the center
6. red circle on a white field
7. two horizontal bands—red on the top and white on the bottom; a crescent moon and five small stars in the top left corner
8. one diagonal black stripe on a red field
9. blue Shield or Star of David on a white field
10. blue with six small yellow stars and one large yellow star

Australia
Canada
France
Israel
Japan
Kenya
Singapore
Switzerland
Trinidad and Tobago
Democratic Republic of the Congo

403